DB2 9 for z/OS
Database Administration
Certification Study Guide

DB2 9 for z/OS
Database Administration
Certification Study Guide

Susan Lawson
Daniel Luksetich

MC PRESS

MC Press Online, LP
Lewisville, TX 75077

DB2 9 for z/OS Database Administration Certification Study Guide
Susan Lawson and Daniel Luksetich

First Edition

First Printing—October 2007

MC Press offers excellent discounts on this book when ordered in quantity for bulk purchases or special sales, which may include custom covers and content particular to your business, training goals, marketing focus, and branding interest.

For information regarding permissions or special orders, please contact:
    MC Press
    Corporate Offices
    125 N. Woodland Trail
    Lewisville, TX 75077 USA

For information regarding sales and/or customer service, please contact:
    MC Press
    P.O. Box 4300
    Big Sandy, TX 75755-4300 USA

ISBN: 978-158347-074-9

Contents

Preface

The purpose of this book is to assist you with preparing for the IBM DB2 Version 9.1 z/OS Certified Database Administrator exam. This book covers all topics on the exam and is written by two members of the team who participated in the actual writing of the exam.

In addition to covering all topics on the test, this book covers much more, reviewing the new features of Version 9 for both database and application development. Below, we describe the objectives of the certification exams and identify the topics covered on the tests.

IBM DB2 Version 9.1 z/OS Certified Database Administrator

To become a DB2 Version 9.1 z/OS Certified DBA, you must pass two exams:

- 730 Exam: DB2 9 Fundamentals

- 732 Exam: DB2 Version 9.1 z/OS Database Administration

The following sections describe these exams in terms of what the objective are for each.

> This book covers 100 percent of the information needed for the 732 exam. It also covers the majority of the 730 exam, except for questions that are specific to non-z/OS DB2 platforms. For more information about these platforms, refer to the DB2 9 Fundamentals Guide published by MC Press.

730 Exam Objectives

Section 1: Planning (14%)

- Knowledge of restricting data access

- Knowledge of the features and functions available in DB2 tools

- Knowledge of database workloads (OLTP vs. warehousing)

- Knowledge of non-relational data concepts (extenders)

- Knowledge of XML data implications (non-shreading)

Section 2: Security (11%)

- Knowledge of DB2 products (client, server, and so on)

- Knowledge of different privileges and authorities

- Knowledge of encryption options (data and network)

- Given a DDL SQL statement, knowledge to identify results (grant/revoke/connect statements)

Section 3: Working with Databases and Database Objects (17%)

- Ability to identify and connect to DB2 servers and databases

- Ability to identify DB2 objects

- Knowledge of basic characteristics and properties of DB2 objects

- Given a DDL SQL statement, knowledge to identify results (ability to create objects)

Section 4: Working with DB2 Data Using SQL (23.5%)

- Given a DML SQL statement, knowledge to identify results

- Ability to use SQL to SELECT data from tables

- Ability to use SQL to SORT or GROUP data

- Ability to use SQL to UPDATE, DELETE, or INSERT data

- Knowledge of transactions (i.e., commit/rollback and transaction boundaries)

- Ability to call a procedure or invoke a user-defined function

- Given an XQuery statement, knowledge to identify results

Section 5: Working with DB2 Tables, Views, and Indexes (23.5%)

- Ability to demonstrate use of DB2 data types

- Given a situation, ability to create a table

- Knowledge to identify when referential integrity should be used

- Knowledge to identify methods of data constraint

- Knowledge to identify characteristics of a table, view, or index

- Knowledge to identify when triggers should be used

- Knowledge of schemas

- Knowledge of data type options for storing XML data

Section 6: Data Concurrency (11%)

- Knowledge to identify factors that influence locking

- Ability to list objects on which locks can be obtained

- Knowledge to identify characteristics of DB2 locks

- Given a situation, knowledge to identify the isolation levels that should be used

732 Exam Objectives

Section 1: Database Design and Implementation (26%)

- Design tables and views

  » Data types

  » XML

  » User-defined data types

- » Temporary tables

- » Clone tables

- » Materialized query tables

- » Automatic creation of objects

- Explain the different performance implications of identity column, row ID, and sequence objects, new row format

- Design XML indexes

- Create and alter objects

  - » Design table spaces

  - » Determine space attributes

- Perform table space and index partitioning

- Use the universal table space

- Normalize data and translate data model into physical model

- Implement user-defined integrity rules

  - » Referential integrity

  - » User-defined functions

  - » Check constraints

  - » Triggers

- Use the appropriate method to create and alter DB2 objects

- Design and alter index structures

  - » Data-partitioned secondary indexes (DPSIs)

  - » VARCHAR column index implications

  - » Backward index scan

  - » Index on expression

Section 2: Operation and Recovery (28%)

- Issue database-oriented commands for normal operational conditions

    » START, STOP, DISPLAY

- Issue database-oriented commands and utility control statements for use in abnormal conditions

    » RECOVER, RESTART

- Identify and perform actions needed to protect databases from planned and unplanned outages and ensure that timely image copies are taken periodically

- Load and unload data into and from created tables

- Reorganize objects when necessary

- Monitor an object by collecting statistics

- Monitor threads

- Identify and respond to advisory/restrictive statuses on objects

- Establish timely checkpoints

- Identify and perform problem determination

    » Traces and other utilities

- Perform health checks

    » Maintenance

    » Check utilities

    » Offline utilities

    » Queries

- Develop backup scenarios

    » Table spaces, indexes

    » Roll forward, roll back, current point in time, prior point in time

    » System point-in-time copy and restore

» Catalog and directory

- Describe the special considerations for recovery in a data-sharing environment

  » Implement disaster recovery

  » Identify options in disaster recovery

  » Plan for disaster recovery

  » Perform disaster recovery (offsite, local)

- Creating LISTDEF and TEMPLATE statements

Section 3: Security and Auditing (10%)

- Protect DB2 objects

  » Establish security profile

  » Define authorization roles

  » Identify the appropriate DB2 privileges required for access to DB2 resources

  » Define and implement authorization and privileges on user and system database objects

    ▪ GRANTs and REVOKEs

- Protect connection to DB2

  » Describe access to the DB2 subsystem (local request, remote request)

  » Coordinate effort between DB2 and RACF team

  » Identify conditions when external security mechanisms (e.g., RACF) should be used in place of DB2 internal security mechanisms

- Audit DB2 activity and resources and identify primary audit techniques

  » Identify and respond appropriately to symptoms from trace output or error messages that signify security problems

- Create and maintain roles and trusted contexts

Section 4: Performance (31%)

- Plan for performance monitoring by setting up and running monitoring procedures (continuous, detailed, periodic, exception)

- Analyze performance (manage and tune CPU requirements, memory, I/O, locks, response time, index and table compression)

- Analyze and respond to RUNSTATS statistics analysis

- Determine when and how to run the REORG utility

- Understand and implement Real-Time Statistics and DSNACCOR

- Analyze cache

  - » Buffer pool tuning (sizes and thresholds)

  - » Sort pool, RID pool, EDM pool (contents and performance)

- Evaluate and set appropriately the performance parameters for different utilities

- Describe the performance concerns for the distributed environment

  - » DDF

  - » DBAT threads

  - » Thread pooling

  - » Connection pooling

- Describe DB2 interaction with WLM (distributed, stored procedures, user-defined functions, RRS)

- Interpret traces (statistics, accounting, performance) and explain the performance impact of different DB2 traces

- Identify and respond to critical performance thresholds (excessive I/O wait times, lock-latch waits and CPU waits; deadlocks, timeouts)

- Review and tune SQL

  - » Interpret EXPLAIN output

  - » Analyze access paths

» Query parallelism

» Indexable, stage 1, and stage 2 predicate types

» Join methods

» Block fetching

- Explain the performance impact of multi-row functionality

» Multi-row insert

» Multi-row fetch

Section 5: Installation and Migration/Upgrade (5%)

- Identify and explain the application of runtime considerations and parameters
- Run catalog health checks using queries and utilities
- Identify the critical DSNZPARMs
- Identify the migration/upgrade modes
- Identify and explain data-sharing components and concepts such as

» Coupling facility structures

» GBP-dependent data sets

CHAPTER 1

DB2 Product Fundamentals

In This Chapter

- ✔ DB2 9 for z/OS
- ✔ DB2 9 for Linux, UNIX, and Windows
- ✔ DB2 middleware, connectivity, and information integration
- ✔ DB2 application development
- ✔ DB2 administration

This chapter introduces you to IBM's DB2 family of products for System z, Linux, UNIX, and Intel platforms. DB2 has the ability to store all types of electronic information—traditional relational data and Extensible Markup Language (XML), as well as structured, semi-structured, and unstructured information; documents and text in many languages; graphics, images, and multimedia (audio and video); and application-related objects, such as engineering drawings, maps, insurance claim forms, and numerical control streams. In this chapter, we introduce IBM's DB2 and related Information Management products and describe some of the features and functions of each offering. All descriptions are based on Version 9 level of function.

The DB2 product family is an important part of IBM's Information Management software portfolio, which integrates data and enterprise content to leverage information on demand. Popular Information Management tools include WebSphere Developer for developing Java, PL/I, or COBOL programs or components, Rational software for architecture management, Service Oriented Architecture (SOA) development (integrated with WebSphere), and Tivoli software for distributed systems management.

As for application server software, IBM offers several types of servers depending on the business requirement, from message queuing with WebSphere MQ to Java-based transaction processing with WebSphere Application Server. Several other products use the WebSphere Application Server infrastructure, including WebSphere Host Access Transformation Services (HATS), WebSphere Portal, and WebSphere Business Modeler. The most popular IBM software servers are its data servers, specifically the DB2 family.

The DB2 family executes on pervasive devices and on Intel, Linux, UNIX, midrange, and mainframe servers. Supported operating environments include Microsoft Windows 2000/2003/XP/Vista, Linux, AIX, Hewlett-Packard's HP-UX, Sun Microsystems' Solaris, OS/400, i5/OS, VSE/VM, and z/OS. To ensure maximum performance, the DB2 code base is optimized for each platform. Common to all platforms is the SQL API, permitting applications written on one platform to access data on any platform. Internally, DB2 on i5/OS, VSE/VM, and z/OS differ from DB2 on the Intel, Linux, and UNIX platforms, but the common SQL API enables applications to work together. The DB2 code base on Intel, Linux, and UNIX platforms is the same. DB2 provides seamless database connectivity using the most popular network communications protocols.

DB2 and the On Demand Business

The DB2 family of database products is part of the IBM DB2 software brand. With respect to leveraging IBM information assets, this group of products has expanded to include Informix, U2, Cloudscape, and Information Management System (IMS) database products; a variety of tools; and new products in the areas of business intelligence (BI), information integration, and content management. In addition, DB2 9 incorporates an optimized management of both relational and XML data.

As a core component of IBM's Service Oriented Architecture direction, DB2 is a catalyst for delivering applications that directly impact a company's operations. SOA technology enables organizations to quickly develop solutions based on loosely coupled software services that can use independent technologies. Common applications in this area include electronic commerce, enterprise resource planning (ERP), customer relationship management (CRM), supply chain management (SCM), and content management (CM). DB2 as the database is an integral part of this service.

Today's companies face several major business challenges, including continuous change, rigorous competition, financial pressures, security and compliance issues, and unpredictable risks. Business integration involves business modeling, process transformation, application and information integration, access, collaboration, security, compliance, and business process management. Implementing these elements lets companies further integrate their people, processes, and information. Infrastructure management, another challenge, includes areas such as availability, security, optimization, business service management, and resource virtualization. Addressing these areas of the business lets companies optimize and simplify their infrastructure.

Focusing on the database, we see business challenges manifested through unpredictable workloads with reduced problem tolerance, business partners of all types with evolving language standards, increased realtime decision making, continuous growth in size and form of data, and skyrocketing systems complexity. Successful management of the integration and infrastructure is critical. How well the organization is able to meet information challenges at the database level will, to a significant degree, determine the success of its application development and its ability to thrive in today's on-demand world. Using IBM's mainframe and DB2 for z/OS, businesses can reduce cost and complexity in their IT infrastructure, simplify compliance, and leverage their core asset: their data.

The DB2 Product Family

The DB2 family of products spans many platforms that can coexist in a distributed environment:

- **DB2 9 for z/OS.** This hybrid relational and XML database management system is the largest of the DB2 family, often serving as an enterprise server handling many transactional systems (including e-business), content management, enterprise resource management, business intelligence, and mission-critical systems. The DB2 for z/OS offering is most often used to support the very largest databases and the highest transaction rates. Using

IBM's largest hardware platform, the System z9, with DB2 and today's innovative programming models, you can derive new value from the data and applications on the mainframe. With the wealth of corporate data on the mainframe, the System z9 platform can leverage open standards and advanced virtualization capabilities in other IBM products to help position the platform as a data hub for the enterprise.

- **DB2 for i5/OS.** DB2 for i5/OS provides for a common database architecture in that many of its features and capabilities are compatible and/or interchangeable with the other members of the DB2 product family. These features include a common SQL language, DB2 tools (such as Extenders), and the ability to connect to other DB2 product family data servers and databases. As with DB2 for z/OS, the ability to connect to other DB2 data servers is built into the DB2 for i5/OS product.

- **DB2 9 for Linux, UNIX, and Windows (LUW).** This DB2 9 offering is the next-generation hybrid data server with optimized management of both XML and relational data on UNIX and Intel platforms. This full-function database product is scalable from single processors to symmetric multiprocessors to massively parallel clusters. DB2 9 for LUW comes in several editions, responding to different processing requirements and applications.

- **DB2 Express 9.** DB2 Express is an ideal entry-level data server, suitable for transaction processing or complex query workloads on servers with up to two processors. DB2 Express 9 provides many capabilities of the DB2 Enterprise 9 Edition (described below) as value-added features to let you to control costs by buying only what you need.

  » **DB2 Express-C 9.** This product is a version of DB2 Express 9 for the community: a no-charge data server for use in developing and deploying applications, including C/C++, Java, .NET, PHP, XML, and more. You can run DB2 Express-C on up to two dual-core CPU servers with up to 4 GB of memory and any storage system setup, with no restrictions on database size or any other artificial restrictions. When combined with the DB2 suite of application development tools, DB2 Express-C 9 enables a powerful and inexpensive development platform.

- **DB2 Workgroup 9.** This product is an ideal data server for deployment in a departmental, workgroup, or midsized business environment, suitable for transaction processing or complex query workloads on servers with up to four processors. Your workload may be smaller, but your business data is as critical to you as to the largest enterprise. Like DB2 Express 9, DB2 Workgroup 9 provides many Enterprise capabilities as value-added features to let you control costs by buying only the capability you need.

- **DB2 Enterprise 9.** DB2 Enterprise is an ideal data server for the most demanding workloads. It easily scales to handle high-volume transaction processing, multi-terabyte data warehouses, and mission-critical applications from vendors such as SAP. It offers many connectivity options and can share data with third-party databases and DB2 on heterogeneous platforms. DB2 Enterprise most often supports very large databases. Popular uses include supporting large data warehouses and Internet applications. DB2 Enterprise 9 can exploit single servers, clusters, or massively parallel hardware architectures, and it supports database and table partitioning.

- **DB2 Everyplace 9.** The Everyplace product features a small-footprint relational database and high-performance data synchronization solution that lets you securely extend enterprise applications and data to mobile devices such as personal digital assistants (PDAs), smart phones, and embedded mobile devices. The database runs on a variety of mobile and embedded platforms, including Embedded Linux, Linux, Microsoft Win32, Palm OS, QNX Neutrino, Symbian, and Windows CE/Pocket PC.

- **DB2 Personal 9.** This single-user, full-function relational database with built-in replication is ideal for desktop or laptop deployments.

- **DB2 Enterprise Developer 9.** This offering lets a single application developer design, build, and prototype applications for deployment on any IBM Information Management client or server platform. The product includes DB2 Workgroup 9 and DB2 Enterprise 9, Informix Dynamic Server (IDS) Enterprise Edition, Cloudscape, DB2 Connect Unlimited Edition for zSeries, and all the DB2 9 features.

- DB2 Warehouse 9. With this single integrated software package, IBM delivers all the capabilities needed to cost-effectively consolidate, manage, deliver, and analyze your business information. The Warehouse edition integrates DB2 Enterprise 9 with a data-mining tool, online analytical processing (OLAP) acceleration, DB2 Query Patroller, and DB2 Alphablox.

In the next sections of this chapter, we take a closer look at the products in the DB2 family.

DB2 for z/OS

The DB2 9 for z/OS relational database management system (RDBMS) is the foundation of many e-business, BI, CRM, and ERP applications and numerous mission-critical systems. The primary focus of this certification guide, DB2 9 for z/OS is the largest member of the DB2 family, often functioning as an enterprise server handling many of the biggest applications in the world. The operating environment furnished by z/OS is IBM's largest and most powerful, providing the most scalable and available platform.

DB2 9 for z/OS delivers large data capacity, high transaction performance, and extensive connectivity. It supports transactions arising from Web servers, Customer Information Control System (CICS), IMS transaction management, and Multiple Virtual Storage (MVS) batch jobs as well as via distributed connections from remote clients on numerous platforms. In addition to being able to handle single tables up to 128 TB, use 64-bit addressability to take advantage of very large amounts of physical memory, process complex SQL (including multi-row operations), handle data storage in Unicode, and offer the highest level of availability, DB2 9 for z/OS expands the value delivered to your business by the industry-leading IBM mainframe data server through innovations in key areas:

- Rich hybrid data server support for both relational and pureXML storage, with the necessary services to support both data structures. This support enables direct XML access to and from the database.

- New data types (BIGINT, DECFLOAT, and VARBINARY).

- Native SQL procedural language. The SQL procedure language has been available for several years but has always resulted in generated C external programs that weren't very compatible when migrating from other relational RDBMSs. Now, these stored procedures run as native runtime structures, eliminating any performance issues related to external program scheduling.

- Improved security, with roles, trusted context, new encryption functions, and Secure Sockets Layer (SSL) support.

- Extensions of DB2 for z/OS Version 8 capabilities to make changes to data.

- Enhancements to large object (LOB) support and performance.

- Volume-based copy and recover.

- Refinements to the DB2 industry-leading optimization.

- Query Management Facility (QMF) interface design changes that provide on-demand access to data, reports, and interactive visual solutions with an optional Web browser.

- Enablement for IBM System z9 Integrated Information Processors (zIIP). With this support, z/OS may be able to free up capacity and help you optimize the resource utilization of general-purpose processors by directing eligible work to this new specialty engine.

Among the highlights of the DB2 9 for z/OS offering are the following features:

- **High performance.** In many ways, DB2 9 for z/OS excels in the area of performance. Designed specifically for, and tightly coupled with, the z/OS operating system, it can exploit operating system functionality specifically for performance. No other database management system vendor owns the platform architecture and operating system, and DB2's synergy with the operating system enables it to exploit the various features of the operating system, as well as the System z platform. Advanced SQL optimization and a highly sophisticated, cost-based optimizer let you construct SQL to solve a variety of business functions as quickly as possible. This capability includes high degrees of query parallelism across single instances (subsystems) or even across multiple members of data-sharing groups and machines. 64-bit addressability enables DB2 to take advantage of the large amounts of available cache on the System z servers.

- **High availability.** The highest levels of availability are obtained with DB2 9 for z/OS and the Parallel Sysplex on the System z architecture with DB2 data sharing. Additional features—such as workload-managed stored procedure address spaces; online utilities (reorganization, load, copy, and so on); and table space, disk volume, and system-level online backup and recovery options—allow for continuous, reliable, and secure operations.

- **Data sharing.** Data sharing enables multiple DB2 subsystems to operate against a single data source. By exploiting the Parallel Sysplex clustering technology, this functionality makes continuous operations possible across outages of a single DB2 subsystem, z/OS operating system, or System z server. This capability enables automated handling of planned and unplanned outages as well as near linear scalability across single servers or clusters of servers. Critical data sets and logs are duplexed, and the server can automatically direct workloads to various members for workload balancing or during outages. SQL queries can be executed across members.

- **Large tables.** DB2 9 for z/OS can manage the storage of very large tables (up to 128 TB) in a variety of ways. Tables can be partitioned by ranges or can grow automatically based on demand. Management of these tables can be automated or can be performed manually according to the application design. Multiple indexing options for tables adapt to the needs of high availability, fast access to data, and ease of database management. The physical storage of the tables is tightly coupled with the operating system's physical storage architecture, enabling the exploitation of advanced storage and I/O features from within the data server.

- **Advanced workload management.** DB2 9 for z/OS is designed to work cooperatively with IBM's z/OS Workload Manager. A typical z/OS configuration supports a variety of applications running batch jobs, online transaction processing (OLTP), ERP applications, BI, and distributed applications. In these complex environments, automated workload management is a necessity. DB2 is fully incorporated into the automated workload management of applications using batch, CICS, Time-Sharing Option (TSO), UNIX System Services, and Web servers. Workload priorities are managed at the transaction or application level, across the Parallel Sysplex.

- **Compression.** The quantity of data that businesses are storing today is growing exponentially. To satisfy analytical needs, regulatory requirements, and historical analysis, we need more and more data. DB2 9 for z/OS takes advantage of System z hardware compression to effectively compress data in the most cost-effective way possible. This compression, combined with the table partitioning options and 128 TB table size, lets organizations store and quickly retrieve extremely large quantities of data.

- **Security.** DB2 9 for z/OS provides a robust set of built-in security features that are tightly coupled with the z/OS operating system software. These additional security features of DB2 and z/OS include SSL, Kerberos, multilevel security, and trusted contexts (which allow a trusted relationship between DB2 and an external entity).

- **Encryption.** With many organizations paying more attention to the security of their data as well as striving to comply with regulatory requirements, the need to protect data goes beyond security. DB2 9 for z/OS uses IBM Data Encryption to further secure data.

- **PureXML.** The DB2 pureXML feature provides simple, efficient access to XML data while furnishing the same levels of security, integrity, and resilience that are available for relational data. DB2 9 for z/OS stores XML data in a hierarchical format that naturally reflects the structure of XML. This storage approach, along with innovative XML indexing techniques, lets DB2 efficiently manage XML data without the complex and time-consuming parsing typically required when storing XML data in a relational database.

DB2 for i5/OS

DB2 for i5/OS is an advanced, 64-bit RDBMS that leverages the On Demand features of IBM's System i5. A member of IBM's leading-edge family of DB2 products, DB2 for i5/OS supports a broad range of applications and development environments at a lower cost of ownership due to its unique autonomic computing (self-managing) features. DB2 for i5/OS is built into i5/OS, the System i's operating system. Because of the tight integration between DB2 and i5/OS and the operating system's unique architecture, many of the traditional, database-specific administration requirements found on other DBMSs either aren't necessary with DB2 for i5/OS or are administered through i5/OS facilities.

DB2 for i5/OS provides for a common database architecture in that many of its features and capabilities are compatible and/or interchangeable with the other members of the DB2 product family. These features include a common SQL language, DB2 tools (such as Extenders), and the ability to connect to other DB2 product family data servers and databases. As with the DB2 for z/OS product offering, the ability to connect to other DB2 data servers is built in to the DB2 for i5/OS product.

The DB2 for i5/OS offering includes the following features and capabilities:

- **Autonomic computing features.** The tight integration of DB2 with i5/OS gives this RDBMS unique attributes. Single-level store and the object-based operating system, i5/OS, minimize the effort required to manage the database while maintaining mainframe-like reliability and security. Automation of many of the common database administrator (DBA) tasks required by other RDBMSs is a cornerstone of DB2 for i5/OS's lower cost of ownership.

- **Open development environments.** DB2 is uniquely suited to support many different development environments through adherence to existing and emerging open standards and continued investment protection of heritage programming interfaces. Whether you develop in traditional environments such as RPG or COBOL, use Java/J2EE or Web Services through IBM's WebSphere suite of products, or develop using many of the application development tools in the marketplace (including Microsoft's .NET Framework), DB2 can simplify the IT infrastructure.

- **Scalability.** DB2 for i5/OS leverages the System i's On Demand capabilities, including Dynamic Logical Partitioning and On/Off Capacity Upgrade on Demand, to simply and quickly respond to changing workloads, thus ensuring business continuity in a dynamic environment. DB2's sophisticated, cost-based query optimizer, unique single-level store architecture, and database parallelism feature let the database scale nearly linearly within a System i's symmetric multiprocessing (SMP) configuration. Recent benchmarks highlight DB2's performance in a real-world, mixed-workload environment.

DB2 9 for Linux, UNIX, and Windows

DB2 9 is the latest release of the DB2 product for Linux, UNIX, and Windows. The LUW offering runs on a wide variety of platforms, and several editions are available. Each edition satisfies a specific business need in addition to opening up the world of DB2 to anyone who wants to use it, even at no cost. These editions, along with an extensive collection of tools and product add-ons, provide for a fully comprehensive database management system. Many of the features of the DB2 9 family are available across editions.

DB2 Express Edition

DB2 Express is the lowest-priced full-function hybrid data server designed specifically to meet the needs of small and medium businesses. DB2 9 Express is available on Linux, Solaris x86, and Windows platforms with one or two CPUs and up to 4 GB of RAM (it may run on machines with more than 4 GB). DB2 Express is perfect as an entry-level data server and can easily meet the needs of application developers or small businesses. It is easily upgradable to other editions. Some advanced features of DB2 Enterprise Edition aren't available with DB2 Express.

Like all the editions of DB2 9, DB2 Express features a simple installation, autonomous self-managing features, and optimized tools and interfaces for application developers. It supports a wide array of development paradigms. Two important features of DB2 Express are *adaptive memory allocation* and *automatic storage management*.

- In adaptive memory allocation, the DB2 9 self-tuning memory manager uses intelligent control and feedback mechanisms to keep track of changes in workload characteristics, memory consumption, and demand for the various shared resources in the database and dynamically adapts their memory use as needed. For example, if more memory is needed for sort operations and some buffer pools have excess memory, the memory tuner frees up the excess buffer pool memory and allocates it to the sort heaps.

- DB2 9 extends the automated storage features first introduced in DB2 V8.2.2. Automatic storage management automatically "grows" the size of your database across disk and file systems. It eliminates the need to manage storage containers while taking advantage of the performance and flexibility of database-managed storage. In DB2 9, automatic storage is now enabled by default when you create new databases.

You can expand the functionality of DB2 Express with the following add-on features:

- **PureXML.** The DB2 pureXML Feature unlocks the latent potential of XML by providing simple, efficient access to XML with the same levels of security, integrity, and resiliency taken for granted with relational data. DB2 9 stores XML data in a hierarchical format that naturally reflects the structure of XML. This structure, along with innovative indexing techniques, lets DB2 efficiently manage the data and eliminate the complex and time-consuming parsing typically required for XML.

- **High availability.** The DB2 High Availability Feature provides 24x7 availability for your DB2 data server through replicated failover support and data recovery modules. The three packages that make up this feature bring one unique aspect of high availability to the data server environment. The feature consists of the High Availability Disaster Recovery (HADR), Online Reorganization, and IBM Tivoli System Automation for Multiplatforms (SAMP) modules.

- **Performance optimization.** The DB2 Performance Optimization Feature includes two critical components, DB2 Performance Expert and DB2 Query Patroller, that can significantly improve the overall responsiveness of your data server and database applications. These two complementary tools improve data server performance, response times, and throughput. While DB2 Query Patroller enables you to focus on queries (with the ability to hold, schedule, cancel, fix, and prioritize queries), DB2 Performance Expert lets you concentrate on overall DB2 system, operating system, and application performance, which you can monitor and analyze over time.

- **Workload management.** The DB2 Workload Management Feature leverages the Connection Concentrator in conjunction with either Query

Patroller or the DB2 Governor to provide a more proactive, fail-safe workload environment for your users.

- **DB2 homogonous federation.** The DB2 Homogeneous Federation Feature delivers the ability to easily manage and access remote DB2 and Informix data servers as local tables. Homogeneous federation meets the needs of customers who require unified access to data managed by multiple data servers. For data sources beyond DB2 and Informix, WebSphere Information Integrator significantly expands the choice of data sources. The DB2 Homogeneous Federation Feature enables applications to access and integrate diverse data—mainframe and distributed, public and private—as if it were a DB2 table, regardless of where the information resides, while retaining the autonomy and integrity of the data sources.

DB2 Express-C Edition

DB2 Express-C is a no-cost, full-function hybrid data server designed to be an entry-level evaluation server or a full-function development database platform. Like DB2 Express, DB2 Express-C is available on Linux, Solaris x86, and Windows platforms with one or two CPUs and up to 4 GB of RAM (it may run on machines with more than 4 GB). Several of the more advanced features of DB2 Express aren't available with DB2 Express-C, including High Availability, Performance Optimization, and Workload Management. However, DB2 Express-C does come with the PureXML Feature already integrated with the product. You can easily upgrade DB2 Express-C to DB2 Express without impacting existing applications or databases.

DB2 Workgroup Edition

The DB2 Workgroup product has all the features of DB2 Express with scalability to larger servers. DB2 Workgroup can run on servers with up to four CPUs and 16 GB of RAM. Supported operating systems include a wide variety of AIX, Linux, UNIX, and Windows 32-bit and 64-bit bit systems. As with DB2 Express, the following add-on features (as described above for DB2 Express) are available for DB2 Workgroup: PureXML, High Availability, Performance Optimization, Workload Management, and DB2 Homogonous Federation. DB2 Workgroup provides the perfect departmental, workgroup, or small enterprise server.

DB2 Enterprise Edition

DB2 9 Enterprise is fully Web-enabled and is scalable from single to many processors and to massively parallel clusters. It supports unstructured data, such as image, audio, video, text, spatial, and XML, with its object relational capabilities. Applications for DB2 Enterprise can scale upward and execute on massively parallel clusters or can scale downward, with applications executing on single-user database systems. The product's scalability, reliability, and availability provide the ideal foundation for building data warehouse, transaction processing, or Web-based solutions as well as providing a back-end for packaged solutions such as ERP, CRM, or SCM. In addition, DB2 Enterprise offers connectivity and integration to other enterprise DB2 and Informix data sources. It also gives you the ability to partition data within a single server or across multiple data servers.

DB2 Enterprise includes all the features of DB2 Workgroup plus features designed to help manage very high transaction volumes, a variety of workloads, and very high availability. These additional features include the following:

- **Tivoli system automation.** Tivoli Automation automates tasks and responds to system events; correlates system and network data to identify business performance issue root causes; helps manage data growth, storage incidents, and data compliance; configures storage management; and more.

- **Table partitioning.** Table partitioning (sometimes referred to as *range partitioning*) is a data organization scheme in which table data is divided across multiple storage objects, called *data partitions* (not to be confused with database partitions or DPF, the Database Partitioning Feature), according to values in one or more table columns. These storage objects can reside in different table spaces, the same table space, or a combination of both. DB2 9 supports data partitions or data ranges based on a variety of attributes. One commonly used partitioning scheme uses the date, letting you clump together data in data partitions by year or by month. You can also use numeric attributes for partitioning—for instance, storing records with IDs from 1 to 1 million in one data partition, IDs from 1 million to 2 million in another data partition, and so on. Or, you might store records for customers whose names start with A through C in the first data partition, D through M in the second, N through Q in the third, and R through Z in the last.

- **Multidimensional data clustering.** This feature lets a relational table be clustered on one or more orthogonal clustering attributes (or expressions) of a table. Many applications (e.g., OLAP, data warehousing) process a table or tables in a database using a multidimensional access paradigm.

- **Materialized query tables.** A materialized query table (MQT) is a table whose definition is based on the result of a query. The data contained in an MQT is derived from one or more tables on which the MQT definition is based.

- **Full intra-query parallelism.** With intra-partition parallelism, the given query is divided into a series of operations such as scanning, joining, and sorting, but all the work for those operations occurs concurrently in the same partition using different processes.

- **Connection Concentrator.** This feature addresses the need to handle a large number of incoming connections that have very short-lived transactions but relatively large delays. With Connection Concentrator, system resources aren't held up by connections that perform no work (idle connections), agents can switch among servicing many client applications because of the multiplexing architecture, and server resource limitations are based on actual transaction load rather than on the number of connections.

You can expand DB2 9 Enterprise with the following value-added features:

- **PureXML.** For an explanation of this feature, see the preceding description of DB2 9 Express. The DB2 pureXML Feature unlocks the latent potential of XML by providing simple, efficient access to XML with the same levels of security, integrity, and resiliency taken for granted with relational data. DB2 9 stores XML data in a hierarchical format that naturally reflects the structure of XML. This structure, along with innovative indexing techniques, lets DB2 efficiently manage the data and eliminate the complex and time-consuming parsing typically required for XML.

- **Storage optimization.** The DB2 Storage Optimization Feature gives you the ability to compress data on disk to decrease disk space and storage infrastructure requirements. Because disk storage systems can often be the most expensive components of a database solution, even a small reduction in the storage subsystem can result in substantial cost savings for the entire database solution.

- **Advanced access control.** Using label-based security, the Advanced Access Control Feature increases the control you have over who can access your data. Label Based Access Control (LBAC) lets you decide exactly who has write access and who has read access to individual rows and individual columns. LBAC controls access to table objects by attaching security labels to them. Users trying to access an object must have its security label granted to them. If there's a match, access is permitted; otherwise, access is denied.

- **Performance optimization.** For an explanation of this feature, see the description of DB2 9 Express.

- **Database partitioning.** You can use the DB2 Database Partitioning Feature to better manage a large database by dividing it into multiple partitions that are physically placed on one or more servers. This solution offers a great deal of flexibility and scalability. From an application or user perspective, this partitioning requires no changes at all—everything still looks and acts like a regular database. The partitioning feature is most often used by customers with very large databases, to partition the database across a cluster of multiple, inexpensive servers instead of undertaking the overhead of a large, expensive server.

- **Geodetic data management.** The Geodetic Data Management Feature provides the ability to store, access, manage, and analyze location-based, round-earth information for weather, defense, intelligence, and natural resource applications for commercial or government use. The feature lets users manage and analyze spatial information with accuracies in distance and area by treating the earth as a continuous, spherical coordinate system.

- **Real-time insight.** Existing infrastructures can easily be overwhelmed when you're trying to manage large volumes of incoming data. Incoming data with message rates of tens to hundreds of thousands of messages per second can make it hard to leverage this high volume of data. The DB2 Real-Time Insight Feature is powered by the DB2 Data Stream Engine, which enables organizations to store and forward high volumes of data from multiple data streams. The data messages from the feed can be aggregated, filtered, and enriched in real time before being stored or forwarded.

- **Homogeneous federation.** For a explanation of this feature, see the description of DB2 9 Express.

DB2 Everyplace Edition

DB2 Everyplace features a small-footprint relational database and high-performance data synchronization that enables you to securely extend enterprise applications and data to mobile devices such as PDAs, smart phones, and other embedded mobile devices. With DB2 Everyplace, the mobile work force in industries such as health care, telecommunications, retail, distribution, transportation, and hospitality can now easily access the information they need to perform their work—from any location, at any time, right from the palm of their hand. DB2 Everyplace is available in two editions: DB2 Everyplace Database Edition and DB2 Everyplace Enterprise Edition. The DB2 Everyplace database is optimized for SAP mobile applications. Supported operating systems include Embedded Linux, Java, Linux, Palm OS, QNX, Symbian EPOC, Windows, and Windows CE.

DB2 Everyplace Enterprise Edition is a comprehensive mobile database and enterprise synchronization solution. Its high-performance synchronization server manages the distribution and synchronization of data to mobile workers. It supports advanced conflict detection with logging and customized resolution, integrates with key RDBMS data sources (such as IBM DB2, Cloudscape, Domino, Informix, Oracle, Microsoft, Sybase, and JDBC-compliant data sources), and supports advanced sync server features such as high availability and load balancing. Supported operating systems include AIX, Linux, Sun Unix, and Windows.

The DB2 Everyplace database is available for the following operating systems:

- Linux and Embedded Linux kernel 2.4 or later, for x86 and StrongARM/XScale architectures
- Palm OS 4.1 for Dragonball, Palm OS 5.0 and 5.2.1 for ARM/XScale architectures
- Neutrino 6.2, for x86 and StrongARM/XScale architectures

- Symbian OS V7s, Symbian OS V7 for x86 and ARM architectures

- Windows 2000, Windows 2003, Windows XP

- Microsoft PocketPC, PocketPC 2000, PocketPC 2002, Handheld PC 2000 for MIPS, x86 and ARM architectures

- Windows Mobile 2003 for Pocket PC, Windows Mobile 2003 Second Edition for Pocket PC, Windows CE .NET for ARM, ARMv4T, x86, XScale, MIPS architectures

- Windows CE v5 for ARM, x86, XScale, MIPS architectures

All supported devices include a command line processor (CLP). The SQL statements supported by the DB2 Everyplace database enable you to create or drop a table or index and to delete, insert, or update rows of a table. DB2 Everyplace includes a 200 K footprint database with zero administration required, industry-leading indexing and query performance with advanced database and SQL functionality, table-level local data encryption in the database, and a secure data synchronization architecture.

DB2 Personal Edition

DB2 Personal 9 is a single-user, full-function relational database with built-in replication, ideal for desktop or laptop deployments. DB2 Personal 9 can be remotely managed, making it the perfect choice for deployment in occasionally connected or remote office implementations that don't require multi-user capability. You can deploy DB2 Personal 9 on Linux or Windows. You need a separate user license for each authorized user of this product.

DB2 Enterprise Developer Edition

The Enterprise Developer edition offers a package for a single application developer to design, build, and prototype applications for deployment on any IBM Information Management client or server platform. This comprehensive developer offering includes DB2 Workgroup 9 and DB2 Enterprise 9, IDS Enterprise Edition, Cloudscape, DB2 Connect Unlimited Edition for zSeries, and all the DB2 9 features, letting customers build solutions that use the latest data server technologies.

The software in this package can't be used for production systems. You must acquire a separate user license for each authorized user of this product.

DB2 Data Warehouse Edition

DB2 Data Warehouse Edition (DWE) includes DB2 9 Enterprise with the Data Partitioning Feature and several other tools and features:

- **DB2 DWE Design Studio.** The Design Studio is a development environment for business intelligence solutions. It includes and extends Rational Data Architect (RDA) modeling functions. The studio integrates the following tasks in a unified graphical environment: physical data modeling (RDA), DB2 SQL-based warehouse construction, OLAP cube modeling, and data-mining modeling.

- **DB2 DWE SQL Warehousing Tool.** The SQL Warehousing Tool solves data integration problems in a DB2 data warehouse environment. Users can model logical flows of higher-level operations, which generate units of code that are organized inside execution plans. The tool provides a metadata system and an integrated development environment (IDE) to create, edit, and manage these flows as well as a code-generation system that understands the source graph and translates it into optimized SQL code for execution.

- **DB2 DWE Administration Console.** The DWE Administration Console is a Web application for managing and monitoring business intelligence applications. Installed with WebSphere Application Server, the DWE admin console uses Web clients to access and deploy data warehouse applications modeled and designed in DWE.

- **DB2 DWE OLAP Acceleration.** The DB2 DWE OLAP Acceleration Feature (formerly DB2 Cube Views) makes the relational database a first-class platform for managing and deploying multidimensional data across the enterprise. Using OLAP acceleration can provide easier-to-manage OLAP solutions more quickly. It can improve performance across the spectrum of analytical applications, regardless of the particular OLAP tools and technologies used.

- **DB2 DWE data mining and visualization.** DB2 Data Warehouse Edition's data-mining features help you discover hidden relationships in your data without exporting data to a special data-mining computer or resorting to small samples of data. The visualization feature provides data-mining model analysis via a Java-based results browser. DB2 DWE lets both experts and non-experts view and evaluate the results of the data-mining process.

- **DB2 Alphablox Analytics.** DB2 Alphablox provides the ability to rapidly create custom Web applications that fit into the corporate infrastructure and reach a wide range of users, inside and outside the corporate firewall. Applications built with the Alphablox platform run in standard Web browsers, allowing realtime, highly customizable, multidimensional analysis from a client computer. Alphablox is tightly integrated with OLAP Acceleration, providing common metadata and database optimization for Alphablox multidimensional analysis.

- **DB2 Query Patroller.** DB2 Query Patroller lets you regulate your database's query workload so that small queries and high-priority queries can run promptly and system resources are used efficiently.

The DB2 Data Warehouse Edition and associated tools help the database administrator and warehouse developer create and manage a database designed specifically in support of queries. This application contrasts with other database features that may be geared more toward OLTP processing, backup and recovery, and security. Although these features are certainly a part of the DB2 DWE offering, the emphasis is on the optimization of large query performance. For example, an OLTP query might request specific data, such as the address or telephone number of a specific customer as of today. In contrast, a warehouse query might request information about the quantity of sales per region for the first quarter of last year. While we tend to retain current information about customers, products, inventory, employees, and so on, in an OLTP-designed database the warehouse may contain vast quantities of information spanning many years. DB2 DWE optimizes access to this sort of data.

DB2 Middleware and Connectivity

DB2 is a very open database and provides a variety of options for connecting to both DB2 and non-DB2 databases. Client code is required on workstations for remote users to access a DB2 database or on servers for remote programs or applications to access a DB2 database. The DB2 Connect product enables applications executing on UNIX and Intel platforms to transparently access DB2 databases in the i5/OS, VSE/VM, z/OS, and Linux on System z environments. Note that you don't need DB2 Connect to access DB2 databases on Intel or UNIX platforms.

DB2 Clients

The DB2 product includes clients that applications or workstations use to communicate with DB2 servers. There are two types of DB2 clients: the DB2 Runtime Client and the DB2 Client.

DB2 Runtime Client

The DB2 Runtime Client provides the ability for applications to connect to remote DB2 databases. It includes the following features and capabilities:

- Support for common database interfaces:
  » Java Database Connectivity (JDBC)
  » ADO.NET
  » Object Linking and Embedding Database (OLE DB)
  » Open Database Connectivity (ODBC)
  » DB2 Command Line Interface (CLI)

This support includes drivers and capabilities to define data sources. For example, installing a DB2 client installs the DB2 ODBC driver and registers the driver. Application developers and other users can use the Windows ODBC Data Source Administrator tool to define data sources.

- Base client support to handle database connections, SQL statements, XQuery statements, and DB2 commands.

- Lightweight Directory Access Protocol (LDAP) exploitation.

- Support for common network communications protocols: TCP/IP and Named Pipe.

- Versions that run on 32-bit and 64-bit operating systems.

- Support for installing multiple copies of a client on the same computer. These copies can be the same or different versions.

- License terms that allow free redistribution of the DB2 Runtime Client with your application.

- A smaller deployment footprint compared with the full DB2 Client (covered next) in terms of install image size and required disk space.

- A catalog that stores information for connecting to DB2 databases and servers.

- The command line processor for issuing DB2 commands. The CLP provides a basic means to remotely administer DB2 servers.

DB2 Client

The DB2 Client includes all the functionality of the DB2 Runtime Client plus functionality for client/server configuration, database administration, and application development. Capabilities include

- Configuration Assistant to assist with cataloging the database and configuring the database server.

- First Steps for new users.

- Control Center and other graphical tools for database implementation and for administration. These tools are available for versions of Windows and Linux.

- Application header files.

- Precompilers for various programming languages.

- Bind support.

The DB2 clients are supported on a variety of platforms, including AIX, HP-UX, Linux, Solaris, and Windows.

DB2 Connect

DB2 Connect 9 for Linux, UNIX, and Windows is the industry-leading solution integrating System z, System i, and other enterprise data with client/server, Web, mobile, and service-oriented architecture applications. DB2 Connect V9.1 is designed to leverage your enterprise information, no matter where it is stored. For enterprises that have made DB2 on System z and System i servers the cornerstone of their On Demand Business solution, DB2 Connect provides application enablement and a robust, highly scalable communications infrastructure for connecting Web, Windows, UNIX, Linux, and mobile applications to data.

Note that DB2 Connect isn't required on the z/OS operating system; DB2 for z/OS includes the ability for applications on the z/OS platform to access remote DB2 data servers.

The DB2 Connect V9.1 product

- enables fast, secure access to legacy data through intranets, extranets, or the public Internet

- simplifies application development through rapid application deployment, providing a lightweight runtime client and tight integration with leading application infrastructures

- integrates new Web-based applications with existing core business applications

- provides the performance, scalability, reliability, and availability needed for the most demanding e-commerce, CRM, BI, and ERP applications

- provides extensive application programming tools for developing client/server and Web applications using industry-standard APIs

- lets you build new Internet applications and extend existing applications— such as data warehousing, data mining, OLTP, and OLAP—to the Web

- integrates with both Java and Microsoft models for developing new Web-based applications and enhanced support for federated data solutions

- energizes mobile PC users and users of the new pervasive computing devices with reliable, up-to-date data from System z and System i database servers

- lets IT staff spend more time supporting the needs of the business instead of installing and deploying database systems

- optimizes management of pureXML and relational data

- reduces cost through adaptive, self-tuning memory allocation and Object Maintenance Policy wizards for DB2 9 for z/OS

DB2 Connect comes in five editions:

- **Personal Edition.** Makes company data available directly to a personal computer. This edition provides access from a single workstation to DB2 databases residing on z/OS, i5/OS, and VSE/VM servers, as well as DB2 databases on Linux, UNIX, and Windows data servers. The edition is available on Linux and Windows operating systems.

- **Enterprise Edition.** Provides connectivity for client/server applications in large-scale, demanding environments. This edition concentrates and manages connections from multiple desktop clients and Web applications to DB2 servers running on System z or System i systems. The edition is available for AIX, HP-UX, Linux, Solaris, and Windows workstations and servers.

- **Unlimited Edition for zSeries.** Provides enterprise connectivity to host data while simplifying product selection and licensing. The product contains both the DB2 Connect Personal Edition and the DB2 Connect Enterprise Edition. This offering is available only for DB2 for z/OS data servers.

- **Unlimited Edition for iSeries.** Provides simplified deployment for development against System i (i5/OS) databases.

- **Application Server Edition.** Provides Web- and application server–based connectivity for multi-tier applications. This is the same offering as DB2 Connect Enterprise Edition with different licensing.

DB2 Application Development

DB2 offers a rich application development environment that lets developers build databases that support requirements for e-business and business intelligence applications. Many of these tools are integrated with the database. In this section, we review the major tools, in particular those that can be used with DB2 for z/OS. They are:

- **DB2 Developer Workbench.** Provides a comprehensive development environment for creating, editing, debugging, deploying, and testing DB2 stored procedures and user-defined functions. You can also use DB2 Developer Workbench to develop SQLJ applications and to create, edit, and run SQL statements and XML queries.

- **DB2 Extenders.** Enable the SQL API to access unstructured data types, including text, image, audio, video, and XML.

- **DB2 Information Center.** Provides comprehensive DB2 documentation for the DB2 product family. The Information Center can be installed on a PC or accessed over the Internet.

- **DB2 Client.** Provides connectivity to DB2 databases as well as a collection of tools for application development and database administration.

- **DB2 Driver for ODBC and CLI.** IBM-supplied middleware providing a library of functions to enable direct access from a variety of programming languages and platforms to DB2 databases.

- **DB2 Driver for JDBC and SQLJ.** A native Java library of functions providing direct connectivity to DB2 databases directly from Java. (This driver was formerly the DB2 Universal Driver.)

- **Query Management Facility.** An integrated, powerful, and reliable query and reporting tool set for DB2 data. There is also an optional QMF for Windows.

DB2 Developer Workbench

DB2 Developer Workbench is an Eclipse-based tool that replaces the Development Center from DB2 UDB for Linux, UNIX, and Windows Version 8 and the DB2 Stored Procedure Builder in Version 7. It is a comprehensive development environment for creating, editing, debugging, deploying, and testing DB2 stored procedures and user-defined functions. You can also use Developer Workbench to develop SQLJ applications and to create, edit, and run SQL statements and XML queries.

With the Developer Workbench, you can develop routines using the SQL procedure language or Java and deploy them on any DB2 data server. You can use the tool to design SQL statements, stored procedures, and user-defined functions. The workbench can run SQL statements in the database and can also be used to debug stored procedures. These routines can be compared and/or migrated between various DB2 data servers, including unlike servers. For example, you can create a routine on a DB2 for an LUW platform and then deploy that routine on a DB2 for z/OS data server. However, not all server combinations are supported.

The Developer Workbench also provides the ability to edit table data and to extract and load table data. You can also run SQL statements and launch the Visual Explain product. The workbench contains support for XML functions, the XML data type, and XML schema registration. You can also create XQueries using the XQuery builder.

In addition, the Developer Workbench provides the ability to develop JDBC and SQLJ applications. In support of SQLJ application, it provides the following capabilities:

- Generate an SQLJ template file by using a wizard
- Translate and compile SQLJ files automatically
- Customize and bind SQLJ profiles by using a wizard
- Print SQLJ profile files
- Edit applications by using code assist and templates
- Debug SQLJ files

DB2 Extenders

The DB2 Extenders can take your database applications beyond traditional numeric and character data to images, XML, videos, voice, spatial objects, complex documents, and more. Using these add-ons, you can bring all these types of data into a database and work with them using SQL.

Some examples of extenders:

- **XML Extender.** DB2's XML Extender provides new data types that let you store XML documents in DB2 databases and adds functions that help you work with these documents in a database. You can store entire XML documents in DB2 or as external files managed by the database; this storage method is known as *XML Columns*. Or you can decompose an XML document into relational tables and then recompose that information to XML on the way out of the database. In essence, this means that your DB2 database can strip the XML out of a document and take just the data, or it can take the data and create an XML document from it. This storage method is known as *XML Collections*.

- **DB2 Net Search Extender.** This extender helps businesses that need fast performance when searching for information in a database. It's likely to be used in Internet applications, where excellent search performance on large indexes and scalability of concurrent queries are critical.

- **DB2 Geodetic Extender.** This extender uses a round earth model to let you store, manage, and analyze spatial data (e.g., location of geographic features) in DB2, along with traditional data for text and numbers. The DB2 Geodetic Extender extends the function of DB2 with a set of advanced spatial data types that represent geometries such as points, lines, and polygons; it also includes many functions and features that interoperate with these new data types.

- **Text, Audio, Image, and Video Extenders.** These extenders let you extend the relational database to use nontraditional forms of data such as text, songs, pictures, and movies. With these extenders, you can work with data via SQL.

Query Management Facility

DB2's Query Management Facility (QMF) is a tightly integrated, powerful, and reliable query and reporting tool set for DB2 databases on distributed and host platforms. With QMF, you can execute queries, format reports, and build procedures to perform multiple activities. QMF stores the queries, forms, and procedures in its own database so you can reuse them. It provides an environment that's easy for a novice to use but also powerful enough for an application programmer.

In brief, QMF also lets you:

- easily build queries and reports via a quick-start interface

- leverage a Java-based query capability to launch queries from your favorite Web browser

- integrate query results with desktop tools such as spreadsheets and personal databases

- rapidly build data access and update applications

- fully exploit DB2 performance, SQL syntax, and advanced database performance techniques, such as static SQL

DB2 QMF has been enhanced with new data-visualization, solution-building, Web-enablement, and solution-sharing capabilities. Visual data appliances such as executive dashboards offer visually rich interactive functionality and interfaces specific to virtually any type of information request.

DB2 Administration

DB2 provides several tools to help you administer the subsystem environment and database objects. Some of these tools are optional and Windows-based. In this section, we look at some of the major tools, in particular those that can be used with DB2 for z/OS:

- **DB2 Client.** A workstation-based tool for managing and administering databases.

- **Visual Explain.** A graphical tool for analyzing the access paths DB2 chooses for SQL queries or statements.

- **Optimization Service Center.** The latest offering from IBM for visually displaying access paths, analyzing subsystem parameters, accessing the dynamic statement cache, viewing statistics, and grouping and modeling statements into transactions to monitor and predict workload.

- **DB2 Control Center.** A workstation-based graphical interface and tools to aid in the creation, administration, development, and monitoring of DB2 data servers and databases.

DB2 Client

The DB2 Client (which you learned about earlier in the chapter) provides the ability for workstations from a variety of platforms to access and administer DB2 databases through the Command Center, Control Center, or Configuration Assistant. Additional tools support monitoring (Event Analyzer, Health Center, and Memory Visualizer) and general administration (Replication Center). DB2 Client includes all the features of the DB2 Runtime Client as well as all the DB2 Administration tools, documentation, and support for thin clients.

The Control Center supports the entire DB2 family, including z/OS. It can serve as a single point of entry for controlling the entire DB2 family. You can use the Control Center to display database objects and their relationships to each other. Its graphical interface lets you easily manage local and remote servers from a single workstation.

Visual Explain

DB2 Visual Explain lets you graphically analyze the access paths DB2 chooses for your SQL queries or statements. It displays the graph of an access path on a Windows workstation, eliminating the need to interpret the EXPLAIN table output manually. The tool offers suggestions for improving the performance of your SQL queries or statements. You can change an SQL statement and dynamically explain it to see whether the change improved the access path. You can also use Visual Explain to browse the current values of subsystem parameters as well as the contents of the dynamic statement cache.

Visual Explain issues Distributed Relational Database Architecture (DRDA) queries through a DB2 client on the workstation to get the information it needs. It helps database administrators and application developers

- graphically see the access path for a given SQL statement

- view statement cost in milliseconds and service units

- tune SQL statements for better performance

- view the current values for subsystem parameters

- view catalog statistics for tables and indexes

- view the SQL dynamic statement cache

- generate RUNSTAT utility statements in support of SQL statements

- generate custom reports

Optimization Service Center

The Optimization Service Center is a workstation-based tool that lets you easily interact with DB2 EXPLAIN and the explain tables to analyze SQL statements, objects, statistics, the statement cache, and workloads. You can automatically gather information from DB2 EXPLAIN and view graphical depictions of the access plans DB2 chooses for your SQL queries and statements. Such graphs eliminate the need to manually interpret EXPLAIN information. The graphs clearly illustrate the relationships between database objects (e.g., tables and indexes) and operations (e.g., table space scans and sorts). You can use this information to help determine the access path DB2 chooses for a query; design databases, indexes, and application programs; and determine when to rebind an application.

The Optimization Service Center also lets you "snap" the information from the statement cache and view the contents of the statement cache table. Queries can be imported into Service Center from the DB2 system catalog as well as from files or programs. You can group statements into workloads and then monitor and analyze those workloads together.

Although the Optimization Service Center is by far the easiest way to view the contents of the explain tables, the explain tables are populated via the EXPLAIN statement for the user executing EXPLAIN. These tables are accessible via normal SQL queries, and while most people are used to querying the PLAN_TABLE table, it doesn't provide the details of the additional explain tables. You can join the additional tables to the plan table for a query; they are indexed via the query number and EXPLAIN timestamp.

DB2 Control Center

The DB2 Control Center provides a graphical interface that gives database administrators and application developers simplified and comprehensive access to DB2 data servers and databases. This support helps facilitate the creation of databases and applications, as well as the administration and monitoring of the data servers and databases. In the Control Center, you can administer all your systems, instances, databases, and database objects. You can also open other centers and tools to help you optimize queries, jobs, and scripts; create stored procedures; and work with DB2 commands. The Control Center's features and capabilities include the following operations:

- Add DB2 systems, existing instances, and existing databases.

- Create database objects that will be added to the object trees.

- View the details of database objects. You can look at a table's constituent columns and see the current state of a database.

- Manage database objects. You can create, alter, and drop databases, table spaces, tables, views, indexes, triggers, and schemas. You can also manage users.

- Manage data. You can load, import, export, and reorganize data. You can also gather statistics.

- Perform preventive maintenance by backing up and restoring databases or table spaces.

- Configure and tune instances and databases.

- Manage database connections, such as DB2 Connect servers and subsystems.

- Manage applications.

- Launch other tools, such as the Command Center and the Health Center.

The Control Center includes interactive access to a variety of graphical interface tools to help you monitor and manage your DB2 data servers and databases. Let's take a brief look at some of these aids.

Health Center

The DB2 Health Center is a graphical interface that provides a front end to collected DB2 health information. The Health Center shows the overall state of the database environment and all its current alerts. The Health Center is a management-by-exception tool, so only health indicators in an alert state are viewable (it doesn't make a lot of sense to grab the valuable attention of a DBA for something that isn't a problem). The center contains several tools that help developers and DBAs monitor and tune DB2 databases and data servers. For example, you can use the SQL Performance Monitor to analyze all the database operations performed by an application against a DB2 for i5/OS database.

Design Advisor

DB2 UDB V8.2 introduced a new tool called the Design Advisor, replacing the Index Advisor with a broadened scope. In addition to indexes, the Design Advisor now provides advice about materialized query tables, multidimensional clustering tables (MDCs), and Data Partitioning Feature partitioning keys. However, even for DBAs interested only in indexes, the Design Advisor is improved over the Index Advisor of the prior release.

Replication Center

You use the Replication Center to administer replication between a DB2 database and another relational database (DB2 or non-DB2). From here, you can define replication environments, apply designated changes from one location to another, and synchronize the data in both locations.

Journal

The Journal displays historical information about tasks, database actions and operations, Control Center actions, messages, and alerts.

Task Center

Use the Task Center to run tasks, either immediately or according to a schedule, and to notify people about the status of completed tasks. The Task Center includes functionality from the Script Center in previous DB2 versions plus new functionality. A task is a script, together with the associated success conditions, schedules, and notifications. You can create a task within the Task Center, create a script within another tool and save it to the Task Center, import an existing script, or save the options from a DB2 dialog or wizard, such as the Load wizard. A script can contain DB2, SQL, or operating system commands. For each task, you can do the following:

- Schedule the task

- Specify success and failure conditions

- Specify actions that should be performed when the task is completed successfully or when it fails

- Specify e-mail addresses (including pagers) that should be notified when the task is completed successfully or when it fails

Activity Monitor

Use the Activity Monitor to monitor application performance and concurrency, resource consumption, and SQL statement usage of a database or database partition. The Activity Monitor provides a set of predefined reports based on a specific subset of monitor data. These reports let you focus monitoring on application performance, application concurrency, resource consumption, and SQL statement use. The Activity Monitor also provides recommendations for most reports. These recommendations can help you diagnose the cause of database performance problems and tune queries for optimal utilization of database resources.

Command Editor

Use the Command Editor to generate, edit, execute, and manipulate SQL statements, IMS commands, and DB2 commands; to work with the resulting output; and to view a graphical representation of the access plan for explained SQL statements. You can execute commands and SQL statements on DB2 databases for Linux, UNIX, and Windows; z/OS and OS/390 systems and subsystems; and IMSplexes.

Summary

The DB2 family of products covers a wide range of platforms, letting users choose the best-performing platform for the job. DB2 is a very scalable product that can run on the smallest platforms to the largest z/OS server. IBM provides a comprehensive set of tools in many different categories to support and use DB2. Many of these tools are included with the base product itself; others are available for optional purchase.

Additional Resources

IBM DB2 9 for Linux, UNIX, and Windows site
http://www-306.ibm.com/software/data/db2/9

Practice Questions

Question 1

Which of the following entry-level DB2 products can be installed and run on a server with up to four CPUs?

○ A. DB2 Express Edition

○ B. DB2 Personal Edition

○ C. DB2 Workgroup Edition

○ D. DB2 Enterprise Edition

Question 2

Which of the following tools can make recommendations for indexes and/or MQTs to improve the performance of DB2 applications?

○ A. Visual Explain

○ B. Tivoli System Automation

○ C. Configuration Assistant

○ D. Design Advisor

Question 3

Which of the following tools can be used to view the result of Control Center actions?

○ A. Journal

○ B. Task Center

○ C. Activity Monitor

○ D. Command Line Processor

Question 4

What is the emphasis and strength of the DB2 Data Warehouse Edition offering?

○ A. Backup and recovery

○ B. Queries

○ C. Transactions

○ D. Security

Question 5

Which of the following products is required for a DB2 for z/OS application to be able to connect to a remote DB2 data server?

○ A. DB2 Run-Time Client

○ B. DB2 Connect Enterprise Edition for z/OS

○ C. DB2 for z/OS

○ D. DB2 Control Center

Answers

Question 1

The answer is **C**, DB2 Workgroup Edition. While both the Express Edition and the Workgroup Edition provide a robust, full-functional data server, the Express Edition is limited to two CPUs, and the Workgroup Edition is limited to four. There is no CPU limit for the Enterprise Edition.

Question 2

The answer is **D**, the Design Advisor. The Configuration Assistant aids in setting up connections to DB2 data servers. Tivoli System Automation helps monitor and configure system settings. Visual Explain can expose an access path and can recommend RUNSTATS, but it doesn't suggest database changes.

Question 3

The answer is **A**, the Journal. You use the Task Center to run or to schedule database operations (scripts) to run at specific times. The Activity Monitor monitors application performance and concurrency. The command line processor provides a simple interface for entering database commands, CLP commands, and SQL statements.

Question 4

The answer is **B**, queries. While a database designed for OLTP focuses on the performance of small units of work and specific granular transactions, a warehouse is designed for optimal query performance of large queries. DB2 DWE provides the tools for this application.

Question 5

The answer is **C**, DB2 for z/OS. The DB2 for z/OS product comes complete with the ability to connect to remote data servers and databases.

CHAPTER 2

Environment

In This Chapter

- ✔ z/OS
- ✔ Address spaces
- ✔ Attachment facilities
- ✔ Installation and migration
- ✔ System parameters
- ✔ Commands
- ✔ Utilities
- ✔ Catalog and directory
- ✔ Distributed data

DB2 operates as a formal subsystem of the z/OS operating system. DB2 utilities run in the batch environment, and applications that access DB2 resources can run in the batch, CICS, IMS, and TSO environments. IBM provides attachment facilities to connect DB2 to each of these environments. In this chapter, we examine the subsystem architecture that supports DB2, and we describe the available attachments. We also discuss some of the key features of the DB2 environment. We also briefly review the installation process of the DB2 subsystem and introduce the subsystem configuration parameters known as DSNZPARMs. In addition, we describe how to execute the DB2 utilities and various commands.

DB2 also has the ability to access other DB2 subsystems and other relational databases. Before concluding this chapter's tour of the DB2 environment, we'll take a look at the methods for accomplishing this access.

z/OS

The IBM System z is part of a family of enterprise servers, and it uses z/OS as its operating system software. z/OS is the next generation of operating system for OS/390. The core of this operating system is the base control program, MVS. Open-standard application server functions that support scalable, secure e-business application are integrated with the MVS base.

The z/OS platform can provide scalable, secure processing for different types of workloads in high-performance environments, such as stock trading. The applications can be batch, OLTP, or decision support systems (DSS). The major strengths of this environment include reliability, manageability, scalability, flexibility, availability, and security.

DB2 for z/OS

The DB2 database management system operates as a formal subsystem of the z/OS operating system. DB2 processes can be executed in several different *address space* regions within z/OS, such as for IMS or CICS. As of DB2 Version 8, which provided a new architecture supporting a 64-bit operating system, the z/OS platform can support many diverse applications with increased availability, scalability, and security.

Address Spaces

The address spaces used in the operation of DB2 are

- internal resource lock manager
- system services address space

- database services address space

- distributed database facility

- stored procedure address space

- allied address spaces

- Workload Manager

Figure 2.1 shows the relationships among the address spaces used by DB2.

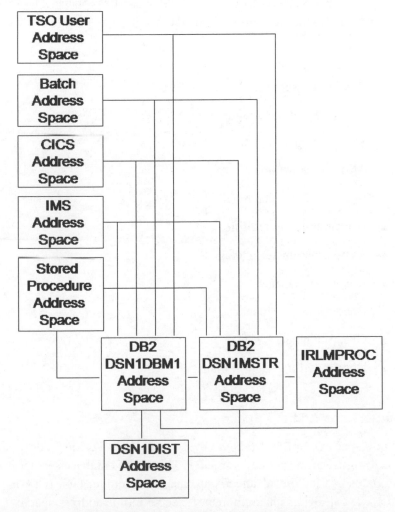

Figure 2.1: Relationship between DB2 users and DB2-related address spaces

Internal Resource Lock Manager Address Space

Each DB2 subsystem has its own internal resource lock manager (IRLM). The IRLM controls access to the application data, and DB2 uses the IRLM address space, IRLMPROC, as the lock manager to ensure the integrity of the data.

System Services Address Space

The system services address space (SSAS), DSN1MSTR (or MSTR for short), is also called the data system control facility (DSCF) address space. The following subcomponents execute in this address space:

- General command processor
- Subsystem support
- Agent services manager
- Storage manager
- Message generator
- Initialization procedures
- Instrumentation facilities
- System parameter manager
- Recovery manager
- Recovery log manager
- Group manager
- Distributed transaction manager

Database Services Address Space

Address space DSN1DBM1 (also known as DBM1) is a critical address because it manages most of the activities in DB2. This is the database services address space (DSAS), also called the advanced database management facility (ADMF) address space. The following subcomponents execute in this address space:

- Service controller

- Data manager

- Large object manager (LOBM)

- Data space manager

- Relational data system (RDS)

- Stored procedures manager

- Utilities (which work with associated code in an allied address space)

- Buffer manager

The DBM1 address space uses memory for several operations in DB2.

Distributed Data Facility Services Address Space

The distributed data facility (DDF) is what enables client applications running in an environment that supports Distributed Relational Database Architecture (DRDA) to access DB2 data. It also lets one DB2 subsystem access data on another DB2 subsystem. Other relational database servers can be accessed as long as they support DRDA. TCP/IP and Systems Network Architecture (SNA) are the supported network protocols.

DDF permits up to 150,000 distributed concurrent threads to be attached to a single DB2 subsystem at a time. The following resource managers execute in the DDF services address space, DSN1DIST:

- Data communications resource manager (DCRM)

- Distributed transaction manager (DTM)

- Distributed relational data system manager (DRDS)

- Distributed data interchange services (DDIS)

Stored Procedure Address Space

Address space DSN1SPAS is the stored procedure address space (SPAS). This DB2-established address space provides an isolated environment in which to execute stored procedures. SPAS goes away in DB2 9 for z/OS, and stored procedures instead execute in a Workload Manager (WLM) address space. The stored procedure address space is required to be managed by WLM.

Allied Address Spaces

The allied address spaces are the address spaces that communicate with DB2. The stored procedure address space, discussed above, actually operates as an allied address space. The following subcomponents execute in allied address spaces:

- CICS attachment facility
- TSO attachment facility
- IMS attachment facility
- Call attachment facility
- Recoverable Resource Services attachment facility
- Utilities (which work with associated code in database services address space)
- Standalone utilities
- Subsystem support
- Message generator (standalone only)

We discuss many of these address spaces in the following sections.

Address Space Priority

There are some general recommendations for how to establish the z/OS address space dispatching priorities. You should place the IRLM address space above IMS, CICS, and DB2, with DB2's MSTR and DBM1 address spaces placed above CICS. The following is the recommended priority listing.

1. MVS monitor with IRLM capabilities

2. IRLM

3. DB2 performance monitors

4. DBM1

5. MSTR

6. CICS

If the IRLM address space isn't at the top of the dispatching priorities, DB2 locks won't be set and released without excessive wait time. (For information about DB2 locks, see Chapter 16.) If the IRLM isn't above DBM1 at DB2 startup, you'll receive a warning message.

It's important to pay attention to the dispatching recommendations of the vendors of the various performance monitors. Each uses one or more address spaces, and the vendors always recommend specific dispatching priorities. If you use a performance monitor that can analyze problems in the IRLM, dispatching IRLM higher than a DB2 and/or MVS monitor could be a problem. If the monitor can't get dispatched ahead of IRLM, you won't be able to find or analyze the problem.

Under z/OS, the DPRTY parameter is no longer valid, and all priorities must be set using the MVS parameters in either the Installation Performance Specification/Installation Control Specification (IPS/ICS) table or the program priority table. If you use the IPS/ICS table to define relative priorities, the system can change the priorities dynamically.

Attachments

DB2 *attachment facilities* provide the interface between DB2 and other environments. Five different attachment facilities can be used, depending on the environment in which a program will execute. Only one attachment can be active within a program at any given time. The attachments are:

- TSO
- CICS
- IMS
- Call attachment facility (CAF)
- Recoverable Resource Services (RRS) attachment facility

Each program runs in an allied address space. The program calls the DB2 attachment facility modules, which execute within the allied address space and establish communications with the DB2 address spaces. Once initialized, the attachment modules link to DB2, and agent control blocks are created in the DSN1MSTR address space to control the program's DB2 processing.

When a program issues an SQL statement, the attachment modules receive control. The attachment programs prepare the request for DB2 and pass it over to the DB2 address space. Results are returned to the attachment programs and copied into the application storage areas.

Let's take a brief look at the different attachment facilities.

Customer Information Control System

CICS is an application server that provides online transaction management for applications. To connect to DB2 from this environment, you can use the CICS attachment facility. This attachment facility permits access to DB2 data from CICS. A CICS application can access both DB2 and CICS data; in the event of a failure, CICS coordinates the recovery between DB2 and CICS.

Once the DB2 subsystem has been started, DB2 can be operated from a CICS terminal. DB2 and CICS can be started independently of each other. The connection can also be made to be automatic. Figure 2.2 portrays the relationship between CICS and DB2.

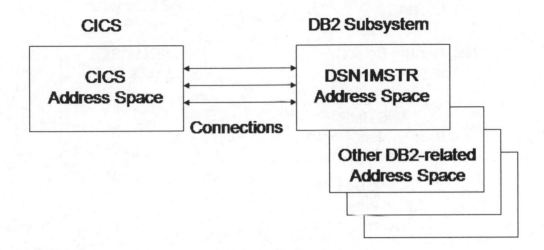

Figure 2.2: Relationship between CICS and DB2

Information Management System

IMS is a database computing system that includes a hierarchical database manager, a transaction manager, and middleware products for access to the IMS databases and transactions. To connect to DB2, you can use the IMS attachment facility. This facility receives and interprets requests for access to DB2 data via exit routines in the IMS subsystems.

IMS can connect automatically to DB2 without operator intervention. You can make DB2 calls from IMS applications by using embedded SQL statements. DB2 also provides the database services for IMS-dependent regions with the IMS attachment facility. In an IMS batch environment, there is support for DL/1 batch jobs to have access to both IMS (DL/1) and DB2 data.

In the event of a failure, IMS coordinates recovery between DB2 and IMS. You can also include DB2 in the IMS Extended Recovery Facility (XRF) recovery scenario. Figure 2.3 depicts the relationship between IMS and DB2.

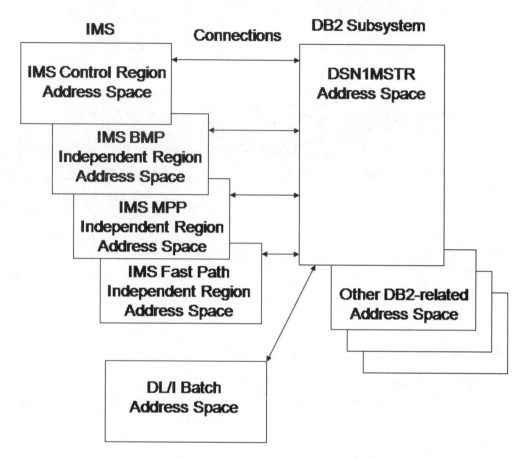

Figure 2.3: Relationship between IMS and DB2

Time Sharing Option

TSO provides interactive time-sharing capabilities from remote terminals. To connect to DB2 in a TSO environment, you can use the TSO attachment facility, the call attachment facility, or the Resource Recovery Services attachment facility.

Using TSO, you can bind application plans and packages and can execute several online functions of DB2. You can create, modify, and maintain application programs and databases via the TSO attach. You can run either in the foreground or in the batch environment when accessing DB2.

When you use TSO, you have access to two different command processors:

- the DSN command processor

- DB2 Interactive (DB2I)

The DSN command processor (DSN stands for "default subsystem name") runs as a TSO command processor using the TSO attachment facility. It provides an alternative way to execute programs that access DB2 in a TSO environment. You can invoke the processor from the foreground by issuing a TSO command or from batch by invoking the terminal monitor program (TMP) from an MVS batch job and passing the commands in the SYSTSIN data set to TMP. When DSN is running and DB2 is up, you can issue DB2 or DSN commands. (We cover both of these command groups later in the chapter.)

The DB2 Interactive command processor presents panels that permit an interactive connection to DB2 and invoke the DSN command processor. With this processor, you can invoke utilities, issue commands, and run SQL statements. We discuss DB2I in more detail later.

Most TSO applications use the TSO attachment facility. Figure 2.4 shows the relationship between TSO and DB2.

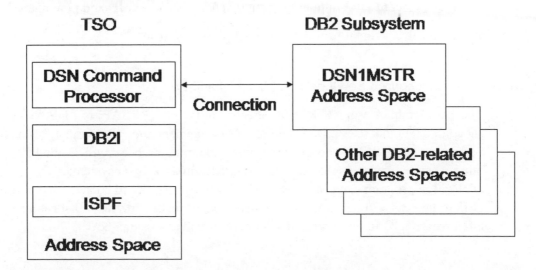

Figure 2.4: Relationship between TSO and DB2

Call Attachment Facility

The call attach facility is a DB2 facility used for application programs that run under TSO or z/OS batch. This facility is an alternative to the DSN command processor that provides greater control over the execution environment. With this facility, your application program can establish and control its own connection to DB2. Programs that run in z/OS batch, TSO foreground, and TSO background can use CAF.

It's also possible for IMS batch applications to access DB2 databases through CAF, although that method doesn't coordinate the commitment of work between the IMS and DB2 systems. For IMS batch applications, we recommend you use the DB2 DL/I batch support.

Programs using CAF can:

- access DB2 from address spaces where there is no CICS, IMS, or TSO

- access the instrumentation facility interface (IFI)

- access DB2 from multiple tasks within an address space

- control the connection to DB2 explicitly

- connect to DB2 implicitly using a default subsystem ID and plan name

- receive a signal from DB2 on startup or shutdown

Recoverable Resource Services Attachment Facility

The Recoverable Resource Services attachment facility (RRSAF) is a DB2 subcomponent that uses z/OS Transaction Management and Recoverable Resource Services (z/OS RRS) to coordinate resource commitment between DB2 and all other resource managers that also use z/OS RRS in a z/OS subsystem. An application program can use the RRSAF attachment facility to connect to and use DB2 to process SQL statements, commands, or IFI calls. Programs that run in z/OS batch, TSO foreground, and TSO background can use RRSAF.

With RRSAF, you can coordinate DB2 updates with updates made by all other resource managers that also use z/OS RRS in a z/OS system.

Programs that use RRSAF can

- run under UNIX System Services

- sign on to DB2 with an alternate user ID

- access DB2 from one or more tasks in an address space

- use the instrumentation facility interface

- exercise control over the exact state of the DB2 connection

- capture DB2 startup and termination events

Programs using RRSAF can be run from almost every environment available under z/OS. You can invoke them from the command prompt in TSO, from a shell prompt under UNIX System Services, and, like any non-DB2 program, on the EXEC card in job control language (JCL).

Each task control block (TCB) can have only one connection to DB2. With RRSAF, this connection can be switched between tasks within the address space.

DB2 and Security

One way to add extra security to your DB2 subsystem is to use the Resource Access Control Facility (RACF), a component of the SecureWay Security Server for z/OS. Equivalent third-party security packages are also available. With RACF, you can prevent unauthorized users from accessing the system. You can use RACF to protect many different resources in DB2 and to check the identity of DB2 users.

An exit routine that runs as an extension to DB2 can also provide central control authorizations to DB2 objects. We provide more information about DB2 security options in Chapter 3.

Parallel Sysplex Support

DB2 has the ability to run in a Parallel Sysplex environment. This environment is a requirement to support DB2 data sharing (for details about data sharing, see Chapter 9). Parallel Sysplex technology lets you configure an environment in which several processors can share data and the DB2 subsystems can have concurrent read/write access to the data. It also gives you the flexibility to add new processors for increased throughput, the ability to seamlessly rout workload away from failed processors, and the capacity to balance diverse work across multiple processors.

Storage Management Subsystem

You can use the Storage Management Subsystem (DFSMS) to manage DB2 data sets automatically and reduce the administrative workload for database and systems administrators. DFSMS enables easier allocation and movement of data, better availability and performance management, and automated space management. The performance benefit is most important: DFSMS lets you set performance goals for each class of data, thereby reducing the need for manual tuning. This environment also uses the cache provided by the storage hardware.

DB2 Interfaces

There are a variety of ways to interface with DB2, such as with programs using TSO, CICS, CAF, and so on. Two of the most common interfaces provided with the DB2 product are DB2I (which you've already learned a bit about) and SQL Processing Using File Input, or SPUFI.

DB2 Interactive

You can use the interactive program DB2I to run application programs and perform many DB2 operations by entering values on panels. DB2I runs under TSO using Interactive System Productivity Facility (ISPF) services. To use DB2I, follow the local procedures for logging on to TSO, and enter **ISPF**. You control each operation by entering the parameters that describe it on the provided panels. Help panels explain how to use each operation and also show syntax and examples of DSN subcommands, DB2 operator commands, and DB2 utility control statements.

Using DB2I, you can perform the following tasks:

- Execute SQL statements using SPUFI

- Perform a DCLGEN (declarations generator command)

- Prepare a DB2 program

- Invoke the DB2 precompiler

- Execute BIND/REBIND/FREE command

- Run an SQL program

- Issue DB2 commands

- Invoke DB2 utilities

- Change DB2I defaults

Figure 2.5 shows the DB2I main menu.

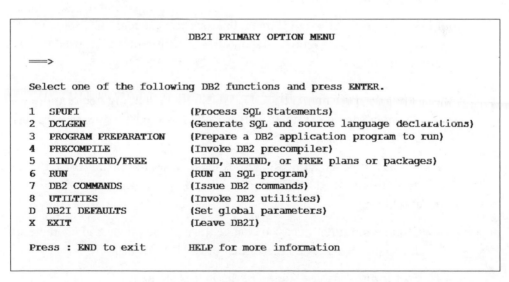

```
                    DB2I PRIMARY OPTION MENU

 ===>

 Select one of the following DB2 functions and press ENTER.

   1   SPUFI                  (Process SQL Statements)
   2   DCLGEN                 (Generate SQL and source language declarations)
   3   PROGRAM PREPARATION    (Prepare a DB2 application program to run)
   4   PRECOMPILE             (Invoke DB2 precompiler)
   5   BIND/REBIND/FREE       (BIND, REBIND, or FREE plans or packages)
   6   RUN                    (RUN an SQL program)
   7   DB2 COMMANDS           (Issue DB2 commands)
   8   UTILTIES               (Invoke DB2 utilities)
   D   DB2I DEFAULTS          (Set global parameters)
   X   EXIT                   (Leave DB2I)


 Press : END to exit       HELP for more information
```

Figure 2.5: DB2I Primary Option menu

The panel in Figure 2.6 shows the default settings for DB2I. You can change these values for each individual's DB2I. Among the parameters you can set are the DB2 subsystem on which to run requests, the application language of choice, the number of rows returned to the session, and which string delimiter to use.

```
                        DB2I DEFAULTS PANEL 1

Command ===> _

Change defaults as desired:

1   DB2 NAME..............  ===> DSN        (Subsystem Identifier)
2   DB2 CONNECTION RETRIES  ===> 0          (How many retries for DB2 connection)
3   APPICATION LANGUAGE...  ===> COB2       (ASM, C, CPP, COBOL, COB2, IBMCOB,
                                             FORTRAN, PLI)
4   LINES/PAGE OF LISTING.  ===> 60         (A number from 5 to 999)
5   MESSAGE LEVEL.........  ===> I          (Information, Warning, Error, Severe)
6   SQL STRING DELIMITER..  ===> DEFAULT    (DEFAULT or ' or ")
7   DECIMAL POINT.........  ===> .          (. or , )
8   STOP IF RETURN CODE >=  ===> 8          (Lowest terminating return code)
9   NUMBER OF ROWS........  ===> 20         (For ISPF Tables)
10  CHANGE HELP BOOK NAMES? ===> NO         (YES to change HELP data set names)


Press : ENTER to process  END to cancel   HELP for more information
```

Figure 2.6: DB2I Defaults panel

SQL Processing Using File Input

SPUFI is an option on the DB2I menu that lets you execute SQL statements interactively with DB2. Figure 2.7 shows the SPUFI main panel, used to set the following options.

- **Input data set name.** Specifies a data set containing one or more SQL statements to be executed. This data set must exist before you can use SPUFI.

- **Output data set name.** Specifies the data set that will receive the output from the executed SQL statement. This data set need not exist before execution.

- **Change defaults.** Lets you change the control values and characteristics of the output data set and the format of SPUFI settings.

- **Edit input.** Enables editing of the SQL statements.

- **Execute.** Indicates to execute the SQL statement in the input file.

- **Autocommit.** Tells DB2 whether to make the changes to the data permanent.

- **Browse output.** Enables browsing of the query output.

- **Connect location.** Specifies the name of the application server to submit the queries to.

```
SPUFI                              SSID: DSN
===>

Enter the input data set name:        (Can be sequential or partitioned)
  1  DATA SET NAME ... ===> ISPF.SQL(RECURS1)
  2  VOLUME SERIAL ... ===>            (Enter if not cataloged)
  3  DATA SET PASSWORD ===>            (Enter if password protected)

Enter the output data set name:       (Must be a sequential data set)
  4  DATA SET NAME ... ===> OUTPUT.DATA

Specify processing options:
  5  CHANGE DEFAULTS   ===> YES        (Y/N - Display SPUFI defaults panel?)
  6  EDIT INPUT ...... ===> YES        (Y/N - Enter SQL statements?)
  7  EXECUTE ......... ===> YES        (Y/N - Execute SQL statements?)
  8  AUTOCOMMIT ...... ===> YES        (Y/N - Commit after successful run?)
  9  BROWSE OUTPUT ... ===> YES        (Y/N - Browse output data set?)

For remote SQL processing:
 10  CONNECT LOCATION  ===>


PRESS:  ENTER to process    END to exit          HELP for more information
```

Figure 2.7: SPUFI main panel

SPUFI lets you include multiple queries in one input data set member for execution. You can stack the queries by using a semicolon (;) delimiter between the statements. If no explicit COMMIT statement exists, all the SQL statements are considered a unit of work.

After the SQL has been executed, SPUFI displays both the SQLCODE and the SQLSTATE.

Installation, Migration, and Conversion

Installation, migration, and conversion represent three distinct processes in the DB2 for z/OS environment. *Installation* is the process of preparing DB2 to operate as a z/OS subsystem. *Migration* is the process of upgrading from Version 8 to DB2 9 compatibility mode. *Conversion* is a process composed of five catalog levels: compatibility mode, compatibility mode*, enabling-new-function mode, enabling-new-function mode*, and new-function mode. (We define these levels later in this section.)

Whether you're installing, migrating, or converting, several of the steps you must perform are the same. This book doesn't cover the details of each migration step; if you require more information, refer to the *IBM DB2 9 for z/OS Installation Guide*.

Before you begin installing or migrating, be sure to plan the amount of direct access storage and virtual storage you'll need. Planning and coordinating with other DB2 subsystems is essential if you intend to install DDF. For more information about estimating storage needs, refer to the *IBM DB2 9 for z/OS Administration Guide*. Review the values needed for the parameters on the installation and migration panels.

DB2 provides a set of tools that automate the process of installing or migrating. These tools include most of the JCL needed to install and migrate the product. This JCL constitutes the *installation and migration jobs*. Each of these jobs helps you perform a task when installing or migrating.

Another tool is the *installation CLIST* (command list), which helps you tailor the installation and migration jobs. Also called the *migration CLIST* or simply the *CLIST*, this tool contains the code necessary to help you customize the jobs to your needs. A series of ISPF and ISPF/Program Development Facility (ISPF/PDF) panels let you pass parameter values to the CLIST, which then uses the values to tailor the installation and migration jobs.

DB2 also provides a set of sample programs and procedures that help you determine whether DB2 is functioning correctly. Because DB2 is distributed as object code, it requires few assemblies. You must perform an assembly to specify DB2 initialization parameters, but this task requires only a few seconds.

DB2 lets you specify many subsystem characteristics during DB2 operation, thereby providing the ability to defer decisions about DB2 characteristics until after the install or migration. Some of these decisions include authorizing users, defining databases and tables, and tuning DB2.

High-Level Overview

Whether installing or migrating DB2, you must perform the following procedures:

1. If using distributed data, install Virtual Telecommunications Access Method (VTAM) and, optionally, TCP/IP.

2. If you're planning implementation in a data sharing Parallel Sysplex environment, you'll need to examine some additional considerations for the Parallel Sysplex installation before installing DB2 or migrating to data sharing.

3. Load the DB2 libraries (do the System Modification Program/Extended, or SMP/E, steps).

4. If you plan to use DB2's Call Level Interface (CLI) or DB2 for z/OS Java Edition, you must execute additional jobs. For details, see the IBM DB2 ODBC Guide and Reference or the IBM DB2 for z/OS Java Edition.

5. Customize the installation or migration jobs.

6. Install or migrate DB2 to compatibility mode.

7. Connect the DB2 attachment facilities.

8. Prepare DB2 for use.

9. Verify installation or migration to compatibility mode.

10. After migration to compatibility mode, verify all is stable.

11. Tailor the enable-new-function jobs.

12. Convert to enable-new-function mode to convert the catalog.

13. Start new-function mode.

DB2 9 Migration and Conversion

The complete process of converting to DB2 9 begins with the migration to compatibility mode. From there, successive modes, or levels, move you closer to a fully converted environment, in which you can take advantage of all the new function available in DB2 9.

- **Compatibility mode.** Compatibility mode is the state of the DB2 catalog after the DB2 9 migration process is complete. In a DB2 data sharing group, members in compatibility mode can coexist with members that are still in Version 8. In compatibility mode, new DB2 9 functions aren't available for use. You can fall back to Version 8 from compatibility mode.

- **Compatibility mode*.** This state is similar to compatibility mode, but the asterisk (*) indicates that at one time the DB2 subsystem or data sharing group was in enabling-new-function mode, enabling-new-function mode*, or new-function mode. Objects that were created in enabling-new-function mode or new-function mode can still be accessed. data sharing groups can't have any Version 8 members. You cannot fall back to Version 8 from compatibility mode* or coexist with a Version 8 system.

- **Enabling-new-function mode.** This mode is a transitional state that indicates that the DB2 subsystem or data sharing group is in the process of enabling new function. New DB2 9 functions aren't available in enabling-new-function mode. You can't return to DB2 9 compatibility mode from here, but you can return to DB2 9 compatibility mode*. You cannot fall back to Version 8 from enabling-new-function mode or coexist with a Version 8 system.

- **Enabling-new-function mode*.** This mode is a transitional state that is similar to enabling-new-function mode, but the * indicates that at one time the DB2 subsystem or data sharing group was in new-function mode. You can still access objects that were created in new-function mode, but you can't create any new objects. You can return to DB2 9 compatibility mode*. You cannot fall back to Version 8 from enabling-new-function mode* or coexist with a Version 8 system.

- **New-function mode.** New-function mode is the state of the catalog after migration is complete. The catalog has been marked as being in new-function mode. All new DB2 9 functions are available in this mode. You can return to DB2 9 compatibility mode* or DB2 9 enabling new-function mode*. You cannot fall back to Version 8 from new-function mode or coexist with a Version 8 system.

To see which mode DB2 is in during the migration process, use the –DISPLAY GROUP command. The MODE attribute value in the command's results gives this information.

MODE value	Current mode
C	Compatibility
C*	Compatibility*
E	Enabling new function
E*	Enabling new function*
N	New function

The following output shows the result of a –DISPLAY GROUP command indicating new-function mode.

```
DSN7100I  +DSN9 DSN7GCMD
 *** BEGIN DISPLAY OF GROUP(........) GROUP LEVEL(...) MODE(N)
                  PROTOCOL LEVEL(2)  GROUP ATTACH NAME(....)
 _____
 DB2                                 DB2 SYSTEM IRLM
 MEMBER    ID  SUBSYS CMDPREF  STATUS  LVL NAME   SUBSYS  IRLMPROC
 _____    __  _____ _____  _____  ___ ____   _____  _____
 ........   0  DSN9   +DSN9    ACTIVE  910 P390   BRLM    BRLMPROC
 _____
 *** END DISPLAY OF GROUP(........)
 DSN9022I  +DSN9 DSN7GCMD 'DISPLAY GROUP ' NORMAL COMPLETION
```

DSNZPARMs

The parameters for which you supply values at installation time, via the install panels, are known as the *DSNZPARMS*. These parameters specify a multitude of details about your operating environment for the installation process. After installation, you can change the DSNZPARMs without having to go back through the install process. You can do so by updating the parameters using the installation CLIST to create a new DSNTIJUZ member, reassembling, and then bouncing the DB2 subsystem to have your changes take effect. We don't advise updating DSNTIJUZ without using the installation CLIST. Do so, and you'll lose your changes when you migrate to a later version of DB2.

Online DSNZPARMs

DB2 also lets you change most of the DSNZPARMs dynamically without having to stop and restart the DB2 subsystem and cause an unwanted outage. The advantage to changing DSNZPARMs dynamically is the ability to tailor parameters to the current workload. For example, you could implement an approved change to the Environmental Descriptor Manager (EDM) pool size sooner without necessitating a DB2 outage. It also might be desirable to change not only buffer pool size but also EDM pool size and checkpoint frequency for overnight batch processing.

The DSNZPARM member is changed dynamically in its entirety by activating a different DSNZPARM member. You issue the –SET SYSPARM command from a z/OS console, a DSN session under TSO, a DB2I panel, or a CICS or IMS terminal or via an application or product using the instrumentation facility. The issuer must have SYSADM, SYSCTRL, or SYSOPR authority (you'll learn more about these authorities in Chapter 3). You can use the following forms of the SET SYSPARM statement to control dynamic DSNZPARM settings.

```
-SET SYSPARM LOAD (modname)
Loads the named parameter module; the default is DSNZPARM.

-SET SYSPARM RELOAD
Loads the last named subsystem parameter module into storage.

-SET SYSPARM STARTUP
Loads the initial parameters from DB2 startup.
```

Table 2.1 lists all the DSNZPARMs and provides a description of each parameter, its allowable values, and whether you can change the parameter online.

Table 2.1: DB2 DSNZPARMs			
Parameter	**Description**	**Acceptable values (defaults appear in bold)**	**Updatable online?**
ABEXP	EXPLAIN processing	**YES**, NO	Yes
ABIND	Auto BIND	**YES**, NO	Yes
ACCUMACC	DDF/RRSAF accumulation data	**NO**, 2–65535	Yes
ACCUMUID	Aggregation fields	**0**–10	Yes
AEXITLIM	Authorization exit limit	0–32676; **10**	Yes
AGCCSID	ASCII coded character set (graphic)	0–65533	—
ALCUNIT	Allocation units	**BLK**, TRK, CYL	Yes
ALL/*dbname*	Start names	**ALL**, *spacenames*	—
AMCCSID	ASCII coded character set (mixed)	0–65533	—
APPENSCH	Application encoding	ASCII, **EBCDIC**, UNICODE, *ccsid*	—
ARCPFX1	Copy 1 prefix	1–34 char	Yes
ARCPFX2	Copy 2 prefix	1–34 char	Yes
ARCRETN	Retention period	0–**9999**	Yes
ARCWRTC	WTOR route code	1–16; **1,3,4**	Yes
ARCWTOR	Write to operator	NO, **YES**	Yes
ARC2FRST	Read copy 2 archive	**NO**, YES	Yes

Table 2.1: DB2 DSNZPARMs *(continued)*			
Parameter	**Description**	**Acceptable values (defaults appear in bold)**	**Updatable online?**
ASCCSID	ASCII coded character set (single-byte)	**0**–65533	—
ASSIST	Assistant	**YES**, NO	No
AUDITST	Audit trace	**NO**, YES, *list*, *	No
AUTH	Use protection	**YES**, NO	No
AUTHCACH	Plan authorization cache	0–4096; **1024**	Yes
BACKODUR	Backout duration	0–255; **5**	No
BINDNV	Bind new package	**BINDADD**, BIND	Yes
BLKSIZE	Block size	8192–**28672**	Yes
BMPTOUT	IMS BMP timeout	1–254; **4**	Yes
CACHEDYN	Cache dynamic SQL	**NO**, YES	Yes
CACHEPAC	Package authorization cache	0–2MB; **32K**	No
CACHERAC	Routine authorization cache	0–2 MB; **32K**	No
CATALOG	Catalog alias	1–8 char; **DSNCAT**	Yes
CDSSRDEF	Current degree	**1**, ANY	Yes
CHARSET	CCSID used	**ALPHANUM**, KATAKANA (if SCCSID = 930 or 5026)	—
CHKFREQ	Checkpoint frequency	200K–16 MB rec (**50K**) or 1–60 minutes	Yes
CHGDC	DROP support	**1**, 2, 3	Yes
CMTSTAT	DDF threads	**ACTIVE**, INACTIVE	No
COMPACT	Compact data	**NO**, YES	Yes
COMPAT	IBM service	**OFF**	—
CONDBAT	Max remote connected	0–25000; **64**	Yes
CONTSTOR	Contract thread storage	**NO**, YES	Yes
COORDNTR	Coordinator	**NO**, YES	No
CTHREAD	Max users	1–2000; **70**	Yes
DBACRVW	DBADM can create view for other authid	YES, **NO**	Yes
DBPROTCL	Database protocol	**DRDA**, PRIVATE	Yes
DATE	Date format	**ISO**, USA, EUR, JIS, LOCAL	—
DB2SUPLD	Serviceability parameter	—	—
DATELEN	Local date length	**0**, 10–254	—
DDF	DDF startup option	**NO**, AUTO, COMMAND	No
DEALLCT	Deallocate period	**0**–1439 min, 0–59 sec, NOLIMIT	Yes

Table 2.1: DB2 DSNZPARMs (continued)			
Parameter	Description	Acceptable values (defaults appear in bold)	Updatable online?
DECARTH	Decimal arithmetic	DEC15, DEC31, 15, 31	—
DECDIV3	Minimum divide scale	**NO**, YES	No
DECIMAL	Decimal point	, .	—
DEF_DECFLOAT_ROUND_MODE	Decfloat rounding mode	ROUND_CELING, ROUND_DOWN, ROUND_FLOOR, ROUND_HALF_DOWN, **ROUND_HALF_EVEN**, ROUND_HALF_UP, ROUND_HALF_EVEN	—
DEFLANG	Language default	ASM, C, CPP, COBOL, COB2, **IBMCOB**, FORTRAN, PL1	—
DEFLTID	Unknown authid	**IBMUSER**, *authid*	No
DELIM	String delimiter	**DEFAULT**, ", '	—
DESCSTAT	Describe for static	**NO**, YES	Yes
DISABSCL	SQLWARN1 and 5 for non-scrollable cursors	**NO**, YES	—
DLDFREQ	Level ID update frequency	0–32767; **5**	Yes
DLITOUT	DL/I batch timeout	1–254; **6**	Yes
DSHARE	Data sharing	**YES**, NO, blank	No
DSMAX	Data set maximum	1–32767; **calculated**	Yes
DSQLDELI	Dist SQL string delimiter	', "	—
DSSTIME	Data set stats time	1–1440; **5**	Yes
DSCVI	Vary DS control interval	**YES**, NO	Yes
DYNRULES	Use for dynamic rules	**YES**, NO	—
EDMBFIT	Algorithm for free chain search	YES, **NO**	Yes
EDMDBDC	EDM DBD cache	**5000K**–2097152K	Yes
EDMPOOL	EDMPOOL storage size	1K–2097152K; **calculated**	Yes
EDMSTMTC	EDM statement cache size	0–1048576K; **5000**	Yes
EDPROP	DROP support	**1**, 2, 3	Yes
ENSCHEME	Default encoding scheme	**EBCDIC**, ASCII	—
EVALUNC	Predicate evaluation with UR and RS	YES, **NO**	Yes
EXTRAREQ	Extra blocks requestor	0–**100**	Yes
EXTRASRV	Extra blocks server	0–**100**	Yes
EXTSEC	Extended security	**NO**, YES	Yes

Parameter	Description	Acceptable values (defaults appear in bold)	Updatable online?
GCCSID	EBCDIC coded character set (graphic byte)	0–65533	—
GRPNAME	Group name	1–8 char; **DSNCAT**	No
HOPAUTH	Authorization at hop site	**BOTH**, RUNNER	No
IDBACK	Max batch connect	1–2000; **40**	Yes
IDFORE	Max TSO connect	1–2000; **40**	Yes
IDTHTOIN	Idle thread timeout	0–9999	Yes
IDXBPOOL	Default buffer pool for user indexes	**BP0**–BP*x*	Yes
IMMEDWRI	Immediate write	**NO**, YES, PH1	Yes
IMPDB	Create implicit database	**YES**, NO	Yes
IMPDSDEF	Define datasets	YES, **NO**	Yes
IMPTSCMP	Use data compression	YES, **NO**	Yes
IMPTSSEG	Tablespace type	SEGMENTED, **PARTITIONED**	Yes
INLISTP	IN list elements	1–5000; **50**	Yes
IRLMAUT	Auto start	**YES**, NO	No
IRLMPRC	Proc name	**IRLMPROC**, IRLM *procedure name*	No
IRLMRWT	Resource timeout	1–3600; **60**	No
IRLMSID	Subsystem name	**IRLM**, *IRLM name*	No
IRLMSWT	Time to autostart	1–3600	Yes
IXQTY	Indexspace default size	**0**–4194304	Yes
LBACKOUT	Postpone backward log processing	**AUTO**, YES, NO	No
LC_CTYPE	Locale LC_CTYPE	Valid locale, 0–50 char	—
LEMAX	Maximum LE tokens	0–50; **20**	No
LOBVALA	User LOB value storage	1–2097152; **2048**	Yes
LOBVALS	User LOB value storage	1–510002; **2048**	Yes
LOGAPSTG	Log apply storage	1MB–100MB; **100**	No
LRDRTHLD	Long-running reader threshold	**0**–1439 minutes	Yes
MAINTYPE	Current maintenance types for MQTs	NONE, **SYSTEM**, USER, ALL	Yes
MAXARCH	Recording max	10–**1000**	No

Table 2.1: DB2 DSNZPARMs (continued)

Table 2.1: DB2 DSNZPARMs (continued)			
Parameter	Description	Acceptable values (defaults appear in bold)	Updatable online?
MAXDBAT	Max remote active	0–1999; **64**	Yes
MAX_NUM_CUR	Max open cursors	0–99999; **500**	Yes
MAXOFILR	Max open file references	0–MAXUSERS value; **100**	Yes
MAXKEEPD	Max kept dynamic statements	0–65535; **5000**	Yes
MAXRBLK	RID pool size	0, 16K–1000000K; **calculated**	Yes
MAXRTU	Read tape units	1–99; **2**	Yes
MAXTEMPS	Max temp/stage agent	**0**–214748364	Yes
MAX_ST_PROC	Max number of stored procedures	0–99999; **2000**	Yes
MAXTYPE1	Max type 1 inactive	**0**–MAX REMOTE CON value	Yes
MCCSID	EBCDIC coded character set (mixed byte)	**0**–65533	—
MEMBNAME	Member name	1–8 char; **DSN1**	No
MGEXTSZ	Optimize extent sizing	YES, **NO**	Yes
MINDVSCL			
MINRBLK	Number of ridlists for each ridmap	**1**, *n*	
MINSTOR	Thread management	YES, **NO**	Yes
MIXED	Mixed data	**NO**, YES	—
MON	Monitor trace	**NO**, YES	No
MONSIZE	Monitor size	**8K** to 1MB	No
NEWFUN			—
NPGTHRSH	Use of index after table growth	**0**, –1, *n*	Yes
NUMLKTS	Locks per tablespace	0–50000; **1000**	Yes
NUMLKUS	Locks per user	0–100000; **10000**	Yes
OFFLOAD	Offload active logs online	NO, **YES**	
OJPERFEH	Outer join performance	YES, **NO**	Yes
OPTPREF		**ON**, OFF	
OPTHINTS	Optimization hints	**NO**, YES	Yes
OUTBUFF	Output buffer	40K–400MB; **400K**	No
PADIX	Pad index by default	YES, **NO**	Yes
PADNTSTR	Pad null-terminated strings	YES, **NO**	Yes
PARAMDEG	Degree of parallelism	**0**–no upper limit	Yes
PARTKEYU	Allow partitioning keys to be updated	**YES**, NO, or SAME	Yes
PCLOSEN	RO switch checkpoints	1–32767; **5**	Yes
PCLOSET	RO switch time	1–32767; **10**	Yes

Parameter	Description	Acceptable values (defaults appear in bold)	Updatable online?
Table 2.1: DB2 DSNZPARMs (continued)			
POOLINAC	Pool thread timeout	0–9999; **120**	Yes
PRIQTY	Primary quantity	**Blank**, 1–9999999	Yes
PROTECT	Archive logs protected with RACF	**NO**, YES	Yes
PTASKROL	Include accounting traces for parallel tasks	**YES**, NO	Yes
QUIESCE	Quiesce period	0–999; **5**	Yes
RECALL	Recall database	**YES**, NO	No
RECALLD	Recall delay	0–32767; **120**	Yes
REFSHAGE	Current refresh age	**0**, ANY	Yes
REOPTEXT	Reopt automatically	YES, **NO**	Yes
RESTART/DEFR	Restart or defer	**RESTART**, DEFER	—
RECVOER_ RESTORE FROMDUMP	Recovery/restore	YES, **NO**	Yes
RESTORE_TAPEU NITS	Maximum tape units	**NOLIMIT**, 1–255	Yes
RESYNC	Resync interval	1–99; **2**	Yes
RETLWAIT	Retained lock timeout	**0**–254	Yes
RETVLCFK	Varchar from index	**NO**, YES	Yes
RGFCOLID	Registration owner	1–8 char; **DSNRGCOL**	No
RGFDBNAM	Registration database	1–8 char; **DSNRGFDB**	No
RGFDEDPL	Control all applications	**NO**, YES	No
RGFDEFLT	Unregistered DDL default	APPL, **ACCEPT**, REJECT	No
RGFESCP	ART/ORT escape character	Non-alphanumeric char	No
RGFFULLQ	Require full names	**YES**, NO	No
RGFINSTL	Install DD control support	**NO**, YES	No
RGFNMORT	OBJT registration table	1–17 char; **DSN_REGISTER_OBJT**	No
RGFNMPRT	APPL registration table	1–17 char; **DSN_REGISTER_APPL**	No
RLF	RLF auto start	**NO**, YES	No
RLFAUTH	Resource authid	**SYSIBM**, *authid*	Yes
RLFERR	RLST access error	**NOLIMIT**, NORUN, 1–50000000	Yes
RLFERRD	RLST access error	**NOLIMIT**, NORUN, 1–50000000	Yes

Table 2.1: DB2 DSNZPARMs (continued)

Parameter	Description	Acceptable values (defaults appear in bold)	Updatable online?
RLFTBL	RLST name suffix	**01**, 2 alphanumeric char	Yes
ROUTCDE	WTO route codes	**1**, 1–14 route codes	No
RRULOCK	U lock for RR/RS	**NO**, YES	Yes
SCCSID	EBCDIC coded character set (single-byte)	0–65533	—
SECQTY	Secondary quantity	**Blank (clist calculated)**, 1–9999999	Yes
SEQCACH	Sequential cache	**BYPASS**, SEQ	Yes
SEQPRES	Utility cache option	**NO**, YES	Yes
SITETYP	Site type	**LOCALSITE**, RECOVERYSITE	No
SJMXPOOL	Star join max pool	0–1024; **20**	Yes
SJTABLES	Number of tables in star join	1–255; **10**	Yes
SKIPUNCI	Skip uncommitted inserts	YES, **NO**	Yes
SMF89	Measured usage pricing	YES, **NO**	Yes
SMFACCT	SMF accounting	NO, **YES(1)**, *list* (1–5,7,8), *	No
SMFSTAT	SMF statistics	**YES (1,3,4)**, NO, list(1–5) , *	No
SMSDCFL	SMS data class for file tablespace	**Blank**, 1–8 char	Yes
SMSDCIX	SMS data class for index tablespace	**Blank**, 1–8 char	Yes
SPRMEDX			Yes
SPRMLTD			
SQLDELI	SQL string delimiter	**Default**, ', "	—
SRTPOOL	Sort pool size	240K–64000K; **2MB**	Yes
SSID	Subsystem name	**DSN**, *SSID*	—
STARJOIN	Enabling star join	**Disable**, enable, 1, 2–32768	Yes
STATHIST	Collect historical statistics	SPACE, **NONE**, ALL, ACCESSPATH	Yes
STATSINT	Time to write RTS stats	1–1440 min; **30**	Yes
STATROLL	Runstats aggregates partition-level statistics	YES, **NO**	Yes
STATIME	Statistics time	1–1440 min; **30**	Yes
STDSQL	Standard SQL language	**NO**, YES	—
STORMXAB	Max abend count	**0**–225	Yes
STORPROC	DB2 procedure name	1–8 char; *ssnm*SPAS	No
STORTIME	Timeout value	5–1800 sec; **180**	Yes
SUPERRS	Suppress Logrec recording during soft errors	**YES**, NO	Yes

Table 2.1: DB2 DSNZPARMs *(continued)*			
Parameter	**Description**	**Acceptable values (defaults appear in bold)**	**Updatable online?**
SVOLARC	Single volume	YES, **NO**	Yes
SYNCVAL	Statistics sync	**NO**, 0–59	Yes
SYSADM	System admin 1	**SYSADM**, *authid*	Yes
SYSADM2	System admin 2	**SYSADM**, *authid*	Yes
SYSOPR1	System operator 1	**SYSOPR**, *authid*	Yes
SYSOPR2	System operator 2	**SYSOPR**; *authid*	Yes
SYSTEM_LEVEL_ BACKUPS	System-level backups	**YES**, NO	Yes
TBSBP8K	Default 8K BP for user data	Any 8K buffer pool; **BP8K0**	Yes
TBSBP16K	Default 16K BP for user data	Any 16K buffer pool; **BP16K0**	Yes
TBSBP32K	Default 32K BP for user data	Any 32K buffer pool; **BP32K0**	Yes
TBSBPOOL	Default buffer pool for user Data	**BP0**–BP*x*	Yes
TCPALVER	TCP/IP already verified	**NO**, YES	Yes
TCPKPALV	TCP/IP keep alive	**ENABLE**, DISABLE, 1–65524	Yes
TIME	Time format	**ISO**, JIS, USA, EUR, LOCAL	—
TIMELEN	Local time length	**0**, 8–254	—
TRACLOC	Size of local trace table	**16** (4K bytes)	
TRACSTR	Trace auto start	**NO**, YES (1–3), list (1–9)	No
TRACTBL	Trace size	4K–396K; **64K**	No
TRKRSITE	Remote tracker site usage	**NO**, YES	No
TSQTY	Default allocation for tablespace	**0**–4194304	Yes
TSTAMP	Timestamp archives	**NO**, YES	Yes
TWOACTV	Number of active copies	**2**, 1	No
TWOARCH	Number of archive copies	**2**, 1	No
TWOBSDS	Number of BSDSs	YES, NO	No
UGCCSID	Unicode CCSID (graphic)	**1208**	—
UIFCIDS	Unicode IFCIDS	YES, **NO**	Yes
UMCCSID	Unicode CCSID (Mixed)	**1208**	—
UNIT	Device type 1	**TAPE**, any device	Yes
UNIT2	Device type 2	**Device or unit name**	Yes
URCHKTH	UR check frequency	**0–255**	Yes
URLGWTH	UR log write check	0K–**1000K**	Yes
USCCSID	Unicode CCSID (single-byte)	**1208**	—
UTILS_DUMP_CL ASS_NAME	Dump class name	**Blank**, valid DFSMS dump class name	

Table 2.1: DB2 DSNZPARMs (continued)			
Parameter	Description	Acceptable values (defaults appear in bold)	Updatable online?
UTIMOUT	Utility timeout	1–254; **6**	Yes
VOLTDEVT	Temporary unit name	**SYSDA**, valid name	Yes
WLMENV	WLM environment	Valid name (1–18 char)	Yes
XLKUPDT	X lock for searched U/D	YES, **NO**	Yes

Commands

Commands in the DB2 environment fall into six categories:

- the DSN command and its subcommands

- DB2 commands

- IMS commands

- CICS attachment facility commands

- MVS IRLM commands

- TSO CLISTs

In this section, we look at the first two groups: the DSN commands and the DB2 commands.

DSN Commands

DSN is the DB2 command processor and executes as a TSO command processor. All its subcommands, except SPUFI, run under DSN in either the foreground or the background, and all except END also run under DB2I. SPUFI runs only in the foreground under ISPF.

Table 2.2 lists the DSN commands and their functions.

Table 2.2: DSN commands	
DSN command (or subcommand)	**Function**
ABEND	Causes the DSN session to terminate with a X'04E'
BIND	Builds an application package or plan
DB2	Executes a DB2 command
DCLGEN	Produces declarations for tables or views
DSN	Starts a DSN session
END	Ends a DSN session
FREE	Deletes an application package or plan
REBIND	Updates an application package or plan
REBIND TRIGGER PACKAGE	Updates an application trigger package
RUN	Executes an application program
SPUFI	Executes the SQL Processing Using File Input facility
*	Comment

DB2 Commands

Table 2.3 lists the DB2 commands and their functions. You can issue the START DB2 command only from a z/OS console (or from an Authorized Program Facility, or APF, authorized program that passes the command to the console). All other DB2 commands can be issued from:

- a z/OS console or z/OS application program
- a TSO terminal session
- a DB2I panel
- an IMS terminal
- a CICS terminal
- an APF-authorized program
- an IFI application program

An application program can issue DB2 commands using the DB2 instrumentation facility interface. DB2 commands issued from a z/OS console are not associated with any secondary authorization IDs.

Table 2.3: DB2 commands	
DB2 command	**Function**
-ACCESS DATABASE(DB2)	Forces a physical open of a table space, index space, or partition or removes group buffer pool (GBP) dependent status for a table space, index space, or partition
-ALTER BUFFERPOOL	Alters attributes for the buffer pools
-ALTER GROUPBUFFERPOOL	Alters attributes for the group buffer pools
-ALTER UTILITY	Alters parameter values of the REORG utility
-ARCHIVE LOG	Enables a site to close a current active log and open the next available log data set
-CANCEL THREAD	Cancels processing for specific local or distributed threads
-DISPLAY ARCHIVE	Displays information about archive log processing
-DISPLAY BUFFERPOOL	Displays information about the buffer pools
-DISPLAY DATABASE	Displays status information about DB2 databases
-DISPLAY DDF	Displays information about the status and configuration of the distributed data facility as well as statistical information regarding connections or threads controlled by DDF
-DISPLAY FUNCTION SPECIFIC	Displays statistics about external user-defined functions
-DISPLAY GROUP	Displays information about the data sharing group to which a DB2 subsystem belongs and reports the mode in which DB2 is operating
-DISPLAY GROUPBUFFERPOOL	Displays status information about DB2 group buffer pools
-DISPLAY LOCATION	Displays status information about distributed threads
-DISPLAY LOG	Displays log information and status of the offload task
-DISPLAY PROCEDURE	Displays status information about stored procedures
-DISPLAY PROFILE	Displays whether a profile is active or inactive
-DISPLAY RLIMIT	Displays status information about the resource limit facility (governor)
-DISPLAY THREAD	Displays information about DB2 threads
-DISPLAY TRACE	Displays information about DB2 traces
-DISPLAY UTILITY	Displays status information about a DB2 utility
-MODIFY TRACE	Changes the IFCIDs (trace events) associated with a particular active trace
-RECOVER BSDS	Reestablishes dual bootstrap data sets
-RECOVER INDOUBT	Recovers threads left in doubt
-RECOVER POSTPONED	Completes back-out processing for units of recovery left incomplete during an earlier restart

Table 2.3: DB2 commands (continued)	
DB2 command	**Function**
-REFRESH DB2, EARLY	Reloads the EARLY modules and rebuilds the EARLY control block
-RESET GENERICLU	Purges information stored by VTAM in the coupling facility
-RESET INDOUBT	Purges information displayed in the in-doubt thread report generated by the -DISPLAY THREAD command
-SET ARCHIVE	Controls the allocation of tape units and the deallocation time of the tape units for archive log processing
-SET LOG	Modifies the checkpoint frequency
-SET SYSPARM	Loads the subsystem parameters specified in the command
-START DATABASE	Makes the specified database available for use
-START DB2	Initializes the DB2 subsystem (can be issued only from a z/OS console)
-START DDF	Starts the distributed data facility
-START FUNCTION SPECIFIC	Activates an external function that is stopped
-START PROCEDURE	Activates the definition of stopped or cached stored procedures
-START PROFILE	Loads or reloads the profile table into a data structure in memory
-START RLIMIT	Starts the resource limit facility (governor)
-START TRACE	Initiates DB2 trace activity 300
-STOP DATABASE	Makes specified databases unavailable for applications
-STOP DB2	Stops the DB2 subsystem
-STOP DDF	Stops the distributed data facility
-STOP FUNCTION SPECIFIC	Stops the acceptance of SQL statements for specified functions
-STOP PROCEDURE	Stops the acceptance of SQL CALL statements for stored procedures
-STOP RLIMIT	Stops the resource limit facility (governor)
-STOP TRACE	Stops trace activity
-TERM UTILITY	Terminates execution of a utility

A DSN9022I message indicates the normal end of DB2 command processing. Message DSN9023I indicates the abnormal end of DB2 command processing.

DB2 Utilities

You can think of DB2 utilities in two general categories: those that execute within the subsystem (online) and those that are standalone and run outside the subsystem (offline). The following list shows the activities that the utilities perform. We discuss each tool in detail in the noted chapter. In this section, we describe how to execute the DB2 utilities and various commands.

- Loading data (Chapter 7)

- Reorganizing data (Chapter 7)

- Gathering statistics (Chapter 7)

- Repairing data (Chapter 7)

- Recovering data and indexes (Chapter 8)

- Rebuilding indexes (Chapter 8)

- Quiescing data (Chapter 8)

Executing the Utilities

The most common way to execute the DB2 utilities is to create JCL with the appropriate control cards. You must execute the utilities on the subsystem where the objects reside (this requirement differs in a data sharing environment; for more information, see Chapter 9). You also have other options for utility execution. Let's look briefly at each alternative.

DB2I

The DB2I interface provides a panel you can use to generate JCL and run utilities. This option doesn't require a great deal of JCL knowledge, and you can save the jobs for future execution and editing. Figure 2.8 shows a sample DB2I panel for DB2 utilities.

```
DB2 UTILITIES                    SSID: DSN
===>

Select from the following:

 1 FUNCTION ===> EDITJCL            (SUBMIT job, EDITJCL, DISPLAY, TERMINATE)
 2 JOB ID   ===> TEMP              (A unique job identifier string)
 3 UTILITY  ===>                   (CHECK DATA, CHECK INDEX, CHECK LOB,
                                    COPY, DIAGNOSE, LOAD, MERGE, MODIFY,
                                    QUIESCE, REBUILD, RECOVER, REORG INDEX,
                                    REORG LOB, REORG TABLESPACE, REPORT,
                                    REPAIR, RUNSTATS, STOSPACE, UNLOAD)

 4 STATEMENT DATA SET ===> UTIL

Specify restart or preview option, otherwise enter NO.

 5 RESTART  ===> NO                (NO, CURRENT, PHASE or PREVIEW)

 6 LISTDEF? (YES|NO) ===>          TEMPLATE? (YES|NO) ===>

 * The data set names panel will be displayed when required by a utility.

PRESS:  ENTER to process     END to exit     HELP for more information
```

Figure 2.8: DB2 Utilities panel

DSNU CLIST Command

You can invoke a DB2 online utility by running the DSNU CLIST command under TSO. The CLIST command generates the JCL data set required to execute the DSNUPROC procedure and to execute online utilities as batch jobs. When you use this command, you needn't concern yourself with details of the JCL data set.

The CLIST command creates a job to perform one utility operation only. To perform multiple utility operations, you can issue the command for each operation you want to perform and then edit and merge the outputs into one job or step.

Control Center

The DB2 Control Center supports utility execution as well. Using its wildcarding capability, you execute utilities against a list of objects that match a specified pattern of matching characters. With this support, you could create a utility procedure that would let you run a mixture of several utilities against several objects with one command, making maintenance much easier for the DBA. There is also support for restarting utilities from the last committed phase (phase) or the last committed point (current). This functionality is available only for utilities originally started in the Control Center. The restart is accessible through the Display Utility dialog.

Support is also available for utility IDs. The Tools Settings notebook provides an option to create a utility ID template using a variety of variables, such as USERID and UTILNAME. You can edit the utility ID to make it more meaningful before executing the utility.

DSNUTILS

DSNUTILS is a DB2-supplied stored procedure that enables execution of utilities from a local or remote application via an SQL CALL. The client application calls DSNUTILS with appropriate parameters. DSNUTILS then analyzes the parameters to create a SYSIN stream and allocate all necessary data sets. After the data sets are allocated, DSNUTILS calls the utility batch module DSNUTILB, which executes the appropriate utility. The utility statements are processed, and DSNUTILS retrieves the data (execution results) from the SYSPRINT file, puts it in the SYSIBM.SYSPRINT temporary table, opens a cursor on the table, and returns control to the client application. The client application then fetches all rows from the result set. Figure 2.9 depicts this execution flow.

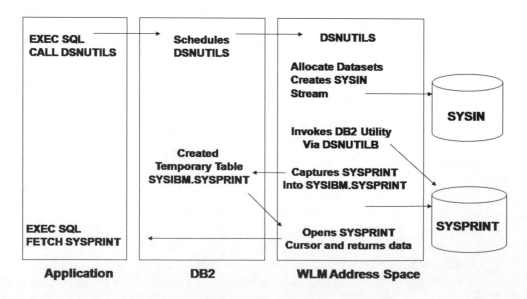

Figure 2.9: DSNUTILS stored procedure execution

For more information about stored procedures, see Chapter 13.

DSNUTILU

Stored procedure DSNUTILU enables you to provide control statements in Unicode UTF-8 characters instead of EBCDIC characters to execute DB2 utilities from a DB2 application program.

Utility Templates

Some DB2 utilities produce data sets as a byproduct or an end result of utility execution. These data sets are referenced on utility control statements by a set of DD name keywords and are specified in detail on the corresponding JCL DD cards.

The DD cards must be coded for each utility, as required, and must be maintained over time as the structure of data changes. Database administrators establish data set policies, refer to those policies on utility control statements, and let DB2 utilities administer the policies at execution time. Many DB2 utilities will accept a template construct in lieu of DD cards to dynamically allocate utility data sets.

Templates contain

- the data set naming convention
- DFSMS parameters
- DASD or TAPE allocation parameters

You can specify a TEMPLATE in the SYSIN data set, ahead of the utility control statement that references it, or in one or more TEMPLATE data sets. You specify the TEMPLATE data set DD name on the OPTIONS utility control statement using the format TEMPLATEDD(*ddname*); this name applies to all subsequent utility control statements until the end of input or until DB2 encounters a new OPTIONS TEMPLATEDD(*ddname*) specification. The default TEMPLATE data set DD name is SYSTEMPL.

TEMPLATE data sets may contain only TEMPLATE utility control statements. Any TEMPLATE defined within SYSIN overrides another TEMPLATE definition of the same name found in a TEMPLATE data set. With this functionality, database administrators can standardize data set allocation and the utility control statements that refer to those data sets, reducing the need to customize and alter utility job streams.

You can't use templates with the REPAIR utility.

You can use the TEMPLATE specification for both DASD and TAPE data set allocation, including the support for data set stacking on tape and generation data group (GDG) base definition. TEMPLATE syntax also allows user-specified DASD SPACE parameters. If you don't specify the SPACE keyword, the size of the data set will be estimated based on formulas that vary by utility and by data set.

The TEMPLATE statement required for a COPY example might look something like this:

```
TEMPLATE tmp1
DSNAME(DB2.&TS..D&JDATE..COPY&ICTYPE.&LOCREM.&PRIBAK.)
VOLUMES(vol1,vol2,vol3)
TEMPLATE tmp2
DSNAME(DB2.&TS..D&JDATE..COPY&ICTYPE.&LOCREM.&PRIBAK.)
VOLUMES(vol4,vol5,vol6)
LISTDEF payroll INCLUDE TABLESPACE CERTTS.*
INCLUDE INDEXSPACE CERTTS.*IX
EXCLUDE TABLESPACE CERTTS.TEMP*
EXCLUDE INDEXSPACE CERTTS.TMPIX*
COPY LIST payroll ...COPYDDN(tmp1,tmp1)RECOVERYDDN(tmp2,tmp2)
```

By using the PREVIEW function, database administrators can check their utility control statements without actual execution. In PREVIEW mode, DB2 expands all TEMPLATE data set names appearing in the SYSIN DD, as well as any from the TEMPLATE DD that are referenced on a utility control statement. DB2 then prints the information to the SYSPRINT data set and halts execution. You can specify PREVIEW in one of two ways: either as a JCL PARM or on the OPTIONS PREVIEW utility control statement.

For more information about templates and the DB2 utilities, see the *IBM DB2 9 for z/OS Utility Guide and Reference.*

Displaying Utilities

You can display DB2 utilities to see important runtime information about the jobs, including jobs running in a data sharing group. The output provides information about

- the type of utility
- how much of the processing the utility has completed
- the status of the utility
- the member on which the utility is executing
- the current phase of the utility

Catalog and Directory

The DB2 catalog and directory act as central repositories for all information about objects, authorizations, and communications related to the support and operations of DB2.

DB2 Catalog

The *DB2 catalog* consists of several DB2 tables and can be accessed via SQL. It contains details about DB2 objects obtained from SQL Data Definition Language (DDL) when an object is created or altered or from the Data Control Language (DCL) when an authorization is granted on an object or group of objects. The DB2 catalog also contains information about communications with other DB2 and non-DB2 databases through the use of the communications database (CDB), which contains information about VTAM and TCP/IP addresses.

Table 2.4 lists the DB2 catalog tables and the types of information each table contains.

For detailed descriptions of all the columns in the DB2 catalog tables, consult Appendix G of the IBM DB2 9 for z/OS SQL Reference.

Table 2.4: DB2 catalog tables	
Catalog table (SYSIBM.*table*)	**Information contents**
IPLIST	Lets multiple IP addresses be specified for a given LOCATION. Insert rows into this table when you want to define a remote DB2 data sharing group. Rows can be inserted, updated, and deleted.
IPNAMES	Defines the remote DRDA servers DB2 can access using TCP/IP. Rows in this table can be inserted, updated, and deleted.
LOCATIONS	Contains a row for each accessible remote server. The row associates a LOCATION name with the TCP/IP or SNA network attributes for the remote server. Requesters are not defined in this table. Rows in this table can be inserted, updated, and deleted.
LULIST	Lets you specify multiple LU names for a given LOCATION. Insert rows into this table when you want to define a remote DB2 data sharing group. The same value for LUNAME column cannot appear in both the SYSIBM.LUNAMES table and the SYSIBM.LULIST table. Rows in this table can be inserted, updated, and deleted.
LUMODES	Each row of the table provides VTAM with conversation limits for a specific combination of LUNAME and MODENAME. The table is accessed only during the initial conversation limit negotiation between DB2 and a remote LU. This negotiation is called *change-number-of-sessions (CNOS)* processing. Rows in this table can be inserted, updated, and deleted.
LUNAMES	Contains a row for each remote SNA client or server that communicates with DB2. Rows can be inserted, updated, or deleted.
MODESELECT	Associates a mode name with any conversation created to support an outgoing SQL request. Each row represents one or more combinations of LUNAME, authorization ID, and application plan name. Rows in this table can be inserted, updated, and deleted.
SYSAUXRELS	Contains one row for each auxiliary table created for a large object (LOB) column. A base table space that is partitioned must have one auxiliary table for each partition of each LOB column.
SYSCHECKDEP	Contains one row for each reference to a column in a table check constraint.
SYSCHECKS	Contains one row for each table check constraint.
SYSCHECKS2	Contains one row for each table check constraint created in or after DB2 for OS/390 V7.
SYSCOLAUTH	Records the UPDATE or REFERENCES privileges held by users on individual columns of a table or view.
SYSCOLDIST	Contains one or more rows for the first key column of an index key. Rows in this table can be inserted, updated, and deleted.

Table 2.4: DB2 catalog tables (continued)	
Catalog table (SYSIBM.*table*)	Information contents
SYSCOLDIST_HIST	Contains rows from table SYSCOLDIST. Whenever rows are added or changed in SYSCOLDIST, the rows are also written to the new history table. Rows in this table can be inserted, updated, and deleted.
SYSCOLDISTSTATS	Contains zero or more rows per partition for the first key column of a partitioning index or Data Partitioned Secondary Index (DPSI). Rows are inserted when RUNSTATS scans index partitions of the partitioning index. No row is inserted if the index is a nonpartitioning index. Rows in this table can be inserted, updated, and deleted.
SYSCOLSTATS	Contains partition statistics for selected columns. For each column, a row exists for each partition in the table. Rows are inserted when RUNSTATS collects either indexed column statistics or nonindexed column statistics for a partitioned table space. No row is inserted if the table space is nonpartitioned. Rows in this table can be inserted, updated, and deleted.
SYSCOLUMNS	Contains one row for every column of each table and view.
SYSCOLUMNS_HIST	Contains rows from table SYSCOLUMNS. Whenever rows are added or changed in SYSCOLUMNS, the rows are also written to the new history table. Rows in this table can be inserted, updated, and deleted.
SYSCONSTDEP	Records dependencies on check constraints or user-defined defaults for a column.
SYSCONTEXT	Contains one row for each trusted context.
SYSCONTEXTAUTHIDS	Contains one row for each authid with which a trusted context can be used.
SYSCOPY	Contains information needed for recovery.
SYSCTXTTRUSTATTRS	Contains one row for each list of attributes for a given trusted context.
SYSDATABASE	Contains one row for each database, except for database DSNDB01.
SYSDATATYPES	Contains one row for each distinct type defined to the system.
SYSDBAUTH	Records the privileges held by users over databases.
SYSDBRM	Contains one row for each DBRM of each application plan.
SYSDEPENDENCIES	Records the dependencies between objects.
SYSDUMMY1	Contains one row. The table is used for SQL statements in which a table reference is required but the table's contents aren't important.
SYSENVIRONMENT	Records the environment variables when an object is created.
SYSFIELDS	Contains one row for every column that has a field procedure.

Table 2.4: DB2 catalog tables (continued)	
Catalog table (SYSIBM.*table*)	**Information contents**
SYSFOREIGNKEYS	Contains one row for every column of every foreign key.
SYSINDEXES	Contains one row for every index.
SYSINDEXES_HIST	Contains rows from table SYSINDEXES. Whenever rows are added or changed in SYSINDEXES, the rows are also written to the new history table. Rows in this table can be inserted, updated, and deleted.
SYSINDEXPART	Contains one row for each nonpartitioning index and one row for each partition of a partitioning index or a DPSI.
SYSINDEXPART_HIST	Contains rows from table SYSINDEXPART. Whenever rows are added or changed in SYSINDEXPART, the rows are also written to the new history table. Rows in this table can be inserted, updated, and deleted.
SYSINDEXSTATS	Contains one row for each partition of a partitioning index. Rows in this table can be inserted, updated, and deleted.
SYSINDEXSTATS_HIST	Contains rows from table SYSINDEXSTATS. Whenever rows are added or changed in SYSINDEXSTATS, the rows are also written to the new history table. Rows in this table can be inserted, updated, and deleted.
SYSJARCLASS_SOURCE	Serves as an auxiliary table for table SYSCONTENTS.
SYSJARCONTENTS	Contains Java class source for installed Java Archive (JAR).
SYSJARDATA	Serves as an auxiliary table for table SYSOBJECTS.
SYSJAROBJECTS	Contains binary large objects representing the installed jar.
SYSJAVAOPTS	Contains build options used during INSTALL_JAR.
SYSJAVAPATHS	Contains the complete JAR resolution path and records the dependencies one JAR has on its JAR in its Java path.
SYSKEYCOLUSE	Contains a row for every column in a unique constraint (primary key or unique key) from the SYSTABCONST table.
SYSKEYS	Contains one row for each column of an index key.
SYSKEYTARGETS	Contains one row for each key-target that is participating in an extended index definition.
SYSKEYTARGETS_HIST	Contains rows from the SYSKEYTARGETS table whenever rows are added or changed.
SYSKEYTARGETSTATS	Contains partition statistics for select key-targets.
SYSKEYTGTDIST	Contains one or more rows for the first key-target of an extended index key.
SYSKEYTGTDIST_HIST	Contains rows from table SYSKEYTGTDIST whenever rows are added or changed in SYSKEYTGTDIST.
SYSKEYTGTDISTSTATS	Contains zero or more rows per partition for the first key-target of a partitioned secondary index.

Table 2.4: DB2 catalog tables (continued)	
Catalog table (SYSIBM.*table*)	**Information contents**
SYSLOBSTATS	Contains one row for each LOB table space.
SYSLOBSTATS_HIST	Contains rows from table SYSLOBSTATS. Whenever rows are added or changed in SYSLOBSTATS, the rows are also written to the new history table. Rows in this table can be inserted, updated, and deleted.
SYSOBJROLEDEP	Lists the dependence object for each role.
SYSPACKAGE	Contains a row for every package.
SYSPACKAUTH	Records the privileges held by users over packages.
SYSPACKDEP	Records the dependencies of packages on local tables, views, synonyms, table spaces, indexes and aliases, functions, and stored procedures.
SYSPACKLIST	Contains one or more rows for every local application plan bound with a package list. Each row represents a unique entry in the plan's package list.
SYSPACKSTMT	Contains one or more rows for each statement in a package.
SYSPARMS	Contains a row for each parameter of a routine or multiple rows for table parameters (one for each column of the table).
SYSPKSYSTEM	Contains zero or more rows for every package. Each row for a given package represents one or more connections to an environment in which the package could be executed.
SYSPLAN	Contains one row for each application plan.
SYSPLANAUTH	Records the privileges held by users over application plans.
SYSPLANDEP	Records the dependencies of plans on tables, views, aliases, synonyms, table spaces, indexes, functions, and stored procedures.
SYSPLSYSTEM	Contains zero or more rows for every plan. Each row for a given plan represents one or more connections to an environment in which the plan could be used.
SYSRELS	Contains one row for every referential constraint.
SYSRESAUTH	Records CREATE IN and PACKADM ON privileges for collections, USAGE privileges for distinct types, and USE privileges for buffer pools, storage groups, and table spaces.
SYSROLES	Contains one row for each role.
SYSROUTINEAUTH	Records the privileges held by users on routines. (A routine can be a user-defined function, cast function, or stored procedure.)
SYSROUTINES	Contains a row for every routine. (A routine can be a user-defined function, cast function, or stored procedure.)
SYSROUTINES_OPTS	Contains a row for each generated routine, such as one created by the DB2 Stored Procedure Builder tool, that records the build options for the routine. Rows in this table can be inserted, updated, and deleted.

Table 2.4: DB2 catalog tables (continued)	
Catalog table (SYSIBM.*table*)	**Information contents**
SYSROUTINES_SRC	Contains source for generated routines, such as those created by the DB2/zOS Procedure Process or DSNTPSMP.
SYSROUTINESTEXT	Serves as an auxiliary table for the TEXT column of table SYSROUTINES and is required to hold the LOB data.
SYSSCHEMAAUTH	Contains one or more rows for each user that is granted a privilege on a particular schema in the database.
SYSSEQUENCEAUTH	Records the privileges held by users over sequences.
SYSSEQUENCES	Contains one row for each identity column.
SYSSEQUENCESDEP	Records the dependencies of identity columns on tables.
SYSSTMT	Contains one or more rows for each SQL statement of each DBRM.
SYSSTOGROUP	Contains one row for each storage group.
SYSSTRINGS	Contains information about character conversion. Each row describes a conversion from one coded character set to another.
SYSSYNONYMS	Contains one row for each synonym of a table or view.
SYSTABAUTH	Records the privileges users hold on tables and views.
SYSTABCONST	Contains one row for each unique constraint (primary key or unique key) created in DB2 for OS/390 Version 7 or later.
SYSTABLEPART	Contains one row for each nonpartitioned table space and one row for each partition of a partitioned table space.
SYSTABLEPART_HIST	Contains rows from table SYSTABLEPART. Rows are added or changed when RUNSTATS collects history statistics. Rows in this table can be inserted, updated, and deleted.
SYSTABLES	Contains one row for each table, view, or alias.
SYSTABLES_HIST	Contains rows from table SYSTABLES. Rows are added or changed when RUNSTATS collects history statistics. Rows in this table can be inserted, updated, and deleted.
SYSTABLESPACE	Contains one row for each table space.
SYSTABSTATS	Contains one row for each partition of a partitioned table space. Rows in this table can be inserted, updated, and deleted.
SYSTABSTATS_HIST	Contains rows from table SYSTABSTATS. Rows are added or changed when RUNSTATS collects history statistics. Rows in this table can be inserted, updated, and deleted.
SYSTRIGGERS	Contains one row for each trigger.
SYSUSERAUTH	Records the system privileges held by users.
SYSVIEWDEP	Records the dependencies of views on tables, functions, and other views.

Table 2.4: DB2 catalog tables (continued)	
Catalog table (SYSIBM.*table*)	**Information contents**
SYSVIEWS	Contains one or more rows for each view.
SYSVOLUMES	Contains one row for each volume of each storage group.
SYSUSERNAMES	Each row in this table is used to carry out one of the following operations: • Outbound ID translation • Inbound ID translation and "come from" checking Rows in this table can be inserted, updated, and deleted.
SYSXSRCOMPONENT	Auxiliary table for BLOB column COMPONENT in table SYSXRSOBJECTCOMPONENTS.
SYSXSROBJECTCOMPONENTS	Contains one row for each component (document) in an XML schema.
SYSXSROBJECTGRAMMER	Serves as an auxiliary table for the BLOB column GRAMMER in table SYSXSROBJECTS.
SYSXSROBJECTHIERARCHIES	Contains one row for each component (document) in an XML schema to record the XML schema document hierarchy relationship.
SYSXSROBJECTPROPERTY	Serves as an auxiliary table for the BLOB column PROPERTIES in table SYSXRSOBJECTS.
SYSXSROBJECTS	Contains one row for each registered XML schema.
SYSXSRPROPERTY	Serves as an auxiliary table for the BLOB column COMPONENT in table SYSXRSOBJECTCOMPONENTS.

Catalog Consistency Queries

To ensure that the data in the catalog is correct, you can execute consistency queries as part of the migration process. The queries, found in the data set *prefix*.SDSNSAMP(DSNTESQ), test logical relationships, such as ensuring that all indexes are created on tables that exist.

You can execute the SQL statements from SPUFI or from a dynamic SQL program such as DSNTEP2. The queries can be run on the actual catalog tables or on copies of the catalog. To ensure the best performance, execute RUNSTATS on the catalog or the copies. In some cases, the queries will perform better when executed on the copies, using the extra indexes as defined for some of the tables.

Here's an example of a catalog consistency query that verifies that all table spaces belong to a defined database. This query will find all databases in table SYSTABLESPACE that lack corresponding rows in SYSDATABASE. The desired (and expected) result is to have no rows returned.

```
SELECT DBNAME, NAME
    FROM SYSIBM.SYSTABLESPACE TS
    WHERE NOT EXISTS
      (SELECT *
          FROM SYSIBM.SYSDATABASE DB
          WHERE DB.NAME = TS.DBNAME);
```

DB2 Directory

The *DB2 directory* stores information about the operation and housekeeping of the DB2 environment. In contrast to the DB2 catalog, the directory cannot be accessed using SQL. The DB2 directory contains information required to start DB2, and there are activities and utilities in the DB2 environment that actually do the updating and deleting of table entries in the directory. The DB2 directory contains five tables; Table 2.5 provides a description of each.

Table 2.5: DB2 directory tables	
Directory table	**Information contents**
SPT01	Referred to as the *skeleton package table (SKPT)*, this table contains information about access paths and the internal form of the SQL for a package at bind time. Entries are made into this table during bind time (BIND PACKAGE) and are deleted when a package is freed (FREE PACKAGE). This table is loaded into memory at execution time (along with the SCT02 table, described next).
SCT02	Referred to as the *skeleton cursor table (SKCT)*, this table contains information about access paths and the internal form of the SQL for an application plan. Entries in the table are made when a plan is bound (BIND PLAN) and are deleted when a plan is freed (FREE PLAN). Like table SPT01, this table is loaded into memory at execution time.
DBD01	This table holds information about database descriptors (DBDs), which are internal control blocks. Each database in DB2 has one DBD for its objects (table spaces, indexes, tables, referential integrity constraints, and check constraints). Updates to the table are made when a database is created or updated. DB2 accesses this information instead of continually using the DB2 catalog. This mechanism allows for faster, more efficient access to the information. The information this directory table is also contained in the DB2 catalog.
SYSLGRNX	Referred to as the *log range table*, this table contains information from the DB2 logs about the Relative Byte Address (RBA) range for updates. This information lets DB2 efficiently find the RBAs it needs from the DB2 logs for recovery purposes. A row is inserted every time a table space or partition is opened or updated and is updated when the object is closed.
SYSUTILX	The system utilities table stores information about the execution of DB2 utilities, including status and execution steps. DB2 uses this information when it needs to restart a utility. Information in this table is added when a utility is started; the entry is removed when the execution has ended.

Distributed Data

Using DB2's distributed data facility, you can access data held by other data management systems or make your DB2 data accessible to other systems. A DB2 application program can use SQL to access data at DBMSs other than the DB2 at which the application's plan is bound. This *local DB2* and the other DBMSs are called *application servers*. Any application server other than the local DB2 is considered a *remote server*, and access to its data is a distributed operation. DB2 uses DRDA to access data at remote application servers.

For application servers that support the two-phase commit process, both methods permit the updating of data at several remote locations within the same unit of work.

You define the location name of the DB2 subsystem during DB2 installation. The communications database records the location name and network address of a remote DBMS. The tables in the CDB are part of the DB2 catalog.

DRDA

With DRDA (the recommended method), an application connects to a server at another location and executes packages that have been previously bound at that server. To access the server, the application uses a CONNECT statement, a three-part name, or an alias (for packages bound with DBPROTOCOL(DRDA)).

Queries can originate from any system or application that issues SQL statements as an *application requester* in the formats required by DRDA. DRDA access supports the execution of dynamic SQL statements and SQL statements that satisfy all the following conditions:

- The static statements appear in a package bound to an accessible server.

- The statements are executed using that package.

- The objects involved in the execution of the statements are at the server where the package is bound. If the server is a DB2 subsystem, three-part names and aliases can be used to refer to another DB2 server.

You can use DRDA access in application programs by coding explicit CONNECT statements or by coding three-part names and specifying the DBPROTOCOL(DRDA) bind option. For more information about bind options, refer to Chapter 11.

DRDA access is based on a set of protocols known as Distributed Relational Database Architecture. (The Open Group Technical Standard documents these protocols in *DRDA Volume 1: Distributed Relational Database Architecture (DRDA)*.) DRDA communications conventions are invisible to DB2 applications and let DB2 bind and rebind packages at other servers and execute the statements in those packages.

For two-phase commit using SNA connections, DB2 supports both presumed abort and presumed nothing protocols defined by DRDA. If you're using TCP/IP, DB2 uses the sync point manager defined in the documentation for DRDA Level 3.

Communications Protocols

DB2's distributed data facility uses TCP/IP or SNA to communicate with other systems. Setting up a network for use by database management systems requires knowledge of both database management and communications. Thus, you must put together a team of people with those skills to plan and implement the network.

TCP/IP

Transmission Control Protocol/Internet Protocol is a standard communications protocol for network communications. Previous versions of DB2 supported TCP/IP requesters, although additional software and configuration was necessary. Native TCP/IP eliminates these requirements, allowing gateway-less connectivity to DB2 for systems running UNIX System Services.

SNA

System Network Architecture describes the logical structure, formats, protocols, and operational sequences for transmitting information through and controlling the configuration and operation of the networks.

VTAM

DB2 also uses Virtual Telecommunications Access Method to communicate with remote databases. To permit this access, you assign two names to the local DB2 subsystem: a *location name* and a *logical unit name (LU name)*. A location name distinguishes a specific DBMS in a network, and applications use this name to direct requests to the local DB2 subsystem. Other systems use different terms for a location name. For example, DB2 Connect calls it the *target database name*. DB2 uses the DRDA term, *RDBNAM*, to refer to non-DB2 relational database names.

Communications Database

The DB2 catalog includes the communications database, which contains several tables that hold information about connections with remote systems:

- SYSIBM.LOCATIONS

- SYSIBM.LUNAMES

- SYSIBM.IPNAMES

- SYSIBM.MODESELECT

- SYSIBM.USERNAMES

- SYSIBM.LULIST

- SYSIBM.LUMODES

Some of these tables must be populated before you can request data from remote systems. If the DB2 system services only data requests, the CDB doesn't have to be populated; you can use the default values.

When sending a request, DB2 uses the LINKNAME column of the SYSIBM.LOCATIONS catalog table to determine which protocol to use.

- To receive VTAM requests, an LUNAME must be selected in installation panel DSNTIPR.

- To receive TCP/IP requests, a DRDA port and a resynchronization port must be selected in installation panel DSNTIP5. TCP/IP uses the server's port number to pass network requests to the correct DB2 subsystem. If the value in the LINKNAME column is found in table SYSIBM.IPNAMES, DB2 uses TCP/IP for DRDA connections. If the value is found in SYSIBM.LUNAMES table, SNA is used.

- If the same name exists in both SYSIBM.LUNAMES and SYSIBM.IPNAMES, DB2 uses TCP/IP to connect to the location.

A requester cannot connect to a given location using both the SNA and TCP/IP protocols. For example, if the SYSIBM.LOCATIONS table specifies a LINKNAME of LU1 and LU1 is defined in both SYSIBM.IPNAMES and SYSIBM.LUNAMES, TCP/IP is the only protocol DB2 uses to connect to LU1 from this requester for DRDA connections. For private protocol connections, the SNA protocols are used. If private protocol connections are being used, the SYSIBM.LUNAMES table must be defined for the remote location's LUNAME.

Subsystem Pools

The DBM1 address space contains many objects critical to the operation of DB2. In this section, we take a brief look at buffer pools, the RID pool, the EDM pool, and the sort pool. For information about tuning these pools for performance, refer to Chapter 17.

Buffer Pools

Buffer pools are database objects used to cache database data pages in memory. If an object's data page is placed in a buffer pool, physical I/O access to disks will be avoided. Buffer pools can be assigned to cache only a particular table space's data. This assignment takes place within the table space definition.

Buffer pools are areas of virtual storage that temporarily store pages of table spaces or indexes. When a program accesses a row of a table, DB2 places the page containing that row in a buffer. When a program changes a row of a table, DB2 must write the data in the buffer back to disk (eventually) — normally either at a checkpoint or a write threshold. A write threshold is set either as a vertical threshold at the page set level or as a horizontal threshold at the buffer pool level. Storage for buffer pools is in real memory above the 2 GB bar.

Up to 80 virtual buffer pools are available, allowing for the following breakdown:

- 50 4K page buffer pools (BP0–BP49)

- 10 32K page buffer pools (BP32K– BP32K9)

- 10 8K page buffer pools

- 10 16K page buffer pools

Creating Buffer Pools

It's easy to create a buffer pool; you do so using the –ALTER BUFFERPOOL command. The following example shows how to create a 3,000-page buffer pool with a sequential threshold of 50 percent. (Fifty percent of the buffer pool can be used for sequentially processed pages, and 50 percent will be used for randomly processed pages.) For information about tuning these parameters, see Chapter 17.

```
-ALTER BUFFERPOOL (BP3) VPSIZE(3000) VPSEQT(50)
```

Each buffer pool can have a different size and different parameter settings. The parameters control activities such as writing changed pages to disk. To change buffer pool sizes and thresholds, you again use the –ALTER BUFFERPOOL command.

EDM Pool

The Environmental Descriptor Manager pool consists of three components, each of which resides in is own separate storage area and contains many items, including the following:

- EDM pool (EDMPOOL)

  » SKCTs: skeleton cursor tables

  » CTs: cursor tables (copies of the SKCTs)

  » SKPTs: skeleton package tables

  » PTs: package tables (copies of the SKPTs)

  » Authorization cache block for each plan

    ■ except those with CACHESIZE set to 0

- EDM database descriptor cache (EDMDBDC)

  » DBDs: database descriptors

- EDM statement cache (EDMSTMTC)

  » Skeletons of dynamic SQL for CACHE DYNAMIC SQL

If the size of first two EDM pools is too small, you'll see increased I/O activity in the following DB2 table spaces, which support the DB2 directory:

- DSNDB01.DBD01

- DSNDB01.SPT01

- DSNDB01.SCT02

Our main goal for these EDM pools is to limit the I/O against the directory and catalog. If a pool is too small, you'll also see increased response times due to the loading of the SKCTs, SKPTs, and DBDs. Also, if your EDM pool is too small, you'll see fewer threads used concurrently because DB2 knows it doesn't have the appropriate resources to allocate/start new threads. If you increase the EDM pool, you may see an immediate increase in the number of threads allowed.

By correctly sizing the EDM pool (EDMPOOL and EDMDBDC), you can avoid unnecessary I/Os from accumulating for a transaction. If a SKCT, SKPT, or DBD has to be reloaded into the EDM pool, additional I/O is required. This can happen if the pool pages are stolen because the EDM pool is too small. Pages in the pool are maintained on an LRU queue, and the least recently used pages are stolen if required.

Efficiency of the EDM pool can be measured using the following ratios:

- CT requests versus CTs not found in EDM pool

- PT requests versus PTs not found in EDM pool

- DBD requests versus DBDs not found in EDM pool

You'd like to see at least an 80 percent hit ratio for objects found in the EDM pool.

By correctly sizing the EDMSTMTC cache, you can potentially help performance for dynamic SQL statements that are using the cache.

RID Pool

The Row Identifier (RID) pool is used for storing and sorting RIDs for operations such as list prefetch, multiple index access, hybrid joins, and enforcing unique keys while updating multiple rows. The optimizer looks at the RID pool for prefetch and RID use.

The full use of the RID pool is possible for any single user at runtime. Runtime operations can result in a table space scan if insufficient space is available in the RID. For example, if you want to retrieve 10,000 rows from a 100,000,000-row table and no RID pool is available, a scan of 100,000,000 rows would occur, at any time and without external notification. The optimizer assumes physical I/O will be less with a large pool.

The RID pool size is set with an installation parameter (16 K to 100,000 MB). The pool is created at startup time, but no space is allocated until RID storage is actually needed.

Sort Pool

At startup, DB2 allocates a sort pool in the private area of the DBM1 address space. DB2 uses a special sorting technique called a *tournament sort*. During the sorting processes, it's not uncommon for this algorithm to produce logical work files called *runs*, which are intermediate sets of ordered data. If the sort pool is large enough, DB2 completes the sort in that area. More often than not, however, the sort cannot be completed in the sort pool, and the runs are moved into the DB2 work files that are used to perform sorts. These runs are later merged to complete the sort. When the DB2 work files are used to hold the pages that make up the sort runs, you may experience performance degradation if the pages are externalized to the physical work files because they will have to be read back in later to complete the sort.

A DSNZPARM defines the sort pool size, which is currently 240 K to 128 MB with a 2 MB default.

Summary

In this chapter, we examined most of the components that make up the DB2 environment. The operating subsystems for DB2 on System z enterprise servers are based on the core operating system of z/OS. Within this structure, several address spaces make up the environment, and each address space is allocated certain functions. The main components of DB2, and all its managers, reside in the DSAS and SSAS. The IRLM address space communicates with DB2 and provides the internal lock manager.

Across the environment, security services act as a total umbrella to provide many levels of security. The highest level is the component called SecureWay Security Server, which houses such components as RACF.

DB2I and SPUFI are only two of several interfaces to DB2, but they provide for most of the direct interface to DB2 for DBAs and developers. SPUFI is used as a batch program; DB2I is used as a realtime interface.

The installation process, whether performed from TSO or the graphical Windows installer, focuses primarily on choosing options for the many DSNZPARMs, the configuration parameters for DB2. At present, you can modify the vast majority of subsystem parameters online, without taking an outage.

Six different categories of commands and many utilities are available in the DB2 environment. The most-used are the DSN commands and the DB2 commands.

The DB2 catalog and directory comprise the control repository for the environment. There are many catalog tables, which are primarily populated by SQL DDL and DCL, for every object creation and modification.

We examined briefly the distributed network architectures of SNA and TCP/IP and looked at how DRDA provides the services on top of those layers. We'll look further at distributed data access in Chapter 14.

We also discussed other subsystem objects—specifically the buffer pools, the EDM pool, the RID pool, and the sort pool—in terms of how DB2 uses them. We'll revisit these objects in Chapter 17 when we cover performance monitoring and tuning.

Additional Resources

DRDA information: *http://www.opengroup.org*
IBM DB2 9 Administration Guide (SC18-9840)
IBM DB2 9 Installation Guide (GC18-9846)
IBM DB2 9 Reference for Remote DRDA Requesters and Servers (SC18-9853)
IBM DB2 9 SQL Reference (SC18-9854)
IBM DB2 9 Utility Guide and Reference (SC18-9855)
Open Group Technical Standard in *DRDA Volume 1: Distributed Relational Database Architecture (DRDA)*
SNA LU 6.2 Peer Protocols Reference (SC31-6808)

Practice Questions

Question 1

A DBA needs to issue a DB2 command. Which of the following options will allow this?

○ A. SPUFI

○ B. Trigger

○ C. z/OS console

○ D. An SQL statement

Question 2

When reviewing a statistics report, a DBA notices that about 20 timeouts occurred in a 24-hour period. The DBA is unsure how long each user is actually waiting before a timeout error message is issued. How can this information be determined?

○ A. By looking at the NUMLKTS DSNZPARM

○ B. By observing the value of the IRLMRWT DSNZPARM

○ C. By selecting from SYSIBM.SYSTABLESPACE and observing the LOCKMAX value

○ D. By looking at the total wait time in the accounting report for each plan

Question 3

What is the recommended priority setting for the DB2 address spaces?

○ A. IRLM, MSTR, DBM1

○ B. DB2 performance monitors, IRLM, MSTR

○ C. IRLM, DBM1, MSTR

○ D. CICS, IRLM, DBM1

Question 4

Which of the following is true for compatibility mode*?

○ A. DB2 can fall back to V8.

○ B. data sharing groups can have V8 members.

○ C. Changes made to the catalog during migration are undone.

○ D. Objects created in DB2 9 new-function mode can still be accessed.

Question 5

What is one main difference between the DB2 catalog and the DB2 directory?

○ A. The directory doesn't need to be backed up.

○ B. The catalog can be accessed using SQL.

○ C. The catalog is in BP0.

○ D. The directory consists of tables.

Answers

Question 1

The correct answer is **C**, a z/OS console. You can issue the command START DB2 only from a z/OS console (or APF-authorized program passing it to the console). All other DB2 commands can be issued from

- a z/OS console or z/OS application program
- a TSO terminal session
- a DB2I panel
- an IMS terminal
- a CICS terminal
- an APF-authorized program
- an IFI application program

Question 2

The correct answer is **B**, by observing the value of the IRLMRWT DSNZPARM. The IRLMRWT parameter specifies the number of seconds an application will wait before it times out.

Question 3

The correct answer is **C**: IRLM, DBM1, MSTR. A complete list or recommended address space prioritization is a follows:

- MVS monitor with IRLM capabilities
- IRLM
- DB2 performance monitors
- DBM1
- MSTR
- CICS

Question 4

The correct answer is **D**, objects created in DB2 9 new-function mode can still be accessed. The * indicates that at one time the DB2 subsystem or data sharing group was in enabling-new-function mode, enabling-new-function mode*, or new-function mode. Objects that were created in enabling-new-function mode or new-function mode can still be accessed. data sharing groups cannot have any Version 8 members, and you cannot fall back to Version 8 from compatibility mode* or coexist with a Version 8 system.

Question 5

The correct answer is **B**, the catalog can be accessed using SQL. You can query the DB2 catalog using standard SQL statements.

CHAPTER 3

Access and Security

In This Chapter

- ✔ Subsystem access
- ✔ Data set protection
- ✔ Authorization IDs
- ✔ Trusted context and roles
- ✔ Authorities and privileges
- ✔ Auditing

Whenever you store data in a relational database management system, security is an important consideration. In this chapter, we discuss controlling data access using many different methods. Access to data within DB2 is controlled at several levels, including the subsystem, database object, and application plan/package. We discuss user ID and password authentication and describe how to configure groups of typical database users, such as database administrators, system administrators, transactional processing personnel, and decision support users. Each of these user types may require different access privileges. As a final piece to our security discussion, we explain how to audit access to DB2 objects so you can monitor access to and manipulation of data.

As Figure 3.1 depicts, there are several routes from a process to DB2 data, with controls on every route.

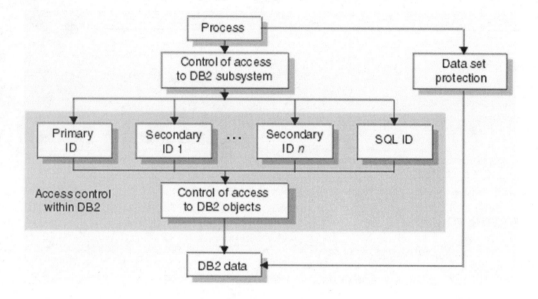

Figure 3.1: DB2 data access control

With each new release, DB2 gets bigger, faster, and more secure. Over the years, it has recognized and addressed the following security problems:

- Privilege theft or mismanagement

- Application or application server tampering

- Data or log tampering

- Storage media theft

- Unauthorized object access

To address these areas, DB2 offers the following security solutions:

- Authentication

- Authorization

- Data integrity

- Confidentiality

- System integrity

- Audit

DB2 Subsystem Access

You can control whether a process can gain access to a specific DB2 subsystem from outside DB2. A common procedure is to grant access only through the Resource Access Control Facility or a similar security system. With this approach, you define profiles for access to DB2 from various environments (and DB2 address spaces) as resources to RACF. You identify these profiles by specifying the subsystem and the environment. Environments include the following:

Environment	Description
MASS	For IMS
SASS	For CICS
DIST	For DDF
RRSAF	For RRSAF
BATCH	For TSO, CAF, utilities

Each request to access DB2 is associated with an identifier. When a request is made, RACF verifies whether this ID is authorized for DB2 resources and either permits or does not permit access to DB2.

The RACF system provides several advantages of its own. For example, it can

- identify and verify the ID associated with a process

- connect those IDs to RACF group names

- log and report unauthorized attempts to access protected resources

The RACF resource class for DB2 is DSNR, and this class is contained in the RACF descriptor table. To control access, you define a profile name as a member of class DSNR for every combination of subsystem and environment you'll be using. You can then issue commands to give authority to groups that are authorized for class DSNR.

For example, the following PERMIT command lets users run batch jobs and utilities on a subsystem.

```
PERMIT DSN.BATCH CLASS(DSNR) ID(DB2USER) ACCESS(READ)
```

You can also use PERMIT to take away DB2 access from a user:

```
PERMIT DSNP.BATCH CLASS(DSNR) ID(DB2USER) ACCESS(NONE)
```

Authorization Control with Exit Routines

You can also control access to DB2 subsystems through exit routines. DB2 provides two exit points for authorization routines, one in connection processing and one in sign-on processing. Both are important for ID assignment. You need a routine for each exit, and IBM supplies default routines for each type: DSN3@ATH for connections and DSN3@SGN for sign-ons.

DB2 provides a third exit point (DSNX@XAC) that lets you furnish your own access-control routines or use RACF (or the equivalent) to perform system authorization checking. When DB2 invokes an authorization routine, it passes three possible functions to it:

- Initialization (DB2 startup)
- Authorization check
- Termination (DB2 shutdown)

The exit routine may not be called in the following situations:

- If the user is Install SYSADM or Install SYSOPR
- If DB2 security has been disabled (i.e., if you specified NO for the USE PROTECTION installation field on the DSNTIPP panel)
- If a prior invocation of the routine indicated the routine should not be called again
- If a GRANT statement is being executed

Local DB2 Access

Even before reaching DB2, a local DB2 user is subject to several checks. For example, if you're running DB2 under TSO and using the TSO logon ID as the DB2 primary authorization ID, that ID is verified with a password when the user logs on. Once the user gains access to DB2, a user-written or IBM-supplied exit routine connected to DB2 can check the authorization ID further, change it, and associate it with secondary IDs (which we discuss later). In providing these functions, DB2 can use the services of an external security system.

Remote Access

Remote users, too, are subject to several checks before reaching your DB2. You can use RACF or a similar security subsystem. RACF can

- verify an identifier associated with a remote attachment request and check it with a password.

- generate PassTickets on the sending side. Used instead of a password, a PassTicket lets a user gain access to a host system without sending the RACF password across the network.

> DB2's communications database does permit some control of authentication in that you can cause IDs to be translated before sending them to the remote system. For more information about accessing DB2 and the CDB, see Chapter 2.

IMS and CICS Security

You can also control DB2 access from within IMS or CICS.

IMS terminal security lets you limit the entry of a transaction code to a particular logical terminal (LTERM) or group of LTERMs in the system. To protect a particular program, you can authorize a transaction code to be entered only from any terminal on a list of LTERMs. As an alternative, you can associate each LTERM with a list of the transaction codes a user can enter from that LTERM. IMS then passes the validated LTERM name to DB2 as the initial primary authorization ID.

CICS transaction code security works with RACF to control the transactions and programs that can access DB2. Within DB2, you can use the ENABLE and DISABLE options of the bind operation to limit access to specific CICS subsystems.

Kerberos Security

Kerberos security is a network security technology developed at the Massachusetts Institute of Technology. DB2 for z/OS can use Kerberos security services to authenticate remote users. With Kerberos security services, remote end users access DB2 when they issue their Kerberos name and password. This same name and password is used for access throughout the network, so a separate z/OS password to access DB2 isn't necessary.

Kerberos security technology doesn't require passwords to flow in readable text, making it secure even in client/server environments. This flexibility is possible because Kerberos employs an authentication technology that uses encrypted tickets that contain authentication information for the end user.

DB2 support for Kerberos security requires the z/OS SecureWay Security Server Network Authentication and Privacy Service and the z/OS SecureWay Security Server (formerly known as RACF), or the functional equivalent. The Network Authentication and Privacy Service provides Kerberos support and relies on a security product (e.g., RACF) to provide registry support. The SecureWay Security Server enables administrators already familiar with RACF commands and RACF ISPF panels to define Kerberos configuration and principal information.

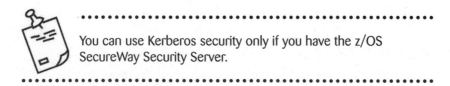

You can use Kerberos security only if you have the z/OS SecureWay Security Server.

Secure Sockets Layer Support

DB2 exploits the z/OS Application Transparent–Transport Layer Security (AT-TLS) function in the TCP/IP stack to provide TLS for DB2 clients that require secure connections. AT-TLS performs TLS on behalf of the application by invoking the z/OS system SSL in the TCP transport layer of the stack. DB2's SSL support provides protected connections between DB2 servers. With SSL support, a DB2 server can optionally listen on a secondary secure port for inbound SSL connections. Similarly, a DB2 requester can optionally send encrypted data across the network through an SSL connection to the server.

Protection Against Denial-of-Service Attacks

In a denial-of-service attack, an attacker tries to prevent legitimate users from accessing information or services. By targeting a DB2 server and its network connection, an attacker might be able to prevent you from accessing data or other services that the server provides. The DB2 server guards against such attacks and provides a more secure operating environment for legitimate users.

Data-Set Protection

The data in a DB2 subsystem is contained in data sets. It's possible to access these data sets without going through DB2 at all. If the data is sensitive, you want to control that route.

If you're using the z/OS SecureWay Security Server (or a similar security system) to control access to DB2, the simplest way to control data-set access outside DB2 is to use RACF for that purpose, too. That means defining RACF profiles for data sets and permitting access to them for certain DB2 IDs.

If the data is very sensitive, you may want to consider encrypting it to protect against unauthorized access to data sets and backup copies outside DB2. You can use DB2 edit procedures or field procedures to encrypt data, and those routines can use the Integrated Cryptographic Service Facility (ICSF) of z/OS. Note that data compression is not a substitute for encryption. In some cases, the compression method doesn't actually shorten the data, and the data is then left uncompressed and readable. If you both encrypt and compress data, be sure to compress it first to obtain the maximum compression; then encrypt the result. When retrieving data, take the steps in reverse order: decrypt the data first, and then decompress the result.

DB2 Object Access

An individual process can be represented by a primary authorization ID, possibly one or more secondary IDs, and an SQL ID. The security and network systems and the DB2 connections that are made all affect the use of IDs.

DB2 controls access to objects by assigning privileges and authorities to either primary or secondary IDs. Object ownership also carries with it a set of related privileges over the object. An ID can own an object it creates, or it can create an object to be owned by another ID. Separate controls govern creation and ownership.

Executing a plan or package exercises implicitly all the privileges that the owner needed when binding it. Hence, granting the privilege to execute can provide a finely detailed set of privileges and can eliminate the need to grant other privileges separately.

● ●

You can use RACF access control to supplement or replace the DB2 GRANT and REVOKE statements.

● ●

In this section, we look at how privileges, authorities, and ownership work together to provide security for access to DB2 objects.

Authorization IDs

Every process that connects to or signs on to DB2 is represented by a set of one or more DB2 identifiers called *authorization IDs*. Authorization IDs can be assigned to a process by default procedures or by user-written exit routines.

Primary Authorization ID

A *primary authorization ID* is assigned to every process. Each process has only one primary authorization ID, and it is the ID that is normally used to uniquely identify the process.

Secondary Authorization ID

A *secondary authorization ID*, which can hold additional privileges, is optional. Secondary authorizations are often used for groups, such as RACF groups. A primary authorization ID can be associated with multiple secondary authorization IDs.

When you add a new user to an RACF group, that user is visible the next time he or she logs on to TSO.

Role

A role is available within a trusted context. You can define a role and assign it to an authorization ID in a trusted context. When associated with a role and using the trusted connection, the authorization ID inherits all the privileges granted to that role. We discuss roles and trusted contexts in more detail later.

Current SQL ID

Either the primary ID or the secondary ID can be the current SQL ID at any given time. Furthermore, one ID (either primary or secondary) is designated as the current SQL ID. You can change the value of the SQL ID during your session. For example, if DB2EXPT is your primary or one of your secondary authorization IDs, you can make it your current SQL ID by issuing the SQL statement

```
SET CURRENT SQLID ='DB2EXPT';
```

An ID with SYSADM authority (described later) can set the *current* SQL ID to any string of up to eight bytes, whether or not the ID is an authorization ID associated with the process that is running.

Trusted Contexts

DB2 9 helps you satisfy the need for data security and accountability by enabling you to create and use *trusted contexts* as another method to manage access to your DB2 servers. Within a trusted context, you can use trusted connections to reuse the authorization and switch users of the connection without the database server needing to authenticate the IDs.

A trusted context is an independent database entity that you can define based on a system authorization ID and connection trust attributes. The trust attributes specify a set of characteristics about a specific connection. These attributes include the IP address, domain name, or SERVAUTH security zone name of a remote client and the job or task name of a local client. A trusted context lets you define a unique set of interactions between DB2 and the external entity, including the following abilities:

- The ability for the external entity to use an established database connection with a different user without the need to authenticate that user at the DB2 server. This support eliminates the need for the external entity to manage end-user passwords. Also, a database administrator can assume the identity of other users and perform actions on their behalf.

- The ability for a DB2 authorization ID to acquire one or more privileges within a trusted context that are not available to it outside that trusted context. You accomplish this by associating a role with the trusted context.

Several client applications support the trusted context:

- The DB2 Driver for JDBC and SQL introduces new APIs for establishing trusted connections and switching users of a trusted connection.

- The DB2 Driver for ODBC and CLI introduces new keywords for connecting APIs to establish trusted connections and switch users of a trusted connection.

- WebSphere Application Server 6.0 exploits the trusted context support through its "propagate client identity" property.

Trusted Connections

A *trusted connection* is a database connection that is established when the connection attributes match the attributes of a unique trusted context defined at the server. You can establish a trusted connection locally or at a remote location.

A trusted context establishes a trusted relationship between DB2 and an external entity, such as a middleware server. To determine whether a specific context can be trusted, DB2 evaluates a series of trust attributes. At this time, the only attribute DB2 considers is the database connection.

The relationship between a connection and a trusted context is established when the connection to the server is first created, and that relationship remains in place as long as that connection exists.

Roles

A *role* is a database entity, available only in a trusted context, that groups together one or more privileges and can be assigned to users. You can define a role and assign it to an authorization ID in a trusted context. When associated with a role and using the trusted connection, the authorization ID inherits all the privileges granted to that role.

A role can own database objects, a fact that helps eliminate the need for individual users to own and control database objects. A role owns objects if the objects are created in a trusted context with the role defined as the owner (by specifying the ROLE AS OBJECT OWNER clause in the trusted context definition). Databases, table spaces, tables, indexes, and views can be implemented in a trusted context with role as the owner of the created objects.

You can assign a role to an individual user or a group of users by defining a trusted context. A role thus offers a mechanism other than authorization IDs through which you can assign privileges and authorities. When you define a role for a trusted context, the role becomes the actual owner of the objects when you specify the ROLE AS OBJECT OWNER clause. As a result, roles give you the flexibility of authorization methods and help simplify the management of authentication.

If objects were created using a ROLE, you can remove the user ID to which the role was assigned without having to redo privileges or drop or re-create objects. For example, say a company creates an APP1 trusted context and an APP1_DBA role to limit exposure to an application and then assigns DBA1 to this role and all the objects. If DBA1 leaves the company and the ID is removed, the objects and privileges of the role remain untouched.

Defining Trusted Contexts

Before you can create a trusted connection, you must define a trusted context by specifying a system authorization ID and connection trust attributes.

A system authorization ID is the DB2 primary authorization ID used to establish the trusted connection. For local connections, the system authorization ID is derived as follows:

Source	System authorization ID
Started task (RRSAF)	USER parameter on JOB or RACF USER
TSO	TSO logon ID
BATCH	USER parameter on JOB

For remote connections, the system authorization ID is derived from the system user ID provided by an external entity, such as a middleware server.

Connection trust attributes identify a set of characteristics about the specific connection. These attributes are required for the connection to be considered a trusted connection. For a local connection, the connection trust attribute is the job or started task name. For a remote connection, the connection trust attribute is the client's IP address, domain name, or SERVAUTH security zone name. Table 3.1 describes the connection trust attributes.

Table 3.1: Connection trust attributes	
Attribute	**Description**
ADDRESS	Specifies the client's IP address or domain name; used by the connection to communicate with DB2. The protocol must be TCP/IP.
SERVAUTH	Specifies the name of a resource in the RACF SERVAUTH class. This resource is the network access security zone name that contains the IP address of the connection to communicate with DB2.
ENCRYPTION	Specifies the minimum level of encryption of the data stream (network encryption) for the connection. **Value** — **Meaning** NONE — No encryption (the default) LOW — DRDA data stream encryption HIGH — SSL encryption
JOBNAME	Specifies the local z/OS started task or job name. The value of JOBNAME depends on the source of the address space. **Source** — **JOBNAME** Started task (RRSAF) — Job or started task name TSO — TSO logon ID BATCH — Job name on JOB statement

You cannot specify the JOBNAME attribute with the ADDRESS, SERVAUTH, or ENCRYPTION attribute.

Performing Tasks on Behalf of Others

If you have DBADM authority (described later), you can assume the identity of other users within a trusted context and perform tasks on their behalf. After successfully assuming the identity of a view owner, you inherit all the privileges from the ID that owns the view and can therefore perform the CREATE, DROP, and GRANT actions on the view.

To perform tasks on behalf of another user:

1. Define a trusted context. Make sure the SYSTEM AUTH ID is the primary authorization ID you use in SPUFI.

2. Specify the primary authorization ID as the JOBNAME for the trusted connection.

3. Specify the primary authorization ID of the user whose identity you want to assume.

4. Log on to TSO using your primary authorization ID.

5. Set the ASUSER option on the DB2I DEFAULTS panel to the primary authorization ID of the user whose identity you want to assume.

6. Perform the desired actions by using privileges of the specified user.

For example, let's assume you have DBADM authority (the minimum authority required), your primary authorization ID is DAN, and you want to drop a view owned by user SUSAN. You can issue the following statement to create and enable a trusted context called CTXLOCAL in which DAN can drop the selected view on SUSAN's behalf:

```
CREATE TRUSTED CONTEXT CTXLOCAL
BASED UPON CONNECTION USING SYSTEM AUTHID DAN
ATTRIBUTES (JOBNAME 'DAN')
ENABLE
ALLOW USE FOR SUSAN;
```

After logging on to TSO, set the ASUSER option to SUSAN in the DB2I DEFAULTS panel, and invoke SPUFI to process SQL statements. DB2 obtains the primary authorization ID DAN and JOBNAME DAN from the TSO log-on session, authenticates DAN, searches for the matching trusted context (CTXLOCAL), and establishes a trusted connection. DB2 then authenticates the primary authorization

ID (SUSAN) and validates all privileges assigned to SUSAN. After successful authentication and validation, you, DAN, can drop the view that is owned by SUSAN.

Explicit Privileges

You can grant several *explicit privileges* to a primary ID, secondary authorization ID, or role to grant that ID the privilege to perform a particular task. Certain granted privileges also provide an inherited authority (e.g., if you grant CREATEDBA to an ID, that ID will become DBADM over the database it creates). The privileges are grouped into several categories:

- Tables and views

- Plans

- Packages

- Collections

- Databases

- Subsystems

- Usage

- Schemas

- Distinct types or JARs

- Routines (functions or procedures)

- Sequences

Table 3.2 lists the available privileges that can be granted to either a primary authorization ID, secondary authorization ID, or role, along with the type of usage associated with each privilege.

No specific authority exists for creating a view. To create a view, you must have the SELECT privilege from the table (or tables) on which the view is being created.

Additional privileges exist for statements, commands, and utility jobs.

Privilege	Provides this usage
Table 3.2: Explicit privileges	
Privilege	**Provides this usage**
Table	
ALTER	The ALTER TABLE statement, to change the table definition.
DELETE	The DELETE statement, to delete rows.
GRANT ALL	SQL statements of all table privileges.
INDEX	The CREATE INDEX statement, to create an index on the table.
INSERT	The INSERT statement, to insert rows.
REFERENCES	The ALTER or CREATE TABLE statement, to add or remove a referential constraint referring to the named table or to a list of columns in the table.
SELECT	The SELECT statement, to retrieve data from the table.
TRIGGER	The CREATE TRIGGER statement, to define a trigger on a table.
UPDATE	The UPDATE statement, to update all columns or a specific list of columns.
Plan	
BIND	The BIND, REBIND, and FREE PLAN subcommands, to bind or free the plan.
EXECUTE	The RUN command, to use the plan when running the application.
Package	
BIND	The BIND, REBIND, and FREE PACKAGE subcommands and the DROP PACKAGE statement, to bind or free the package and, depending on the installation option BIND NEW PACKAGE, to bind a new version of a package.
COPY	The COPY option of BIND PACKAGE, to copy a package.
EXECUTE	Inclusion of the package in the PKLIST option of BIND PLAN.
GRANT ALL	All package privileges.
Collection	
CREATE IN	Naming the collection in the BIND PACKAGE subcommand.
Database	
CREATETAB	The CREATE TABLE statement, to create tables in the database.
CREATETS	The CREATE TABLESPACE statement, to create table spaces in the database.
DISPLAYDB	The DISPLAY DATABASE command, to display the database status.
DROP	DROP and ALTER DATABASE, to drop or alter the database.

Table 3.2: Explicit privileges (continued)	
Privilege	**Provides this usage**
IMAGCOPY	The QUIESCE, COPY, and MERGECOPY utilities, to prepare for, make, and merge copies of table spaces in the database; and the MODIFY RECOVERY utility, to remove records of copies.
LOAD	The LOAD utility, to load tables in the database.
RECOVERDB	The RECOVER, REBUILD INDEX, and REPORT utilities, to recover objects in the database and report their recovery status.
REORG	The REORG utility, to reorganize objects in the database.
REPAIR	The REPAIR and DIAGNOSE utilities (except REPAIR DBD and DIAGNOSE WAIT) to generate diagnostic information about, and repair data in, objects in the database.
STARTDB	The START DATABASE command, to start the database.
STATS	The RUNSTATS, CHECK, LOAD, REBUILD INDEX, REORG INDEX, and REORG TABLESPACE utilities, to gather statistics and check indexes and referential constraints for objects in the database and delete unwanted statistics history records from the corresponding catalog tables.
STOPDB	The STOP DATABASE command, to stop the database.
Subsystem	
ARCHIVE	The ARCHIVE LOG command, to archive the current active log; the DISPLAY ARCHIVE command, to give information about input archive logs; the SET LOG command, to modify the checkpoint frequency specified during installation; and the SET ARCHIVE command, to control allocation and deallocation of tape units for archive processing.
BINDADD	The BIND subcommand with the ADD option, to create new plans and packages.
BINDAGENT	The BIND, REBIND, and FREE subcommands and the DROP PACKAGE statement, to bind, rebind, or free a plan or package, or to copy a package, on behalf of the grantor. The BINDAGENT privilege is intended for separation of function, not for added security. A bind agent with the EXECUTE privilege might be able to gain all the authority of the grantor of BINDAGENT.
BSDS	The RECOVER BSDS command, to recover the bootstrap data set.
CREATEALIAS	The CREATE ALIAS statement, to create an alias for a table or view name.
CREATEDBA	The CREATE DATABASE statement, to create a database and have DBADM authority over it.
CREATEDBC	The CREATE DATABASE statement, to create a database and have DBCTRL authority over it.
CREATESG	The CREATE STOGROUP statement, to create a storage group.
CREATETMTAB	The CREATE GLOBAL TEMPORARY TABLE statement, to define a created temporary table.
DEBUGSESSION	The DEBUGINFO connection attribute, to control debug session activity for native SQL and Java stored procedures.

Table 3.2: Explicit privileges (continued)	
Privilege	**Provides this usage**
DISPLAY	The DISPLAY ARCHIVE, DISPLAY BUFFERPOOL, DISPLAY DATABASE, DISPLAY LOCATION, DISPLAY LOG, DISPLAY THREAD, and DISPLAY TRACE commands, to display system information.
MONITOR1	Receive trace data that is not potentially sensitive.
MONITOR2	Receive all trace data.
RECOVER	The RECOVER INDOUBT command, to recover threads.
STOPALL	The STOP DB2 command, to stop DB2.
STOSPACE	The STOSPACE utility, to obtain data about space usage.
TRACE	The START TRACE, STOP TRACE, and MODIFY TRACE commands, to control tracing.
Usage	
USE OF BUFFERPOOL	A buffer pool.
USAGE ON JAR	A Java class.
USAGE ON SEQUENCE	A sequence.
USE OF STOGROUP	A storage group.
USE OF TABLESPACE	A table space.
Schema	
CREATEIN	Create distinct types, user-defined functions, triggers, and stored procedures in the designated schemas.
ALTERIN	Alter user-defined functions or stored procedures, or specify a comment for distinct types, user-defined functions, triggers, and stored procedures in the designated schemas.
DROPIN	Drop distinct types, user-defined functions, triggers, and stored procedures in the designated schemas.
Distinct type	
USAGE ON DISTINCT TYPE	A distinct type.
Routine	
EXECUTE ON FUNCTION	A user-defined function.
EXECUTE ON PROCEDURE	A stored procedure.
Sequence Object	
ALTER	A sequence object.

GRANTing and REVOKEing Privileges

The privileges in Table 3.2 must be GRANTed to an authorization ID or role. The GRANT and REVOKE statements are part of the SQL language known as *Data Control Language* (*DCL*). Let's take a look at some examples of granting and revoking privileges.

To grant the ID DB2EXPT the ability to select data from a particular table, you would execute the following SQL statement:

```
GRANT SELECT ON DSN8910.EMP TO DB2EXPT
```

To grant DB2EXPT the ability to BIND packages to the DB2SAMPL collection, you would execute this statement:

```
GRANT BIND ON PACKAGE DB2SAMPL.* TO DB2EXPT
```

To grant everyone the ability to select, update, insert, or delete data from a particular table, you'd execute this statement:

```
GRANT ALL ON DSN8910.EMP TO PUBLIC
```

Note that the keyword PUBLIC lets any user have the granted privilege.

To take away everyone's delete authority from a particular table, you would execute this statement:

```
REVOKE DELETE ON DSN8910.EMP FROM PUBLIC
```

Revoking a privilege from a user can also cause that privilege to be revoked from other users. This type of revoke is called a *cascade revoke*.

Related and Inherited Privileges

DB2 defines sets of related privileges that are identified by administrative authorities (which we examine the next). This grouping makes it easier to administer authority because instead of having to grant several individual privileges to an ID, you can simply grant the administrative authority—which includes all applicable privileges. Some privileges are also inherited with object ownership.

Authorities

An *administrative authority* is a set of privileges, often covering a related set of objects. Authorities often include privileges that aren't explicit, have no name, and cannot be specifically granted—for example, the ability to terminate any utility job, which is included in the SYSOPR authority. The nine DB2 administrative authorities are:

- Installation SYSADM

- SYSCTRL

- SYSADM

- SYSOPR

- Installation SYSOPR

- PACKADM

- DBMAINT

- DBCTRL

- DBADM

Table 3.3 describes the capabilities and privileges of each authority.

The DBCTRL authority provides a good way to assign all the necessary privileges a DBA needs to perform his or her duties without granting the ability to access the data itself.

Table 3.3: DB2 administrative authorities		
Authority	**Capabilities**	**Privileges**
Installation SYSADM	Assigned during DB2 installation, this authority has all the privileges of the SYSADM authority. In addition: • Authority is *not* recorded in the DB2 catalog. The catalog need not be available to check installation SYSADM authority. (The authority outside the catalog is crucial. If the catalog table space SYSDBAUT is stopped, for example, DB2 can't check the authority to start it again. Only an installation SYSADM can start it.) • No ID can revoke this authority; it can be removed only by changing the module that contains the subsystem initialization parameters (typically DSNZPARM). SYSADM IDs can also • run the CATMAINT utility • access DB2 when the subsystem is started with ACCESS(MAINT) • start databases DSNDB01 and DSNDB06 when they are stopped or in restricted status • run the DIAGNOSE utility with the WAIT statement • start and stop the database containing the application registration table (ART) and the object registration table (ORT)	All privileges of all the authorities.
SYSCTRL	This authority has almost complete control of the DB2 subsystem but *cannot* access user data directly unless granted the privilege to do so. Designed for administering a system containing sensitive data, SYSCTRL can • act with installation SYSOPR authority (when the catalog is available) or with DBCTRL authority over any database • run any allowable utility on any database • issue a COMMENT ON, LABEL ON, or LOCK TABLE statement for any table • create a view for itself or others on any catalog table • create tables and aliases for itself or others • bind a new plan or package, naming any ID as the owner	System privileges: • BINDADD • BINDAGENT • BSDS • CREATEALIAS • CREATEDBA • CREATEDBC • CREATESG • CREATETMTAB • MONITOR1 • MONITOR2 • STOSPACE Privileges on all tables: • ALTER • INDEX • REFERENCES • TRIGGER

Table 3.3: DB2 administrative authorities (continued)		
Authority	**Capabilities**	**Privileges**
	Without additional privileges, SYSCTRL cannot • execute SQL Data Manipulation Language (DML) statements on user tables or views • run plans or packages • set the current SQL ID to a value that is not one of its primary or secondary IDs • start or stop the database containing the ART and ORT • act fully as SYSADM or as DBADM over any database • access DB2 when the subsystem is started with ACCESS(MAINT) • revoke a privilege granted by another ID *Note*: SYSCTRL authority is intended for separation of function, not for added security.	Privileges on catalog tables: • DELETE • INSERT • SELECT • UPDATE Privileges on all plans: • BIND Privileges on all packages: • BIND • COPY Privileges on all collections: • CREATE IN Privileges on all schemas: • ALTERIN • CREATE IN • DROPIN Use privileges on: • BUFFERPOOL • STOGROUP • TABLESPACE
SYSADM	This authority includes SYSCTRL, plus access to all data. SYSADM can • use all privileges of the DBADM authority over any database • use EXECUTE and BIND on any plan or package and use COPY on any package • use privileges over views owned by others • set the current SQL ID to any valid value, whether it is currently a primary or secondary authorization ID • create and drop synonyms and views for others on any table • use any valid value for OWNER in BIND or REBIND • drop database DSNDB07 • grant any of the privileges listed above to others Holders of SYSADM authority can also drop or alter any DB2 object except system databases, issue a COMMENT ON or LABEL ON statement for any table or view, and terminate any utility job; however, SYSADM cannot specifically grant these privileges.	All privileges held by SYSCTRL and DBADM Plan privileges: • EXECUTE Package privileges: • BIND • COPY Routine privileges: • EXECUTE Distinct type and sequence privileges: • USAGE Debug privileges: • DEBUGSESSION

Table 3.3: DB2 administrative authorities (continued)		
Authority	**Capabilities**	**Privileges**
SYSOPR	This authority can • issue most DB2 commands except ARCHIVE LOG, START DATABASE, STOP DATABASE, and RECOVER BSDS • terminate any utility job • execute the DSN1SDMP utility	System privileges: • DISPLAY • RECOVER • STOPALL • TRACE Privileges on routines: • START DISPLAY • STOP
Installation SYSOPR	This authority is assigned during DB2 installation and has the following privileges in addition to those of SYSOPR: • Authority is not recorded in the DB2 catalog. The catalog need not be available to check installation SYSOPR authority. • No ID can revoke the authority; it can be removed only by changing the module that contains the subsystem initialization parameters (typically DSNZPARM). The SYSOPR authority can • access DB2 when the subsystem is started with ACCESS(MAINT) • run all allowable utilities on the directory and catalog databases (DSNDB01 and DSNDB06) • run the REPAIR utility with the DBD statement • start and stop the database containing the ART and ORT • issue dynamic SQL statements that aren't controlled by the DB2 governor • issue a START DATABASE command to recover objects that have logical page list (LPL) entries or group buffer pool recovery-pending status SYSOPR IDs cannot change the access mode.	All privileges held by SYSOPR System privileges: • ARCHIVE • STARTDB (cannot change access mode)
PACKADM	This authority has all package privileges on all packages in specific collections, or on all collections, plus the CREATE IN privilege on those collections. If the installation option BIND NEW PACKAGE is set to BIND, PACKADM also has the privilege to add new packages or new versions of existing packages.	Privileges on a collection: • CREATE IN Privileges on all packages in the collection: • BIND • COPY • EXECUTE

Table 3.3: DB2 administrative authorities (continued)		
Authority	**Capabilities**	**Privileges**
DBMAINT	This authority is granted for a specific database, in which the ID can create certain objects, run certain utilities, and issue certain commands. It can use the TERM UTILITY command to terminate all utilities except DIAGNOSE, REPORT, and STOSPACE on the database.	Privileges on one database: • CREATETAB • CREATETS • DISPLAYDB • IMAGCOPY • STARTDB • STATS • STOPDB
DBCTRL	In addition to DBMAINT privileges, the DBCTRL authority can run utilities that can change the data.	All privileges held by DBMAINT on a database Privileges on one database: • DROP • LOAD • RECOVERDB • REORG • REPAIR
DBADM	In addition to the privileges held by DBCTRL over a specific database, DBADM has privileges to access any of its tables through SQL statements. It can also drop and alter any table space, table, or index in the database and issue a COMMENT ON, LABEL ON, or LOCK TABLE statement for any table. If the value of field DBADM CREATE VIEW on installation panel DSNTIPP was set to YES during DB2 installation, a user with DBADM authority can create a view for another user ID on any table or combination of tables and views in a database.	All privileges held by DBCTRL on a database Privileges on tables and views in one database: • ALTER • DELETE • INDEX • INSERT • REFERENCES • SELECT • TRIGGER • UPDATE

GRANTing and REVOKEing Authorities

The authorities in Table 3.3 must be GRANTed to an authorization ID. Just as with privileges, you can accomplish this task using the GRANT and REVOKE statements. Let's look at a couple of examples of granting and revoking authorities.

To grant DBADM authority on the DSN8D91A database to ID DB2EXPT, you'd issue this statement:

```
GRANT DBADM ON DSN8D91A TO DB2EXPT
```

To remove PACKADM authority from DB2EXPT, you'd issue this statement:

```
REVOKE PACKADM FROM DB2EXPT
```

WITH GRANT OPTION

If you GRANT an authority using the WITH GRANT option, the holder can GRANT the privileges contained in that authority to others. To grant DB2EXPT DBADM authority on the DSN8D91A database and permit DB2EXPT to give this authority to others, you'd issue this statement:

```
GRANT DBADM ON DSN8D91A TO DB2EXPT WITH GRANT OPTION
```

if the DBADM authority is ever revoked from DB2EXPT, any ID that has been granted DBADM from this ID will also be revoked automatically.

Ownership

Implicit privileges are included with ownership of an object. When you create DB2 objects (other than plans and packages) by issuing SQL CREATE statements in which you name the object, you establish ownership. The owner implicitly holds certain privileges over the owned object.

The privileges inherent in the ownership of an object cannot be revoked.

Unqualified Objects

If an object name is unqualified, the object ownership established depends on the type of object. Ownership of tables, views, indexes, aliases, and synonyms with unqualified names is established differently from ownership of user-defined functions, stored procedures, distinct types, sequences, and triggers with unqualified names.

If the name of a table, view, index, alias, or synonym is unqualified, you establish the object's ownership in these ways:

- If the CREATE statement is issued dynamically (via SPUFI or the Query Management Facility), the owner of the created object is the current SQL ID of the issuer. That ID must have the privileges necessary to create the object.

- If the CREATE statement is issued statically (by executing a plan or package that contains it), the ownership of the created object depends on the option used for the bind operation. You can bind the plan or package with the QUALIFIER option, the OWNER option, or both.

  » With the QUALIFIER option only, the QUALIFIER is the owner of the object. The QUALIFIER option lets the binder name a qualifier to use for all unqualified names of tables, views, indexes, aliases, or synonyms that appear in the plan or package.

  » With the OWNER option only, the OWNER is the owner of the object.

  » With both the QUALIFIER option and the OWNER option, the QUALIFIER is the owner of the object.

  » If neither option is specified, the binder of the plan or package is implicitly the object owner.

••
The plan or package owner must have all required privileges on the objects designated by the qualified names.
••

You establish the ownership of a user-defined function, stored procedure, distinct type, sequence, or trigger in the following ways:

- If the CREATE statement is issued dynamically, the owner of the created object is the current SQL ID of the issuer. That ID must have the privileges necessary to create the object.

- If the CREATE statement is issued statically (by running a plan or package that contains it), the owner of the object is the plan or package owner. You can use the OWNER bind option to explicitly name the object owner. If the OWNER bind option is not specified, the binder of the package or plan is implicitly the object owner.

The implicit qualifier is determined for an unqualified user-defined function, stored procedure, distinct type, sequence, or trigger by the name in the dynamic statements or the PATH bind option in static statements. The owner of a JAR that is used by a stored procedure or user-defined function is the current SQL ID of the process that performs the INSTALL_JAR function.

Qualified Objects

If an object name is qualified, the way ownership of the object is established depends, again, on the type of object.

For tables, views, indexes, aliases, or synonyms created with a qualified name, the qualifier is the owner of the object and is the schema name. The schema name identifies the schema to which the object belongs. All objects qualified by the same schema are related.

If you create a distinct type, user-defined function, stored procedure, sequence, or trigger with a qualified name, the qualifier will also be the schema name. The schema name identifies the schema to which the object belongs. You can think of all objects that are qualified by the same schema name as a group of related objects. Unlike with other objects, however, this qualifier doesn't identify the owner of the object. You establish ownership of a distinct type, user-defined function, stored procedure, or trigger as follows:

- If you issue the CREATE statement dynamically, the owner of the created object is your current SQL ID. That ID must have the privileges necessary to create the object.

- If you issue the CREATE statement statically (by running a plan or package that contains it), the owner of the object is the plan or package owner. You can use the OWNER bind option to explicitly name the object owner. If the OWNER bind option is not used, the binder of the package or plan is the implicit object owner.

For more information about schemas, see Chapter 15.

Objects Within a Trusted Context

Roles can help simplify administration by serving as owners of objects. If the owner of an object is an authorization ID and you need to transfer the ownership to another ID, you must first drop the object first and then re-create it with the new authorization ID as the owner. If the owner is a role, these steps are unnecessary because all the users that are associated with that role have the owner privilege.

The definition of a trusted context determines the ownership of objects that are created in the trusted context. Assume you issue the CREATE statement dynamically and define the trusted context using the ROLE AS OBJECT OWNER clause. In this case, the associated role is the owner of the objects, regardless of whether the objects are explicitly qualified.

In contrast, assume you issue the CREATE statement statically and the plan or package is bound in the trusted context with the ROLE AS OBJECT OWNER clause. In this case, the role that owns the plan or package also owns the created objects, regardless of whether the objects are explicitly qualified.

Privileges of Ownership by Object

Table 3.4 lists the privileges that are inherited with ownership of an object.

Table 3.4: Privileges inherited with object ownership	
Object type	**Implicit privileges of ownership**
Storage group	• ALTER or DROP the storage group • Name the storage group in the USING clause of a CREATE INDEX or CREATE TABLESPACE statement
Database	• DBCTRL or DBADM authority over the database, depending on the privilege (CREATEDBA or CREATEDBC) used to create the database. DBCRTL authority does not include the privilege to access data in tables in the database
Table space	• ALTER or DROP the table space • Name the table space in the IN clause of a CREATE TABLE statement
Table	• ALTER or DROP the table or any indexes on it • Use LOCK TABLE, COMMENT ON, or LABEL on the table • CREATE an index or view on the table • SELECT or UPDATE any row or column • INSERT or DELETE any row • Use the LOAD utility for the table • Define referential constraints on any table or set of columns • CREATE a trigger on the table
Index	• ALTER or DROP the index
View	• DROP, COMMENT ON, or LABEL the view, or SELECT any row or column • UPDATE any row or column • INSERT or DELETE any row (if the view is not read-only)
Synonym	• USE or DROP the synonym
Trusted context	• CREATE, ALTER, COMMIT, REVOKE, or COMMENT ON the trusted context
Package	• BIND, REBIND, FREE, COPY, DROP, EXECUTE, or DROP the package
JAR	• REPLACE, USE, or DROP the JAR
Plan	• BIND, REBIND, FREE, or EXECUTE the plan
Alias	• DROP the alias
Distinct type	• USE or DROP a distinct type
Role	• CREATE, ALTER, COMMIT, DROP, or COMMENT ON the role
Sequence	• ALTER, COMMENT ON, USE, or DROP the sequence
User-defined functions	• EXECUTE, ALTER, DROP, START, STOP, or DISPLAY a user-defined function
Stored procedure	• EXECUTE, ALTER, DROP, START, STOP, or DISPLAY a stored procedure

Plan or Package Ownership

An application plan or a package can take many actions on many tables, all of them requiring one or more privileges. The owner of the plan or package must hold every required privilege. Another ID can execute the plan with just the EXECUTE privilege. In this way, another ID can exercise all the privileges used in validating the plan or package, but only within the restrictions imposed by the SQL statements in the original program.

The executing ID can use some of the owner's privileges, within limits. If the privileges are revoked from the owner, the plan or the package is invalidated; it must be rebound, and the new owner must have the required privileges.

The BIND and REBIND subcommands create or change an application plan or package. On either subcommand, use the OWNER option to name the owner of the resulting plan or package. When naming an owner, keep the following points in mind.

- If you use the OWNER option:
    - » Any user can name the primary or any secondary ID.
    - » An ID with the BINDAGENT privilege can name the grantor of that privilege.
    - » An ID with SYSADM or SYSCTRL authority can name any authorization ID on a BIND command, but not on a REBIND command.
- If you omit the OWNER option:
    - » On a BIND command, the primary ID becomes the owner.
    - » On a REBIND command, the previous owner retains ownership.

Unqualified Names

A plan or package can contain SQL statements that use unqualified table and view names. For static SQL, the default qualifier for these names is the owner of the plan or package. However, you can use the QUALIFIER option of the BIND command to specify a different qualifier.

For plans or packages that contain static SQL, using the BINDAGENT privilege and the OWNER and QUALIFIER options gives you considerable flexibility in performing bind operations. For plans or packages that contain dynamic SQL, the DYNAMICRULES behavior determines how DB2 qualifies unqualified object names.

For unqualified distinct types, user-defined functions, stored procedures, sequences, and trigger names in dynamic SQL statements, DB2 finds the schema name to use as the qualifier by searching schema names in the CURRENT PATH special register. For static statements, the PATH bind option determines the path that DB2 searches to resolve unqualified distinct types, user-defined functions, stored procedures, and trigger names.

However, an exception exists for ALTER, CREATE, DROP, COMMENT ON, GRANT, and REVOKE statements. For static SQL, specify the qualifier for these statements in the QUALIFIER bind option. For dynamic SQL, the qualifier for these statements is the authorization ID of the CURRENT SQLID special register.

Trusted Context

You can issue the BIND and REBIND commands in a trusted context with the ROLE AS OBJECT OWNER clause to specify the ownership of a plan or package. In this trusted context, you can specify only a role, not an authorization ID, as the OWNER of a plan or package. If you specify the OWNER option, the specified role becomes the owner of the plan or package. If you don't specify the OWNER option, the role that is associated with the binder becomes the owner. If you omit the ROLE AS OBJECT OWNER clause for the trusted context, the current rules for plan and package ownership apply.

If you want a role to own the package at a remote DB2 data server, you need to define the role ownership in the trusted context at the remote server. Be sure to establish the connection to the remote DB2 as trusted when binding or rebinding the package at the remote server.

If you specify the OWNER option in a trusted connection during the remote BIND processing, the outbound authorization ID translation is not performed for the OWNER.

If the plan owner is a role and the application uses a package bound at a remote DB2 for z/OS data server, the privilege of the plan owner to execute the package is not considered at the remote DB2 server. The privilege set of the authorization ID (either the package owner or the process runner, depending on the DYNAMICRULES behavior) at the DB2 for z/OS data server must have the EXECUTE privilege on the package at the DB2 data server.

Plan Execution Authorization

The plan or package owner must have authorization to execute all static SQL statements that are embedded in the plan or package. These authorizations do not need to be in place when the plan or package is bound, nor do the objects that are referred to need to exist at that time.

A bind operation always checks whether a local object exists and whether the owner has the required privileges on it. Any failure results in a message. To choose whether the failure prevents the bind operation from being completed, use the VALIDATE option of the BIND PLAN and BIND PACKAGE subcommands and also the SQLERROR option of BIND PACKAGE. If you permit the operation to be completed, the checks occur again at runtime. The corresponding checks for remote objects are always made at runtime.

Authorization to execute dynamic SQL statements is also checked at runtime.

To include a package in a plan's PKLIST, the owner will need to be given execute authority on the package.

For more information about plans and packages, see Chapter 11.

Catalog Table Information for Object Access

Table 3.5 provides information about the authorities and privileges currently held on various objects in the DB2 subsystem.

Table 3.5: DB2 catalog table authorities and privileges	
DB2 catalog table	**Authorities/Privileges**
SYSIBM.SYSCOLAUTH	Update column authority
SYSIBM.SYSDBAUTH	Database privileges
SYSIBM.SYSPACKAUTH	Package privileges
SYSIBM.SYSPLANAUTH	Plan privileges
SYSIBM.SYSRESAUTH	Buffer pool, storage group, collection, table space, and distinct type use privileges
SYSIBM.SYSROUTINEAUTH	User-defined functions and stored procedure privileges
SYSIBM.SYSSCHEMAAUTH	Schema privileges
SYSIBM.SYSEQUENCEAUTH	Sequence object privileges
SYSIBM.SYSTABAUTH	Tables and view privileges
SYSIBM.SYSUSERAUTH	System authorities

Controlling Access with Views

By using views, you can control what data a user can see, whether it be certain columns, certain rows, or even a combination of rows and columns. Views thus give you a way, in addition to granting privileges and authorities, to further restrict access to data. You implement this type of access control by creating a view that lets users see only certain columns or rows and then permitting them access to only the view, not the base table.

The following example permits the user of the view to see the names of employees who work in department D01.

```
CREATE VIEW EMPVIEW
AS
SELECT FIRSTNME, LASTNAME
FROM DSN8910.EMP
WHERE WORKDEPT = 'D01'
```

Multilevel Security

Multilevel security enables a more granular approach to setting security, combining hierarchical and categorical security schemes. Organizations can use this type of security to prevent individuals from accessing data at a higher security level or from declassifying data.

DB2 supports multilevel security at the row level. With row-level security, the system restricts individual user access to a specific set of rows in a table. This security method requires z/OS 1.5 RACF at a minimum.

The security enforcement occurs automatically at statement runtime and lets you perform new security checks that are difficult to express using SQL views or queries. Multilevel security doesn't rely on special views or database variables, and the controls are consistent and integrated across the system.

User security classification is maintained in the RACF security database only.

To support multilevel security, the DB2 tables require a new column, defined as SECURITY LABEL. This column contains the security label. Every row has a specific security label; these values correspond to security label definitions. For each accessed row, DB2 calls the RACF Security Exit to check authorization. If access is authorized, normal data access is permitted; otherwise, data is not returned. To reduce overhead, the security labels are cached.

Security Function DB2_SECURE_VAR

DB2 provides a way to feed external security information into SQL. The variables are set by the connection/sign-on exit routines. Built-in function DB2_SECURE_VAR lets you retrieve the value for a variable. You can use this variable in views, triggers, stored procedures, functions, and constraints to enforce security policies.

Here's an example of using function DB2_SECURE_VAR in a view.

```
CREATE VIEW MY_DATA AS
      SELECT *
        FROM SHARED_DATA
       WHERE COL_OWNER
           = DB2_SECURE_VAR('SEC_OWNER')
```

Auditing

This chapter answers some fundamental auditing questions, the following two before foremost among them:

- Who is privileged to access what objects?

- Who has actually accessed the data?

The DB2 catalog holds the answer to the first question: it contains a primary audit trail for the DB2 subsystem. Most of the catalog tables describe the DB2 objects, such as tables, views, table spaces, packages, and plans. Several other tables (those with "AUTH" in their name) hold records of every grant of a privilege or authority on different types of objects. Each grant record contains the name of the object, the ID that received the privilege, the ID that granted it, the time of the grant, and other information. You can retrieve data from the catalog tables by writing SQL queries.

Audit Trace

Another primary audit trail for DB2 is the audit trace. The trace can record changes in authorization IDs for a security audit as well as changes made to the structure of data (e.g., dropping a table) or to data values (e.g., updating or inserting records) for an audit of data access. You can also use the audit trace to track access attempts by unauthorized IDs, the results of GRANT and REVOKE statements, the mapping of Kerberos security tickets to RACF IDs, and other activities of interest to auditors.

The audit trace can answer the question of who has accessed data. When started, the trace creates records of actions of certain types and sends them to a named destination. From these records, you can obtain information such as:

- the ID that initiated an activity

- the LOCATION of the ID that initiated the activity (if the access was initiated from a remote location)

- the type of activity and the time it occurred

- the DB2 objects affected

- whether access was denied

- who owns a particular plan and package

Using the audit trace, you can also determine which primary ID is responsible for the action of a secondary ID when that information might not appear in the catalog.

Whether a request comes from a remote location or from the local DB2, it can be audited. For a remote request, the authorization ID on a trace record is the ID that is the final result of any outbound translation, inbound translation, or activity of an authorization exit routine — that is, it is the same ID to which you've granted access privileges for your data. Requests from your location to a remote DB2 are audited only if an audit trace is active at the remote location. The trace output appears only in the records at that location.

Trace Details

The audit trace doesn't record everything. The actual changed data is recorded in the DB2 log. If an agent or transaction accesses a table more than once in a single unit of recovery, the trace records only the first access, and then only if you've started the audit trace for the appropriate class of events.

Some utilities are not audited. The first access of a table by the LOAD utility is audited, but access by COPY, RECOVER, and REPAIR is not. Access by standalone utilities, such as DSN1CHKR and DSN1PRNT, is not audited. (For more information about these DB2 utilities, see Chapter 7.)

Everything comes at a cost. Auditing does impose some overhead and can produce more data than necessary.

When you start the trace, you choose the events to audit by supplying one or more numbers to identify classes of events. Trace records are limited to 5,000 bytes, so descriptions that contain long SQL statements may be truncated. Table 3.6 lists the available classes and the events they include. (For more information about trace classes, see Chapter 17.)

The audit trace does not audit DB2 commands.

Table 3.6: Audit trace event classes	
Class	**Events traced**
1	Access attempts that DB2 denies because of inadequate authorization. This class is the default.
2	Explicit GRANT and REVOKE statements and their results. This class does not include implicit grants and revokes.
3	CREATE, ALTER, and DROP operations affecting audited tables, and their results. This class includes the dropping of a table caused by DROP TABLESPACE or DROP DATABASE and the creation of a table with AUDIT CHANGES or AUDIT ALL. The trace audits ALTER TABLE statements only when they change the AUDIT option for the table.
4	Changes to audited tables. Only the first attempt to change a table, within a unit of recovery, is recorded. (If the agent or the transaction issues more than one COMMIT statement, the number of audit records increases accordingly.) The changed data isn't recorded, only the attempt to make a change. If the change is not successful and is rolled back, the audit record remains; it is not deleted. This class includes access by the LOAD utility. The trace also audits accesses to a dependent table that are caused by attempted deletions from a parent table. The audit record is written even if the delete rule is RESTRICT, which prevents the deletion from the parent table. The audit record is also written when the rule is CASCADE or SET NULL, which can result in deletions cascading to the dependent table.
5	All read accesses to tables identified as AUDIT ALL. As in class 4, only the first access within a DB2 unit of recovery is recorded, and references to a parent table are audited.
6	The bind of static and dynamic SQL statements of the following types: • INSERT, UPDATE, DELETE, CREATE VIEW, and LOCK TABLE statements for audited tables. Except for the values of host variables, the audit record contains the entire SQL statement. • SELECT statements to tables identified as AUDIT ALL. Except for the values of host variables, the audit record contains the entire SQL statement.
7	Assignment or change of an authorization ID through an exit routine (default or user-written) or SET CURRENT SQLID statement, through an outbound or inbound authorization ID translation, or because the ID is being mapped to an RACF ID from a Kerberos security ticket.
8	The start of a utility job, and the end of each phase of the utility.
9	The writing of various types of records to IFCID 0146 by the IFI WRITE function.
10	CREATE and ALTER TRUSTED CONTEXT statements, establish trusted connection information, and switch user information.

Auditing Specific IDs or Roles

You can start the audit trace for a particular plan name, a particular primary authorization ID, or a combination of both. Having audit traces on at all times can be useful for IDs with SYSADM authority, for example, because they have complete access to every table. If you have a network of DB2 subsystems, you might need to trace multiple authorization IDs for those users whose primary authorization ID is translated several times.

By using the ROLE and XROLE filters, you can also start traces for a particular role in a trusted context.

Starting/Stopping the Trace

To start the audit trace, you execute the –START TRACE command. The following example starts a trace that audits data changes and captures the text of any dynamic SQL.

```
-START TRACE (AUDIT) DEST (SMF)
COMMENT ('Trace data changes; include text of dynamic DML statements.')
```

To stop this trace, issue the –STOP TRACE command:

```
-STOP TRACE (AUDIT)
```

This command simply stops the last trace started. If more than one trace is executing, you can use the –DISPLAY TRACE command to identify a particular trace by number. (For more information about DB2 commands, see Chapter 2.)

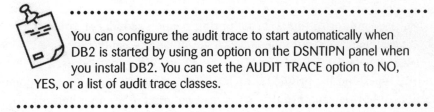

You can configure the audit trace to start automatically when DB2 is started by using an option on the DSNTIPN panel when you install DB2. You can set the AUDIT TRACE option to NO, YES, or a list of audit trace classes.

Auditing a Table

For the audit trace to be effective at the table level, you must first choose, by specifying an option of the CREATE or ALTER statement, whether to audit the table. This example shows how to indicate that you want to audit changes.

```
CREATE TABLE DSN8910.EMP
(EMPNO CHAR(6) NOT NULL
  ...
IN DSN8D91A.DSN8S91E
AUDIT CHANGES
```

Possible AUDIT values are CHANGES, ALL, and NONE, with the default being NONE (no auditing). To turn off auditing at the table level, you'd simply perform an ALTER specifying AUDIT NONE.

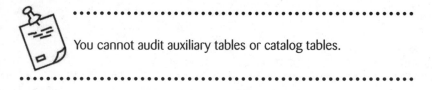

You cannot audit auxiliary tables or catalog tables.

Summary

In this chapter, we discussed several topics related to data access. We covered security with respect to the subsystem, data sets, and DB2. DB2 lets you control subsystem security in a variety of ways, such as via CICS, IMS, and Kerberos and RACF. In some situations, you also need to consider securing access at the data-set level because DB2 stores its data into individual data sets that can be accessed outside DB2.

We discussed authorization IDs (both primary and secondary), roles, and how both are assigned. DB2 provides several administrative authority levels: SYSADM, SYSCTRL, DBADM, DBCTRL, PACKADM, and so on. We discussed each of these authority types and the privileges they possess. Object ownership also comes with inherited authorities and privileges that can be granted to other authorization IDs.

We examined the granting and revoking of database object privileges using the GRANT and REVOKE SQL statements.

We talked in detail about the DB2 audit trace, which lets you carefully monitor critical tables to see who is manipulating data or, in some very sensitive cases, who is simply trying to access data.

The trusted context and roles are new to DB2 9 and provide another level of security and manageability for your databases and applications. All these levels of security can work together to keep your data and your subsystem safe.

Additional Resources

IBM DB2 9 Administration Guide (SC18-9840)
IBM DB2 9 SQL Reference (SC18-9854)

Practice Questions

Question 1

DBA1 needs to be able to create tables in a database and be able to run periodic REORGs. However, DBA1 is not permitted to access the data or manipulate it. Which of the following authorities would be the most appropriate?

○ A. SYSADM

○ B. DBADM

○ C. DBCTRL

○ D. DBMAINT

Question 2

To limit exposure for an application, a company creates an APP1 trusted context and an APP1_DBA role. DBA1 was assigned to this role and all the objects. What happens if DBA1 leaves the company and the ID is removed?

○ A. The objects and privileges of the role are untouched.

○ B. All privileges need to be re-granted.

○ C. All dependent privileges are cascade revoked.

○ D. The objects need to be dropped and re-created.

Question 3

A user ID is required to attach a client to the current application/process connection to enable client application testing of native SQL or Java procedures that are executed within the session. Which of the following system privileges is required?

○ A. TRACE

○ B. MONITOR1

○ C. MONITOR2

○ D. DEBUGSESSION

Question 4

A DBA wants to create a new plan using the BIND PLAN PKLIST option and specifying individual packages. What authority/privilege must the DBA have for the operation to be successful?

○ A. COPY to copy the individual packages

○ B. EXECUTE authority on each package specified in the PKLIST

○ C. CREATE IN to name the collection containing the individual packages

○ D. BINDAGENT to bind all the individual packages on behalf of their owner

Question 5

Which level of authority is required to revoke a privilege that another ID has granted?

○ A. DBADM

○ B. DBCTRL

○ C. SYSOPR

○ D. SYSCTRL

Answers

Question 1

The correct answer is **C**, DBCTRL. This authority will let DBA1 create tables in a specified database as well as run some utilities, such as REORG, on the table spaces in the database. This authority does not permit SQL Data Manipulation Language (DML) to be executed against the objects in the database.

Question 2

The correct answer is **A**, the objects and privileges of the role are untouched. One benefit of roles is the fact that if the ID assigned to the role is removed, nothing happens to the objects or privileges assigned to the role.

Question 3

The correct answer is **D**, DEBUGSESSION. This is a new privilege with DB2 9 that provides the ability to control debug session activity for native SQL and Java stored procedures.

Question 4

The correct answer is **B**, EXECUTE authority on each package specified in the PKLIST. To be able to create a new plan with packages, you must have EXECUTE authority on the packages in the PKLIST.

Question 5

The correct answer is **D**, SYSCTRL. This is the only level of authority that can revoke a privilege granted by another ID.

CHAPTER 4

Database Objects

In This Chapter

- ✔ Creating database objects
- ✔ Data types
- ✔ Tables and table spaces
- ✔ Aliases and synonyms
- ✔ Constraints
- ✔ Views
- ✔ Indexes
- ✔ Sequence objects

DB2 is a relational database that consists of one or more tables made up of rows and columns. You create and access DB2 tables using the industry-standard Structured Query Language (SQL). The data in DB2 tables is accessed via content, not location. In this chapter, we look at the structures in a DB2 subsystem and those that make up a DB2 database. Many DB2 objects can be referenced directly from an SQL statement; it's therefore important to understand their purpose.

SQL is divided into three major parts:

- You use SQL *Data Definition Language (DDL)* to create, change, and drop database objects.

- You use SQL *Data Manipulation Language (DML)* to select, insert, update, and delete database data (records).

- You use SQL *Data Control Language (DCL)* to provide data-object access control.

As SQL has evolved, it has adopted many new statements to provide a more complete set of data access methods.

Understanding Data Structures

A database is an organized collection of related objects. Throughout the database industry, SQL is used as a common method of issuing database queries. SQL is considered a language, composed of statements, functions, and data types. You use SQL statements to access database objects using relational operations.

Before we examine the SQL language, you need to understand some DB2 terminology. We'll be referring to the basic data structures or objects that are defined for each DB2 database. These objects include the following:

- Tables
- Aliases
- Synonyms
- Views
- Indexes
- Table spaces
- Index spaces
- Databases
- Storage groups

Figure 4.1 depicts the relationship among DB2 objects.

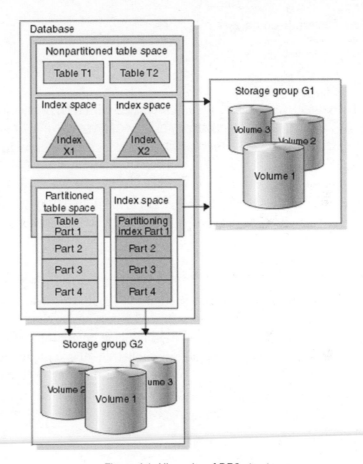

Figure 4.1: Hierarchy of DB2 structures

Tables

A *table* is an unordered set of data records. It consists of columns—each based on a data type—and rows. Once you create a table and populate it with data, you reference it either in the FROM clause of the SQL statements or in automatic query rewrite (a feature associated with materialized query tables, or MQTs). DB2 supports several types of tables:

- Permanent (or base) tables
- Auxiliary tables
- Temporary (declared or global) tables

- Materialized query tables

- Clone tables

- XML tables

In this chapter, we discuss only tables created with a DDL statement. You use the CREATE TABLE, CREATE AUXILIARY TABLE, or CREATE GLOBAL TEMPORARY TABLE statement to create these tables, and each is a logical representation of the way the data is physically stored on disk. You'll also learn how to define MQTs and clone tables, but we'll defer discussion of their use and the declared temporary tables to Chapters 6 and 12. XML table spaces are created implicitly when you create a column with an XML data type.

Aliases

An *alias* is basically a pointer to another table and is a substitute for the three-part name of a table or view. DB2 on z/OS is the only server that supports three-part name syntax, and aliases are often used in place of any three-part named table to make the references portable. You can qualify an alias with an owner ID, and the referenced table can be on the local site or on a remote site. If the table pointed to by an alias is dropped, the alias is not dropped.

Synonyms

You use *synonyms* to refer to a table using a different name or to refer to another owner's table as if you were the owner. A synonym is basically a private pointer to a table. Only the synonym's owner can reference the synonym, and the synonym is not allowed to be qualified.

Unlike an alias, a synonym can be used to refer only to a table in the same subsystem in which it was defined. If the table is dropped, so is the synonym.

Views

Views provide alternative ways of viewing data in one or more base tables or other views. A view is not a physical object and does not store actual data. It is an entry in the DB2 catalog that, when accessed, executes an SQL statement that retrieves data from other tables or views. You can use views to limit access to certain kinds of data, create customized views of data for users, or permit alterations of tables without affecting application programs. Views can be read-only if necessary, or they can be UPDATEable, INSERTable, or DELETEable. Some restrictions apply to using views.

Indexes

Indexes are ordered sets of pointers associated with a table. You can create indexes on permanent tables or on declared temporary tables. An index is based on the values of one or more columns in a table. The index values can be ascending, descending, or random. Each table can have one or more indexes, and you can use indexes to enforce uniqueness in the data values and clustering sequence. You can also use indexes to improve performance when accessing data; with an index, large scans of data can be avoided.

DB2 supports two types of indexes: partitioned and non-partitioned. A partitioned index is created on a partitioned table space and can be partitioning or secondary. A non-partitioned index is used on tables defined in segmented or simple table spaces or as an alternate index on a partitioned table space.

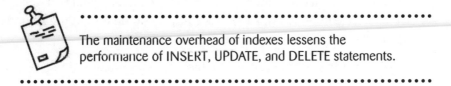

The maintenance overhead of indexes lessens the performance of INSERT, UPDATE, and DELETE statements.

Keys

A *key* is a named, ordered set of columns on one table. A composite key is a key made of several columns. Many keys can be defined on a table. Each key will play a particular role for a given table.

Table Spaces

Table spaces are objects that consist of one or more data sets used to store DB2 data. Tables are created in table spaces, and you can have one or many tables in a table space, depending on the type of table space defined. DB2 provides six types of table spaces: simple, segmented, partitioned, universal, large object (LOB), and XML.

- **Simple table spaces.** These table spaces can contain one or more tables; however, the rows of the different tables aren't kept on separate database pages, which can cause concurrency and space usage issues. As of DB2 9, you can no longer create a simple table space. However, the use of existing simple table spaces is still supported.

- **Segmented table spaces.** Segmented table spaces can contain one or more tables, and the space is divided into same-sized segments. Each segment will contain rows from only one table.

- **Partitioned table spaces.** A partitioned table space divides the data into several separate data sets (partitions). Only one table can exist in a partitioned table space. You can have up to 4,096 partitions of up to 64 GB each. Each partition can have different characteristics, such as volume placement and free space.

- **Universal table spaces.** A universal table space is created as either a range-partitioned table space or a partition-by-growth table space, depending on the setting specified in the CREATE TABLESPACE statement. Like partitioned table spaces, universal table spaces can contain up to 4,096 partitions. Many newer DB2 features require universal table spaces.

- **LOB table spaces.** Large object table spaces are required to hold large object data. LOB table spaces are associated with the table space that holds the logical LOB column. LOB table spaces can be explicitly defined.

- **XML table spaces.** XML table spaces are used to hold XML data that is stored in XML data type columns. Unlike LOB table spaces, which you can define explicitly, the XML table spaces are created implicitly by DB2 when you define an XML column.

Both simple and segmented table spaces can contain multiple tables, but due to the many performance issues associated with simple table spaces, it's best to use only segmented table spaces. We examine the various types of table spaces in more detail later in the chapter.

Index Spaces

When you create an index, an *index space* is also created. Index spaces are a set of virtual storage access method (VSAM) linear data sets that hold index data, and they are implicitly associated with the database that contains the table on which the index is defined.

Databases

Databases in DB2 are collections of table spaces and index spaces. The database on the z/OS platform doesn't have any physical storage characteristics but acts more like an umbrella over all its dependent objects. It enables defaults to be established for the table space and indexes within it.

Storage Groups

You use *storage groups* to define a list of volumes to DB2 for its use when creating physical objects such as table spaces and index spaces. The system allocates the storage when you load the tables with data. You create storage groups using DDL.

Materialized Query Tables

Materialized query tables are objects that are created to allow whole or partial queries to be pre-computed so that the computed results can be used to answer future queries. MQTs provide a way to save the results of prior queries and reuse the common results in subsequent queries. This feature helps avoid redundant scanning, aggregating, and joins.

Clone Tables

You create a *clone table* by specifying the ADD CLONE keywords on an ALTER TABLE statement. The clone table receives a distinct name from the base table on which it is defined, but it is defined within the same schema and has the same structure as the base table, and it exists within the same universal table space as the base table. The clone table inherits the column names, data types, null attributes, check constraints, indexes, and before triggers of the base table. Once created, a clone table can be manipulated independently of the base table, and you can use an

SQL EXCHANGE statement to exchange data between the base table and the clone table. Clone tables thus provide the functional equivalent of an online LOAD REPLACE utility (which doesn't exist).

Sequence Objects

A *sequence object* is a user-defined object that generates a sequence of numeric values according to the specifications that create the object. Sequence objects are standalone objects that provide an incremental counter generated by DB2.

Schemas

Schemas are names used to fully identify database objects. They relate to creator name for a table or index and are used to fully qualify database objects such as sequences, user-defined functions, triggers, user-defined data types, and stored procedures. Schemas are implicitly created when you define one of these objects, but you can also define a schema using a CREATE SCHEMA statement (which can be processed only by something called the Schema Processor).

Managing Database Objects

To create, modify, or delete objects in a database, you use SQL DDL. The DDL contains four main SQL statements: CREATE, DECLARE, DROP, and ALTER. We examine each of these statements in the following sections.

The CREATE Statement

```
CREATE  <database object>
```

You use the CREATE statement to define a database object. Database objects serve different purposes. Some define a condition or relationship (index, trigger), and others are a logical representation of data as it is physically stored on disk (table, table space). You can create the following types of database objects using the CREATE statement:

- Alias
- Auxiliary table (LOB)

- Database

- Function (user-defined function)

- Global temporary table

- Index

- Materialized query table

- Procedure (stored procedure)

- Role

- Sequence object

- Stogroup (storage group)

- Synonym

- Table

- Table space

- Trigger

- Trusted context

- Type (user-defined data type)

- View

The creation of any database object using DDL results in an update to the DB2 system catalog tables. You need special database authorities or privileges to create database objects (for more information about authorities and privileges, see Chapter 3).

The DECLARE Statement

```
DECLARE  <database object>
```

The DECLARE statement is similar to the CREATE statement except that the object it can create is a temporary table. Temporary tables are used only for the duration of an application, stored procedure, or connection. Temporary tables cause no logging or contention against the system catalog tables, and they're useful for working with intermediate results. This type of table is materialized in the work files.

The creation of a temporary table doesn't result in any update to the system catalog tables, so you avoid locking, logging, and other forms of contention with this object.

You can drop and alter declared tables, but no other database objects (e.g., views, triggers) can be created to act against them. Temporary tables do allow for the specification of a partitioning key.

Once you declare a table, you can reference it like any other SQL table. You'll learn more about declared temporary tables in Chapter 12.

The DROP Statement

DROP *<database object>*

You use the DROP statement to remove definitions from the system catalog tables (and hence from the database itself). You can't delete objects directly from the system catalog tables, so you use the DROP statement to remove data records from these tables. Database objects can be dependent on other database objects, and the act of dropping a particular object results in dropping any object that directly or indirectly depends on that object. Any plan or package that depends on the object deleted from the catalog on the current server will be invalidated.

You can drop any object that was created with the CREATE *<database object>* statement or the DECLARE *<table>* statement.

The ALTER Statement

ALTER *<database object>* . . .

The ALTER statement lets you change some characteristics of database objects. Any object being altered must already exist in the database. The following database objects can be altered:

- Database

- Function

- Index

- Procedure

- Sequence object

- Stogroup

- Table

- Table space

- Trusted context

Every time you issue a DDL statement, the system catalog tables are updated. The update includes a creation or modification timestamp and the authorization ID of the creator (modifier).

Later in the chapter, we'll look in detail at some of the objects you can create. We'll cover tables, sequence objects, table spaces, views, materialized query tables, clone tables, indexes, databases, and storage groups. Before discussing tables or other objects, though, you need to understand the various data types available with DB2.

Data Types

When you create a table, you use *data types* to specify the attributes of the table's columns. Data types define the type of data that will occupy each column in a DB2 table and provide the length of the column. Data that doesn't match the data type defined for a column won't be allowed in that column. Different types of data exist, including string, numeric, date, time, ROWID, large object, XML, and user-defined distinct data types. Depending on the data type, the column length may be fixed or varying.

DB2's data types fall into two distinct groups: built-in and user-defined. The built-in data types are those defined by DB2. The other group, user-defined, lets you define your own type of data to be stored in a column. The user-defined data types are based on existing built-in data types.

DB2-Supplied Data Types

When implementing the database design, you can use any DB2-supplied data type. Every DB2-supplied type belongs to one of three major categories:

- Numeric

- String (binary, single-byte, double-byte)

- Date-time

More specialized data types for row ID and XML values also exist. Table 4.1 lists the valid built-in data types in DB2.

Table 4.1: Built-in DB2 data types		
Data type	**Description**	**DB2 data type**
Signed numeric types		
Exact	Binary integer: 16-bit	SMALLINT
	Binary integer: 32-bit	INTEGER
	Binary integer: 64 bit	BIGINT
	Decimal: packed	DECIMAL, DEC, NUMERIC
Approximate	Single-precision floating point	REAL
	Double-precision floating point	DOUBLE, FLOAT
Decimal floating point	Decimal floating point	DECFLOAT
String types		
Character	Fixed-length	CHAR
	Varying-length	VARCHAR, CLOB
Graphic	Fixed-length	GRAPHIC
	Varying-length	VARGRAPHIC, DBCLOB
Binary	Fixed-length	BINARY
	Varying-length	VARBINARY, BLOB

Table 4.1: Built-in DB2 data types (continued)		
Data type	**Description**	**DB2 data type**
Date-time types		
Time		TIME
Timestamp		TIMESTAMP
Date		DATE
Row identifier		ROWID
XML		XML

Numeric Data Types

The seven DB2 data types available to store numeric data are:

- SMALLINT

- INTEGER

- BIGINT

- DECIMAL/DEC/NUMERIC

- REAL

- DOUBLE/FLOAT

- DECFLOAT

You use these data types to store different numeric types and precisions. The *precision* of a number is the number of digits used to represent its value. The data is stored in the DB2 database using a fixed amount of storage for all numeric data types. The amount of storage required increases as the precision of the number goes up.

When manipulating numeric fields, you must be aware of the range limits of the data types and the corresponding application programming language. Some data values, such as the number of employees, are of the integer type by nature. It would be impossible to have a number that contains fractional data (i.e., numbers to the right of the decimal) representing a number of people. On the other hand, some values, such as bonus (in the DB2 employee sample table), require decimal places to accurately reflect their value. These two examples should use different DB2 data types to store their values (INTEGER and DECIMAL, respectively).

You don't enclose numeric values in quotation marks; do so, and DB2 will treat the value as a character string. Even if a field contains numbers in its representation, you should use a DB2 numeric data type to represent the data only if arithmetic operations should be allowed.

Let's look at the details of the different numeric data types available in DB2.

Small Integer (SMALLINT)

A small integer uses the least amount of storage in the database for each value. An integer allows no digits to the right of the decimal. The data value range for a SMALLINT is –32,768 to 32,767. The precision for a SMALLINT is five digits (to the left of the decimal). Each SMALLINT column value uses two bytes of database storage.

Integer (INTEGER)

An INTEGER takes twice as much storage as a SMALLINT but has a greater range of possible values. The range value for an INTEGER data type is –2,147,483,648 to 2,147,483,647. The precision for an INTEGER is 10 digits to the left of the decimal. Each INTEGER column value uses four bytes of database storage.

Big Integer (BIGINT)

A BIGINT takes twice as much storage as an INTEGER but provides an even greater range of possible values. The range value for a BIGINT data type is –9,223,372,036,854,775,808 to 9,223,372,036,854,775,807; the precision is 19 digits to the left of the decimal. Each BIGINT column value uses eight bytes of database storage.

Decimal (DECIMAL/NUMERIC)

You use the DECIMAL or NUMERIC data type for numbers that have fractional and whole parts. The DECIMAL data is stored in a packed format. When you use a decimal data type, you must provide the precision and scale. The precision is the total number of digits (range from 1 to 31), and the scale is the number of digits in the fractional part of the number. For example, a decimal data type to store currency values of up to $1 million would require a definition of DECIMAL(9,2).

You can use the term DECIMAL, DEC, or NUMERIC to declare a decimal or numeric column. If you plan to use a decimal data type in a C program, you must declare the host variable as a double. A DECIMAL number takes up to $p/2 + 1$ bytes of storage, where p is the precision used. For example, DEC(8,2) would take up five bytes of storage ($8/2 + 1$), whereas DEC(7,2) would take up only four bytes (truncate the division of $p/2$).

Single-Precision Floating Point (REAL)

A REAL data type is an approximation of a number. The approximation requires 32 bits or four bytes of storage. To specify a single-precision number using the REAL data type, you must define the length between 1 and 24. (You can also use FLOAT(n), where n represents a value between 1 and 24, to define a REAL data type.)

Double-Precision Floating Point (DOUBLE/FLOAT)

A DOUBLE or FLOAT data type is an approximation of a number. The approximation requires 64 bits or eight bytes of storage. To specify a double-precision number using the FLOAT data type, you must define the length between 25 and 53 or not specify a length at all.

Decimal Floating Point (DECFLOAT)

A DECFLOAT value is an IEEE 754r (floating-point) number with a decimal point. The position of the decimal point is stored in each decimal floating-point value. The maximum precision is 34 digits. The range of a decimal floating-point number is either 16 or 34 digits of precision, with an exponent range of, respectively, 10^{-383} to 10^{+384} or 10^{-6143} to 10^{+6144}.

In addition to the finite numbers, decimal floating-point numbers can represent one of the following named special values.

Special value	Description
Infinity	A value that represents a number whose magnitude is infinitely large
Quiet NaN	A value that represents undefined results but will not cause an invalid number condition
Signaling NaN	A value that represents undefined results and will cause an invalid-number condition if used in any numerical operation

When a number has one of these special values, its coefficient and exponent are undefined. The sign of an infinity is significant (that is, it's possible to have both positive and negative infinity). For arithmetic operations, the sign of a NaN (NaN stands for "Not a Number") has no meaning. In place of INFINITY, you can use INF.

String Data Types

DB2 supports the following string data types:

- CHAR
- VARCHAR
- CLOB
- GRAPHIC
- VARGRAPHIC
- DBCLOB
- BINARY
- VARBINARY
- BLOB

Although the syntax of LONG VARCHAR and LONG VARGRAPHIC are still supported, the alternative syntaxes of VARCHAR(integer) and VARGRAPHIC(integer) are preferred. DB2 will translate the LONG definitions into the other format before actually defining the table. Therefore, you should use only the VARCHAR() and VARGRAPHIC() definitions.

Fixed-Length Character String (CHAR)

Fixed-length character strings are stored in the database using the entire defined amount of storage. If the data being stored always has the same length, you should use a CHAR data type.

Using fixed-length character fields can potentially waste disk space within the database if the data isn't using the defined amount of storage. However, storing varying-length character strings imposes some overhead. The length of a fixed-length string must be between 1 and 255 characters. If you don't supply a value for the length, DB2 assumes a value of 1.

Varying-Length Character String (VARCHAR)

Varying-length character strings are stored in the database using only the amount of space required to store the data and a two-byte prefix to hold the length. The employee last names in the DB2 sample database, for example, are stored as varying-length strings (VARCHAR) because each person's name has a different length (up to a maximum length of 15 characters).

If a varying-length character string is updated and the resulting value is larger than the original, it may not fit on the same database page; in that case, the row will be moved to another page in the table, leaving a marker in the original place. These marker data records are known as *indirect reference rows*. Too many of these records can significantly degrade performance because multiple pages (and possibly I/Os) are required to return a single data record.

A VARCHAR column has the restriction that it must fit on one database page. This means that a 4 K page would allow a VARCHAR up to 4,046 characters long (defined as VARCHAR(4046)), an 8 K page would be up to 8,128 characters long, and so on up to a 32 K page with the maximum column length of 32,704 bytes. This means that you must create a table space for this table that can accommodate the larger page size, and you must have sufficient space in the row to accommodate this string.

Beginning with DB2 9, DB2 has the ability to efficiently organize data physically in a row of a table based on whether a column is varying or fixed in length. In previous versions, the rows of a column were stored in the physical order in which they were defined in the CREATE TABLE statement—a format called *basic row format*. This physical format had certain inefficiencies because DB2 had to search for any columns after the varying-length columns in a physical row, depending on the length of the varying-length columns. Any tables that contained varying-length columns before DB2 9 are still stored in basic row format. However, any new tables created in new table space after migration to DB2 9 will use something called *reordered row format*. With this physical row format, the variable-length columns will be placed physically in the row after any fixed-length columns.

Character strings on z/OS are stored in the database without a termination character. Depending on the non-z/OS development environment or programming language used, a null terminator may or may not be appended to the end of a character string when the data is stored or retrieved.

Updates to variable character fields can cause the row length to change and may cause indirect references.

Character Large Object (CLOB)

CLOBs are varying-length, single-byte character set (SBCS) or multi-byte character set (MBCS) character strings that are stored in the database. CLOB columns are used to store greater than 32 K of text. The maximum size for each CLOB column is 2 GB (2 gigabytes minus 1 byte). Because this data type is of varying length, the amount of data in each record determines the amount of disk space allocated.

For this reason, you should specify the length of the longest string when creating the column.

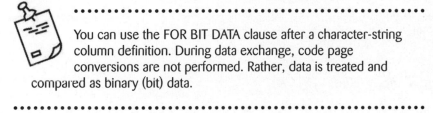

You can use the FOR BIT DATA clause after a character-string column definition. During data exchange, code page conversions are not performed. Rather, data is treated and compared as binary (bit) data.

Double-Byte Character Strings (GRAPHIC)

The GRAPHIC data types represent a single character using two bytes of storage. These data types are GRAPHIC (fixed length, maximum 127 DBCS characters), VARGRAPHIC (varying length, maximum 32,704 DBCS characters for 32 K pages), and DBCLOB.

VARCHAR data types over 255 bytes are similar to CLOB data types. (Both types have usage restrictions.)

Double-Byte Character Large Objects (DBCLOB)

DBCLOBs are varying-length character strings that are stored in the database using two bytes to represent each character. A code page is associated with each column. DBCLOB columns are used for large amounts (greater than 32 K) of double-byte text data, such as Japanese text. You should specify the maximum length when defining the column because each data record will be variable in length.

Fixed-Length Binary Strings (BINARY)

Binary strings are a sequence of bytes and aren't associated with any coded character set identifier (CCSID). BINARYs are fixed-length binary strings that can be between 1 and 255 bytes in length. For a BINARY column, all values have the same length.

Varying-Length Binary Strings (VARBINARY)

VARBINARYs are varying-length binary strings that can be between 1 and 32,704 bytes in length. For a VARBINARY column, all values have the same length. VARBINARYs have the same length restrictions as VARCHARs.

Binary Large Object (BLOB)

BLOBs are variable-length binary strings. The data is stored in a binary format in the database. Restrictions apply when using this data type, including the inability to sort using this type of column. The BLOB data type is useful for storing nontraditional relational database information. The maximum size of each BLOB column is 2 GB (2 gigabytes minus 1 byte). Because this data type is of varying length, the amount of data in each record, not the defined maximum size of the column in the table definition, determines the amount of disk space allocated.

Large Object Considerations

Traditionally, large unstructured data was stored somewhere outside the database. Therefore, you couldn't access this data using SQL. In addition to the traditional database data types, DB2 implements data types that can store large amounts of unstructured data. These data types are known as *large objects*, or LOBs.
You can define multiple LOB columns for a single table. DB2 provides special considerations for handling these large objects. For example, you can choose not to log the LOB values to avoid large amounts of data being logged.

There is a LOG option you can specify on the CREATE TABLESPACE statement for each AUXILIARY TABLE that will hold LOB column data to avoid logging any modifications. If you'd like to define a LOB column greater than 1 GB, you must specify the LOG NO option.

In a database, you can choose to use BLOBs for the storage of pictures, images, or audio or video objects, along with large documents. BLOB columns will accept any binary string without regard to the contents. To manipulate textual data that is greater than 32 K in length, you'd use a CLOB data type. For example, if each test candidate were required to submit his or her resume, you could store the resume in a CLOB column along with the rest of the candidate's information. Many SQL functions can be used to manipulate large-character data columns.

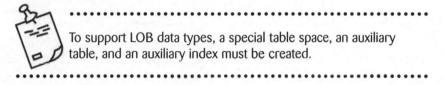

To support LOB data types, a special table space, an auxiliary table, and an auxiliary index must be created.

String Encoding Schemes

An *encoding scheme* is a set of rules used to represent character data. All string data stored in a DB2 table must use the same encoding scheme, and all tables within a table space must use the same encoding scheme, except for global temporary tables, declared temporary tables, and work file table spaces. DB2 supports three encoding schemes for string data:

- ASCII
- EDCDIC
- Unicode

Even within each encoding scheme, there can be different CCSIDs. For Unicode, there are two; for ASCII and EBCDIC, there are many. Within the encoding scheme, the CCSID determines how the strings are stored (the hexadecimal value of the characters). This approach permits great flexibility in dealing with special characters and various languages.

You can set the encoding scheme during the CREATE TABLE statement. User application data under z/OS is typically stored in EBCDIC, but in special situations it can be stored in ASCII or Unicode. All the data in a table is stored in the same encoding scheme. The encoding scheme can impact comparisons and other database operations (e.g., sorting), especially across platforms, because DRDA performs character translations (for some columns) across different platforms and encoding schemes. This can get complicated. The important things to remember are the operations that are performed on the data server versus on the client or remote platform. For example, in the following example, a Unicode string is compared with a column of a table defined with an ASCII encoding scheme.

```
SELECT * FROM TEST.TABLE1 WHERE COL1 = UX'4E2F';
```

The comparison in this case takes place in ASCII; that is, the Unicode string is converted to ASCII for the comparison.

The encoding scheme can also influence the sort order. In the next statement, TABLE1 is stored with an ASCII encoding scheme. Even though the request could be coming from a remote application that uses an EBCDIC encoding scheme, the sort actually happens on the server, and the returned data will be ordered according to the ASCII encoding scheme.

```
SELECT * FROM TEST.TABLE1 ORDER BY COL1, COL2;
```

The whole issue of encoding schemes and character sets can become quite complicated. The best source for information about this topic is the *SQL Reference Guide*. We provide more details about DB2's Unicode support later in the chapter.

Date and Time Data Types

Three DB2 data types are specifically used to represent dates and times:

- **DATE.** This data type is stored internally as a (packed) string of four bytes. Externally, the string has a length of 10 bytes (MM-DD-YYYY—this representation can vary and depends on the country code).

- **TIME.** This data type is stored internally as a (packed) string of three bytes. Externally, the string has a length of eight bytes (HH.MM.SS—this representation may vary).

- **TIMESTAMP.** This data type is stored internally as a (packed) string of 10 bytes. Externally, the string has a length of 26 bytes (YYYY-MM-DD.HH.MM.SS.NNNNNN).

From the user perspective, these data types can be treated as character or string data types. Every time you need to use a date-time attribute, you need to enclose it in quotation marks. However, date-time data types aren't stored in the database as fixed-length character strings.

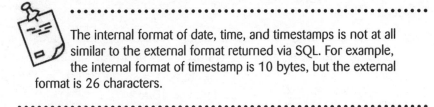

The internal format of date, time, and timestamps is not at all similar to the external format returned via SQL. For example, the internal format of timestamp is 10 bytes, but the external format is 26 characters.

DB2 provides special functions that let you manipulate the date-time data types. These functions let you extract the month, hour, or year of a date-time column. The date and time formats correspond to the site default. Therefore, the string that represents a date value will change depending on the default format. In some countries, the date format is DD/MM/YYYY, whereas in other countries it is YYYY-MM-DD. You should be aware of the default format used by your site to use the correct date string format. If you use an incorrect date format in an SQL statement, an SQL error will be reported. Scalar functions are available to return date, time, and timestamp columns in formats other than the default.

As a general recommendation, if you're interested in a single element of a date string—say, the month or year—always use the SQL functions provided by DB2 to interpret the column value. By using the SQL functions, you can make your application more portable.

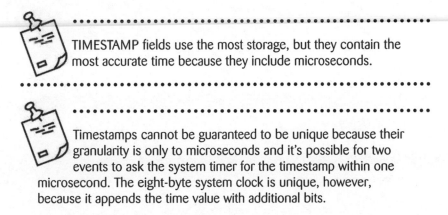

TIMESTAMP fields use the most storage, but they contain the most accurate time because they include microseconds.

Timestamps cannot be guaranteed to be unique because their granularity is only to microseconds and it's possible for two events to ask the system timer for the timestamp within one microsecond. The eight-byte system clock is unique, however, because it appends the time value with additional bits.

We stated that all date-time data types have an internal and external format. The external format is always a character string. Let's examine the various date-time data type formats available in DB2.

Date String (DATE)

DB2 provides several valid ways to represent a Date as a string. You can use any of the string formats shown in Table 4.2 to store dates in a DB2 database. When the data is retrieved (via a SELECT statement), the output string will be in one of these formats, or it can be returned in any format specified.

Table 4.2: Date string formats	
Standard	**String format**
International Standards Organization (ISO)	YYYY-MM-DD
IBM USA Standard (USA)	MM/DD/YYYY
IBM European Standard (EUR)	DD.MM.YYYY
Japanese Industrial Standard (JIS)	YYYY-MM-DD

In addition, many scalar functions in DB2 return date information:

- ADD_MONTHS
- DATE
- DAY
- DAYOFMONTH
- DAYOFWEEK
- DAYOFWEEK
- DAYOFYEAR
- DAYS
- JULIAN_DAY
- LAST_DAY
- MONTH
- MONTHS_BETWEEN
- NEXT_DAY
- QUARTER
- WEEK

- WEEK_ISO

- YEAR

Time String (TIME)

Several valid methods also exist for representing a time as a string. To store times in a DB2 database, you can use any of the string formats in listed in Table 4.3. When data is retrieved, the external format of the time will be one of the formats shown in the table.

Table 4.3: Time string formats	
Standard	Format
International Standards Organization (ISO)	HH.MM.SS
IBM USA Standard (USA)	HH:MM AM or PM
IBM European Standard (EUR)	HH.MM.SS
Japanese Industrial Standard (JIS)	HH:MM:SS

In addition, several scalar functions in DB2 return time information:

- HOUR

- MINUTE

- SECOND

- TIME

Timestamp String (TIMESTAMP)

The timestamp data type has a single default external format: YYYY-MM-DD-HH.MM.SS.NNNNNN (year-month-day-hour-minute-second-microsecond). However, several scalar functions can manipulate this output format. Of particular note is the TIMESTAMP_FORMAT function, which can return any type of string, up to 255 characters, based on a user-defined template.

In addition, many scalar functions in DB2 return timestamp information (besides all those listed for DATE and TIME), including:

- MICROSECOND

- TIMESTAMP

- TIMESTAMP_FORMAT

ROWID

The ROWID data type defines a value that uniquely identifies a row in a table. A ROWID column lets you write queries that navigate directly to a row in the table. ROWID column values are generated by DB2 unless you supply them, but they must be unique. If you supply a value, it must be a valid DB2-generated value. The internal format is 17 bytes and contains bit data. The external length is 40 bytes.

If you use a ROWID column in a query, the access method is referred to as *direct row access* because DB2 accesses the row directly, without a scan of the index or the table space. This type of access appears as a D in the ACCESS_PATH column in the PLAN_TABLE. (For information about the PLAN_TABLE and access paths, refer to Chapter 17.) However, even though the ROWID provides this access path, direct row access is not guaranteed. If you use ROWID access extensively, consider creating an index on the ROWID column to avoid a table space scan.

The best guarantee that DB2 will use ROWID access for queries is to perform the ROWID access in the same unit of work in which the ROWID value was generated by DB2. In other words, perform a "SELECT from INSERT" to obtain the ROWID value, and then subsequently access the row using the ROWID value for update or delete without committing in between. This technique guarantees ROWID access.

XML

The XML data type is new in DB2 9. An XML value represents well-formed XML in the form of an XML document, XML content, or a sequence of XML nodes. An XML value that is stored in a table as the value of a column defined with the XML data type must be a well-formed XML document. XML values are processed in an internal representation that is not comparable to any string value. Using functions, however, you can transform XML values into or from a serialized string value that represents the XML.

The XML data type has a variable length and allows for a wide range of sizes. DB2 treats XML string data in a similar manner to LOB data to be able to accommodate very large XML values. Thus, XML values are constrained by the same maximum length limit as LOB data.

Whenever you add an XML column to a table, DB2 implicitly builds additional objects, including an XML table and table space, where the XML data will be stored separately from the base table. Also created in the base table are a BIGINT DOCID column that identifies the XML document and an index on the DOCID column.

User-Defined Data Types

User-defined data types, or UDTs, let a user extend the data types that DB2 understands in a database. DB2 for z/OS supports only the user-defined *distinct type*. You can create user-defined data types based on existing data types or on other user-defined data types. You use UDTs to further define the types of data being represented in the database. If columns are defined using different UDTs that are based on the same base data type, the UDTs can't be directly compared. This property, known as *strong typing*, helps avoid end-user mistakes during the assignment or comparison of different types of real-world data. Chapter 15 provides information about how to create and use UDTs.

Null Values

A *null value* represents an unknown state. Therefore, when columns containing null values are used in calculations, the result is unknown. All the data types we've discussed support the presence of null values. During the table definition, you can specify that a valid value must be provided; you do so by adding a phrase to the column definition. Specify NOT NULL after the definition of each column in the CREATE TABLE statement to ensure that the column contains a known data value.

Special considerations are required to properly handle null values when coding a DB2 application. DB2 treats a null value differently than it treats other data values.

To define a column not to accept null values, add the NOT NULL phrase to the end of the column definition. For example:

```
CREATE TABLE t1 (c1 CHAR(3) NOT NULL)
```

In this example, DB2 will not allow any null values to be stored in the c1 column. In general, you should avoid using nullable columns unless they're necessary to implement the database design. There is also overhead storage you must consider. An extra byte per nullable column is required if you permit null values.

● ●

Relational databases allow null values. It's important to remember that such values can be appropriate for your database design.

● ●

NOT NULL WITH DEFAULT

When you insert a row into a table and omit the value of one or more columns, those columns may be populated using either a null value (if the column is defined as nullable) or a defined default value (if you've specified this to be used). If the column is defined as not nullable, the insert will fail unless the data has been provided for the column. DB2 has a defined default value for each DB2 data type, but you can provide a default value for each column in the CREATE TABLE statement. By defining your own default value, you can ensure that the data value is populated with a known value.

Unicode Support

The Unicode character encoding scheme assists with support across multinational boundaries, enabling a representation of codepoints and characters of several different geographies and languages that allows for the exchange of data internationally. Unicode provides the ability to encode all characters used for the written languages of the world, and it treats alphabetic characters, ideographic characters, and symbols equivalently because it specifies a numeric value and a name for each of its characters. It includes punctuation marks, mathematical symbols, technical symbols, geometric shapes, and dingbats. DB2 supports two encoding forms:

- *UTF-8: Unicode Transformation Format*, an eight-bit encoding form designed for ease of use with existing ASCII-based systems. A UTF-8 character is 1, 2 , 3, or 4 bytes in length. A UTF-8 data string can contain any combination of SBCS and MBCS data. The CCSID value for data in UTF-8 format is 1208.

- *UTF-16: Unicode Transformation Format*, a 16-bit encoding form designed to provide code values for more than a million characters and a superset of UCS-2 (Universal Character Set). UTF-16 can encode any of the Unicode characters. In UTF-16 encoding, characters are two bytes in length, except for supplementary characters, which require two two-byte string units per character. The CCSID value for data in UTF-16 format is 1200.

DB2 UDB supports UCS-2 as a new multi-byte code page. CHAR, VARCHAR, LONG VARCHAR, and CLOB data are stored in UTF-8, and GRAPHIC, VARGRAPHIC, LONG VARGRAPHIC, and DBCLOB data are stored in UCS-2.

By default, databases are created in the code page of the application creating them. As an alternative, you can specify UTF-8 as the CODESET name with any valid two-letter TERRITORY code:

```
CREATE DATABASE dbname USING CODESET UTF-8 TERRITORY US
```

A UCS-2 database allows connection from every supported single-byte and multi-byte code page. DB2 automatically performs code-page character conversions between a client's code page and UTF-8. Data in graphic string types is always in UCS-2 and does not go through code-page conversions. Although some client workstations have a limited subset of UCS-2 characters, the database allows the entire repertoire of UCS-2 characters.

All supported data types are also supported in a UCS-2 database. In a UCS-2 database, all identifiers are in multi-byte UTF-8. Therefore, it's possible to use any UCS-2 character in identifiers where DB2 permits the use of a character in the extended character set. This feature also lets you specify UCS-2 literals either in GRAPHIC string constant format, using the G'...' or N'....' format, or as a UCS-2 hexadecimal string, using the UX'....' or GX'....' format.

Choosing the Correct Data Type

Selecting the correct data type to use requires knowledge of the possible data values and their usage. Specifying an inappropriate data type when defining tables can result in wasted disk space, improper expression evaluation, and performance considerations. Table 4.4 provides a small checklist for data type selection.

Table 4.4: Data type selection	
Usage	Data type(s) to use
Is the data variable in length?	VARCHAR, VARBINARY
If the data is variable in length, what is the maximum length?	VARCHAR, VARBINARY
Do you need to sort (order) the data?	CHAR, VARCHAR, NUMERIC
Is the data going to be used in arithmetic operations?	DECIMAL, NUMERIC, REAL, DOUBLE, FLOAT, INTEGER, SMALLINT, BIGINT
Does the data element contain decimals?	DECIMAL, NUMERIC, REAL, DOUBLE,FLOAT,DECFLOAT
Is the data fixed in length?	CHAR, BINARY
Does the data have a specific meaning (beyond DB2 base data types)?	USER DEFINED TYPE
Is the data larger than what a character string can store, or do you need to store nontraditional data?	CLOB, BLOB, DBCLOB, XML

Remember that you need to create page sizes that are large enough to contain the length of a row in a table. This point is particularly important for tables with large character columns. When you use character data types, the range of lengths of the columns determines the choice between CHAR and VARCHAR. For example, if the range of column length is relatively small, use a fixed CHAR with the maximum length. This selection will reduce the storage requirements and could improve performance.

Identity Columns

Previously, we discussed how columns can be populated with data values if no value was supplied by the user. It's also possible to have DB2 generate sequence numbers or other values as part of a column during record insertion.

In most applications, a single column within a table represents a unique identifier for that row. Often, this identifier is a number that is updated sequentially as new records are added. In DB2, a feature exists that will automatically generate this value on behalf of the user. The following example shows a table definition that causes the EMPNO field to be generated automatically as a sequence.

```
CREATE TABLE EMP
    (EMPNO INT GENERATED ALWAYS AS IDENTITY,
     NAME CHAR(10));

INSERT INTO EMP(NAME) VALUES 'SMITH','LAWSON';

SELECT * FROM EMP;

EMPNO        NAME
----------- ----------
          1 SMITH
          2 LAWSON
```

If you define the column with GENERATED ALWAYS, the INSERT statement can't specify a value for the EMPNO field. By default, the numbering will start at 1 and be incremented by 1. You can change the starting and increment values as part of the column definition:

```
CREATE TABLE EMP
    (EMPNO INT GENERATED ALWAYS AS
        IDENTITY(START WITH 100, INCREMENT BY 10)),
     NAME CHAR(10));

INSERT INTO EMP(NAME) VALUES 'SMITH','LAWSON';

SELECT * FROM EMP;

EMPNO        NAME
----------- ----------
        100 SMITH
        110 LAWSON
```

In addition, the default value can be GENERATED BY DEFAULT, which means that the user can optionally supply a value for the field. If no value is supplied (using the DEFAULT keyword), DB2 will generate the next number in sequence.

One additional keyword is available as part of identity columns. You can decide how many numbers should be "pre-generated" by DB2. This practice can help reduce catalog contention because you can instruct DB2 to store the next *n* numbers in memory rather than go back to the catalog tables to determine which number to generate next.

Identity columns are restricted to numeric values (integer or decimal) and can be used in only one column in the table definition. In the following example, the EMPNO column is generated as an identity column.

```
CREATE TABLE EMP
    (EMPNO INT GENERATED ALWAYS AS IDENTITY,
    NAME CHAR(10),
    SALARY INT,
    BONUS INT,
    PAY INT);

    INSERT INTO EMP(NAME, SALARY, BONUS) VALUES
    ('SMITH',20000,2000),
    ('LAWSON',30000,5000);

  SELECT * FROM EMPLOYEE;

EMPNO   NAME        SALARY       BONUS       PAY
-------  ----------  -----------  ----------- ----------
      1 SMITH          20000         2000       22000
      2 LAWSON         30000         5000       35000
```

Table 4.5 describes the values used for identity column definition.

Table 4.5: Identity column values	
Value	**Description**
GENERATED	DB2 generates values for the column. The column must specify GENERATED if the column is to be considered an identity column (or if the data type is a ROWID or a distinct type that is based on a ROWID).
ALWAYS	DB2 will always generate a value for the column when a row is inserted into the table.
BY DEFAULT	DB2 generates a value for the column when a row is inserted into the table, unless a value is specified. Use of BY DEFAULT is recommended only when using data propagation.
AS IDENTITY	This value specifies that the column is an identity column for the table. A table can have only one identity column. You can specify AS IDENTITY only if the data type for the column is an exact numeric type with a scale of zero (SMALLINT, INTEGER, DECIMAL with a scale of zero, or a distinct type based on one of these types). An identity column is implicitly not null.
START WITH *n*	This is a numeric constant that provides the first value for the identity column. The value can be a positive or a negative value that could be assigned to the column. No nonzero digits are allowed to the right of the decimal point. The default is 1.

Table 4.5: Identity column values (continued)	
Value	**Description**
INCREMENT BY *n*	This is a numeric constant that provides the interval between consecutive values of the identity column. This value can be any positive or negative value that is not 0, and the default is 1. With a positive value, the sequence of values for the identity column will ascend; if the value is negative, the sequence of identity column values will descend.
CACHE*	Indicates whether pre-allocated values will be kept in memory. Caching these values will help improve performance when inserting rows into a table that has an identity column.
CACHE *n**	Provides the number of values of the identity column sequence that DB2 pre-allocates and keeps in memory. The default is 20. If a system fails, all cached identity column values will never be used. The value specified for CACHE also represents the maximum number of identity column values that may be lost during a system failure. With a data sharing environment, each member has its own range of consecutive values to use. For instance, if using CACHE 30, DB2T may get values 1 to 30, and DB2U may use values 31 to 60. The values assigned might not be in the order in which they are requested if transactions from different members generate values for the same identity column.
NO CACHE*	Caching is not to be used. Use NO CACHE if you need to guarantee that the identity values are generated in the order in which they are requested for non-affinity transactions in a data sharing environment.
CYCLE*	Specifies whether the identity column should continue to generate values after reaching either the maximum or minimum value of the sequence. If the column values are ascending, it will start with the lowest value. If the column values are descending, it will start with the highest value. MAXVALUE and MINVALUE are used to determine these ranges. Note that when CYCLE is in effect, duplicate values can occur. If a unique index exists, an error will result.
ORDER/NO ORDER*	Specifies that the values are generated in order of the request. Specifying ORDER might disable the caching of values. ORDER applies only to a single-application process. CACHE and NO ORDER will cause multiple caches to be active in a data sharing environment.
MAXVALUE*	Specifies the maximum value that can be generated for the identity column. Value can be positive or negative but must be greater than MINVALUE.
MINVALUE*	Specifies the minimum value generated for the identity column. Can be positive or negative but must be less than MAXVALUE.
RESET WITH*	Allows for the identity column values to be reset.

* These values are ALTERable.

If the data needs to be unloaded and reloaded while preserving previously generated numbers, the GENERATED option can be altered.

Some restrictions apply when you use identity columns. You cannot specify an identity column on a table that has an edit procedure defined. You cannot define an identity column with the FIELDPROC clause or the WITH DEFAULT clause. When updating an identity column, you cannot update the value of an identity column defined as GENERATED ALWAYS. If you're executing an ALTER TABLE statement to add an identity column to a table that is not empty, the table space that contains the table is placed in the REORG-pending state. When the REORG utility is then executed, DB2 generates the values for the identity column for all existing rows and removes the REORG-pending status. The values are guaranteed to be unique, and the system determines their order.

When defining another table using the LIKE clause (to create a table with the columns and attributes of another table), you have some options for picking up the identity column attributes. For an identity column, the newly created table will inherit only the data type of the identity column; no other column attributes are inherited unless you use the INCLUDING IDENTITY COLUMN ATTRIBUTES clause.

Row Change Timestamp

A row change timestamp, like an identity column, specifies a column whose values are generated automatically by DB2. In the case of a row change timestamp, that value is a timestamp data type that corresponds to the insert or update time of a row. If multiple rows are inserted or updated with a single statement, the value for the row change timestamp column might be different.

A table can have only one row change timestamp column. A row change timestamp cannot have a default value, nor can it be nullable. The row change timestamp can be generated always by DB2 or generated by default, and it can also be hidden. A hidden row change timestamp column is not visible to a SELECT statement unless the column is explicitly specified in the SELECT clause. For example, SELECT * would not return a hidden row change timestamp.

You can use row change timestamps to assist with the implementation of optimistic locking, a technique we describe further in Chapter 12. In the following example, the UPD_TSP column of the employee table is a row change timestamp:

```
CREATE TABLE EMP
    (EMPNO INT NOT NULL,
    NAME CHAR(10),
    SALARY INT,
    BONUS INT,
    PAY INT
    UPD_TSP NOT NULL GENERATED ALWAYS FOR EACH ROW
            AS ROW CHANGE TIMESTAMP,
     );
```

Tables

As you learned earlier in the chapter, DB2 tables consist of columns and rows that store an unordered set of data records. Tables can have *constraints* to guarantee the uniqueness of data records, maintain the relationships between and within tables, and so on. A constraint is a rule that the database manager enforces. DB2 supports three types of constraints:

- A *unique constraint* ensures the unique values of a key in a table. Any changes to the columns that make up the unique key are checked for uniqueness.

- A *referential constraint* enforces referential integrity on insert, update, and delete operations. Referential integrity is the state of a database in which all values of all foreign keys are valid.

- A *check constraint* verifies that changed table data doesn't violate conditions specified when the table was created or altered.

Unique Constraints

A unique constraint is the rule that the values of a key are valid only if they are unique within the table. You can place a unique constraint on an individual column, in which case you must define the column as NOT NULL. A unique constraint can also be defined within the context of a table definition. In the case of a unique constraint definition, multiple columns can be specified, and each of those columns must be defined as NOT NULL.

You define unique constraints in the CREATE TABLE or ALTER TABLE statement by using the PRIMARY KEY clause or the UNIQUE clause. When you specify either of these clauses, DB2 marks the table as unavailable until you explicitly create an index for any key specified as PRIMARY KEY or UNIQUE (unless the CREATE TABLE statement is processed by the schema processor, in which case DB2 implicitly creates all necessary indexes).

A table can have any number of unique constraints; however, it cannot have more than one unique constraint on the same set of columns. The constraint is enforced through a unique index. Once you establish a unique constraint on a column, DB2 defers the check for uniqueness during multiple row updates until the end of the update (*deferred unique constraint*). You can also use a unique constraint as the parent key in a referential constraint.

Referential Constraint

Referential integrity (RI) lets you define required relationships between and within tables. The database manager maintains these relationships, which are expressed as referential constraints, and requires that all values of a given attribute or table column also exist in some other table column. Figure 4.2 shows an example of the referential integrity between two tables. The constraint portrayed in the figure requires that every employee in the EMP (employee) table must be in a department that exists in the DEPT (department) table. No employee can be in a department that does not exist.

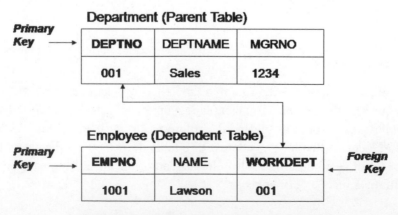

Figure 4.2: Referential integrity between two tables

A *unique key* is a set of columns in which no values are duplicated in any other row. You can define only one unique key as a primary key for each table. The unique key may also be known as the parent key when referenced by a foreign key.

A *primary key* is a special case of a unique key. Each table can have only one primary key. In the example, DEPTNO and EMPNO are the primary keys of the DEPT and EMP tables, respectively.

A *foreign key* is a column or set of columns in a table that refer to a unique key or primary key of the same or another table. You use a foreign key to establish a relationship with a unique key or a primary key and to enforce referential integrity among tables. The column WORKDEPT in the EMP table is a foreign key because it refers to the primary key, column DEPTNO, in the DEPT table.

A *parent key* is a primary or unique key of a referential constraint. A parent table is a table containing a parent key that is related to at least one foreign key in the same or another table. A table can be a parent in an arbitrary number of relationships. In the example, the DEPT table, which has a primary key of DEPTNO, is a parent of the EMP table, which contains the foreign key WORKDEPT.

A *dependent table* is a table containing one or more foreign keys. A dependent table can also be a parent table. A table can be a dependent in an arbitrary number of relationships. In the example, the EMP table contains the foreign key WORKDEPT and is dependent on the DEPT table, which has a primary key.

A *referential constraint* is an assertion that non-null values of a designated foreign key are valid only if they also appear as values of a unique key of a designated parent table. The purpose of referential constraints is to guarantee that database relationships are maintained and data entry rules are followed.

Enforcement of referential constraints has special implications for some SQL operations that depend on whether the table is a parent or a dependent. The database manager enforces referential constraints across systems based on the RI rules: the INSERT rule, the DELETE rule, and the UPDATE rule. Only the DELETE rules are explicitly defined.

INSERT Rules

An INSERT rule is implicit when you specify a foreign key. You can insert a row at any time into a parent table without any action being taken in the dependent table. You cannot insert a row into a dependent table unless a row in the parent table has a parent key value equal to the foreign key value of the row being inserted or the foreign key value is null. If an atomic or mass insert operation fails for one row during an attempt to insert multiple rows, all rows inserted by the statement are removed from the database.

DELETE Rules

When you delete a row from a parent table, the database manager checks to see whether the dependent table contains any dependent rows with matching foreign key values. If any dependent rows are found, several actions can be taken. You determine which action is taken by specifying a DELETE rule when you create the dependent table:

- **RESTRICT or NO ACTION**: This rule prevents any row in the parent table from being deleted if any dependent rows are found. If you need to remove both parent and dependent rows, delete the dependent rows first.

- **CASCADE**: This rule automatically deletes the row from the dependent table when the parent row is deleted.

- **SET NULL**: This option sets the value of the foreign key to NULL (provided it allows nulls). Other parts of the row remain unchanged.

UPDATE Rules

The database manager prevents the update of a unique key of a parent row. When you update a foreign key in a dependent table and the foreign key is defined with the NOT NULL option, the updated value must match some value of the parent key of the parent table.

Check Constraints ·

Check constraints enforce data integrity at the table level. Once you've defined a check constraint for a table, every UPDATE and INSERT statement will involve checking the restriction or constraint. If the constraint is violated, the data record won't be inserted or updated, and an SQL error will be returned.

You can define a check constraint at table creation time or later using the ALTER TABLE statement. Check constraints can help implement specific rules for the data values contained in a table by specifying the values allowed in one or more columns in every row of the table. They can save application developers time because the database, rather than each application that accesses the database, can validate each data value.

When you create or add a check constraint, DB2 performs a syntax check on it. A check constraint cannot contain host variables or special registers.

DB2 stores the check constraint definition in the system catalog tables, specifically in tables SYSIBM.SYSCHECKS and SYSIBM.SYSCHECKDEP.

Adding Check Constraints

To define a check constraint on an existing table, you specify the ADD CONSTRAINT *constraint-name* CHECK clause of the ALTER TABLE statement. If the table is empty, the constraint is added to the table's description. If the table is not empty, the value of the CURRENT RULES special register determines what happens. If the value is STD, the check constraint is enforced immediately when it is defined. If a row doesn't conform, the constraint is not added to the table, and an error occurs. If the value is DB2, the check constraint is added to the table description but its enforcement is deferred. Because some rows in the table might violate the check constraint, the table is placed in check-pending (CHKP) status.

It's a good idea to appropriately label every constraint (trigger, check, or referential integrity). This practice is particularly important for diagnosing errors that might occur.

The best way to remove the CHKP status is to run the CHECK DATA utility. For more information about the CHKP status and the CHECK DATA utility, see Chapter 7.

To remove a check constraint from a table, use the DROP CONSTRAINT or DROP CHECK clause of the ALTER TABLE statement. You must not use DROP CONSTRAINT in the same ALTER TABLE statement as DROP FOREIGN KEY, DROP CHECK, or DROP.

Here's an example of adding a check constraint to a table to ensure that the JOB is valid.

```
ALTER TABLE EMP
ADD CONSTRAINT check_job
CHECK (JOB IN ('Engineer','Sales','Manager'));
```

Modifying Check Constraints

Because check constraints implement business rules, you may need to modify them from time to time as the business rules change in your organization. There's no special command to modify a check constraint. Whenever you need to change a check constraint, you must drop it and create a new one. You can drop check constraints at any time; this action won't affect your table or the data in it.

When you drop a check constraint, be aware that data validation performed by the constraint will no longer be in effect. To drop a constraint, you use the ALTER TABLE statement. The following example shows how to modify an existing constraint. After dropping the constraint, you must re-create it with the new definition.

```
ALTER TABLE EMP
DROP CONSTRAINT check_job;

ALTER TABLE EMP
ADD CONSTRAINT check_job
CHECK (JOB IN ('OPERATOR','CLERK'));
```

Creating Tables

You can use the CREATE TABLE statement to define a new table. The definition must include the table's name and the attributes of its columns. The definition may include additional attributes of the table, such as its primary key or check constraints.

Once you've defined the table, its column names can't be modified. However, you can change some column data types as well as add new columns to the table (be careful when doing so, however, because DB2 will use default data values for existing records).

The RENAME TABLE statement lets you change the name of an existing table.

The maximum number of columns a table can consist of is 750. This limit does not vary based on the data page size on z/OS. DB2 supports 4 K, 8 K, 16 K, and 32 K data page sizes. Table 4.6 lists the maximum number of columns in a table and maximum row length by page size.

Table 4.6: Maximum table columns and row lengths				
	4 K page	8 K page	16 K page	32 K page
Max columns*	750	750	750	750
Max row length** (in bytes)	4,056	8,138	16,330	32,714

*If the table is a dependent table in a referentially intact structure, the maximum number of columns is 749.
**If an EDITPROC is defined on the table, the maximum row size is 10 bytes smaller in each case.

Tables are always created within a table space. You can specify the name of the table space in which a table will be created or have DB2 create one implicitly. In the following example, DB2 implicitly creates a table space in the DSN8D91A database because the CREATE TABLE statement provides no table space name. The name of the table space is derived from the table.

```
CREATE TABLE DSN8910.DEPT
        (DEPTNO    CHAR(3)       NOT NULL,
         DEPTNAME VARCHAR(36)    NOT NULL,
         MGRNO    CHAR(6)                 ,
         ADMRDEPT CHAR(3)        NOT NULL,
         LOCATION CHAR(16)                ,
         PRIMARY KEY(DEPTNO))
IN DATABASE DSN8D91A
CCSID EBCDIC;
```

•••

An index has its own index space, which is created when the index is created.

•••

Once you create a table, you can place user data into it using one of these methods:

- INSERT statement

- LOAD utility

- DSN1COPY

•••

If you really need a temporary table for use only for the duration of a program, use the DECLARE GLOBAL TEMP TABLE statement instead of CREATE TABLE. Doing so causes no catalog contention, logging, or lock contention.

••

Let's look at some more sample CREATE TABLE statements.

The next example creates two tables. The definition includes unique constraints, check constraints, and referential integrity. This example is derived from the DB2 sample database that is delivered as part of the product. In this example:

- The DEPT table has a primary key that consists of column DEPTNO.

- The EMP table has a check constraint that says the PHONE extension value should be between '0000' and '9999'.

- The default value is defined for the column HIREDATE in the EMP table.

- EMP table has a primary key that consists of column EMPNO.

- A referential constraint is defined between the DEPT table and the EMP table.

- The EMP table is created in the DSN8S91E table space in the DSN8D91A database.

```
CREATE TABLE DSN8910.DEPT
       (DEPTNO    CHAR(3)        NOT NULL,
        DEPTNAME VARCHAR(36)     NOT NULL,
        MGRNO     CHAR(6)                 ,
        ADMRDEPT CHAR(3)         NOT NULL,
        LOCATION CHAR(16)                 ,
        PRIMARY KEY(DEPTNO))
IN DSN8D91A.DSN8S91D
CCSID EBCDIC;

  CREATE TABLE DSN8910.EMP
       (EMPNO      CHAR(6)        NOT NULL,
        FIRSTNME   VARCHAR(12)    NOT NULL,
        MIDINIT    CHAR(1)        NOT NULL,
        LASTNAME   VARCHAR(15)    NOT NULL,
        WORKDEPT   CHAR(3)                 ,
        PHONENO    CHAR(4) CONSTRAINT NUMBER CHECK
          (PHONENO >= '0000' AND PHONENO <= '9999'),
        HIREDATE   DATE WITH DEFAULT       ,
        JOB        CHAR(8)                 ,
        EDLEVEL    SMALLINT                ,
        SEX        CHAR(1)                 ,
        BIRTHDATE DATE                     ,
        SALARY     DECIMAL(9, 2)           ,
        BONUS      DECIMAL(9, 2)           ,
        COMM       DECIMAL(9, 2)           ,
        PRIMARY KEY(EMPNO),
        FOREIGN KEY RED (WORKDEPT) REFERENCES DSN8910.DEPT
           ON DELETE SET NULL)
EDITPROC  DSN8EAE1
IN DSN8D91A.DSN8S91E
CCSID EBCDIC;
```

Auxiliary Tables

Large object data is not actually stored in the table in which it is defined. The defined LOB column holds information about the LOB, while the LOB itself is stored in another location. The normal place for this data storage is a LOB table space that defines the physical storage that will hold an auxiliary table related to the base column and table.

Because the actual LOB is stored in a separate table, if you have a large variable character column in use (that is infrequently accessed), you may be able to convert it to a LOB so it is kept separately. This technique could speed up table space scans on the remaining data because fewer pages would be accessed.

Null is the only supported default value for a LOB column, and if the value is null, the LOB won't take up space in the LOB table space. The following examples show how to create a base table with LOBs and the auxiliary tables to support it.

```
CREATE TABLE  DSN8910.EMP_PHOTO_RESUME
       (EMPNO        CHAR( 06 )   NOT NULL,
        EMP_ROWID    ROWID NOT NULL GENERATED ALWAYS,
        PSEG_PHOTO   BLOB( 500K ),
        BMP_PHOTO    BLOB( 100K ),
        RESUME       CLOB(   5K ),
        PRIMARY KEY  ( EMPNO ) )
IN  DSN8D91L.DSN8S91B
CCSID  EBCDIC;

CREATE AUX TABLE  DSN8910.AUX_PSEG_PHOTO
IN  DSN8D91L
STORES  DSN8910.EMP_PHOTO_RESUME
COLUMN  PSEG_PHOTO;

CREATE UNIQUE INDEX  DSN8910.XAUX_PSEG_PHOTO
ON  DSN8910.AUX_PSEG_PHOTO;

CREATE AUX TABLE  DSN8910.AUX_BMP_PHOTO
IN  DSN8D91L
STORES  DSN8910.EMP_PHOTO_RESUME
COLUMN  BMP_PHOTO;

CREATE UNIQUE INDEX  DSN8910.XAUX_BMP_PHOTO
ON  DSN8910.AUX_BMP_PHOTO;

CREATE AUX TABLE  DSN8910.AUX_EMP_RESUME
IN  DSN8D91L
STORES  DSN8910.EMP_PHOTO_RESUME
COLUMN  RESUME;

CREATE UNIQUE INDEX  DSN8910.XAUX_EMP_RESUME
ON  DSN8910.AUX_EMP_RESUME;
```

Copying a Table Definition

It's possible to create a table using the same characteristics of another table (or a view). You do so using the CREATE TABLE LIKE statement. The name specified after LIKE must identify a table or view that exists at the current server, and the privilege set must implicitly or explicitly include the SELECT privilege on the identified table or view. An identified table must not be an auxiliary table. An identified view must not include a column that is considered a ROWID column or an identity column.

The use of LIKE is an implicit definition of *n* columns, where *n* is the number of columns in the identified table or view. The implicit definition includes all attributes of the *n* columns as they're described in the SYSCOLUMNS catalog table with a few exceptions, such as identity attributes (unless you use the INCLUDING IDENTITY clause).

The implicit definition does not include any other attributes of the identified table or view. For example, the new table won't have a primary key, foreign key, or check constraint. The table is created in the table space that is implicitly or explicitly specified by the IN clause, and it has any other optional clause only if the optional clause is specified.

Here's a sample CREATE TABLE LIKE statement:

```
CREATE TABLE NEW_DEPT LIKE DEPT
IN DATABASE DSN8D91A
```

Modifying a Table

The ALTER TABLE statement enables you to change existing tables. ALTER TABLE modifies existing tables by:

- adding one or more columns to a table

- adding or dropping a primary key

- adding or dropping one or more unique or referential constraints

- adding or dropping one or more check constraint definitions

- altering the data type length (an increase is permitted only within numeric or character data types)

- altering the data type

- altering identity column attributes

- renaming a column

- adding or dropping a clone table

- changing the table to or from a materialized query table

- enabling auditing of the table

If you drop a table's primary key, the dependent tables will no longer have foreign keys.

You cannot use ALTER TABLE to change the database in which a table has been created.

The following example shows how to add a check constraint to the DEPT table.

```
ALTER TABLE DEPT ADD CHECK (DEPTNO > 'L99')
```

The next example shows how to change the data type of a column. In this case, we assume that the data type was originally CHAR and was less than 30.

```
ALTER TABLE DEPT ALTER COLUMN DEPTNAME SET DATA TYPE CHAR(35)
```

With a change such as an increase to a data type, you must not forget to relay the information to the application programmer because this type of change may impact code (i.e., host variable definitions).

Removing a Table

When you want to remove a table, issue the DROP TABLE statement:

```
DROP TABLE EMP;
```

Any objects that are directly or indirectly dependent on a dropped table (e.g., indexes, triggers, views) are deleted or made inoperative. Whenever a table is deleted, its description is deleted from the catalog, and any packages that reference the object are invalidated.

Sequence Objects

A sequence object is a user-defined object that generates a sequence of numeric values according to the specifications in which it was created. Sequence objects provide an incremental counter generated by DB2 and are similar to identity columns. You can think of an identity column as a special kind of sequence object; however, the sequence object is separate from the table. Sequence objects support all the same attributes that identity columns do, including CACHE, CYCLE, INCREMENT BY, MINVAL, MAXVAL, and RESTART WITH.

Applications use sequence object values for a variety of reasons, and these objects provide several benefits:

- No waits for incrementing values
- Standalone sequential-number-generating object (not tied to a table)
- Ascending or descending number generation
- Useful for application porting from other DBMSs
- Can help generate keys that can be used to coordinate keys across multiple tables (referential integrity or application related)

Creating Sequence Objects

A sequence name consists of two parts: the 128-byte schema name and the 128-byte identifier. You create both pieces using the new CREATE SEQUENCE statement, and all attributes are completely user-defined (or defaults). The values in the sequence object can be of any exact numeric data type. You define the starting value with a START WITH value and define advances with INCREMENT BY (ascending or descending). The values can be cached, and DB2 generates them in the order of request.

The following example shows a creation and simple use of a sequence object.

```
CREATE SEQUENCE ACCOUNT_SEQ
  AS INTEGER
  START WITH 1
  INCREMENT BY 10
  CYCLE
  CACHE 20
```

Using Sequence Objects

Some additional advantages to using sequence objects over other methods of number generation include the use of the NEXT VALUE FOR and PREVIOUS VALUE FOR expressions. NEXTVAL FOR generates and returns the next value for the sequence object. PREVVAL FOR generates and returns the previous value for the sequence object. You can use these expressions with the following SQL elements:

- SELECT and SELECT INTO statements

- INSERT, DELETE, or UPDATE statement within a SELECT clause of fullselect

- UPDATE statement within the SET clause (searched or positioned)

- SET *host-variable* statement

- VALUES or VALUES INTO statement

- CREATE PROCEDURE, CREATE FUNCTION, or CREATE TRIGGER statement

For more information about using sequence objects, see Chapter 12.

Modifying Sequence Objects

You can ALTER sequence objects. The following ALTERs are allowed:

- Changing whether to cycle the generated sequence values

- Changing the MAXVALUE or the MINVALUE

- Changing the starting value

- Changing the increment value

- Changing whether to cache the values

You can't change the data type or length of the values generated by a sequence object. To do so, you'd need to drop and re-create the sequence object.

Removing Sequence Objects

You use the DROP statement to remove sequence objects:

```
DROP SEQUENCE <sequence-name>
```

Table Spaces

DB2 stores data in table spaces composed of one or many VSAM data sets. Six types of table spaces exist:

- Simple

- Segmented

- Partitioned

- Large object

- Universal

- XML

Simple Table Space

Simple table spaces are fairly outdated and not the optimal choice. With a simple table space, you can have more than one table in the table space. If you have several tables in the table space, rows from different tables may be interleaved on the same page; therefore, when you lock a page, you're potentially locking rows of other tables. Simple table spaces are no longer the default as in previous DB2 versions. In fact, you can't create a simple table space in DB2 9. However, existing simple table spaces are still supported.

Segmented Table Space

Normally, in the cases where a table is not partitioned, a segmented, not simple, table space is used. A segmented table space organizes pages of the table space into segments, and each segment contains the rows of only one table. Segments can consist of four to 64 pages each, and each segment has the same number of pages. The default for a table space definition is a segmented table space with a segment size of four pages.

Using segmented table spaces provides several advantages. Because the pages in a segment contain rows from only one table, there is no locking interference with other tables. In simple table spaces, rows are intermixed on pages, and if one table page is locked, it can inadvertently lock a row of another table just because it's on the same page. When you have only one table per table space, this locking isn't an issue; however, using a segmented table space for one table still offers benefits, such as the following:

- If a table scan is performed, the segments belonging to the table being scanned are the only ones accessed; empty pages aren't scanned.

- If a mass delete or a DROP TABLE occurs, segment pages are available for immediate reuse (after the commit), and you don't need to run the REORG utility.

- Mass deletes are much faster for segmented table spaces, and they produce less logging.

- The COPY utility doesn't have to copy empty pages left by a mass delete.

- When you insert records, you can avoid some read operations by using the more comprehensive space map of the segmented table space.

- By being able to safely combine several tables in a table space, you can reduce the number of open data sets necessary, which lessens the amount of memory required in the subsystem.

When you use a segmented table space to hold more than one table, make sure the tables have similar characteristics in all categories, including size, volatility, locking needs, compression, and backup/recovery strategies.

There are some guidelines for how many tables to have in a segmented table space based on the number of pages in the table space, but number of pages isn't the only consideration. Table 4.7 lists very generic thresholds.

Table 4.7: Table page thresholds	
Number of pages	**Table space design**
>100,000	Consider partitioning
>10,000	One-table segmented table space
>128 to <10,000	Multiple-table segmented table spaces
<128	Multiple-table segmented table spaces

The SEGSIZE clause tells DB2 how large to make each segment for a segmented table space, and it determines how many pages are contained in a segment. SEGSIZE will vary, depending on the size of the table space. Table 4.8 lists recommendations.

Table 4.8: Table segment size recommendations	
Number of pages	**SEGSIZE**
28 or less	4 to 28
28 to 128	32
128 or more	64

A segmented table space is limited to 64 GB.

The following example shows how to create a segmented table space with a segment size of 4.

```
CREATE TABLESPACE DSN8S91C
   IN DSN8D91P
   USING STOGROUP DSN8G910
             PRIQTY 160
             SECQTY 80
   SEGSIZE 4
   LOCKSIZE TABLE
   BUFFERPOOL BP0
   CLOSE NO
   CCSID EBCDIC;
```

••

You cannot ALTER the SEGSIZE parameter.

••

Partitioned Table Space

Partitioning a table space has several advantages. For large tables, partitioning provides the only way to store large amounts of data. But partitioning also offers benefits for tables that aren't necessarily large. DB2 lets you define up to 4,096 partitions of up to 64 GB each. (However, total table size is limited to 16 TB when using a 4 K page size, and the number of partitions depends on the value specified for the DSSIZE parameter.) Non-partitioned table spaces are limited to 64 GB of data. You can execute utilities on separate partitions in parallel, and you can access data in certain partitions while utilities are executing on others. In a data-sharing environment, you can split workloads by spreading partitions among several members. You can spread data over multiple volumes without having to use the same storage group for each data set that belongs to the table space; with this capability, you have the option to place frequently accessed partitions on faster devices.

The following example creates a partitioned table space with four partitions.

```
CREATE TABLESPACE DSN8S91E
   IN DSN8D91A
   USING STOGROUP DSN8G910
             PRIQTY 20
             SECQTY 20
```

```
            ERASE NO
     NUMPARTS 4
        (PART 1 USING STOGROUP DSN8G910
                          PRIQTY 12
                          SECQTY 12,
         PART 3 USING STOGROUP DSN8G910
                          PRIQTY 12
                          SECQTY 12)
     LOCKSIZE PAGE LOCKMAX SYSTEM
     BUFFERPOOL BP0
     CLOSE NO
     COMPRESS YES
     CCSID EBCDIC;
```

> It's possible to use the ALTER statement to change the partitioning key ranges and/or to add partitions for rebalancing. The REORG utility's REBALANCE option also provides this capability during a REORG.

Adding Partitions

Many database designs are outgrowing the bounds of some partitioned table spaces and require more partitions. To address this need, the ALTER statement provides the ability to add partitions to a table space:

```
ALTER TABLE table1 ADD PARTITION
```

DB2 chooses the partition number based on the next available partition. If the partitions are stogroup-defined, the data set is allocated for the table space and partitioning index with a PRIQTY value being picked up from the previous partition. You may need to alter the table space to provide new parameters that better suit the new partition (e.g., primary allocations, freespace). If your underlying data sets are VCAT-defined, you'll need to define the data set up front, before the ALTER is performed. The new partitions will be available immediately after the ALTER. For the change to take effect, the table space must be stopped and then started again. All affected plans, packages, and cached SQL statements are invalidated because the SQL may be optimized to read certain partitions, and the new number of partitions may change the access path.

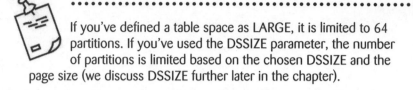

If you've defined a table space as LARGE, it is limited to 64 partitions. If you've used the DSSIZE parameter, the number of partitions is limited based on the chosen DSSIZE and the page size (we discuss DSSIZE further later in the chapter).

Rotating Partitions

The archiving of data, or rolling of partitions, has often involved a large outage and a lot of planning. Even though tables can support up to 4,096 partitions, they still have their limits. In addition, you may not want to support that much historical data in the primary table space.

You can rotate partitions to move the first partition to last. This feature lets you make the lowest logical partition the last logical partition and specify new partition values to enforce the values of the last partition. The RESET option permits a partition to be reset, at which time the data is deleted (which can impact the performance of the feature and the availability of the data). Before the rotation, the partition holds the oldest data; afterward, it holds the newest.

As we mentioned, rotation deletes the data from old partitions. Depending on the partition size, this may become a performance issue due to the logging impacts of the deletes. You may want to consider using the LOAD utility to delete the data from the partition before the ALTER. You can do so easily using LOAD...PART x REPLACE with a dummy SYSREC. This practice will help lessen the duration of the outage during the rotation of the partitions.

During the rotate, a database descriptor (DBD) lock will be taken as the DDL is completed, and all activity will be quiesced immediately when the ALTER is issued.

Note that all keys for deleted rows must be deleted from non-partitioned secondary indexes (NPSIs), and if multiple NPSIs exist on a table, the scans are executed serially to perform the deletes—definitely something to consider, especially when large NPSIs are involved.

If physical DB2-enforced RI relationships or triggers exist, the deletes occur a row at a time. Again, this is a situation where you may want to consider unloading the data first. If a DELETE RESTRICT relationship is in place, the rotate may not work.

The ALTER PART ROTATE command can change partition order. To account for this, the LOGICAL_PART keyword has been added to the SYSTABLEPART and SYSCOPY catalog tables. This information will also be visible in the –DISPLAY DATABASE output.

Figure 4.3 illustrates the ALTER of a three-partition CUSTOMER table in which we're rotating off the first physical partition (P1), which will now become the last logical partition (P3).

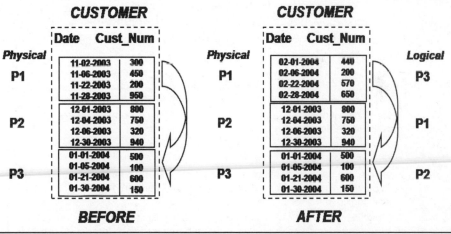

ALTER TABLE CUSTOMER ALTER PART ROTATE VALUES('02/29/2004') RESET

Figure 4.3: Rotating partitions

Table-Controlled Partitioning

The ability to partition can be handled by the table creation, not just by the index as was the case in the past. The next example uses the CREATE TABLE statement to handle the partitioning of a table:

```
CREATE TABLE ACCOUNTS
   (ENTER_DATE  DATE,
    ACCOUNT     INTEGER,
    STATUS      CHAR(3))
   IN TSP1
        PARTITION BY (ENTER_DATE)
           (PARTITION 1 ENDING AT ('2007-02-28'),
            PARTITION 2 ENDING AT ('2007-03-31'));
```

Instead of the PARTITION ENDING AT clause, you could use the PART VALUES clause; however, PARTITION ENDING AT is preferred.

Once a partitioned table has been created, it's ready to be used. There is no requirement to create a separate partitioning index; in fact, doing so is not allowed. Catalog tables SYSTABLES, SYSCOLUMNS, and SYSTABLEPART store the information about the limit keys for the partitions.

IBM recommends you use table-controlled partitioning instead of index-controlled partitioning. Table 4.9 spells out the differences between the two partitioning methods.

Table 4.9: Table-controlled vs. index-controlled partitioning	
Table-controlled partitioning	**Index-controlled partitioning**
A partitioning index is not required; a clustering index is not required.	A partitioning index is required; a clustering index is required.
Multiple partitioned indexes can be created in a table space.	Only one partitioned index can be created in a table space.
A table space partition is identified by both a physical partition number and a logical partition number.	A table space partition is identified by a physical partition number.
The high-limit key is always enforced.	The high-limit key is not enforced if the table space is non-large.
A nullable column can be used as part of the partitioning key. However, DB2 does limit inserts of null key values to descending keys only.	Nullable columns cannot be part of the partitioning key.

Table-controlled partitioning is a replacement for index-controlled partitioning. The change from index-controlled partitioning to table-controlled partitioning can take place when any of the following occur:

- DROP *partitioning-index*
- ALTER INDEX NOT CLUSTER

- ALTER TABLE ADD PART
- ALTER TABLE ALTER PART ROTATE
- ALTER TABLE ALTER PART *partno*
- CREATE INDEX PARTITIONED
- CREATE INDEX VALUES (with no CLUSTER keyword)

Universal Table Spaces

DB2 9 introduces a new type of table space. A *universal table space* is a table space that is both segmented and partitioned. Two types of universal table spaces are available: the partition-by-growth table space and the range-partitioned table space.

A universal table space offers the following benefits:

- **Better space management relative to varying-length rows.** A segmented space map page provides more information about free space than a regular partitioned space map page.

- **Improved mass delete performance.** Mass delete in a segmented table space organization tends to be faster than table spaces that are organized differently. In addition, you can immediately reuse all or most of the segments of a table.

Before DB2 9, partitioned tables required key ranges to determine the target partition for row placement. Partitioned tables provide more granular locking and parallel operations by spreading the data over more data sets. Now, in DB2 9, you have the option to partition according to data growth, which means you can partition segmented tables as they grow, without the need for key ranges. As a result, segmented tables benefit from increased table space limits and SQL and utility parallelism that formerly were available only to partitioned tables. In addition, you no longer need to reorganize a table space to change the limit keys.

You can implement partition-by-growth table space organization in two ways:

- Use the new MAXPARTITIONS clause on the CREATE TABLESPACE statement to specify the maximum number of partitions that the partition-by-growth table space can accommodate. DB2 uses the value you specify in the MAXPARTITIONS clause to protect against runaway applications that perform an insert in an infinite loop.

- Use the MAXPARTITIONS clause on the ALTER TABLESPACE statement to change the maximum number of partitions to which an existing partition-by-growth table space can grow. This ALTER TABLESPACE operation acts as an immediate ALTER.

A range-partitioned table space is a type of universal table space that is based on partitioning ranges and contains a single table. The new range-partitioned table space doesn't replace the existing partitioned table space, and operations supported on regular partitioned or segmented table spaces are supported on range-partitioned table spaces. You can create a range-partitioned table space by specifying both SEGSIZE and NUMPARTS keywords on the CREATE TABLESPACE statement.

With a range-partitioned table space, you can also control the partition size, choose from a wide array of indexing options, and take advantage of partition-level operations and parallelism capabilities. Because the range-partitioned table space is also a segmented table space, you can run table scans at the segment level. As a result, you can immediately reuse all or most of the segments of a table after dropping the table or performing a mass delete.

Range-partitioned universal table spaces follow the same partitioning rules as partitioned table spaces in general. That is, you can add, rebalance, and rotate partitions. As with partitioned table spaces, the DSSIZE and page size control the maximum number of partitions possible for both range-partitioned and partition-by-growth universal table spaces (as indicated in later in the chapter).

LOB Table Spaces

Each column (or each column of each partition) of a base LOB table (i.e., a table with a LOB column) requires a LOB table space. This table space must exist in the same database as the base table, and it will contain the auxiliary table. This storage model is used only for LOB table spaces. The LOB table space is basically implemented in the same fashion as pieces are implemented for NPSIs (discussed later in this chapter). You can have 254 partitions of 64 GB each, allowing a total of 16 TB, and there will be one LOB table space for each LOB column (up to 254 partitions), which makes up to 4,000 TB possible. You can create a LOB table space in normal 4 K, 8 K, 16 K, or 32 K buffer pools. Figure 4.4 depicts physical LOB storage.

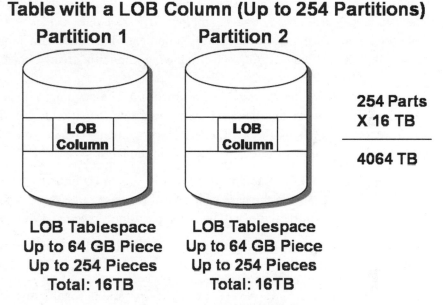

Figure 4.4: Physical LOB storage

Partitioned base tables can each have different LOB table spaces. A LOB value can be longer than a page in a LOB table space and can also span pages. Here's an example of creating a LOB table space:

```
CREATE LOB TABLESPACE DSN8S91L
    USING STOGROUP SGROUP1
    PRIQTY 3200
    SECQTY 1600
LOCKSIZE LOB
BUFFERPOOL BP16K1
GBPCACHE SYSTEM
LOG NO
CLOSE NO;
```

If you don't explicitly define the database, it defaults to DSNDB04.

XML Table Spaces

When you create an XML column in a table, DB2 implicitly creates an XML table space and an XML table to store the XML data, along with a node ID. The XML table spaces are similar to LOB table spaces. Each XML column has its own table space. The XML table space does not have limit keys. The XML data resides in a partition that corresponds in number to the partition number of the base row. Tables containing XML columns also have the following implicitly created objects:

- A hidden column to store the document ID. The document ID is a DB2-generated value that uniquely identifies a row. It is used to identify documents within the XML table. The document ID is common for all XML columns, and its value is unique within the table.

- A unique index on the document ID (document ID index). The document ID index points to the base table RID. If the base table space is partitioned, the document ID index will be a non-partitioned secondary index.

The base table will have an indicator column for each XML column containing a null bit, invalid bit, and a few reserved bytes.

The XML table space inherits several attributes from the base table space:

- LOG
- CCSID
- LOCKMAX
- DSSIZE

Creating Table Spaces

To define a segmented, partitioned, universal, or LOB table space on the current server, you use the CREATE TABLESPACE statement. Table space creation involves many parameters, with significant options depending on the type of table space. The major table space parameters are as follows:

- **DSSIZE.** Specifies that the maximum size of any partition in a partitioned table space can exceed the 2 GB limit, up to a size of 64 GB.

- **LOB.** Specifies that the table space is a LOB table space, used to hold only LOB values.

- **USING clause.** Specifies whether storage groups or a user-defined table space is being defined.

- **USING STOGROUP.** Specifies that DB2 will manage the data sets; there will also be a PRIQTY and SECQTY to define the allocations for the data sets.

- **USING VCAT.** Specifies that the data sets will be user-defined.

- **FREEPAGE and PCTFREE.** Specify the amount of free space to be left when a table space is loaded or reorganized.

- **MAXROWS.** Specifies the maximum number of rows DB2 will consider placing on each data page. This value is considered for INSERT operations and the LOAD and REORG utilities.

- **DEFINE.** Specifies whether a physical VSAM data set(s) supporting the table space should be created upon defining the table space. If you defer the definition by specifying DEFINE NO, any physical data sets won't be created until a LOAD or INSERT is performed on any table in the table space.

- **GBPCACHE.** Used in data sharing to specify which pages of a table space or partition are written to the group buffer pools.

- **NUMPARTS.** Specifies the number of partitions in a partitioned table space, with a maximum of 4,096 allowed. If specified with SEGSIZE, this parameter designates a range-partitioned universal table space.

- **MAXPARTITIONS.** Specifies that the table space is a universal table space. Also indicates the maximum number of partitions to which a partition-by-growth table space can grow.

- **SEGSIZE.** Specifies the number of pages in a segment for segmented table spaces. If you specify SEGSIZE in combination with the NUMPARTS parameter, it defines the number of pages per segment of a range-partitioned universal table space.

- **BUFFERPOOL.** Specifies the buffer pool to which the table space is assigned. You can set a default buffer pool with the DSNZPARM TBSBPOOL.

- **LOCKSIZE.** Specifies the size of locks used within the table space. In certain cases, LOCKSIZE can also specify the threshold at which lock escalation occurs. The allowable lock sizes are:

» ANY

» TABLESPACE

» TABLE

» PAGE

» ROW

» LOB

- **MAXROWS.** Specifies the maximum number of rows allowed on a page, up to a maximum of 255.

- **COMPRESS.** Specifies whether data compression is used for rows in the table space or partition.

- **(NOT) LOGGED.** Specifies whether data changes to data in the table space will be written to the log.

- **TRACKMOD.** Specifies whether DB2 tracks modified pages in the space map pages in the table space or partition.

Page Sizes

Table 4.10 lists the four page sizes available for use.

Table 4.10: Table page sizes	
Buffer pool	**Page size**
BP0–BP49	4 K
BP8K0–BP8K9	8 K
BP16K0–BP16K9	16 K
BP32K0–BP32K9	32 K

The larger page sizes help you achieve better hit ratios and reduce I/O because you can fit more rows on a page. For instance, if you have a 2,200-byte row (maybe for a data warehouse), a 4 K page can hold only one row. But if you use an 8 K page, three rows can fit on a page, and one less lock is required.

The buffer pool chosen for the table space defines the page size. For example, BP8K0 supports 8 K pages.

DSSIZE

Depending on the DSSIZE and the page size, there are limitations to the number of partitions a table space can have. Table 4.11 shows these limits.

Table 4.11: DSSIZE and partition limitations				
DSSIZE	4K	8K	16K	32K
4 GB	4,096	4,096	4,096	4,096
8 GB	2,048	4,096	4,096	4,096
16 GB	1,024	2,048	4,096	4,096
2 GB	512	1,024	2,048	4,096
4 GB	256	512	1,024	2,048

Therefore, a table's maximum size is limited by the DSSIZE and the number of partitions. For example, the maximum size of a table with a 4 K page size and 4,096 partitions with a DSSIZE of 4 GB is 16 TB. The largest table space possible is one with a 32 K page size, a DSSIZE of 64 GB, and 2,048 partitions, resulting in a total of 128 TB of storage.

Free Space

The FREEPAGE and PCTFREE clauses can help improve the performance of updates and inserts by letting free space exist on table spaces or index spaces. Performance improvements include improved access to the data through better data clustering, less index page splitting, faster inserts, fewer row overflows, and fewer required REORGs. Tradeoffs include an increase in the number of pages (and therefore the amount of storage needed), fewer rows per I/O, less efficient use of buffer pools, and more pages to scan.

It's therefore important to achieve a good balance for each individual table space and index space when deciding on free space, and that balance will depend on the processing requirements of each table space or index space. When inserts and updates are performed, DB2 will use the free space defined; by doing so, it can keep records in clustering sequence as much as possible. When the free space is used up, the records must be located elsewhere, and this is when performance can begin to suffer. Read-only tables don't require any free space, and tables with a pure insert-at-end strategy generally don't require free space. Exceptions to this rule are tables with VARCHAR columns and tables using compression that are subject to updates.

The FREEPAGE amount represents the number of full pages inserted between each empty page during a LOAD or REORG of a table space or index space. The tradeoff is between how often you can perform reorganization and how much disk you can allocate for an object. You should use FREEPAGE for table spaces so that inserts can be kept as close to the optimal page as possible. For indexes, you should use FREEPAGE for the same reason, except the improvements will be in terms of keeping index page splits near the original page instead of placing them at the end of the index. FREEPAGE is useful when inserts are sequentially clustered.

PCTFREE specifies the percentage of a page left free during a LOAD or REORG. This option is useful when you can assume an even distribution of inserts across the key ranges. It's also needed in indexes to avoid all random inserts causing page splits.

Allocation

The PRIQTY and SECQTY clauses of the CREATE TABLESPACE and ALTER TABLESPACE SQL statements specify the space to be allocated for the table space if DB2 manages the table space. These settings influence how the operating system allocates the underlying VSAM data sets in which table space and index space data is stored.

PRIQTY specifies the minimum primary space allocation for a DB2-managed data set of the table space or partition. You specify the primary space allocation in kilobytes, up to a maximum of 64 GB. DB2 will request a data set allocation corresponding to the primary space allocation, and the operating system will try to allocate the initial extent for the data set in one contiguous piece.

SECQTY specifies the minimum secondary space allocation for a DB2-managed data set of the table space or partition. DB2 will request secondary extents in a size according to the secondary allocation. However, the actual primary and secondary data set sizes depend on a variety of settings and installation parameters.

You can specify the primary and secondary space allocations for table spaces and indexes, or you can let DB2 choose them. Having DB2 choose the values, especially for the secondary space quantity, increases the possibility of reaching the maximum data set size before running out of extents. In addition, the MGEXTSZ subsystem parameter influences the SECQTY allocations; when set to YES (NO is the default), it changes the space calculation formulas to help use all the potential space allowed in the table space before running out of extents.

Compression

The COMPRESS clause of the CREATE TABLESPACE and ALTER TABLESPACE SQL statements permits the compression of data in a table space or in a partition of a partitioned table space.

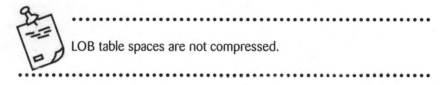

LOB table spaces are not compressed.

In many cases, using COMPRESS can significantly reduce the amount of DASD space needed to store data, but the compression ratio achieved depends on the characteristics of the data.

Compression lets you get more rows on a page and therefore gain many of the following performance benefits, depending on the SQL workload and the amount of compression:

- Higher buffer pool hit ratios
- Fewer I/Os
- Fewer getpage operations
- Reduced CPU time for image copies

Some considerations in terms of processor cost apply when using compression, but that cost is relatively low.

- Depending on the SQL workload, compressing data can result in a higher processor cost.

- The processor cost to decode a row using the COMPRESS clause is significantly less than the cost to encode that same row. This rule applies regardless of whether the compression uses the synchronous data compression hardware or the software simulation built into DB2.

- The data access path DB2 uses affects the processor cost for data compression. In general, the relative overhead of compression is higher for table space scans and is less costly for index access.

The following example shows a table space created with compression.

```
CREATE TABLESPACE DSN8S91S
   IN DSN8D91A
   USING STOGROUP DSN8G910
           PRIQTY 144000
           SECQTY 1400
           ERASE NO
   LOCKSIZE PAGE LOCKMAX SYSTEM
   BUFFERPOOL BP0
   CLOSE NO
   COMPRESS YES
   CCSID EBCDIC;
```

Type of Table Space Created

The combination of the SEGSIZE, MAXPARTITONS, and NUMPARTS clauses dictates whether the created table space will be a segmented, partitioned, partition-by-growth universal, or a range-partitioned universal table space. Table 4.12 indicates the various combinations of these settings and the resultant table space type.

Table 4.12: SEGSIZE, MAXPARTITONS, and NUMPARTS combinations			
SEGSIZE clause	MAXPARTITIONS clause	NUMPARTS clause	Resulting table space type
Specified	Specified	Not specified	Partition-by-growth
Specified	Not specified	Not specified	Segmented
Specified	Not specified	Specified	Range-partitioned
Not specified	Not specified	Not specified	Segmented
Not specified	Not specified	Specified	Partitioned

Modifying Table Spaces

The ALTER TABLESPACE statement lets you change existing table spaces. This statement can modify many of the table space parameters, letting you

- change the buffer pool assignment
- change the lock size or the lock escalation threshold
- change the specifics for a single partition
- change any of the space definitions
- turn compression off and on
- change how pages are cached in group buffer pools
- change whether or not to perform logging
- rotate partitions
- add partitions
- change the primary or secondary allocations
- change the USING VCAT clause

This example uses the ALTER TABLESPACE statement to change the buffer pool assignment and lock size:

```
ALTER TABLESPACE DSN8D91A.DSN8S91S
    BUFFERPOOL BP4
    LOCKSIZE ROW;
```

You can alter the primary and secondary space allocations for a table space. The new secondary space allocation will take effect immediately. However, because the primary allocation happens when the data set is created, that allocation won't take affect until a data set is added (depends on the type of table space) or until the data set is re-created via utility execution (e.g., REORG, LOAD REPLACE).

Removing Table Spaces

When you want to remove a table space, use the DROP TABLESPACE statement to delete the object. Doing so removes any objects that are directly or indirectly dependent on the table space. It also invalidates any packages or plans that refer to the object and removes its descriptions and all related data from the catalog.

```
DROP TABLESPACE DSN8D91A.DSN8S91S;
```

Views

Views are logical tables that you create using the CREATE VIEW statement. Once you define a view, it can be accessed using DML statements (e.g., SELECT, INSERT, UPDATE, DELETE) as if it were a base table. A view is a (logical) temporary table, and the data in the view is available only during query processing.

With a view, you can make a subset of table data available to an application program and validate data that is to be inserted or updated. A view can have column names that differ from the names of corresponding columns in the original tables. The use of views provides flexibility in the way application programs and end-user queries look at table data.

Let's look at a sample CREATE VIEW statement. The original table, EMP, has columns named SALARY and COMM. For security reasons, this view is created from the EMPNO, LASTNAME, WORKDEPT, JOB, and HIREDATE columns. In addition, the view restricts access to the WORKDEPT column. The definition will show the information only of employees who belong to the department whose WORKDEPT is C01.

```
CREATE VIEW EMP_VIEW1
(EMPNO,LASTNAME, DEPT,JOB,HIREDATE)
  AS SELECT ID,NAME,WORKDEPT,JOB,HIREDATE
     FROM    EMP
     WHERE   WORKDEPT='C01';
```

Once you create the view, you can specify the access privileges. This approach provides data security because it makes a restricted view of the base table accessible. As the example shows, a view can contain a WHERE clause to restrict access to certain rows or can contain a subset of the columns to restrict access to certain columns of data.

The column names in the view needn't match the column names of the base table. The table name has an associated schema, as does the view name. Once you define the view, it can be used in DML statements such as SELECT, INSERT, UPDATE, and DELETE (with restrictions). The database administrator can decide to give a group of users a higher-level privilege on the view than on the base table.

A view provides an alternative way to look at data in one or more tables. It's basically an SQL SELECT statement that is effectively executed whenever the view is referenced in a SQL statement. Because the view is not materialized until execution, operations such as ORDER BY, the WITH clause, and the OPTIMIZE FOR clause have no meaning.

Views with Check Option

If the view definition includes conditions (e.g., a WHERE clause) and your intent is to ensure that any INSERT or UPDATE statement referencing the view will have the WHERE clause applied, you must define the view using WITH CHECK OPTION. This option can ensure the integrity of the data being modified in the database. An SQL error will be returned if the condition is violated during an INSERT or UPDATE operation.

The following view definition uses the WITH CHECK OPTION. The option is required to make sure the condition is always checked. You want to ensure that the WORKEPT is always C01. This will restrict the input values for the DEPT column. When a view is used to insert a new value, the WITH CHECK OPTION is always enforced.

```
CREATE VIEW EMP_VIEW1
(EMPNO,LASTNAME,DEPT,JOB,HIREDATE)
   AS SELECT  ID,NAME,WORKDEPT,JOB,HIREDATE
      FROM    EMP
      WHERE   WORKDEPT='C01'
WITH CHECK OPTION;
```

If the view in this example is used in an INSERT statement, the row will be rejected if the WORKDEPT column is not the value C01. It's important to remember that no data validation takes place during modification unless you specify WITH CHECK OPTION. If this view is used in a SELECT statement, the conditional WHERE clause will be invoked, and the resulting table will contain only the matching rows of data.

In other words, WITH CHECK OPTION doesn't affect the result of a SELECT statement. Do not specify WITH CHECK OPTION for views that are read only.

Nested View Definitions

If a view is based on another view, the number of predicates that must be evaluated is based on the WITH CHECK OPTION specification. If a view is defined without the WITH CHECK OPTION, the definition of the view is not used in the data validity checking of any insert or update operations. However, if the view directly or indirectly depends on another view defined with WITH CHECK OPTION, the definition of that super view is used in the checking of any insert or update operation.

Read-Only Views

A view classified as read-only allows no inserts, updates, or deletes. A view is considered read-only if any of the following conditions is met:

- The first FROM clause identifies more than one table or view, a table function, or a read-only view.

- The outer select contains a GROUP BY or HAVING clause.

- The outer select contains a column function or DISTINCT.

- The view contains a subquery with the same table as the outer select.

Chapter 5 provides examples and a further discussion of read-only views.

Modifying a View

To modify a view, you simply drop and re-create it. The view definition cannot be altered.

Removing a View

To remove a view:

```
DROP VIEW EMP_VIEW2;
```

Materialized Query Tables

Decision-support queries are often difficult and expensive. They typically operate over a large amount of data and may have to scan or process terabytes of data and possibly perform multiple joins and complex aggregations. With these types of queries, traditional optimization and performance isn't always optimal.

One solution can be the use of materialized query tables. MQTs let you pre-compute whole queries or parts of multiple queries and then use the computed results to answer future queries. MQTs thus help avoid redundant scanning, aggregating, and joins. MQTs are useful for data warehouse applications.

MQTs don't completely eliminate optimization problems but rather move optimization issues to other areas. Some challenges include finding the best MQT for an expected workload, maintaining the MQTs when underlying tables are updated, recognizing the usefulness of MQT for a query, and being able to decide to actually use an MQT for a query. OLAP tools address most of these problems, but MQTs are the first step.

Defining MQTs

MQTs work with two "tables": a source table and the materialized query table. The source table is the base table, view, table expression, or table function. The materialized query table is the table used to contain materialized data derived from one or more source tables in a fullselect. A materialized query table is similar to a view, but a view is logical, whereas an MQT contains materialized data of the query result. You could think of an MQT as a "materialized view."

You use the CREATE TABLE statement to create an MQT, and the MQT's columns can be specified explicitly or derived from the fullselect associated with the table. The columns are physically stored the same way as with declared temporary tables. The following example shows the syntax used to create an MQT. This example creates an MQT called SALESMQT.

```
CREATE TABLE SALESMQT (CUSTID, STOREID, LOCID, MTH) AS (
  SELECT CUSTID, STOREID, LOCID, MTH, COUNT(*)
  FROM SALES
  GROUP BY CUSTID, STOREID, LOCID, MTH)
DATA INITIALLY DEFERRED
REFRESH DEFERRED
MAINTAINED BY SYSTEM
ENABLE QUERY OPTIMIZATION;
```

Next, let's review the options available for defining MQTs.

MQT Options

The DATA INITIALLY DEFERRED option states that when a materialized query table is created, it won't be populated by the result of the query. The REFRESH DEFERRED option says that the data in the materialized query table is not refreshed immediately when the MQT's based tables are updated.

You can refresh an MQT at any time using the REFRESH TABLE statement. You can also use this statement for the initial population of the MQT. The statement deletes all rows with a mass delete on the MQT and then executes the fullselect in the MQT definition to recalculate the data from the base tables. It then inserts the calculated result into the MQT and updates the catalog for the refresh timestamp and cardinality of the MQT. This all occurs in a single commit scope. The following statement refreshes SALESMQT.

```
REFRESH TABLE SALESMQT;
```

Another option is MAINTAINED BY SYSTEM, which indicates that the MQT is system-maintained; you'll need to use the SQL statement REFRESH TABLE to perform this update. This option doesn't permit user updates by load, insert, update, or delete; thus, it is by nature read-only. The MAINTAINED BY USER option indicates that the MQT is user-maintained by either triggers or batch updates. It allows for user updates via load, insert, update, or delete. When you specify MAINTAINED BY USER, the MQT can also be updated by the REFRESH TABLE statement, which can be EXPLAINed if necessary.

ENABLE QUERY OPTIMIZATION lets the DB2 optimizer choose the MQT for use during the process of establishing an access path. DISABLE QUERY OPTIMIZATION prevents the optimizer from rewriting a query against the base table to automatically consider the MQT.

Changing MQTs

You can use the ALTER TABLE statement to change a materialized query table to a base table and to change a base table into a materialized query table. You can use this statement to enable or disable automatic query rewrite and to switch between system-maintained and user-maintained refresh. If you need to change the attributes of an MQT, you have two options: drop and re-create the MQT with a different definition or use ALTER TABLE to change the MQT to a base table and then change it back with an equivalent SELECT for the MQT query that matches the new definition.

Clone Tables

You can create a clone table on an existing base table at the current server by using the ALTER TABLE statement. Although you ALTER TABLE syntax to create a clone table, the authorization granted as part of the clone creation process is the same as you'd get during regular CREATE TABLE processing. The schema for the clone table will be the same as for the base table.

● ●
You can create a clone table only if the base table is in a universal table space.
● ●

To create a clone table, issue an ALTER TABLE statement with the ADD CLONE option:

```
ALTER TABLE base-table-name ADD CLONE clone-table-name
```

The creation or drop of a clone table does not impact applications accessing base table data. No base object quiesce is necessary, and this process does not invalidate plans, packages, or the dynamic statement cache.

Some restrictions apply to the use of clone tables:

- No statistics are kept for a clone table (for example, you can't use RUNSTATS on a clone table). When a data exchange takes place, realtime statistics that existed for the former base table are invalidated.

- Catalog and directory tables can't be cloned.

- Indexes cannot be created on the clone table (although they can be created on the base table). Indexes created on the base table apply to both the base and the clone tables.

- Before triggers can't be created on the clone table. Before triggers created on the base table apply to both the base and clone tables.

- You cannot rename a base table that has a clone relationship.

- You cannot clone a Real Time Statistics (RTS) table.

- You cannot drop an AUX (auxiliary) table or AUX index on an object involved in cloning.

- You cannot alter any table or column attributes of a base table or a clone table when the objects are involved with cloning.

- The maximum number of partitions cannot be altered when a clone table resides in a partition-by-growth table space.

You can exchange the base and clone data by using the EXCHANGE statement. To exchange table and index data between the base and clone tables, issue an EXCHANGE statement using the following syntax.

```
EXCHANGE DATA BETWEEN TABLE table-name1 AND table-name2
```

After a data exchange, the base and clone table names remain the same as they were before the exchange. No data movement actually takes place. The instance numbers in the underlying VSAM data sets for the objects (tables and indexes) do change, and this has the effect of changing the data that appears in the base and clone tables and their indexes. For example, say a base table exists with the data set name *I0001.*. You clone the table, and the clone's data set is initially named *.I0002.*. After an exchange, the base objects are named *.I0002.* and the clones are named *I0001.*. Each time an exchange happens, the instance numbers that represent the base and clone objects change, which immediately changes the data contained in the base and clone tables and indexes.

Indexes

An index is a list of the locations of rows sorted by the contents of one or more specified columns. We typically use indexes to improve query performance. However, indexes can also serve a logical data design purpose. For example, a unique index does not allow the entry of duplicate values in columns, thereby guaranteeing that no rows of a table are the same. You can create indexes to specify ascending or descending order by the values in a column. The indexes contain a pointer, known as a record ID (RID), to the physical location of the rows in the table. There are three main reasons to create indexes:

- To ensure uniqueness of values

- To improve query performance

- To ensure a physical clustering sequence

You can define more than one index on a particular base table, a technique that can improve the performance of queries. However, the more indexes there are, the more the database manager must work to keep the indexes up-to-date during update, delete, and insert operations. Creating a large number of indexes for a table that receives many updates can slow processing.

Indexes are also stored in underlying VSAM data sets, just like table spaces. To make a correlation between the index that you (or DB2) created, you can look in the INDEXSPACE column in the SYSINDEXES catalog table.

Let's take a look at some of the most important parameters of the CREATE INDEX statement:

- **UNIQUE.** Prevents the table from containing two or more rows with the same value as the index key.

- **USING clause.** Specifies whether you're defining storage groups or a user-defined index space.

  » USING STOGROUP indicates that DB2 will manage the data sets and that a PRIQTY and SECQTY will be specified to define the allocations for the data sets.

  » USING VCAT specifies that the data sets will be user-defined and that no space allocations are defined in this statement.

- **FREEPAGE and PCTFREE.** Specify the amount of free space to be left when an index space is built or reorganized. You should use these settings to leave space for inserts.

- **GBPCACHE.** Used in data sharing to specify which pages of an index space are written to the group buffer pools.

- **COMPRESS.** Specifies whether index compression will be used.

- **DEFINE.** Specifies whether to create the underlying data sets.

- **CLUSTER.** Specifies whether the index is a clustering index.

- **PARTITIONED.** Specifies whether the index is partitioned (primary or secondary).

- **PART.** Identifies the partition number.

- **VALUES.** Identifies the values of the keys to be contained in the partition.

- **BUFFERPOOL.** Specifies the buffer pool to which the table space is assigned. You can assign a default buffer pool with DSNZPARM IDXBPOOL.

- **PIECESIZE.** Identifies the size of the pieces (data sets) used for a non-partitioning secondary index.

- **NOT PADDED.** Permits an index with a VARCHAR column to not be padded with blanks. This option reduces the size of the index and lets it be used for index-only access. NOT PADDED applies only to indexes that contain variable-length character columns.

- **COPY.** Specifies whether the index can be image copied.

Deferring Physical Definition

You can define an index with the DEFINE NO option (DEFINE YES is default) to specify an index but defer its actual physical creation. The data sets won't be created until data is inserted into the index. This option is helpful for reducing the number of physical data sets.

Index Compression

You can define an index with the COMPRESS YES option (COMPRESS NO is the default) to reduce the amount of disk space an index consumes. We recommend index compression for applications that perform sequential insert operations with few or no delete operations. Random inserts and deletes can adversely affect compressions. Index compressions is also recommended for applications in which the indexes are created primarily for scan operations.

A buffer pool that is used to create the index must be 8 K, 16 K, or 32 K in size. The physical page size for the index on disk will be 4 K. The reason the buffer pool size is larger than the page size is that index compression saves space only on disk; the data in the index page is expanded when read into the pool.

Clustering Index

In general, it's important to control the physical sequence of the data in a table. You use the CLUSTER option on one, and only one, index on a table to specify the physical sequence. Without this option, the first index defined on the table in a non partitioned table space is used for the clustering sequence.

•••

When you use the CLUSTER keyword, the index is referred to as the explicit clustering index. If no index is defined with the CLUSTER keyword, the index DB2 chooses for clustering is referred to as the implicit clustering index.

•••

The best clustering index is one that supports the majority of the sequential access to the data in the table. For example, if a large batch process reads data based on an input key in a specific order, it may be best to make the column corresponding to that input sequence the clustering key.

There is also an option in defining table spaces called MEMBER CLUSTER. When you use this option, DB2 ignores the clustering sequence specified by the clustering index. In that case, DB2 will choose to locate the data based on available space when an SQL INSERT statement is used. The same is true if you specify the APPEND YES option on a CREATE TABLE or ALTER TABLE statement. The MEMBER CLUSTER option is mainly used in a data-sharing environment to avoid excessive p-lock negotiation on the space map when inserts are coming in by the clustering index on multiple members.

The clustering index can also be changed. You can ALTER this attribute to change whether an index is the clustering index. For instance, the following statement indicates that index CUSTIX should no longer be the clustering index.

```
ALTER INDEX CUSTIX NO CLUSTER;
```

After a NO CLUSTER index is established, the inserts will still occur according to the implicit clustering index. You'll need to define a new clustering index or ALTER an existing index to make it the new clustering index. The following syntax demonstrates the latter method.

```
ALTER INDEX CUSTIX2 CLUSTER;
```

Once you've defined the new clustering index, inserts will use the new index. Obviously, for performance reasons, it's wise to perform a REORG right after the ALTER to create the new clustering index so that inserts can now use the new clustering index.

Partitioning Index

The PARTIONED keyword on the CREATE INDEX statement specifies that the index is data partitioned (that is, partitioned according to the partitioning scheme of the underlying data). The types of partitioned indexes are partitioning and secondary.

An index is considered a partitioning index if the specified index key columns match or constitute a superset of the columns specified in the partitioning key, are in the same order, and have the same ascending or descending attributes. A secondary index is any index defined on a partitioned table space that does not meet the definition of the partitioning index.

The following example defines a partitioning index using index-controlled partitioning.

```
CREATE UNIQUE INDEX DSN8910.XEMP1
       ON DSN8910.EMP
          (EMPNO    ASC)
       USING STOGROUP DSN8G910
               PRIQTY 12
               ERASE NO
       CLUSTER
         (PART 1 VALUES('099999'),
          PART 2 VALUES('199999'),
          PART 3 VALUES('299999'),
          PART 4 VALUES('999999'))
       BUFFERPOOL BP0
       CLOSE NO;
```

When table-controlled partitioning is in place, the index definition simply needs to include the PARTITIONED keyword to indicate that the index is a partitioned index:

```
CREATE UNIQUE INDEX DSN8910.XEMP1
       ON DSN8910.EMP
          (EMPNO    ASC)
       USING STOGROUP DSN8G910
               PRIQTY 12
               ERASE NO
       CLUSTER
       PARTITIONED
       BUFFERPOOL BP0
       CLOSE NO;
```

Just like the partitioned table space, the partitioned index consists of several data sets. Each partition can have different attributes (i.e., some may have more free space than others).

Unique Index and Non-Unique Index

A unique index guarantees the uniqueness of the data values in a table's columns. During query processing, a unique index provides faster retrieval of data. The uniqueness is enforced at the end of the SQL statement that updates rows or inserts new rows. The uniqueness is also checked during execution of the CREATE INDEX statement. If the table already contains rows with duplicate key values, the index is not created. The previous example of the partitioned index definition is for a unique index as well.

A non-unique index can also improve query performance by maintaining a sorted order for the data. Depending on how many columns you use to define a key, you can have one of the following types:

- An *atomic key* is a single-column key.

- A *composite key* is composed of two or more columns.

The following key types are used to implement constraints:

- A *unique key* is used to implement unique constraints. A unique constraint does not allow two different rows to have the same values on the key columns.

- A *primary key* is used to implement entity integrity constraints. A primary key is a special type of unique key. There can be only one primary key per table. The primary key column must be defined with the NOT NULL option.

- A *foreign key* is used to implement referential integrity constraints. Referential constraints can reference only a primary key or a unique constraint. The values of a foreign key can have values defined only in the primary key or unique constraint they are referencing or null values. (A foreign key is not an index.)

DB2 uses unique indexes and the NOT NULL option to maintain primary and unique key constraints.

Unique Where Not Null Index

This is a special form of a unique index. Normally in a unique index, any two null values are taken to be equal. Specifying WHERE NOT NULL lets any two null values be unequal.

Null Values and Indexes

It's important to understand the difference between a primary key and a unique index. DB2 uses two elements to implement the relational database concept of primary and unique keys: unique indexes and the NOT NULL constraint. Therefore, unique indexes don't enforce the primary key constraint by themselves because they can allow a null value. Null values are unknown, but when it comes to indexing, a null value is treated as equal to all other null values (except when you use UNIQUE WHERE NOT NULL INDEX). You cannot insert a NULL value twice if the column is a key of a unique index because this would violate the uniqueness rule for the index.

Expressions and Indexes

As of DB2 9, you can use scalar expressions in place of columns in the definition of a unique or non-unique index. Expressions are results derived from calculations and/or functions. You can specify a key-expression in place of a column list in a CREATE INDEX statement. DB2 can then use the index on the expression to match predicates in SQL statements that include the expression. The key-expression must contain at least one column from the referenced table that is not a LOB, XML, or DECFLOAT column. In addition, the key-expression must not include

- a subquery
- an aggregate function
- a user-defined function
- a sequence reference
- a special register
- a CASE expression

If a unique constraint exists on the index (i.e., the index was defined as unique), the uniqueness will be enforced on the result of the expression.

DB2 considers the index on an expression during access path selection. It's possible to collect statistics on the expression; system catalog tables SYSKEYTARGETS, SYSKEYTARGETSTATS, SYSKEYTGTDIST, and SYSKEYTGTDISTSTATS support these statistics.

Non-Partitioning Secondary Indexes

NPSIs are indexes that are used on partitioned tables. They are not the same as the partitioning key, which DB2 uses to order and partition the data; rather, they are for access to the data. While partitioning and partitioned indexes have one index partition per table space partition, one NPSI references the entire table space, spanning all partitions. NPSIs can be unique or non-unique.

You can break NPSIs apart into multiple pieces (data sets) by using the PIECESIZE clause on the CREATE INDEX statement. Pieces can vary in size from 254 K to 64 GB; the best size will depend on how much data you have and how many pieces you want to manage. If you have several pieces, you can achieve more parallelism on processes (such as heavy INSERT batch jobs) by alleviating the bottlenecks caused by contention on a single data set. The following example shows how to create an NPSI with pieces.

```
CREATE INDEX DSN8910.XEMP2
      ON DSN8910.EMP
         (WORKDEPT ASC)
      USING STOGROUP DSN8G910
            PRIQTY 144000
            SECQTY 14400
            ERASE NO
      BUFFERPOOL BP0
      CLOSE NO
      PIECESIZE 512K;
```

Data Partitioned Secondary Indexes

The data partitioned secondary index (DPSI) provides many advantages for secondary indexes on a partitioned table space over the traditional NPSIs in terms of availability and performance.

The partitioning scheme of the DPSI will be the same as the table space partitions, and the index keys in index partition x will match those in partition x of the table space. Figure 4.5 shows how a DPSI is physically structured. The CUST_NUMX index is a DPSI.

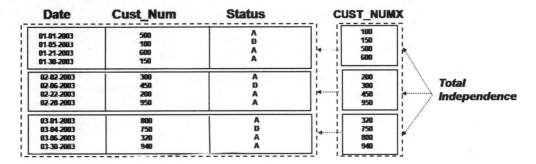

Date	Cust_Num	Status		CUST_NUMX	
01-01-2003	500	A		100	
01-05-2003	100	D		150	
01-21-2003	600	A		500	
01-30-2003	150	A		600	
02-02-2003	300	A		200	
02-06-2003	450	D		300	*Total*
02-22-2003	200	A		450	*Independence*
02-28-2003	950	A		950	
03-01-2003	800	A		320	
03-04-2003	750	D		750	
03-06-2003	320	A		800	
03-30-2003	940	A		940	

Figure 4.5: DPSI physical layout

Among the benefits a DPSI provides are

- clustering by a secondary index
- the ability to easily rotate partitions
- efficient utility processing on secondary indexes
- reduced overhead in data sharing (affinity routing)

Drawbacks of DPSIs

Although DPSIs further partition independence, some queries may not perform as well. Queries with predicates that reference columns in a single partition and therefore are restricted to a single partition of the DPSI will benefit from this new organization. To achieve this benefit, the queries will have to be designed to allow for partition pruning through the predicates. This means that at least the leading column of the partitioning key must be supplied in the query for DB2 to prune (eliminate) partitions from the query access path. However, if a predicate references only columns in the DPSI, it may not perform very well because it may need to probe several partitions of the index. Figure 4.6 shows how applications will need to code predicates for DPSIs.

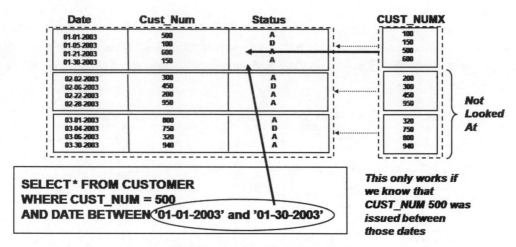

Figure 4.6: Coding predicates for DPSIs

Other limitations to using DPSIs include the facts that they cannot be completely unique (can only be unique within a partition) and they may not be the best candidates for ORDER BYs.

LOB Indexes

An index must be created on an auxiliary table for a LOB. The index itself consists of 19 bytes for the ROWID and five bytes for the RID. Due to this fact, a LOB index is always unique. No LOB columns are allowed in the index. The following example shows the CREATE statement for an auxiliary index. (No columns are specified because the auxiliary indexes have implicitly generated keys.)

```
CREATE AUX TABLE
DSN8910.AUX_BMP_PHOTO
IN      DSN8D91L.DSN8S91M
STORES  DSN8910.EMP_PHOTO_RESUME
COLUMN  BMP_PHOTO;

CREATE UNIQUE INDEX
DSN8910.XAUX_BMP_PHOTO
ON      DSN8910.AUX_BMP_PHOTO;
```

XML Indexes

An XML index can improve the efficiency of queries on XML documents that are stored in an XML column. In contrast to traditional relational indexes, where index keys consist of one or more table columns that you specify, an XML index uses a particular XML pattern expression to index paths and values in XML documents stored within a single column. The data type of that column must be XML.

Instead of providing access to the beginning of a document, index entries in an XML index provide access to nodes within the document by creating index keys based on XML pattern expressions. Because multiple parts of a XML document can satisfy an XML pattern, DB2 might generate multiple index keys when it inserts values for a single document into the index.

You create an XML index using the CREATE INDEX statement and drop an XML index using the DROP INDEX statement. The GENERATE KEY USING XMLPATTERN clause you include with the CREATE INDEX statement specifies what you want to index. Some of the keywords used with the CREATE INDEX statement for indexes on non-XML columns do not apply to indexes over XML data. The UNIQUE keyword also has a different meaning for indexes over XML data.

Suppose we want to create an XML index in the Info column of the sample Customer table. The following document shows the format of documents in the Info column.

```
<customerinfo xmlns='http://posample.org' Cid='1000'>
<name>Kathy Smith</name>
<addr country='Canada'>
<street>5 Rosewood</street>
<city>Toronto</city>
<prov-state>Ontario</prov-state>
<pcode-zip>M6W-1E6</pcode-zip>
</addr>
<phone type='work'>416-555-1358</phone>
</customerinfo>
```

Users of the CUSTOMER table often retrieve customer information using the customer ID. You might use an index like this one to make that retrieval more efficient.

```
CREATE UNIQUE INDEX CUST_CID_XMLIDX ON CUSTOMER(INFO)
GENERATE KEY USING XMLPATTERN
'declare default element namespace 'http://posample.org';
/customerinfo/@Cid'
AS SQL VARCHAR(4);
```

General Indexing Guidelines

Indexes consume disk space. The amount of disk space will vary depending on the length of the key columns, compression option specified, and whether the index is unique or non unique. Index size increases as you add more data into the base table. Therefore, consider the disk space required for indexes when planning the size of the database. Some of the indexing considerations include the following:

- Primary and unique key constraints will require a unique index.

- It's usually beneficial to create indexes on foreign key constraint columns.

- PCTFREE and FREEPAGE will greatly help insert performance.

- It's beneficial to always create a clustering index.

Modifying an Index

The ALTER INDEX statement lets you change many of the characteristics of an index. You can

- add a column to the index

- change the buffer pool assignment

- change the specifics for a single partition

- change any of the space definitions

- change whether the index is to be copied

- change the clustering index

- choose to not pad the index if it contains a VARCHAR

- change whether the index is compressed

The following statement shows how to change the buffer pool assignment for an index.

```
ALTER INDEX DSN8910.XEMP2 BUFFERPOOL BP1;
```

Not all the index attributes can be changed via an ALTER. For example, you can't change the order of columns in an index. To do that, you must drop the index and then re-create it.

Removing an Index

Use the DROP statement to remove an index:

```
DROP INDEX DSN8910.XEMP2;
```

A drop of an index may not always be successful. When a primary or unique constraint is defined on the table and the index is a unique index supporting that primary or unique constraint, the drop isn't allowed until the primary or unique constraint is altered off the table.

Renaming an Index

The RENAME statement lets you rename an index or a table. Simply code a statement similar to the following example:

```
RENAME INDEX DSN8910.XEMP2 TO XEMP9;
```

The original index name can be implicitly or explicitly qualified. The new index name must be implicitly qualified, and it inherits the qualifying of the original index.

Databases

A database is a collection of table spaces, index spaces, and the objects with them. There is also a database used for special purposes: a WORKFILE database The work file database is used as storage for DB2 work files for processing SQL statements that require working space (such as that required for a sort) and as storage for created global temporary tables and declared global temporary tables. For this special database, you can also specify which data-sharing member it is for because each member must have its own. You can also specify the coding scheme for the data in the database (ASCII, CCSID, EBCDIC, UNICODE).

Creating a Database

Following is an example of the creation of the DSN8D91A database. We use the BUFFERPOOL parameter to specify that any objects created in this database without an assigned buffer pool will default to buffer pool BP8. The DSNZPARM INDEXBP serves the same purpose but provides a default buffer pool for indexes.

```
CREATE DATABASE DSN8D91A
    STOGROUP DSN8G910
    BUFFERPOOL BP8
    CCSID EBCDIC;
```

Modifying a Database

You can change the default buffer pools, encoding scheme, and storage group for a database. Here is a sample ALTER DATABASE statement:

```
ALTER DATABASE DSN8D91A
    BUFFERPOOL BP4;
```

Removing a Database

Removing a database is easy; it's a matter of a simple DROP statement (provided all the appropriate authorities are in place). When you drop a database, all dependent objects are also dropped.

```
DROP DATABASE DSN8D91A;
```

Storage Groups

Storage groups list the DASD volumes that will be used to store data. They can contain one or many volumes. Storage groups can work with or without system-managed storage (SMS). If table spaces or index spaces are defined using a storage group (identified in the USING clause in the CREATE TABLESPACE or CREATE INDEX statement), they're considered to be DB2-managed, and DB2 will create them, letting you specify PRIQTY and SECQTY for the data-set allocations. Otherwise, these objects are considered user-managed and must be defined explicitly through the Integrated Catalog Facility (ICF).

Creating a Storage Group

You use the CREATE STOGROUP statement to create a storage group:

```
CREATE STOGROUP DSN8G910
   VOLUMES (*)
   VCAT  DSNC910;
```

The asterisk (*) in this example indicates that SMS will manage the volumes to be used. SMS storage constructs may also be used by specifying the DATACLAS, MGMTCLAS, or STORCLAS keywords.

Modifying a Storage Group

Use ALTER to add or remove volumes within a storage group or change the SMS constructs:

```
ALTER STOGROUP DSN8G91X ADD VOL1;
```

Removing a Storage Group

To remove a storage group, use the DROP statement. You can drop a storage group only if no table spaces or index spaces are using it.

```
DROP STOGROUP DSN8G910;
```

Database Design and Implementation

When implementing a DB2 relational database, you have many facets to work on, as Figure 4.7 illustrates.

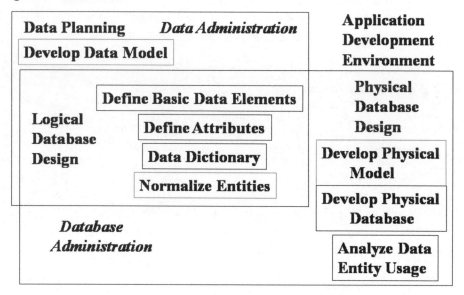

Figure 4.7: Designing relational database applications

We're going to focus on a couple of general design steps you need to perform: development of a logical model and development/implementation of a physical model.

Logical Design

Logical design is the process of determining entities, entity attributes, relationships between entities, and degrees of the relationships and then representing these elements in a fully keyed, normalized data model or entity relationship diagram. The normalized data model can then be used to define the tables needed for the relational database. Performing the logical design also involves identifying primary keys and foreign keys.

A *data model* is a graphic, conceptual model that identifies the entity types of the business and the business interactions between them. The data model provides a static, rather than a dynamic, view of data, in which the data appears as if frozen in time. Two basic approaches exist to designing a data model:

- A "bottom-up" approach produces a composite or global view of an organization's data based on the combination of many users' views of the problem requirements. It does not depict the inherent structure of the data, nor does it reflect the entire set of business activities of the organization. A bottom-up approach is most often used in data analysis.

- A "top-down" approach produces an organizational view of the data before the application views are identified. This type of approach takes into account the business activities of the entire organization and is independent of any particular application.

A logical data model consists of three basic components: entities, relationships, and attributes.

Entities

An *entity* is an object about which you store data for the purpose of answering a query or making a decision. It may be a person, place, thing, or event of interest to the enterprise (or application). Occurrences of an entity are uniquely identified by one or more attributes that make up the key to the data entity. An entity is often named with a singular noun (e.g., Customer). There is also an association between two or more data entities that represents an action and may be defined in an English sentence (subject, verb). This interaction is directional.

Relationships

Many types of *relationships* can exist between entities:

- One to one
- One to many
- Many to many
- Zero to one
- Zero to many

Attributes

Attributes are the values or characteristics associated with an entity. Every occurrence of an entity has associated attributes. Each attribute can be represented as a field. Domains are also used to convey a specific property of an object. If an attribute has attributes, it should be considered as a possible entity.

Attributes are the data items required to make process work. When identifying attributes, consider characteristics such as data type, size, how used, and entities to which related.

Normalization

Normalization is the process of non-loss decomposition of data relations. Normalization is performed during logical database design and promotes the formalization of simple ideas such as, "Domains must contain atomic values (single values)." The concept of functional dependence plays a key role. Normalization is a helpful tool for physical design; however, it's not an absolute and does not result in a physical design (final table design). Many process considerations must be accounted for before a physical design is considered done.

A normalized design can

- minimize the amount of space required to store data by forcing the storage of non-key information in a single place

- minimize the risk of data inconsistencies and improve the logical data integrity within a database by storing data items only once where possible

- minimize several types of possible update and delete errors, again by storing data only in one place where possible

- maximize the stability of the data structures by focusing on the properties of the data rather than on how the applications will use the data

Some of the objectives of data normalization include

- eliminating all data "anomalies" (i.e., update, insert, and delete)

- avoiding redundancy of data

- avoiding potential inconsistency among data

- preserving all relevant information

- maintaining maximum flexibility in the database design

- accommodating changes easily

- providing non-loss decomposition of data elements

Normal Forms

There are several degrees of normalization, or *normal forms*. The exact number varies depending on the interpretation of the relational model, but in general there are five. We look at only three normal forms here because most normalized designs are in third normal form.

First normal form, illustrated in Figure 4.8, has the following characteristics.

Not in First Normal Form:

Customer

ID	CITY	DATE	AMT	DATE	AMT	DATE	AMT
202Smith	Chicago	2/90	20.00	3/90	40.00	4/90	22.00

Solution:

Customer

NBR	NAME	CITY
202	Smith	Chicago

Payment

CUST-NBR	DATE	AMT
202	2/9	20.00

Figure 4.8: First normal form

- First normal form (1NF)

  » The data entity is in first normal form if for any specific value of the unique identifier (unique key), each attribute has only one value.

  » No repeating groups or arrays exist. (These belong in child tables.)

» Each attribute has a unique meaning and name.

» All attributes contain atomic values.

» Several data fields must not be grouped as a single value for a column.

» A true relational table satisfies 1NF.

» There will still be a high degree of redundancy.

Second normal form, illustrated in Figure 4.9, has the following characteristics.

● Second normal form (2NF)

» The data relation must first be in 1NF.

» Every non-key attribute must be fully dependent on the primary key.

» No data elements are dependent on a component of the primary key.

» Non-key attributes cannot be assigned to entities in which a part of the primary key can determine the non-key attributes.

Not in Second Normal Form:

Line Item

INV_NBR	LINE_NB	CUST_NM	CUST_CTY	ITEM	AMT
175	1	Lawson	Springfield	123	500.00
175	2	Lawson	Springfield	5445	100.00

Solution:

Invoice

INV_NBR	NAME	CITY
175	Lawson	Springfield

Line Item

INV_NBR	LINE_NB	ITEM	AMT
175	1	123	500.00
175	2	544	100.00

Figure 4.9: Second normal form

Third normal form, illustrated in Figure 4.10, has the following characteristics.

- Third normal form (3NF)

  » The data relation must first be in 2NF.

  » No data elements are dependent on other non-key data elements.

  » Every non-key attribute is non-transitively dependent on the primary key.

  » 3NF is considered to be an optimal form for most tables.

Not in Third Normal Form:

Invoice

INV_NBR	NAME	CITY
175	Smith	Chicago

Solution:

Invoice

INV_NBR	NAME
175	Smith

Customer

CUST-NAME	CITY
Smith	Chicago

Figure 4.10: Third normal form

Anomalies

Data anomalies can occur when the data is not stored in at least third normal form. A *data anomaly* is a condition in which the value for a specific occurrence of an attribute occurs in more than one location and the value in one location differs from that in the other location. For example, if you repeat the customer name on every occurrence of a customer order and a customer changes his or her name, you would need to change the name on every order; otherwise, you'll have a data anomaly.

When data anomalies are introduced into a database design, they can lower productivity in application design and create useless data. Anomalies need to be eliminated to accomplish the following goals:

- Achieve semantic clarity.

- Increase productivity and consistency among data.

- Create a design that requires the least amount of knowledge to achieve results.

Some of the problems anomalies cause include the following:

- Integrity problems (i.e., duplication, inconsistencies)

- Loss of conceptual clarity

- Unnecessary programming complexity

- Questionable growth and stability

Figure 4.11 shows what an update anomaly is and a problem that could result. Figure 4.12 shows how a normalized design would fix the issue.

If the value of an attribute changes, it must be changed in multiple places

PK

Customer Order

Order #	Order_Cost	Customer #	Customer_Name	Phone
1001	600.00	400	Joe Smith	555-1212
1002	150.00	540	Sam Jones	555-4444
1003	749.00	390	Harry Harris	555-1111
1004	22.00	489	Mary Mitchell	555-9990
1005	100.00	489	Mary Mitchell	555-9990

What if Mary Mitchell changes her name ?

Figure 4.11: Update anomaly

Order Table

PK

Order #	Order_Cost	Customer #
1001	600.00	400
1002	150.00	540
1003	749.00	390
1004	22.00	489
1005	100.00	489

Customer Table

PK

Customer #	Customer_Name	Phone
400	Joe Smith	555-1212
540	Sam Jones	555-4444
390	Harry Harris	555-1111
489	Mary Mitchell	555-9990

It would now only have to be changed once.

Figure 4.12: Normalized design to solve update anomaly

Physical Design

The physical data model is similar to the logical data model, but now the objects are identified as actual physical objects ready to be implemented in a DB2 environment. All elements of the logical model should transform into an object on the physical model. At this point, the model should be normalized.

Transforming Logical to Physical

There are some general guidelines for transforming a logical model to a physical one (you must still consider performance and DBMS specifics afterward). These general transformations include:

- creating a physical table for each entity

- defining unique index for each primary key

- defining a non-unique index for each foreign key

- defining other non-unique and unique indexes

- documenting processing needs to be considered before actual implementation

Sample Implementation

The best way to understand data type selection is to design a database and implement the design using DB2. In this sample implementation, we'll create a database for use in scheduling and tracking the results of a certification program. We'll use this database to illustrate many aspects of SQL and features of DB2. You'll find examples from this database throughout this book.

The database used in most of our examples will be the DB2 sample database that comes as part of the product installation. In most cases, we'll use this sample database as is, but in some situations we'll modify it to demonstrate a particular feature.

The sample database represents data for a fictional company, mostly revolving around employees working for the company. The employees are grouped into departments and are assigned projects. Departments are responsible for projects, and one employee manages each department. Employees can also be responsible for projects. As employees work on projects, the time they spend on those projects is recorded.

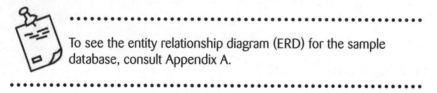

To see the entity relationship diagram (ERD) for the sample database, consult Appendix A.

DB2 Sample Database Table Descriptions

The following sample tables will be used in the examples:

- The DEPT table stores information about each department in the company. Each department has a manager, a name, a location, and a department that administers it.

- The EMP table stores information about employees. This data includes employee name, birth date, hire date, salary, and the department each employee works in, among other things.

- The PROJ table stores information about the projects being worked on. This data includes project number, project name, responsible employee, and any projects that are above these projects in a hierarchy.

- The PROJACT table defines the relationship between a project and an activity.

- The EMPROJACT table contains information about the timc employees have spent working on projects.

- The ACT table contains information about the activities.

Member DSNTEJ1 of the SDSNSAMP installation library contains the sample table definitions. Member DSNTEJ7 contains LOB definitions.

It's beneficial to have a primary key defined for each table; this practice ensures uniqueness of the data records. The attributes that are underlined in the ERD will be used as primary keys. We'll also create unique keys to illustrate their use.

Defining Tables and Columns

Designing a database involves many considerations, only a few of which we discuss in this book.

The first step in creating a database is to run a CREATE DATABASE statement, such as this one:

```
CREATE DATABASE DSN8D91A
  STOGROUP DSN8G910
  BUFFERPOOL BP0
  CCSID EBCDIC;
```

Once the database has been created, you can create the dependent physical objects. Tables can be created (if you plan to use explicit table spaces, you'll need to create them first), but for this example we'll assume the tables are already created. (For more table space creation methods, see Appendix A.)

The database design includes a number of attributes. Each of these attributes will be a column in the table definitions. Every DB2 table contains one or more columns. The tables and their corresponding columns are given names. In the previous sections, we discussed all the data types available for column definitions.

You place data in a DB2 table using SQL's INSERT, MERGE, or UPDATE statement. (The LOAD utility is also an option.) It's usually desirable for each column, or data value, to have a value. Sometimes, the INSERT statement provides no value for a column. If that column is defined as NOT NULL, the INSERT statement will fail. If a default value has been defined, that value will be stored for the column.

The table being created in the following DDL is called DSN8910.PROJ, and it contains eight columns. Each column is given a name and a data type. For some of the columns, the CREATE TABLE statement defines referential constraints. For example, no projects can be created unless they are in a valid department and have an existing responsible employee. (These are foreign keys, which we describe a little later in the chapter.) In addition, if no project name is specified, a default value of 'PROJECT NAME UNDEFINED' will be assigned.

```
CREATE TABLE DSN8910.PROJ
      (PROJNO   CHAR(6) PRIMARY KEY NOT NULL,
       PROJNAME VARCHAR(24)     NOT NULL WITH DEFAULT
        'PROJECT NAME UNDEFINED',
       DEPTNO   CHAR(3)         NOT NULL REFERENCES
         DSN8910.DEPT ON DELETE RESTRICT,
       RESPEMP  CHAR(6)         NOT NULL REFERENCES
         DSN8910.EMP ON DELETE RESTRICT,
       PRSTAFF  DECIMAL(5, 2)          ,
       PRSTDATE DATE                   ,
       PRENDATE DATE                   ,
       MAJPROJ  CHAR(6))
IN DSN8D91A.DSN8S91P
CCSID EBCDIC;
```

Keys

Keys are a special set of columns defined on a table. They can be used to uniquely identify a row or to reference a uniquely identified row from another table. Keys can be classified either by the columns they are composed of or by the database constraint they support.

As we described earlier in the chapter, a key can be one of the following types, depending on how many columns you use to define the key:

- An atomic key is a single-column key.

- A composite key is composed of two or more columns.

Three types of keys are used to implement constraints:

- A unique key is used to implement unique constraints. A unique constraint does not allow two different rows to have the same values in the key columns.

- A primary key is used to implement entity integrity constraints. A primary key is a special type of unique key. There can be only one primary key per table. The primary key column must be defined with the NOT NULL option.

- A foreign key is used to implement referential integrity constraints. Referential constraints can reference only a primary key or a unique key. The values of a foreign key can have values defined only in the primary key or unique key they are referencing or the null value. When the foreign key in a child table becomes the leading columns of the primary key of that child table, that is considered an identifying relationship between the child and the parent table.

Defining Primary Keys

It's sometimes beneficial to define a primary key for each of your DB2 tables; this practice guarantees the uniqueness of a column value or group of column values (composite key). In the sample CREATE statement, the primary key for the table project is defined as the column PROJNO (project number). Because we've specified this column as a primary key, DB2 will force the creation of a unique index. If the schema processor creates the table, or if DB2 implicitly creates the table space, the unique index supporting the primary key will be defined automatically; otherwise, you'll need to create an index to support the primary key before the table can be used.

The following two statements define the activity and employee project activity tables:

```
CREATE TABLE DSN8910.ACT
     (ACTNO      SMALLINT      NOT NULL,
      ACTKWD    CHAR(6)       NOT NULL,
      ACTDESC  VARCHAR(20)   NOT NULL,
       PRIMARY KEY(ACTNO))
IN DSN8D91A.DSN8S91P
CCSID EBCDIC;
```

```
CREATE TABLE DSN8910.EMPPROJACT
      (EMPNO       CHAR(6)         NOT NULL,
       PROJNO      CHAR(6)         NOT NULL,
       ACTNO       SMALLINT        NOT NULL,
       ACTPROJEMPNO INTEGER        NOT NULL,
       EMPTIME   DECIMAL(5, 2)           ,
       EMSTDATE DATE                     ,
       EMENDATE DATE                     ,
        FOREIGN KEY REPAPA (PROJNO, ACTNO, EMSTDATE)
        REFERENCES DSN8910.PROJACT
        ON DELETE CASCADE,
        FOREIGN KEY REPAE (EMPNO) REFERENCES DSN8910.EMP
        ON DELETE RESTRICT,
        CONSTRAINT EMAUNIQUE UNIQUE(ACTPROJEMPNO))
IN DSN8D91A.DSN8S91P
CCSID EBCDIC;
```

You cannot define a foreign key on a table until the primary key and unique index have been defined in the parent table.

Defining Unique Keys

You can use unique keys to enforce uniqueness on a set of columns. A table can have more than one unique key (index) defined. The EMPPROJACT table definition (modified for our example above) uses a unique constraint (EMAUNIQUE) on column ACTPROJEMPNO to ensure that one of these special assignment IDs is not used twice.

Having unique constraints on more than one set of columns of a table is different from defining a composite unique key that includes the whole set of columns. For example, if we define a composite primary key on the columns EMPNO, PROJNO, and ACTNO, a chance still exists that an activity number will be duplicated using a different project number and/or employee number.

A unique index must always be created for primary (if one does not already exist) or unique key constraints (unless using the schema processor). Also, if you want to drop the only unique index that supports a primary key, you must drop the primary key first.

Defining Foreign Keys

A foreign key is a reference to the data values in another table. Different types of foreign key constraints exist. Looking at the previous table definition for EMPPROJACT, you can see that it is a relationship table between projects, activities, and employees. This table is recording the time employees have spent on each project.

The foreign key constraints will perform the following functions:

- If a record in the PROJACT table is deleted, all matching records in the EMPPROJACT table will be deleted (DELETE CASCADE).

- If a test in the EMP table is deleted and there are matching records in the EMPPROJACT table, the DELETE statement will result in an error (DELETE RESTRICT).

A foreign key constraint always relates to a primary key or unique key constraint of the table in the references clause.

Defining parent–child relationships between tables is known as *declarative referential integrity* because the child table refers to the parent table. You define these constraints during table creation or by using the ALTER TABLE SQL statement. DB2 enforces referential constraints for all insert, update, and delete activity.

This database implementation created only some of the sample tables. You can find the complete DDL for the storage group, databases, table spaces, tables, and indexes in Appendix A.

Summary

In this chapter, we concentrated on the SQL Data Definition Language (DDL), which you use to create, modify, and remove database objects. Three main statements occur in DDL: CREATE, ALTER, and DROP. We covered some of the options in the CREATE and ALTER statements. If you want to use a DB2 database, you may need to learn DDL first to create some database objects. A DB2 database contains many kinds of objects. Some are created by a DB2 command; others, by DDL statements.

Among the database objects created by DDL, we focused primarily on data types, tables, views, and indexes. You use data types to specify the attributes of columns in a table. DB2 has two kinds of data types: built-in and user-defined. The built-in data types are DB2-supplied types and fall into three main categories:

- Numeric

- String (including large object, or LOB)

- Date-time

We also discussed DB2's support for Unicode, as well as various encoding schemes and character sets.

A table consists of columns and rows and stores an unordered set of records. Each column has a data type as one of its attributes. A table itself can have some rules, called constraints, to guarantee the uniqueness of records or maintain the relationships between and within tables. Constraints help application programmers evaluate the records or maintain the consistency between tables.

Views can also reduce some application development workload. A view is a logical table based on the physical table or other views. You can create a view to limit access to sensitive data while allowing more general access to other data.

An index is one of the most important objects in terms of performance. You can also use an index to guarantee the uniqueness of each record.

Additional Resources

IBM DB2 9 Administration Guide (SC18-9840)
IBM DB2 9 SQL Reference (SC18-9854)

Practice Questions

Question 1

Which of the following options is the most plausible reason for a DROP INDEX failing?

○ A. The table was defined with restrict on drop.

○ B. The index has no extents left.

○ C. A unique key constraint exists.

○ D. The DEFER keyword was not specified.

Question 2

Which clause would be used to create a partition-by-growth table space?

○ A. The DSSIZE MAX clause

○ B. The NUMPARTS MAX clause

○ C. The NUMPARTS 4096 clause

○ D. The MAXPARTITIONS clause

Question 3

The primary space allocation on a DB2-managed segmented table space named MYTS1 in database MYDB needs to be increased from 50 MB to 60 MB. Which of the following sequences of steps should you take to change the primary space quantity and allocate the additional space?

○ A. `ALTER TABLESPACE MYDB.MYTS1 PRIQTY 60000;`

○ B. `ALTER TABLESPACE MYDB.MYTS1 PRIQTY 60000;`
      `REORG TABLESPACE MYDB.MYTS1`

○ C. `-STOP DATABASE(MYDB) SPACENAM(MYTS1`
      `ALTER TABLESPACE MYDB.MYTS1 PRIQTY 60000;`

○ D. `-STOP DATABASE(MYDB) SPACENAM(MYTS1)`
      `ALTER TABLESPACE MYDB.MYTS1 PRIQTY 60000;`
      `REORG TABLESPACE MYDB.MYTS1 REUSE`

Question 4

Which of the following is the name of the type of relationship between two tables in which the primary key columns of the parent table are inherited by and become a subset of the primary key columns of the child table?

○ A. Recursive

○ B. Identifying

○ C. Independent

○ D. Associative

Question 5

Given that an environment that uses EBCDIC as the default encoding scheme doesn't support mixed and graphic data and has a table TEST.TABLE1 in ASCII format, the DBA issues the following SQL statement:

```
SELECT * FROM TEST.TABLE1 WHERE COL1 = X'26'
```
Which of the following encoding schemes will be used for the value that is compared with COL1?

○ A. CCSID

○ B. EBCDIC

○ C. ASCII

○ D. UNICODE

Answers

Question 1

The answer is **C**, a unique constraint exists. Whenever a primary key constraint or a unique key constraint is defined on a table, a unique index must exist to support the constraint. If the index being dropped is the last unique index in support of a unique constraint or primary key, that index cannot be dropped until the primary key is dropped or the unique constraint is dropped.

Question 2

The answer is **D**, the MAXPARTITIONS clause. Two types of universal table spaces exist: partition-by-growth and range-partitioned. While the MAXPARTITIONS clause designates a partition-by-growth table space, the combination of NUMPARTS and SEGSIZE designates a range-partitioned universal table space. NUMPARTS alone creates a partitioned table space, and SEGSIZE alone creates a segmented table space.

Question 3

The answer is **B**. The primary space allocation indicates the initial size of the VSAM data set (or sets) supporting the table space. Once this initial space is allocated, it can be changed, but the change won't be effective until the primary space is reallocated. This will happen only if the underlying VSAM data set is deleted and redefined. This will happen during a REORG or LOAD REPLACE, but only if the data set isn't reused.

Question 4

The answer is **B**, identifying.

Question 5

The answer is **C**, ASCII. Comparisons on the data server are always in the encoding scheme defined for the table. Likewise, sorting on columns in an ORDER BY depend on the encoding scheme of the table.

Retrieving and Manipulating Database Objects

In This Chapter

- ✔ Data Manipulation Language
- ✔ Selecting data
- ✔ Inscrting data
- ✔ Updating data
- ✔ Deleting data
- ✔ Merging data

In Chapter 4, we discussed the definitions of various database objects using SQL's Data Definition Language. In this chapter, we start manipulating the database objects using the part of SQL known as Data Manipulation Language, or DML. We'll be populating (inserting) data into the database and retrieving the data using many powerful methods. Depending on the sophistication of the database users, SQL can be used to query the database, access advanced functions, manipulate the data, answer complex questions, access legacy data stores, and return XML documents. We cover a good deal of this information in Chapters 6, 13, and 15, but here we start with the basics.

Most SQL statements in a DB2 application involve DML statements. Therefore, application developers need to understand the various methods of inserting, updating, and retrieving data from the database. We'll begin with simple retrieval statements and gradually introduce more complex methods of data manipulation. Most of the examples use the DB2 sample database. We'll consider five main SQL DML statements: SELECT, INSERT, UPDATE, MERGE, and DELETE.

Data Retrieval

SQL is based on mathematical principles, specifically on set theory and relational algebra. The data is stored in the database as unordered sets of data records. SQL is a set-oriented language, and many of its language elements are directly related to relational algebraic terms, such as "permutation," "projection," "restriction," and "join."

A set of data is represented in a DB2 database as a table or a view and is stored in a DB2 table without regard to order. To retrieve data in a particular order, you must add an ORDER BY phrase to a SELECT statement. Similarly, if the data is to be grouped, you must add a GROUP BY phrase to the statement.

Let's review the DB2 sample database design defined in the previous chapter and manipulate some data using various SQL statements. Recall that there are three main tables: DEPT, EMP, and PROJ. Each table represents a set of records that correspond, respectively, to a department, employee, and project in our fictitious

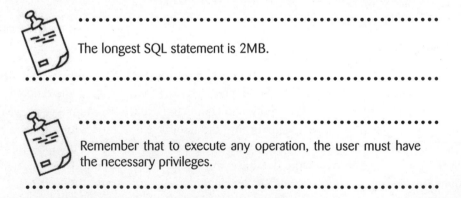

The longest SQL statement is 2MB.

Remember that to execute any operation, the user must have the necessary privileges.

company. An associative table, known as the EMPPROJACT table, is used to relate activities to projects and employees. This table records the amount of time each employee spends on activities in projects.

The Major Components of a SELECT Statement

A query consists of a *select-statement*. The select-statement contains components called *fullselects* and *subselects*. A subselect specifies a result table that is derived from the tables or views that are identified in the FROM clause. A fullselect is a component of the select-statement, as well as of the CREATE VIEW, CREATE TABLE, and INSERT statements; the ALTER TABLE statement for a definition of a materialized query table; and the DECLARE GLOBAL TEMPORARY TABLE statement. A fullselect can also be a component of certain predicates that are components of a subselect. A fullselect that is a component of a predicate is called a *subquery*. A *scalar-fullselect*, which returns a table of one row and one column, can be a component of an expression as well as a component of the assignment clause of a DELETE, UPDATE, or MERGE statement.

Confused? The subselect is the basic form of data retrieval. It specifies the input in the FROM clause, the output in the SELECT clause, filtering in the WHERE clause, grouping with filtering after grouping in the GROUP BY and HAVING clauses, ordering in the ORDER BY clause, and limitation of rows in the result table in the FETCH FIRST clause. Subselects are a component of a fullselect, and there can be many subselects within a fullselect. A fullselect can contain many subselects and fullselects and can include DISTINCT, UNION, EXCEPT, INTERSECT, as well as ORDER BY and FETCH FIRST clauses. You can specify a select-statement directly in a DECLARE CURSOR statement or in SPUFI or the command-line processor. The select-statement is the result of the fullselect contained within the select-statement.

The SQL language is *orthogonal*. This means that, for the most part, you can specify any component of the language—fullselect, subselect, expression, and so on—within any other component of the language. The result is an extremely dynamic and advanced query language that is relatively easy to code.

Retrieving the Entire Table

The most basic of all SQL retrieval commands involves the SELECT statement with no operators other than the name of the table. The following SQL statement retrieves all the information about the amount of time employees spent working on project activities.

```
SELECT * FROM DSN8910.EMPPROJACT
```

SQL is a data access language that consists of language statements and clauses. Many optional clauses are available to modify the output. The output of a SELECT statement is known as a *result set* or a *result table*.

Let's look at the results of the sample SELECT statement. This example uses the asterisk, or star, character (*) for column selection, and the columns are returned to the user in the order in which they were defined when the table was created. (To conserve space, we present only a portion of the actual result set here.)

```
EMPNO   PROJNO ACTNO EMPTIME EMSTDATE   EMENDATE
_____  _____ _____ _____ _____ _____
000010 MA2100    10    0.50 1982-01-01 1982-11-01
000010 MA2110    10    1.00 1982-01-01 1983-02-01
000010 AD3100    10    0.50 1982-01-01 1982-07-01
000020 PL2100    30    1.00 1982-01-01 1982-09-15
000030 IF1000    10    0.50 1982-06-01 1983-01-01
000030 IF2000    10    0.50 1982-01-01 1983-01-01
000050 OP1000    10    0.25 1982-01-01 1983-02-01
000050 OP2010    10    0.75 1982-01-01 1983-02-01
000070 AD3110    10    1.00 1982-01-01 1983-02-01
000090 OP1010    10    1.00 1982-01-01 1983-02-01
000100 OP2010    10    1.00 1982-01-01 1983-02-01
000110 MA2100    20    1.00 1982-01-01 1982-03-01
000130 IF1000    90    1.00 1982-01-01 1982-10-01
000130 IF1000   100    0.50 1982-10-01 1983-01-01
000140 IF1000    90    0.50 1982-10-01 1983-01-01
000140 IF2000   100    1.00 1982-01-01 1982-03-01
000140 IF2000   100    0.50 1982-03-01 1982-07-01
000140 IF2000   110    0.50 1982-03-01 1982-07-01
000140 IF2000   110    0.50 1982-10-01 1983-01-01
000150 MA2112    60    1.00 1982-01-01 1982-07-15
...
```

In SQL, you use the * character to indicate that you're referencing all columns of a table. In this case, the SQL statement refers to all the columns defined for the DSN8910.EMPPROJACT table. If you altered the table and added a new column to the table definition, the result set would contain the new column.

You use the * character to refer to all the columns defined for a table. The order of the columns in the result table is the same as the order specified in the CREATE TABLE or CREATE VIEW statement.

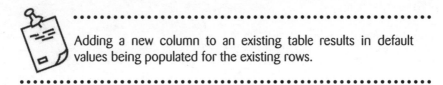

Adding a new column to an existing table results in default values being populated for the existing rows.

As we noted, the data returned to the user is known as the result set. If the result set is large, it's advisable to filter the data using a WHERE predicate.

Because the output of an SQL statement that uses the * character varies according to the table definition, the recommendation is to specify each column name you want to see in the SELECT statement. The list of columns following the SELECT keyword is known as the *select list*. We can obtain the same result as the preceding statement by using the following SQL statement.

```
SELECT EMPNO, PROJNO, ACTNO, EMPTIME, EMSTDATE, EMENDATE
FROM DSN8910.EMPPROJACT;
```

The FROM clause in the SQL DML statement describes the location (table or view) of the data. Our example references a single table called DSN8910.EMPPROJACT. All data retrieval statements must include the SELECT and FROM clauses.

Projecting Columns from a Table

Projection is a relational operation that lets you retrieve a subset of the defined columns from a table. The next example restricts the output from the SELECT statement so that only the employee number, name, and department attributes from the EMP table are shown.

```
SELECT EMPNO, FIRSTNME, MIDINIT, LASTNAME, WORKDEPT FROM DSN8910.EMP
```

Here is a portion of the output of this SELECT statement:

```
EMPNO   FIRSTNME  MIDINIT  LASTNAME   WORKDEPT
_____  _____  _____  _____   _____
000010  CHRISTINE I        HAAS       A00
000020  MICHAEL   L        THOMPSON   B01
000030  SALLY     A        KWAN       C01
000050  JOHN      B        GEYER      E01
000060  IRVING    F        STERN      D11
000070  EVA       D        PULASKI    D21
000090  EILEEN    W        HENDERSON  E11
```

```
000100 THEODORE  Q        SPENSER   E21
000110 VINCENZO  G        LUCCHESSI A00
000120 SEAN               O'CONNELL A00
000130 DOLORES   M        QUINTANA  C01
000140 HEATHER   A        NICHOLLS  C01
...
```

The order of the columns in the result table will always match the order in the select list. DB2 ignores the order of the columns as they were defined in the CREATE TABLE or CREATE VIEW statement when the SQL statement provides a select list. In the example, the column order resembles the order in the CREATE TABLE statement (which you can view in Appendix A) because this statement defines the EMPNO column before defining the name and department columns.

Changing the Order of the Columns

Permutation is the relational operation that lets you change the order of the columns in a result table. You use permutation every time you select columns in an order different from the order defined in the CREATE TABLE statement. For example, to display the name before the employee number, we could execute the following:

```
SELECT FIRSTNME, MIDINIT, LASTNAME, EMPNO, WORKDEPT
FROM DSN8910.EMP
```

This SELECT statement specifies the select list in a different order than was defined in the table definition and produces the following result table:

```
FIRSTNME  MIDINIT LASTNAME  EMPNO  WORKDEPT
————————  ——————— ————————  —————— ————————
CHRISTINE I       HAAS      000010 A00
MICHAEL   L       THOMPSON  000020 B01
SALLY     A       KWAN      000030 C01
JOHN      B       GEYER     000050 E01
IRVING    F       STERN     000060 D11
EVA       D       PULASKI   000070 D21
EILEEN    W       HENDERSON 000090 E11
THEODORE  Q       SPENSER   000100 E21
VINCENZO  G       LUCCHESSI 000110 A00
SEAN              O'CONNELL 000120 A00
DOLORES   M       QUINTANA  000130 C01
HEATHER   A       NICHOLLS  000140 C01
...
```

We refer to the output of a SELECT statement as the result table because the output of all SELECT statements can be considered a relational table.

Restricting Rows from a Table

Restriction is a relational operation that filters the resulting rows of a table. To accomplish restriction, you can use *predicates* defined in an SQL WHERE clause. A predicate is a condition placed on the data. The result of the condition is TRUE, FALSE, or UNKNOWN. To restrict our sample result set, we need to add a WHERE clause to the SQL statement.

The WHERE clause specifies conditions or predicates that DB2 must evaluate before returning the result table to the user. Many valid types of predicates can be used. The following example uses the equality (=) predicate to restrict the records to only those employees who work in department C01.

```
SELECT FIRSTNME, MIDINIT, LASTNAME, EMPNO, WORKDEPT
FROM DSN8910.EMP
WHERE WORKDEPT = 'C01';
```

The WHERE clause accepts other comparison operators, such as greater than (>), less than (<), greater than or equal to (>=), less than or equal to (<=), and not equal to (<>). The preceding statement is an example of a *basic predicate*. A basic predicate simply compares two values. More complex predicates, such as LIKE, BETWEEN, and IN, are also valid; we discuss these predicates later.

Restricting Rows Using Multiple Conditions

It's possible to combine multiple conditions (predicates) in a single SQL statement. You can combine predicates by using Boolean operators, such as AND and OR. The order of the predicate evaluation does not affect the result set (a property known as *set closure*).

The following SQL statement uses multiple predicates to retrieve the records for employees who work in department C01 and whose salary exceeds $30,000. The rows that satisfy the predicates are known as the *qualifying rows*.

```
SELECT FIRSTNME, MIDINIT, LASTNAME, EMPNO, WORKDEPT
FROM DSN8910.EMP
WHERE WORKDEPT = 'C01'
AND   SALARY > 30000;
```

Selecting Columns from Multiple Tables

There are basically two operations that combine columns from multiple tables in a single SQL statement. These operations are the Cartesian product and the join.

Cartesian Products

A *Cartesian product* is a relational operation that merges all the values from one table with all the values from another table. This operation isn't used frequently because its result table can be very large. The number of rows in the result table is always equal to the product of the number of qualifying rows in each table being accessed.

> The DB2 optimizer may choose to use a Cartesian product of unrelated tables if it deems this method to be an efficient way to access multiple tables. An example would be two single-row tables that are joined with a large table. The cross-product of 1 x 1 = 1; thus, the large table access is deferred as late as possible, with a potential increase in the restrictive predicates that can be applied without incurring the overhead of a large Cartesian result. This method of table access is typical in processing queries against a star schema data model.

The following example represents a Cartesian product of all employees in department C01 with all projects owned by that department. First, we select the employees in department C01:

```
SELECT FIRSTNME, MIDINIT, LASTNAME, EMPNO, WORKDEPT
FROM DSN8910.EMP
WHERE WORKDEPT = 'C01'
```

```
FIRSTNME  MIDINIT  LASTNAME  EMPNO   WORKDEPT
--------  -------  --------  ------  --------
SALLY     A        KWAN      000030  C01
DOLORES   M        QUINTANA  000130  C01
HEATHER   A        NICHOLLS  000140  C01
KIM       N        NATZ      200140  C01
```

Then, we select from all projects for department C01:

```
SELECT PROJNO, PROJNAME, DEPTNO
FROM DSN8910.PROJ
WHERE DEPTNO = 'C01';

PROJNO  PROJNAME         DEPTNO
------  --------------   ------
IF1000  QUERY SERVICES   C01
IF2000  USER EDUCATION   C01
```

Now, we combine the two tables to form a Cartesian product result table:

```
SELECT FIRSTNME, MIDINIT, LASTNAME, EMPNO, WORKDEPT,
       PROJNO, PROJNAME, DEPTNO
FROM DSN8910.EMP,

DSN8910.PROJ
WHERE DEPTNO = 'C01'
AND   WORKDEPT = 'C01';

FIRSTNME  MIDINIT  LASTNAME  EMPNO   WORKDEPT  PROJNO  PROJNAME         DEPTNO
--------  -------  --------  ------  --------  ------  --------------   ------
SALLY     A        KWAN      000030  C01       IF1000  QUERY SERVICES   C01
SALLY     A        KWAN      000030  C01       IF2000  USER EDUCATION   C01
DELORES   M        QUINTANA  000130  C01       IF1000  QUERY SERVICES   C01
DELORES   M        QUINTANA  000130  C01       IF2000  USER EDUCATION   C01
HEATHER   A        NICHOLLS  000140  C01       IF1000  QUERY SERVICES   C01
HEATHER   A        NICHOLLS  000140  C01       IF2000  USER EDUCATION   C01
KIM       N        NATZ      200140  C01       IF1000  QUERY SERVICES   C01
KIM       N        NATZ      200140  C01       IF2000  USER EDUCATION   C01
```

The FROM clause of this query references two tables. The tables are separated by a comma, a notation called an *implicit join*. The WHERE clause contains no relationship expression. This type of query results in a Cartesian product.

The result table is a representation of all possible combinations of the input tables. The EMP table, after filtering on the department, has four rows, and the PROJ table, after filtering, has two rows. Therefore, the SELECT statement shown above returns eight rows.

Adding a WHERE clause to your query doesn't always provide the desired result. In the preceding example, we want to know all the projects that are in the departments where these employees work. However, the query only coincidentally returns the combinations because both tables have been filtered on department C01. Had we not filtered the PROJ table on department C01, the query would have returned 80 rows, joining each of the three employees to every project. When referencing multiple tables, you normally should include a cross-table relationship using a table merge or join method, as the following example shows. We'll examine table join methods further in the next section.

```
SELECT FIRSTNME, MIDINIT, LASTNAME, EMPNO, WORKDEPT,
       PROJNO, PROJNAME, DEPTNO
FROM DSN8910.EMP,

DSN8910.PROJ
WHERE
WORKDEPT = 'C01'
AND WORKDEPT = DEPTNO;
```

FIRSTNME	MIDINIT	LASTNAME	EMPNO	WORKDEPT	PROJNO	PROJNAME	DEPTNO
SALLY	A	KWAN	000030	C01	IF1000	QUERY SERVICES	C01
SALLY	A	KWAN	000030	C01	IF2000	USER EDUCATION	C01
DELORES	M	QUINTANA	000130	C01	IF1000	QUERY SERVICES	C01
DELORES	M	QUINTANA	000130	C01	IF2000	USER EDUCATION	C01
HEATHER	A	NICHOLLS	000140	C01	IF1000	QUERY SERVICES	C01
HEATHER	A	NICHOLLS	000140	C01	IF2000	USER EDUCATION	C01
KIM	N	NATZ	200140	C01	IF1000	QUERY SERVICES	C01
KIM	N	NATZ	200140	C01	IF2000	USER EDUCATION	C01

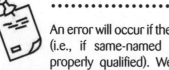

An error will occur if the columns being referenced are ambiguous (i.e., if same-named columns from different tables are not properly qualified). We discuss how to qualify column names when we cover correlation names.

Joins

To avoid data redundancy, database tables should be normalized. After a normalization process, multiple related tables will exist. To satisfy some of the required queries, the result tables containing the desired data must be reconstructed. You can reconstruct the tables temporarily by using a table join strategy to produce a single-result table.

The result tables in the previous examples usually provided department numbers and not the complete name of each department. The sample database stores the department numbers in the EMP and PROJ table, while the DEPT table holds the full department names. To obtain the name of a department, we must retrieve the data from the DEPT table using a relationship or join strategy.

Consider an example that lists the departments D01 and D21 along with the names of the employees who work in those departments. Our query involves the following tables:

- DSN8910.EMP

- DSN8910.DEPT

First, let's retrieve the employee names from the EMP table. These names are stored in multiple columns to allow for easy retrieval by last name.

```
SELECT EMPNO, FIRSTNME, MIDINIT, LASTNAME, WORKDEPT
FROM    DSN8910.EMP;
```

The output of this example follows. Pay special attention to the values in the WORKDEPT column. We'll use this column as the *join column* in the next example.

EMPNO	FIRSTNME	MIDINIT	LASTNAME	WORKDEPT
000010	CHRISTINE	I	HAAS	A00
000020	MICHAEL	L	THOMPSON	B01
000030	SALLY	A	KWAN	C01
000050	JOHN	B	GEYER	E01
000060	IRVING	F	STERN	D11
000070	EVA	D	PULASKI	D21
000090	EILEEN	W	HENDERSON	E11
000100	THEODORE	Q	SPENSER	E21
000110	VINCENZO	G	LUCCHESSI	A00
000120	SEAN		O'CONNELL	A00
000130	DELORES	M	QUINTANA	C01
000140	HEATHER	A	NICHOLLS	C01
000150	BRUCE		ADAMSON	D11
000160	ELIZABETH	R	PIANKA	D11
000170	MASATOSHI	J	YOSHIMURA	D11
000180	MARILYN	S	SCOUTTEN	D11

```
000190 JAMES     H     WALKER     D11
000200 DAVID           BROWN      D11
000210 WILLIAM   T     JONES      D11
000220 JENNIFER  K     LUTZ       D11
000230 JAMES     J     JEFFERSON  D21
000240 SALVATORE M     MARINO     D21
000250 DANIEL    S     SMITH      D21
000260 SYBIL     P     JOHNSON    D21
000270 MARIA     L     PEREZ      D21
000280 ETHEL     R     SCHNEIDER  E11
000290 JOHN      R     PARKER     E11
... continues for a total of 43 rows
```

Now, let's retrieve the department names for departments D01 and D21:

```
SELECT DEPTNO, DEPTNAME
FROM   DSN8910.DEPT
WHERE  DEPTNO = 'D01'
OR     DEPTNO = 'D21';

DEPTNO DEPTNAME
_____ _____

D01    DEVELOPMENT CENTER
D21    ADMINISTRATION SYSTEMS
```

Each department number in the EMP table must correspond to a department number in the DEPT table because of declarative referential integrity constraints. The parent table in the relationship is the DEPT table, and the child (dependent) table is the EMP table. After all, employees work in departments.

We need to join the two result tables based on the department number values. This column is known as the join column.

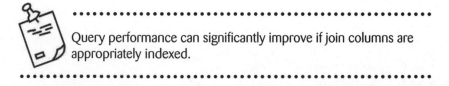

Query performance can significantly improve if join columns are appropriately indexed.

The following single query satisfies the end-user requirement.

```
SELECT DEPTNO, DEPTNAME
       EMPNO, FIRSTNME, MIDINIT, LASTNAME, WORKDEPT
FROM   DSN8910.DEPT,
       DSN8910.EMP
WHERE  (DEPTNO = 'D01' OR DEPTNO = 'D21')
AND    DEPTNO = WORKDEPT;
```

A table join requires a predicate that includes an expression based on columns from the tables referenced in the FROM clause. This expression is known as a *join predicate*.

> An alternative form of the FROM clause for joins involves explicitly coding the JOIN keyword between the tables (rather than using a comma) and coding the join predicates in the ON clause rather than in the WHERE clause. We cover this method of coding in more detail in Chapter 6.

The join query above is not typical in modern database design due to the naming of the columns. Notice that the join columns are WORKDEPT from the EMP table and DEPTNO from the DEPT table. In typical database designs that follow standardized naming conventions, these columns would have the same name. If this were the case, we'd have to take measures to fully qualify the column names. When a single query accesses multiple tables, any selected columns that occur in more than one table must be qualified with the table name. Imagine that the department number column in both tables had the same name. We'd then have to write the query in the following manner.

```
SELECT  DSN8910.DEPT.DEPTNO, DEPTNAME
        EMPNO, FIRSTNME, MIDINIT, LASTNAME,
        DSN8910.EMP.DEPTNO
FROM    DSN8910.DEPT,
        DSN8910.EMP
WHERE   (DSN8910.DEPT.DEPTNO = 'D01'
        OR DSN8910.DEPT.DEPTNO = 'D21')
AND     DSN8910.DEPT.DEPTNO = DSN8910.EMP.DEPTNO;
```

DEPTNO	EMPNO		FIRSTNME	MIDINIT	LASTNAME	WORKDEPT
D21	ADMINISTRATION SYSTEMS	EVA	D	PULASKI	D21
D21	ADMINISTRATION SYSTEMS	JAMES	J	JEFFERSON	D21
D21	ADMINISTRATION SYSTEMS	SALVATORE	M	MARINO	D21
D21	ADMINISTRATION SYSTEMS	DANIEL	S	SMITH	D21
D21	ADMINISTRATION SYSTEMS	SYBIL	P	JOHNSON	D21
D21	ADMINISTRATION SYSTEMS	MARIA	L	PEREZ	D21
D21	ADMINISTRATION SYSTEMS	ROBERT	M	MONTEVERDE	D21

The maximum number of base tables referenced in a single SQL statement is 225.

The kind of join operation shown in the preceding example is also called an inner join. An inner join displays only the rows that are present in both of the joined tables. Notice that department D01 isn't in the join result. It has no employees!

Using Correlation Names

If you had to fully qualify every column with the table name (e.g., *tableschema.tablename.columnname*), queries would become very large and cumbersome to work with. Fortunately, there's an easier way to qualify the ambiguous columns that result from a multi-table SELECT statement.

You can use a *correlation name* to qualify the columns. A correlation name is a temporary alias for a table referenced in an SQL statement. We can rewrite the previous query using correlated names as follows:

```
SELECT  D.DEPTNO, DEPTNAME
        EMPNO, FIRSTNME, MIDINIT, LASTNAME,
        E.DEPTNO
FROM    DSN8910.DEPT D,
        DSN8910.EMP E
WHERE   (D.DEPTNO = 'D01' OR D.DEPTNO = 'D21')
AND     D.DEPTNO = E.DEPTNO;
```

The correlation name immediately follows the name of the table as stated in the FROM clause. In this example, the correlated name for the DEPT table is D, and the correlated name for the EMP table is E.

You can optionally prefix correlation names with the AS keyword—for example, DSN8910.EMP AS E. This technique is purely for readability.

Once you've defined a correlation name, you can reference it in the rest of the query in place of the table name. (You can still reference the table name itself, as well.) The correlated names are accessible within the SQL statement only. After the execution of the statement, the correlation name is no longer defined.

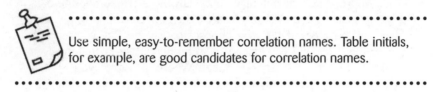

Use simple, easy-to-remember correlation names. Table initials, for example, are good candidates for correlation names.

Sorting Your Output

Up to now, we've been retrieving data from one or more tables. None of our SQL statements has specified the order of the result table. Without an ORDER BY clause in the SQL statement, DB2 retrieves the data in an undetermined order.

The only guaranteed way to return data in the required sequence is to use the ORDER BY clause. Any data retrieval that is currently returned in sequence without this clause is purely based on the data retrieval method at the time. A future access path change may not return the data in the same sequence.

The following example produces a list of employees and their departments, in alphabetical (ascending) order by last name, for the employees who work in department C01.

```
SELECT  D.DEPTNO, D.DEPTNAME
        E.EMPNO, E.FIRSTNME, E.MIDINIT, E.LASTNAME,
        E.WORKDEPT
FROM    DSN8910.DEPT D,
        DSN8910.EMP E
WHERE   D.DEPTNO = 'C01'
AND     D.DEPTNO = E.WORKDEPT
ORDER BY E.LASTNAME ASC;
```

As you can see, this example contains a new clause, ORDER BY. You use the ORDER BY clause to list the columns that specify the sort order and the type of sort. In this case, the ASC keyword specified after the LASTNAME column in the ORDER BY clause indicates that DB2 should sort the result table in ascending order based on last name.

Appropriate indexing may permit DB2 to avoid sorting the data to match the ORDER BY clause. If the data is already sequenced via the index, DB2 may choose to use the index and avoid sorting the data. DB2 can't avoid a sort for an ORDER BY that involves columns from more than one table. Where possible, you should include columns from only one table in an ORDER BY clause to give DB2 greater opportunity for sort avoidance.

Let's modify the SQL to change the output to descending order by last name, with a secondary order column on first name in ascending order:

```
SELECT  D.DEPTNO, D.DEPTNAME
        E.EMPNO, E.FIRSTNME, E.MIDINIT, E.LASTNAME,
        E.WORKDEPT
FROM    DSN8910.DEPT D,
        DSN8910.EMP E
WHERE   D.DEPTNO = 'C01'
AND     D.DEPTNO = E.WORKDEPT
ORDER BY E.LASTNAME DESC, E.FIRSTNME;
```

Here, the DESC keyword in the ORDER BY clause indicates that the result table should be sorted in descending order by last name.

More than one record can have the same last name; in fact, this situation is quite common. Our ORDER BY clause therefore specifies a second column, FIRSTNME, to sort on. Because no keyword defines the sort sequence for this column, DB2 will use the default ordering sequence (ascending).

You can reference the column that DB2 should use to sort the data by specifying either the column's name (as we've done above) or its position in the select list. Using the column position is helpful when the column in the select list is made up of derived (calculated) columns that have no explicit name.

Our next example involves three columns: LASTNAME, FIRSTNME, and PHONENO. Here, we specify the sort order using the column position:

```
SELECT  D.DEPTNO, D.DEPTNAME
        E.EMPNO, E.FIRSTNME, E.MIDINIT, E.LASTNAME,
        E.WORKDEPT, E.PHONENO
FROM    DSN8910.DEPT D,
        DSN8910.EMP E
WHERE   D.DEPTNO = 'C01'
AND     D.DEPTNO = E.WORKDEPT
ORDER BY 6 DESC, 4, 8;
```

Although useful, coding a column position rather than a column (or renamed column) in the ORDER BY clause can lead to a different sequence if you inadvertently add a column that alters the column positioning to the query.

Another option is to assign an alternative column name using *column renaming*. With this technique, you can reference the assigned name in the ORDER BY clause, and this name will appear as the column heading where appropriate.

```
SELECT  D.DEPTNO, D.DEPTNAME
        E.EMPNO, E.FIRSTNME as "first name", E.MIDINIT,
        E.LASTNAME as "last name",
        E.WORKDEPT, e.phoneno as phone_number
FROM    DSN8910.DEPT D,
        DSN8910.EMP E
WHERE   D.DEPTNO = 'C01'
AND     D.DEPTNO = E.WORKDEPT
ORDER BY "LAST NAME" DESC, "FIRST NAME", PHONE_NUMBER;
```

The ORDER BY clause can be used in subselects within a SELECT statement as long as the subselect is enclosed in parentheses or is the outermost fullselect of the SELECT statement.

Derived Columns

In some cases, you'll need to perform calculations on the data. The SQL language has some basic mathematical and string functions built into it. Mathematical operations include standard addition, subtraction, multiplication, and division.

You can define a calculation in the WHERE clause of the SQL statement or in the select list. Suppose we want to calculate the total compensation for an employee (the total of salary, bonus, and commission). The following SQL statement accomplishes this for us for employee 000010:

```
SELECT EMPNO, SALARY + BONUS + COMM
FROM DSN8910.EMP
WHERE EMPNO = '000010';
```

In this example, the second column of the output list is a calculated column (SALARY + BONUS + COMM). Remember that you must specify the column position if you want to use this calculated column in the ORDER BY clause, unless you name it (as we discuss next).

Naming Derived/Calculated Columns

You can specify a column name for any expression. When you give a derived (calculated) column a name, the ORDER BY clause can reference the derived name, providing a more readable SQL statement.

The following SQL calculates the total compensation for all employees and then sorts the result in the order of the derived column in descending sequence.

```
SELECT EMPNO, SALARY + BONUS + COMM AS COMPENSATION
FROM DSN8910.EMP
ORDER BY COMPENSATION DESC;
```

You use the AS clause to rename the default name of an element in the select list. In this example, we assign the name COMPENSATION to the result of the addition of the SALARY, BONUS, and COMM columns. The query uses the assigned column name to specify the column to use for sorting the output. You could also code the expression itself in the ORDER BY clause:

```
SELECT EMPNO, SALARY + BONUS + COMM AS COMPENSATION
FROM DSN8910.EMP
ORDER BY SALARY + BONUS + COMM DESC;
```

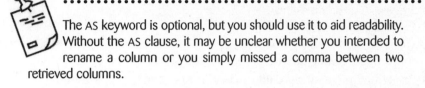

The AS keyword is optional, but you should use it to aid readability. Without the AS clause, it may be unclear whether you intended to rename a column or you simply missed a comma between two retrieved columns.

Functions

SQL provides different types of functions to operate on data in a DB2 table. Among these are scalar and column functions. (A third type, table function, is discussed in Chapter 15.)

- *Scalar functions* (also known as *row functions*) provide a result for each row of the result table. You can use a scalar function anyplace an expression is allowed.

- *Column functions* (also known as *vector functions*) work with a group of rows to provide a result. You specify the group using a result table and optionally group the results using the GROUP BY clause.

In this section, we introduce you to some of the SQL functions provided with DB2. SQL functions are categorized by their implementation type. Either the functions are built-in or they are extensions of DB2 known as user-defined functions (UDFs).

- *Built-in functions* are defined within the SQL standards and are provided by DB2. They can be either scalar or column functions.

- *User-defined functions* are not defined within the SQL standards because they are extensions of the current SQL language. These functions can be developed by a DB2 administrator or application developer. UDFs can be either scalar or table functions, but not column functions. Once a UDF has been created, any end user with the proper privileges can invoke it. For more information about UDFs, see Chapter 15.

Scalar Functions

Scalar functions are applied to each row of data to produce a per-row result. If you wanted to retrieve only the first initial of the employees along with their last name, you could use a scalar function—one called SUBSTR. The SUBSTR function's arguments include a string data type column, a starting position, and a length. The output data type and attribute of the function depend on the input data type and attribute. The following example retrieves the first initial for the column FIRSTNME.

```
SELECT LASTNAME, SUBSTR(FIRSTNME,1,1) AS FIRST_INIT
FROM DSN8910.EMP;
```

In this example, the SUBSTR scalar function returns a character string of one character. The result string corresponds to the first character of the FIRSTNME column value. SUBSTR is known as a *string function* because it works with any string data type. To give the output column a meaningful name, we provide an alias, FIRST_INIT.

In the example, the substring starts at the beginning of the string because we indicate 1 (one) as the second parameter of the function. The third argument indicates the length of the resulting string. In this case, the length is 1.

The following query uses the MONTH scalar function to report the month when each employee was born. The input for this function is a BIRTHDATE column of the date data type, and the output is an integer.

```
SELECT LASTNAMR, MONTH(BIRTHDATE)
FROM DSN8910.EMP;
```

Column Functions

Column functions provide a single result for a group of qualifying rows for a specified table or view. You can use column functions to satisfy many common queries, such as finding the smallest value, the largest value, or the average value for a group of data records. The following example uses the MAX column function to obtain the maximum salary of any of the employees (i.e., the highest salary paid to an employee).

```
SELECT MAX(SALARY) FROM DSN8910.EMP;
```

If we added a WHERE clause to this example, the maximum would represent the maximum salary for the qualifying rows because DB2 uses the predicate to filter the data before applying the MAX function.

The next example calculates the average salary of the employees in the company. Notice the use of the column function AVG in this example.

```
SELECT AVG(SALARY) FROM DSN8910.EMP;
```

DB2 provides many more built-in functions. If you're interested in calculating statistical information, you can use statistical functions, such as VARIANCE, STDDEV, or a sampling of these functions.

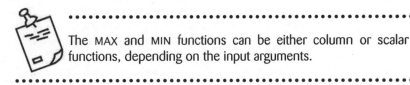

The MAX and MIN functions can be either column or scalar functions, depending on the input arguments.

Grouping Values

Many queries require some level of aggregated data within logical groups. You accomplish this in SQL through use of the GROUP BY clause. GROUP BY conceptually rearranges the table represented by the FROM clause into partitions, such that within any one group all rows have the same value for the GROUP BY field (or fields).

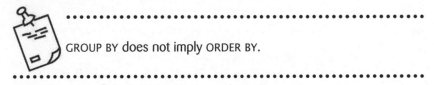

GROUP BY does not imply ORDER BY.

The following SQL obtains the average salary for each department.

```
SELECT WORKDEPT, AVG(SALARY)
FROM   DSN8910.EMP
GROUP BY WORKDEPT;
```

This statement first retrieves the department number and salary for all employees. The GROUP BY clause tells DB2 to group together rows that have the same value in the column indicated in the group by list. In the example, we're grouping departments into subsets. As it creates the groups or subsets, DB2 calculates the average of each group, in this case for each department.

When you combine column functions and other elements—such as column names, scalar functions, or calculated columns—you must use the GROUP BY clause. In this case, the group by list must include every element that is not a column function. The only elements you can omit in the GROUP BY list are constant values.

The next SQL statement obtains a list that includes the department number and salary for employees. The result is then grouped by department, and the average and minimum salary is determined by department.

```
SELECT WORKDEPT, AVG(SALARY), MIN(SALARY)
FROM    DSN8910.EMP
GROUP BY WORKDEPT;
```

Appropriate indexing can enable DB2 to avoid performing a sort to group the data rows to match the GROUP BY clause.

It's possible to sort the output of the previous example using an ORDER BY clause.

The GROUP BY clause may return data in the same order as an ORDER BY, but this result is based on the access path and not guaranteed. The only way to guarantee data sequence is by using an ORDER BY.

In addition to grouping by columns, it's possible to group by expressions in a query. To do so, you simply repeat the expression in the GROUP BY clause. In the following example, we analyze the average salary of employees according to the number of years they've worked for the company. We must calculate the number of years of employment for display and also for the grouping.

```
SELECT  YEAR(CURRENT DATE - HIREDATE) AS "YEARS",
        AVG(SALARY) AVERAGE_SALARY
FROM    DSN8910.EMP
GROUP BY YEAR(CURRENT DATE - HIREDATE);
```

Restricting the Use of Sets of Data

Up to now, we've discussed how to restrict output based on row conditions. With SQL, it's also possible to restrict that output using column functions and the GROUP BY clause. Suppose you want a list of all the departments that pay their employees a total of more than $300,000, along with the number of employees in each department. To make this assignment easier to understand, let's first get the total employee salary and number of employees for each department.

```
SELECT  WORKDEPT, SUM(SALARY), COUNT(*)
FROM    DSN8910.EMP
GROUP BY WORKDEPT;
```

We use the SUM column function to calculate the total salary of the employees and use the COUNT column function to determine the number of employees. When you use an asterisk with COUNT, you're indicating that you want the number of rows in a table that meet the criteria established in the SQL statement. In this example, we're grouping by WORKDEPT because we have a number of occurrences for all the departments in the EMP table. As the last step, we restrict the output to departments that pay their employees a total of more than $300,000:

```
SELECT  WORKDEPT, SUM(SALARY), COUNT(*)
FROM    DSN8910.EMP
GROUP BY WORKDEPT
HAVING  SUM(SALARY) > 300000;
```

This example introduces the HAVING clause, which is equivalent to a WHERE clause for groups and column functions. The HAVING clause restricts the result set to only the groups that meet the condition specified in it. In the example, only the departments that issue more than $300,000 in total salary to their employees will be displayed.

Eliminating Duplicates

When you execute a query, you might get duplicate rows in the answer set. The SQL language provides a special clause to remove duplicate rows from your output. The following SQL generates a list of employees who have worked on projects. In this example, we eliminate the duplicate rows from our output list by using the DISTINCT clause.

```
SELECT DISTINCT E.LASTNAME, E.FIRSTNME
FROM   DSN8910.EMPPROJACT EPA,
       DSN8910.EMP E
WHERE E.EMPNO = EPA.EMPNO;
```

You can also use the DISTINCT clause with the COUNT function. When you use DISTINCT inside a COUNT function, it will not count duplicate entries for a particular column. The following example lets us count how many different departments have employees.

```
SELECT COUNT(DISTINCT WORKDEPT) FROM EMP;
```

Make sure you understand the difference between COUNT(*), COUNT(*colname*), and COUNT(DISTINCT *colname*). They are very similar in syntax but differ in function. COUNT(*) returns a count of all rows that qualify against the WHERE clause. COUNT(*colname*) returns a count of all rows that qualify against the WHERE clause, with null occurrences of *colname* removed. COUNT(DISTINCT *colname*) counts distinct occurrences of *colname*, with nulls removed.

Searching for String Patterns

SQL has a powerful predicate, LIKE, that lets you search for patterns in character string columns. Suppose you want to generate a list of employees whose first name starts with the letter G.

```
SELECT EMPNO, FIRSTNME, MIDINIT, LASTNAME
FROM   DSN8910.EMP
WHERE  FIRSTNME LIKE 'G%';
```

In this query, we use a wildcard character with the LIKE predicate. In SQL, the percent character (%) is a substitute for zero or more characters. The search string 'G%' will match to names such as Gary, George, Ginger, and so on. (Because the percent character can represent zero or more characters, the search string can also match the single letter G.)

You can use the percent character anywhere in the search string and as many times as you need it. The percent sign isn't case-sensitive, so it can represent uppercase or lowercase letters. Constant characters included in your search string, however, are case-sensitive.

Another wildcard character used with the LIKE predicate is the underscore character (_). This character represents one and only one character. The underscore can take the place of any character; however, it cannot substitute for an empty character.

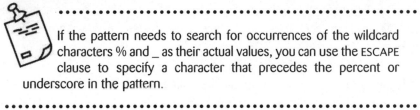

If the pattern needs to search for occurrences of the wildcard characters % and _ as their actual values, you can use the ESCAPE clause to specify a character that precedes the percent or underscore in the pattern.

We can modify the preceding SQL to include all employees whose last name has the letter A as its second letter.

```
SELECT EMPNO, FIRSTNME, MIDINIT, LASTNAME
FROM    DSN8910.EMP
WHERE   LASTNAME LIKE '_A%';
```

This example uses two wildcard characters with the LIKE predicate. The first character of the string can be any character, the letter A is the second character in the string, and the string can end with any number of characters. The search string in this case can include names such as PAUL, RANDY, and JACKSON.

When the pattern in a LIKE predicate is a fixed-length host variable, you must specify the correct length for the string to be returned. 'G%' assigned to an eight-byte variable (LIKE :variable) will search for all occurrences of 'G%' (G, followed by any character, followed by six blank characters). To find rows that begin with a G, you should assign 'G%%%%%%%' to the fixed-length variable.

Searching for Data in Ranges

SQL also offers us a range operator. You use this operator to restrict result set rows to a particular range of values. Consider the requirement to list those employees whose salary is between $50,000 and $80,000.

```
SELECT  EMPNO, FIRSTNME, MIDINIT, LASTNAME
FROM    DSN8910.EMP
WHERE   SALARY BETWEEN 50000 AND 80000;
```

The BETWEEN predicate includes the values that you specify for searching your data. An important fact about BETWEEN is that it can work with character ranges as well.

In addition to the salary requirement, the next example modifies the SQL to include only those employees whose last name begins with a letter between B and G.

```
SELECT  EMPNO, FIRSTNME, MIDINIT, LASTNAME
FROM    DSN8910.EMP
WHERE   SALARY BETWEEN 50000 AND 80000
AND     LASTNAME BETWEEN 'B' AND 'GZ';
```

In this example, the second BETWEEN predicate contains character values. We need to specify the 'GZ' value to include all possible names that start with the letter G. The assumption is that the letter Z is the last possible value in the alphabet. Comparing the single character 'G' with the full-length last name column will pad the 'G' with blanks. Assuming an encoding scheme of EBCDIC, a blank is a lower value than any alphabetic character.

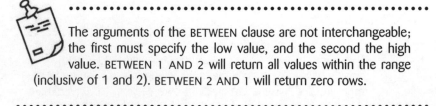

The arguments of the BETWEEN clause are not interchangeable; the first must specify the low value, and the second the high value. BETWEEN 1 AND 2 will return all values within the range (inclusive of 1 and 2). BETWEEN 2 AND 1 will return zero rows.

Searching for Null Values

Null values represent an unknown value for a particular occurrence of an attribute. You can use a null value in cases where you don't know a particular value of a column. Let's say you want a list of all the departments that don't have a manager. You can represent this condition with a null value.

```
SELECT  DEPTNO, DEPTNAME
FROM    DSN8910.DEPT
WHERE   MGRNO IS NULL;
```

This example uses the IS NULL predicate to search for the null value. Remember that the null value means "unknown." Because null has no particular value, it can't be compared with other values. You can't use conditional operands, such as equal (=) or greater than (>), with null values.

Searching for Negative Conditions

The BETWEEN, IS, and LIKE predicates always look for the values that meet a particular condition. You can also use these predicates to look for values that *don't* meet a particular criterion. Combined with the LIKE, BETWEEN, or NULL predicate, the NOT logical operator lets you look for the opposite condition to accomplish negative searches.

The following example uses a LIKE predicate combined with the NOT logical operator to produce a list of departments managed by an employee number that does not begin with 00001.

```
SELECT  DEPTNO, DEPTNAME
FROM    DSN8910.DEPT
WHERE   MGRNO NOT LIKE '00001%';
```

The next example combines a BETWEEN predicate with the NOT logical operator to list the employees whose salary is not between $50,000 and $80,000.

```
SELECT  EMPNO, FIRSTNME, MIDINIT, LASTNAME
FROM    DSN8910.EMP
WHERE   SALARY NOT BETWEEN 50000 AND 80000;
```

In this example, the NOT logical operator will exclude all values that are in the range of $50,000 and $80,000.

You can also apply negation to the null value. The following SQL produces a report that identifies those departments that have a manager assigned. We express this condition with a NOT NULL value.

```
SELECT DEPTNO, DEPTNAME
FROM   DSN8910.DEPT
WHERE  MGRNO IS NOT NULL;
```

 You can also use the NOT logical operator to negate the standard comparison operators =, <, <=, >, and >=.

When you work with nulls, NOT or negation may not return the opposite of the positive logic. For example, WHERE MGRNO = '000010' returns only the rows for the departments that employee 000010 manages. Any value other than '000010' is discarded because these rows are FALSE, including nulls because these are UNKNOWN. WHERE MGRNO <> '000010' excludes rows where the manager number is '000010' and also discards nulls because these are UNKNOWN. This may not be the desired result.

To consider the nulls in the comparison, you have two coding options. The first is to add a second predicate to test for the presence of nulls:

```
SELECT DEPTNO, DEPTNAME
FROM   DSN8910.DEPT
WHERE  MGRNO <> '000010'
OR     MGRNO IS NOT NULL;
```

The second way is to use the IS DISTINCT FROM or IS NOT DISTINCT FROM clause. These clauses consider nulls in a comparison; that is, the nulls no longer evaluate to UNKNOWN. A null will equal a null, and a null won't be equal to a value instead of evaluating to UNKNOWN. These clauses can be confusing, but if you replace the word DISTINCT with the word "different," understanding becomes easier. In this regard, IS DISTINCT FROM is the "not equals" and IS NOT DISTINCT FROM is the "equals." The following query produces exactly the same result as the previous one.

```
SELECT DEPTNO, DEPTNAME
FROM   DSN8910.DEPT
WHERE  MGRNO IS DISTINCT FROM '000010';
```

Searching for a Set of Values

In SQL, it's possible to establish a restriction condition based on a set of values. Suppose you need a list of the employees in departments A01 and C01. You can query this with the following statement.

```
SELECT EMPNO, FIRSTNME, MIDINIT, LASTNAME
FROM    DSN8910.EMP
WHERE   (WORKDEPT = 'A01' OR WORKDEPT = 'C01');
```

To simplify building multiple OR conditions when comparing multiple values for the same column, you can rewrite the statement using the IN clause:

```
SELECT EMPNO, FIRSTNME, MIDINIT, LASTNAME
FROM    DSN8910.EMP
WHERE   WORKDEPT IN ('A01', 'C01');
```

You use the IN clause to denote a set of values. In this example, we use a constant set of values.

You can also use the NOT logical operator with the IN clause. In this case, the condition will be true when a value is not present in the set of values provided to the IN clause. You can use as many values as you like in the IN clause, within the defined limits of the size of an SQL statement.

Advanced Selection Functionality

In Chapter 6, we'll look at more of the functionality and power of the SELECT statement, covering topics such as

- subqueries

- unions

- excepts

- intersects

- nested table expressions

- common table expressions

- data change tables

- inner and outer joins

- CASE expressions

- row expressions

- XQuery and XPath

Data Modification

Up to now in this chapter, we've discussed basic SELECT statements. The SELECT statement lets you retrieve data from your database tables and assumes that data has been previously loaded into the tables. Now, we concentrate on getting the data into the database tables using SQL. Four main statements let you add and change data stored in a DB2 database table:

- INSERT

- UPDATE

- MERGE

- DELETE

To perform these operations, you must have the required privileges on the tables being accessed. These privileges are usually more strictly enforced because they can permit an end user to modify data records.

Inserting Data Records

To initially populate a DB2 table with data, you can use the INSERT statement to store one row at a time, or you can insert more than one row at a time if you use a subselect within an INSERT statement. You can target the statement to insert data directly into a base table, or you can use a view instead. When using a view as the target, remember that the base table is where the actual data will be stored.

Every row that is populated using the INSERT statement must adhere to data type validation, table check constraints, unique constraints, referential integrity constraints, and dynamic (trigger) constraints. An SQL error will occur if any of these conditions is violated during the processing of the INSERT statement.

Remember that you must have the necessary table or view privileges to perform an INSERT statement.

Our first example is a simple INSERT statement. The following statement inserts the data for a new department into the DEPT table.

```
INSERT INTO DSN8910.DEPT
(DEPTNO, DEPTNAME, MGRNO, ADMRDEPT, LOCATION)
 VALUES ('Z99','CERTIFICATION DEPARTMENT','000010','D01',);
```

In this example, we've specified all the column names and their corresponding values for the data record. In the VALUES portion of the statement, we include the actual data values for the record.

The number and order of the inserted elements specified in the VALUES clause must match the number and order of the column names defined in the INSERT statement. (However, the column order needn't match the order in which the columns are defined in the table.) For columns that don't require a value, you can indicate null or default values. In the example, we've supplied the null value for the LOCATION column.

The number of elements following the VALUES clause must match the number of names in the insert column list.

Depending on your column definition, the DEFAULT keyword can cause a default value to be inserted into a column. The default might be a system-defined default, a user-defined default, or null. Be aware that if the column doesn't accept nulls (NOT NULL) and wasn't defined as WITH DEFAULT, you'll receive an error message if you use the DEFAULT keyword. The error occurs because the default value for columns not using the WITH DEFAULT option is the null value.

When you want to insert values into all the columns of a table, you can omit the column names in the INSERT statement:

```
INSERT INTO DSN8910.DEPT
  VALUES ('Z99','CERTIFICATION DEPARTMENT','000010','D01',DEFAULT);
```

This method works only if you specify a value for each column of the table. If you miss one of the columns, DB2 won't let you insert the row into the table. The DEFAULT keyword used in this example causes DB2 to insert the default value for the LOCATION column.

••

Remember that, depending on the column definition, the default value could be a user-defined default value, a system-defined default value, an identity value, or NULL.

••

Inserting Data into Specific Columns

There are times when you need to add data to specific columns. In these cases, every column that is not included in the INSERT statement will receive its default value.

You can accomplish this operation only if the omitted columns accept nulls or have a default value definition. This means you must specify a value for the columns defined as NOT NULL. This restriction excludes columns defined as NOT NULL WITH DEFAULT.

Let's insert a row into the employee sample table. We'll insert data only for the columns EMPNO, WORKDEPT, LASTNAME, and EDLEVEL.

```
INSERT INTO DSN8910.EMP
(EMPNO, WORKDEPT, LASTNAME, EDLEVEL)
  VALUES ('011000','D01','RADY',16);
```

Remember that columns defined using WITH DEFAULT that are not listed in the INSERT statement will receive the null value or a default value.

The EMP table has some referential integrity with other tables. If you want to insert a record into this table, you should insert the appropriate values into the other tables in advance.

Inserting a Set of Values

Using SQL, you can insert the result of a SELECT statement into a different table. The SQL statement that generates the resulting set must follow several rules:

- The number of columns specified in the SELECTstatement must equal the number of columns in the insert column list.

- The data type of each column in the select list must be compatible with the data type of the columns in the insert list.

- You can omit column names from the insert list only if you're inserting values into all the columns in the table.

- Only columns defined to allow null or defined as NOTNULL WITH DEFAULT can be omitted from the insert list.

In some situations, it might be useful to create tables that are duplicates of others so that you can perform multiple calculations against them. The next example uses a table called EMP2, which is a copy of the EMP table. We'll use this new table to extract information about employees who are paid more than $80,000.

```
INSERT INTO DSN8910.EMP2
(EMPNO, WORKDEPT, LASTNAME, EDLEVEL, SALARY)
SELECT EMPNO, WORKDEPT, LASTNAME, EDLEVEL, SALARY
FROM DSN8910.EMP
WHERE SALARY > 80000;
```

If you include all the columns in the insert column list (or if you omit the insert list), you can substitute a select asterisk for the select list used in the fullselect. However, to keep the query isolated from future table modifications, it's best to use the select list instead of the asterisk.

Inserting Large Amounts of Data

Using the INSERT statement, or INSERT with a subselect, to insert data into a table can be very useful. However, loading large amounts of data into a table using INSERT isn't recommended because the transaction logging overhead can become unmanageable. Instead, consider using DB2's LOAD utility, which is designed to move large amounts of data into a table.

Updating Data Records

So far, we've looked at the INSERT statement as a method of moving data into your DB2 table. You may want to update only a column with values for a group of data records. SQL's UPDATE statement performs this task, letting you specify the column and its new values. You can reference a table or a view as the target for the UPDATE statement.

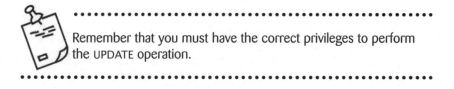

Remember that you must have the correct privileges to perform the UPDATE operation.

You can use the UPDATE statement in two forms:

- A *searched update* updates one or more rows in a table. It requires a WHERE clause to establish the update condition (i.e., to indicate which rows are to be updated).

- A *positioned update* is always embedded into a program. It uses cursors to update the row where the cursor is positioned. As the cursor is repositioned via a FETCH statement, the target row for the UPDATE statement changes.

In this chapter, we focus on searched updates. As with the INSERT statement, DB2 enforces all the database constraint mechanisms during an UPDATE statement. There can be specific update constraint triggers and referential integrity constraints that might differ from the insert constraints.

The following statement updates the birthday of employee 000010, making a correction to add three days.

```
UPDATE DSN8910.EMP
SET BIRTHDATE=BIRTHDATE + 3 days
WHERE EMPNO='000010';
```

In this example, we use an operation known as a *labeled duration* to add three days to the original date.

DB2 labeled durations for date-time data types include years, months, days, hours, minutes, seconds, and microseconds.

It's important to provide the proper WHERE clause to avoid updating unintended data records. In this example, we needed to specify the employee number to avoid changing the birth date of any of the other employees.

You can also use the UPDATE statement with fullselects. In this case, the fullselect must return a row with exactly the same number of columns and compatible data types as the row that will be updated. Observe that this fullselect must return only one row.

Let's update a row using a SELECT statement to set the new value. All employees in department C01 have been assigned a bonus and commission of the company averages.

```
UPDATE DSN8910.EMP
SET (BONUS,COMM)=
(SELECT AVG(BONUS), AVG(COMM)
 FROM DSN8910.EMP)
WHERE WORKDEPT = 'C01';
```

In this example, we update two different columns in the same operation. We indicate these columns in the parentheses following the SET clause. After specifying which columns are going to be updated, we use a SELECT statement to retrieve the average bonus and commission for the company. Notice that the WHERE clause in the statement restricts the rows that will be updated.

If you forget the WHERE clause in a searched update, all the data in your table will be updated.

The SQL statement that updates the bonus and commission columns is known as a *row fullselect*. This name is given because the statement returns only one row. Observe that the scalar fullselect can be considered a special case of a row fullselect.

Updating Large Amounts of Data

There are times when you need to update a large number of rows of a particular table. You can accomplish this by issuing a searched update, but this type of update also can allocate a large amount of transactional log space. Using positioned updates to perform large updates lets you easily control the commit frequency.

Merging Data

A MERGE statement updates a target (table, view, or underlying tables or views of a fullselect) using specified input data. Rows in the target that match the input data are updated as specified, and rows that don't exist in the target are inserted.

A MERGE is combination of an UPDATE and an INSERT. Any row that matches will be updated, and ones that don't will be inserted. We describe MERGE in further detail in Chapter 12.

Removing Data

Many methods are available to remove data from a DB2 database. To remove all the data within a database, perform the DROP DATABASE command. Note, though, that this action may remove more data than you intend because the entire database, including its configuration, will be physically removed.

It's also possible to remove data using the DROP TABLESPACE or DROP TABLE statement. Usually, only the SYSADM or DBADM issues these statements because the statements remove large amounts of data. If you want to remove all the data records from a table, it's easier and quicker to use DROP TABLE. This statement removes the table definition as well as the data. An even easier, and less destructive, method is to use the LOAD utility with the REPLACE option, specifying an empty input file (or perhaps using the TRUNCATE statement).

A mass delete from a segmented table space limits logging and improves performance by merely updating the space map pages to indicate the deletion rather than deleting each data row.

If you drop a table, it must be re-created before any data can be populated again in the table.

The DELETE Statement

To remove a single data record or a group or records from a table, use SQL's DELETE statement. The syntax of the DELETE statement differs from the SELECT and INSERT statements because you can't delete individual columns; only rows can be deleted.

You can also use the DELETE statement with views. However, there are restrictions on the type of views that can be used within a DELETE statement.

Remember that you must have the necessary privileges over a table to perform the DELETE operation.

In general, there are two kinds of DELETE statements:

- A *searched delete* deletes one or multiple rows from a table. It can use a WHERE clause to establish the delete condition.

- A *positioned delete* is always embedded into a program. It uses cursors to delete the row where the cursor is positioned.

In this section, we focus on the searched delete. The following SQL statement deletes departments that have no manager. We use a searched delete to accomplish this task.

```
DELETE FROM DSN8910.DEPT
WHERE MGRNO IS NULL;
```

This example uses a WHERE clause to delete the data that meets a specific criterion. To verify the result of the DELETE statement, you can issue a SELECT statement with the same WHERE clause. If the DELETE was successful, the SELECT will return an empty set.

You can perform a more sophisticated delete by using subselects. The next SQL statement deletes all the employees who are not responsible for projects.

```
DELETE FROM DSN8910.EMP
WHERE EMPNO NOT IN (SELECT RESPEMP FROM DSN8910.PROJ);
```

In this example, we use a subselect to retrieve the RESPEMP values (i.e., the employee numbers in the project table) of the employees responsible for projects. DB2 will use this list to search for the employees we want to delete.

Deleting All the Rows in a Table

You can delete all the rows in a table by specifying no search condition in your DELETE statement. You can also delete all the rows in a table if all the rows meet the search condition.

You must be aware of the implications of this type of statement. Deleting all the rows in a table by using a DELETE statement may not be the most efficient method. When your tables are large, this kind of statement can consume a lot of log space.

As an alternative to DELETE, you can use a TRUNCATE statement to perform a mass delete. TRUNCATE offers two distinct advantages. First, it does not activate triggers. Second, you have the option to immediately commit the deletion of all the data in the table outside the commit scope of the transaction.

The following TRUNCATE statement deletes all project activity time, immediately commits the deletion outside the unit of work, and causes the freed space to be immediately available for reuse.

```
TRUNCATE DSN8910.EMPPROJACT
REUSE STORAGE
IMMEDIATE;
```

View Classification

Now that we've examined various SQL DML statements, let's take a closer look at views. We've already discussed creating views. Here, we consider the different types of views. Views are classified by the operations they allow but are generally referred to as either *read-only* or *non-read-only* (updatable) views.

Referential and check constraints are treated independently; they don't affect the view classification. For example, you may not be able to insert a value into a table because of a referential constraint. If you create a view using that table, you also can't insert that value using the view. However, if the view satisfies the rules for a non-read-only view, it will still be considered an insertable, updatable, or deletable view because the insert restriction is located on the base table, not on the view definition.

Read-Only Views

Depending on how it is defined, a view can be read-only or it can be the object of a DELETE, UPDATE, or INSERT. A view is read-only if one (or more) of the following statements is true of its definition:

- The first FROM clause identifies more than one table or view or identifies a table function.

- The first select specifies the keyword DISTINCT.

- The outer fullselect contains a GROUP BY clause.

- The outer fullselect contains a HAVING clause.

- The first SELECT clause contains a column function.

- The view contains a subquery such that the base object of the outer fullselect and of the subquery is the same table.

- The first FROM clause identifies a read-only view.

A read-only view cannot be the object of an INSERT, UPDATE, or DELETE statement, but it can have an INSTEAD OF trigger defined on it (as described in Chapter 15). A view that includes GROUP BY or HAVING cannot be referred to in a subquery of a base predicate. The following is an example of a read-only view.

```
CREATE VIEW read_only_view
(NAME, PHONE, DEPTNO, DNAME)
AS
SELECT DISTINCT E.LASTNAME, E.PHONENO, D.DEPTNO, D.DEPTNAME
FROM DSN8910.EMP e, DSN8910.DEPT D
WHERE E.WORKDEPT = D.DEPTNO;
```

This view is a read-only view because it uses the DISTINCT clause and the SQL statement involves more than one table.

Non-Read-Only Views

A view must meet the rules listed above to be considered a non-read-only view; that is, none of the listed statements can be true for the view. Here's an example of a view that can be used for a DELETE statement:

```
CREATE VIEW deletable_view
(EMPNO, FIRSTNME, MIDINIT, LASTNAME, WORKDEPT, PHONENO, HIREDATE, JOB,
EDLEVEL, SEX, BIRTHDATE, SALARY, BONUS, COMM)
AS
SELECT EMPNO, FIRSTNME, MIDINIT, LASTNAME, WORKDEPT, PHONENO, HIREDATE,
JOB, EDLEVEL, SEX, BIRTHDATE, SALARY, BONUS, COMM
FROM DSN8910.EMP
WHERE WORKDEPT = 'C01';
```

A view that can be the object of an UPDATE statement is a special case of a non-read-only view because at least one of its columns must be updatable. A column of a view can be updated when all the following rules are true:

- The view is not a read-only view.

- The column resolves to a column of a base table.

- Neither the FOR READ ONLY nor the FOR FETCH ONLY option is specified.

Even though the following view definition uses constant values that cannot be updated, it's a non-read-only view, and you can update at least one of its columns. Therefore, it can be the object of an UPDATE statement.

```
CREATE VIEW updatable_view
(DEPTNO, DEPTNAME, MGRNO, ADMRDEPT, LOCATION, TDATE)
AS
SELECT DEPTNO, DEPTNAME, MGRNO, ADMRDEPT, 'unknown', current date
FROM DSN8910.DEPT;
```

A view can be the object of an INSERT statement when all its columns are updatable. Also, all columns that don't have a default value must be specified in the INSERT statement. The row being inserted must contain a value for each column in the view definition. The following is a view that can be used to insert rows.

```
CREATE VIEW insertable_view
(EMPNO, LASTNAME, EDLEVEL)
AS
SELECT EMPNO, LASTNAME, EDLEVEL;
```

Remember, the constraints defined on the base table are independent of the operations that can be performed using a view.

Summary

In this chapter, we discussed SQL's Data Manipulation Language. DML has five primary statements: SELECT, UPDATE, INSERT, MERGE, and DELETE. These statements enable database object data manipulation.

The knowledge of basic SQL is mandatory for a DB2 database administrator and application developer. However, SQL is very powerful language, and the level of SQL skill required will vary depending on the user's primary activity.

In this chapter, we covered many of the basic functions of SQL statements, including how to

- retrieve rows
- sort the result set
- restrict the result with some conditions
- retrieve rows from more than one table at a time
- add a row to a table
- remove a record (or records)
- change the value of the table

If you're a business analyst, you may expect more analytical, statistical information from DB2. DB2 supports very powerful SQL functions for various business needs. We'll talk about some advanced SQL topics in the next chapter.

Additional Resources

IBM DB2 9 Application Programming and SQL Guide (SC18-9841)
IBM DB2 9 SQL Reference (SC18-9854)

Practice Questions

Question 1

A view is considered to be "read-only" if the view definition

○ A. contains an ORDER BY clause

○ B. contains a scalar fullselect

○ C. references more than one table in the first FROM clause

○ D. contains a subquery referencing a table in the first FROM clause

Question 2

Assume the following table definition:

```
CREATE TABLE DSN8910.DEPT
        (DEPTNO    CHAR(3)        NOT NULL,
         DEPTNAME VARCHAR(36)     NOT NULL,
         MGRNO     CHAR(6)                 ,
         ADMRDEPT CHAR(3)         NOT NULL,
         LOCATION CHAR(16)                 ,
         PRIMARY KEY(DEPTNO))
IN DSN8D91A.DSN8S91D
CCSID EBCDIC;
```

If the manager is being replaced and the location reset in every department with a department number that starts with the letter D, which of the following statements would be correct?

○ A. UPDATE DEPT SET (MGRNO = NULL; LOCATION=NULL) WHERE
       DEPTNO LIKE 'D%'

○ B. UPDATE DEPT SET (MGRNO, LOCATION) = (NULL, NULL) WHERE
       DEPTNO LIKE 'D%'

○ C. UPDATE DEPT SET MGRNO = NULL, SET LOCATION = NULL WHERE
       DEPTNO LIKE 'D%'

○ D. UPDATE DEPT SET (MGRNO = NULL), (LOCATION = NULL) WHERE
       DEPTNO LIKE 'D%'

Question 3

Assume the following query:

```
SELECT FIRSTNME, MIDINIT, LASTNAME, EMPNO, WORKDEPT, PROJNO, PROJNAME,
DEPTNO
FROM DSN8910.EMP, DSN8910.PROJ
```

If the EMP table contains two rows and the PROJ table contains four rows, how many rows does this query return?

- ○ A. Four
- ○ B. Eight
- ○ C. Six
- ○ D. Two

Question 4

Which of the following statements will count only the unique occurrences of the department number in the employee table?

- ○ A. SELECT COUNT(UNIQUE WORKDEPT) FROM EMP
- ○ B. SELECT COUNT(DISTINCT WORKDEPT) FROM EMP
- ○ C. SELECT COUNT(WORKDEPT) UNIQUE FROM EMP
- ○ D. SELECT COUNT(WORKDEPT) DISTINCT FROM EMP

Question 5

Which of the following clauses will sort the EMP table in order of department descending and then last name ascending:

- ○ A. SORT BY WORKDEPT, LASTNAME
- ○ B. SORT BY WORKDEPT DESC, LASTNAME ASC
- ○ C. ORDER BY WORKDEPT DESC, LASTNAME ASC
- ○ D. ORDER BY LASTNAME, WORKDEPT DESC

Answers

Question 1

The answer is **C**, references more than one table in the first FROM clause.

Question 2

The answer is **B**. This statement demonstrates the proper representation of a row expression.

Question 3

The answer is **B**, eight rows will be returned. The query contains no join predicate, so it is a Cartesian product, which is every row from the first table joined to every row from the second table.

Question 4

The answer is **B**. The DISTINCT clause will eliminate null values as well as any duplicate values for the WORKDEPT column, so the COUNT function will count only the resulting distinct (i.e., unique) values.

Question 5

The answer is **C**. The order of the columns specified in the ORDER BY clause dictates the order of the columns in the sort, so you must specify the WORKDEPT column first. The default ordering is ASC (ascending).

Advanced SQL Coding

In This Chapter

- ✔ Subqueries
- ✔ Unions, excepts, and intersects
- ✔ Joins
- ✔ Nested and common table expressions
- ✔ Data change tables
- ✔ CASE expressions
- ✔ Row expressions
- ✔ ORDER BY and FETCH FIRST
- ✔ Predicates and filtering
- ✔ XPath and XQuery

This chapter covers some of the more advanced features found in DB2's SQL. Our discussions begin with the constructs of subqueries, unions, and joins. Next, we'll examine nested table expressions, data change tables, the CASE expression with its if-then-else logic, row expressions, and OLAP features.

Efficient query coding also requires knowledge of how DB2 processes predicates. We'll look at how predicates are classified and how data is filtered during query processing. Last, we'll provide an overview of the XML query features of DB2 for z/OS.

Subqueries

A *subquery* is an SQL statement specifying a search condition that contains either a subselect or a fullselect and is used inside another SQL statement. A subquery can include search conditions of its own. Each search condition can also contain subqueries. Any SQL statement can contain a hierarchy of subqueries. The SQL query block that contains the subqueries is at a higher level than the subqueries it contains. The query level is important because it affects how columns are referenced between levels.

A subquery can contain search conditions that reference not only columns of the tables identified by its FROM clause but also columns of tables identified at any higher level. The reverse, however, is not true. A query at a higher level cannot reference columns from a subquery, although outer query columns can be compared with the resultant columns from a subquery. A reference within a subquery to a column of a table from a higher level is called a *correlated reference* (or *correlation predicate*).

When specified in a search condition, subqueries can use many operands and are generally categorized as single-result, IN list, or existence (EXISTS) subqueries.

> ●
>
> Quantified predicates are another form of subquery that compare a value (or values) with a collection of values by preceding the comparison operator (e.g., =, >, <) with ANY, SOME, or ALL. To avoid confusion, we ignore quantified predicates in this text.
>
> ●

The following example demonstrates a single-result subquery to return the employee with the highest salary.

```
SELECT EMPNO, FIRSTNME, LASTNAME
FROM DSN8910.EMP
WHERE SALARY =
(SELECT MAX(SALARY) FROM DSN8910.EMP)
```

This subquery can return only one result: either a null if the subquery table contains no qualifying rows or a value that represents the maximum value of the SALARY column in the EMP table. The subquery compares this value with the outer table rows and returns only those rows that equal the maximum value for SALARY.

This type of subquery is known as a *non-correlated subquery* because no correlation exists between the subquery and the outer query. The subquery is independent of the outer query and merely returns a single result to the outer query for comparison.

To demonstrate an IN list subquery, consider the difficulty of producing a report on the departments that have projects without including the department names. The following SQL produces a report that provides the department names for the departments that have projects.

```
SELECT DEPTNAME
FROM DSN8910.DEPT D
WHERE D.DEPTNO IN
(SELECT P.DEPTNO FROM DSN8910.PROJ P)
```

In this example, the subquery appears as part of the IN clause. In the subquery, we retrieve all the department numbers from the project table. Note that you'll never see the output of this subquery. Its purpose is merely to create a list of values for use by the outer SELECT statement.

Both of our examples have demonstrated a non-correlated subquery. The most common forms of non-correlated subqueries are the single-result and the IN list subqueries.

The third alternative, an EXISTS (existence) subquery, generally isn't coded for a non-correlated subquery. Because an EXISTS subquery returns true or false, it will be either true for every row of the outer table or false for every row of the outer table.

In contrast, a *correlated subquery* is a query in which the subquery references values of the immediate outer SELECT or any subselect at a higher level. The most common forms are the single-result and the EXISTS correlated subquery. Whereas a non-correlated subquery is evaluated once and a result returned to the outer query, a correlated subquery is potentially evaluated once for every outer row processed.

The IN subquery generally isn't coded for a correlated subquery due to the potential for the IN list to be built numerous times.

Like the non-correlated example, a single-result correlated subquery returns a single result for every execution. The difference is that a non-correlated subquery is executed once rather than many times.

Consider a query to return the employees with the highest salary in each department. The following correlated subquery returns the desired result.

```
SELECT FIRSTNME, LASTNAME
FROM    DSN8910.EMP E
WHERE   SALARY =
(SELECT MAX(SALARY)
  FROM    DSN8910.EMP E2
  WHERE   E2.WORKDEPT = E.WORKDEPT)


FIRSTNME   LASTNAME
---------  ---------
CHRISTINE  HAAS
MICHAEL    THOMPSON
SALLY      KWAN
JOHN       GEYER
IRVING     STERN
EVA        PULASKI
EILEEN     HENDERSON
THEODORE   SPENSER
```

For each outer row, the department number for that row is passed to the subquery, and the maximum salary for that department is returned to the outer query for comparison. If the maximum salary equals the salary of the current row, that row is returned; otherwise, the row is discarded. It's possible for the outer query to return more than one row for each department if more than one person has the maximum salary.

The next example demonstrates an EXISTS subquery in which we rewrite the previous non-correlated IN list SQL example as a correlated subquery. This query produces a report that includes the department names for all departments that have projects. To match the problem description to the query, we can express the problem as follows: Produce a report that includes the names of all departments where there exists a project assigned to that department.

```
SELECT DEPTNAME
FROM DSN8910.DEPT D
WHERE EXISTS
(SELECT 1
 FROM DSN8910.PROJ P
 WHERE P.DEPTNO = D.DEPTNO)
```

As with standard WHERE clause predicates, you can achieve the reverse condition by prefixing a specified condition with the NOT keyword, such as NOT EXISTS or NOT IN. Remember, however, that a null will not qualify against either an IN or a NOT IN condition.

Observe the WHERE clause in the subquery in this example. It references a table that is listed in the outer FROM clause.

The EXISTS subquery returns a true or a false to the outer query. If true, the outer row is considered a match, and the row is returned to the application. The correlated EXISTS subquery terminates after the first true condition is found or when a false can be determined, because the requirement is only to return a true or false condition, not to list how many occurrences match.

Because DB2 "prunes" the SELECT list for EXISTS subqueries, it's not important for the access path or performance which columns you list in the subquery select list of an EXISTS subquery. Therefore, whether you specify SELECT * or SELECT 1, DB2 still will return a true or false and will not retrieve all columns, as an outer query would if you specified SELECT *.

Unions

The UNION operation lets you combine the results of two or more SQL statements into one answer set. You can combine many different tables or SQL statements using the UNION (or UNION ALL) operator; the only restriction is that every table or SQL statement must have the same type, number, and order of columns. The term used to describe this requirement is that the tables or statements must be *UNION-compatible*.

Suppose we want to combine the minimum and maximum salary for employees by department on different output rows and add a string constant that indicates which values are the maximum and minimum.

```
SELECT WORKDEPT,'Minimum:', MIN(SALARY)
FROM DSN8910.EMP
GROUP BY WORKDEPT
UNION
SELECT WORKDEPT,'Maximum:', MAX(SALARY)
FROM DSN8910.EMP
GROUP BY WORKDEPT
ORDER BY WORKDEPT,2
```

The UNION operator shows you the results of two or more separate queries as a single result. In this example, the first query calculates the minimum salary by department of the EMP table. Then, the second query calculates the maximum salary by department value. Both queries have the same type, order, and number of columns.

In this example, the two SQL statements are very similar. However, you can combine very different queries using the UNION operator. Just remember the restriction about the resulting rows.

The UNION (optionally UNION DISTINCT) operator removes duplicate rows from the result set. However, there will be times when you'll need to list all the rows processed by your SQL statements or times when duplicates aren't possible. SQL provides an operator clause, the ALL clause, that lets you keep all the rows involved in a UNION operation. Because the previous example can never produce duplicate rows, we can add the ALL clause to the UNION:

```
SELECT WORKDEPT,'Minimum:', MIN(SALARY)
FROM DSN8910.EMP
GROUP BY WORKDEPT
UNION ALL
SELECT WORKDEPT,'Maximum:', MAX(SALARY)
FROM DSN8910.EMP
GROUP BY WORKDEPT
ORDER BY WORKDEPT,2
```

•••

Always try to code a UNION ALL rather than UNION. Code a UNION only when duplicates are possible and are not desired. UNION ALL offers better performance because a UNION always invokes a sort to remove duplicates and a UNION ALL does not. Be aware, though, that, you can't always substitute a UNION with a UNION ALL.

•••

•••

You can use UNION (and UNION ALL) between any combination of subselects and fullselects and in subqueries, views, and table expressions.

•••

UNION ALL in a View

The ability to perform a UNION within a view provides an alternative for table design. Perhaps a partitioned table has grown beyond DB2's 16 TB limit for a 4 K page size. Or maybe the complications of large partitioned table spaces (such as large BUILD2 phases with non-partitioned secondary indexes for SHRLEVEL REFERENCE REORGs) has become too much of an obstacle for 24x7 availability. By using UNION ALL in a view, you can combine several tables together, making it appear to applications using the view that there is one single table. This technique offers many benefits, including independence of the tables and no need for large NPSIs. However, to best use this feature, there are some coding practices you should follow.

Let's assume the following design: five independent tables (AC1–AC5), each holding data for different accounts. We could develop a view (ACCOUNT_VIEW) to UNION all five tables together to appear as one larger table. Here is the view definition:

```
CREATE ACCOUNT_VIEW(ACCT_ID)
SELECT ACCT_ID FROM AC1 WHERE ACCT_ID BETWEEN 1 AND 10000000
UNION  ALL
SELECT ACCT_ID FROM AC2 WHERE ACCT_ID BETWEEN 10000001 AND 20000000
UNION  ALL
SELECT ACCT_ID FROM AC3 WHERE ACCT_ID BETWEEN 20000001 AND 30000000
UNION  ALL
SELECT ACCT_ID FROM AC4 WHERE ACCT_ID BETWEEN 30000001 AND 40000000
UNION  ALL
SELECT ACCT_ID FROM AC5 WHERE ACCT_ID BETWEEN 40000001 AND 50000000
```

Queries written against the ACCOUNT_VIEW must repeat the predicate defined in the view for DB2 to use subquery pruning. Subquery pruning applies to UNION ALL queries and requires you to code redundant predicates in the view definition to compare distributed predicates with defined predicates in the definition. DB2 then removes unnecessary query blocks at bind time or runtime. This mechanism essentially limits the number of tables that are accessed to satisfy the query.

Using the preceding view definition, assume table AC1 contains values where ACCT_ID is between 1 and 10,000,000, table AC2 contains values where ACCT_ID is between 10,000,001 and 20,000,000, and so on. The predicate ACCT_ID = 10,340,576 will be distributed to each subselect in the view, and therefore only the necessary tables will be accessed. Figure 6.1 shows how the predicate in the select works with the tables in the view. In the example, only table AC2 will be accessed.

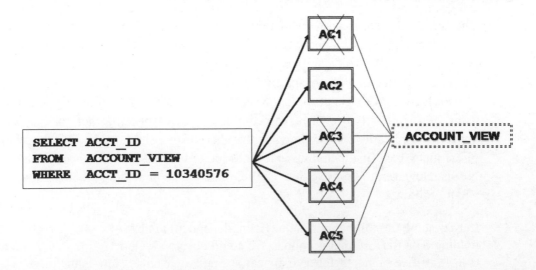

Figure 6.1: Predicates for subquery pruning

After the predicates are distributed, DB2 can then prune unnecessary query blocks—that is, those where the distributed predicates combined with the original view definition predicates evaluate to false. The original view definition must contain the predicates to allow pruning to occur, even if redundant.

Excepts

You use the EXCEPT operator to specify the difference set operator. Like UNION, EXCEPT operates on two or more result sets. You can combine many different tables or SQL statements using the EXCEPT (or EXCEPT ALL) operator; the only restriction is that every table or SQL statement must have the same type, number, and order of columns. The effect of EXCEPT (or EXCEPT ALL) is that only the rows of the first table or subselect that do not match the second table or subselect are returned. EXCEPT eliminates duplicate rows from the result; EXCEPT ALL does not.

Suppose we want a list of project names that are not major projects. There are many ways to obtain this information. One way is to use an EXCEPT ALL to produce the list. The first subselect obtains the project numbers and names. The second subselect does the same for the major projects. The result is a list of rows from the first result set that don't match any row in the second.

```
SELECT PROJNO, PROJNAME
FROM   DSN8910.PROJ
EXCEPT ALL
SELECT P1.MAJPROJ, P2.PROJNAME
FROM   DSN8910.PROJ P1
INNER JOIN
       DSN8910.PROJ P2
ON P1.MAJPROJ = P2.PROJNO;


1      PROJNAME
_____ _____
AD3113 ACCOUNT PROGRAMMING
OP2012 APPLICATIONS SUPPORT
OP2013 DB/DC SUPPORT
OP1010 OPERATION
AD3111 PAYROLL PROGRAMMING
AD3112 PERSONNEL PROGRAMMING
IF1000 QUERY SERVICES
OP2011 SCP SYSTEMS SUPPORT
IF2000 USER EDUCATION
MA2113 W L PROD CONT PROGS
MA2111 W L PROGRAM DESIGN
MA2112 W L ROBOT DESIGN
PL2100 WELD LINE PLANNING
```

Intersects

You use the INTERSECT operator to specify the intersection set operator. Like UNION, INTERSECT operates on two or more result sets. You can combine many different tables or SQL statements using INTERSECT (or INTERSECT ALL); the only restriction is that every table or SQL statement must have the same type, number, and order of columns. The effect of INTERSECT (or INTERSECT ALL) is that only the matching rows of the result sets are returned. INTERSECT eliminates duplicate rows from the result; INTERSECT ALL does not.

Suppose you need a list of department names that have employees and also have projects. There are many ways to do this; INTERSECT ALL provides one method. The first subselect obtains the department names for the departments that have projects. The second subselect does the same for departments that have employees. The result is a list of department names that have both employees and projects.

```
SELECT DEPTNAME
FROM    DSN8910.DEPT D
WHERE   EXISTS
        (SELECT 1
          FROM    DSN8910.EMP E
          WHERE   E.WORKDEPT = D.DEPTNO)
INTERSECT
SELECT DEPTNAME
FROM    DSN8910.DEPT D
WHERE   EXISTS
        (SELECT 1
          FROM    DSN8910.PROJ P
          WHERE   P.DEPTNO = D.DEPTNO);
```

Nested Table Expressions

A *nested table expression* is a special kind of fullselect that is used in the FROM clause of an SQL statement. Nested table expressions create logical temporary tables that are known only in the SQL statement that defines them. They may or may not result in a physically materialized local table being created because the SQL may be merged with the outer SQL statement (the statement selecting from the nested table expression).

You can think of these subqueries as temporary views, and they are also sometimes referred to as *inline views*. You can use nested table expressions to select from a grouped table or to obtain the same results you expect from a view.

Consider the problem of obtaining the maximum average salary for the departments. To gather this result, you must first obtain the averages and then select the maximum value from that list. In the following example, we use a nested table expression to accomplish this request.

```
SELECT MAX(AVG_SALARY)
FROM (
    SELECT WORKDEPT,
    AVG(SALARY) AS AVG_SALARY
    FROM DSN8910.EMP
    GROUP BY WORKDEPT) AS AVERAGES
```

In this example, the nested table expression creates a temporary table that the outer SELECT will use to obtain the maximum average salary for departments. This temporary table is called AVERAGES.

An advantage of using nested table expressions over views is that nested table expressions exist only during the execution of the query, so you don't have to worry about their maintenance. They reduce contention over the system catalog tables, and because they're created at execution time, you can define them using host variables. They also give the SQL programmer more information about the SQL statement. Because views are hidden, it's possible to introduce redundancy if the programmer isn't aware of the full view description.

Nested table expressions give us the ability to answer complex business problems within single SQL statements. Take, for example, the combination of line item and summary information in the same statement. In the following example, we obtain information about our sales reps (line item) along with information about the salary and number of employees in the departments in which the sales reps work (summary information).

```
SELECT  TAB1.EMPNO, TAB1.SALARY,
        TAB2.AVGSAL,TAB2.HDCOUNT
FROM
  (SELECT        EMPNO, SALARY, WORKDEPT
   FROM          DSN8910.EMP
   WHERE JOB='SALESREP') AS TAB1
```

```
  LEFT OUTER JOIN
    (SELECT      AVG(SALARY) AS AVGSAL, COUNT(*) AS HDCOUNT,
                 WORKDEPT
     FROM        DSN8910.EMP
    GROUP BY WORKDEPT) AS TAB2
  ON TAB1.WORKDEPT = TAB2.WORKDEPT;
```

We can express the same statement using a correlated nested table expression. In this statement, we use the TABLE keyword to designate to DB2 that the nested table expression is going to make a correlated reference to a table outside the nested table expression. Without the TABLE keyword, the statement would fail. The statement is logically equivalent to the previous statement but operates very differently in that the fullselect within the nested table expression will be executed once for each qualifying row of the first table specified in the FROM clause (TAB1).

```
SELECT  TAB1.EMPNO, TAB1.SALARY,
        TAB2.AVGSAL,TAB2.HDCOUNT
FROM          DSN8910.EMP TAB1,
TABLE(SELECT AVG(SALARY) AS AVGSAL,
            COUNT(*) AS HDCOUNT
      FROM   DSN8910.EMP
      WHERE  WORKDEPT = TAB1.WORKDEPT) AS TAB2
WHERE   TAB1.JOB = 'SALESREP';
```

> You can also use the TABLE clause to denote that the fullselect following it is a nested table expression. This keyword is mandatory if the nested table expression contains a correlated reference to a prior FROM clause table. The TABLE keyword is also used to denote a user-defined TABLE function (UDF). For more information about UDFs, see Chapter 15.

Common Table Expressions

Common table expressions can provide performance improvements by computing a value once, rather than multiple times, during the execution of a query. You can use common table expressions in SELECT, CREATE VIEW, and INSERT statements. The expressions may also contain references to host variables. Here's an example of a common table expression:

```
WITH DEPTOTAL (WORKDEPT, MAXSALARY) AS
(SELECT WORKDEPT, SUM(SALARY+COMM)
  FROM DSN8910.EMP
  GROUP BY WORKDEPT)
SELECT WORKDEPT FROM DEPTOTAL
WHERE MAXSALARY =
  (SELECT MAX(MAXSALARY)
          FROM DEPTOTAL);
```

In this example, the DEPTOTAL common table expression is established by calculating the sum of the salaries plus commissions for each department. The WITH clause identifies the common table expression, followed by the name of the common table expression and the column names. The fullselect within the parentheses following the WITH clause defines the data for the common table expression. This data can then be used in the remainder of the query.

Data Change Tables

A *data-change-table-reference clause* specifies an intermediate result table based on the rows that are directly changed by the SQL data-change statement (insert, merge, update, or delete) that is contained in the clause. A data-change-table-reference must be the only table reference in the FROM clause of the outer fullselect used in a SELECT statement, and that fullselect must be in a subselect or a SELECT INTO statement. A data-change-table-reference in a SELECT statement of a cursor makes the cursor read-only. The target table or view of the SQL data-change statement is a table or view referenced in the query. The privileges held by the authorization ID of the statement must include the SELECT privilege on the target table or view. Expressions in the select list of a view in a table reference can be selected only if you specify OLD TABLE or if the expression includes none of the following objects:

- A function that is defined to read or modify SQL data

- A function that is defined as not deterministic or that has an external action

- A NEXT VALUE expression for a sequence

The data-change-table-reference gives you the ability to select data from a change to a table. That is, you can SELECT from an INSERT, UPDATE, MERGE, or DELETE statement. This capability lets you gather information that DB2 generated automatically from a DML modification statement, such as identity columns, sequence objects, default values, and values set by triggers. You can access data values as they look before or after the change, depending on the statement in the data-change-table-reference.

The FINAL TABLE clause specifies that the rows of the intermediate result table represent the set of rows changed by the SQL data-change statement as they appear at the completion of that statement. If AFTER triggers result in further operations on the table that is the target of the SQL data-change statement, an error is returned. If the target of the SQL data-change statement is a view defined with an INSTEAD OF trigger for the type of data change, an error is returned.

The OLD TABLE clause specifies that the rows of the intermediate result table represent the set of affected rows as they exist before the application of the SQL data-change statement. If you specify OLD TABLE, the select list cannot contain an XML column.

The following three examples demonstrate a SELECT from INSERT, UPDATE, and DELETE, respectively. In the first example, an insert statement places a row into the activity table. The ACT table has a primary key of ACTNO that is automatically generated via an identity column. Because the ACT table has child tables, we'll need the ACTNO for other inserts. The statement retrieves ACTNO from the FINAL TABLE.

```
SELECT ACTNO
FROM FINAL TABLE
 (INSERT INTO DSN8910.ACT (ACTKWD, ACTDESC)
         VALUES ('TASK32', 'PROGRAMMING LEGACY') );
```

In the next example, we obtain the new salary from an update statement. If our application requires the new salary to be displayed after an update, this statement retrieves that new salary after the update without having to perform an additional read of the table.

```
SELECT  SALARY
FROM FINAL TABLE UPDATE DSN8910.EMP
SET SALARY = SALARY + 5000
WHERE EMPNO = '000010';
```

In this last example, an old employee row is being removed from the database. However, auditing requirements dictate that the deleted employee must be retrieved for archiving in a separate database. This statement accesses the last salary and job for the employee from the image of the employee row before deleting the employee. This technique permits the delete and the retrieval to happen in the same statement.

```
SELECT  SALARY, JOB
FROM OLD TABLE
DELETE FROM DSN8910.EMP
WHERE EMPNO = '000010';
```

Joins

The heart of SQL in a relational system is the ability to perform relational joins. You specify joins by using more than one table name in the FROM clause of a query. A joined table specifies an intermediate result table that is the result of either an inner join or an outer join.

DB2 supports up to 225 tables in a query, including subqueries.

Inner Joins

The join operation used most often is known as an *inner join*. An inner join combines each row of the left table with each row of the right table, keeping only the rows where the join condition is true. The result table may be missing rows from either or both of the joined tables.

The following example shows an inner join using implicit join syntax, which means that the inner join is implicitly defined. To indicate the join, we separate the tables in the FROM clause with a comma. This type of syntax is valid only for inner joins. The example retrieves the department name and employee names for departments A00 and C01.

```
SELECT E.EMPNO, E.FIRSTNME, E.LASTNAME, D.DEPTNAME
FROM   DSN8910.EMP E, DSN8910.DEPT D
WHERE  E.WORKDEPT = D.DEPTNO
AND    E.WORKDEPT IN ('A00', 'C01')
```

If the inner join used the explicit syntax, it would appear as

```
SELECT E.EMPNO, E.FIRSTNME, E.LASTNAME, D.DEPTNAME
FROM   DSN8910.EMP E
INNER  JOIN
       DSN8910.DEPT D
ON     E.WORKDEPT = D.DEPTNO
WHERE  E.WORKDEPT IN ('A00', 'C01')
```

For the explicit join syntax, the keyword INNER is optional; if you omit it, an inner join is implied. Deciding whether to code the explicit join syntax or to separate the joined tables with commas is purely a matter of preference and is unrelated to performance.

> The explicit join syntax has the following benefits: compatibility with the outer join syntax, improved readability of large SQL statements (because each join is followed by its join predicate), and increased likelihood that all join predicates will be coded correctly (the ON clause is required)

In the example, the ON clause determines the join predicates between the tables, and the WHERE clause applies the local, or table access, predicates. For an inner join, it actually doesn't matter whether the local predicates appear in the WHERE or the ON clause. With explicit join syntax, the ON clause is required. For consistency with outer joins, we recommend you specify join predicates only in the ON clause and use local predicates only in the WHERE clause. For outer joins, the placement of predicates in these clauses can change the result dramatically. We'll demonstrate this point in the section on outer joins.

Each join must be followed by its ON clause, which dictates the two tables being joined. The joined tables must appear in the FROM clause before being referenced by join predicates in the ON clause. In the following example, the first join is between tables EMP and DEPT. The second join is between tables EMP and PROJ, as dictated by the ON clause. This query not only retrieves the names of the departments employees work in but also the projects they're responsible for.

```
SELECT E.EMPNO, E.FIRSTNME, E.LASTNAME, D.DEPTNAME, P.PROJNO
FROM   DSN8910.EMP E
INNER  JOIN
       DSN8910.DEPT D
ON     E.WORKDEPT = D.DEPTNO
INNER  JOIN
       DSN8910.PROJ P
ON     E.EMPNO = P.RESPEMP
WHERE  E.WORKDEPT IN ('A00', 'C01');
```

There is one exception to the rule that an ON clause must follow each join, and that is when you're nesting joins within other joins. For simplicity, we don't recommend this syntax, and you can recode easily to suit the rule.

Outer Joins

Next, we look at a different kind of join operation, the *outer join*. As you've learned, the result set of an inner join consists of only those matched rows that are present in both joined tables. What happens when you need to include the values that are present in one or another joined table, but not in both of them? In this case, you need to use an OUTER JOIN operation. Outer joins are designed to generate an answer set that includes those values that are present in joined tables as well as those that are not. This type of optional relationship between tables is very common. There are three types of outer joins: left outer join, right outer join, and full outer join.

Figure 6.2 depicts the best way to visualize outer joins. The diagram shows the data from each table that is included or excluded in each type of join.

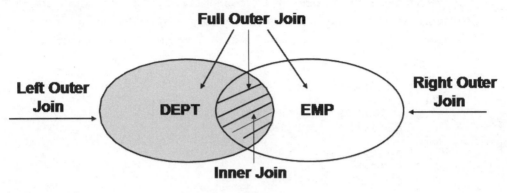

Figure 6.2: Outer joins

Left Outer Join

A LEFT OUTER JOIN operation, also known as a *left join*, produces an answer set that includes the matching values of the joined tables (the inner join rows) as well as the values that are present only in the left joined table (the rows exclusive to the left table). The left joined table is the one specified on the left side of the LEFT OUTER JOIN operator when you code the join operation in the FROM clause.

In a left outer join, we refer to the left table as the *preserved row table*. If a row is unmatched between the two joined tables, it is still returned (preserved) from the left table. The opposite (right) table is the *null-supplying table*. When a row is unmatched from the left to the right table in the join, the row from the right table is supplied with nulls.

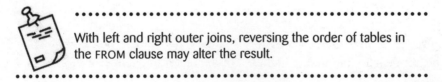

With left and right outer joins, reversing the order of tables in the FROM clause may alter the result.

Let's assume we've been asked to generate a report that includes the names of all departments along with the names and hire dates of the employees who work in the departments. If we use an inner join, the report will include data only for those departments that have employees, but some departments don't have any employees. Therefore, if we want to list all departments, this query requires a left join.

Without using the outer join syntax, we could solve this request using some SQL statements we've already discussed; however, the construction would be complex. Instead, we'll use a left outer join to satisfy the request, as the following example shows.

```
SELECT D.DEPTNAME, E.FIRSTNME, E.LASTNAME, E.HIREDATE
FROM DSN8910.DEPT D
    LEFT OUTER JOIN
      DSN8910.EMP E
ON D.DEPTNO = E.WORKDEPT;
```

The keyword OUTER is optional. Provided the JOIN is preceded by either LEFT, RIGHT, or FULL, OUTER is implied.

Observe the syntax used to indicate a left outer join. We use the LEFT OUTER JOIN operator to indicate the join operation. In the example, the answer set includes those departments that have no employees. In those cases, the employee information will be null.

When you code outer joins, it's important to note the difference between WHERE and ON clause predicates. From the preceding example, say we want to retrieve only the information for departments A00, C01, and D01.

```
SELECT D.DEPTNAME, E.FIRSTNME, E.LASTNAME, E.HIREDATE
FROM DSN8910.DEPT D
    LEFT OUTER JOIN
      DSN8910.EMP E
ON D.DEPTNO = E.WORKDEPT
WHERE D.DEPTNO IN ('A00', 'C01', 'D01');
```

DEPTNAME	FIRSTNME	LASTNAME	HIREDATE
SPIFFY COMPUTER SERVICE DIV.	CHRISTINE	HAAS	1995-01-01
SPIFFY COMPUTER SERVICE DIV.	VINCENZO	LUCCHESSI	1988-05-16
SPIFFY COMPUTER SERVICE DIV.	SEAN	O'CONNELL	1993-12-05
SPIFFY COMPUTER SERVICE DIV.	DIAN	HEMMINGER	1995-01-01
SPIFFY COMPUTER SERVICE DIV.	GREG	ORLANDO	2002-05-05
INFORMATION CENTER	SALLY	KWAN	2005-04-05
INFORMATION CENTER	DELORES	QUINTANA	2001-07-28
INFORMATION CENTER	HEATHER	NICHOLLS	2006-12-15
INFORMATION CENTER	KIM	NATZ	2006-12-15
DEVELOPMENT CENTER	NULL	NULL	NULL

The WHERE clause predicate in this example is applied to the left, or preserved, row table. DB2 is able, therefore, to apply this predicate before the join to the EMP table and join only departments A00, C01, and D01 to the EMP table. Department D01, the Development Center, ends up having its employee first name, last name, and hire date values set to null because this department has no employees; therefore, no rows are found in the EMP table.

Consider the result if we write the query to also exclude those employees who have been hired in the past 10 years (given that today is 3/30/2007).

```
SELECT D.DEPTNAME, E.FIRSTNME, E.LASTNAME, E.HIREDATE
FROM DSN8910.DEPT D
    LEFT OUTER JOIN
      DSN8910.EMP E
ON D.DEPTNO = E.WORKDEPT
WHERE D.DEPTNO IN ('A00', 'D01', 'C01')
AND    E.HIREDATE < CURRENT DATE - 10 YEARS;

DEPTNAME                     FIRSTNME  LASTNAME  HIREDATE
_____ _____  _____  _____

SPIFFY COMPUTER SERVICE DIV. CHRISTINE HAAS      1995-01-01
SPIFFY COMPUTER SERVICE DIV. VINCENZO  LUCCHESSI 1988-05-16
SPIFFY COMPUTER SERVICE DIV. SEAN      O'CONNELL 1993-12-05
SPIFFY COMPUTER SERVICE DIV. DIAN      HEMMINGER 1995-01-01
```

Only four rows qualify from this query. The WHERE clause predicate on the preserved row table—WHERE D.DEPTNO IN ('A00', 'D01', 'C01')—can be applied before the join to limit the number of rows that must be joined. The additional WHERE clause predicate—AND E.HIREDATE < CURRENT DATE – 10 YEARS—is applied after the join because it's not known until after the join what the value of HIREDATE will be. This predicate is applied to each row, with the following results:

- Is Christine's hire date less than the current date minus 10 years? TRUE.

- Is Vincenzo's hire date less than the current date minus 10 years? TRUE.

- Is Sean's hire date less than the current date minus 10 years? TRUE.

- Is Dian's hire date less than the current date minus 10 years? TRUE.

- Is Greg's hire date less than the current date minus 10 years? FALSE.

- Is Sally's hire date less than the current date minus 10 years? FALSE.

- Is Delores's hire date less than the current date minus 10 years? FALSE.

- Is Heather's hire date less than the current date minus 10 years? FALSE.

- Is Kim's hire date less than the current date minus 10 years? FALSE.

- Is the NULL hire date less than the current date minus 10 years? UNKNOWN.

Remember that for a row to be returned, the WHERE clause must evaluate to TRUE. Because the nulls introduced by the outer join are discarded by the WHERE clause applied to the null-supplying table, DB2 will actually rewrite the left join to an INNER JOIN, thus letting the WHERE clause predicates be applied to both tables before the joining of the rows occurs.

```
SELECT D.DEPTNAME, E.FIRSTNME, E.LASTNAME, E.HIREDATE
FROM DSN8910.DEPT D
    INNER JOIN
       DSN8910.EMP E
ON D.DEPTNO = E.WORKDEPT
WHERE D.DEPTNO IN ('A00', 'D01', 'C01')
AND   E.HIREDATE < CURRENT DATE - 10 YEARS;
```

If you want to maintain the null-supplied rows, you must include an additional IS NULL predicate, as shown in the following example.

DB2 records the outer join simplification in the JOIN_TYPE column of the plan table. If a left, right, or full join has been simplified to an inner join, the JOIN_TYPE value will be blank.

```
SELECT D.DEPTNAME, E.FIRSTNME, E.LASTNAME, E.HIREDATE
FROM DSN8910.DEPT D
    INNER JOIN
       DSN8910.EMP E
ON D.DEPTNO = E.WORKDEPT
WHERE D.DEPTNO IN ('A00', 'D01', 'C01'
AND   (E.HIREDATE < CURRENT DATE - 10 YEARS
      OR E.HIREDATE IS NULL);
```

```
DEPTNAME                      FIRSTNME  LASTNAME   HIREDATE
----------------------------  --------  ---------  ----------
SPIFFY COMPUTER SERVICE DIV.  CHRISTINE HAAS       1995-01-01
SPIFFY COMPUTER SERVICE DIV.  VINCENZO  LUCCHESSI  1988-05-16
SPIFFY COMPUTER SERVICE DIV.  SEAN      O'CONNELL  1993-12-05
SPIFFY COMPUTER SERVICE DIV.  DIAN      HEMMINGER  1995-01-01
DEVELOPMENT CENTER            NULL      NULL       NULL
```

In this case, DB2 doesn't simplify the left outer join to an inner join because the null-supplied row isn't discarded by the WHERE clause predicate. Thus, the row for the development center is included in the result set because the hire date is null.

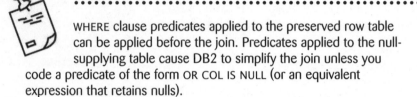

WHERE clause predicates applied to the preserved row table can be applied before the join. Predicates applied to the null-supplying table cause DB2 to simplify the join unless you code a predicate of the form OR COL IS NULL (or an equivalent expression that retains nulls).

We've looked at WHERE clause predicates applied to either the preserved row or null-supplied tables. The next objective is to demonstrate the impact of coding local predicates in the ON clause. The following example displays the output if we specify the department numbers (A00, C01, and D01) in the ON clause rather than in the WHERE clause.

```
SELECT D.DEPTNAME, E.FIRSTNME, E.LASTNAME, E.HIREDATE
FROM DSN8910.DEPT D
   LEFT OUTER JOIN
     DSN8910.EMP E
ON   D.DEPTNO = E.WORKDEPT
AND D.DEPTNO IN ('A00', 'D01', 'C01');
```

```
DEPTNAME                      FIRSTNME  LASTNAME   HIREDATE
----------------------------  --------  ---------  -----------
SPIFFY COMPUTER SERVICE DIV.  CHRISTINE HAAS       1995-01-01
SPIFFY COMPUTER SERVICE DIV.  VINCENZO  LUCCHESSI  1988-05-16
SPIFFY COMPUTER SERVICE DIV.  SEAN      O'CONNELL  1993-12-05
SPIFFY COMPUTER SERVICE DIV.  DIAN      HEMMINGER  1995-01-01
SPIFFY COMPUTER SERVICE DIV.  GREG      ORLANDO    2002-05-05
PLANNING                      NULL      NULL       NULL
INFORMATION CENTER            SALLY     KWAN       2005-04-05
INFORMATION CENTER            DELORES   QUINTANA   2001-07-28
INFORMATION CENTER            HEATHER   NICHOLLS   2006-12-15
```

INFORMATION CENTER	KIM	NATZ	2006-12-15
DEVELOPMENT CENTER	NULL	NULL	NULL
MANUFACTURING SYSTEMS	NULL	NULL	NULL
ADMINISTRATION SYSTEMS	NULL	NULL	NULL
SUPPORT SERVICES	NULL	NULL	NULL
OPERATIONS	NULL	NULL	NULL
SOFTWARE SUPPORT	NULL	NULL	NULL
BRANCH OFFICE F2	NULL	NULL	NULL
BRANCH OFFICE G2	NULL	NULL	NULL
BRANCH OFFICE H2	NULL	NULL	NULL
BRANCH OFFICE I2	NULL	NULL	NULL
BRANCH OFFICE J2	NULL	NULL	NULL

Because there are no WHERE clause predicates to restrict the result, this query returns all rows of the DEPT table, plus the rows from the EMP for some of the departments. Columns from the EMP table are supplied only when the ON clause is true. Remember, WHERE clause predicates restrict the result, whereas ON clause predicates determine the criteria for the join. For the rows not matching the full ON clause—D.DEPT NOT IN ('A00', 'C01', 'D01')—DB2 will preserve the row from the left table and supply nulls from the right table. Rows matching the ON clause—D.DEPT IN ('A00', 'C01', 'D01')—will match and thus will return columns from both tables (as long as there are rows matching in the EMP table; otherwise the query will still return nulls for the right table).

> If DB2 can determine that the ON clause will fail before joining the rows, it will automatically supply nulls for the null-supplied columns without attempting the join. This behavior improves performance because rows aren't joined unnecessarily if the final result will not match regardless.

Right Outer Join

A RIGHT OUTER JOIN operation, also known as *right join*, produces an answer set that includes the matching values of both joined tables as well as those values present only in the right joined table. The right joined table is the one specified on the right side of the RIGHT OUTER JOIN operator when you code the join operation.

For a right join, the right table is the preserved row table, and the left table is the null-supplied table for unmatched rows. This is the opposite of a left join. The next example uses a right outer join.

```
SELECT  E.LASTNAME, P.PROJNO
FROM    DSN8910.PROJ P
RIGHT   JOIN
        DSN8910.EMP E
ON      E.EMPNO = P.RESPEMP
WHERE   E.WORKDEPT IN ('A00', 'C01');
```

This query requests all employees for departments A00, and C01, along with the numbers of the projects for which those employees are responsible, if they are responsible for a project. Notice that there may be some employees who are not responsible for any projects.

As with a left join, the order of the tables in the FROM clause for a right join can impact the result. However, a right join can be converted to a left join by reversing the order of the tables in the FROM clause and also by changing the RIGHT keyword to LEFT.

● ●

DB2 converts all right joins to left joins at bind time. The JOIN_TYPE column of the plan table will show an L for a right or a left join unless DB2 has simplified the join to an inner join. For this reason, the recommendation is to avoid coding right joins to minimize confusion when evaluating the access path.

● ●

Full Outer Join

The FULL OUTER JOIN operation produces an answer set that includes the matching values of both joined tables along with those values not present in one or the other of the tables. Thus, it returns the inclusive inner join rows plus the exclusive left and right outer rows.

To show a FULL OUTER JOIN operation, we'll use two nested table expressions. One expression calculates the number of employees and total salary by department from the employee table. The other calculates the number of projects per department. Because a department may not have employees and a department may not have projects, only a full outer join will return all the results. The contents of both table expressions are as follows.

```
SELECT WORKDEPT, SUM(SALARY) AS TOTSAL
       ,COUNT(*) AS NUMEMP
FROM   DSN8910.EMP
GROUP  BY WORKDEPT;

WORKDEPT TOTSAL     NUMEMP
_____ _____  _____
A00      354250.00       5
B01       94250.00       1
C01      308890.00       4
D11      646620.00      11
D21      358680.00       7
E01       80175.00       1
E11      317140.00       7
E21      282520.00       6

SELECT DEPTNO, COUNT(*) AS NUMPROJ
FROM   DSN8910.PROJ
GROUP  BY DEPTNO;

DEPTNO NUMPROJ
_____ _____
B01          1
C01          2
D01          2
D11          4
D21          4
E01          2
E11          1
E21          4
```

We want to show all the employee information, as well as all the project information, for all departments whether or not they are missing either piece of information. Therefore, we use a full outer join, as shown here:

```
SELECT E.WORKDEPT, E.TOTSAL, E.NUMEMP,
       P.DEPTNO, P.NUMPROJ
FROM
 (SELECT WORKDEPT, SUM(SALARY) AS TOTSAL,
        COUNT(*) AS NUMEMP
 FROM   DSN8910.EMP
 GROUP  BY WORKDEPT) AS E
FULL OUTER JOIN
 (SELECT DEPTNO, COUNT(*) AS NUMPROJ
 FROM    DSN8910.PROJ
 GROUP   BY DEPTNO) AS P
ON E.WORKDEPT = P.DEPTNO;
```

WORKDEPT	TOTSAL	NUMEMP	DEPTNO	NUMPROJ
A00	354250.00	5	NULL	NULL
B01	94250.00	1	B01	1
C01	308890.00	4	C01	2
D11	646620.00	11	D11	4
D21	358680.00	7	D21	4
E01	80175.00	1	E01	2
E11	317140.00	7	E11	1
E21	282520.00	6	E21	4
NULL	NULL	NULL	D01	2

As you can see, the rows that have a null value were added by the outer join operation. The department number column (WORKDEPT/DEPTNO) appears twice so we can see those departments present in the E table expression that are not present in the P table expression, and vice versa.

As the full join example shows, both tables can preserve rows and also supply nulls for unmatched rows. Because WHERE clause predicates applied to null-supplied tables may cause DB2 to perform simplification of the outer join, predicates that are to be applied before the join to limit the result set must be coded within nested table expressions.

> DB2 can simplify a full join to either a left or an inner join if the WHERE clause predicates discard nulls from one or both tables, respectively. This information appears in the JOIN_TYPE column of the plan table as either an L for left or a blank for inner join, rather than an F for a full join.

Consider the following example, where we want to list the information only for project and employee counts greater than one. For purposes of this example, we've used additional nested table expressions and WHERE, but we could have used HAVING as well.

```
SELECT E.WORKDEPT, E.TOTSAL, E.NUMEMP,
       P.DEPTNO, P.NUMPROJ
FROM
 (SELECT WORKDEPT, TOTSAL, NUMEMP
 FROM
  (SELECT WORKDEPT, SUM(SALARY) AS TOTSAL,
       COUNT(*) AS NUMEMP
```

```
    FROM    DSN8910.EMP
      GROUP  BY WORKDEPT) AS X
  WHERE X.NUMEMP > 1) AS E
FULL OUTER JOIN
  (SELECT DEPTNO, NUMPROJ
  FROM
    (SELECT DEPTNO, COUNT(*) AS NUMPROJ
      FROM    DSN8910.PROJ
      GROUP    BY DEPTNO) AS Y
  WHERE Y.NUMPROJ > 1) AS P
ON E.WORKDEPT = P.DEPTNO;

WORKDEPT TOTSAL     NUMEMP DEPTNO NUMPROJ
_____ _____  _____ _____ _____
C01      308890.00       4 C01         2
D11      646620.00      11 D11         4
D21      358680.00       7 D21         4
E21      282520.00       6 E21         4
NULL          NULL    NULL E01         2
NULL          NULL    NULL D01         2
A00      354250.00       5 NULL     NULL
E11      317140.00       7 NULL     NULL
```

Because the department number can return null from either table, it's common to code the COALESCE or VALUE function to ensure that the value is always supplied (and not null). The select list for this example would be

```
SELECT COALESCE(E.WORKDEPT, P.DEPTNO), E.TOTSAL, E.NUMEMP,
       P.NUMPROJ
```

COALESCE returns the first element in the list that is not null.

Combining Outer Joins

Up until now, we've discussed each outer join operation separately. Now, we'll look at a more complex example that combines two outer joins in a single query. Let's display all the employee last names and the project numbers of the projects for which the employees are responsible, if they are responsible. Then, let's also display the number of subprojects that a project is immediately responsible for, even if the employees listed don't match.

To create this query, we need two outer joins. The first obtains all employees and the projects they're responsible for (for departments A00, and C01, only, to limit the results), including any employees who are not responsible for projects. The second outer join retrieves all the projects that have subprojects and counts the subprojects, regardless of whether we returned any employee information.

```
SELECT TAB1.LASTNAME,
       COALESCE(TAB1.PROJNO, TAB2.MAJPROJ) AS PROJNO,
       TAB2.MINOR_PROJS
FROM
 (SELECT E.LASTNAME, P.PROJNO
  FROM    DSB8910.PROJ P
  RIGHT JOIN
          DSN8910.EMP E
  ON      E.EMPNO = P.RESPEMP
  WHERE   E.WORKDEPT IN ('A00', 'C01')) AS TAB1
FULL OUTER JOIN
 (SELECT MAJPROJ, COUNT(*) AS MINOR_PROJS
   FROM   DSN8910.PROJ
   WHERE  MAJPROJ IS NOT NULL
   GROUP BY MAJPROJ) AS TAB2
ON TAB1.PROJNO = TAB2.MAJPROJ;
```

LASTNAME	PROJNO	MINOR_PROJS
HAAS	AD3100	1
NULL	AD3110	3
HAAS	MA2100	2
NULL	MA2110	3
NULL	OP1000	1
NULL	OP2000	1
NULL	OP2010	3
KWAN	IF1000	NULL
KWAN	IF2000	NULL
LUCCHESSI	NULL	NULL
HEMMINGER	NULL	NULL
NICHOLLS	NULL	NULL
QUINTANA	NULL	NULL
ORLANDO	NULL	NULL
O'CONNELL	NULL	NULL
NATZ	NULL	NULL

Take care when joining the result of an outer join to subsequent tables. If the join predicate refers to columns from a null-supplied table, the join predicate must also handle the occurrence of nulls. Where possible, code the join predicate from the preserved row table, and if the preceding join was a full join, use the COALESCE function to ensure that the join predicate cannot be null.

Joins vs. Denormalization

One issue we need to examine when discussing joins is that of *denormalization*. Denormalization is the process of pulling normalized tables back together into a single table to avoid joins. Denormalization is often done in an effort to minimize joins and improve performance.

Because denormalization is generally applied to tables in a one-to-many relationship, it results in multiple occurrences of the same data. This introduces update anomalies—the situation where a single piece of data occurs multiple times. When an attempt to update that data takes place, all occurrences must be found, and there is no fixed way to determine the number or location of the multiple occurrences.

There are legitimate reasons for some denormalization in certain environments, such as in read-only data warehouses, but each situation must be evaluated carefully. For more information about normalization/denormalization and update anomalies, refer to Chapter 4.

ORDER BY and FETCH FIRST in Subselects and Fullselects

Before DB2 9, the ORDER BY and FETCH FIRST clauses were allowed at the statement level only as part of a SELECT statement or a SELECT INTO statement. DB2 9 extends this functionality to support the specification of ORDER BY and FETCH FIRST as part of a subselect or a fullselect. This support gives you the ability to include these clauses in subqueries, nested table expressions, and so on.

The ORDER BY clause specified in a subselect affects the order of rows returned by the query only if the subselect is the outermost fullselect. The exception is when a nested subselect includes an ORDER BY clause and the outermost fullselect specifies that the ordering should be retained. You accomplish this using the ORDER OF clause within the ORDER BY.

This type of flexibility can affect problems such as finding the first row of data for a certain condition or perhaps finding the latest version of a status within a history table:

```
SELECT   A.ACCT_BAL, H.ACCT_STATUS
FROM     ACCOUNT A,
TABLE    (SELECT ACCT_STATUS
                 FROM ACCT_STS_HIST X
                 WHERE  A.ACCT_ID = X.ACCT_ID
                 ORDER BY STATUS_DTE DESC
                 FETCH FIRST 1 ROW ONLY) AS H
WHERE    A.ACCT_ID = 'A000010';
```

The ORDER OF clause enables a prior sort sequence to be retained. Consider the following example. In this case, we could specify the ORDER BY clause in the nested table expression to force materialization and force the join to table T1 to be more efficient. The sort order for the intermediate sort is also desired in the output, and the ORDER OF clause is used for that designation.

```
SELECT T1.C1, T1.C2, TEMP.CY, TEMP.CX
FROM   T1,
          (SELECT T2.C1, T2.C2 FROM T2 ORDER BY 2) AS TEMP(CX, CY)
WHERE  CY = T1.C1
ORDER BY ORDER OF TEMP;
```

CASE Expressions

You can add if-then-else logic to your SQL statements and output using CASE expressions. Consider the education level of the employees. The education level represents the number of years of education, but suppose you'd like to categorize this into the level of schooling employees have achieved. The following SQL statement uses a CASE expression to solve this problem.

```
SELECT FIRSTNME, LASTNAME,
    CASE
        WHEN EDLEVEL < 15 THEN 'SECONDARY'
        WHEN EDLEVEL <= 19 THEN 'COLLEGE'
        ELSE 'POST GRADUATE'
    END AS SCHOOLING
FROM DSN8910.EMP
WHERE WORKDEPT IN ('A00', 'C01');
```

This SQL statement provides string messages based on the conditions of the CASE expression. In this example, the education level column features a numeric value, but we use it to produce a character string. The column derived from the CASE expression has been assigned the name SCHOOLING.

The order of the conditions for the CASE expression is important. DB2 processes the first condition first, then the second, and so on. If you don't pay attention to the order in which the conditions are processed, you might retrieve the same result for every row in your table. For example, if you coded the <= 19 option before the < 15, all the data that is lower than 19, even 13 or 14, will display the COLLEGE value.

You can use CASE expressions in places other than select lists, such as in WHERE, ON, and HAVING clauses. You can also nest CASE expressions within other CASE expressions.

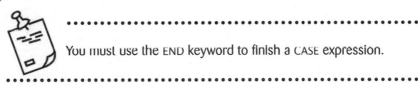

You must use the END keyword to finish a CASE expression.

Using CASE Expressions in Functions

CASE expressions can be embedded as function parameters. This technique lets you supply different parameters to a function in a single pass of the data. Suppose the EMP table is very large and we have a requirement to count the following:

- The number of employees with a salary less than $40,000

- The number of employees with a salary between $40,000 and $50,000

- The number of employees with a salary greater than $50,000

Without the use of CASE expressions, this assignment will require four different queries that potentially will read the entire table. We want to do the work in a single pass of the data because the table is very large. Our query uses three SUM functions, each one evaluating different criteria using a CASE expression:

```
SELECT
    SUM (CASE WHEN SALARY < 40000 THEN 1 ELSE NULL END)
      AS LESS_THAN_40K,
    SUM (CASE WHEN SALARY >= 40000 AND SALARY <=50000
          THEN 1 ELSE NULL END)
      AS BETWEEN_40K_TO_50K,
    SUM (CASE WHEN SALARY > 50000 THEN 1 ELSE NULL END)
      AS MORE_THAN_50K
FROM DSN8910.EMP;
```

This type of query may be useful when you're performing data inspection analysis. Notice that the three different requirements are solved in a single pass of the data. The query was created using a different SUM function for each one of the conditions presented as a requirement. The conditions are evaluated in the CASE expression inside each function. When the condition evaluates true, it returns a value of 1, and the row is summed. When the condition evaluates false, the CASE expression returns a null value, and the row is not summed.

Row Expressions

Row expressions are an extension to predicates. They allow more than one set of comparisons in a single predicate, using a subquery that returns more than one column and even more than one row. In the following example, the WHERE clause predicate will be true when all three columns on the left equal the three values in any single row returned in the result set from the subquery. You can also use quantified predicates (such as = ANY, = SOME, or <> ALL) with row expressions.

```
SELECT * FROM TABLE
WHERE (col1, col2, col3) IN
    (SELECT cola, colb, colc
     FROM TABLE
     UNION ALL
     SELECT colx, coly, colz
     FROM ANOTHER_TABLE)
```

XPath and XQuery

PureXML, the DB2 for z/OS support for XML, lets you manage XML data in DB2 tables. You can store well-formed XML documents in their hierarchical form and retrieve all or parts of those documents. You can retrieve entire XML documents from XML columns using an SQL SELECT statement, or you can use SQL with XML extensions (SQL/XML), specifying XPath expressions, to retrieve portions of documents. The SQL/XML function that supports retrieval of parts of XML documents is XMLQUERY. To filter table rows by XML document content, you use the SQL/XML XMLEXISTS predicate.

Retrieval of an entire XML document from an XML column is similar to retrieval of a value from a LOB column (covered in Chapter 15), with the following differences:

- LOB values can have locators, but XML values cannot. This means you need to allocate enough application storage to retrieve entire XML values, use file reference variables, or use the SQL FETCH WITH CONTINUE statement.

- XML values can have internal encoding as well as external encoding. With LOB values, you need to consider only whether differences exist between the database server encoding and the application encoding when you retrieve data.

For these examples, we'll use the CUSTOMER table defined here:

```
CREATE TABLE DSN8910.CUSTOMER
(CID                      BIGINT NOT NULL,
 INFO                     XML)
IN DSN8D91X.DSN8S91X;
```

Retrieving the data from the table, including the XML column INFO in its entirety, is as easy as using SQL to select from the table:

```
SELECT *
FROM    DSN8910.CUSTOMER
WHERE   CID = 1000;

CID    INFO
----   ------------------------------------------------------------------------
1000   <customerinfo xmlns="http://posample.org" Cid="1000"><name>Kathy
       Smith</name><addr country="Canada"><street>5
       Rosewood</street><city>Toronto</city><prov-state>Ontario</prov-
       state><pcode-zip>M6W 1E6</pcode-zip></addr><phone type="work">
       416-555-1358</phone></customerinfo>
```

XPath Exressions

To retrieve portions of an XML document, you need to use *XPath expressions*. XPath is an expression language designed by the World Wide Web Consortium to allow processing of XML data that conforms to the XQuery 1.0 and XPath 2.0 data model. You can use DB2 XPath in the following contexts:

- As an argument to the XMLQUERY SQL built-in function, which extracts data from an XML column

- As an argument to the XMLEXISTS SQL predicate, which is used for evaluation of data in an XML column

- In an XML index, to determine the nodes in an XML document that are to be indexed

The basic building block of XPath is the expression. DB2 XPath provides several kinds of expressions for working with XML data:

- *Primary expressions*, which include the basic primitives of the language, such as literal, variable references, and function calls

- *Path expressions* for locating nodes within a document tree

- *Filter expressions,* which are primary expressions followed by zero or more predicates that filter the result of the primary expression

- *Arithmetic expression*s for addition, subtraction, multiplication, division, and modulus

- *Comparison expressions* for comparing two values

- *Logical expressions* for using Boolean logic

In DB2 XPath, an XPath expression consists of an optional *prolog* followed by an expression. The prolog contains a series of declarations that define the processing environment for the expression. The path expression consists of an expression that defines the result of the XPath expression.

To invoke XPath expressions, you use the SQL/XML XMLQUERY function. This scalar function returns the result of an XPath expression as an XML sequence. When you execute XPath expressions from within an XMLQUERY function, you can

- retrieve parts of stored XML documents, instead of entire XML documents

- enable XML data to participate in SQL queries

- operate on both relational and XML data in the same SQL statement

To prevent naming collisions, DB2 XPath uses XML namespaces. An *XML namespace* is a collection of names that is identified by a namespace Uniform Resource Identifier (URI). Namespaces provide a way to qualify names used for elements, attributes, data types, and functions in XPath.

The XPath expression can include path expressions and filter expressions. Path expressions locate nodes within an XML tree. In DB2 XPath, path expressions are based on the syntax of XPath 2.0.

A path expression consists of a series of one or more steps that are separated by a slash character (/) or two slash characters (//). The path can begin with one slash, two slashes, or a step. Two slash characters in a path expression are expanded as

```
/descendant-or-self::node()/
```

which leaves a sequence of steps separated by a slash character.

A step generates a sequence of items. DB2 evaluates the steps in a path expression from left to right. The sequence of items that a step generates are used as context nodes for the step that follows. For example, in the expression

```
description/name
```

the first step generates a sequence of nodes that includes all description elements. The second step evaluates the name element once for each description item in the sequence. Each time a name element is evaluated, it is evaluated with a different focus, until all name elements have been evaluated. The sequences that result from each evaluation of the step are combined, and duplicate nodes are eliminated based on node identity.

A slash character at the beginning of a path expression means that the path is to begin at the root node of the tree that contains the context node. That root node must be a document node. Because the slash can be both an operator and an operand, you should use parentheses to clarify the meaning of the slash character if you use it is as the first character of an operator. For example, to specify an empty path expression as the left operand of a multiplication operation, use (/)*5 instead of /*5. The latter expression causes an error; path expressions have the higher precedence, so DB2 interprets this expression as a path expression with a wildcard for a name test (/*) followed by the token 5.

Two slash characters at the beginning of a path expression establish an initial node sequence that contains the root of the tree in which the context node is found and all nodes descended from this root. This node sequence is used as the input to subsequent steps in the path expression. That root node must be a document node.

The value of the path expression is the combined sequence of items that results from the final step in the path. This value is a sequence of nodes or an atomic value. A path expression that returns a mixture of nodes and atomic values results in an error.

A filter expression consists of a primary expression followed by zero or more predicates. The predicates, if present, filter the result of the primary expression. The result of a filter expression consists of all the items that are returned by the primary expression for which all the predicates are true. If no predicates are specified, the result is the result of the primary expression. The result can contain nodes, atomic values, or a combination of nodes and atomic values. The ordering of the items returned by a filter expression is the same as their order in the result of the primary expression. Context positions are assigned to items based on their ordinal position in the result sequence.

XPath is case-sensitive, so you need to ensure that the case of variables you specify in an XMLQUERY function and in its XPath expression match.

The XMLQUERY function returns an XML value from the evaluation of an XPath expression using supported XPath language syntax. For example, if we're just interested in the telephone number for customer 1000, we could issue the following query (which contains a prolog and a path expression):

```
SELECT XMLQUERY('declare default element namespace
  "http://posample.org"; $d/customerinfo/phone' passing INFO as "d") as
  PHONE
FROM    DSN8910.CUSTOMER
WHERE   CID = 1000;

PHONE
<phone xmlns="http://posample.org" type="work">416-555-1358</phone>
```

The XMLEXISTS predicate lets you specify XPath variables for searching XML documents. You pass values into these variables through the passing clause. The values specified are SQL expressions that can be cast either implicitly or explicitly to the XPath variable. In the next example, we pass an SQL expression—in this case, a literal value representing the telephone number—into an XML XPath variable and then use that variable to search for our customer using the telephone number:

```
select cid, xmlquery('declare default element namespace
"http://posample.org"; $d/customerinfo/name' passing INFO as "d")
from dsn8910.customer where xmlexists('declare default element namespace
"http://posample.org"; $d//customerinfo[phone=$phone]' passing INFO
as "d", '416-555-1358' as "phone")

CID    2
____   _____
1000   <name xmlns="http://posample.org">Kathy Smith</name>
```

While DB2 for z/OS provides XQuery functionality within the SQL language, DB2 for Linux, UNIX, and Windows provides the same capability plus XQuery language support that includes DB2 access functions. For example, the db2-fn:xmlcolumn function takes a string literal argument that identifies an XML column in a table or view and returns a sequence of XML values that are in that column. The argument must be an XML column. This function permits a whole column of XML data to be returned without applying a search condition. For example, the following XQuery returns all our customer telephone numbers as separate rows:

```
XQUERY: declare default element namespace "http://posample.org";
db2-fn:xmlcolumn ('CUSTOMER.INFO')/customerinfo/phone
```

The data is returned as well-formed XML values, such as

```
<phone xmlns="http://posample.org" type="work">416-555-1358</phone>
```

To add data to XML columns, you use the SQL INSERT statement. The data you insert into an XML column must be a well-formed XML document. When you insert the data into the XML column, it must be converted to its XML hierarchical format. The DB2 data server performs this operation implicitly if the application data type is not an XML data type. You can also invoke the XMLPARSE function explicitly when you perform the insert operation to convert the data to the XML hierarchical format. To avoid character set conversions, it's important for applications to use the BLOB data type for host variable storage and not pass XML documents as literals. The data values must be well-formed XML documents. For example:

- `<a xml:space="preserve"><b> <c>c</c>b </b></a>`

- `<employee/>`

No size is specified for an XML column upon definition.

DB2 also provides the ability to store XML data in a relational database. This functionality involves the process of *decomposition*, also known as *shredding*. DB2 provides a stored procedure called XDBDECOMPXML that uses an XML schema to perform the decomposition and storage into relational tables. An XML schema is a mechanism for describing and constraining the content of XML files by indicating which elements are allowed and in which combinations. DB2 provides an XML schema repository. Shredding can be beneficial when the XML data is naturally tabular in structure.

Predicates and Filtering

In this chapter and the preceding one, you've seen "how" to code predicates using the WHERE, HAVING, and ON clauses. Predicates describe the attributes of the data. They are usually based on the columns of a table and either qualify rows (through an index) or reject rows (returned by a scan) when the table is accessed. The resulting qualified or rejected rows are independent of the access path chosen for the table.

We've discussed several different classifications of predicates:

- A compound predicate is the result of two predicates, whether simple or compound, connected by AND or OR Boolean operators.

- A local predicate references only one table. The predicate is local to that table and restricts the number of rows returned for the table.

- A join predicate involves more than one table or correlated reference. This type of predicate determines the way rows are joined from two or more tables.

- Any predicate that is not contained by a compound OR predicate structure is a Boolean term. If a Boolean term predicate evaluates to false for a particular row, the whole WHERE clause is considered false.

- A simple predicate is a predicate that is not compound, join, or Boolean term.

In addition to these types, predicates are further classified as indexable, stage 1, or stage 2.

Indexable predicate types can match index entries. Assuming an index on EMPNO, the following predicate is indexable.

```
SELECT  FIRSTNME, LASTNAME
FROM    DSN8910.EMP
WHERE   EMPNO = '000010';
```

The following predicate is not a matching predicate and is not indexable.

```
SELECT  FIRSTNME, LASTNAME
FROM    DSN8910.EMP
WHERE   JOB <> 'MANAGER';
```

To make your queries as efficient as possible, use indexable predicates in your queries and create suitable indexes on your tables. Indexable predicates allow the possible use of a matching index scan, which is often a very efficient access path.

Rows retrieved for a query go through two stages of processing:

1. *Stage 1* predicates (sometimes called *sargable*) can be applied at the first stage.

2. *Stage 2* predicates (sometimes called *nonsargable* or *residual*) cannot be applied until the second stage.

Some general rules apply regarding predicate evaluation:

- In terms of resource usage, the earlier a predicate is evaluated, the better.

- Stage 1 predicates are better than stage 2 predicates because they disqualify rows earlier and reduce the amount of processing needed at stage 2.

- When possible, try to write queries that evaluate the most restrictive predicates first. When predicates with a high filter factor are processed first, DB2 screens unnecessary rows as early as possible, which can reduce processing cost at a later stage. However, a predicate's restrictiveness is effective only among predicates of the same type and the same evaluation stage.

When DB2 evaluates the predicates, there are essentially two sets of rules that determine the order. The first set of rules describes the order of initial evaluation:

1. Indexable predicates are applied first. All matching predicates on index key columns are applied first and evaluated when the index is accessed. Next, stage 1 predicates that have not been picked as matching predicates but still refer to index columns are applied to the index. This process is called index screening.

2. Other stage 1 predicates are applied next. After data page access, stage 1 predicates are applied to the data.

3. Last, the stage 2 predicates are applied on the returned data rows.

The second set of rules describes the order of predicate evaluation within each of the stages:

1. All equal predicates (including "*column* IN *list*", where the list has only one element, or "*column* BETWEEN *value1* AND *value1*") are evaluated.

2. All range predicates and predicates of the form column IS NOT NULL are evaluated.

3 All other predicate types are evaluated.

After both sets of rules are applied, predicates are evaluated in the order in which they appear in the query. Because you specify that order, you have some control over the order of evaluation. One exception here is the fact that regardless of coding order, noncorrelated subqueries are evaluated before correlated subqueries, unless DB2 transforms the subquery into a join.

Table 6.1 shows whether predicates are indexable and whether they are processed at stage 1.

Any predicate associated with a DECFLOAT data type is neither indexable nor stage 1. An XMLEXISTS predicate is stage 2 unless an XML index exists to support the predicate. An expression may be indexable if an index exists on that expression. Also, subqueries may change between stage 1 and stage 2 if DB2 decides to correlate them, de-correlate them, or transform them into a join.

Table 6.1: Indexable and stage 1 predicates		
Predicate type	**Indexable**	**Stage 1**
COL = *value*	Y	Y
COL = *noncol expr*	Y	Y
COL IS NULL	Y	Y
COL *op value*	Y	Y
COL *op noncol expr*	Y	Y
COL BETWEEN *value1* AND *value2*	Y	Y
COL BETWEEN *noncol expr1* AND *noncol expr2*	Y	Y
value BETWEEN COL1 AND COL2	N	N
COL BETWEEN COL1 AND COL2	N	N
COL BETWEEN *expression1* AND *expression2*	Y	Y
COL LIKE '*pattern*'	Y	Y
COL IN (*list*)	Y	Y
COL <> *value*	N	Y
COL <> *noncol expr*	N	Y
COL IS NOT NULL	Y	Y
COL NOT BETWEEN *value1* AND *value2*	N	Y
COL NOT BETWEEN *noncol expr1* AND *noncolexpr2*	N	Y
value NOT BETWEEN COL1 AND COL2	N	N
COL NOT IN (*list*)	N	Y
COL NOT LIKE '*char*'	N	Y
COL LIKE '%*char*'	N	Y
COL LIKE '_*char*'	N	Y
COL LIKE *host variable*	Y	Y
T1.COL = T2 *col expr*	Y	Y

Table 6.1: Indexable and stage 1 predicates (continued)		
Predicate type	**Indexable**	**Stage 1**
T1.COL *op* T2 *col expr*	Y	Y
T1.COL <> T2 *col expr*	N	Y
T1.COL = T2 *col expr*	Y	Y
T1.COL *op* T2 *col expr*	Y	Y
T1.COL <> T2 *col expr*	N	Y
T1.COL1 = T1.COL2	N	N
T1.COL1 *op* T1.COL2	N	N
T1.COL1 <> T1.COL2	N	N
COL=(*noncor subq*)	Y	Y
COL = ANY (*noncor subq*)	N	N
COL = ALL (*noncor subq*)	N	N
COL op (*noncor subq*)	Y	Y
COL*op* ANY (*noncor subq*)	Y	Y
COL*op* ALL (*noncor subq*)	Y	Y
COL <> (*noncor subq*)	N	Y
COL <> ANY (*noncor subq*)	N	N
COL <> ALL (*noncor subq*)	N	N
COL IN (*noncor subq*)	Y	Y
(COL1,...COLn) IN (*noncor subq*)	Y	Y
COL NOT IN (*noncor subq*)	N	N
(COL1,...COLn) NOT IN (*noncor subq*)	N	N
COL = (*cor subq*)	N	N
COL = ANY (*cor subq*)	N	N
COL = ALL (*cor subq*)	N	N
COL op (*cor subq*)	N	N
COL <> ANY (*cor subq*)	N	N
COL <> ALL (*cor subq*)	N	N
COL IN (*cor subq*)	N	N
(COL1,...COLn) IN (*cor subq*)	N	N
COL NOT IN (*cor subq*)	N	N
(COL1,...COLn) NOT IN (*cor subq*)	N	N
COL IS DISTINCT FROM *value*	N	Y
COL IS NOT DISTINCT FROM *value*	Y	Y
COL IS DISTINCT FROM *noncol expr*	N	Y
COL IS NOT DISTINCT FROM *noncol expr*	Y	Y

Table 6.1: Indexable and stage 1 predicates (continued)		
Predicate type	**Indexable**	**Stage 1**
T1.COL1 IS DISTINCT FROM T2.COL2	N	N
T1.COL1 IS NOT DISTINCT FROM T2.COL2	N	N
T1.COL1 IS DISTINCT FROM T2 *col expr*	N	Y
T1.COL1 IS NOT DISTINCT FROM T2 *col expr*	Y	Y
COL IS DISTINCT FROM *(noncor subq)*	N	Y
COL IS NOT DISTINCT FROM *(noncor subq)*	Y	Y
COL IS DISTINCT FROM ANY *(noncor subq)*	N	N
COL IS NOT DISTINCT FROM ANY *(noncor subq)*	N	N
COL IS DISTINCT FROM ALL *(noncor subq)*	N	N
COL IS NOT DISTINCT FROM ALL *(noncor subq)*	N	N
COL IS NOT DISTINCT FROM *(cor subq)*	N	N
COL IS DISTINCT FROM ANY *(cor subq)*	N	N
COL IS DISTINCT FROM ANY *(cor subq)*	N	N
COL IS NOT DISTINCT FROM ANY *(cor subq)*	N	N
COL IS DISTINCT FROM ALL *(cor subq)*	N	N
COL IS NOT DISTINCT FROM ALL *(cor subq)*	N	N
EXISTS *(subq)*	N	N
NOT EXISTS *(subq)*	N	N
Expression = *value*	N	N
expression <> *value*	N	N
expression op *value*	N	N
expression op *(subq)*	N	N
XMLEXISTS	Y	N
NOT XMLEXISTS	N	N

Summary

In this chapter, we looked at some of the advanced features of SQL, including all the different types of joins: inner, left outer, right outer, and full outer.

SQL can be very useful for solving complex business problems, thanks to features such as CASE expressions, nested table expressions, unions, and subqueries. These features let you push a lot of business logic into the SQL statement.

This chapter also looked at the different classifications of predicates and how to most efficiently code them to minimize the amount of data returned.

Additional Resources

IBM DB2 9 Application Programming and SQL Guide (SC18-9841)
IBM DB2 9 SQL Reference (SC18-9854)

Practice Questions

Question 1

Given the following join coded with implicit join syntax, which of the four choices represent
the correct explicit join syntax supporting the same query?

```
SELECT    E.EMPNO, E.FIRSTNME, E.LASTNAME, D.DEPTNAME
FROM      DSN8910.EMP E, DSN8910.DEPT D
WHERE     E.WORKDEPT = D.DEPTNO
AND       E.WORKDEPT IN ('A00', 'C01')
```

○ A. SELECT E.EMPNO, E.FIRSTNME, E.LASTNAME, D.DEPTNAME
   FROM   DSN8910.EMP E
   FULL OUTER JOIN
           DSN8910.DEPT D
   ON   E.WORKDEPT = D.DEPTNO
   WHERE   E.WORKDEPT IN ('A00', 'C01')

○ B. SELECT E.EMPNO, E.FIRSTNME, E.LASTNAME, D.DEPTNAME
   FROM   DSN8910.EMP E
   LEFT JOIN
           DSN8910.DEPT D
   ON   E.WORKDEPT = D.DEPTNO
   WHERE   E.WORKDEPT IN ('A00', 'C01')

○ C. SELECT E.EMPNO, E.FIRSTNME, E.LASTNAME, D.DEPTNAME
   FROM   DSN8910.EMP E
   INNER JOIN ON E.WORKDEPT = D.DEPTNO
           DSN8910.DEPT D
   WHERE   E.WORKDEPT IN ('A00', 'C01')

○ D. SELECT E.EMPNO, E.FIRSTNME, E.LASTNAME, D.DEPTNAME
   FROM   DSN8910.EMP E
   INNER JOIN
           DSN8910.DEPT D
   ON   E.WORKDEPT = D.DEPTNO
   AND   E.WORKDEPT IN ('A00', 'C01')

Question 2

Given the CASE expression

```
CASE
        WHEN EDLEVEL < 15 THEN 'SECONDARY'
        WHEN EDLEVEL <= 19 THEN 'COLLEGE'
        ELSE
        'POST GRADUATE'
END AS SCHOOLING
```

and the values 19, 10, 15, and 22 for EDLEVEL, what will the resulting rows contain?

○ A. COLLEGE, SECONDARY, SECONDARY, POST GRADUATE

○ B. POST GRADUATE, COLLEGE, SECONDARY, POST GRADUATE

○ C. COLLEGE, SECONDARY, COLLEGE, POST GRADUATE

○ D. COLLEGE, SECONDARY, SECONDARY, POST GRADUATE

Question 3

Which of the following queries will return data from the first table, TABLE1, only when those rows don't exist in the second table, TABLE2, also eliminating any duplicates in the resulting rows?

○ A. SELECT COL1, COL2
   FROM   TABLE1
   UNION
   SELECT COL1, COL2
   FROM   TABLE2

○ B. SELECT COL1, COL2
   FROM   TABLE1
   EXCEPT ALL
   SELECT COL1, COL2
   FROM   TABLE2

○ C. SELECT COL1, COL2
   FROM   TABLE1
   NOT EXISTS
   SELECT COL1, COL2
   FROM   TABLE2

○ D. SELECT COL1, COL2
   FROM   TABLE1
   EXCEPT
   SELECT COL1, COL2
   FROM   TABLE2

Question 4

Given the following XML document and XPath expression in an XMLQUERY function, what will the output look like?

```
<customerinfo xmlns="http://posample.org" Cid="1000"><name>
Kathy Smith</name><addr country="Canada"><street>5
Rosewood</street><city>Toronto</city><prov-state>Ontario</
prov-state><pcode-zip>M6W 1E6</pcode-zip></addr><phone
type="work">416-555-1358</phone></customerinfo>

SELECT XMLQUERY('declare default element namespace
"http://posample.org"; $d/customerinfo/phone' passing
INFO as "d") as PHONE
FROM     DSN8910.CUSTOMER
WHERE    CID = 1000;
```

○ A. 416-555-1358

○ B. <phone xmlns="http://posample.org" type="work">
       416-555-1358</phone>

○ C. <416-555-1358/>

○ D. Nothing is returned.

Question 5

Given that you need to return a list of sales reps, along with the number of employees and total salary for the departments in which they work, which of the following statements would actually be successful?

```
○ A.  SELECT    TAB1.EMPNO, TAB1.SALARY,
                TAB2.AVGSAL,TAB2.HDCOUNT
      FROM      DSN8910.EMP TAB1,
      (SELECT   AVG(SALARY) AS AVGSAL,
                COUNT(*) AS HDCOUNT
        FROM    DSN8910.EMP
       WHERE    WORKDEPT = TAB1.WORKDEPT) AS TAB2
       WHERE    TAB1.JOB = 'SALESREP';
○ B.  SELECT    TAB1.EMPNO, TAB1.SALARY,
                TAB2.AVGSAL,TAB2.HDCOUNT
      FROM      DSN8910.EMP TAB1,
      TABLE(SELECT   AVG(SALARY) AS AVGSAL,
                COUNT(*) AS HDCOUNT
            FROM   DSN8910.EMP
            WHERE  WORKDEPT = TAB1.WORKDEPT) AS TAB2
       WHERE   TAB1.JOB = 'SALESREP';
```

```
○ C. SELECT   TAB1.EMPNO, TAB1.SALARY,
              TAB2.AVGSAL,TAB2.HDCOUNT
       FROM   DSN8910.EMP TAB1,
       (SELECT   AVG(SALARY) AS AVGSAL,
              COUNT(*) AS HDCOUNT
         FROM   DSN8910.EMP
         WHERE  WORKDEPT = (SELECT WORKDEPT
                                   FROM    DSN8910.EMP
                                   WHERE   WORKDEPT=TAB1.WORKDEPT)
       ) AS TAB2
       WHERE   TAB1.JOB = 'SALESREP';

○ D. SELECT   TAB1.EMPNO, TAB1.SALARY,
              TAB2.AVGSAL,TAB2.HDCOUN
       FROM   DSN8910.EMP TAB1,
       TABLE(SELECT   AVG(SALARY) AS AVGSAL,
                 COUNT(*) AS HDCOUNT
             FROM DSN8910.EMP E) AS TAB2
       WHERE   TAB1.JOB = 'SALESREP'
       AND     TAB1.WORKDEPT = E.WORKDEPT;
```

Answers

Question 1

The answer is **D**. The proper format for an explicit join is table name, JOIN clause, ON clause. This pattern continues until all joins are specified; a WHERE clause can then be used. An implicit join can be only an inner join, and so the explicit format should specify INNER JOIN or, optionally, just the word JOIN, which implies inner.

Question 2

The answer is **C**: COLLEGE, SECONDARY, COLLEGE, POST GRADUATE. CASE expressions are powerful tools for performing data conversions, whether it be report writing, data analysis, grouping, or even for performance to avoid multiple passes through the data.

Question 3

The answer is **D**. The EXCEPT will return only those rows in the first subselect that are not in the second subselect. In addition, EXCEPT ALL allows duplicate values to be returned, while EXCEPT or EXCEPT DISTINCT eliminates the duplicates.

Question 4

The answer is **B**. The XMLQUERY or XQuery db-fn:xmlcolumn function returns a well-formed XML element pulled out of a document.

Question 5

The answer is **B**. To make a correlated reference from inside a nested table expression to outside the nested table expression, the nested table expression must be preceded with the TABLE keyword. Also, the correlated reference only works from inside the table expression to outside the table expression. You cannot make references outside the table expression to tables inside the table expression.

Maintaining Data

In This Chapter

- ✔ Loading data
- ✔ Unloading data
- ✔ Reorganizing data
- ✔ Gathering statistics
- ✔ Checking data consistencies
- ✔ Resolving exceptions

In this chapter, we examine the techniques for populating and extracting DB2 data using DB2's LOAD and UNLOAD utilities. We review the different options for using these utilities and discuss some of the performance options.

We also take a close look at the REORG utility. A variety of options are available with REORG, and we'll go over many of these. We'll also examine the parallelism available for objects involved in the REORG process.

Additional maintenance topics include gathering statistics via the RUNSTATS utility and examining the data and statistics of the database management system. In addition, we cover the CHECK utilities, which help ensure that the data is always in a consistent state, and we discuss how to resolve restrictive and advisory states.

Data Movement

To get data into the DB2 tables, you can perform DML INSERTs, but for large amounts of data, INSERT isn't a feasible option. To populate tables with large amounts of data, you need to use the LOAD utility.

Similarly, to remove data from a DB2 table, you have the option of doing DML DELETEs, but, again, this method isn't optimal for large amounts of data. For unloading data, you have a few different options: the DSNTIAUL program, the UNLOAD utility, and REORG UNLOAD EXTERNAL or REORG DISCARD.

Load Utility

The LOAD utility loads data into one or more tables of a table space. The utility loads records into the tables and builds or extends any indexes defined on them. If the table space already contains data, you can choose whether you want to add the new data to the existing data or replace the existing data. The loaded data is processed by any edit or validation routine associated with the table and by any field procedure associated with any column of the table. The LOAD utility loads data coming from a sequential data set into one or more tables in the same table space. Because data is coming in from a non-DB2 source, all integrity checking must be performed, including checks for entity integrity, referential integrity, and check integrity.

The output from a LOAD DATA operation consists of a loaded table space or partition, a discard file of rejected records, and a summary report of errors encountered during processing (generated only if you specify ENFORCE CONSTRAINTS or if the LOAD involves unique indexes).

LOAD Phases

The LOAD utility consists of 10 phases:

1. **UTILINIT.** Performs initialization and startup.

2. **RELOAD.** Loads the record types and writes temporary file records for indexes and foreign keys. Check constraints are checked for each row. One pass through the sequential input data set is made. Internal commits

are taken to provide commit points at which to restart in case operation should halt in this phase. If you specified the COPYDDN or RECOVERYDDN keyword, the RELOAD phase creates inline copies.

3. If you use the SORTKEYS option, a subtask is started at the beginning of the RELOAD phase to handle the work of sorting the keys. The sort subtask initializes and waits for the main RELOAD phase to pass its keys to the SORT phase. The RELOAD phase loads the data, extracts the keys, and passes them in memory for sorting. At the end of the RELOAD phase, the last key is passed to SORT, and record sorting is completed. PREFORMAT for table spaces occurs at the end of the RELOAD phase.

4. **SORT.** Sorts temporary file records before creating indexes or validating referential constraints, if indexes or foreign keys exist. The SORT phase is skipped if all the following conditions apply for the data processed during the RELOAD phase:

   » There is not more than one key per table.

   » All keys are the same type (index key, index foreign key, nonindexed foreign key).

   » The data being loaded or reloaded is in key order (if a key exists).

   » The data being loaded or reloaded is grouped by table, and each input record is loaded into one table only.

   » If the SORTKEYS keyword is used, SORT passes the sorted keys in memory to the BUILD phase, which builds the indexes.

5. **BUILD.** Creates indexes from temporary file records for all indexes defined on the loaded tables, detects any duplicate keys, and performs preformatting of indexes.

6. **SORTBLD.** If you specified a parallel index build, all activities that normally occur in both the SORT and the BUILD phases occur in the SORTBLD phase instead.

7. **INDEXVAL.** Corrects unique index violations from the information in SYSERR, if any exist.

8. **ENFORCE.** Checks referential constraints, corrects violations, and reports them to SYSERR.

9. **DISCARD.** Copies error-causing records from the input data set to the discard dataset.

10. **REPORT.** Generates a summary report if you specified ENFORCE CONSTRAINTS or if load index validation is performed.

11. **UTILTERM.** Performs any necessary clean-up.

Loading Data

To load data into a DB2 table, you must supply an input data set and a target table. The input data set must match the target table. The following example loads data from the data set specified by the SYSREC01 DD statement into the DSN8910.EMP table.

```
LOAD DATA INDDN SYSREC01
    INTO TABLE DSN8910.EMP
```

Rules can also be selectively added to the LOAD criteria to LOAD only those rows that meet a specified criteria. Here's an example:

```
LOAD DATA INDDN SYSREC01
    INTO TABLE DSN8910.EMP
    WHEN (39:39)='C01'
```

To map the position in the file to the columns in the table:

```
LOAD DATA INDDN SYSRECEM CONTINUEIF(72:72)='X'
    INTO TABLE DSN8910.EMP
        (EMPNO      POSITION( 1)  CHAR(6),
         FIRSTNME   POSITION( 8)  VARCHAR,
         MIDINIT    POSITION(21)  CHAR(1),
         LASTNAME   POSITION(23)  VARCHAR,
         WORKDEPT   POSITION(36)  CHAR(3),
         PHONENO    POSITION(40)  CHAR(4),
         HIREDATE   POSITION(45)  DATE EXTERNAL,
         JOB        POSITION(56)  CHAR(8),
         EDLEVEL    POSITION(65)  INTEGER EXTERNAL(2),
         SEX        POSITION(68)  CHAR(1),
```

```
BIRTHDATE  POSITION(80)   DATE EXTERNAL,
SALARY     POSITION(91)   INTEGER EXTERNAL(5),
BONUS      POSITION(97)   INTEGER EXTERNAL(5),
COMM       POSITION(103)  INTEGER EXTERNAL(5))
```

This example shows how to identify the table that is to be loaded, the fields within the input record, and the format of the input record. The fields must be mapped to the columns of the table being loaded; otherwise, errors will result.

Add To or Replace

The LOAD utility's LOAD REPLACE option lets you replace data in a single-table table space or in a multiple-table table space. Using LOAD REPLACE, you can replace all the data in the table space. If you want to preserve the records that already exist in the table, use the LOAD RESUME option.

If an object is in REORG-pending status, you can perform a LOAD REPLACE of the entire table space (which resets REORG-pending status). In this situation, no other LOAD operations are allowed.

The following example shows how to replace data in one table in a single-table table space.

```
LOAD DATA
    REPLACE
       INTO TABLE DSN8710.DEPT
       (DEPTNO POSITION (1)CHAR(3),
        DEPTNAME POSITION (5)VARCHAR,
  . . .
  . . .
       )
    ENFORCE NO
```

Take care when using LOAD REPLACE on a multiple-table table space because LOAD works on an entire table space at a time. To replace all rows in a LOAD multiple-table table space, you must work with one table at a time, using the RESUME YES option on all but the first table. For example, if you have two tables in a table space, you need to perform the following steps. First, use LOAD REPLACE on the first table. This step empties out the table space and replaces just the data for the first table. Next, use LOAD with RESUME YES on the second table. This step adds the records for the second table without destroying the data in the first table.

If you need to replace just one table in a multi-table table space, then all rows need to be deleted from the table, so use LOAD with RESUME YES. If you need to add data to a table rather than replace it, again use LOAD with RESUME YES.

The RESUME keyword specifies whether data is to be loaded into an empty or a non-empty table space. RESUME NO loads records into an empty table space. RESUME YES loads records into a non-empty table space. If you specify RESUME NO and the target table space isn't empty, no data is loaded. If you specify RESUME YES and the target table space is empty, data is loaded.

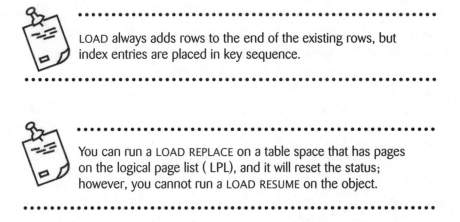

LOAD always adds rows to the end of the existing rows, but index entries are placed in key sequence.

You can run a LOAD REPLACE on a table space that has pages on the logical page list (LPL), and it will reset the status; however, you cannot run a LOAD RESUME on the object.

To delete all the data in a table space, specify LOAD REPLACE without loading any records. This technique provides an efficient way to clear a table space. To use this method, specify the input data set in the JCL as DD DUMMY. The LOAD REPLACE method is efficient for the following reasons:

- LOAD REPLACE doesn't log any rows.

- LOAD REPLACE redefines the table space.

- LOAD REPLACE retains all views and privileges associated with a table space or table.

- You can use LOG YES to make the LOAD REPLACE recoverable.

- LOAD REPLACE replaces all tables in the table space.

Logging

The LOAD utility's LOG parameter indicates whether logging is to occur during the RELOAD phase of the load process. The default value is YES, which specifies normal logging during the load process. All records that are loaded are logged. If the table space has the NOT LOGGED attribute, DB2 performs the LOAD with no logging. If LOG NO is set, no logging of data occurs during the load process. If the table space has the LOGGED attribute, the NO option sets the COPY-pending restriction against the table space or partition where the loaded table resides. No table or partition in the table space can be updated by SQL until this restriction is removed. To ensure recoverability without using the log, a COPY SHRLEVEL REFERENCE is the recommended next step.

If you load a single partition of a partitioned table space and the table space has a secondary index, some logging might occur during the build phase as DB2 logs any changes to the index structure. This logging allows recoverability of the secondary index in case an abend occurs, and it also permits concurrency. DB2 treats table spaces that were created as NOT LOGGED as if you specified LOG NO. If you specify LOG NO without specifying COPYDDN, the base table space is placed in COPY-pending status. If XML columns are nullable and not loaded, only the base table space is placed in COPY-pending status. A LOB table space affects logging while DB2 loads a LOB column, regardless of whether the LOB table space was defined with LOG YES or LOG NO.

Loading Ordered Rows

The LOAD utility loads records into a table space in the order in which they exist in the input stream. LOAD doesn't sort the input stream, and it doesn't insert records in sequence with existing records, even if a clustering index exists. To achieve clustering when loading an empty table or replacing data, sort the input stream.

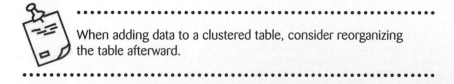

When adding data to a clustered table, consider reorganizing the table afterward.

Loading Partitions

When you specify the PART clause of the LOAD utility's INTO TABLE option, only the specified partitions of a partitioned table are loaded. If you omit the PART keyword, DB2 loads the entire table. You can specify the REPLACE and RESUME options separately by partition.

The following example loads data into the first and second partitions of the employee table. Records with '0' in column 1 replace the contents of partition 1, and records with '1' in column 1 are added to partition 2; all other records are ignored. (This example, simplified to illustrate the point, does not list field specifications for all columns of the table.)

```
LOAD DATA INDDN SYSRECEM
INTO TABLE DSN8910.EMP PART 1 REPLACE WHEN (1)= '0'
        (EMPNO     POSITION( 1)  CHAR(6),
         FIRSTNME  POSITION( 8)  VARCHAR,
         MIDINIT   POSITION(21)  CHAR(1),...
)
INTO TABLE DSN8910.EMP PART 2 RESUME YES WHEN (1)='1'
        (EMPNO     POSITION( 1)  CHAR(6),
         FIRSTNME  POSITION( 8)  VARCHAR,
         MIDINIT   POSITION(21)  CHAR(1),...
)
```

If you're not loading columns in the same order as defined by the CREATE TABLE statement, you must code field specifications for each INTO TABLE statement.

The next example assumes that the data is in separate input data sets. The data is already sorted by partition, so the WHEN clause of INTO TABLE is unnecessary. Placing the RESUME YES option before the PART option will prohibit concurrent partition processing during execution of the utility.

```
LOAD DATA INDDN EMP1 CONTINUEIF(72:72)='X'
RESUME YES
INTO TABLE DSN8910.EMP REPLACE PART 1
LOAD DATA INDDN EMP2 CONTINUEIF(72:72)='X'
RESUME YES
INTO TABLE DSN8910.EMP REPLACE PART 2
```

The following example allows partitioning independence when loading more than one partition concurrently.

```
LOAD DATA INDDN SYSREC LOG NO
INTO TABLE DSN8910.EMP PART 2 REPLACE
```

Delimited Load

The LOAD utility can accept delimited files. A delimited file is a file with row and column delimiters. The utility's FORMAT DELIMITED syntax supports the COLDEL, CHARDEL, and DECPT options for specifying the column delimiter, character delimiter, and decimal point character, respectively, on the input file. The following example uses LOAD DATA with delimited input.

```
LOAD DATA RESUME YES FORMAT DELIMITED COLDEL ';'
```

Concurrent Access

If another table needs to access data during a LOAD operation, you can specify SHRLEVEL CHANGE on a LOAD RESUME with the LOG YES option. This setting effectively combines the speed and performance of the LOAD utility with the availability and access offered by INSERT processing. This solution operates similarly to an SQL INSERT program. It claims instead of draining for best concurrent access.

This type of LOAD is LOG YES only (it will not require a COPY afterward). The solution avoids locking problems through internal monitoring of the commit scope. You can also run it in parallel for partitioned table spaces.

Referential Integrity

The LOAD utility will not load a table that has an incomplete definition. If the table has a primary key, a unique index on that key must exist. If any table named to be loaded has an incomplete definition, the LOAD job terminates.

By default, LOAD enforces referential constraints (via the ENFORCE CONSTRAINTS option). During this process, several errors can occur, including the following:

- The input file may have duplicate values of a primary key.

- The input file may have invalid foreign key values (values not in the primary key of the corresponding parent table).

- The target table might lack primary key values (values of foreign keys in dependent tables).

A primary index must be a unique index and must exist if the table definition is complete. Therefore, when a parent table is loaded, there must be at least a primary index.

You'll need an error data set, and probably also a map data set and a discard data set, for the LOAD utility to handle referential integrity errors.

A dependent table has the constraint that the values of its foreign keys must be values of the primary keys of corresponding parent tables. By default, LOAD enforces this constraint in much the same way it enforces the uniqueness of key values in a unique index. First, it loads all records to the table; subsequently, it checks their validity with respect to the constraints, identifies any invalid record by an error message, and deletes the record. The record can optionally be copied to a discard data set.

If a record fails to load because it violates a referential constraint, any of its dependent records in the same job also fail. For example, suppose that the sample project table and the project activity table belong to the same table space, that you load them both in the same job, and that some input records for the project table have an invalid department number. Then, that record fails to be loaded and doesn't appear in the loaded table; the summary report identifies it as causing a primary error.

But the project table has a primary key: the project number. In this case, the record rejected by LOAD defines a project number, and any record in the project activity table that refers to the rejected number is also rejected. The summary report identifies those records as causing secondary errors. If you use a discard data set, both types of error records are copied to it.

The deletion of invalid records does not cascade to other dependent tables already in place. Suppose now that the project and project activity tables exist in separate table spaces and that they are both currently populated and possess referential integrity. Further, suppose that the data in the project table is now to be replaced (using LOAD REPLACE) and that the replacement data for some department was inadvertently not supplied in the input data. Records referencing that department number might already exist in the project activity table. LOAD, therefore, automatically places the table space containing the project activity table (and all table spaces containing dependent tables of any table being replaced) into CHECK-pending (CHKP) status.

The CHECK-pending status indicates that the referential integrity of the table space is in doubt; the table space might contain records that violate a referential constraint. DB2 severely restricts the use of a table space in CHECK-pending status; typically, you run the CHECK DATA utility to reset this status.

ENFORCE NO

When you use the ENFORCE NO option, the LOAD utility does not enforce referential constraints. But the result is that the loaded table space might violate the constraints. The following example illustrates running without enforcing constraints.

```
LOAD DATA INDDN SYSREC01 ENFORCE NO
INTO TABLE DSN8910.EMP
```

● ●

LOAD places the loaded table space in CHECK-pending status. If you use REPLACE, all table spaces containing any dependent tables of the tables that were loaded are also placed in CHECK-pending status.

● ●

Correcting Violations

The referential integrity checking in LOAD can only delete incorrect dependent rows that were input to LOAD. Deletion isn't always the best strategy for correcting referential integrity violations.

For example, the violations may occur because parent rows don't exist. In this case, it's better to correct the parent table than to delete the dependent rows. Therefore, in this case ENFORCE NO would be more appropriate than ENFORCE CONSTRAINTS. After correcting the parent table, you can use the CHECK DATA utility to reset the CHECK-pending status.

Note that LOAD ENFORCE CONSTRAINTS is not equivalent to CHECK DATA. LOAD ENFORCE CONSTRAINTS deletes any rows that are causing referential constraint violations. CHECK DATA detects violations and optionally deletes such rows. CHECK DATA checks a complete referential structure, while LOAD checks only the rows being loaded. We provide more information about the CHECK DATA utility later in this chapter.

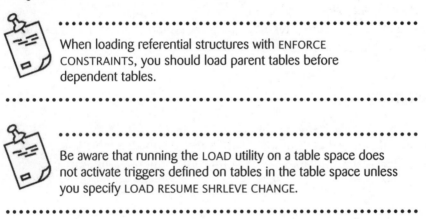

When loading referential structures with ENFORCE CONSTRAINTS, you should load parent tables before dependent tables.

Be aware that running the LOAD utility on a table space does not activate triggers defined on tables in the table space unless you specify LOAD RESUME SHRLEVE CHANGE.

Loading ROWID Columns

You can designate columns defined as ROWID as input fields using the LOAD field specification syntax diagram. If the ROWID column is part of the partitioning key, LOAD PART is not allowed. You can designate columns defined as ROWID as GENERATED BY DEFAULT or GENERATED ALWAYS. With GENERATED ALWAYS, DB2 always generates a row ID.

Columns defined as ROWID GENERATED BY DEFAULT can be set by the LOAD utility from input data. The input field must be specified as a ROWID. No conversions are allowed. The input data for a ROWID column must be a unique, valid value for a row ID. If the value of the row is not unique, a duplicate key violation occurs. In the event of such an error, the load fails. In this case, you'll need to discard the duplicate values and retry the load with a new, unique value or let DB2 generate the value of the row ID.

You can use the DEFAULTIF attribute with the ROWID keyword. If the specified condition is met, the column will be loaded with a value generated by DB2. The NULLIF attribute cannot be used with the ROWID keyword because row ID columns cannot be null.

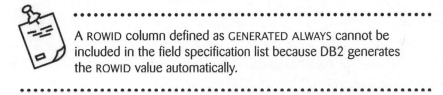

A ROWID column defined as GENERATED ALWAYS cannot be included in the field specification list because DB2 generates the ROWID value automatically.

Free Space

When loading into a non-segmented table space, LOAD leaves one free page after reaching the FREEPAGE limit, regardless of whether the records loaded belong to the same or different tables.

When loading into a segmented table space, LOAD leaves free pages, and free space on each page, in accordance with the current values of the FREEPAGE and PCTFREE parameters. These values can be set by the CREATE TABLESPACE, ALTER TABLESPACE, CREATE INDEX, or ALTER INDEX statement. LOAD leaves one free page after reaching the FREEPAGE limit for each table in the table space.

Inline Copies

Another feature of the LOAD utility is the ability to perform an inline copy. An inline copy is, for the most part, equivalent to a full image copy taken with SHRLEVEL REFERENCE. The only differences between an inline copy and a regular full image copy are that data pages and space map pages may be out of sequence or repeated, and if a compression dictionary was built during the LOAD, the pages will be duplicated. These differences, however, should be negligible in terms of the amount of space required for the copy data set, and the copy is still valid for recovery.

The inline copy increases the availability of your data because after the data has been loaded and the inline copy taken, the table space isn't left in a COPY-pending status (even if you specify LOG NO), and the data is ready to be accessed. You can take multiple image copies with this feature as well (with a maximum of two primary and two secondary image copies allowed).

Inline copies are highly recommended from a performance perspective over taking a separate copy.

Inline Statistics

Statistics can be collected as the LOAD utility executes. This feature eliminates the need to execute the RUNSTATS utility after the LOAD. Use the STATISTICS keyword to gather catalog statistics for the table space:

```
LOAD STATISTICS
INTO TABLE DSN8910.EMP
```

If the LOAD fails and has to be restarted, inline statistics are not collected, and you'll need to execute the RUNSTATS utility after the LOAD is completed.

We discuss the RUNSTATS utility further later in this chapter.

SORTKEYS

The SORTKEYS keyword improves the performance of the index key sort. SORTKEYS is the default if one of the following conditions is true:

- SHRLEVEL is not NONE.

- SHRLEVEL is NONE, and the target table has one or more indexes.

With SORTKEYS, index keys are passed in memory rather than written to work files. Avoiding this I/O to the work files improves LOAD performance. You also reduce disk space requirements for the SYSUT1 and SORTOUT data sets, especially if you provide an estimate of the number of keys to sort. If you omit this estimate or specify it as 0, LOAD writes the extracted keys to the work data set, which reduces the performance improvement of using SORTKEYS.

The SORTKEYS option reduces the elapsed time from the start of the RELOAD phase to the end of the BUILD phase. However, if the index keys are already in sorted order, or if no indexes exist, SORTKEYS provides no advantage. You can reduce the elapsed time of a LOAD job for a table space or partition with more than one defined index by specifying the parameters to invoke a parallel index build.

PREFORMAT

When DB2's preformatting delays impact the performance or execution-time consistency of high INSERT applications and you can predict the table size for a business processing cycle, LOAD PREFORMAT or REORG PREFORMAT might be a technique to consider. This technique will be of value only if DB2's preformatting imposes a measurable delay on the INSERT processing or causes inconsistent elapsed times for INSERT applications. The recommendation is to conduct a performance assessment before and after using LOAD PREFORMAT or REORG PREFORMAT to quantify the technique's value in your environment.

The PREFORMAT technique eliminates the need for DB2 to preformat new pages in a table space during execution time. Although this measure can eliminate execution-time delays, it adds the preformatting cost as setup before the application's execution. LOAD or REORG PREFORMAT primes a new table space and prepares it for INSERT processing. When the preformatted space is used and DB2 must extend the table space, normal data-set extending and preformatting occurs.

Preformatting for INSERT processing may be desirable for high INSERT tables that will receive a predictable amount of data, because the technique can pre-allocate all the required space before the application's execution. This would be the case for a table that acts as a repository for work items coming into a system that are subsequently used to feed a back-end task that processes the work items.

Preformatting of a table space containing a table used for query processing may cause a table space scan to read additional empty pages, extending the elapsed time for these queries. LOAD or REORG PREFORMAT is not recommended for tables that have a high ratio of reads to inserts if the reads result in table space scans.

You can also use the PREFORMAT option on the REORG utility.

Parallel Index Builds

LOAD builds all the indexes defined for any table being loaded. At the same time, it checks for duplicate values of any unique index key. If any duplicate values exist, none of the corresponding rows are loaded. Error messages identify the input records that produce duplicates, and the records are optionally copied to a discard data set. At the end of the job, a summary report lists all errors found. For unique indexes, any two null values are taken to be equal unless the index was created with the UNIQUE WHERE NOT NULL clause. In that case, if the key is a single column, it can contain any number of null values, although its other values must be unique.

Neither the loaded table nor its indexes contain any of the records that might have produced an error. Using the error messages, you can identify faulty input records, correct them, and load them again. If you use a discard data set, you can correct the records there and add them to the table using LOAD RESUME.

A *parallel index build* reduces the elapsed time for a LOAD job by sorting the index keys and rebuilding multiple indexes in parallel rather than sequentially. Optimally, a pair of subtasks processes each index; one subtask sorts extracted keys, while the other builds the index. LOAD begins building each index as soon as the corresponding sort emits its first sorted record. LOAD uses parallel index build when there is more than one index to be built and the LOAD utility specifies the SORTKEYS keyword (along with a non-zero estimate of the number of keys) in the utility statement. You can choose to have the utility dynamically allocate the data sets needed by SORT, or you can provide the necessary data sets in the job.

LOAD Parallelism for Partitioned Table Spaces

LOAD parallelism helps when you're dealing with short windows in which to load a lot of data. This feature lets you LOAD multiple partitions of a partitioned table space in parallel in the same job.

Large loads have posed a problem in the past when they involved nonpartitioned secondary indexes, often causing the DBA to have to drop and recreate the NPSIs to get large data loads done. With LOAD parallelism, you can use multiple tasks within a single job to load the partitions in parallel and submit a single job with several input files to be loaded in parallel. The performance is fast, and contention on the NPSI is eliminated. The number of CPUs and virtual storage available, as well as the number of available threads, will determine the number of parallel load tasks.

The following example illustrates the necessary syntax. In this example, we're loading two partitions in parallel, and part 1 is also being preformatted:

```
LOAD INTO TABLE tab1 PART 1 INDDN infile1 PREFORMAT
     INTO TABLE tab1 PART 2 INDDN infile2
```

To get LOAD parallelism on the initial load in the case where the data set definitions have been deferred (the DDL was run with DEFINE NO), do a LOAD with an empty data file on the first partition; you can then load the other partitions in parallel.

Cursors

The LOAD utility also permits you to define a cursor for the input data using the EXEC SQL and INCURSOR parameters. You can use this cursor to invoke the DB2 family's cross-loader function, which lets you load data from any DRDA remote server. A few restrictions apply. For example, you can't load into the same table as the defined cursor, use SHRLEVEL CHANGE, or use field specifications or discard processing.

Here's an example of using a cursor in a LOAD utility:

```
EXEC SQL
  DECLARE C1 CURSOR
        FOR SELECT * FROM DSN8910.EMP
ENDEXEC
LOAD DATA
INCURSOR(C1)
REPLACE
INTO DSN8910.EMP2
```

Unloading Data

As we noted at the beginning of the chapter, DB2 provides several alternatives to DML DELETEs for removing large amounts of data from DB2 tables. Let's turn our attention now to the three techniques: the DSNTIAUL program, the UNLOAD utility, and REORG UNLOAD EXTERNAL or REORG DISCARD.

DSNTIAUL

You can use the DB2 unload program DSNTIAUL to unload data. DSNTIAUL can also create control statements for use with the DB2 LOAD utility. You can find this program in the SDSNSAMP target installation data set, which is created as part of the Installation Verification Procedure (IVP).

UNLOAD Utility

DB2's UNLOAD utility unloads data from one or more source objects to one or more Basic Sequential Access Method (BSAM) sequential data sets in external formats. The source of the data can be

- DB2 table spaces
- DB2 image copy data sets (full or incremental)
  - » Image copies that were taken with the CONCURRENT keyword aren't usable as input to the UNLOAD utility.
- Copies taken with DSN1COPY

The UNLOAD utility supports unloading rows from an entire table space, from specific partitions, or from individual tables. It can also just unload specific columns of a table through the use of a field specification list. If a table space is partitioned, you can unload all the selected partitions into a single data set, or you can unload each partition in parallel into physically distinct data sets. Multiple tables from the same table space can be unloaded in the same job; however, the unload doesn't have the ability to perform joins on tables. If you don't specify the tables to be unloaded, the utility unloads all tables in the table space.

The UNLOAD utility provides other capabilities, including the ability to change the data types of selected columns, change the order of the columns, use sampling to obtain a cross section of data, specify conditions for row selection, and limit the number of rows to be unloaded.

The output records written by the UNLOAD utility are compatible as input to the LOAD utility. This fact gives you the ability to reload the original table or different tables with the data from the UNLOAD.

Output from UNLOAD consists of one or more of the following:

- An unloaded table space or partition

- A discard file of rejected records

- SYSPUNCH output that contains the LOAD control statements

The UNLOAD utility has three phases:

1. **UTILINIT.** Initialization and setup.

2. **UNLOAD.** Unloading records to sequential data sets.

3. **UTILTERM.** Cleanup.

During the UNLOAD phase, DB2 makes one pass through the input data set. If UNLOAD is processing a table space or a partition, DB2 takes internal commits to provide commit points at which to restart in case operation should halt in this phase.

Here's a sample use of the UNLOAD utility:

```
UNLOAD TABLESPACE DSN8D91A.DSNS910E
FROM TABLE DSN8910.EMP
WHEN (WORKDEPT = 'C01' AND SALARY > 50000)
```

Delimited Unload

Paralleling the LOAD utility, the UNLOAD utility can produce a delimited output file. The DELMITED syntax on UNLOAD supports the COLDEL, CHARDEL, and DECPT options for specifying the column delimiter, character delimiter, and decimal point character, respectively, on the output file.

Using REORG to Remove Data

The REORG utility gives you the option of unloading or discarding data during REORG utility execution. REORG's UNLOAD EXTERNAL option unloads selected data and places it into a data set that you can then load into a table. The DISCARD option permits selected removal of rows during REORG utility execution. We provide more information about the REORG utility and these options in the next section.

Data Maintenance

The physical distribution of the data stored in tables has a significant effect on the performance of applications that use those tables. The way the data is stored in a table is affected by the update, insert, and delete operations on the table. For example, a delete operation may leave empty pages of data that may not be reused later. Also, updates to variable-length columns may result in a new column value not fitting in the same data page. This situation can cause the row to be moved to a different page and so produce internal gaps or unused space in the table. As a consequence, DB2 may have to read more physical pages to retrieve the information the application requires.

These scenarios are almost unavoidable. However, as the database administrator, you can use the data maintenance utilities provided in DB2 to optimize the physical distribution of the data stored in your tables. Two related utilities or commands can help you organize the data in your tables: REORG and RUNSTATS.

Analyzing Data's Physical Organization

As we mentioned, certain SQL operations can produce internal gaps in tables. So the question you may ask is, how can you determine the state of the physical organization of your tables or indexes? How can you know how much space is currently being used and how much is free?

With the information collected from the system catalog tables, you can generally determine the state of any table space or index space.

You should establish a data maintenance policy to ensure that the data in your table is stored as efficiently as possible. If you don't, you may discover that your application performance starts to suffer. Poor physical organization of the data can cause performance to degrade, so you need to perform preventive maintenance on the tables to avoid this problem.

REORG Utility

The REORG utility reorganizes data in table spaces and in indexes. Let's first take a look at how you use REORG with tables spaces.

Reorganizing Table Spaces

During a reorganization of a table space, the following activities occur:

- The data in the table space and the corresponding indexes defined on the table in the table space are reorganized.

- The space of dropped tables is reclaimed (if it wasn't reclaimed before).

- Free space is provided.

- New allocation units become effective.

- Segments are realigned, and the rows of the tables are rearranged in clustering-index sequence (except for simple table spaces with multiple tables).

- Overflow pointers are eliminated.

- The corresponding indexes are rebuilt from scratch.

- The version number of each row is updated to the current version number.

The REORG TABLESPACE utility operates in the following phases.

1. **UTILINIT.** This phase is the initialization phase. It performs the setup operations for the utility.

2. **UNLOAD.** This phase unloads the rows of the table space and writes to the unload data set specified in the UNLDDN parameter in the utility.The default DD name for the unload data set is SYSREC, and the unload data set is also known as the SYSREC data set. The type of table space, the number of tables in the table space, and whether the tables have explicit clustering indexes will affect the sequence in which the utility unloads the rows.

3. **RELOAD.** During this phase, the rows are reloaded from the unload data set into the table space. The sequence in which the rows are unloaded will be the sequence in which they are contained in the unload data set and subsequently the sequence in which they will be reloaded. For a segmented table space, all rows for a table are unloaded together and then restored together, resulting in the segments for the table being contiguous. Free space is reserved in the pages, and free pages are provided for future insertions during the reloading, according to the active PCTFREE and FREEPAGE values for the table space.

4. **SORT.** In this phase, the key/RID pairs for the various indexes are sorted using the DFSORT program by index, key, and RID. At the end of this phase, DB2 passes the sorted key/RID pairs in memory to the BUILD phase.

5. **BUILD.** In this phase, DB2 uses the output of the SORT phase (the sorted key/RID pairs for the different indexes) to build the indexes for the tables in the table space.

6. **SORTBLD.** If parallel index build occurs, all activities that normally take place in both the SORT phase and the BUILD phase occur in the SORTBLD phase instead.

7. **LOG.** This phase processes the log iteratively and appends changed pages to the full image copies. The LOG phase occurs only if you specify SHRLEVEL CHANGE or SHRLEVEL REFERENCE PART *x*.

8. **SWITCH.** The SWITCH phase switches access to a shadow copy of table space or partition. This phase occurs only if you specify SHRLEVEL CHANGE or SHRLEVEL REFERENCE.

9. **UTILTERM.** This final phase performs cleanup operations, such as releasing virtual storage.

The phases of the REORG utility are performed sequentially, one after the other. Exploiting other features of REORG causes many of the phases to be performed in parallel.

Segmented Table Space

If the target table space is segmented, REORG unloads and reloads by table. If an explicit clustering index exists on a table in a segmented table space, the utility unloads that table in clustering sequence. If no explicit clustering index exists, the table is unloaded in physical row and segment order.

For segmented table spaces, REORG does not normally have to reclaim space from dropped tables. Space freed by dropping tables in a segmented table space is immediately available if the table space can be accessed when the DROP TABLE statement is executed. If the table space cannot be accessed when DROP TABLE is executed, REORG reclaims the space for dropped tables. After execution of the REORG, the segments for each table are contiguous.

Partitioned Table Space

If a table space is partitioned, you don't need to reorganize the entire table space. You can choose to simply reorganize one partition if necessary. If you reorganize a single partition or a range of partitions, all indexes of the table space are affected. Depending on how disorganized the nonpartitioning indexes are, they may need to be reorganized as well. The following example shows how to reorganize a partition of a table space.

```
REORG TABLESPACE DSN8D91A.DSN8S91E
PART 3
SORTDATA
SORTDEVT SYSDA
```

Ranges of partitions can also be REORGed. The following syntax reorganizes parts 3, 4, 5, and 6.

```
REORG TABLESPACE DSN8D91A.DSN8S91E
PART 3:6
```

LOB Table Space

Reorganizing a large object table space is a separate task from reorganizing the base table space. A LOB table space defined with LOG YES or LOG NO will affect logging while a LOB column is reorganized. To avoid leaving the LOB table space in COPY-pending status after the REORG, specify LOG YES and SHRLEVEL NONE when you reorganize a LOB table space.

A LOB REORG has four phases: UTILINIT, REORGLOB, SWITCH, and UTILTERM.

For SHRLEVEL NONE, the utility rebuilds the LOB table space in place. The utility does not unload or reload LOBs. The LOB table space is set to RECOVER-pending status at the start of processing; this status is reset when the REORGLOB phase is completed. If the REORGLOB phase fails, the LOB table space remains in RECOVER-pending status.

For SHRLEVEL REFERENCE, the utility unloads LOBs to a shadow data set. RECOVER-pending is not set on the LOB table space. Any error during this phase will leave the original data set intact. The utility will remove embedded free space and try to make the LOB pages contiguous. As a result, prefetch should be more effective. REORG also reclaims physical space if available.

REORG Options

Let's take a look at some of the most important parameters of the REORG utility and talk about how some of them help to achieve parallelism in the REORG phases.

SHRLEVEL

The SHRLEVEL parameter determines the level of access allowed during the REORG. Option NONE states that during the unload phase applications can read but not write to the affected area and that during the reload phase applications have no access to the data. The REFERENCE option allows read access during the unload and reload phases. SHRLEVEL CHANGE allows reading and writing during both the unload and reload phases.

If you need a more restrictive access (e.g., no access at all by applications or by end users), start the table space in UT (utility mode). These are all offline REORGs. The following example does not allow concurrent writes during the reload.

```
REORG TABLESPACE DSN8D91A.DSN8S91E
SHRLEVEL REFERENCE
```

If an object is in REORG-pending (REORP) status, you'll need to execute a REORG SHRLEVEL NONE on the affected data.

SORTDATA

The SORTDATA parameter specifies that the data is to be unloaded by a table space scan and sorted in clustering order. The default is SORTDATA YES unless you specify UNLOAD ONLY or UNLOAD EXTERNAL; if you specify one of these options, the default is SORTDATA NO. The NO option specifies that the data is to be unloaded in the order of the clustering index. You cannot specify SORTDATA NO with SHRLEVEL CHANGE.

Specify SORTDATA NO if either of the following conditions is true:

- The data is in or near perfect clustering order, and the REORG utility is used to reclaim space from dropped tables.
- The data is very large, and insufficient disk space is available for sorting.

DB2 ignores SORTDATA YES for some of the catalog and directory table spaces.

The following example uses the SORTDATA keyword on the REORG of a partitioned table space.

```
REORG TABLESPACE DSN8D91A.DSN8S91E
PART 3
SORTDATA
SORTDEVT SYSDA
```

Parallel Index Build

When you use SORTKEYS (this option is on by default), DB2 performs many operations in parallel. These operations can be multiple sort and index build operations or multiple SORT and BUILD phases performed in parallel by the subtasks of the allocated task groups. When these operations occur in parallel, they take place in the SORTBLD phase. This phase encompasses the sort and build activities for all indexes involved in the reorganization.

The SORTBLD phase, which the allocated task groups jointly perform, overlaps partially with the RELOAD phase. Each index is constructed by a predefined task group. The task group can process multiple indexes. The proper SORT tasks for the indexes pass the key/RID pairs to the DFSORT program for sorting as the keys for the indexes are extracted from the rows and the new RIDs for the rows are determined. This procedure lets the sorting of the key/RID pairs be performed in parallel with the RELOAD phase. If multiple tasks groups are used, the key/RID pairs for the various indexes are then sorted in parallel.

When DFSORT emits the sorted key/RID pairs, the BUILD tasks of the index begin constructing the index. The building of the indexes will partially overlap with the reloading of the table space and the sorting of the key/RID pairs (even of those for the same index). DB2 constructs the various indexes in parallel if multiple task groups are used.

The construction of an index finishes only after the table space has been reloaded completely, despite the fact that the building of the indexes happens in parallel with the reloading of the table space. The task groups have three subtasks if you've requested inline statistics. The third subtask, STATISTICS, collects the requested statistics as the rows are reloaded and the indexes are built.

Each SORT task requires a sort work data set and a message data set. The message data set can be common to all task groups. It is assigned to SYSOUT.

Logging

The REORG utility's LOG option specifies whether records are logged during the reload phase of REORG. If the records are not logged, the table space is recoverable only after an image copy has been taken. If you specify COPYDDN, RECOVERYDDN, SHRLEVEL REFERENCE, or SHRLEVEL CHANGE, an image copy is taken in parallel during REORG execution.

When you specify LOG YES, DB2 logs records during the reload phase. This option is not allowed for any table space in DSNDB01 or DSNDB06 or if you use the SHRLEVEL REFERENCE or SHRLEVEL CHANGE option. If you specify SHRLEVEL NONE (explicitly or by default), the default is LOG YES. However, if you specify LOG NO with SHRLEVEL NONE, previous image copies may not be candidates for use during certain recoveries.

With LOG NO, DB2 does not log records. This puts the table space in COPY-pending status if either of two conditions is true:

- REORG is executed at thc local site, and the REORG does not specify COPYDDN, SHRLEVEL REFERENCE, or SHRLEVEL CHANGE.

- REORG is executed at the remote site, and RECOVERYDDN is not specified.

Online Reorganization

Most reorganizations limit or restrict access to the table space that is being reorganized. This is especially true if you use SHRLEVEL NONE. Write access is prohibited during the UNLOAD phase, and no type of access is allowed during the RELOAD phase. With today's increasing demand for 24-hour service, it becomes less and less acceptable to block access for longer periods of time or at all. To deal with this issue, DB2 supports *online reorganization (OLR)*—that is, a reorg during which online processes can access the table space for most of the time. Online reorg comes in two flavors.

If you specify SHRLEVEL REFERENCE, you'll have read access to the table space and access via the associated indexes for most of the time. There will be only a small window within the SWITCH phase during which no access is allowed. SHRLEVEL REFERENCE reorganizations are also referred to as *read-only online reorgs*.

If you specify SHRLEVEL CHANGE, you'll have read/write access to the table space and access via the indexes associated with the table space for most of the time. During a small period at the end of the LOG phase, you'll have read access only, and during a small period within the SWITCH phase, no access at all is allowed. SHRLEVEL CHANGE reorgs are known as *read/write online reorgs*. The LOG and SWITCH phases exist only for online reorganizations.

Read-Only OLR

Online REORG uses shadow data sets for the table space and the indexes being reorganized. Collectively, the shadow data sets for a table space are called the *corresponding shadow table space*. Similarly, the shadow data sets for an index are known as the *corresponding shadow index* or *shadow index space*. These data sets never exist in the catalog.

During an online reorganization, the rows of the original tables space (i.e., of the space being reorganized), are unloaded (UNLOAD phase) and then reloaded into the shadow table space (RELOAD phase). The reorganized indexes for the table space aren't constructed in the original index spaces but in the shadow indexes spaces (SORTBLD phase or SORT/BUILD phases). During the SWITCH phase, the shadow data sets for the table/index spaces replace the original data sets, and all access is directed to them. As part of the switching process, the original data sets for the table/index spaces are renamed, and the shadow data sets receive their former names. Because the original table space doesn't change during a read-only online reorganization, these four phases are sufficient.

For DB2-managed table/index spaces, DB2 automatically creates the shadow data sets in the respective storage groups with the respective active space parameters. It also deletes the original data sets after a successful switch. For user-managed table/index spaces, you must define, using Access Method Services (AMS), the data sets for the shadow tables/index spaces yourself. During the UTILTERM phase, the REORG utility completes the switch by renaming the original data sets again. They now receive the data set names that the respective shadow data sets had before the reorganization. It's your responsibility to delete these data sets.

During all phases except the SWITCH phase, the rows of the table space can be read, and the indexes of the table space can be used. However, during the SWITCH phase, no access to the table space or through the indexes is allowed.

FASTSWITCH

The FASTSWITCH keyword (on by default) reduces the time that data is unavailable during the SWITCH phase. When you use this option, the online reorg no longer renames data sets, replacing the approximately three-second outage associated with the renaming of original and shadow data set copies with a memory-speed switch of MVS catalog entries. The utility also doesn't have to invoke AMS to rename the data set.

You cannot use the FASTSWITCH keyword on catalog or directory objects.

A point-in-time (PIT) recovery works in spite of the changed data set name, even when using concurrent copies.

Read/Write OLR

Read/write online REORG (SHRLEVEL CHANGE) doesn't let you specify parameter SORTDATA, NONSYSREC, or SYSKEYS; the reorg always operates as if these parameters were specified. Thus, it uses DFSORT to sort the rows during the UNLOAD phase and does not use the unload data set. This method sorts the key/RID pairs for the indexes in parallel with the RELOAD phase and with the building of the indexes in the shadow index spaces. If the sort work data sets are dynamically allocated or explicitly allocated for multiple task groups, DB2 builds the indexes in parallel with each other.

The algorithm for read/write online reorg is basically the same as for read-only online reorg. However, the fact that changes are allowed during the UNLOAD, RELOAD, and SORTBLD phases is reflected by an additional phase, the LOG phase. During the switch, DB2 applies the changes performed throughout these phases to the shadow table/index spaces. Even during most of the LOG phase, the user has full read/write access. Only at the end of the LOG phase must the REORG utility limit access to read-only to guarantee that the reorganization comes to an end.

During a read/write online reorg, no access is allowed during the SWITCH phase. Also, a read/write online REORG always creates an inline copy for the table space being reorganized. Therefore, you don't need to create a full image copy after the reorganization of the table space.

If a –TERM UTIL command is issued during the SWITCH phase, you can simply restart the REORG utility.

Mapping Table

During the LOG phase of a read/write online reorg, changes to the original table space in the DB2 log are applied to the shadow table space and, consequently, to the shadow index. The RIDs for the DB2 records in the DB2 log point to the original table space. To map the changes to the shadow table space, the REORG utility uses a mapping table (actually a unique index over the mapping table). This table and index must be created before the REORG utility execution.

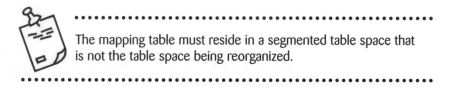

The mapping table must reside in a segmented table space that is not the table space being reorganized.

The following sample DDL shows the four columns in the mapping table.

```
CREATE TABLE MAP_TABLE
   (TYPE CHAR(1) NOT NULL,
    SOURCE_RID CHAR(5) NOT NULL,
    TARGET_XRID CHAR(9) NOT NULL,
    LRSN CHAR(6) NOT NULL)
IN DSN8910.MAPTS;

CREATE UNIQUE INDEX MAPINX1 ON MAP_TABLE
   (SOURCE_RID ASC,
    TYPE,
    TARGET_XRID,
    LRSN);
```

The SOURCE_RID contains the RIDs for the rows in the original table space, whereas the column and the TARGET_XRID contain the (extended) RIDs for the rows in the shadow table space. The key of the mapping table index has the same four columns as the mapping table, but in a different sequence.

You must specify the name of the mapping table via the MAPPING TABLE parameter for the REORG utility; it can be any name you choose. Here's an example that uses the mapping table:

```
    REORG TABLESPACE DSN8D91A.DSN8S91D
    SHRLEVEL CHANGE
    ...
  MAPPING TABLE DB2USER1.MAP_TABLE
```

DELETE, INSERT, SELECT, and UPDATE authorization is required on the mapping table.

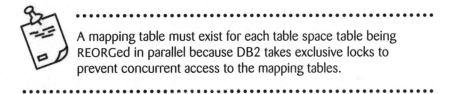

A mapping table must exist for each table space table being REORGed in parallel because DB2 takes exclusive locks to prevent concurrent access to the mapping tables.

Only the index over the mapping table is filled; therefore, it's sufficient to allocate as little space as possible to the mapping table. Assuming the entire table space is being reorganized, you should assign at least the following space for this index:

```
  1.1 * num_rows_in_TS * 27 bytes
```

For reorgs of partitions of the table space only, use the number of rows in the partitions instead of the number of rows in the table space.

Controlling Log Iterations

During read/write online reorganizations, application programs or end users may change the data in the original table space up to the end of the LOG phase.

In a first step, the LOG phase applies the changes made during the UNLOAD, RELOAD, and SORTBLD phases to the shadow table space and the shadow indexes. During most of the LOG phase, read/write access to the original table space is allowed. Because the data in the original table space may have changed during the first iteration, the second iteration must apply the changes made during the first iteration, a third iteration must apply the changes made during the second iteration, and so on. This cycle could potentially cause the LOG phase to never end.

Ideally, fewer and fewer changes must be applied with each iteration. However, it's conceivable that an endless number of iterations may be necessary. Therefore, the REORG utility must ultimately limit the access during the LOG phase to read, only to come to a final iteration. Once this is done, it must then apply only the changes accumulated during the previous iteration before it can enter the SWITCH phase.

Because switching to read-only access impacts the operating environment, the REORG utility gives you the ability to specify for how long a period this can be tolerated. You use the MAXRO parameter to define this period.

REORG estimates how long the next iteration will take based on the changes for the previous iteration. If its estimate is lower than or equal to the value specified via the MAXRO parameter, the utility switches to read-only access, or even to no access depending on what you requested, and the last iteration takes place. The actual time of the last iteration may be larger than the estimate or the value you specified; however, it should not be substantially larger.

If you specified DRAIN WRITERs (either explicitly or by default), the REORG utility drains all writers (i.e., waits until all units of recovery accessing the table space have been committed) and does not allow new units of recovery to begin. In the case of DRAIN ALL, REORG drains all the users (i.e., waits until all readers and writers are off the table space and prevents further read or write access). Readers may have locks (CLAIMs) not being released before they commit. Therefore, it's imperative that even long-running read-only programs commit from time to time to allow online reorganizations to succeed.

The default value for the MAXRO parameter is 300 seconds. MAXRO DEFER causes log processing to continue indefinitely until you change MAXRO by means of the ALTER UTILITY command, until a different condition forces the last iteration (LONGLOG), or until the reorganization is terminated.

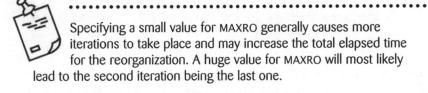

Specifying a small value for MAXRO generally causes more
iterations to take place and may increase the total elapsed time
for the reorganization. A huge value for MAXRO will most likely
lead to the second iteration being the last one.

Controlling Long Log Situations

If you specify a small value for MAXRO, the log processing of the REORG utility
may not catch up with the change activities performed for the table space. This
situation is referred to as the *long log condition*. REORG raises a long log condition
if the number of log records processed by the next iteration won't be sufficiently
lower than the number of log records for the previous iteration and the next log
iteration will take longer than the specified MAXRO value (the next iteration won't
be the last one).

There is an option you can use to specify what should happen in the case of long
log situations. After message DSNU3771 is issued and the time specified through
the DELAY parameter has passed, DB2 performs the action specified by the
LONGLOG parameter. The action can be CONTINUE (continue log processing
iterations), TERM (terminate the REORG), or DRAIN (drain writers to force the last
log iteration—that is, wait until all units of recovery involving the table space have
been committed and prevent new units of recovery for the table space).

If necessary, you can change the time specified on the DELAY
parameter and the actions specified in LONGLOG parameter by
using the ALTER command.

REORG DEADLINE

The REORG utility also lets you control when a reorg must be completed. Using
the DEADLINE parameter, you can specify a deadline at which time the reorg must
finish. The deadline can be an absolute time (a timestamp) or a relative time
(a labeled duration expression using CURRENT DATA or CURRENT TIMESTAMP).

If REORG estimates that the SWITCH phase won't be completed before the specified deadline, it issues the message that the DISPLAY UTILITY command would issue and terminates the reorganization.

You can change the DEADLINE using the ALTER UTILITY command if it appears that the reorg won't finish before its deadline and you don't want the reorg to be terminated.

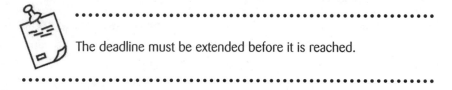

The deadline must be extended before it is reached.

Inline Statistics During REORG

After reorganization, the old statistics for the reorganized table space, index, or partitions are no longer valid. Neither are the old statistics for the indexes associated with a table space being reorganized. You need to establish new statistics for these objects to make sure the DB2 optimizer has the proper statistics for access path determination. (For more information about access paths, see Chapter 17.)

You can execute the RUNSTATS utility after the reorganization to collect new statistics, but you can also have the REORG utility do this work for all the associated objects. To request these *inline statistics*, you specify the STATISTICS clause on the REORG. The REORG utility will update the DB2 catalog tables accordingly and/or report the statistics in its output listing.

Here's an example that requests inline statistics during a REORG:

```
REORG TABLESPACE DSN8D91A.DSN8S91E
SORTDATA STATISTICS PART 3
```

By letting REORG perform inline statistics saves, you avoid the need to run the RUNSTATS utility after the REORG. Running the statistics inline is faster because the work is performed in parallel by subtasks during the REORG.

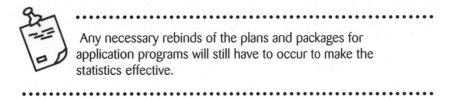

Any necessary rebinds of the plans and packages for application programs will still have to occur to make the statistics effective.

The keywords you can specify as a part of the STATISTICS clause are the same as those you can specify for RUNSTATS, and the provided functions are the same. These functions include statistics sampling, a topic we discuss later in the chapter.

REORG DISCARD and REORG UNLOAD

You can use the REORG utility to remove other rows that are no longer needed. The utility lets you select the rows you want to remove (in addition to those that must be discarded because they no longer belong to any partition) by means of the DISCARD clause. The DISCARD clause can contain one or more FROM TABLE specifications identifying the tables from which the rows should be removed.

In the FROM TABLE specification, you name a table of the table space from which rows should be removed and specify the selection condition (WHEN condition) for the removal of the rows. In the WHEN condition, you can combine basic predicates using AND and OR to select the rows to be discarded. The predicates must refer to columns of the specified table.

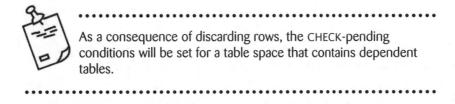

As a consequence of discarding rows, the CHECK-pending conditions will be set for a table space that contains dependent tables.

REORG also lets you unload data using the UNLOAD options. There are various forms of UNLOAD, including CONTINUE, PAUSE, ONLY, and EXTERNAL.

CONTINUE tells REORG to continue processing after the data is unloaded, and ONLY says to stop and terminate after the unload.

PAUSE tells REORG to stop after the UNLOAD phase. One common use for REORG UNLOAD PAUSE is to unload the data from the table space and then remove the extents from user-defined data sets using Access Method Services. The REORG status is recorded in the SYSUTIL directory table. You could then restart the utility at the next phase (RESTART(PHASE)).

The UNLOAD EXTERNAL option lets you unload data into a data set that will be in a format that the LOAD utility can use.

The following examples demonstrate UNLOAD EXTERNAL and DISCARD.

```
REORG TABLESPACE DSN8D91A.DSN8S91D
   UNLOAD EXTERNAL
   FROM TABLE DSN8910.DEPT
   WHEN (MGRNO = '000010')

REORG TABLESPACE DSN8D91A.DSN8S91D
   DISCARD
   FROM TABLE DSN8910.DEPT
   WHEN (MRGNO = '000010')
```

Reorganizing Indexes

Reorganizing an index reclaims fragmented space and improves access performance. You can sometimes improve performance simply by reorganizing the index and not necessarily the table space. The REORG INDEX statement supports options similar those of REORG TABLESPACE, including degree of access to the data during reorganization, inline statistics, preformatting of pages, and online reorg features.

The REORG INDEX statement reorganizes the entire index (all parts if partitioned). REORG INDEX PART *n* reorganizes PART *n* of a partitioned index.

The execution phases of REORG INDEX are fairly similar to those of REORG TABLESPACE:

1. **UTILINIT.** Performs initialization and setup.

2. **UNLOAD.** Unloads the index space and writes keys to a sequential data set.

3. **BUILD.** Builds indexes and updates index statistics.

4. **LOG.** Processes the log iteratively (used only if you specify SHRLEVEL CHANGE).

5. **SWITCH.** Switches access to a shadow copy of the index space or partition (used only if you specify SHRLEVEL REFERENCE or SHRLEVEL CHANGE).

6. **UTILTERM.** Performs any necessary cleanup.

The following is an example of executing the REORG INDEX utility with inline statistics.

```
REORG INDEX DSN8910.XEMP2
SHRLEVEL REFERENCE STATISTICS
```

Triggering Reorganizations

Data that is organized well physically can improve the performance of access paths that rely on index or data scans. Well-organized data can also help reduce the amount of disk storage used by an index or table space. If your main reason for reorganizing is performance, the best way to determine when to reorganize is to watch your statistics for increased I/O, getpages, and processor consumption. When performance degrades to an unacceptable level, analyze the statistics described in the guidelines in this section to develop your own rules for when to reorganize in your particular environment. Note, though that running the REORG utility can be quite expensive and disruptive, so it's desirable to run REORG only when a table space or index absolutely requires it.

We can offer some general guidelines for determining when to reorganize. There are a couple of ways to make the determination: by querying the catalog to manually determine the need to run a REORG or by using the REORG utility to trigger REORGs when necessary.

Catalog Queries

Sample job DSNTESP in data set SDSNSAMP includes several catalog queries that can help you determine when to reorganize You can use these queries, shown below, as input to SPUFI.

List table spaces that are candidates for reorganization.

```
SELECT DBNAME, TSNAME
 FROM SYSIBM.SYSTABLEPART
  WHERE ((CARD > 0 AND (NEARINDREF + FARINDREF) * 100 / CARD > 10)
  OR PERCDROP  > 10);
```

Indirect references (growth in the NEARINDREF and FARINDREF values) can be caused by updates to columns defined with VARCHARs where the lengths of the rows change.

List index spaces that are candidates for reorganization.

```
SELECT IXNAME, IXCREATOR
 FROM SYSIBM.SYSINDEXPART
   WHERE LEAFDIST > 200;
```

Return the number of varying-length rows in a table space that were relocated to other pages because of an update. This information provides an indication of how well DASD space is being used.

```
SELECT CARD, NEARINDREF, FARINDREF
   FROM SYSIBM.SYSTABLEPART
   WHERE DBNAME = 'xxx'
   AND TSNAME = 'yyy';
```

Return the percentage of unused space in a nonsegmented table space. In such table spaces, the space used by dropped tables isn't reclaimed until you reorganize the table space.

```
SELECT PERCDROP
   FROM SYSIBM.SYSTABLEPART
   WHERE DBNAME = 'xxx'
   AND TSNAME = 'yyy';
```

Determine whether the rows of a table are stored in the same order as the entries of its clustering index. A large FAROFFPOS value indicates that clustering is degenerating. A large NEAROFFPOS value might also indicate that the table space needs reorganizing, but the value of FAROFFPOS is a better indicator.

```
SELECT NEAROFFPOS, FAROFFPOS
  FROM SYSIBM.SYSINDEXPART
  WHERE IXCREATOR = 'zzz'
  AND IXNAME = 'www';
```

Return LEAFDIST, which is the average distance (multiplied by 100) between successive leaf pages during sequential access of an index. If LEAFDIST increases over time, you should reorganize the index.

```
SELECT LEAFDIST
  FROM SYSIBM.SYSINDEXPART
  WHERE IXCREATOR = 'zzz'
  AND IXNAME = 'www';
```

List the LOB table spaces that should be reorganized. A value greater than 2 for ORGRATIO generally indicates a LOB table space that needs reorganization.

```
SELECT DBNAME, NAME, ORGRATIO
  FROM SYSIBM.SYSLOBSTATS
  WHERE ORGRATIO > 2;
```

REORG Triggers

If the statistics are current in the DB2 catalog tables, the REORG utility can determine whether it needs to actually perform a reorganization. The utility lets criteria, known as REORG triggers, be specified to indicate when reorganization should be performed. This feature saves the DBA from having to analyze the statistics and determine whether to schedule a reorg.

To provide this functionality, the REORG utility embeds the function of catalog queries. If a query returns a certain result (you can accept the default or supply your own), REORG will either reorganize or not. You can optionally have REORG run a report instead of actually doing the reorganization.

The following example shows how to specify the OFFPOSLIMIT and INDREFLIMIT conditional REORG triggers.

```
REORG TABLESPACE DSN8D91A.DSN8S91D
   SORTDATA NOSYSREC SORTKEYS
   COPYDDN SYSCOPY1
   OFFPOSLIMIT
```

```
INDREFLIMIT
STATISTICS TABLE(ALL)INDEX(ALL)
```

The OFFPOSLIMIT, INDREFLIMIT, and LEAFDISTLIMIT options can also be described by the following SQL.

```
SELECT CARDF,
    (NEAROFFPOSF + FAROFFPOSF) * 100 / CARDF
FROM SYSIBM.SYSINDEXPART
WHERE CARDF > 0
AND (NEAROFFPOSF + FAROFFPOSF) * 100
  / CARDF > :offposlimit

SELECT CARD,
    (NEARINDREF + FARINDREF) * 100 / CARD
FROM SYSIBM.SYSTABLEPART
WHERE CARD > 0
AND (NEARINDREF + FARINDREF * 100
  / CARD > :indreflimit

SELECT LEAFDIST
FROM SYSIBM.SYSINDEXPART
WHERE LEAFDIST > :leafdistlimit
```

The REORG utility does not embed any function to help you determine when to reorganize LOB table spaces.

Table ALTERs

Another time to consider reorganizing data to improve performance is when ALTER TABLE statements have been used to add a column to a table or to change the data types or lengths of existing columns. Such changes cause the table space to be placed in advisory REORG-pending (AREO*) status.

In the case of changing the definition of an existing column, the table space is placed in AREO* status because the existing data isn't immediately converted to its new definition. Reorganizing the table space causes the rows to be reloaded with the data converted to the new definition. Until you reorganize the table space, DB2 must track the changes and apply them as the data is accessed, possibly degrading performance. For example, depending on the number of changes, you may see decreased performance for dynamic SQL queries, updates and deletes, and other ALTER statements (especially those that are run concurrently).

In addition, running multiple REORG and LOAD utilities concurrently may perform more slowly or create timeouts. It may also take longer to unload a table that has undergone many changes before being reorganized.

Reorganizing Table Spaces

The SYSIBM.SYSTABLEPART catalog table contains the information about how the data in a table is physically stored. Consider running REORG TABLESPACE in the following situations:

- FAROFFPOSF/CARDF is greater than 10 percent or, if the index is a clustering index, the CLUSTERRATIOF column of SYSIBM.SYSINDEXES is less than 90 percent.

- (NEARINDREF + FARINDREF)/CARDF is greater than 10 percent.

- PERCDROP is greater than 10 percent for a simple table space. If you're reorganizing the table space because of this value, consider using the REUSE option to improve performance.

- The data set has multiple extents. Keeping the number of extents to less than 50 is a general guideline.

- The table space is in AREO* status as the result of an ALTER TABLE statement.

Reorganizing LOB Table Spaces

SYSIBM.SYSLOBSTATS contains information about how the data in a table space is physically stored. Consider running REORG on a LOB table space when the value in the ORGRATIO column is 2. In addition, you can use realtime statistics to identify DB2 objects that should be reorganized, have their statistics updated, or be image-copied.

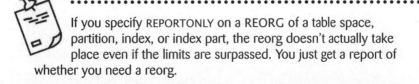

If you specify REPORTONLY on a REORG of a table space, partition, index, or index part, the reorg doesn't actually take place even if the limits are surpassed. You just get a report of whether you need a reorg.

Reorganizing Indexes

The LEAFNEAR and LEAFFAR columns of the SYSIBM.SYSINDEXPART catalog table measure the disorganization of physical leaf pages by indicating the number of pages that are not in an optimal position. You should consider performing a REORG INDEX in the following cases:

- LEAFFAR/NLEAF is greater than 10 percent. (NLEAF is a column in SYSIBM.SYSINDEXES.)

- PSEUDO_DEL_ENTRIES/CARDF is greater than 10 percent. If you're reorganizing the index because of this value, consider using the REUSE option to improve performance.

- The data set has multiple extents. Keeping the number of extents to less than 50 is a general guideline. (Many secondary extents can detract from performance of index scans.)

- The index is in advisory REORG-pending status (AREO*) or advisory-REBUILD-pending status (ARBDP) as the result of an ALTER statement.

- ((REORGINSERTS + REORGDELETES) ×100)/TOTALENTRIES is greater than RRIInsertDeletePct.

- (REORGAPPENDINSERT × 100)/TOTALENTRIES is greater than RRIInsertDeletePct.

- Mass delete occurred.

DBA Analysis for REORG Determination

The DBA can choose not to use the REORG triggers and opt instead to analyze the statistics manually to determine whether a REORG is necessary. For any table space, a REORG is called for if any of the following apply (using statistics from the clustering index):

- Any data set behind the tablespace has too many (more than 20) extents.

- The CLUSTERRATIO value is always greater that 90 percent. However:

  » Keep very small tables 100 percent clustered (inexpensive and easy).

» Reorg medium tables below 98 percent.

» Reorg large tables below 95 percent.

» A 90 to 95 percent CLUSTERRATIO can cause very poor performance.

- (NEARINDREF + FARINDREF)/CARD is greater than 10 percent.

- FAROFFPOS/CARD is greater than 5 percent.

- NEAROFFPOS/CARD is greater than 10 percent.

- Database descriptor (DBD) growth occurs after successive drops/re-creates in a table space.

To check whether your index space needs to be reorganized, review the LEAFDIST column in the SYSINDEXPART catalog table. Large numbers in this column indicate that several pages exist between successive leaf pages, and using the index will result in additional overhead. In this situation, DB2 may turn off prefetch usage, as well. Reorganizing the index space will solve these problems.

Reorganizing the Catalog and Directory

You can also determine when to reorganize the DB2 catalog table space and index spaces by using the same techniques used to determine when to reorganize application table spaces and index spaces. First, you'll want to ensure that statistics are kept current by using RUNSTATS based on the frequency of changes in the catalog so your decisions about reorganizations are based on current numbers. A reorganization would also be necessary if the objects are in extents or if unused space needs to be reclaimed.

Every table space in the DSNDB06 database is eligible for reorganization, but you cannot reorganize DSNDB06.SYSPLAN with SHRLEVEL CHANGE.

DB2 directory reorganizations are also important because the directory contains critical information about internal DB2 control and structures. This information is important to DB2 processing because it affects application plans and package execution, utility execution, and database access. If we permit these items to become disorganized, transaction and utility performance can be affected.

Be aware that relationships exist between the DB2 catalog and some of the DB2 directory tables. For instance, you'll want to reorganize directory table DBD01 when you reorganize catalog table SYSDBASE. Directory tables SCT01 and SCT02 should be reorganized with SYSPLAN and SYSPACKAGE, respectively.

Rebalancing Partitions

You can change the limit keys for the partitions of a partitioned table space if the partitions become unbalanced. You do so using the ALTER INDEX SQL statement, specifying the PART clause and the VALUES parameter.

This step changes only the definition in the DB2 catalog; it doesn't actually move any rows in the partitioned table space or any index entries in the partitioned index. DB2 also sets the REORP status for those partitions because they may no longer contain the correct rows. The affected partitions (all those in the range affected by the ALTER) are no longer accessible.

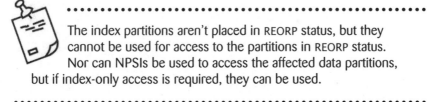

The index partitions aren't placed in REORP status, but they cannot be used for access to the partitions in REORP status. Nor can NPSIs be used to access the affected data partitions, but if index-only access is required, they can be used.

To redistribute the rows for the affected partitions, you must reorganize all these partitions at the same time by specifying a range in the PART *n:m* parameter of the REORG utility control statement. The following example REORGs parts 1 through 3:

```
REORG TABLESPACE DSN8D91A.DSN8S91E PART 1:3
```

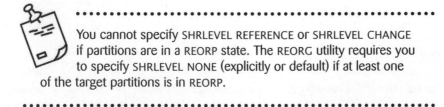

You cannot specify SHRLEVEL REFERENCE or SHRLEVEL CHANGE if partitions are in a REORP state. The REORG utility requires you to specify SHRLEVEL NONE (explicitly or default) if at least one of the target partitions is in REORP.

If you reduce the limit key for the last partition in key sequence for a large table space (created with LARGE or DSSIZE), a discard data set is required, even if some of the partition's former rows no longer belong to the key range. DB2 places the rows no longer belonging to any key range into the discard data set. You can specify the DD name for the discard data set using the DISCARDDN parameter, or you can accept the default DD name of SYSDISC.

> The REORG utility always establishes an inline copy for at least one of the partitions being reorganized that is in REORP status. This is a single inline copy that includes all partitions of the specified range. The DD name for the local primary copy data set must be specified via the COPYDDN parameter, or you can provide a DD statement with the DD name SYSCOPY.

You can also use the REORG utility to rebalance partitions by using the REBALANCE keyword. DB2 automatically rebalances the keys over the specified partitions. The following example rebalances partitions 3 and 4.

```
REORG TABLESPACE DSN8910.EMP PART(3:4) REBALANCE
```

Data Statistics

The system catalog tables contain information about columns, tables, and indexes. They contain information such as the number of rows in a table, the use of space by a table or index, and the number of different values in a column. However, this information is not automatically kept current. It must be generated periodically by a utility called RUNSTATS. The statistics collected by the RUNSTATS utility can be used in two ways: to describe the physical organization of the data and to provide information that the DB2 optimizer needs to select the best access path for executing SQL statements.

To ensure efficient access paths to data, current statistics must exist that reflect the actual state of your tables, columns, and indexes. Whenever you issue a dynamic SQL statement, the DB2 optimizer reads the system catalog tables to review the available indexes, the size of each table, the characteristics of columns, and other information to choose the best access path for executing the query. If the statistics don't reflect the current state of the tables, the DB2 optimizer won't have the correct information to make the best choice in selecting an access path to execute your query. This becomes more crucial as the complexity of the SQL statements increases. When only one table is accessed without indexes, fewer choices are available to the optimizer. However, when the SQL statement involves several tables, each with one or more indexes, the number of choices available to the optimizer increases dramatically.

Choosing the correct access path can lessen the response time considerably by reducing the amount of I/O needed to correctly retrieve the data. Depending on the size of the tables, the indexes available, and other considerations, the selected access path can affect the response time, which varies from minutes to hours.

The next step in improving performance involves the use of the RUNSTATS utility. It is recommended to you execute RUNSTATS on a frequent basis on tables that have a large number of updates, inserts, or deletes. For tables with a great deal of insert or delete activity, you may decide to run statistics after a fixed period of time or after the insert or delete activity.

An important feature of DB2 is that it lets you reorganize and use the RUNSTATS utility on the system catalog tables. This feature can improve the access plans generated when querying the system catalog tables. DB2 may access these tables when you issue an SQL statement even though you are referencing only user tables. Therefore, it's very important to have current statistics on the system catalog tables.

● ●

You should use the RUNSTATS utility after a REORG of a table or use inline statistics during the REORG.

● ●

RUNSTATS Utility

RUNSTATS is a utility that is critical to a properly tuned DB2 environment. It gathers statistics about DB2 objects—table spaces and indexes. RUNSTATS can also be embedded in other utilities, such as REORG and LOAD, giving you the ability to collect statistics during the execution of a given utility (as we discussed earlier in this chapter).

The RUNSTATS utility can be executed on a table space and its indexes, or for each object independently, or even for a specific column. RUNSTATS should initially be run on all columns after the data is loaded and reorganized. In addition, there are some general guidelines for RUNSTATS execution. You should run the utility

- after a table space or index has been reorganized and the statistics have changed significantly

- after adding a new index

- after any heavy update, insert, or delete processing has occurred

The statistics should also be run before any binding/rebinding of packages or plans and before any performance tuning that would require monitoring of the statistics in the catalog.

Let's look at an example of the RUNSTATS utility. Our example runs the utility on the table for all columns, and it also collects statistics for the indexes on the table (only the statistics on the first column of each index). It updates all necessary statistics in the catalog, produces a report, and collects history.

```
RUNSTATS TABLESPACE DSN8D91A.DSN8S91D
TABLE (MYTABLE1) COLUMN(ALL)
INDEX
REPORT YES
UPDATE ALL
HISTORY ALL
```

Reporting and Performing Catalog Updates

You can have RUNSTATS report on the statistics it gathers by using the REPORT NO|YES parameter. You can also control whether RUNSTATS updates the DB2 catalog, and what it updates, by using the following UPDATE options:

- **ALL.** The utility includes both space and access path statistics.

- **NONE.** The utility performs no updating of the DB2 catalog.

- **SPACE.** The utility updates only statistics related to space management (i.e., free space).

- **ACCESSPATH.** The utility updates only statistics used by the optimizer.

The following example executes the RUNSTATS utility and updates the catalog with only the statistics that are collected for access path selection. This example also uses the REPORT option to route the collected statistics to SYSPRINT.

```
RUNSTATS TABLESPACE DSN8D91A.DSN8S91D
REPORT YES
UPDATE ACCESSPATH
```

Access During RUNSTATS Execution

A RUNSTATS operation that uses SHRLEVEL CHANGE runs without any locking or interference to other processes. This option lets you execute RUNSTATS as often as necessary.

Sampling

The RUNSTATS sampling feature lets you choose the percent of nonindexed column statistics gathered and will help RUNSTATS to execute more quickly. The sampling technique can affect the optimizer's choice in access path selection because the sampling must be representative of the data. In the absence of true representation, it would assume a linear distribution of data, which would affect the filter factor and costing done by the optimizer. Here's an example that uses sampling of 25 percent.

```
RUNSTATS TABLESPACE DSN8D91A.DSN8S91D
    TABLE(ALL)SAMPLE 25
    INDEX(ALL)
    SHRLEVEL CHANGE
```

Key Correlation Statistics

Key correlation statistics give DB2 the ability to gather statistics when one column's value is related to the value of another column. Without these statistics, only the FIRSTKEYCARD and FULLKEYCARD columns provide calculated information, and the correlation is on columns for FULLKEYCARD only. Without key correlation statistics, no second or third key cardinality is calculated, and multikey cardinality is computed independently, often leading to inaccurate estimation of filter factors and inaccurate estimation of join size, join sequencing, and join methods, which in turn can result in inefficient access path selection.

RUNSTATS collects key correlation statistics with minimal additional overhead, and these statistics can provide CPU and elapsed-time reductions through improved cost and resources estimations. Key correlation statistics play a major role in access path selection by giving the optimizer information about multicolumn cardinalities and multicolumn frequent values.

This feature gives you the ability to specify the number of columns (NUMCOLS) on which to collect statistics as well as the number of values (COUNT). The KEYCARD parameter indicates that RUNSTATS is to collect cardinalities for each column, concatenated with all previous key columns. This option provides more information for the optimizer when the related columns are used in a compound WHERE clause.

Using this RUNSTATS feature gives you the option to build the frequency values for critical concatenated key columns, such as the first and second columns, or maybe the first, second, and third columns.

The following example shows how to update statistics on frequently occurring values. For a given index, we can use the KEYCARD option to indicate that the utility is to collect cardinality statistics for the index. If the index is a three-column index, RUNSTATS will collect cardinality statistics for the first column, the first and second, and the first, second, and third. Because we've specified the NUMCOLS option, RUNSTATS will also collect the 10 most frequently occurring values for the first group and the 15 most frequently occurring values for the second group.

```
RUNSTATS INDEX (DSN8910.XEMP2)
   KEYCARD
   FREQVAL NUMCOLS 1 COUNT 10
   FREQVAL NUMCOLS 2 COUNT 15
```

Frequency Distribution Statistics

Many performance problems can be attributed to skewed distribution of data. The optimizer assumes that the data is uniformly distributed. When this is not the case, the result can be poor join sequences, increased synchronous I/O, and longer application response times. These outcomes can occur if the optimizer chooses an incorrect access path because it has incorrectly estimated the number of matching rows for a qualified predicate.

DB2 maintains distribution (frequency) statistics in the catalog table SYSIBM.SYSCOLDIST. If you use these statistics with the cardinality statistics in

SYSIBM.SYSCOLUMNS, performance may improve. You can expand this optimization effort further by holding frequency and cardinality statistics not just for single columns but for skewed combinations of columns. You may also need to gather distribution statistics for non-leading indexed columns or non-indexed columns to give DB2 more information for better optimization. The RUNSTATS utility can help with all these tasks. By considering these statistics, you can improve DB2's index selections for screening predicates or matching in-list/in-subquery predicates.

Let's consider a quick example of skewed data. The following table shows the distribution of values for a column called DB2_SKILLS.

DB2_SKILLS	Frequency
Guru	5%
Senior	20%
Junior	40%
Trainee	10%
Needs-new-job	25%

If we don't collect this frequency information, DB2 assumes 1/COLCARDF (the value in SYSCOLUMNS that contains frequency information) is 20 percent. In the case of a predicate such as

```
WHERE DB2_SKILLS = 'Junior'
```

this assumption would be incorrect.

To determine whether the data values are skewed, you can run a simple query to obtain counts on the distinct values. For example, the following query returns the count of the distinct values for the DB2_SKILLS column. In this case, you may want to collect frequency statistics in RUNSTATS.

```
SELECT DB2_SKILLS, COUNT(*)
FROM IT_EMP
GROUP BY DB2_SKILLS

DB2_SKILLS    COUNT
----------    -----
Guru              5
Junior           55
Senior           20
Trainee           8
Not skilled      24
```

You can also collect information about the LEAST and MOST frequently occurring values, for both index and non-index columns as well as for groups of columns. For static values, you'd need to collect this information just once.

The next example shows how to update the statistics for a group of columns. We use the COLGROUP keyword to group the columns. The distribution statistics for the group will be stored in SYSCOLDIST.

```
RUNSTATS TABLESPACE (DSN8D91A.DSN8S91E)
   TABLE (DSN8910.EMP)
   COLGROUP (JOB, EDLEVEL)
```

By using the FREQVAL option with COLGROUP, you can collect frequency distribution statistics for a specific group of non-index columns. Adding the COUNT keyword, as shown here, lets you specify the number of frequently occurring values to be collected from the specified column group.

```
RUNSTATS TABLESPACE (DSN8D91A.DSN8S91E)
   TABLE (DSN8910.EMP)
   COLGROUP (JOB, EDLEVEL) FREQVAL COUNT 10
```

Collection of data correlation information and skewed data distributions can improve access path selection and may help reduce RID list size.

The values for frequency distribution statistics are stored in the following columns of catalog tables SYSCOLDIST and SYSCOLDISTSTATS:

Column	Column definition	Description
TYPE	CHAR(1) NOT NULL DEFAULT 'F'	Indicates the type of statistic (cardinality or frequent value)
CARDF	FLOAT NOT NULL DEFAULT–1	Identifies the number of distinct values for the column group
COLGROUPCOLNO	VARCHAR(254) NOT NULL WITH DEFAULT	Identifies the set of columns
NUMCOLUMNS	SMALLINT NOT NULL DEFAULT 1	Indicates the number of columns in the group

••

The COLCARDF column in SYSCOLUMNS contains the number of distinct values for a single column.

••

Histogram Statistics

Histogram statistics enable DB2 to improve access path selection by estimating predicate selectivity from value-distribution statistics that are collected over the entire range of values in a data set. This information aids filtering estimation when certain data ranges are heavily populated and others are sparsely populated. (RUNSTATS cannot collect histogram statistics on randomized key columns.)

DB2 chooses the best access path for a query based on predicate selectivity estimation, which in turn relies heavily on data distribution statistics. Histogram statistics summarize data distribution on an interval scale by dividing the entire range of possible values within a data set into a number of intervals.

DB2 creates equal-depth histogram statistics, meaning that it divides the whole range of values into intervals that each contain about the same percentage of the total number of rows. The following columns in a histogram statistics table define an interval:

- **QUANTILENO.** An ordinary sequence number that identifies the interval.

- **HIGHVALUE.** A value that serves as the upper bound for the interval.

- **LOWVALUE.** A value that serves as the lower bound for the interval.

Note the following characteristics of histogram statistics intervals:

- Each interval includes approximately the same number, or percentage, of the rows. A highly frequent single value might occupy an interval by itself.

- A single value is never broken into more than one interval, meaning that the maximum number of intervals is equal to the number of distinct values on the column. The maximum number of intervals cannot exceed 100, the maximum number DB2 supports.

- Adjacent intervals sometime skip values that don't appear in the table, especially when doing so avoids a large range of skipped values within an interval.

- HIGHVALUE and LOWVALUE can be inclusive or exclusive, but an interval typically represents a non-overlapped value range.

- NULL values, if any exist, occupy a single interval.

- Because DB2 cannot break any single value into two different intervals, the maximum number of intervals is limited to the number of distinct values in the column and cannot exceed the DB2 maximum of 100 intervals.

RUNSTATS on the DB2 Catalog

The frequency with which you need to execute the RUNSTATS utility on the DB2 catalog depends on the amount of DDL, DML, and other activities occurring that insert and delete rows in the DB2 catalog tables. DB2 won't be able to appropriately optimize queries against the catalog without having current statistics on the table spaces and index spaces. The same principle applies here as with DB2 user-defined objects; you need a current view of all DB2 objects to determine the need for and frequency of reorganization of DB2 catalog table spaces and index spaces.

Inline Statistics

To avoid having to run a separate RUNSTATS job, you can collect inline statistics when running the REORG, LOAD, or REBUILD INDEX utility. Establishing inline statistics is faster than running RUNSTATS after these operations because separate subtasks of these utilities establish the inline statistics as a by-products of running the utilities. You can choose to request a statistics report and/or update the DB2 catalog for the objects involved. For REORG, you can request the statistics for the table space, for the indexes associated with the tables of the table space, or for the indexes being reorganized.

For the LOAD utility, you can request inline statistics only for REPLACE or RESUME operations; for REBUILD INDEX, inline stats are available only for indexes being built.

You request inline statistics using the STATISTICS clause of the REORG, LOAD, or REBUILD utility. The same parameters used with the RUNSTATS utility are available for inline statistics.

Inline statistics cannot be collected

- for DB2 catalog or directory tables with links

- for non-partitioned secondary indexes if the load or reorganization is on only individual partitions (because DB2 wouldn't know how to apply the partial values to the existing totals for the non-partitioned indexes)

- if you restart the REORG utility using RESTART (CURRENT)

- if you restart the LOAD or REBUILD INDEX utility

Inline statistics established during LOAD may include information about rows that have been discarded. If only a few rows have been discarded, this behavior isn't a concern, but if many rows have been discarded, the inline stats may be very inaccurate, and you might be better off executing a separate RUNSTATS utility.

SQL Cache Invalidation Using RUNSTATS

The only way to invalidate (remove) statements in the dynamic SQL cache is to execute the RUNSTATS utility on the objects on which the prepared cached statements rely.

If you update statistics, affected dynamic SQL statements that are cached are invalidated so they can be re-prepared. Cache invalidation occurs at the table space and index space levels. To invalidate the dynamic SQL cache, you can specify RUNSTATS REPORT YES; however, this method can take a fair amount of time. You also have the option to run RUNSTATS with REPORT NO and UPDATE NONE. This alternative lets you invalidate dynamic SQL cache statements without the overhead of collecting the actual stats, generating a report, or updating catalog tables.

```
RUNSTATS TABLESPACE DSN8D91A.DSN8S91D
         REPORT NO UPDATE NONE
```

Historical Statistics

DB2 provides the ability to keep a history of statistics for better performance analysis capabilities. This feature helps you better monitor objects in terms of change over time and furnishes other information to help determine whether objects need to change. You use the HISTORY keyword on the RUNSTATS, REORG, LOAD, and REBUILD utilities to identify that you want historical statistics to be collected:

```
REORG INDEX.....HISTORY
   RUNSTATS TABLESPACE.....HISTORY
```

Nine different DB2 catalog tables store the historical statistics:

- SYSIBM.SYSCOLDIST_HIST

- SYSIBM.SYSCOLUMNS_HIST

- SYSIBM.SYSINDEXES_HIST

- SYSIBM.SYSINDEXPART_HIST

- SYSIBM.SYSINDEXSTATS_HIST

- SYSIBM.SYSLOBSTATS_HIST

- SYSIBM.SYSTABLEPART_HIST

- SYSIBM.SYSTABLES_HIST

- SYSIBM.SYSTABSTATS_HIST

As the statistics age and are no longer needed, you can delete them using the MODIFY STATISTICS utility, described later in this chapter.

STOSPACE Utility

The STOSPACE utility collects space information from the Integrated Catalog Facility (ICF) catalogs for storage groups and related table spaces and indexes. This utility then updates the DB2 catalog with information about the amount of space in use. You execute the utility against a storage group. (For more information about storage groups, see Chapter 4.)

Here's an example that illustrates the STOSPACE utility syntax:

```
STOSPACE STOGROUP DSN8G910
```

Real Time Statistics

DB2's Real Time Statistics (RTS) facility lets DB2 collect data about table spaces and index spaces and then periodically write this information into two catalog tables. The statistics can then be used by user-written queries or programs, the DB2-supplied stored procedure DSNACCOR, or the Control Center to make decisions for object maintenance (i.e., REORG, RUNSTATS, COPY).

Statistics Collection

DB2 is always generating realtime statistics for database objects. It keeps these statistics in virtual storage and calculates and updates them asynchronously upon externalization.

Two catalog tables hold the statistics:

- SYSIBM.SYSTABLESPACESTATS

- SYSIBM.SYSINDEXSPACESTATS

DB2 populates these tables with one row per table space, index space, or partition.

Some of the important statistics collected for table spaces include total number of rows, number of active pages, and time of last COPY, REORG, or RUNSTATS execution. Some statistics that may help determine when a REORG is needed include space allocated; extents; number of inserts, updates, or deletes (singleton or mass) since the last REORG or LOAD REPLACE; number of unclustered inserts, number of disorganized LOBs, and number of overflow records created since the last REORG. Also available are statistics to help you decide when RUNSTATS should be executed, such as number of inserts/updates/deletes (singleton and mass) since the last RUNSTATS execution. Statistics collected to help with COPY determination include distinct updated pages, changes since the last COPY execution, and the Relative Byte Address/Log Record Sequence Number (RBA/LRSN) of the first update since the last COPY.

Statistics are also gathered on indexes. Basic index statistics include total number of entries (unique or duplicate), number of levels, number of active pages, space allocated, and extents. Statistics that help to determine when an index REORG is needed include time when the last REBUILD, REORG, or LOAD REPLACE occurred. Statistics also report the number of updates, deletes (real or pseudo, singleton or mass), and inserts (random and those that were after the highest key) since the last REORG or REBUILD. These statistics are, of course, very helpful for determining how your data physically looks after certain processes (e.g., batch inserts) have occurred so you can take appropriate actions if necessary.

Externalizing and Using Realtime Statistics

Different events can trigger the externalization of the statistics. Several processes affect the realtime statistics, including SQL, utilities, and the dropping or creating of objects. To control the externalization of the statistics at a subsystem level, you can use DSNZPARM STATSINST (default 30 minutes).

Once the statistics are externalized, you can write queries to read from the tables. For example, you could write a query against the SYSTABLESPACESTATS table to identify when a table space needs to be copied because more than 30 percent of its pages have changed since the last image copy was taken:

```
SELECT NAME
  FROM SYSIBM.SYSTABLESPACESTATS
    WHERE DBNAME = 'DB1' and
    ((COPYUPDATEDPAGES*100)/NACTIVE)>30
```

This next query compares the last RUNSTATS timestamp to the timestamp of the last REORG on the same object to determine when RUNSTATS is needed. If the date of the last REORG is more recent than the last RUNSTATS, it may be time to execute RUNSTATS.

```
SELECT NAME
FROM SYSIBM.SYSTABLESPACESTATS
WHERE DBNAME = 'DB1' and
   (JULIAN_DAY(REORGLASTTIME)>JULIAN_DAY(STATSLASTTIME))
```

The next example may be useful if you want to monitor the number of records inserted since the last REORG or LOAD REPLACE that are not well-clustered with respect to the clustering index. Ideally, "well-clustered" means the record was inserted into a page that was within 16 pages of the ideal candidate page (determined by the clustering index). You can use the SYSTABLESPACESTATS table value REORGUNCLUSTINS to determine whether you need to run REORG after a series of inserts.

```
SELECT NAME
FROM SYSIBM.SYSTABLESPACESTATS
WHERE DBNAME = 'DB1' and
    ((REORGUNCLUSTINS*100)/TOTALROWS)>10
```

A DB2-supplied stored procedure, DSNACCOR, can assist with this process and possibly even help you work toward automating the whole determination/utility execution process. DSNACCOR is a sample procedure that queries the RTS tables to determine which objects need to be reorganized, image copied, or updated with current statistics, as well as those that have taken too many extents or may in a restricted status. DSNACCOR creates and uses its own declared temporary tables and must run in a workload-managed address space. The procedure's output provides recommendations by using a predetermined set of criteria in formulas that use the RTS and user input for their calculations. DSNACCOR can make recommendations for everything (COPY, REORG, RUNSTATS, EXTENTS, and RESTRICT) or for one or more utilities of your choice, as well as for specific object types (table spaces and/or indexes).

Data Maintenance Process

The data maintenance process starts with the RUNSTATS utility. After executing RUNSTATS, a DBA can analyze the statistics to determine whether a REORG is necessary. As an alternative, the REORG utility can review the collected statistics and use the REORG triggers to determine whether a REORG is needed.

If reorganization is necessary, run the REORG utility on the selected objects and then execute RUNSTATS and REBIND. You must perform a REBIND on any packages affected by the preceding operations so they can take advantage of the benefits of the new physical organization and updated statistics. After performing subsequent update, insert, and delete operations as part of the data maintenance process, repeat these steps by first executing the RUNSTATS utility.

Establish a routine for RUNSTATS and the REBIND processes. Updated statistics will give you precise information about your database state.

Rebinds

You should rebind packages in any of the following cases, based on current statistics from the catalog:

- Changes > 20 percent (NLEAF, NPAGES, NACTIVE)
- CLUSTERRATIO < 80 percent, NLEVELS increases > 2
- HIGH2KEY and LOW2KEY ranges change > 10 percent
- Cardinality and row count change > 20 percent

For more information about packages and rebinds, see Chapter 11.

Modeling a Production Environment

To model a production environment, the DBA can update several columns in the DB2 catalog so that the access paths against production data can be determined even if the data doesn't physically exist. For more information about the catalog tables, see Chapter 2. For information about updating catalog columns to help predict access paths, see Chapter 17.

Other Data Maintenance Utilities

DB2 provides several other tools to help you perform various data maintenance functions: the CHECK and MODIFY utilities and the REPAIR utility.

CHECK Utilities

Three CHECK utilities let you check the integrity of data and indexes. These utilities are often required to remove restrictive statuses.

- CHECK DATA

- CHECK INDEX

- CHECK LOB

CHECK DATA

CHECK DATA is an online utility that checks table spaces for violations of referential and table check constraints and reports information about any violations detected during its execution. You should run the CHECK DATA utility after a conditional restart or a point-in-time recovery on all table spaces whose parent and dependent tables might not be synchronized. (For more information about recovery, see Chapter 8.) You can also execute CHECK DATA against a base table space (but not against a LOB table space).

At your option, the utility can delete rows that violate referential or table check constraints. Any row that violates one or more constraints can also be copied, once, to an exception table.

If CHECK DATA finds any violation of constraints, it puts the table space being checked into the CHECK-pending status.

The CHECK DATA utility proceeds through the following phases:

1. **UTILINIT.** This phase initializes the utility.

2. **SCANTAB.** Foreign keys are extracted. CHECK DATA uses the foreign key index for this task if it exists; otherwise, it performs a table scan.

3. **SORT.** The foreign keys are sorted if they weren't extracted from the foreign key index.

4. **CHECKDAT.** This phase looks in primary indexes for foreign key parents and issues messages to report any errors it detects. For each constraint violation, it reports the RID of the row, the table that contained the row, and the constraint name that was violated.

5. **REPORTCK.** This phase copies the error rows into exception tables. If you specified the DELETE YES option, it then deletes these rows from the source table.

6. **UTILTERM.** Any necessary cleanup operations are performed.

The following example uses the CHECK DATA utility to check for and delete all constraint violations in table space DSN8D91A.DSN8S91E.

```
CHECK DATA TABLESPACE DSN8D91A.DSN8S91E
  FOR EXCEPTION IN DSN8910.EMP
  USE DSN8910.EXCP_TT
  DELETE YES
```

After a successful execution, CHECK DATA resets the CHECK-pending status.

CHECK INDEX

The CHECK INDEX online utility tests whether indexes are consistent with the data on which each index is created. The utility issues warning messages when it finds an inconsistency. You should execute CHECK INDEX after a conditional restart or a point-in-time recovery on all table spaces whose indexes may not be consistent with the data.

Also use CHECK INDEX before CHECK DATA to ensure that the indexes used by CHECK DATA are valid. This step is especially important before using CHECK DATA with DELETE YES. When checking an auxiliary table index, CHECK INDEX verifies that each LOB is represented by an index entry and that an index entry exists for every LOB.

The CHECK INDEX utility generates several messages that show whether the indexes are consistent with the data. For unique indexes, any two null values are taken to be equal, unless the index was created with the UNIQUE WHERE NOT NULL clause. In that case, if the key is a single column, it can contain any number of null values, and CHECK INDEX does not issue an error message. If two or more null values exist and the unique index was not created with UNIQUE WHERE NOT NULL, CHECK INDEX issues an error message.

The phases of execution of the CHECK INDEX are very simple. The utility starts with the initialization and setup; then it unloads the index entries, sorts them, and performs a scan of data to validate index entries. As a final step, it performs any necessary cleanup.

This example uses CHECK INDEX to check all indexes in table space DSN8D91A.DSN8S91D.

```
CHECK INDEX (ALL)TABLESPACE DSN8D91A.DSN8S91D
   SORTDEVT SYSDA
```

The CHECK INDEX utility can be executed on user objects and the DB2 catalog and directory.

CHECK LOB

You can run the CHECK LOB online utility against a LOB table space to identify any structural defects in the LOB table space and any invalid LOB values. Run CHECK LOB against a LOB table space that is marked CHECK-pending (CHKP) to identify structural defects. If no defects are found, the utility turns off the CHKP status.

Run the CHECK LOB online utility against a LOB table space that is in auxiliary warning (AUXW) status to identify invalid LOBs. If none exists, the utility turns off the AUXW status.

Run CHECK LOB after a conditional restart or a point-in-time recovery on all table spaces where LOB table spaces might not be synchronized.

The execution phases of the CHECK LOB utility are as follows:

1. **UTILINIT.** This phase initializes the utility.

2. **CHECKLOB.** This phase scans all active pages of the LOB table space.

3. **SORT.** This phase sorts four types of records from the CHECKLOB phase; it reports four times the number of rows sorted.

4. **REPRTLOB.** This phase examines records produced by the CHECKLOB phase and sorted by the SORT phase and issues error messages.

5. **UTILTERM.** During this phase, any necessary cleanup is performed.

Here's an example of executing the CHECK LOB utility against the DSN8S91N table space to will check for structural defects or invalid LOBs.

```
CHECK LOB TABLESPACE DSN8D91L.DSN8S91N
    EXCEPTIONS 3 WORKDDN SYSUT1,
    SORTOUT SORTDEVT SYSDA
    SORTNUM 4
```

After a successful execution of the utility, the CHKP and AUXW statuses are reset.

MODIFY

DB2 provides two different MODIFY utilities: MODIFY RECOVERY and MODIFY STATISTICS. Both are considered maintenance utilities because you use them to remove unwanted (aged) data from the catalog tables. Let's take a look at the purpose of each one and when to run them.

Modify Recovery

The MODIFY online utility with the RECOVERY option deletes records from the SYSIBM.SYSCOPY catalog table, related log records from the SYSIBM.SYSLGRNX directory table, and entries from the DBD. Records can be removed if they were written before a specific date (DATE), or they can be removed if they are of a specific age (AGE). You can delete records for an entire table space, partition, or data set. You should run this MODIFY utility regularly to clear outdated information from SYSIBM.SYSCOPY and SYSIBM.SYSLGRNX. These tables, and particularly SYSIBM.SYSLGRNX, can become very large and take up considerable amounts of space. By deleting outdated information from these tables, you can improve performance for processes that access data from them.

The MODIFY RECOVERY utility automatically removes the SYSIBM.SYSCOPY and SYSIBM.SYSLGRNX recovery records that meet the AGE and DATE criteria for all indexes over the table space that were defined with the COPY YES attribute. It can also remove a specific copy.

The utility deletes image copy rows from SYSIBM.SYSCOPY and SYSIBM.SYSLGRNX. For each full and incremental SYSCOPY record deleted from SYSCOPY, the utility returns a message giving the name of the copy data set.

If MODIFY RECOVERY deletes all the SYSCOPY records, causing the target table space or partition to not be recoverable, the utility places the target object in COPY-pending status.

The MODIFY RECOVERY has three execution phases: the UTILINIT phase, for initialization and setup; the MODIFY phase, which deletes records; and the UTILTERM phase, which performs cleanup.

The following example shows how to use MODIFY RECOVERY to delete SYSCOPY records by date for a specific table space.

```
MODIFY RECOVERY TABLESPACE DSN8D91A.DSN8S91D
DELETE DATE(20070414)
```

You can also use the MODIFY RECOVERY utility to reclaim space in the DBD after a user table has been dropped. To reclaim the DBD space, perform the following steps:

1. Commit the drop.

2. Run the REORG utility.

3. Run the COPY utility to make a full image copy of the table space.

4. Run MODIFY RECOVERY with the DELETE option to delete all previous image copies.

You can also use MODIFY RECOVERY to improve REORG performance after adding a column to a table. When you add a column to a table space, the next REORG of the table space materializes default values for the added column by decompressing all rows of the table space during the UNLOAD phase and then compressing them again during the RELOAD phase. Subsequently, each REORG job for the table space repeats this processing in the UNLOAD and RELOAD phases. The following procedure helps to avoid repeating the compression cycle with each REORG:

1. Run the REORG utility on the table space.

2. Run the COPY utility to make a full image copy of the table space.

3. Run MODIFY RECOVERY with the DELETE option to delete all previous image copies. MODIFY RECOVERY changes the alter added column status only if there are SYSCOPY rows to delete.

Modify Statistics

The MODIFY STATISTICS online utility deletes unwanted statistics history records from the corresponding catalog tables. You can remove statistics history records that were written before a specific date or remove those of a specific age. You can specify delete records for an entire table space, index space, or index.

You should run MODIFY STATISTICS regularly to clear outdated information from the statistics history catalog tables. By deleting outdated information from these tables, you can improve performance for processes that access data from them.

The MODIFY STATISTICS utility deletes rows from the following catalog tables:

-   SYSIBM.SYSCOLDIST_HIST
-   SYSIBM.SYSCOLUMNS_HIST
-   SYSIBM.SYSINDEXES_HIST
-   SYSIBM.SYSINDEXPART_HIST
-   SYSIBM.SYSINDEXSTATS_HIST
-   SYSIBM.SYSLOBSTATS_HIST
-   SYSIBM.SYSTABLEPART_HIST
-   SYSIBM.SYSTABSTATS_HIST

These are the tables used to collect historical statistics from a RUNSTATS execution. For more information about this process, refer to the RUNSTATS discussion earlier in this chapter.

You must specify the DELETE ALL option to delete rows from the SYSIBM.SYSTABLES_HIST catalog table.

The phases for MODIFY STATISTICS are the same as for MODIFY RECOVERY: UTILINIT, MODIFY, and UTILTERM.

The following example illustrates using MODIFY statistics to remove rows for the DSN8S91D table space that are older than 90 days.

```
MODIFY STATISTICS TABLESPACE DSN8D91A.DSN8S91D
  DELETE ALL
  AGE 90
```

Repair

The REPAIR online utility repairs data. The data can be your own data or data you normally would not access, such as space map pages and index entries.

REPAIR is intended as a means of replacing invalid data with valid data. Be extremely careful using REPAIR. Improper use can damage the data even further. You can use the REPAIR utility to

- test DBDs

- repair DBDs

- reset a pending status (e.g., COPY-pending) on a table space or index

- verify the contents of data areas in table spaces and indexes

- replace the contents of data areas in table spaces and indexes

- delete a single row from a table space

- produce a hexadecimal dump of an area in a table space or index

- reset the level ID

- change the page set identifier (PSID) in the header page

- delete an entire LOB from a LOB table space

- dump LOB pages

- rebuild object descriptors (OBDs) for a LOB table space

The potential output from the REPAIR utility consists of a modified page or pages in the specified DB2 table space or index and a dump of the contents.

Execution phases of REPAIR are simply initialization, performing the repair, and terminating the utility. REPAIR cannot be restarted or used at a tracker site (for information about tracker sites, see Chapter 8.)

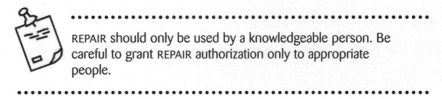

REPAIR should only be used by a knowledgeable person. Be careful to grant REPAIR authorization only to appropriate people.

Diagnose Utility

Another helpful DB2 utility, DIAGNOSE, generates information useful in detecting and correcting problems. Information such as the following can be output from the DIAGNOSE utility.

- OBD of the table space and/or index space

- Records from SYSIBM.SYSUTIL

- Module entry point lists (MEPLs)

- Available utilities on the subsystem

- Database exception table (DBET)

This example uses the DIAGNOSE utility to view MEPLs that can be used to find the service level (including most recent APAR and PTF and when they were installed) of a specific DB2 module.

```
DIAGNOSE DISPLAY MEPL
```

Standalone Utilities

Next, we look at several useful utilities that you can execute outside DB2. These tools are often referred to as *standalone utilities* or *offline utilities*.

DSNJLOGF (Preformat Active Log)

When writing to an active log data set for the first time, DB2 must preformat a VSAM control area before writing the log records. Utility DSNJLOGF avoids this delay by preformatting the active log data sets before bringing them online to DB2.

DSNJU003 (Change Log Inventory)

Utility DSNJU003 changes the bootstrap data sets (BSDSs). You can use this utility to

- add or delete active or archive log data sets

- add or delete checkpoint records

- create a conditional restart control record to control the next start of the DB2 subsystem

- change the VSAM catalog name entry in the BSDS

- modify the communication record in the BSDS

- modify the value for the highest-written log RBA value (relative byte address within the log) or the highest-off loaded RBA value

- delete the CCSID value so it can be changed for the system

DSNJU004 (Print Log Map)

Utility DSNJU004 utility lists the following information:

- Log data set name, log RBA association, and log LRSN for both copy 1 and copy 2 of all active and archive log data sets

- Active log data sets that are available for new log data

- Status of all conditional restart control records in the bootstrap data set

- Contents of the queue of checkpoint records in the bootstrap data set

- The communication record of the BSDS, if one exists

- Contents of the quiesce history record

- System and utility time stamps

- Contents of the checkpoint queue

For example, you could use this utility to determine the actual checkpoint frequency and the start and end RBA for the most current checkpoints.

In a data-sharing environment, DSNJU004 can list information from any or all BSDSs of a data-sharing group.

DSN1CHKR

Utility DSN1CHKR verifies the integrity of DB2 directory and catalog table spaces. The utility scans the specified table space for broken links, broken hash chains, and records that are not part of any link or chain. In other words, it helps to find orphaned records in the catalog and directory.

Use DSN1CHKR on a regular basis to promptly detect any damage to the catalog and directory.

DSN1COMP

Utility DSN1COMP estimates the space savings to be achieved by DB2 data compression in table spaces and indexes. (For more information about compression, see Chapter 4.) You can run the utility on the following types of data sets containing uncompressed data:

- DB2 full image copy data sets

- VSAM data sets that contain DB2 table spaces

- Sequential data sets that contain DB2 table spaces (e.g., DSN1COPY output)

DSN1COMP does not estimate savings for data sets that contain LOB table spaces.

Here's an example of the type of output produced by the DSN1COMP utility:

```
DSN194 I DSN1COMP COMPRESSION REPORT
301 KB WITHOUT COMPRESSION
224 KB WITH COMPRESSION
25 PERCENT OF THE BYTES WOULD BE SAVED
1,975 ROWS SCANNED TO BUILD DICTIONARY
4,665 ROWS SCANNED TO PROVIDE COMPRESSION ESTIMATE
4,096 DICTIONARY ENTRIES
81 BYTES FOR AVERAGE UNCOMPRESSED ROW LENGTH
52 BYTES FOR AVERAGE COMPRESSED ROW LENGTH
16 DICTIONARY PAGES REQUIRED
110 PAGES REQUIRED WITHOUT COMPRESSION
99 PAGES REQUIRED WITH COMPRESSION
10 PERCENT OF THE DB2 DATA PAGES WOULD BE SAVED
```

DSN1COPY

With the DSN1COPY standalone utility, you can copy

- DB2 VSAM data sets to sequential data sets

- DSN1COPY sequential data sets to DB2 VSAM data sets

- DB2 image copy data sets to DB2 VSAM data sets

- DB2 VSAM data sets to other DB2 VSAM data sets

- DSN1COPY sequential data sets to other sequential data sets

You can then use the copies to restore data. The restore can occur on the same DB2 or another DB2 subsystem. DSN1COPY thus provides one way to move data between subsystems.

DSN1COPY also provides the ability to

- print hexadecimal dumps of DB2 data sets and databases

- check the validity of data or index pages (including dictionary pages for compressed data)

- translate database object identifiers (OBIDs) to enable moving data sets between different systems and reset to 0 the log RBA recorded in each index page or data page

DSN1COPY is compatible with LOB table spaces when you specify the LOB keyword and omit the SEGMENT and INLCOPY keywords.

DSN1LOGP

Utility DSN1LOGP formats the contents of the recovery log for display. Two recovery log report formats are available:

- A detail report of individual log records helps IBM Support Center personnel analyze the log indetail. (This book doesn't include a full description of the detail report.)

- A summary report helps you

  - » perform a conditional restart

  - » resolve indoubt threads with a remote site

  - » detect problems with data propagation

You can specify the range of the log to process and select criteria within the range to limit the records in the detail report. For example, you can specify

- one or more units of recovery identified by unit of recovery ID (URID)

- a single database

By specifying a URID and a database, you can display recovery log records that correspond to the use of one database by a single unit of recovery.

DSN1PRNT

With the DSN1PRNT standalone utility, you can print

- DB2 VSAM data sets that contain table spaces or index spaces (including dictionary pages for compressed data)

- image copy data sets

- sequential data sets that contain DB2 table spaces or index spaces

Using DSN1PRNT, you can print hexadecimal dumps of DB2 data sets and databases. If you specify the FORMAT option, DSN1PRNT formats the data and indexes for any page that contains no error that would prevent formatting. If DSN1PRNT detects such an error, it prints an error message just before the page and dumps the page without formatting. Formatting resumes with the next page.

The utility prints compressed records in compressed format.

DSN1PRNT is especially useful when you want to identify the contents of a table space or index. You can run DSN1PRNT on image copy data sets as well as table spaces and indexes. DSN1PRNT accepts an index image copy as input when you specify the FULLCOPY option.

DSN1PRNT is compatible with LOB table spaces when you specify the LOB keyword and omit the INLCOPY keyword.

DSN1SDMP (IFC Selective Dump)

Under the direction of the IBM Support Center, you can use the DSN1SDMP utility to

- force dumps when selected DB2 trace events occur

- write DB2 trace records to a user-defined MVS data set

Displaying Utilities

By displaying the DB2 utilities, you can view important runtime information about the jobs, including jobs running in a data sharing group. You'll find information such as the following in the output.

- Type of utility

- How much of the processing the utility has completed

- Status of the utility

- Member on which the utility is executing

- Current phase of the utility

The following output shows the results of issuing a DISPLAY UTILITY command.

```
-DB1G DISPLAY UTILITY (*)

DSNU100I -DB1G DSNUGDIS USER = SAMPID
MEMBER = DB1G
UTILID = RUNTS
PROCESSING UTILITY STATEMENT 1
UTILITY = RUNSTATS
PHASE = RUNSTATS COUNT = 0
STATUS = STOPPED
DSNU100I -DB1G DSNUGDIS USER = SAMPID
MEMBER = DB2G
UTILID = CHKIX1
PROCESSING UTILITY STATEMENT 8
UTILITY = CHECK
PHASE = UNLOAD COUNT = 0
STATUS = STOPPED
DSN9022I -DB1G DSNUGCC '-DB1G DISPLAY UTILITY' NORMAL COMPLETION
```

The status field may show STOPPED, ACTIVE, INACTIVE, or TERMINATED (except for online utilities, which cannot have a status of INACTIVE).

Resolving Restrictive and Advisory States

DB2 sets a restrictive or advisory status on an object to control access and help ensure data integrity. You can use the –DISPLAY DATABASE command to display the current status for an object. Here's an example of using –DISPLAY DATABASE to display the objects that are in a restrictive state.

```
-DISPLAY DATABASE(DBASE1) SPACE(*) RESTRICT
```

The following output results for objects in a restrictive state.

```
DSNT360I  +DSN9 ********************************
DSNT361I  +DSN9 *   DISPLAY DATABASE SUMMARY
                *     RESTRICTED
DSNT360I  +DSN9 ********************************
```

```
DSNT362I  +DSN9     DATABASE = DBASE1   STATUS = RW
                     DBD LENGTH = 4028
DSNT397I  +DSN9
NAME     TYPE PART  STATUS             PHYERRLO PHYERRHI CATALOG  PIECE
-------- ---- ----- ------------------ -------- -------- -------- -----
TS001    TS         RW,RESTP
******* DISPLAY OF DATABASE DBASE1  ENDED    **********************
DSN9022I  +DSN9 DSNTDDIS 'DISPLAY DATABASE' NORMAL COMPLETION
```

You can also use the –DISPLAY DATABASE command to display objects in an advisory state:

```
-DISPLAY DATABASE(DBASE1) SPACE(*) ADVISORY
```

The following output results for objects in an advisory state.

```
DSNT360I  +DSN9 ***********************************
DSNT361I  +DSN9 *   DISPLAY DATABASE SUMMARY
                 *      ADVISORY
DSNT360I  +DSN9 ***********************************
DSNT362I  +DSN9     DATABASE = DBASE1   STATUS = RW
                     DBD LENGTH = 4028
DSNT397I  +DSN9
NAME     TYPE PART  STATUS             PHYERRLO PHYERRHI CATALOG  PIECE
-------- ---- ----- ------------------ -------- -------- -------- -----
TS002    TS         RW,ICOPY
******* DISPLAY OF DATABASE DBASE1  ENDED *********************
DSN9022I  +DSN9 DSNTDDIS 'DISPLAY DATABASE' NORMAL COMPLETION
```

You can specify options to find only those objects that are in a particular status. For example, the following output shows objects in LPL status.

```
DSNT360I  +DSN9 ***********************************
DSNT361I  +DSN9 *   DISPLAY DATABASE SUMMARY
                 *      GLOBAL LPL
DSNT360I  +DSN9 ***********************************
DSNT362I  +DSN9     DATABASE = DBASE1   STATUS = RW
                     DBD LENGTH = 4028
DSNT397I  +DSN9
NAME     TYPE PART  STATUS             LPL PAGES
-------- ---- ----- ------------------ ------------------
TS002    TS         RW                 000039-00003C
******* DISPLAY OF DATABASE DBASE1  ENDED  ********************
DSN9022I  +DSN9 DSNTDDIS 'DISPLAY DATABASE' NORMAL COMPLETION
```

Table 7.1 lists all the restrictive and advisory states (by status code), the objects affected by each state, and the corrective actions to take.

Table 7.1: Restrictive and advisory states			
Status code	**Status name**	**Affected objects**	**Corrective action(s)**
ACHKP	Auxiliary CHECK pending	Base table space, LOB table spaces	1. Update or delete invalid LOBs and XML objects using SQL. 2. Run CHECK DATA with appropriate SCOPE option to verify the validity of LOBs and XML objects.
AUXW	Auxiliary warning	Base table space	1. Update or delete invalid LOBs and XML using SQL. 2. If an orphan LOB or a version mismatch exists between the base table and the auxiliary index, use REPAIR to delete the LOB from the LOB table space. 3. Run CHECK DATA to verify the validity of LOBs and XML objects.
		LOB table space	1. Update or delete invalid LOBs and XML using SQL. 2. If an orphan LOB or a version mismatch exists between the base table and the auxiliary index, use REPAIR to delete the LOB from the LOB table space. 3. Run CHECK LOB to verify the validity of the LOBs and XML objects.
CHECKP	CHECK pending	Table space, base table space	Check and correct RI constraints using CHECK DATA. If a table space is in both REORG-pending and CHECK-pending (or auxiliary CHECK-pending) status, run REORG first and then use CHECK DATA.
		Partitioning index, non-partitioning index, index on auxiliary table	1. Run CHECK INDEX on the index. 2. If errors, run REBUILD INDEX.
		LOB table space	Run CHECK LOB. If errors: 1. Correct defects found in LOB table space with REPAIR. 2. Run CHECK LOB again.
COPY	COPY pending	Table space, table space partition	Take an image copy (best action), use – START DATABASE(*db*) SPACENAM(*ts*) ACCESS FORCE, or run REPAIR and reset COPY flag.
DBETE	Database exception table (DBET) error	Table space, partition, index, index partition, logical index partition	Contact IBM support.

Status code	Status name	Affected objects	Corrective action(s)
\multicolumn{4}{l}{*Table 7.1: Restrictive and advisory states (continued)*}
GRECP	Group buffer pool (GBP) recover pending	Table space, index space	RECOVER the object, or use the START DATABASE command.
ICOPY	Informational COPY pending	Partitioned index, non-partitioned index, index on auxiliary table	Copy the affected index.
		NOT LOGGED table space	Copy the affected table space.
LPL	Logical page list	Table spaces, index space	• START DATABASE ACCESS R/W or R/O • Run RECOVER or REBUILD INDEX utility. • Run LOAD REPLACE. • DROP the object.
RBDP	REBUILD pending	Physical or logical index partition	Run REBUILD or RECOVER on the affected index partition.
RBDP*		Logical partitions of non-partitioned secondary indexes	Run REBUILD INDEX PART or RECOVER on the affected logical partitions.
PSRBD		Non-partitioned secondary index, index on auxiliary table	Run REBUILD INDEX ALL, RECOVER, or REBUILD INDEX.
			Note: The following actions also reset the REBUILD status. • LOAD REPLACE with table space or partition • REPAIR SET INDEX with NORBDPEND on index part (however, this action doesn't correct inconsistencies). • Start database ACCESS FORCE (however, this action doesn't correct inconsistencies). • REORG INDEX SORTDATA on the index
RECP	RECOVER pending	Table space	Run the RECOVER utility on the affected object.
		Table space partition	Recover the logical partition.
		Index on auxiliary table	Run REBUILD INDEX, RECOVER INDEX, or REORG SORTDATA.

Table 7.1: Restrictive and advisory states (continued)			
Status code	Status name	Affected objects	Corrective action(s)
		Index space	Run one of the following utilities on the affected index space: • REBUILD INDEX • RECOVER INDEX • REORG INDEX SORTDATA
		Any	The following actions also reset the RECOVER status: • LOAD REPLACE with table space or partition. • REPAIR SET TABLESPACE or INDEX with NORCVRPEND on index part (however, this action doesnít correct inconsistencies). • Start database ACCESS FORCE (however, this action doesnít correct inconsistencies).
REFP	Refresh pending	Table space, index space	Run a LOAD REPLACE. The object will also be in RECP or RBDP status and will need appropriate action taken.
REORP	REORG pending	Table space	Perform one of the following: • LOAD REPLACE on entire table space • REORG TABLESPACE SHRLEVEL NONE • REORG TABLESPACE PART *n:m* SHRLEVEL NONE
		Partitioned table space	*For rows <= 32 K:* Run REORG TABLESPACE SHRLEVEL NONE SORTDATA. *For rows > 32 K:* 1. Run REORG TABLESPACE UNLOAD ONLY. 2. Run LOAD TABLESPACE FORMAT UNLOAD.
AREO*	Advisory REORG	Table space	Run one of the following utilities: • REORG TABLESPACE • LOAD REPLACE • REPAIR TABLESPACE
		Index space	Run one of the following utilities: • REORG TABLESPACE • LOAD REPLACE • REORG INDEX • REPAIR INDEX
RESTP	Restart pending	Table space, partition, index space, physical index partition	Objects are unavailable until back-out work is complete or until restart is canceled and a conditional restart or cold start is performed.

Table 7.1: Restrictive and advisory states (continued)			
Status code	Status name	Affected objects	Corrective action(s)
STOPE	Stop error	Table space, index space	RECOVER the table space or index space.
WEPR	Write error page range	Page range in error	Run a RECOVER utility on affected data.

Summary

This chapter dealt with the issues of data movement, organization, and placement in your database. We reviewed various utilities in DB2 that load data into database tables and unload data from tables, including the LOAD, UNLOAD, and DSNTIAUL utilities. We looked at various options for LOAD.

Having data in your tables is only the first step. We also reviewed the utilities and commands in DB2 that let you maintain the data in your environment. This data maintenance includes analyzing data in tables and indexes by executing REORG with available conditions. If the conditions are met, REORG is executed, resulting in physical changes to the organization of your table and index data.

We also looked at how to update the statistics of table and index data using the RUNSTATS utility. An important component of the data maintenance process is making sure your applications are aware of the updated statistics in your environment.

Many of the utilities, or particular circumstances, can put your data into a restrictive or advisory state. We concluded the chapter by looking at each of these states and how to resolve them.

Additional Resources

IBM DB2 9 Administration Guide (SC18-9840)
IBM DB2 9 Command Reference (SC18-9844)
IBM DB2 9 Utility Guide and Reference (SC18-9855)

Practice Questions

Question 1

A DBA wants to know the object descriptor (OBD) of a table space. Which utility provides this information?

- ○ A. REPAIR
- ○ B. DSN1PRNT
- ○ C. DSN1COMP
- ○ D. DIAGNOSE

Question 2

Which of the following utilities can be used to check the data consistency of indexes on the DB2 catalog?

- ○ A. DSN1CHKR
- ○ B. DSN1COPY
- ○ C. CHECK DATA
- ○ D. CHECK INDEX

Question 3

Which of the following utilities would you use to identify orphaned records in DSNDB06.SYSGROUP?

- ○ A. DSN1CHKR
- ○ B. DSN1PRNT
- ○ C. DIAGNOSE
- ○ D. CHECK DATA

Question 4

Which statistics does the following statement collect?

```
RUNSTATS TABLESPACE DSN8D81A.DSN8S81E
REPORT YES
UPDATE ALL
```

○ A. Table space statistics

○ B. Table space and index statistics

○ C. Table space and column statistics

○ D. Table space and histogram statistics

Question 5

Which of the following options is not a phase of the DB2 REORG utility?

○ A. LOG

○ B. SORT

○ C. UNLOAD

○ D. ENFORCE

Answers

Question 1

The correct answer is **D**, DIAGNOSE. The DIAGNOSE utility generates information useful in diagnosing problems. Some of the information this utility can output includes the following:

- OBD of the table space and/or index space
- Records from the SYSIBM.SYSUTIL catalog table
- Module entry point lists (MEPLs)
- Utilities available on the subsystem
- Database exception table (DBET)

Question 2

The correct answer is **D**, CHECK INDEX. You can use this utility to check the data consistency of the indexes in the DB2 catalog.

Question 3

The correct answer is **A**, DSN1CHKR. The DSN1CHKR utility verifies the integrity of DB2 directory and catalog table spaces. The utility scans the specified table space for broken links, broken hash chains, and records that aren't part of any link or chain. In other words, it helps find orphaned records in the catalog and directory.

Question 4

The correct answer is **A**, table space statistics. Only the statistics for the table space will be collected with the given syntax because the INDEX parameter and the COLUMN parameters were excluded. Also, the example does not specify use of histogram statistics with the HISTOGRAM option.

Question 5

The correct answer is **D**, ENFORCE. The ENFORCE phase is not included in the REORG utility. The phases in the REORG utility are as follows:

- UTILINIT

- UNLOAD

- RELOAD

- SORT

- BUILD

- SORTBLD

- LOG

- SWITCH

- UTILTERM

Recovery and Restart

In This Chapter

- ✔ Database recovery concepts
- ✔ Logging
- ✔ Image copies
- ✔ Data recoveries
- ✔ Disaster recoveries
- ✔ System-level backup/recovery
- ✔ DB2 restart
- ✔ Recovering postponed URs

Database Recovery Concepts

DB2 provides several methods for recovering data in the event of failure, error, or disaster. You can recover data to the current state or to a state at an earlier point in time.

Many of the objects in DB2 can be recovered using various methods. You can recover

- table spaces

- index spaces

- indexes

- partitions of a table space

- individual data sets

- pages within an error range

- individual pages

To ensure consistent operation and integrity to data, a DBA must develop strategies for several different recovery scenarios. These scenarios can include but aren't limited to

- hardware failures

- recovery from application failures

- z/OS failures

- space failures

Thanks to current technology, hardware failures hardly ever happen anymore. The most likely reason you'll need to perform a recovery is because data was logically corrupted. For example, errors in program logic may have deleted too much data, or perhaps update runs were mistakenly run twice.

You can recover from such failures only if you've taken the proper backups (image copies and log records). DB2's COPY utility lets you save your data by producing an image copy. If you save all data, the copy is called a *full copy*. If you save only the changes since the last copy, the copy is an *incremental copy*.

It's possible to recover the DB2 catalog, directory, data, and objects to what is termed a *point of consistency*. This point can be the situation that is most current (called *recovery to current* or *to the end of the log*) or a prior point in time when the data was still consistent.

DB2 for z/OS performs its backup and recovery on either a table space level or an index space level. Therefore, if you perform a recovery to a table space and go back in time, *all* tables in the table space go back in time. Backup and recovery at the table level is not possible (unless the table exists in its own table space), but you can recover at a more granular level, down to an individual page.

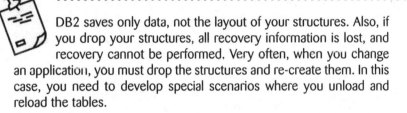

DB2 saves only data, not the layout of your structures. Also, if you drop your structures, all recovery information is lost, and recovery cannot be performed. Very often, when you change an application, you must drop the structures and re-create them. In this case, you need to develop special scenarios where you unload and reload the tables.

Unit of Work

A *unit of work* is a series of recoverable changes within an application sequence. We also refer to a unit of work as a *unit of recovery (UR)* or a *commit scope*.

An application can have several units of work within it. If an error occurs, you can perform a rollback (backing out of changes) of all the changes within the unit of work. The only rollback that DB2 can perform is on a unit of work. Once a unit of work is committed, it cannot be rolled back in time.

Logging

When changes are made to the data in tables, causing a subsequent change to the table space and index spaces, DB2 writes one or more records to its log so that it can back out the changes if the unit of work fails. DB2 can also use this information to "reapply" changes that may have been lost when recovering to a previous point in time. The primary purpose of the active log is to record all changes (inserts, updates, and deletes) made to DB2 objects. DB2 records the DML statements in the log as follows:

- On an insert, the entire after-image of the record is logged. This image is called a *redo record*.

- On a delete, the before-image is recorded. This image is called an *undo record*.

- On an update, both the before and after images (undo and redo records) are recorded.

Each log record has its own unique identifier. In a Parallel Sysplex DB2 data sharing environment, this identifier is known as the *Log Record Sequence Number (LRSN)*. In a non–data sharing environment, the identifier is known as the log *Relative Byte Address (RBA)*—basically, the offset of the record in the log from the beginning of the log. In a data sharing environment, the LRSN helps track the sequence of events that happen over multiple members in the data sharing group. Each member has its own log, and if multiple members are updating the same data, the logs must be merged during a recovery. The LRSN is unique across the sysplex, making this type of merging possible.

Log Data Sets

DB2 physically records changes in log data sets. Each DB2 subsystem has a predefined set of active logs on disk. The log records are then written to these active log data sets. When the active log data sets become full, DB2 automatically switches to the next available log data set. After all the active log data sets have been used DB2, wraps around to the first active log. However, because we don't want to lose log records (because we may want to use them for recovery or backout), the active log data sets are offloaded when they become full. Offloaded active logs are called *archive log data sets* and can be stored on disk or on cartridge tapes. As with the active log, you can have multiple copies of your archive data sets to protect yourself against failure. Using a DSNZPARM, you can specify the medium (disk or cartridge) for archive storage and how many archive copies you want to create.

Recovery from active logs is faster than recovery from archive logs, and recovery from disk archive data sets is much faster recovery than tape archive logs because you can take advantage of DB2's ability to process the logs in parallel.

DB2 allows many archive log data sets, and you'll want to keep archive log data sets in case a recovery is necessary. The retention period of the archive log data sets depends on your image copy frequency and how far you want to go back in time during a point-in-time recovery. You can keep up to 10,000 archive logs.

DB2 also provides a dual-logging capability to ensure two copies of the active log data sets exist; in the event that one is lost, the other can be used for recovery. During a recovery, DB2 applies the changes recorded in the active log that are required to recover to the specified point in time. If the records required for recovery are no longer on the active log, DB2 calls for the appropriate archive log(s).

All production systems should be using dual logs to ensure data can be recovered successfully. As a best practice, you should size the active logs to keep 24 to 48 hours of log data.

BSDS

The *bootstrap data set (BSDS)* is a VSAM key-sequenced data set that contains information about the DB2 logs, the records contained in those logs, and other information. The DB2 system records all the current active log data sets in the BSDS. During offload processing, DB2 dynamically allocates a new data set with a unique name. After a successful offload, this data set is recorded in the BSDS, and DB2 creates a copy of the BSDS. In the case where the archive log is placed on a cartridge, this BSDS copy is placed on the same cartridge. During a recovery, DB2 uses the BSDS to find all the available archive logs.

The DSNZPARM parameter MAXARCH determines the number of records the BSDS can contain. The BSDS should be large enough to record all archive logs. The proper setting for MAXARCH depends on how large your archive logs are and on the oldest point in time to which an application is allowed to recover. Be sure to set the MAXARCH parameter high enough for your environment, and retain your archive log data sets long enough so that you'll have them if a recovery requires you to go back through older archive logs.

If a data set is no longer recorded in the BSDS but is still physically available, it's possible to place its entry in the BSDS by using the standalone utility DSNJU003 (Change Log Inventory). However, you can do so only when the DB2 subsystem is stopped, thereby causing an outage.

DB2 should always be operating with dual bootstrap data sets (dual BSDS operation). If for some reason one is lost, you'll need to restore it using the following general steps.

1. Rename the damaged BSDS.

2. Define a new BSDS.

3. Use the REPRO command to copy the BSDS from the non-damaged BSDS to the new one.

4. Run standalone utility DSNJU004 (Print Log Map) to list the contents of the replacement BSDS.

You must perform these steps to restore dual BSDS operation because if DB2 has to be stopped, it can't be restarted until dual BSDS operation is re-established.

SYSIBM.SYSLGRNX

Table SYSIBM.SYSLGRNX in the DB2 directory gives DB2 the ability to determine the log records for a table space and recoverable indexes by recording the periods of updates for these objects. The SYSLGRNX table contains a row for each time period during which update activity occurred for a table space or index spaces. This row records the following information.

- Database object identifier (DBID) and object identifier (OBID) of the object

- Partition number

- LRSN and local log RBA of the first update after open

- LRSN and local log RBA when a pseudo-close occurred (no more update activity)

- If data sharing, the member which performed the updates

This information helps DB2 determine which log data sets (or parts of the log) it will need in the event of a recovery. It speeds up the recovery process by enabling DB2 to skip the logs that contain no updates for the object being recovered.

If you need to recover SYSLGRNX to a prior point in time, and an application needs to recover to the current point in time, the application must use the TOLOGPOINT option on the RECOVER utility to be sure to apply all the necessary logs.

Removing Rows from SYSLGRNX

The MODIFY utility lets you delete outdated information from the tables that store image copy information. You should execute MODIFY often and on a scheduled basis, depending on system activity. This practice helps improve the performance of several different processes that access the SYSIBM.SYSLGRNX and SYSIBM.SYSCOPY catalog tables. Due to the nature of the data they contain, these tables can grow in size considerably and require a good deal of space.

If your SYSLGRNX and SYSCOPY tables are very large, the recommendation is to delete outdated information by using MODIFY to delete entries by age. For example, it might be best to have one run of the utility remove rows older than 20 months. If you want to keep information longer for recovery, you're advised to unload the tables that have this requirement and keep the DDL to recreate these tables. This approach lets you recreate very old data, possibly under a different name. The DB2 recovery information is not intended for these scenarios.

Image Copies

To be able to recover data when a problem occurs, you need a solid recovery plan and a strategy in place for each of the many situations that can arise. A key part of your plan should include performing image copies on a regular basis. You create image copies of your table spaces and selected index spaces.

Frequency of Image Copies

How often image copies should be taken depends on the allowable down time for the primary user of an application. You should determine this clock-time requirement ahead of time in case you have to recover your data. If an application can't be unavailable for more than two hours, for example, you'll need to take image copies more frequently than if the application can be unavailable for a complete day.

Depending on the currency of data required in the recovery, you'll need to determine when image copies can be taken and what types of image copies to take. You may need to take incremental image copies throughout the day, or you may need to do only one full copy at the end of the day's processing. In some situations, especially where long-running batch processes are involved, the practice is to take an image copy at the beginning of a batch window. This procedure enables a restore in case something goes wrong during the batch cycle.

Some technical considerations also play a role in determining image copy frequency. The minimum time you should allow is half the retention period of the archive log less one day (*[retention period / 2] – 1 day*). This formula guarantees that two valid image copies of the table spaces exist at any moment. You always want two valid copies because of possible media failure, as well as to reduce the risk of inconsistent data on the image copy. After a drop and recreate of an object, all system-retained recovery information is gone. After running utilities that re-create data (e.g., REORG, LOAD REPLACE without the LOG YES option), you must take an image copy to establish a new base for recovery.

Dual Image Copies

It's a good idea to have multiple copies of an image copy in case one copy becomes damaged. You can easily make additional copies (dual) by using the COPYDDN parameter on the COPY utility control card. Here, you can specify a primary copy and a secondary (or backup) copy by providing the DD names for the two copy data sets. The backup copy is intended to be a local backup copy, available for use during a recovery should the primary copy be unusable. Many installations create this local backup copy in addition to a copy made for remote site recovery.

When making image copy data sets, take note of two recommendations:

- Consider using generation data groups (GDGs) for backups to generate unique data set names for the image copy.

- Use DISP=(MOD, CATLG) to provide the ability to restart the COPY utility.

Remember that GDGs are cataloged at the end of a job (not job step). If a job fails, the data set name is already recorded in SYSIBM.SYSCOPY but not in the z/OS catalog. The next run will result in the COPY utility rejecting duplicate names.

In addition to using dual copies, you can make two sets of copies: so that you can have two copies on-site (local) and two off-site (remote). Using just the second copy of a dual copy for off-site backup isn't the best choice because if your on-site copy is bad, obtaining the off-site copy after a failure may be inconvenient, depending on where the off-site storage is located. Keeping two copies at the primary site ensures that you have an immediate backup available to use if one copy is bad. The same concept applies when recovering from image copies at a disaster recovery site (you should maintain two copies there as well).

To create two sets of dual image copies, execute the COPY utility like this:

```
COPY TABLESPACE DSN8D91A.DSN8S91S COPYDDN(DD1, DD2)
   RECOVERYDDN(DD3,DD4)...
```

This statement instructs DB2 to take two copies for the primary site and two for the recovery site.

By default, the COPY utility also performs page validity checking. This check takes place one page at a time during the copy and is set with the CHECKPAGE parameter.

COPYTOCOPY

DB2's COPYTOCOPY utility lets you make additional image copies from a primary image copy. The copies are registered in the DB2 catalog with the following information.

- Original values from the source copy:

    » ICDATE

    » ICTIME

    » START_RBA

- Additional values for COPYTOCOPY:

    » DSNAME

    » GROUP_MEMBER

    » JOBNAME

    » AUTHID

The target object is left in read/write access mode (UTRW), which lets SQL statements and some utilities run concurrently with the same target objects. You can take a maximum of three copies at once using COPYTOCOPY, for a total of four copies: local primary, local backup, remote site primary, and remote site backup.

COPYTOCOPY provides about a 5 percent performance benefit over the COPY utility, and it helps minimize the time needed for copying critical options to create additional remote site copies. The following example illustrates the syntax.

```
COPYTOCOPY TABLESPACE DSN8D91A.DSN8S91S
FROM LASTFULLCOPY RECOVERY DDN(rempri)
```

Tape vs. Disk Image Copies

The fastest recoveries occur when the input data sets reside on disk. This principle applies both to recoveries that use image copies and to those that use archive logs. However, because disk space is more expensive than cartridges, you face a trade-off between the cost of an unavailable application versus the cost of disk space. Mounting, remounting, and winding of cartridges can take a long time.

If you use the cartridge method and stack the files, be sure to specify the proper JCL options during image copy and recovery so that the cartridge stays mounted and positioned. You can automate the handling of stacked files on cartridge by using TEMPLATE statements in the utility parameters. In V9, a new feature lets you specify that the COPY operation use disk up to a certain size and allocate to tape if the image copy exceeds that size.

Full and Incremental Image Copies

DB2 provides two different types of backups: full copies and incremental copies. A full image copy copies all the pages in the table space, whether or not they contain data that has changed since the last full copy (FULL YES is the utility default). Incremental image copies copy only the pages that have changed since the last image copy (FULL NO). You can view the type of copy in the ICTYPE column of the SYSCOPY catalog table, along with the database name, table space name, time of the copy, start RBA/LRSN, data set name, and volume serial number (if the image copy isn't cataloged). A full image copy will have an ICTYPE of F; an incremental image copy will have an ICTYPE of I.

Incremental copies of data can be useful, but the procedures involved in taking these copies are more complex than those for full image copies, involving decisions such as how often to take the copies and when to run the MERGECOPY utility (covered shortly). Many database administrators therefore choose to take only full image copies.

When you use incremental image copies, you run the risk of losing data or extending the recovery time. Incremental copies are a substitute for the log. During the log apply phase, DB2 tries to mount the incremental image copies so it can skip large parts of the log. If this attempt fails, DB2 notes the RBA or LOGPOINT of the last successful incremental copy and uses the archive log from that point on. If the archive log from that point in time no longer exists, the recovery will fail.

Some administrators use the incremental copy utility for its speed and then run the MERGECOPY utility to merge the last full copy and the latest incremental copy into a new full copy. This procedure combines the best of both worlds: ease of recovery and the speed of incremental image copies.

You might want to reconsider the use of incremental copies if your data is very volatile and more than 5 percent of the pages are updated between copies. In this type of environment, the run time of the incremental image copy will be longer than that for a full copy. If run time isn't an issue and the size of the image copy data set is, an incremental copy might be the best solution. Using Real Time Statistics is especially useful in this case. (For information about RTS, see Chapter 7.)

If you've turned off the feature that tracks space map changes (TRACKMOD NO) in the table space definition, incremental copies must perform a table space scan to find the individual pages that have changed and must be copied. In this case, you should avoid incremental copies and use only full image copies.

The image copy utility provides parameters that let you determine, by setting user-defined thresholds, whether DB2 makes an incremental or a full image copy. You can use these thresholds to control subsequent steps taken by the utility, depending on whether an incremental copy or a full copy is done.

Both full and incremental copies are important for creating backups in a 24x7 environment, and both must be able to meet an acceptable recovery window. You should take full copies when

- a table is newly loaded using LOAD LOG NO

- a table is loaded with LOAD RESUME LOG NO

- a table is reorganized with REORG LOG NO

- table data has been modified extensively

> DB2 enforces an image copy in the first three of these instances by setting the image copy pending (COPY) condition for the object. Ignoring this status (e.g., by using the REPAIR utility to turn it off) is unwise unless you never intend to update the data again and you keep the original input of the utility (e.g., a load in a data warehouse environment).

Take incremental copies when changes have been made to the table since the last full image copy and processing the log would take too much time during the recovery. During recovery, DB2 requires access to all incremental copies at the same time. If the incremental copies reside on cartridge, this could be a problem because of the number of available units. If DB2 cannot mount all incremental image copies, it ignores them and starts processing the log data again. You can prevent this situation by running the MERGECOPY utility to merge incremental image copies into a single set.

Copy of Partitions or Data Sets

For both table spaces and index spaces, you can back up individual partitions with the COPY utility by specifying the partition number in the DSNUM keyword on the utility control statement. You cannot copy logical partitions of non-partitioning indexes, and if the PIFCESIZE keyword was used when an index was created, the pieces of the index cannot be individually image copied. The DSNUM value is recorded in the SYSCOPY table for each partition or data set copied.

If you image copy by partition, you must also recover by partition. If you image copy the entire partitioned table space (no use of DSNUM), you can recover the entire table space or one or more partitions.

Multiple Copy Data Sets

You can specify multiple objects in a single COPY statement. This feature lets you take image copies of multiple objects (e.g., table spaces, partitions) in one job step and enables the use of parallelism. To specify multiple objects, you simply repeat the object clause as many times as needed:

```
COPY TABLESPACE DSN8D91A.DSN8S91S COPY DDN dsname1
 TABLESPACE DSN8D91A.DSN8S91C COPY DDN dsname2
 INDEX DSN8910.XEMP1 COPY DDN dsname3
PARALLEL (3)
```

This example copies multiple objects using three parallel streams (PARALLEL (3)). DB2 will attempt three streams, although storage constraints may cause this number to be reduced or ignored. Note that the PARALLEL option doesn't work if you're using a cartridge and the copies are stacked. In this case, the copies are still taken in a serial fashion, and DB2 ignores the PARALLEL keyword.

CHANGELIMIT

By using the COPY utility's CHANGELIMIT feature, you can tell DB2 to take an image copy (full or incremental) only if a specified percentage of changed pages is reached in a table space or partition. The value (or values) you provide in the CHANGELIMIT parameter specify when the copy should be taken.

For example, the following COPY statement causes DB2 to recommend an incremental image copy if the percentage of changed pages is greater than 5 percent but less than 30 percent. The statement instructs DB2 to take a full image copy if the percentage of changed pages is 30 percent or greater.

```
COPY TABLESPACE DSN8D91A.DSN8S91S CHANGELIMIT (5,30)
```

Another COPY utility feature, REPORTONLY, lets you observe whether DB2 recommends an image copy due to the CHANGELIMIT values being met. This feature could help to report whether any changes occurred against an object, possibly for auditing purposes.

The following example demonstrates use of the CHANGELIMIT and REPORTONLY features.

```
COPY TABLESPACE DSN8D91A.DSN8S91S CHANGELIMIT (5,30) REPORTONLY
```

Because this COPY statement specifies REPORTONLY, DB2 won't actually take an image copy but will simply recommend it if the specified values dictate it.

When you use the CHANGELIMIT option, there's a possibility that an image copy won't actually be taken, thus creating an empty copy data set. This result is undesirable, especially with GDGs, because you could lose previous image copies. Using the REPORTONLY option sets the condition code for this job step. The condition code depends on the advice given and can be used with conditional JCL (e.g., full copies go to cartridge, incremental copies go to DISK). You can use the REPORTONLY option to prevent an empty copy data set.

Access During Image Copy Process

During the taking of an image copy, you can choose whether to allow concurrent access. You can do this using either of two alternative methods.

Utility Mode

The first method is simply to start the object in utility mode. To do so, issue the –START DATABASE command using the ACCESS(UT) option. You can specify utility access for both table spaces and index spaces. Choosing this option lets only utilities be executed against the objects. If any other concurrent processes try to access the objects, they will be rejected.

SHRLEVEL

The other way to control concurrent access is through the SHRLEVEL parameter on the COPY utility. The options are REFERENCE and CHANGE.

- SHRLEVEL REFERENCE forces the COPY utility process to wait until no writers are using the table space or index space. The writers must commit their changes before the utility can continue. The benefit to this option is that readers are permitted against the objects being copied during the utility execution. However, no updating is allowed. This option also guarantees that the copies are created in a single run of the COPY utility and have no incomplete units of work.

- SHRLEVEL CHANGE permits applications to update the objects during the image copy. This means that some changes made during the copy may be in the log but not necessarily in the copy itself. An image copy created by this method is often called a *fuzzy copy*.

Regardless of which SHRLEVEL setting you use, DB2 associates a log RBA or LRSN with the image copy and records it in SYSIBM.SYSCOPY. This value indicates the point in the DB2 log from which DB2 would then need to apply log records during a recovery process.

Inline Copies

After loading a table space using LOAD REPLACE or reorganizing a table space, you must establish a full image copy to avoid long log apply phases in the event a recovery is necessary. Taking a copy inline during the LOAD or REORG utility execution is much faster than executing the COPY utility afterward, and it avoids setting the COPY-pending status, thereby increasing the availability of the table space.

An inline copy taken during a LOAD REPLACE or REORG utility execution is equivalent to a full image copy taken with SHRLEVEL REFERENCE, with a few minor differences (e.g., out-of-order pages, multiple versions) that might cause the inline copy to be slightly larger that a normal full copy. Regardless, the inline copy works just fine for recoveries. It can be processed by all DB2 utilities and can be the basis for future incremental image copies.

You request inline copies on the COPYDDN keyword in the LOAD or REORG utility. The syntax also supports use of the RECOVERYDDN keyword to request inline copies for the remote site.

```
LOAD....REPLACE
  COPYDDN (local-primary,(local-backup))
  (RECOVERYDDN (remote-primary,(remote-backup))

REORG
  COPYDDN (local-primary,(local-backup))
  (RECOVERYDDN (remote-primary,(remote-backup))
```

DFSMS Concurrent Copy

A Data Facility Storage Management System (DFSMS) concurrent copy can copy a data set concurrently with other processes. There are two ways to use concurrent copy:

- Execute the COPY utility with the CONCURRENT keyword. DB2 records the copy in SYSIBM.SYSCOPY. The RECOVER utility can use these copies and the logs for recovery.

- Make copies outside DB2. To recover, you'll need to restore the data sets; the logs can then be applied.

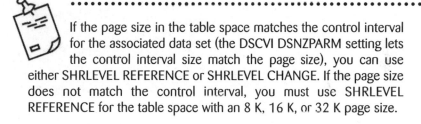

If the page size in the table space matches the control interval for the associated data set (the DSCVI DSNZPARM setting lets the control interval size match the page size), you can use either SHRLEVEL REFERENCE or SHRLEVEL CHANGE. If the page size does not match the control interval, you must use SHRLEVEL REFERENCE for the table space with an 8 K, 16 K, or 32 K page size.

MERGECOPY Utility

The MERGECOPY utility merges existing incremental image copies into a single incremental copy or a new full copy to help lessen recovery time. You should execute this utility based on the amount of exposure perceived in your environment and on the amount of downtime allowed in a recovery. For recover-to-current to be effective, running MERGECOPY frequently is beneficial. If point-in-time recoveries are more likely, MERGECOPY is not beneficial.

MERGECOPY improves performance for to-current recoveries because DB2 needs just the full copy and possibly one incremental copy to recover, instead of having to read through multiple incremental copies. However, for a point-in-time recovery (TORBA or TOCOPY), MERGECOPY may not provide any benefit.

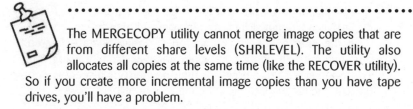

The MERGECOPY utility cannot merge image copies that are from different share levels (SHRLEVEL). The utility also allocates all copies at the same time (like the RECOVER utility). So if you create more incremental image copies than you have tape drives, you'll have a problem.

Let's consider an example that assumes the image copy schedule depicted in the following table.

Copy type	Copy date
Full	May 1
Incremental	May 10
Incremental	May 20
Incremental	May 30
Merge	June 5

If you want to recover to May 20 and the MERGECOPY scheduled for June 5 has not yet been done, the incremental from May 20 will still be in SYSCOPY and can be used to recover to. After the MERGECOPY, the May 20 copy will no longer be in SYSCOPY; DB2 must then go back to the full image copy taken on May 1 and do a forward log apply to May 20. Recovery time will be longer because more of the log will have to be applied.

You can use the NEWCOPY keyword on the MERGECOPY utility to specify whether you want to take a new full copy or just merge all the incremental copies into one new incremental copy:

```
MERGECOPY...NEWCOPY YES
```

or

```
MERGECOPY...NEWCOPY NO
```

When you perform a MERGECOPY and create a new incremental copy, DB2 deletes all the rows in SYSIBM.SYSCOPY for the merged copies.

Another important reason to merge copies frequently is that if DB2 can't mount all incremental copies during a recovery (e.g., if the incremental copies are on cartridge and there aren't enough units), it will choose to apply changes from the log. This procedure increases the amount of time needed for a recovery and could cause the recovery to fail if the log is unavailable.

REPORT Utility

To obtain a report that identifies all referential relationships to a given table, run the REPORT utility with the TABLESPACESET option. You can use the resulting information to determine which table spaces should be quiesced and image copied together. Keep in mind that the report covers only relationships defined in DB2. There may be other, application-defined relationships between tables that belong in the same recovery scope.

The TABLESPACESET option is available for all utilities in combination with templates. You can use this feature to automate utilities if you use DB2-enforced referential integrity.

Index Copy

It's not necessary to have an image copy of an index to recover the index; you can rebuild the index from the data in the table using the REBUILD INDEX utility. You can also recover the index from an image copy. In some cases, it may be faster to recover an index from an image copy versus rebuilding, especially if the index has little or no change activity. When you recover an index from an image copy, DB2 can perform the index recovery in parallel with the table space recovery.

Once you enable an index for image copies (by specifying the COPY YES option on the CREATE INDEX or ALTER INDEX DDL statement), DB2 records recovery information about the index in both SYSIBM.SYSCOPY and SYSIBM.SYSLGRNX. No changes to the log occur because indexes are always logged to enable the rollback of a unit of work. Index copies can only be full image copies because indexes have no space map to determine updated pages. The concept of incremental image copies does not exist for an index.

Copying the Catalog and Directory

You start a DB2 system-wide recovery by first recovering the catalog and directory, and no other recoveries are possible until you complete this process. Therefore, you should image copy the catalog and directory often to make the recovery process for these objects as fast as possible.

If you lose your catalog and/or directory, you won't have an operational DB2 subsystem.

The time required to recover the catalog and directory is crucial and must be minimized. Because DB2 performs the log apply for the catalog and directory, it doesn't matter when you take the image copy of the catalog. However, it helps if you take a SHRLEVEL REFERENCE image copy just before cutting your last archive; then, store both this image and the archive logs in a vault or off-site. In this way, you ensure that the DB2 catalog contains all updates and that it remains valuable without the archive logs.

It's also important to keep the Integrated Catalog Facility in sync with your DB2 catalog. For example, in a disaster recovery scenario, if the ICF catalog has yesterday's image, your DB2 catalog will reference data sets (e.g., image copies, table spaces) that according to the ICF catalog don't exist. To avoid this problem, make sure the recovery procedures of the ICF catalog match the DB2 catalog.

Establishing a Point of Consistency

To make sure it's possible to recover to a point in time where everything is consistent and in sync, you must establish a *point of consistency*, or common quiesce point. The purpose of this point of consistency is to establish a recovery set so that DB2 can recover related objects to a consistent point in time.

You establish a point of consistency by executing the QUIESCE utility. QUIESCE "quiets" the system and writes to the log the time when no activity was occurring and everything was in sync. It does this by waiting for current units of work to be completed and preventing any new ones from beginning. After the last unit of work is completed, the utility establishes a quiesce point. It notes this point for each table space and index space in a recovery set by recording the START_RBA value of the quiesce point in SYSIBM.SYSCOPY. This row has an ICTYPE of Q. These objects then have a common point to which they can be recovered.

You determine which objects will be together in establishing this common point by using the TABLESPACESET keyword on the QUIESCE utility:

```
QUIESCE TABLESPACESET
        TABLESPACE dbname1.tsname1
        TABLESPACE dbname2.tsname2
```

You can also specify particular partitions of a partitioned table space.

•••

By specifying WRITE YES (the default), you can ensure that all changed pages of the table space are written to DISK.

•••

•••

The QUIESCE utility drains the table spaces one by one. In a system that is heavily updated and on which long-running units of recovery can be in the way, QUIESCE can cause a serious outage because it keeps those table spaces that it is able to drain locked, causing SQL to fail.

•••

Another way to establish a consistent point for your data is to establish a copy set. If you perform a single copy of multiple objects using the COPY utility with SHRLEVEL REFERENCE, those objects will have the same START_RBA value, thereby constituting a recovery copy set.

Recovery Concepts

Now that we've discussed how to make proper backups for our DB2 objects and how the DB2 log functions, let's turn our attention to how you use these objects in the event of a recovery. We'll also examine the various types of recoveries. You can recover a single object, a system-level backup, or a list of objects.

Table Space Recovery

To recover a table space, you use the RECOVER utility, which operates in two major phases: RESTORE and LOGAPPLY.

In the RESTORE phase, the RECOVER utility determines which full image copy it needs by looking at the rows in the SYSIBM.SYSCOPY table. It takes the appropriate full image copy and merges it with any incremental copies found in SYSCOPY, replacing any updated pages in the full copy. This updated copy then provides the basis for restoring the table space.

Once the utility brings the full image copy up to current by merging the incremental image copies, it enters the LOGAPPLY phase. Here, RECOVER applies any changes recorded in the DB2 log that were made after the image copies were taken. The utility reads the log and applies the changes to the restored table space. It uses the SYSLGRNX table to identify the range in the DB2 log that pertains to the table space being recovered. It also uses the START_RBA value in SYSCOPY to identify the latest image copy used during the RESTORE phase and to know the point in the log from which the records must be applied. The LOGAPPLY phase is very efficient because it can sort the log on page number and then on RBA/LRSN.

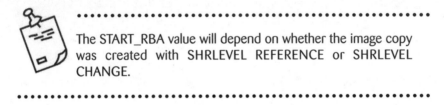

The START_RBA value will depend on whether the image copy was created with SHRLEVEL REFERENCE or SHRLEVEL CHANGE.

It's possible to use backups that weren't created by DB2; however, in that case restoring any object becomes your own responsibility and you should have the RECOVER utility perform a LOGAPPLY only.

Index Recovery

As we noted earlier, you can also recover indexes if they were enabled for image copies in the DDL definition (CREATE INDEX...COPY YES). When you use image copies, DB2 recovers the index rather than rebuilding it from the table using the REBUILD INDEX utility. Only full image copies are permitted on indexes—no incremental copies. The RECOVER utility's LOGAPPLY phase works the same way, applying the necessary changes from the log since the time of the last image copy.

Even if an index is marked as recoverable, you can still rebuild. The REBUILD INDEX utility extracts the index keys from the data, sorts the keys, and builds the index again, ignoring all recovery information available.

Other Object Recovery

You can recover smaller objects as well, performing recoveries against

- a partition

- a data set of a non-partitioned index (NPI)

- a partition of a data-partitioned secondary index (DPSI)

- a single page

- an error page range

• •

You cannot recover a single table independently.

• •

Multiple Object Recovery

Just as it's possible to back up multiple objects in the same job execution, you can also recover multiple objects at the same time. Using a single RECOVER statement, you can recover multiple table spaces, index spaces, partitions, or data sets. To do so, you simply repeat the TABLESPACE, INDEXSPACE, or INDEX clause:

```
RECOVER  TABLESPACE dbname1.tsname1
         TABLESPACE dbname2.tsname2
         INDEXSPACE creator1.ixname1
         (PARALLEL (2))
```

When you specify the PARALLEL option, DB2 performs the RESTORE phases in parallel. This example attempts two streams of parallelism. DB2 will start and execute the RESTORE phases for the specified objects in parallel. One task reads the pages from the image copy, the other tasks write the pages that are read, and all this occurs in parallel.

DB2 reads the log only once during the LOGAPPLY phase. This phase is common for all the objects being recovered; it does not use parallelism, but it can sort the log to improve performance.

If insufficient storage exists to support multiple streams, DB2 will lessen the parallel degree or even serialize the recoveries.

In the past, parallel recovery was possible only if the image copies were on DISK; if the copies were stacked on cartridge, the recovery processes were serialized. As of DB2 8, stack copies on tape can be recovered in parallel. This enhancement improves usability and performance by implicitly RETAINing mounted volumes for input data sets used by the RECOVER and COPYTOCOPY utilities. It also enables dynamic allocation access for data sets stacked onto a tape volume. No unnecessary unload and remount of tapes occurs between access.

If objects in the list require a system-level backup that has been dumped to tape as its recovery base (i.e., you've specified the FROMDUMP option), the RECOVER utility invokes DFSMShsm to restore the data sets for the objects in parallel, with the degree of parallelism being capped by the maximum number of tasks that RECOVER can start. DFSMShsm restores the data sets in parallel based on its install options.

Recovery Using Database Copy Pool

It's possible to perform a recovery of a table space by restoring data sets from the database copy pool. The RECOVER utility's FROMDUMP keyword specifies that only dumps of the database copy pool are to be used to restore the data sets. The DUMPCLASS (*dcl*) keyword then indicates the DFSMShsm dump class to use to restore the data sets. The FROMDUMP and DUMPCLASS options that you specify for the RECOVER utility override the RESTORE/RECOVER FROM DUMP and DUMPCLASS NAME install options specified on installation panel DSNTIP6.

We provide more information about system-level backups and the database copy pool later in the chapter.

Recovery Involving NOT LOGGED Tables

When you create or alter a table space, you can suppress logging by specifying the NOT LOGGED option. Because recovery generally relies on logs, the recovery of NOT LOGGED table spaces requires some extra planning. In particular, you should have a data recovery source that does not depend on a log record to re-create any lost data, or you should limit unlogged modifications to easily repeatable changes that can be re-created quickly.

In addition, avoid actions that place a table space in a RECOVER-pending status during data recovery. Such actions include

- issuing a ROLLBACK or a ROLLBACK TO SAVEPOINT after modifying a table in a NOT LOGGED table space

- causing duplicate keys or referential integrity violations when you modify a NOT LOGGED table space

You should also avoid duplicate key or referential constraint violations in NOT LOGGED table spaces. If these violations occur, the table space will be unavailable until you fix it manually.

Recovering NOT LOGGED LOB or XML Table Spaces

To make sure you're prepared to recover NOT LOGGED table spaces that have associated LOB or XML table spaces, take image copies as a recovery set. This practice ensures that DB2 copies the base table space and all associated LOB or XML table spaces at the same point in time. A subsequent RECOVER TO LASTCOPY operation for the entire set will then result in consistent data across the base table space and the associated LOB and XML table spaces.

Fallback Recovery

Things sometimes go wrong in recoveries, as when an image copy is unavailable, defective, or simply deleted. DB2 has a few choices in these cases:

- Local copies

  » If the local primary copy can't be used, DB2 tries to use the local backup copy. DB2 won't try to use the remote copies because it assumes you're keeping those copies off-site.

- Incremental copies

  » If an incremental copy can't be used, DB2 merges all prior incremental copies with the full copy, ignoring the defective incremental and all subsequent incremental image copies. It then starts the LOGAPPLY phase at the START_RBA of the last merged incremental copy.

- Invalid full copies

  » If the full copy can't be used, DB2 falls back to a previous full image copy and merges it with the incremental image copies (if available). If no good full copy exists at all, either the table space is recovered from the log or a DSNU510I error message is issued and the RECOVER utility terminates in error.

- Index space invalid copies

  » If no valid index space copies exist, a DSNU510I error message is issued, and the RECOVER utility terminates. In this case, you must rebuild the index from the table using the REBUILD INDEX utility.

••

If a REORG LOG NO or LOAD LOG NO was performed after the image copy was created, fallback processing will fail.

••

REPORT RECOVERY

The REPORT RECOVERY utility can aid recovery planning by providing information about

- recovery history from SYSIBM.SYSCOPY

- log ranges from SYSIBM.SYSLGRNX

- VOL-SER numbers where archive logs and BSDS reside

- VOL-SER numbers where image copy data sets reside

The information from this utility helps you identify the image copies, active logs, and archive logs needed to recover a table space.

Using Fast Log Apply

The RECOVER utility can use the standard log apply process during recoveries, or it can use a *fast log apply (FLA)* if this feature has been enabled. The FLA process is enabled if the size of the log apply storage in the DBM1 address space is a non-zero value. This setting, specified by DSNZPARM LOGAPSTG on the DSNTIPL installation panel, has a default value of 100.

The FLA process uses two buffers, known as *FLA buffers*. DB2 uses one buffer to read the log records and uses the other to apply the log records to the table space or index space. When the read buffer fills, the pages are sorted and then applied (making this now the write buffer); then, the older write buffer becomes the new read buffer and begins to fill. The two buffers continue this flipping process until all records have been read and applied.

FLA also takes advantage of parallelism by using one task per object being recovered to apply the logs while an additional task reads the next set of log records at the same time.

Point-in-Time Recovery

You can use the TOLOGPOINT parameter in your RECOVER job to recover to any previous point in time. You specify this parameter to provide the log RBA or LRSN of the point in time for the recovery. The value should be a quiesce point that was established for the copy recovery set. You can obtain this information from the SYSIBM.SYSCOPY table or by using the REPORT RECOVERY utility.

After performing a point-in-time recovery, DB2 inserts a row into SYSIBM.SYSCOPY with an ICTYPE of P for each recovered object to permit future recoveries to skip the associated log ranges.

Uncommitted work by units of work that are active at the specified RBA or LRSN will be backed out, and the objects will be left in a consistent state. This process will work even if the chosen point is not a quiesce point.

In a non–data-sharing environment, you can use the TORBA keyword, but TOLOGPOINT is the recommended choice. In a distributed environment, you can also use TORBA to recover two table spaces in two separate subsystems to the same point in time.

To avoid any pending conditions when you recover a table space set to a prior point in time, be sure to specify all the related table spaces in the same RECOVER control statement. You can use the TABLESPACESET keyword in the table space statement to accomplish this.

When a point-in-time recovery is performed for multiple objects in a single RECOVER utility control statement with TOCOPY, there is no LOGAPPLY phase, only a RESTORE phase to the last image copy. Therefore, you must use multiple control statements to prevent a CHKP status from being set on the objects where referential integrity relationships exist. Using TOCOPY will also cause DB2 to set a RBDP or CHKP status on the indexes. It's wiser to specify a common START_RBA for a recovery copy set via the TOLOGPOINT parameter.

Another option is to use RESTOREBEFORE. The RESTOREBEFORE X'*byte-string*' option specifies that RECOVER is to search for an image copy, concurrent copy, or system-level backup (if you've specified YES for SYSTEM-LEVEL BACKUPS on install panel DSNTIP6) with an RBA or LRSN value earlier than the specified X'*byte-string*' value to use in the RESTORE phase. To avoid specific image copies, concurrent copies, or system-level backups with matching or more recent RBA or LRSN values in START_RBA, the RECOVER utility applies the log records and restores the object to its current state or to the specified TORBA or TOLOGPOINT value. The utility compares the RESTOREBEFORE value with the RBA or LRSN value in the START_RBA column in the SYSIBM.SYSCOPY record for those copies. For system-level backups, it compares the RESTOREBEFORE value with the data complete LRSN. If you specify a TORBA or TOLOGPOINT value with the RESTOREBEFORE option, the RBA or LRSN value for RESTOREBEFORE must be lower than the specified TORBA or TOLOGPOINT value. If you specify RESTOREBEFORE, you cannot specify TOCOPY, TOLASTCOPY, or TOLASTFULLCOPY.

Pending Conditions

A point-in-time recovery can result in a variety of pending conditions:

- Rebuild pending (RBDP)

  » This status results for indexes that existed on tables that were part of a table space that was recovered. This applies to indexes that were not copy-enabled. A copy-enabled index receives this status only if it was not included in the recovery set.

  » Recovering only certain partitions can result in RBDP* status for a non-partitioning index, rendering the index inaccessible.

- Check pending (CHKP)

  » This status results when you recover a table space containing tables that have referential integrity relationships with tables that were not recovered.

  » This status also results when you recover indexes for table spaces that were not also recovered.

To resolve these statuses, you must take certain actions. For a RBDP condition, you must run the REBUILD INDEX utility to rebuild the index. You'll also need to rebuild the index if the RBDP* status is set for a logical partition of a non-partitioning index.

For a CHKP status, you must perform the CHECK DATA utility. CHECK DATA finds any violations of referential integrity constraints and can optionally resolve them by removing the offending rows and any directly or indirectly dependent rows. CHKP conditions on an index may indicate that the index is inconsistent with the data in the table. The CHECK INDEX utility can help resolve such inconsistencies by determining whether there are any; if so, you can run the REBUILD INDEX utility to rebuild the index and get it back in sync with the data.

CHECK INDEX resets the CHKP flag if no inconsistencies are detected. If inconsistencies exist between the index and the data, you may want to run the REBUILD INDEX utility immediately to resolve problems in a timely way.

If you encounter any unexpected pending conditions (especially recovery pending, or RECP), carefully review the utility output. Utilities set and resolve pending conditions while they are processing. If by the end of the utility pending conditions still exist, something may be wrong.

CHECK DATA

Run the CHECK DATA utility to check the recovered table space for violations of table check constraints or referential constraints. Check constraints would be violated only if they were added after the recovery, so only referential constraints should show up as violated. You can execute CHECK DATA on an entire table space or on individual partitions. The utility provides options for handling various violations.

Unless you specify the FOR EXCEPTION clause when you run CHECK DATA, violations are simply reported in the utility output listing. If you specify the FOR EXCEPTION clause and DELETE NO, the utility reports the violations and copies the violators to a provided exception (shadow) table. If you specify DELETE YES, the violators are removed after being moved to the exception tables. You'll need to move the rows back to the original tables after correcting them, but by telling DB2 to delete the violators, you permit the CHECK-pending flag to be reset.

It's necessary to rebuild indexes before running the CHECK DATA utility because the utility uses the primary index and, if available, the index on the foreign key.

Exception Tables

The exception tables used by CHECK DATA must be created before the utility's execution. These tables must have the same columns, in the same order, with the same data type, as the original table, although the column names can differ. The easiest way to create the exception tables is using the CREATE TABLE LIKE statement to create an exception table exactly like the original. You can define two additional columns for this table: a five-character column that provides the RID of the original row and a timestamp column that gives the starting date and time for the CHECK DATA utility.

••

If you want a TIMESTAMP column, a RID column must already exist. However, you can have the RID column even without the TIMESTAMP column.

••

Recover Pending

The RECOVER-pending (RECP) state can be set on table spaces and index spaces. When set, this status prevents access to the affected objects. The RECP status can result on indexes following execution of a recovery utility to TOCOPY and TORBA on a table space or from utility abends or terminations of the RECOVER, LOAD, or REORG utility. To reset the condition, execute a RECOVER, LOAD REPLACE, or REPAIR operation.

System-Level Backup and Recovery

DB2 provides a fast and flexible way to recover by permitting a system-level backup and recovery. This technology can be useful for disaster recovery and subsystem cloning. The feature is implemented with two utilities: BACKUP SYSTEM and RESTORE SYSTEM.

The two utilities perform the backups and restores of volumes defined to a copy pool in Hierarchical Storage Management (HSM) and the Storage Management Subsystem (SMS). The copy pool is a set of SMS groups that can be backed up and restored in one command. This capability, introduced in z/OS 1.5, invokes a new HSM service to back up and restore a subsystem.

Every subsystem defines two COPYPOOLs:

- one for data (database copy pool)

- one for logs (log copy pool)

HSM and SMS determine which volumes belong to the copy pool and are needed for backup/restore. The database copy pool should contain volumes of associated databases and ICF catalogs. The log copy pool should contain volumes with BSDS, active logs, and ICF catalogs.

There are two methods for performing the copies and restores:

- A FULL copy copies the database and log copy pools. You can then use these copies to recover the entire system using normal restart recovery or the RESTORE SYSTEM utility.

- A DATA ONLY copy copies only the database copy pool. You can use these copies with the RESTORE SYSTEM utility to recover the system to a point in time.

You can execute the RESTORE SYSTEM utility from any member in a data sharing group.

After the RESTORE SYSTEM execution is complete, you'll need to recover any objects that are in RECP or RBDP status. These may include objects affected by a REORG or LOAD with LOG NO after the last copy was taken. If a NOT LOGGED table space was updated after the point at which the system-level copy was taken, the table space or partition is marked RECP.

You also have two options for backing up the entire subsystem. The first method, BACKUP SYSTEM FULL, copies both log and database SMS storage groups to produce a "full system backup." You can then restore the system using normal DB2 restart recovery.

DB2 logs and their ICF catalogs should be in the same SMS storage group.

The second method, BACKUP SYSTEM DATA ONLY, copies only database storage groups and produces a "data-only system backup." You can use the RESTORE SYSTEM utility to recover the system to an arbitrary point between system copies. RESTORE SYSTEM uses the backups made by the BACKUP SYSTEM utility.

ICF catalogs for databases should be separate and reside with the data.

When you use RESTORE SYSTEM at a disaster site, the DFSMShsm environment must be restored to a point in time that is synchronized with the restore of the BSDS data sets.

Using the DSNJU003 job, you can create a conditional restart control record to truncate the logs at the desired point in time.

```
CRESTART CREATE SYSPITR=log-point
```

You can use the same point in time for each member of a data sharing group. When DB2 restarts, it will enter System Recover Pending mode, and every DB2 member of the data sharing group must be restarted. At this point, you must run the RESTORE SYSTEM utility and then stop DB2 to reset the System Recover Pending mode. For data sharing, all members must be stopped. You can then start DB2.

Object-Level Recoveries with System-Level Backups

If you're on z/OS V1.8 and DB2 V9 (any mode) and you've chosen a system-level backup as a recovery base for an object, the RECOVER utility invokes DFSMShsm to restore the data sets for the object from the system-level backup of the database copy pool. The following features are included:

- The DUMP, DUMPONLY, and FORCE keywords of the BACKUPSYSTEM utility.

- The FROMDUMP and TAPEUNITS keywords of the RESTORESYSTEM utility.

- The FROMDUMP and TAPEUNITS keywords of the RECOVER utility.

- The ability to restore objects from a system-level backup with the RECOVER utility. You need to set subsystem parameter SYSTEM_LEVEL_BACKUPS to YES so that the RECOVER utility will consider system-level backups.

- If the system-level backup resides on DASD, it is used for the restore of the object.

- If the system-level backup no longer resides on DASD and has been dumped to tape, the dumped copy is used for the restore of the object if you specified FROMDUMP.

DB2 issues message DSNU1520I to indicate that a system-level backup was used as the recovery base.

If you specify YES for the RESTORE/RECOVER FROM DUMP install option on installation panel DSNTIP6, or if you specify the FROMDUMP option on the RECOVER utility statement, only dumps on tape of the database copy pool are used in restoring the data sets. In addition, if you specify either a dump class name on installation panel DSNTIP6 or the DUMPCLASS option on the RECOVER utility statement, the data sets are restored from the system-level backup that was dumped to that particular DFSMShsm dump class. If you do not specify a dump class name on installation panel DSNTIP6 or on the RECOVER utility statement, the RESTORE SYSTEM utility issues the DFSMShsm LIST COPYPOOL command and uses the first dump class listed in the output.

Use the output from LISTCOPY POOL and PRINT LOG MAP to see the system-level backup information. Use the output from the REPORT RECOVERY utility to determine whether the objects to be recovered have image copies, concurrent copies, or a utility LOG YES event that can be used as a recovery base.

You can take system-level backups using the BACKUP SYSTEM utility. However, if any of the following utilities were run since the system-level backup that was chosen as the recovery base, the use of the system-level backup is prohibited for object-level recoveries to a prior point in time.

- LOAD REPLACE
- REBUILD INDEX
- RECOVER from image copy or concurrent copy
- REORG INDEX
- REORG TABLESPACE

Backup and Recovery of the DB2 Catalog and Directory

Because the DB2 catalog and directory are also made up of table spaces and index spaces, they can be subject to failures, such as a media failure. There may thus be instances where you need to recover these objects.

A specific order must be followed in recovering catalog data sets, due to relationships and dependencies in the catalog. This order is as follows:

1. DSNDB01.SYSUTILX
2. SYSUTILX indexes
3. DSNDB01.DBD01
4. DSNDB06.SYSCOPY
5. SYSCOPY indexes
6. DSNDB01.SYSLGRNX
7. SYSLGRNX indexes
8. DSNDB06.SYSALTER

9. SYSALTER indexes

10. DSNDB06.SYSDBAUT

11. SYSDBAUT indexes

12. DSNDB06.SYSUSER

13. DSNDB06.SYSDBASE

14. SYSDBASE and SYSUSER indexes

15. All other catalog and directory table spaces and indexes

16. Catalog indexes (user-defined indexes that have not yet been rebuilt/recovered)

17. System utility table spaces, such as Query Management Facility

18. Real Time Statistics Objects, Application Registration Table/Object Registration Table (ART/ORT), Resource Limit Specification Tables

You can recover the objects listed in step 15 together. Basically, after the indexes for SYSDBASE and SYSUSER have been rebuilt, you can recover all remaining catalog and directory table spaces in a single RECOVER utility statement.

If you don't cover steps 1 to 15 in order, you risk receiving error messages such as the following:

```
DSNT501I  ) DSNIDBET RESOURCE UNAVAILABLE 392
CORRELATION-ID=SYSOPRR                    CONNECTION-ID=UTILITY
LUWID=USIBMSY.SYEC1DB2.BFA18578FD77=0
          REASON 00C90081
          TYPE 00000200
          NAME DSNDB06 .SYSUSER
DSNT500I  ) DSNUGRAR RESOURCE UNAVAILABLE 393
          REASON 00C90081
          TYPE 00000200
          NAME DSNDB06 .SYSUSER
```

This message indicates that that the recovery of SYSDBASE is dependent on the existence of SYSUSER.

Never recover the catalog and directory to a point in time unless all user data is also recovered to the same point in time; otherwise, you'll introduce an inconsistency that will corrupt data and can cause DB2 to fail systemwide.

Disaster Recovery

Another type of recovery you need to prepare for is a disaster recovery. Organizations always face the possibility of losing an entire data center and having to recover at another site, usually known as the disaster or recovery site. This recovery can only be successful with careful planning and practice.

To ensure a success for a disaster recovery, regular backups of the data and log must be available at the disaster site. The more current the backups are, the better, to minimize data loss and update processing. Your goal is to be restored and running as soon as possible.

Preparation

Preparing for disaster recovery at a recovery site involves many steps. Among the basic information needed at this site are the copies of the data, including the catalog and directory, and the archive log data sets.

To prepare a recovery site to be able to recover to a fixed point in time, a weekly copy of the data, possibly with a DFSMS logical volume dump, must be available. Send this copy to the recovery site where it can be restored.

To perform a recovery through the last archive copy, the following objects should be sent to the recovery site in a timely manner:

- Image copies of all user data
- Image copies of the catalog and directory
- Archive logs

- ICF EXPORT and list

- BSDS lists

You can also ready a disaster site by using the log capture exit to capture log data in real time and then periodically sending that data to the recovery site. Often, however, this is not a viable option due to the overhead of using the log capture in high-volume environments.

 You may be using special facilities that you've become dependent on (e.g., DFSMS/HSM). Make sure these facilities are in working order at the recovery site and completely up-to-date. If these facilities go back in time, you might be forced to go back in time, too. If you use these facilities, be sure to include them in your recovery scenarios.

Items Needed for Disaster Recovery

The following items are necessary for a successful disaster recovery and should all be made available at the disaster recovery site.

Image Copies

Image copies of the application data are required. In the event of a disaster recovery, it is assumed that a copy of the local copies are available at the disaster site. An option on the COPY utility lets you make copies to be sent regularly to the remote recovery site. You can create a remote primary and a remote backup copy like the local primary and backup by specifying the data set names in the DD statements for the RECOVERYDDN parameter in the COPY utility control cards. You can use these copies for recovery on a subsystem that has the RECOVERYSITE DSNZPARM enabled or if you run a RECOVER using the RECOVERYSITE parameter.

You'll also need image copies of the catalog and directory and a listing of the contents of SYSCOPY, which you can obtained using an SQL SELECT statement.

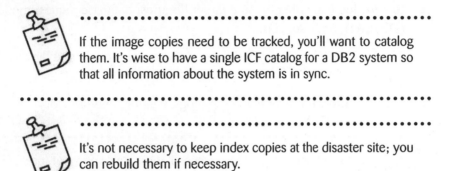

If the image copies need to be tracked, you'll want to catalog them. It's wise to have a single ICF catalog for a DB2 system so that all information about the system is in sync.

It's not necessary to keep index copies at the disaster site; you can rebuild them if necessary.

Archive Logs

Make copies of the archive logs and take them to the disaster recovery site. To create these copies, issue the ARCHIVE LOG command to archive the current active DB2 log. Create a BSDS report by using the DSNJU004 (Print Log Map) utility to generate a listing of the archive logs. DB2 will use the BSDS to find all the available archive logs during a recovery. The BSDS will be found in the first file of the most recent archived log.

ICF

You also need to back up the ICF catalog by executing the VSAM EXPORT command and record a list of DB2 entries using the VSAM LISTCAT command. Perform these tasks daily and send the results to the recovery site.

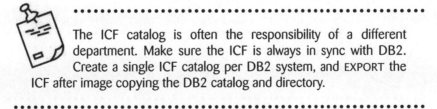

The ICF catalog is often the responsibility of a different department. Make sure the ICF is always in sync with DB2. Create a single ICF catalog per DB2 system, and EXPORT the ICF after image copying the DB2 catalog and directory.

DB2 Libraries

The DB2 libraries need to be backed up to tape if they are changed. These are as follows:

- SMP/E load, distribution, and target libraries; database request modules (DBRMs); and user applications

- The DSNTIJUZ job, which builds the DSNZPARM module and the DECP module

- Data set allocations for the BSDS, logs, catalog, and directory

It's good practice to record when all these items arrive at the recovery site and to have backups of all documentation.

Minimizing Data Loss

Volume dumps and restores are practiced often as a disaster recovery scenario. Significant data loss can occur with these operations. To minimize the data loss, you'll want to perform a dump of all the table spaces, the logs, and the BSDS while DB2 is up—after issuing the following command:

```
-ARCHIVE LOG MODE(QUIESCE)
```

The ARCHIVE LOG command is very useful when you're performing a DB2 backup in preparation for a remote site recovery. It lets the DB2 subsystem quiesce all users after a commit point and capture the resulting point of consistency in the current active log before the archive is taken. Therefore, when the archive log is used with the most current image copy (during an off-site recovery), the number of data inconsistencies will be minimized.

If a –STOP DB2 MODE (FORCE) operation is in progress, the ARCHIVE command is not allowed.

Taking the Table Spaces Offline

During a disaster recovery, you can have the table space taken offline (making it unavailable) until the recovery is complete. To do so, set the DSNZPARM DEFER to ALL (on install panel DSNTIPB). This setting lets the necessary log process continue.

LOB Recovery

Special recovery considerations apply to large objects due to the way LOBs are stored and maintained.

Logging

You can choose whether to log changes made to LOB columns. You set this option when creating the LOB table space by using the LOG option (LOG YES is the default). LOBs larger than 1 GB cannot be logged. If you have a LOB defined as LOG NO, and you decide you want to ALTER it to be LOG YES, DB2 places the LOB in COPY-pending status. For LOBs defined as LOG NO, the force-at-commit protocol ensures that the LOB values persist once committed. Even with LOG NO, the changes to the system pages and the auxiliary indexes are logged.

Point-in-Time Recovery

Although no referential constraints exist between the LOB table space and its associated base table, the LOB table space belongs to the same table space set as the associated base table. A point-in-time recovery must recover both the base table and the LOB table space to a common point of consistency. To accomplish this, you need to establish a point of consistency by quiescing the table space set or by using the COPY utility to generate a set of SHRLEVEL REFERENCE image copies for the table space set. The table space set will then need to be recovered to either the RBA or the quiesce point or image copy set. A QUIESCE WRITE YES operation records the point for the index on the auxiliary table if the index was defined with COPY YES.

AUXW Status

When you use the LOG NO option to specify no logging for LOBs, any log apply processing required during a recovery will invalidate the LOB values that were recorded after the last restored image copy of the table space because DB2 still records when the LOB values were changed, even though the update itself does not. The result is that the LOB table space is placed in AUXW (auxiliary warning) status, and SQL won't read be able to read the invalid LOB values.

You'll need to recover the table space defined with LOG NO to current by running the CHECK LOB utility on the LOB table space to determine the invalid rows. The rows are identified by their ROWID. Then, use SQL on the base table to update the invalid LOB values or delete any row that contains the invalid LOB value. Last, make a second run of the CHECK LOB utility to verify the LOB value and reset the AUXW status. If the LOB table space is in AUXW status, DML statements can be used on the base table, but they will fail with SQLCODE –904 when they try to read an invalid LOB.

Tracker Site Recovery

The Tracker Site option enables the creation of a separate DB2 subsystem (or data sharing group) that exist only for keeping shadow copies of the primary site's data. The primary full image copies need to be sent to the site after undergoing a point-in-time recovery to ensure they're up-to-date. You support the tracker site by transferring the BSDS and archive logs from the primary site to the tracker site. The tracker site periodically runs LOGONLY recoveries to keep shadow data current. If a disaster occurs at the primary site, the tracker site becomes the takeover site. Figure 8.1 illustrates this recovery mechanism.

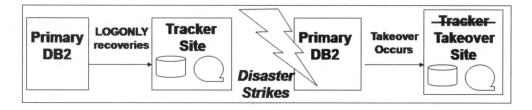

Figure 8.1: Tracker Site recovery

With the tracker site shadowing activity on the primary site, you no longer need to constantly ship image copies. This lets the tracker site take control more quickly than a traditional remote site could.

There are two main reasons to use a tracker site:

- To minimize data loss during a disaster

- To minimize the amount of time required to get access to data during a disaster

You're advised to use a tracker site if it's important to recover data quickly at a disaster recovery site with minimal data loss. DSNZPARM TRKRSITE on the DSNTIPO install panel must be set to be set to support the Tracker Site option; the default setting is NO. After installing the tracker site subsystem, set TRKRSITE to YES to enable the tracker site support.

To start tracker site support, both sites must be brought in sync. To do this, you must shut down the primary DB2 subsystem, take a DISK dump of everything, and then restore this dump on the tracker site. After starting the tracker site, you can restart the primary site. If the sites stay connected, they will stay in sync, but if the connection is lost, the primary site cannot queue the log data and you'll need to bring both sites in sync again using manual intervention.

It's important to ensure that both sites never lose their connection if you choose to use a tracker site. A situation to watch for when using this option is table spaces becoming out of sync due to utilities using the LOG NO option.

Due to the nature of the tracker site, some operations are not allowed:

- Some SQL statements: ALTER, CREATE, DELETE, DROP, GRANT, INSERT, REVOKE, and UPDATE
- Read-only SELECTs: allowed but not recommended
- Binds
- Many utilities, including COPY, RUNSTATS, and REPAIR

DB2 Restart

DB2 can be stopped normally, or it may experience an abnormal termination for a variety of reasons. To bring the DB2 subsystem back up, you must perform the restart process.

Stopping DB2

DB2 can be stopped normally by using the operator command –STOP DB2. If DB2 stops for other reasons, the termination is considered abnormal. The STOP DB2 command has two modes: FORCE and QUIESCE. The FORCE option rolls back all active threads and does not allow any new connections or work. QUIESCE lets new threads be allocated for an application that is currently running and permits existing threads to be completed, but it does not allow new connections.

The following example illustrates stopping DB2 with the QUIESCE mode.

```
-STOP DB2 MODE (QUIESCE)
```

Restarting DB2

DB2 uses its recovery log and the bootstrap data set to determine what to recover when restarting. The BSDS identifies the active and archive log data sets, the location of the most recent DB2 checkpoint on the log, and the high-level qualifier of the ICF catalog name. The restart process executes in four phases.

1. Log initialization

2. Current status rebuild

3. Forward log recovery

4. Backward log recovery

If you're using NOT LOGGED table spaces, these will have a COPY-pending status set during phase 4 because there are no log records to read for these objects.

Many controls in DB2 help minimize the time necessary to restart DB2. We discuss some of these controls in the following paragraphs.

Conditional Restart

A *conditional restart* is a DB2 restart that is directed by a user-defined conditional restart control record (CRCR).

If you want to skip some portion of the log processing during DB2 restart, you can use a conditional restart. However, if a conditional restart skips any database change log records, data in the associated objects becomes inconsistent, and any attempt to process them for normal operations might cause unpredictable results. The only operations that can safely be performed on the objects are recovery to a prior point of consistency, total replacement, or dropping.

Use the DSNJU003 utility to create a conditional restart control record. You can use the CRESTART statement in either of two forms. In the following form, *nnnnnnnnn*000 equals a value that is 1 (one) more than the ENDRBA of the latest archive log.

```
CRESTART CREATE,ENDRBA=nnnnnnnnn000
```

In the following form, *nnnnnnnnnnnn* is the end time of the log record. Log records with a timestamp later than *nnnnnnnnnnnn* are truncated.

```
CRESTART CREATE,ENDTIME=nnnnnnnnnnnn
```

With the conditional restart, DB2 discards any log information in the BSDS and the logs with an RBA greater than the ENDRBA specified in the CRESTART statement. Therefore, to determine the conditional restart RBA to use at the disaster recovery site to enable recovery to the most current point, you would find the most recent archive log in the BSDS listing and add 1 to its ENDRBA value.

Restart Implication with NOT LOGGED Tables

If DB2 did not terminate normally, and a NOT LOGGED table space was open for update at the time DB2 terminated, the subsequent restart places that table space on the LPL (Logical Page List) and marks it with RECOVER-pending status.

Set Log Suspend/Resume

You can use the –SET LOG SUSPEND/RESUME command to temporarily freeze all DB2 activity. This command permits a fast copy of an entire DB2 subsystem to be accomplished via Flash Copy (a hardware feature of the storage device). You can use these copies for remote site recovery or point-in-time recovery.

If you execute the –SET LOG SUSPEND command, a system checkpoint is taken (non–data-sharing only), log buffers are flushed, a log-write latch is obtained, the BSDS is updated with the highest-written RBA, and a message is issued to the console that DB2 update activity has been suspended.

The –SET LOG RESUME command releases the log-write latch, deletes the suspended message, and issues a log-resumed message.

Checkpoint Interval

The checkpoint interval is important for DB2 recovery processing. The greater the amount of time between checkpoint intervals, the more likely your DB2 applications will be exposed to a longer restart time in case of a system failure. You set the checkpoint interval with the CHKFREQ parameter in the DSNZPARMs. You can also change this setting dynamically with the –SET LOG command by specifying either the number of log records written between checkpoints (LOGLOAD) or a number of minutes (CHKFREQ).

The following example sets the checkpoint time to 10 minutes.

```
-SET LOG CHKTIME (10)
```

To immediately force a system checkpoint, you can issue the following statement.

```
-SET LOG LOGLOAD(0)
```

Minimizing Outages

DB2 can optionally issue a warning message when a unit of work has written more log records than a defined threshold without a commit. This feature lets you identify those applications that would require a long backout and/or recovery in case of system or application failure. The URCHKTH DSNZPARM sets this option. To minimize the amount of time it takes to recover from a system failure, make sure your applications are taking frequent commits.

Postponed Units of Recovery

If a DB2 system fails during backout of a postponed abort unit of recovery, subsequent restart of the DB2 system will cause the postponed abort backout to resume starting with the last log record applied during the last postponed abort recovery.

When you use system parameters LBACKOUT=AUTO and BACKODUR=1, any incomplete UR older than 1 checkpoint found during restart of a failed DB2 system will be processed after end restart as a postponed abort UR. By delaying such backout work, you can restart the DB2 subsystem more quickly.

If you specify

```
(LBACKOUT=AUTO) LIMIT BACKOUT = YES
```

you must use the RECOVER POSTPONED command to resolve postponed units of recovery. Use of the –RECOVER POSTPONED CANCEL command while postponed abort threads are backing out causes all data base objects that were in use by postponed abort URs to be put in recover pending.

Use the RECOVER POSTPONED command to complete postponed backout processing on all units of recovery.

You cannot specify a single unit of work for resolution.

This command might take several hours to complete, depending on the content of the long-running job. In some circumstances, you can elect to use the CANCEL option of the RECOVER POSTPONED command. This option leaves the objects in an inconsistent state (REFP) that you must resolve before using the objects. However, you might choose the CANCEL option for the following reasons:

- You determine that the complete recovery of the postponed units of recovery will take more time than you have available and it is faster to either recover the objects to a prior point in time or run the LOAD utility with the REPLACE option.

- You want to replace the existing data in the object with new data.

- You decide to drop the object. To drop the object successfully, take the following steps:

  » Issue the RECOVER POSTPONED command with the CANCEL option.

  » Issue the DROP TABLESPACE statement.

- You don't have the DB2 logs to successfully recover the postponed units of recovery.

Here's an example of the command to recover the postponed units of recovery quickly:

```
-RECOVER POSTPONED CANCEL
```

Viewing Threads Affected by a Failure

If DB2 experiences an abnormal termination while transactions are running, you may need to determine which transactions were affected. This information is important because these threads may be holding resources if they were making database changes when DB2 came down. The status of these units of recovery during the termination will be based on the point in time of the failure. There are four states:

- Indoubt
- In-commit
- In-abort
- Postponed-abort

To view the status of a thread, issue the –DISPLAY THREAD command. The following example uses the command to find threads that are indoubt after a termination and were not resolved during startup.

```
-DISPLAY THREAD(*) TYPE(INDOUBT)
```

RESET INDOUBT

DB2's RESET INDOUBT command purges the information that is displayed in the indoubt thread report generated by the DISPLAY THREAD command. The RESET INDOUBT command *must* be used to purge indoubt thread information in the following situations:

- For threads where DB2 has a coordinator responsibility that it cannot fulfill because of participant cold start, sync point protocol errors, or indoubt resolution protocol errors

- For indoubt threads that were resolved with the RECOVER INDOUBT command, where subsequent resynchronization with the coordinator shows heuristic damage

The RESET column of a display thread report for indoubt threads indicates whether information in the report must be purged using this command.

You can also use the RESET INDOUBT command to purge indoubt thread information in the following situations:

- DB2 has a coordinator responsibility even when no errors have been detected that preclude automatic resolution with the participants. Specify the FORCE keyword to purge this information. Resynchronization with affected participants is not performed.

- DB2 has a participant responsibility even when no errors have been detected that preclude automatic resolution with the coordinator. Resynchronization with the coordinator will not be performed.

Here's an example of the command:

```
-RESET INDOUBT
```

Data-Sharing Recovery

For information about data-sharing recovery, see Chapter 9.

Summary

We've looked at what it takes to back up and recover objects in DB2. As DBA, you must account for many scenarios and know that a successful recovery can come only from careful planning. Setting up and practicing the steps for recovery is key to knowing whether you can achieve your availability requirements in some cases.

Additional Resources

DB2 on MVS Platform: Data Sharing Recovery (SG24-2218)
DB2 UDB Version 8 for z/OS and Continuous Availability (SG24-5486)
IBM DB2 9 Administration Guide (SC18-9840)
IBM DB2 9 Command Reference (SC18-9844)
IBM DB2 9 Installation Guide (GC18-9846)
IBM DB2 9 Utility Guide and Reference (SC18-9855)
Using RVA and SnapShot for BI with OS/390 and DB2 (SG24-5333)

Practice Questions

Question 1

A non-partitioned index in RECP status has pages from the logical partition in the logical page list. Which command or utility could you use to manually resolve the pages in the logical page list?

○ A. -RECOVER INDOUBT ACTION(COMMIT) ID(*)

○ B. RECOVER INDEXSPACE db1.ix1 ERROR RANGE

○ C. -START DATABASE(db1) SPACENAM(ix1) ACCESS(RO)

○ D. REBUILD INDEXSPACE (db1.ix1 PART 3) SCOPE PENDING

Question 2

Consider the following scenario for application table space DB1.TS1.

1. Full copy made at RBA 0010000
2. Updates
3. Full copy made at RBA 0040000
4. Updates
5. Incremental copy made at RBA0070000
6. Updates

The full copy made at point 3 has an I/O error and cannot be used. Which of the following RECOVER statements will recover the DB1.TS1 table space to the current point in time?

○ A. RECOVER TABLESPACE DB1.TS1 TOLASTCOPY

○ B. RECOVER TABLESPACE DB1.TS1 TOLOGPOINT CURRENT

○ C. RECOVER TABLESPACE DB1.TS1 TOLOGPOINT X'0070000'

○ D. RECOVER TABLESPACE DB1.TS1 RESTOREBEFORE X'0040000'

Question 3

Which of the following statements is correct regarding the recovery of the DB2 catalog and directory at a disaster recovery site?

○ A. SYSADM authority is required to RECOVER DSNDB06.SYSUSER.

○ B. RECOVER will not use the logs when recovering DSNDB06.SYSCOPY if it was not updated after the image copy was made.

○ C. DSNDB01.DBD01 must be recovered after DSNDB06.SYSCOPY for the RECOVER utility to obtain the image copy information.

○ D. After the indexes for SYSDBASE and SYSUSER have been rebuilt, all remaining catalog and directory table spaces can be recovered in a single RECOVER utility statement.

Question 4

Which of the following statements is true regarding postponed units of recovery?

○ A. Individual URs being processed by postponed recovery cannot be canceled separately.

○ B. Use of the –RECOVER POSTPONED CANCEL command while postponed abort threads are backing out causes all data base objects that were in use by postponed abort URs to be put in recover pending.

○ C. Using system parameters LBACKOUT=AUTO and BACKODUR=1, any incomplete UR older than 1 checkpoint found during restart of a failed DB2 system will be processed after end restart as a postponed abort UR.

○ D. If a DB2 system fails during backout of a postponed abort UR, subsequent restart of the DB2 system will cause the postponed abort backout to pick up starting with the last log record applied during the last postponed abort recovery.

Question 5

When the RECOVER utility is recovering a list of objects and the recovery base is created by the BACKUP SYSTEM utility, which of the following will occur?

○ A. Objects that have a dump copy will be recovered in parallel.

○ B. RECOVER will do backup processing in order to use a dump copy if the FlashCopy isn't usable.

○ C. Some objects will be recovered from a FlashCopy, and some will be recovered from a dump copy.

○ D. Objects will be restored from a FlashCopy, if it exists, even if the FROMDUMP keyword is specified.

Answers

Question 1

The correct answer is **C**. The –START DATABASE command is the way to remove pages from the logical page list.

Question 2

The correct answer is **D**. RESTOREBEFORE X'*byte-string*' specifies that RECOVER is to search for an image copy, concurrent copy, or system-level backup (if YES has been specified for SYSTEM-LEVEL BACKUPS on install panel DSNTIP6) with an RBA or LRSN value earlier than the specified X'*byte-string*' value to use in the RESTORE phase. To avoid specific image copies, concurrent copies, or system-level backups with matching or more recent RBA or LRSN values in START_RBA, the RECOVER utility applies the log records and restores the object to its current state or to the specified TORBA or TOLOGPOINT value. DB2 compares the RESTOREBEFORE value with the RBA or LRSN value in the START_RBA column in the SYSIBM.SYSCOPY record for those copies. For system-level backups, the RESTOREBEFORF value is compared with the data complete LRSN. If you specify a TORBA or TOLOGPOINT value with the RESTOREBEFORE option, the RBA or LRSN value for RESTOREBEFORE must be lower than the specified TORBA or TOLOGPOINT value. If you specify RESTOREBEFORE, you cannot specify TOCOPY, TOLASTCOPY, or TOLASTFULLCOPY.

Question 3

The correct answer is **D**. There is a predetermined order for recovery of the catalog and directory due to dependencies. However, after SYSDBASE and SYSUSER have had their indexes rebuilt, all table spaces/indexes after that can be handled in single RECOVER statement.

Question 4

The correct answer is **A**. The individuals URs being processed by postponed recovery cannot be canceled separately.

Question 5

The correct answer is **A**, objects that have a dump copy will be recovered in parallel. If objects in a list to be recovered require a system-level backup that has been dumped to tape as its recovery base (i.e., the FROMDUMP option has been specified), the DB2 RECOVER utility invokes DFSMShsm to restore the data sets for the objects in parallel, with the degree of parallelism being capped by the maximum number of tasks that can be started by the RECOVER. DFSMShsm restores the data sets in parallel based on its install options.

CHAPTER 9

Data Sharing

In This Chapter

✔ Data-sharing components

✔ Maintaining data integrity

✔ Migration

✔ Workload management

✔ Sysplex query parallelism

✔ Recovery considerations

DB2 *data sharing* lets an application run on one or more DB2 subsystems in a Parallel Sysplex environment. The applications can read and write to the same data at the same time. Before the introduction of data sharing, we used Distributed Data Facility (DDF) to access data on other subsystems, or we employed other, more creative means, such as replication between subsystems.

The subsystems that can share data must belong to a *data-sharing group*. The subsystems in the group are known as *members*. A data-sharing group can have up to 32 members. Only members in the group can share data, and each member can belong to only one group.

DB2 data sharing operates in a Parallel Sysplex environment, which is a cluster of z/OS systems that can communicate with each other. Some important components enable this communication to occur and ensure the consistency and coherency of the data being shared between the subsystems in the group. All members share the same DB2 catalog and directory and the same user data, which must reside on shared DASD. Figure 9.1 depicts a basic data-sharing environment.

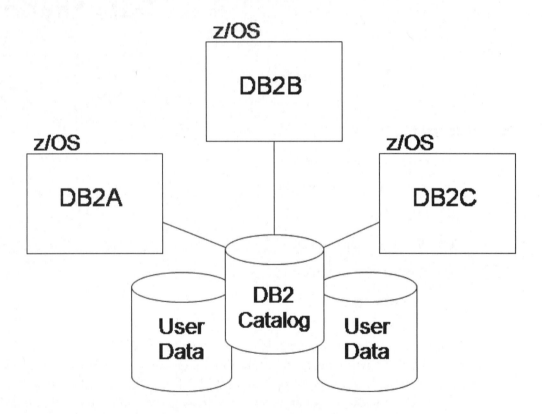

Figure 9.1: Data sharing

Data Sharing Benefits

The advantages made possible by DB2 data sharing are numerous. They include the following benefits:

- Increased capacity, with more power and a higher degree of inter-transaction parallelism available

- Continuous availability, through the ability to hide unplanned and planned outages (e.g., rolling maintenance) and to keep running if a member is lost (after releasing any retained locks)

- Incremental (horizontal) growth, because processors can be added without any disruption

- Configuration flexibility, including the ability to start and stop members as required and to separate subsystems by function (e.g., batch, ad hoc, OLTP)

- The ability to split large queries across all central processor complexes (CPCs) by using sysplex query parallelism

- The flexibility to schedule existing workloads by cloning a CICS region on another MVS and removing the restriction that a CICS application can run on only one MVS

- The ability to run applications concurrently on several subsystems, thereby increasing throughput

- A reduced need for distributed processing because applications needn't use DRDA to communicate to share data, thus eliminating the overhead of DRDA for this purpose

- The ability to have affinity and non-affinity workloads in the same group, run workloads on different processors, or run a workload on a particular processor because data is shared

Shared Data Architecture (SDA) is the architecture behind DB2 data sharing. SDA is based on coupling technology that enables the use of high-speed coupling facility channels, reduced system-to-system communications (message passing), multiple paths to the data for higher availability, and dynamic workload routing based on capacity rather than location. SDA doesn't require data partitioning for growth, and it doesn't rely on node-to-node communications for resources.

Data Sharing Components

A data-sharing environment involves some additional hardware components with which you should be familiar. Most are simply components in the Parallel Sysplex, but they are vital to the operation and success of data sharing. It's important to know what each component is responsible for and how to configure and properly tune it. Many performance and availability issues in a data-sharing environment lie with these components.

Coupling Facility

One of the most important components of a data-sharing environment is the *coupling facility (CF)*. This specialized piece of hardware provides dedicated high-speed links to each DB2 member in the data-sharing group. It is the center for communications and sharing of data between the subsystems.

It's important to have at least two coupling facilities for each data-sharing group, although only one is actually required. We make this recommendation mainly for availability and capacity reasons. It's also ideal to make at least one of the coupling facilities a dedicated processor running only the coupling facility control code (CFCC). We recommend this strategy for both availability and performance.

There are microprocessors available that you can use as a dedicated coupling facility. Such processors provide a CPC that runs only as a coupling facility in a logical partition, with dedicated processor resources. This configuration is optimal because the failure of a coupling facility and a connected MVS image (which is more likely when these are on the same CPC) can lead to extended recovery times. Using dedicated hardware also gives you better performance as well as better connectivity to the coupling facility.

Internal Coupling Facilities (ICFs) are also an option for coupling facility configurations. An ICF is an IBM machine that you can configure with an internal coupling facility. It can use one or more engines, depending on the generation of the machine. An ICF is an attractive alternative to a dedicated microprocessor mainly due to its lower cost. However, having at least one external coupling facility is still desirable for high availability.

The coupling facility is usually one of the top items in this environment that is significantly undersized in terms of storage. The recommendation is to start with at least 1 GB on each facility. Trying to support a data-sharing group with anything less can be difficult, if not impossible.

Your main coupling facility will need enough storage to hold all the necessary coupling facility structures. In addition, it should have enough space available to hold the structures from the data-sharing group's other coupling facility (or it should support duplexed structures) in case you need to rebuild the structures from a failing coupling facility or one you've taken offline for maintenance.

Coupling Facility Structures

A coupling facility consists of three types of structures (storage areas) that are critical for DB2 data sharing: the shared communications area (SCA), lock structure, and group buffer pool (GBP). When you configure a coupling facility, the recommended practice is often to put the SCA and lock structures in one coupling facility and the group buffer pools in the other. Figure 9.2 shows this configuration.

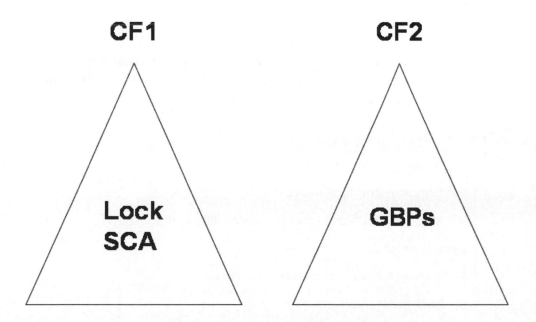

Figure 9.2: Structure placement in coupling facilities

Shared Communications Area

The SCA structure, also known as the *list structure*, holds all database status and system information and any critical information required for a recovery situation. It contains a list (actually an array of lists) that may include the following:

- Database exception table
- Bootstrap data set information
- Stopped page sets
- Logical page list entries
- Group buffer pool recovery pending (GRECP) entries
- Group buffer pool checkpoints
- Global commit log sequence number (GCLSN)
- Environmental Descriptor Manager (EDM) pool invalidations
- Indoubt XA transactions

Lock Structure

The lock structure controls inter-system locking and serialization on records, pages, table spaces, and so on. It also holds all the global locks (more about these later). The lock structure has two parts:

- Lock list
  - » Names of modified resources
  - » Lock status of the resource
  - » Modify and retained locks (discussed later in this chapter)
- Lock hash table
  - » Owning members of modified resources
  - » Lock status information
  - » Quick inter-system lock contention detection

The lock structure is connected by each DB2 member's internal resource lock manager (IRLM) during the member startup. Sizing the lock structure isn't too difficult. You can normally start with 32 MB; for above-average workloads (e.g., high-volume DML), you could start with 64 MB. If the lock structure is too small, you may experience increased lock contention because there are only so many entries for locks to be held.

Group Buffer Pools

The group buffer pools, or *cache structures*, provide high-performance access to shared data, data coherency, and serialization of data updates on DASD. The GBPs are shared by all DB2 subsystems for which a corresponding local buffer pool has been defined. In other words, if objects are defined in local buffer pool BP1 and group buffer pool GBP1 exists, the systems can share these objects. You enable this sharing by defining a corresponding group buffer pool in the coupling facility.

Because you can have up to 80 virtual, or local, buffer pools, you can also have up to 80 group buffer pools. You are, of course, limited by the size of the coupling facility because the group buffer pools take up space there. Sizing group buffer pools is more of an art that a science. It requires knowledge of how the data in each buffer pool is accessed and a good breakout of objects into individual pools.

A GBP is allocated the first time it's needed, and all the pages in it can be shared. The GBP registers data pages and also handles the invalidation of data pages cross-system. We provide more information about group buffer pools later in the chapter.

Structures and Policies

To define the aforementioned coupling facility structures to the coupling facility, you use policies (also known as *couple data sets*). Different policies enforce various definitions in the Parallel Sysplex environment. Policies store information about the systems in the sysplex, Cross System Coupling Facility (XCF) groups, member definitions, and general status information. They are formatted using the MVS IXCL1DSU utility in SYS1.MIGLIB and must be accessible to all members (i.e., reside on shared DASD). Let's take a look at some of the policies that are key to the operation of a data-sharing environment.

Coupling Facility Resource Management

The Coupling Facility Resource Management (CFRM) policy defines the structures to the coupling facility. This is where you define the SCA, lock, and GBP structures. When you define the policies to the coupling facility, it's important to remember to leave room for growth of the structures and to carefully plan what the size should be, according to the space available in your coupling facility, to account for failover conditions. The PREFLIST shows the initial coupling facility for the structure and the failover coupling facility. Listing 9.1 shows a sample CFRM policy.

```
/*----------------------------------------------------*/
/* DB2 DATA SHARING GROUP: DSNDSGA / LIST STRUCTURE    */
/*----------------------------------------------------*/
        STRUCTURE NAME(DSNDSGA_SCA)
              INITSIZE(4000)
              SIZE(10000)
              PREFLIST(CF01,CF02)
              REBUILDPERCENT(5)
  /*----------------------------------------------------*/
  /* DB2 DATA SHARING GROUP: DSNDSGA / CACHE STRUCTURE(S)*/
  /*----------------------------------------------------*/
        STRUCTURE NAME(DSNDSGA_GBP0)
              INITSIZE(8000)
              SIZE(16000)
              PREFLIST(CF02,CF01)
              REBUILDPERCENT(5)

        STRUCTURE NAME(DSNDSGA_GBP1)
              INITSIZE(8000)
              SIZE(16000)
              PREFLIST(CF02,CF01)
              REBUILDPERCENT(5)
```

Listing 9.1: Sample CFRM policy

Sysplex Failure Management

The Sysplex Failure Management (SFM) policy is one to be familiar with because it holds information about the importance of each subsystem in the sysplex. During a coupling facility failure and subsequent structure rebuilds, the REBUILDPERCENT value contained in the CFRM policy is compared with the WEIGHT value in the SFM policy to determine whether to rebuild a structure. Listing 9.2 shows a sample SFM policy.

```
DATA TYPE(SFM)
DEFINE POLICY NAME(POLICY1) CONNFAIL(NO) REPLACE(YES)
   SYSTEM NAME(*)
        ISOLATETIME(0)
DEFINE POLICY NAME(POLICY2) CONNFAIL(YES) REPLACE(YES)
   SYSTEM NAME(*)
        ISOLATETIME(0)
        WEIGHT(5)
   SYSTEMNAME(SYS1)
        PROMPT
        WEIGHT(25)
```

Listing 9.2: Sample SFM policy

Automatic Restart Manager

Automatic Restart Manager (ARM) is an optional, but highly recommended, policy. It is ARM's job to keep specific workloads running in the event of a failure. The more quickly you can restart DB2 after a hardware failure or abend, the better. For availability, it's important to resolve all retained locks (discussed later) quickly, and the only way to do so is to restart the failing member. This is where ARM is critical.

Links

In a data-sharing environment, high-speed links are the components that connect the coupling facilities to the processors running the operating systems and the DB2 members. One link between the coupling facility and processor will suffice, but for performance and, of course, availability reasons, this minimum is not recommended. Use two links between the coupling facility and each processor. Coupling facility links provide high-speed communications between MVS systems and the coupling facility via Cross System Extended Services (XES).

Sysplex Timer

The Sysplex Timer is a required component of the data-sharing Parallel Sysplex environment. You must have at least one timer, and two are highly recommended. The Sysplex Timer keeps timestamps of the z9-109 and System z processors synchronized for the DB2s in the data-sharing group. The timer determines the order of events, regardless of which processor in the Sysplex performs them. For example, the LRSNs can be guaranteed to order events for recovery because they are based on the Time of Day (TOD) clock generated by the timer.

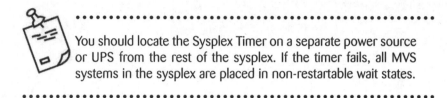

You should locate the Sysplex Timer on a separate power source or UPS from the rest of the sysplex. If the timer fails, all MVS systems in the sysplex are placed in non-restartable wait states.

XES

Cross System Extended Services is a component of z/OS that provides the authorized services for accessing coupling facility structures. XES gives application and subsystems (i.e., DB2) access to the CF and provides the sysplex services that support data sharing through controls for data coherency, concurrency, and communications. XES also provides a set of services for each CF structure type as well as the connection service to the structures.

XCF

The Cross System Coupling Facility (XCF) is also a component of z/OS. All DB2 members join an XCF group when they join a data-sharing group. Each IRLM joins another XCF group. XCF handles communications between the IRLM and XES and is used to notify other members to retrieve database or system status or control information changes made to SCA. DB2 also uses XCF for some intersystem communications and to process DB2 commands and utilities within the group. Figure 9.3 depicts the two XCF groups.

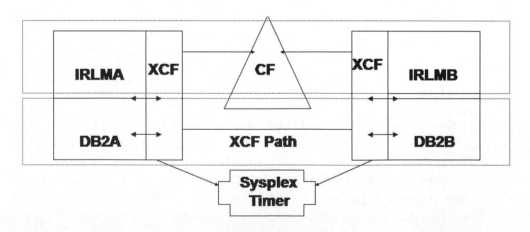

Figure 9.3: XCF groups

There are three categories of XCF services:

- *Group services* provide a way to request information about other members in the same XCF group via SETXCF commands.

- *Signaling services* provide a way to communicate between members of the group.

- *Status monitoring services* let members check their own status and relay this information to others in the group. These services also enable the monitoring of other members in the sysplex.

Shared Data

In a data-sharing environment, the members in the group share many items. For these items to be available for each member of the group, they must reside on shared DASD. The following items must meet this requirement.

- MVS catalog

- DB2 catalog

- DB2 directory

- Couple data sets (CFRM, SFM, ARM)

- Shared databases

- Integrated Catalog Facility user catalog for shared databases

- Log data sets (must be shared for read access, but a log exists for each member)

- BSDS data sets (must be shared for read access, but a BSDS exists for each member)

- Work files

  » Support queries that use sysplex query parallelism

  » Keep DB2 connected to its work files regardless of where the DB2 has to be restarted

  » No longer DSNDB07 (you can only have one work file named DSNDB07)

To Share or Not to Share

Just because you're in a data-sharing environment doesn't mean all data must be shared. You can dedicate some data to one subsystem. These non-shared objects are defined as unique to one member. Figure 9.4 shows how a DB2 member can exist in a data-sharing group yet not share data.

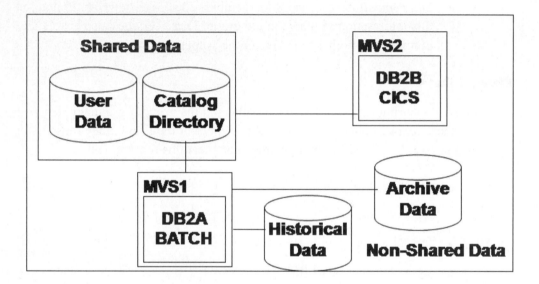

Figure 9.4: Shared and non-shared data

Dedicating objects to a single subsystem is easy: you simply put the object in a virtual buffer pool that is not backed by a group buffer pool in the coupling facility.

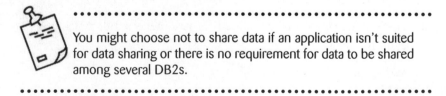

You might choose not to share data if an application isn't suited for data sharing or there is no requirement for data to be shared among several DB2s.

Maintaining Data Integrity

Data defined as "sharable" can be accessed by any DB2 in the group. Several subsystems can read and write simultaneously against the same data. This ability is controlled via something called *inter-DB2 read/write (R/W) interest*. Changed data, or data with inter-DB2 R/W interest, is always cached in the group buffer pool; this data then becomes *group buffer pool–dependent*. The coupling facility controls the invalidations of changed pages in all members' local buffer pools.

Two types of controls protect the consistency of data among the DB2 members in the data-sharing group:

- Concurrency controls
- Coherency controls

To provide concurrency controls among the members, we need a different type of locking structure. Controlling locks is extremely critical to performance in a data-sharing environment, and it's important to understand how it works.

Locking

Locking in a data-sharing environment differs a bit from single-subsystem locking. With data sharing, we introduce *explicit hierarchical locking (EHL)*.

As you may or may not know, before data sharing, you used implicit hierarchical locking. The only difference with EHL is that EHL keeps a token that identifies parent/child relationships. A parent lock is a table space/partition lock, and a child lock is a page/row lock. Figure 9.5 depicts the parent and child locks.

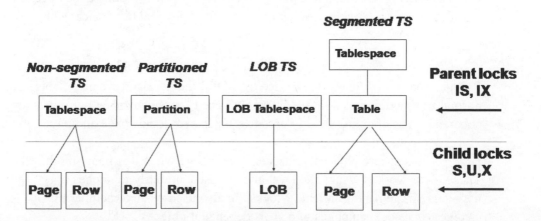

Figure 9.5: Parent/child locks

EHL's benefit lies in the fact that only the most restrictive lock moves to the coupling facility. By reducing the number of calls to the coupling facility, EHL controls concurrency, which can create a great deal of overhead. Lock avoidance also works with EHL. (This doesn't change the fact that you should consider the use of uncommitted read wherever possible.)

With EHL, only the most restrictive parent lock is propagated (recorded in the coupling facility) until the time when it is necessary for the child to be propagated, thus lessening the amount of lock activity.

Let's examine the various types of locks that you may encounter in a data-sharing environment.

Local Locks

Local locks are the locks we know in a single-subsystem environment. These locks are requested on the local subsystem and provide only intra-DB2 concurrency control.

Global Locks

Global locks are the locks that a DB2 subsystem must make known to the data-sharing group through the coupling facility. Global locks can be propagated to the coupling facility, and they provide both intra-DB2 and inter-DB2 concurrency control. In a data-sharing environment, almost all locks are global. Whether a lock becomes global depends on whether the lock request is for a physical or a logical lock.

P-Locks

Physical locks, or P-locks, are owned by a DB2 member and are negotiable. Unlike normal transaction locks, these locks aren't used for concurrency but rather for coherency. The coupling facility uses two types of P-locks: page and page set.

Page P-locks ensure physical consistency of a page when it is being modified. These locks work at a subpage level and are used similarly to latches in a non–data-sharing environment. P-locks are also used when a member makes changes to space map pages of a GBP-dependent object.

Page set P-locks track intersystem interest between DB2 members and determine when a page set becomes GBP-dependent. These locks have different modes depending on the level of R/W interest in the page set among the DB2 members. A P-lock can't be negotiated if it is retained. It is released when the page set or partitioned data set is closed. Few page set P-locks are taken, and they usually are held for long periods of time.

Page set P-lock negotiation takes place when P-locks are noted as being incompatible. The two members with the incompatible lock then negotiate the lock so that both members can still use the object. Because the P-lock's purpose is coherency, not concurrency, this negotiation does not sacrifice any data integrity.

P-lock negotiation reduces the amount of locks that are propagated to the coupling facility. The most restrictive P-lock is taken first; then, if necessary, it is negotiated so another process can access the page set. The coupling facility uses page set P-locks to track interest in a page set and know when it is necessary to begin propagating child locks because of the level of interest among the DB2 members for the page set. You can basically think of P-locks and negotiation as, "I need to know what you are doing. Here is what I am doing. Let's find a way to work together, or do we have to take turns?" A P-lock can also be thought of as an indicator.

L-Locks

Logical locks, or L-locks, occur in both data-sharing and non–data-sharing subsystems. These locks are transaction- or program-owned. They are non-negotiable locks that work like the normal locks in a single-subsystem environment to serialize access to objects. L-locks are controlled by the IRLM of the member and are held from update to commit. There are two types of L-locks: parent and child (as we discussed).

Modify Locks

DB2 data sharing introduces two additional types of locks: modify locks and retained locks. *Modify locks* identify a lock on a resource that is being shared (updated)—an active X-type (X, IX, SIX) P-lock or L-lock. This lock is kept in a *modified resource list* in the lock structure of the coupling facility and is held regardless of the object's group buffer pool dependency. These locks are used to create retained locks if the DB2 member holding the modify lock fails.

Retained Locks

Retained locks are modify locks that are converted to retained locks if a member of the group fails. They are necessary to preserve the data integrity in the event of a failure. This type of lock is held when a DB2 subsystem fails, and the locks belonging to the failing member must be resolved before access to the locked object is allowed by other members.

Retained locks can present a performance or availability bottleneck if you don't have proper procedures in place for recovering a failed DB2 member. These locks are held at the Global Lock Manager (GLM) level and owned by the Local Lock Manager (LLM), not a transaction. This means that only the DB2 member that had the lock can resolve it, so the subsystem *must* come up to resolve the lock. So, regardless of where a transaction may resume (i.e., another subsystem), the locks are retained, and the data remains inaccessible to any process (readers using uncommitted read can still view the data). The DB2 member can be restarted on the same MVS or another one in the same group; it doesn't matter, as long as it comes up.

Each local IRLM also keeps a local copy of retained locks for fast reference so that retained locks can survive a coupling facility failure.

It's critically important to resolve retained locks immediately. The RESTART LIGHT(YES) command can help you with this work. The RESTART LIGHT option brings the DB2 subsystem up just enough to resolve the retained locks.

Lock Contention

Three types of locking contention can occur in a data-sharing environment:

- *Global lock contention* (IRLM or real) occurs when there is real contention against two resources.

- *False lock contention* occurs when two locks hash to the same entry in the lock table but the actual locks are not in contention.

- *XES contention* occurs because XES interprets locks as only X or S; therefore, some locks that are in contention according to XES are actually compatible because they are really intent locks.

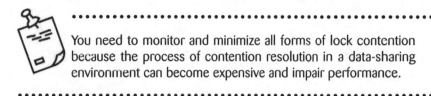

You need to monitor and minimize all forms of lock contention because the process of contention resolution in a data-sharing environment can become expensive and impair performance.

Group Buffer Pools

The group buffer pools are the coupling facility structures that enable the sharing of data between multiple subsystems in a data-sharing environment. When a member reads a page, the page is read into that member's virtual buffer pool and is registered in the group buffer pool. If the page is updated, a force-at-commit caches the changed page in the group buffer pool and invalidates the page in any other member's virtual buffer pool. This process, known as *cross-invalidation*, ensures that everyone is working with the most current page. Figure 9.6 shows how the registration of pages works.

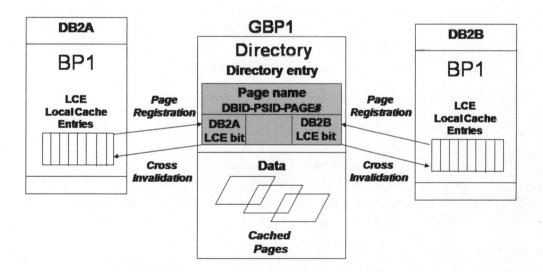

Figure 9.6: Group buffer pool page registration

Page directory entries are used to check for the existence of a page copy in the group buffer pool. They are also used to determine which members will need to be sent XI (cross-invalidation) messages. Only one directory entry is needed for a page, regardless of how many virtual buffer pools the page is cached in.

Interest for a page is registered either in the page directory when a member reads a page into the local buffer pool from disk or in the group buffer pool for a GBP-dependent page set. DB2 prefetch can register up to 64 pages with a single CF interaction; otherwise, registration occurs on a page-by-page basis. When a page set or partition becomes GBP-dependent, all changed pages in the local buffer pool are moved synchronously into the GBP. All these pages, clean and changed, are registered in the directory in the GBP.

The ratio between directory entries and data entries is a setting on the group buffer pool that establishes the number of directory entries to the number of data entries in the GBP. One entry is made for each page read on any DB2 member, with only one page registered regardless of the number of members with interest. If a new page needs to be registered and you don't have enough directory entries, a directory entry will be reclaimed so that the new page can be registered. The process requiring the new page must then go to disk to reread and register that page. Depending on how often this scenario takes place, it can add up to significant overhead. Use the –DISPLAY GROUPBUFFERPOOL command to determine how many times it occurs in your environment. To change the ratio, you can issue the –ALTER GROUPBUFFERPOOL command. The following example changes the ratio to 20:1 (20 directory entries for every data entry).

```
-ALTER GROUPBUFFERPOOL (GBP3) RATIO (20)
```

A few situations can cause the deregistration of a page. If buffers are stolen from the local buffer pool of a GBP-dependent page set, the page is deregistered. If this behavior is occurring, it indicates there may be a problem with the size and/or threshold in the virtual buffer pool because the pages are falling off the LRU queue. This isn't a problem if the page isn't referenced, but if the page is needed and has to be read back into the virtual buffer pool, it must also be reregistered.

If an existing directory entry must be reclaimed for new work, the page is marked invalid and deregistered and, as a result, must then be reread in from disk. This can happen if the group buffer pool is too small or if the ratio is set incorrectly.

Sizing GBPs

Sizing group buffer pools is not like sizing normal virtual buffer pools. The GBPs are defined as structures in the coupling facility and are given an initial size when they are defined in the CFRM policy. For performance and availability reasons, you normally create them in a coupling facility separate from the coupling facility that holds the lock and SCA structures.

Some standard rules of thumb provide guidance about GBP sizing, but most are generic at best. For the best sizing of your group buffer pools, you're going to have to have a good understanding of the amount of sharing that will be occurring against the objects in the group buffer pool. In other words, you need to worry about object separation in virtual buffer pools even more so when implementing group buffer pools; otherwise, your initial sizing estimates will be rather difficult.

Castout

Because no connection exists between the coupling facility and disk, DB2 needs a way to move changed pages out to disk. It does this through a process called *castout*. The castout process (performed by castout engines) moves the changed pages from the group buffer pool to a private area in the DBM1 address space (*not* a virtual buffer pool), and from there they are written to disk. Figure 9.7 depicts the castout process.

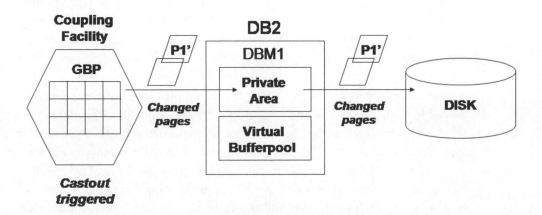

Figure 9.7: Castout process

The castout process is triggered if the number of changed pages exceeds the CLASST threshold or the GBPOOLT threshold or if a psuedo/physical close is performed on a data set by the last updating member. The CLASST threshold is similar to the VDWQT threshold on local buffer pools, and GBPOOLT is similar to the DWQT threshold. Castout can also be triggered if the GBPCHKPT threshold is reached and a group buffer pool checkpoint is taken.

Performance

Data sharing adds new opportunities for DB2 performance and tuning. From application selection to post-implementation troubleshooting, you have several new places to look to discover problems. Old performance problems that were acceptable or tolerable in the past in a single-subsystem environment may be magnified in the data-sharing environment. Monitoring and tuning for overall performance demands additional skills in diverse areas.

What is different about operating in a data-sharing environment is the introduction of additional hardware and rules. Contrary to popular belief, data sharing isn't just an install option! The introduction of the coupling facility in the Parallel Sysplex data-sharing architecture brings a whole new set of factors to think about in terms of performance. The coupling facility is unique to DB2 data sharing and provides many performance benefits over other sharing architectures used by other DBMSs. But it must be cared for. You need to concern yourself with activity involving the coupling facility due to the number of accesses DB2 will have to issue to the facility in terms of LOCK/UNLOCK requests, physical directory reads, cache updates, and reads of buffer invalidated data to maintain the consistency and coherency of the shared data.

In an ideal world, with more processors in the complex, the transaction rate achieved by a single DB2 would be multiplied by the number of available processors. However, due to the requirements of additional buffer management and global locking capability, DB2 and IRLM processing costs are increased, and, as a result, the overall transaction rate attainable may decrease. Typical overhead seen for data sharing has been around 5 percent after defining the second member as data sharing. As each member is added, overhead is generally low but depends greatly on the amount of sharing among the members.

Understanding the overhead involved, and gaining an appreciation of the tuning efforts required to minimize its impact, is essential to estimating data-sharing performance. First, you must set realistic goals, define performance objectives, and, most important, tune your current single-subsystem environment. Keep in mind that bad performers will become worse performers in a data-sharing environment, and new problems will surface. The key to a successful implementation is education of those involved in the migration and support of the data-sharing environment. This preparation will make the monitoring, tuning, and troubleshooting much less painful.

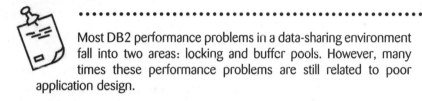

Most DB2 performance problems in a data-sharing environment fall into two areas: locking and buffer pools. However, many times these performance problems are still related to poor application design.

Processing Costs

Processing costs for data sharing will vary according to the degree of data sharing, locking factors, workload characteristics, hardware/software configurations, application design, physical design, and various application options. You can control the processing costs to a degree through application and system tuning.

Data-sharing costs are a function of the processing required, in addition to the normal processing necessary to achieve concurrency control for inter-DB2 interest and data coherency. Hardware/software costs are influenced by processor speed, the level of the coupling facility control code, coupling facility structure sizes and link configurations, hardware level, software maintenance, and the number of members in the data-sharing group. Workload characteristics can include real, false, and XES contention, disk contention, workload dynamics, thread reuse, and application use of lock avoidance.

Movement to Data Sharing

In general, moving to a DB2 data-sharing environment can be approached in two different ways. You can perform a new install of DB2, which gives you the opportunity to start with a clean subsystem when moving applications. This method also makes the monitoring of initial data-sharing performance easier and gives you a chance to implement new naming standards. However, while a new install is less painful, it usually is not practical.

Your other option is to migrate existing subsystems together by enabling a DB2 subsystem as a data-sharing subsystem and then adding members to the group. This approach is much easier if you need to move very large applications, and it has less impact on distributed processing. It is also the more common scenario for moving to a data-sharing environment. Complications, of course, accompany the catalog merge process and the measuring of application performance as the migration occurs.

Whether you decide to do a new install or to enable/migrate existing subsystems, effectively measuring the performance of data sharing and its impact on the overall environment will be an issue you face. Keep in mind that not all applications belong in a data-sharing environment; some will still benefit from isolation.

Application Analysis

Application analysis, or selection, is the process of evaluating which applications will benefit from data sharing and thus belong in a data-sharing environment. To set performance objectives, you'll need to determine the application objectives for data sharing, asking such questions as the following:

- What is the overall goal to accomplish with the implementation of data sharing?

- Do we want to offload CPU cycles?

- Will we benefit from transaction routing capabilities?

- Is 24x7 availability the driving requirement?

- Are there any application affinities?

These are just a few of several questions you should address to implement data sharing with the goal of achieving maximum performance benefit.

Current Environment Evaluation

Before moving to data sharing, evaluate your current DB2 environment in terms of both system and applications. A movement to even one-way data sharing can expose missed performance problems (although likely few because interaction with the coupling facility is minimal), and two-way sharing can further magnify them. The time to fix known application and system performance issues is before any movement into the data-sharing environment. Of course, you'll still need to investigate these same items as workload and other factors change in the new data-sharing environment. Items to evaluate include locking activity, application commit frequency, bind parameters, use of standard rule-of-thumb recommendations, DSNZPARMs, maintenance schedule/HIPER application, buffer pools, and recovery/restart procedures.

Migration Issues

There are many issues to consider when migrating to a data-sharing environment, but with careful planning and testing, you can assure that the process goes smoothly. Let's look a few of the issues that scem to require the most planning.

Catalog Merging

Most shops merge existing subsystems. There are some pros and cons with this approach. The pros include easier movement of large applications and fewer distributed processing implications. However, the cons include complications with the catalog merge process because no completely automated way (i.e., tool) exists to help with this process. Depending on the number of objects and the method used, the catalog merge can be laborious and error-prone. Namingconvention issues will arise with some objects because you must deal with existing names.

Merging subsystems that don't need shared data is not advised, nor is merging test and production subsystems. If subsystems are split out only because of capacity constraints, because they need common data, or because they currently rely on distributed connections or replication, they may certainly benefit from being merged into a single data-sharing group. When merging subsystems, be sure to evaluate the security schemas for the subsystems and make sure the same level of security will be in place after the merge.

The actual migration of the catalog isn't too bad (compared with the migration of the data, that is!). The first step is to decide which catalog to migrate all the other objects to, keeping the aforementioned considerations in mind. Query the catalog to determine which databases, table spaces, and indexes must be defined in the target system. Then, using DDL, define the objects in the target catalog. Depending on the number of objects you need to define, this process could become cumbersome, especially if the DDL isn't current. Normally, when you merge two subsystems into a data-sharing group, the larger subsystem should be the originating member.

Naming Conventions

The establishment of a flexible naming convention is one of the most important planning events in the process of migrating to a data-sharing environment. When done properly, it will reduce operational and administrative errors by reducing confusion and allowing easy extension to the sysplex. There is a benefit to planning names carefully because some names can't be changed at all, and making changes is difficult and often error-prone.

The names you use must be unique within the sysplex, and you have several categories of names to decide on, including group-level names, DB2 member-level names, IRLM group and member names, subsystem data sets (DB2), and ICF catalog names. Many shops have to change from their current naming convention. Of course, this will depend on migration options, in particular whether this is a new data-sharing group starting from scratch or a migration of existing systems into the group. For a complete list of items to consider, consult the *DB2 9 Data Sharing: Planning and Administration* guide.

Workload Management and Affinity Processing

One of the biggest advantages of the data-sharing environment is the ability to balance the workload across the members in the group. The DB2 subsystems work very closely with the workload manager (WLM) component of z/OS, which provides the ability to optimally balance incoming work across the subsystems in the group. WLM manages workloads based on predefined parameters according to the characteristics and priorities of the work.

This functionality lets you assign OLTP transactions a higher priority than long-running batch queries. WLM balances these workloads by ensuring that the long-running batch queries don't consume the resources that the online transactions need, letting the OLTP transactions achieve the desired response times.

Deciding how to distribute the workload across the data-sharing group will affect the sizing of coupling facility structures as well as certain aspects of hardware configurations.

Data sharing lets you move parts of a DB2 application workload across processors in the sysplex, assuring each processor efficient and direct access to the same DB2 data. It's up to you to decide how that workload is going to use its resources.

In a data-sharing environment, you can move workloads away from processors with capacity constraints. This is probably one of the best and quickest benefits to be realized by organizations that are constrained and having problems completing their workload because they have simply outgrown their processor capacity.

You can permit all members in the data-sharing group to process the same data concurrently by letting transactions that access the data run on any member in the group, or you can allow just one member to access the data. This decision directly affects the amount of data-sharing overhead you'll experience due to the control of inter-DB2 read/write interest among members to maintain coherency and concurrency. By using *affinity processing*, you can force an application to run on only one DB2 subsystem. With this approach, you could let OLTP run on one subsystem, batch on another, and ad-hoc on a third. Many configuration options are available.

Distributed Processing

The DB2 data-sharing group configuration should be transparent to SQL users and programs. When they connect, there is no awareness that a DB2 sysplex exists, and the system selects which DB2 member will process the SQL request. Three methods support distributed access:

- **Group-generic.** Using VTAM generic resources, the client requester connects to a generic LU name representing all members. VTAM then controls which DB2 member LU is selected, and the workload is balanced at the client level.

- **Member-specific.** This method uses the DDF Sysplex Support for distributed workload distribution. A client requester can connect to one or more real DB2 LU names, and the MVS Workload Manager then tells the client which DB2 LU names to use. The workload is balanced at the thread level and can be stopped and started on an individual member basis.

- **Hard-coded.** With this option, the client connects to a single, specified DB2 member LU name.This way, the client controls which DB2 member is selected, and the workload is balanced at the client level.

Sysplex Query Parallelism

Sysplex query parallelism gives you the ability to split a single query over several members of a data-sharing group, providing a very scalable solution for complex queries involved in decision support. Sysplex query parallelism works in much the same multitasking way as CPU parallelism, adding the capability to take a complex query and run it across multiple members, as Figure 9.8 illustrates.

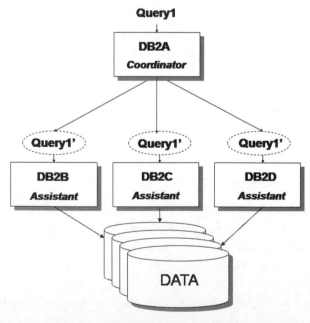

Figure 9.8: Sysplex query parallelism

A query is issued by a *coordinator*, which then sends the query to the *assistant* members in the group. The assistants process the data and then return it to the coordinator, either via a work file (causing the coordinator to read each of the assistant's work files) or using XCF links if a work file is unnecessary.

Good candidates for sysplex query parallelism are long-running, read-only queries, static and dynamic, local and remote, private and DRDA protocols, table space scan and index scan, joins (nested loop, merge scan, hybrid without sort on new table), and sorts. To avoid excess lock propagation to the coupling facility, this solution is best used with isolation-level uncommitted read (UR).

> Some additional considerations apply with sysplex query parallelism because it uses resources (buffer pools and work files) in the subsystems in which it runs. If these resources are unavailable (or insufficient), the degree (i.e., number of members used to process the query) may be decreased for the query.

Recovery Considerations

Recovery in a data-sharing environment is a little different than usual, and a few considerations are necessary.

Each DB2 member writes to its own recovery logs and BSDSs—sort of a striping effect. Each member also needs to be able to read the logs and BSDSs of every other member in the group, so these objects must reside on shared DASD with appropriate access granted. This accessibility is necessary because a media recovery may require logs from multiple DB2s. A group restart also requires access to all logs (as we discuss later).

The SCA structure contains information about all members' logs and BSDSs. During the backward log-recovery phase of DB2 startup, each member updates the SCA with new log information, which each DB2 member then reads during a recovery. The BSDSs back up the SCA. Every members' BSDSs contain the same information that is held in the SCA because the SCA can fail (because it is a cache in the coupling facility).

Logs and Recovery

In a recovery situation, you may need to merge the logs from several DB2s. The LRSN provides common log record sequencing across members and is used to control REDO/UNDO records for data sharing. The LRSN is a six- byte value derived from the Sysplex Timer timestamp and based on a store clock instruction. For non–data-sharing data, DB2 still uses the RBA.

You should avoid storing archive logs on tape because recovery time increases according to the number of members whose archive logs must be processed (unless you use Virtual Tape Storage, or VTS). Depending on where you keep these logs, the recovery process can become a lengthy one. Minimize the number of archive logs needed by having large active logs, incremental copies, and frequent commits. Archiving to DASD is best, but if you must use tape, never archive logs for more than one DB2 in the data-sharing group to the same tape.

During a recovery, DB2 accesses the logs of all DB2 subsystems in the group and merges the log records in sequence by the LRSNs. Figure 9.9 illustrates this recovery process.

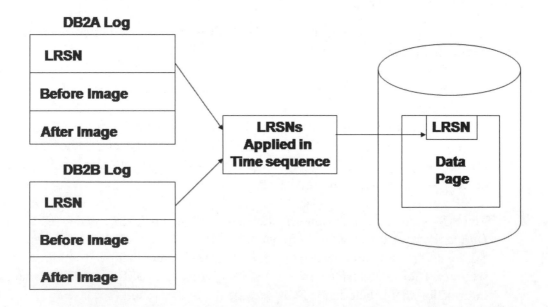

Figure 9.9: LRSNs and recovery

Recovery Scenarios

Let's take a brief look now at what it takes to recover from various failure scenarios.

DASD Failure

When recovering from a DASD failure, you will execute the RECOVER utility to restore to the most recent image copy and then apply log records from the LRSN (at time of image copy) to the end of the logs. This process will require merging logs from all updating members, the logs must be on DASD. If tape archives must be read, you will need enough available drives for all RECOVER operations, and there must be no deallocation delay to avoid tape not being accessible to other members.

DB2 Failure

When a DB2 subsystem fails, the locks are retained, and the other members remain active. When that DB2 is restarted, forward processing of the log begins from the unit of recovery of the oldest indoubt UR and the oldest pending write from the virtual pool to GBP. This is not as bad as non–data-sharing because only the checkpoint forces data to DASD, and data sharing has updated pages forced-at-commit to GBP. Retained locks are freed at the end of subsequent restart. You can restart a DB2 subsystem on the same or a different MVS subsystem. Use the RESTART LIGHT option here to bring up the DB2 subsystem quickly and then back down again to conserve resources.

Coupling Facility Failure

If a coupling facility fails with LOCK or SCA, or if there is a loss of connectivity to the structure, a dynamic rebuild of the lock or SCA structure is triggered. This rebuild is triggered only if the involved system exceeds the rebuild threshold in CFRM (or via an operator command). When a rebuild is caused by a storage failure and the rebuild fails, a group restart is necessary. All DB2 members must be brought down and a coordinated restart of all members performed to rebuild the SCA or lock from the logs.

Some pages—those that were in the GBP when the coupling facility failed—may be marked GRECP (group buffer pool recover pending) and require page set recovery. This recovery requires a LOGONLY recovery and no image copy is needed. A –START DATABASE command will start the recovery. The GBP checkpoint determines how far back in the log to process.

Structure Failures

There are cases when you can lose a structure in the coupling facility. Different recovery needs apply for each type of structure.

- Lock structure

  » This structure failure is detected by all active members at the time of failure, and all members initiate rebuild, although only one rebuild occurs. The structure is rebuilt into the backup coupling facility. The rebuild uses the active members to rebuild the locks from local information. If a loss of connectivity to the coupling facility occurs, the weights from the Sysplex Failure Management policy will determine whether the structure is rebuilt.

- SCA structure

  » This failure is also detected by all members, and attempts are made to rebuild into the backup coupling facility. During the rebuild, the remaining active members rebuild the SCA from local information. If a loss of connectivity to the coupling facility occurs, the weights from the SFM determine whether the structure is rebuilt.

- Group buffer pool structures

  » The GBP will be rebuilt in the backup coupling facility. If there were pages in the GBP, they will be marked GRECP, unless the GBP was defined with AUTOREC(YES), in which case the pages will be recovered automatically. To recover page sets marked GRECP, you can issue either

```
-START DATABASE() SPACENAM() ACCESS(RO)
```

or

```
-START DATABASE() SPACENAM() ACCESS(RW)
```

DB2 merges logs from the oldest modified page LRSN or the oldest pending write to DASD from the GBP to the end of the logs. Running a RECOVER utility, LOAD REPLACE utility, or DROP TABLE statement also removes GRECP status. If connectivity is lost, DB2 will quiesce GBP-dependent page sets, and the result will be an SQLCODE –904 to a requesting application. Writes will then go on the LPL list, and GBP-dependent page sets will be marked GRECP.

Structure Duplexing

If the structures are duplexed (i.e., a primary exists in one coupling facility and an active secondary exists in the other), during a failure the activity is switched from the primary to the secondary without the rebuild process. Duplexing the group buffer pools is recommended to avoided prolonged outages. The rebuild time for a lock or SCA structure is normally minimal; therefore, duplexing these structures is unnecessary unless the lock and SCA structures reside in an ICF.

Summary

Data sharing provides many benefits and is being used in many shops throughout the world to support some very high-volume and highly available databases and applications. Migration to a data-sharing environment is relatively easy and can be done with few or no application changes. Data sharing gives you some new components to become familiar with and some new tuning opportunities as well.

Additional Resources

Batch Processing in a Parallel Sysplex (SG24-5329)
DB2 9 Data Sharing: Planning and Administration (SC18-9845)
DB2 for MVS/ESA V4 Data Sharing Performance Topics (SG24-4611)
DB2 for MVS/ESA Version 4 Data Sharing Implementation (SG24-4791)
DB2 on MVS Platform: Data Sharing Recovery (SG24-2218)
OS/390 Parallel Sysplex Configuration, Volume 1: Overview (SG24-5637)
OS/390 Parallel Sysplex Configuration, Volume 2: Cookbook (SG24-5638)
OS/390 Parallel Sysplex Configuration, Volume 3: Connectivity (SG24-5639)
Parallel Sysplex Continuous Availability – Case Studies (SG24-5346)
Parallel Sysplex Performance Health Case Study (SG24-5373)

Practice Questions

Question 1

A data-sharing environment contains two members (DB21 and DB22) on separate LPARs (L1 and L2) with two coupling facilities (CF1 and CF2). CF1 contains the lock and SCA structures, and CF2 contains the group buffer pool structures. The GBPs are not duplexed. Assume that all the structures can reside on either CF1 or CF2 based on the CRFM policy PREFLIST and parameter AUTOREC is set to YES.

CF2 fails and is no longer available to DB21 or DB22. What action is necessary to minimize loss of data availability to the application?

○ A. Manually rebuild the GBP structures on CF1.

○ B. Stop members DB21 and DB22 and initiate a group restart.

○ C. No action is needed. Each member performs automatic GRECP recovery.

○ D. No action is needed. The GBP structures are automatically rebuilt in CF2.

Question 2

Which of the following structures should *not* exist in the coupling facility of a data-sharing group?

○ A. Lock structure

○ B. Global buffer pool(s)

○ C. Virtual buffer pool(s)

○ D. Shared communications area (SCA)

Question 3

If a coupling facility that contains the group buffer pool structures fails, which is the best option to help lessen the duration of the outage?

○ A. Use ARM.

○ B. Use group buffer pool duplexing.

○ C. Use lock structure duplexing.

○ D. Remove the pages.

Question 4

Which of the following items are registered in the coupling facility in a data-sharing environment?

○ A. Logs

○ B. Work files

○ C. EDM pool entries

○ D. Locks

Question 5

Which of the following is *not* a benefit of a data-sharing environment?

○ A. Continuous availability

○ B. Configuration flexibility

○ C. Concurrent read/write access to the same data

○ D. No need for image copies

Answers

Question 1

The correct answer is **C**, no action is needed because each member performs automatic GRECP recovery. The members will perform automatic GRECP recovery of the pages that existed in the group buffer pools when CF2 became unavailable. Because GBP duplexing was not turned on and CF1 was listed in the PREFLIST with AUTOREC on, the rebuild will occur automatically in the surviving coupling facility (CF1).

Question 2

The correct answer is **C**, virtual buffer pool(s). Virtual buffer pools still exist on each DB2 subsystem (member). The other options are all structures defined in the coupling facility.

Question 3

The correct answer is **B**, use group buffer pool duplexing. By enabling this feature, you can minimize the outage in the event of a coupling facility failure because you won't have to wait for the primary structure to be rebuilt in the surviving coupling facility. The secondary structure will take over.

Question 4

The correct answer is **D**, locks. Locks can be registered in the coupling facility. The other items—logs, work files, and EDM pool entries—are all still associated with a single subsystem and are not found in the coupling facility.

Question 5

The correct answer is **D**, no need for image copies. A data-sharing environment can provide the means for continuous availability, configuration flexibility, and concurrent read/write access to data. However, it does not have the ability to replace normal backup and recovery practices, including the need to do image copies.

Using SQL in an Application Program

In This Chapter

✔ Application environment

✔ Embedded SQL

✔ Host variables

✔ Error checking

✔ Using cursors

✔ Using dynamic SQL

✔ DB2 application developmentenvironment

Suppose you are writing an application program to access data in a DB2 database. When your program executes an SQL statement, the program needs to communicate with DB2. When DB2 finishes processing an SQL statement, DB2 sends back a return code, and your program should test the return code to examine the results of the operation.

To communicate with DB2, you need to choose one of these methods:

● Static SQL

● Dynamic SQL

- Open Database Connectivity (ODBC)

- Java Database Connectivity (JDBC) application support

ODBC lets you access data through ODBC function calls in your application. You execute SQL statements by passing them to DB2 through an ODBC function call. ODBC eliminates the need for precompiling and binding your application and increases the portability of your application by using the industry-standard ODBC interface, but the ODBC processor does issue dynamic SQL.

If you're writing your applications in Java, you can use the industry-standard JDBC application support to access DB2. JDBC is similar to ODBC but is designed specifically for use with Java and is therefore a better choice than ODBC for making DB2 calls from Java applications.

Delimiting SQL in a Program

To distinguish SQL calls from the rest of the program, you use delimiters. Although used in all languages, the actual delimiters and methods differ considerably by language. For all languages that use the standard DB2 precompiler, however, the methods are very similar. For example, you use EXEC SQL and END-EXEC to delimit an SQL statement in a COBOL program:

```
EXEC SQL
an SQL statement
END-EXEC.
```

For REXX, precede the statement with EXEC SQL. If the statement is in a literal string, enclose it in single or double quotation marks.

Declaring Table and View Definitions

Before your program issues SQL statements that retrieve, update, delete, or insert data, you should declare the tables and views your program accesses. To do this, include an SQL DECLARE statement in the program.

You don't have to declare tables or views, but there are advantages to doing so. One advantage is documentation. For example, the DECLARE statement specifies the structure of the table or view you're working with and declares the data type of each column. You can refer to the DECLARE statement to find the column names and data types in the table or view.

Another advantage is that the DB2 precompiler uses your declarations to make sure you've used correct column names and data types in your SQL statements. If the column names and data types don't correspond to the SQL DECLARE statements in your program, the precompiler issues a warning message.

One way to declare a table or view is to code a DECLARE statement in the working-storage section or linkage section within the data division of your COBOL program. Specify the name of the table, and list each column and its data type.

When you declare a table or view, you specify the table name in the DECLARE TABLE statement regardless of whether the table name refers to a table or a view. For example, the DECLARE TABLE statement for the DB2USER1.TEST table looks like this:

```
EXEC SQL
DECLARE DB2USER1.TEST_TABLE
   (NUMBER        CHAR(6)         NOT NULL,
    NAME          VARCHAR(50)     NOT NULL,
    TYPE          CHAR(1)         NOT NULL,
    CUT_SCORE     DECIMAL(6,2),
    LENGTH        SMALLINT        NOT NULL,
    TOTALTAKEN    SMALLINT        NOT NULL)
END-EXEC.
```

An alternative to coding the DECLARE statement manually is to use DCLGEN, the declarations generator supplied with DB2. We cover DCLGEN later in this chapter.

> When you declare a table or view that contains a column with a distinct type, it's best to declare that column with the source type of the distinct type rather than with the distinct type itself. When you declare the column with the source type, DB2 can check embedded SQL statements that reference the column at precompile time.

Host Variables and Host Structures

A *host variable* is a data item declared in the host language for use within an SQL statement. Using host variables, you can

- retrieve data into a host variable for your application program's use

- place data into a host variable to insert into a table or to change the contents of a row

- use the data in a host variable when evaluating a WHERE or HAVING clause

- assign the value in a host variable to a special register, such as CURRENT SQLID and CURRENT DEGREE

- insert null values in columns using a host indicator variable that contains a negative value

- use the data in a host variable in statements that process dynamic SQL, such as EXECUTE, PREPARE, and OPEN

A *host structure* is a group of host variables that an SQL statement can refer to using one name. You can use host structures in all languages except REXX. Use the host language statements to define the host structures.

Using Host Variables

You can use any valid host variable name in an SQL statement. Host variables must be declared to the host program before you can use them. DB2 uses host variables to

- retrieve data and put it into host variables for use by the application program

- insert data into a table or update the table using the data in a host variable

- evaluate a WHERE or HAVING clause using the data in a host variable (however, you can't use host variables to represent a table, column, or view)

To optimize performance, make sure the host language declaration maps as closely as possible to the data type of the associated data in the database. You can specify table, view, or column names at runtime when using dynamic SQL. (We discuss dynamic SQL later in the chapter.)

Host variables follow the naming conventions of the host language. A colon (:) must precede a host variable name used in SQL to tell DB2 that the variable is not a column name. A colon must not precede host variables outside SQL statements.

In the following example, :PHONE and :EMPNO are host variables. Their values will be supplied at runtime.

```
EXEC SQL
   UPDATE EMP
      SET PHONENO = :PHONE
      WHERE EMPNO = :EMPNO
END-EXEC.
```

You can use the host variables to specify a program data area to contain the column values of a retrieved row or rows.

Using Host Structures

You can use a host structure in place of one or more host variables. In the next example, assume that a COBOL program includes the following SQL statement.

```
EXEC SQL
   SELECT  LASTNAME, FIRSTNME
   INTO    :LNAMEHV,:FNAMEHV
   FROM    DSN8910.EMP
   WHERE   EMPNO =:EMPNO
END-EXEC.
```

If you want to avoid listing host variables, you can substitute the name of a structure, say :EMPHS, that contains :LNAMEHV, and :FNAMEHV. The example then reads

```
EXEC SQL
   SELECT   LASTNAME, FIRSTNME
   INTO     :EMPHS
   FROM     DSN8910.EMP
   WHERE    EMPNO =:EMPNO
END-EXEC.
```

You can declare host structures manually or use DCLGEN to generate a C structure declaration, COBOL record description, or PL/I structure declaration that corresponds to the columns of a table.

DCLGEN

DCLGEN, the declarations generator supplied with DB2, produces a DECLARE statement for use in a C, COBOL, or PL/I program so that you don't need to code the declares for the tables manually. DCLGEN generates a table declaration and puts it into a member of a partitioned data set that you can include in your program.

When you use DCLGEN to generate a table's declaration, DB2 obtains the relevant information from the DB2 catalog, which contains information about the table's definition and the definition of each column in the table. DCLGEN uses this information to produce a complete SQL DECLARE statement for the table or view and a matching C or PL/I structure declaration or COBOL record description.

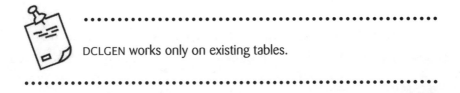

DCLGEN works only on existing tables.

The DCLGEN must be used, and the DCLGEN name of the table or view supplied, before program precompilation. To use the declarations generated by DCLGEN in the program, you code the SQL INCLUDE statement. The following example shows the INCLUDE statement for the EMP DCLGEN:

```
EXEC SQL
    INCLUDE EMP
END-EXEC.
```

DB2 must be active before you can use DCLGEN. You can start the DCLGEN utility in several ways:

- *From ISPF through DB2 I:* Select the DCLGEN option on the DB2 I Primary Option menu panel. Fill in the DCLGEN panel with the information it needs to build the declarations. Then press Enter.

- *Directly from TSO:* Sign on to TSO, issue the TSO command DSN, and then issue the subcommand DCLGEN.

- *From a CLIST:* Run a CLIST in the TSO foreground or background that issues DSN, and then run DCLGEN.

- *With JCL:* Supply the required information, using JCL, and run DCLGEN in batch.

Listing 10.1 shows an example of the output from a DCLGEN.

```
***************************************************************
*      DCLGEN TABLE(DSN8910.EMP)
*          LIBRARY(DB2U01.DCLGEN.LIB(EMP))
*          LANGUAGE(COBOL)
*          APOST
***************************************************************
   EXEC SQL DECLARE DSN8910.EMP
       (EMPNO      CHAR(6)          NOT NULL,
        FIRSTNME   VARCHAR(12)      NOT NULL,
        MIDINIT    CHAR(1)          NOT NULL,
        LASTNAME   VARCHAR(15)      NOT NULL,
        WORKDEPT   CHAR(3)                   ,
        PHONENO    CHAR(4)                   ,
        HIREDATE   DATE                      ,
        JOB        CHAR(8)                   ,
        EDLEVEL    SMALLINT                  ,
        SEX        CHAR(1)                   ,
        BIRTHDATE  DATE                      ,
        SALARY     DECIMAL(9, 2)             ,
        BONUS      DECIMAL(9, 2)             ,
        COMM       DECIMAL(9, 2)
       END-EXEC.
```

Listing 10.1: Sample DCLGEN output (part 1 of 2)

```
***********************************************************************
* COBOL DECLARATION FOR TABLE DSN8910.EMP
***********************************************************************
    01  EMP.
        10 EMPNO                  PIC X(6).
        10 FIRSTNME.
            49 FIRSTNME-LEN        PIC S9(4) USAGE COMP.
            49 FIRSTNME-TEXT       PIC X(12).
        10 MIDINIT                PIC X(1).
        10 LASTNAME.
            49 LASTNAME-LEN        PIC S9(4) USAGE COMP.
            49 LASTNAME-TEXT       PIC X(15).
        10 WORKDEPT               PIC X(3).
        10 PHONENO                PIC X(4).
        10 HIREDATE               PIC X(10).
        10 JOB                    PIC X(8).
        10 EDLEVEL                PIC S9(4) USAGE COMP.
        10 SEX                    PIC X(1).
        10 BIRTHDATE              PIC X(10).
        10 SALARY                 PIC S9(7)V9(2) USAGE COMP-3.
        10 BONUS                  PIC S9(7)V9(2) USAGE COMP-3.
        10 COMM                   PIC S9(7)V9(2) USAGE COMP-3.

***********************************************************************
*    THE NUMBER OF COLUMNS DESCRIBED BY THIS DECLARATION IS 14
***********************************************************************
```

Listing 10.1: Sample DCLGEN output (part 2 of 2)

Retrieving a Single Row of Data

The INTO clause of the SELECT statement names one or more host variables to contain the column values returned. The named variables correspond one-to-one with the list of column names in the SELECT list. In the following example, we retrieve LASTNAME and FIRSTNME from the EMP table and populate the host variables. (Notice that a colon precedes each host variable.) In your program, you can define a data area to hold each column and then name the data areas in the INTO clause, as is done here.

```
EXEC SQL
    SELECT LASTNAME, FIRSTNME
    INTO   :LNAMEHV,:FNAMEHV
    FROM   DSN8910.EMP
    WHERE  EMPNO =:EMPNO
END-EXEC.
```

In the program's data division, host variables EMPNO, LNAMEHV, and FNAMEHV must be declared and need to be compatible with the data types in the columns EMPNO, LASTNAME, and FIRSTNME, respectively, of the DSN8910.EMP table.

If the SELECT statement returns more than one row, an -811 error code results, and any returned data is undefined and unpredictable.

Retrieving Multiple Rows of Data

If the number of rows returned by DB2 is unknown, or if you expect more than one row to be returned, you must use an alternative to the SELECT...INTO statement. A cursor enables an application to process a set of rows and retrieve one row at a time from the result table. We take a look at cursors later in this chapter.

Inserting and Updating Data

You can set or change a value in a DB2 table to the value of a host variable. To do so, you use the host variable name in the SET clause of an UPDATE statement or in the VALUES clause of an INSERT statement. The following example changes an employee's home telephone number.

```
EXEC SQL
   UPDATE DSN8910.EMP
   SET    PHONENO =:HPHONEHV
   WHERE  EMPNO   =:EMPNO
END-EXEC.
```

Searching Data

You can use a host variable to specify a value in the predicate of a search condition or to replace a constant in an expression. For example, if you've defined a field called EMPNO that contains an employee number, you can retrieve the name of the employee whose number is 000010 with

```
MOVE '000010' TO EMPNO.
EXEC SQL
   SELECT LASTNAME
   INTO   :LNAMEHV
   FROM   DSN8910.EMP
   WHERE  EMPNO =:EMPNO
END-EXEC.
```

SQL Execution Validation

A program that includes SQL statements needs to have an area set apart for communications with DB2: an SQL communication area (SQLCA). When DB2 processes an SQL statement in a program, it places return codes in the SQLCODE and SQLSTATE host variables or in the corresponding fields of the SQLCA. The return codes indicate whether the executed statement succeeded or failed.

Because the SQLCA is a valuable problem-diagnosis tool, it's a good idea to include instructions to display some of the information contained in the SQLCA in your application programs. For example, the contents of field SQLERRD(3) — which indicates the number of rows that DB2 updates, inserts, or deletes — could be useful. If SQLWARN0 contains W, DB2 has set at least one of the SQL warning flags (SQLWARN1 through SQLWARNA). Table 10.1 describes the fields of the SQLCA.

Table 10.1: SQL communication area fields		
Name	**Data type**	**Purpose**
SQLCAID	CHAR(8)	An "eye catcher" for storage dumps, containing the text 'SQLCA'.
SQLCABC	INTEGER	Contains the length of the SQLCA: 136.
SQLCODE	INTEGER	Contains the SQL return code: **Code** — **Means** 0 — Successful execution (although there might have been warning messages) Positive — Successful execution, with an exception condition Negative — Error condition
SQLERRML	SMALLINT	Length indicator for SQLERRMC, in the range 0–70. Value 0 means that the value of SQLERRMC is not pertinent.
SQLERRMC	VARCHAR(70)	Contains one or more tokens, separated by X'FF', that are substituted for variables in the descriptions of error conditions. It may contain truncated tokens. A message length of 70 bytes indicates a possible truncatlon.
SQLERRP	CHAR(8)	Provides a product signature and, in the case of an error, diagnostic information such as the name of the module that detected the error. In all cases, the first three characters are 'DSN' for DB2 for z/OS.

Table 10.1: SQL communication area fields (continued)		
Name	**Data type**	**Purpose**
SQLERRD(1)	INTEGER	For a sensitive static cursor, contains the number of rows in a result table when the cursor position is after the last row (that is, when SQLCODE is equal to +100). Can also contain an internal error code.
SQLERRD(2)	INTEGER	For a sensitive static cursor, contains the number of rows in a result table when the cursor position is after the last row (that is, when SQLCODE is equal to +100). Can also contain an internal error code.
SQLERRD(3)	INTEGER	Contains the number of rows that qualified to be deleted, inserted, or updated after an INSERT, MERGE, UPDATE, or DELETE statement. The number excludes rows affected by either triggers or referential integrity constraints. For the OPEN of a cursor for a SELECT with a data change statement or for a SELECT INTO, SQLERRD(3) contains the number of rows affected by the embedded data change statement. The value is 0 if the SQL statement fails, indicating that all changes made in executing the statement canceled. For a DELETE statement, the value will be −1 if the operation is a mass delete from a table in a segmented table space and the DELETE statement did not include selection criteria. If the delete was against a view, neither the DELETE statement nor the definition of the view included selection criteria. For a TRUNCATE statement, the value will be −1. For a REFRESH TABLE statement, SQLERRD(3) contains the number of rows inserted into the materialized query table. For a rowset-oriented FETCH, it contains the number of rows fetched. For SQLCODES −911 and −913, SQLERRD(3) contains the reason code for the timeout or deadlock. When an error is encountered in parsing a dynamic statement, or when parsing, binding, or executing a native SQL procedure, SQLERRD(3) will contain the line number where the error was encountered. The sixth byte of SQLCAID must be 'L' for this to be a valid line number. This value will be meaningful only if the statement source contains new line control characters. This information is not returned for an external SQL procedure.
SQLERRD(4)	INTEGER	Generally contains a timeron, a short floating-point value that indicates a rough relative estimate of resources required. The value does not reflect an estimate of the time required. When preparing a dynamically defined SQL statement, you can use this field as an indicator of the relative cost of the prepared SQL statement. For a particular statement, this number can vary with changes to the statistics in the catalog. It is also subject to change between releases of DB2 for z/OS.
SQLERRD(5)	INTEGER	Contains the position or column of a syntax error for a PREPARE or EXECUTE IMMEDIATE statement.
SQLERRD(6)	INTEGER	Contains an internal error code.

Table 10.1: SQL communication area fields (continued)		
Name	Data type	Purpose
SQLWARN0	CHAR(1)	Contains a W if at least one other indicator also contains a W; otherwise, contains a blank.
SQLWARN1	CHAR(1)	Contains a W if the value of a string column was truncated when assigned to a host variable. Contains an N for non-scrollable cursors or an S for scrollable cursors after the OPEN CURSOR or ALLOCATE CURSOR statement. If subsystem parameter DISABSCL is set to YES, the field will not be set to N for non-scrollable cursors.
SQLWARN2	CHAR(1)	Contains a W if null values were eliminated from the argument of a column function; is not necessarily set to W for the MIN function because its results don't depend on the elimination of null values.
SQLWARN3	CHAR(1)	Contains a W if the number of result columns is larger than the number of host variables. Contains a Z if the ASSOCIATE LOCATORS statement provided fewer locators than the stored procedure returned.
SQLWARN4	CHAR(1)	Contains a W if a prepared UPDATE or DELETE statement does not include a WHERE clause. For scrollable cursor, contains a D for sensitive dynamic cursors, I for insensitive cursors, and S for sensitive cursors after the OPEN CURSOR or ALLOCATE CURSOR statement; blank if not scrollable. If DSNZPARM DISABSCL is set to YES, the field will be set to N for non-scrollable cursors.
SQLWARN5	CHAR(1)	Contains a W if the SQL statement was not executed because it is not a valid SQL statement in DB2 for z/OS. Contains a character value of 1 (read only), 2 (read and delete), or 4 (read, delete, and update) to reflect the capability of the cursor after the OPEN CURSOR or ALLOCATE CURSOR statement. If subsystem parameter DISABSCL is set to YES, the field will not be set to N for non-scrollable cursors.
SQLWARN6	CHAR(1)	Contains a W if the addition of a month or year duration to a DATE or TIMESTAMP value results in an invalid day (e.g., June 31). Indicates that the value of the day was changed to the last day of the month to make the result valid.
SQLWARN7	CHAR(1)	Contains a W if one or more nonzero digits were eliminated from the fractional part of a number used as the operand of a decimal multiply or divide operation.
SQLWARN8	CHAR(1)	Contains a W if a character that could not be converted was replaced with a substitute character.
SQLWARN9	CHAR(1)	Contains a W if arithmetic exceptions were ignored during COUNT DISTINCT processing. Contains a Z if the stored procedure returned multiple result sets.
SQLWARNA	CHAR(1)	Contains a W if at least one character field of the SQLCA or the SQLDA names or labels is invalid due to a character conversion error.
SQLSTATE	CHAR(5)	Contains a return code for the outcome of the most recent execution of an SQL statement.

SQLCODE and SQLSTATE

Whenever an SQL statement is executed, the SQLCODE and SQLSTATE fields of the SQLCA receive a return code. Although both fields serve basically the same purpose (indicating whether the statement was executed successfully), the two fields differ in some ways.

SQLCODE

DB2 returns the following codes in SQLCODE:

- If SQLCODE = 0, execution was successful.
- If SQLCODE > 0, execution was successful with a warning.
- If SQLCODE < 0, execution was not successful.
- SQLCODE 100 indicates no data was found.

The meaning of SQLCODEs other than 0 and 100 varies with the particular product implementing SQL.

SQLSTATE

SQLSTATE lets an application program check for errors in the same way for different IBM database management systems. An advantage to using the SQLCODE field is that it can provide more specific information than SQLSTATE. Many of the SQLCODEs have associated tokens in the SQLCA that indicate, for example, which object incurred an SQL error.

To conform to the SQL standard, SQLCODE and SQLSTATE (SQLCOD and SQLSTA in FORTRAN) can be declared as standalone host variables. If you've specified the STDSQL(YES) precompiler option, these host variables receive the return codes, and you needn't include an SQLCA in your program.

GET DIAGNOSTICS

The GET DIAGNOSTICS statement lets you retrieve diagnostic information about the last SQL statement that was executed. Requests can be made for all diagnostic items or for individual items of diagnostic information from the following categories:

- Statement items, which contain information about the SQL statement as a whole

- Condition items, which contain information about each error or warning that occurred during the execution of the SQL statement

- Connection items, which contain information about the SQL statement if it was a CONNECT statement

You can use the GET DIAGNOSTICS statement to handle multiple SQL errors that might result from the execution of a single SQL statement. As a first step, check SQLSTATE (or SQLCODE) to determine whether diagnostic information should be retrieved using GET DIAGNOSTICS. This method is especially useful for diagnosing problems that result from a multiple-row INSERT that is specified as NOT ATOMIC CONTINUE ON SQLEXCEPTION.

Even if you use GET DIAGNOSTICS in an application program to check for conditions, you must either include the instructions needed to use the SQLCA or declare SQLSTATE (or SQLCODE) separately in the program.

When you use the GET DIAGNOSTICS statement, DB2 assigns the requested diagnostic information to host variables. Declare each target host variable with a data type that is compatible with the data type of the requested item. Then, to retrieve condition information, the number of condition items must first be retrieved.

Table 10.2 shows the data types for GET DIAGNOSTICS items that return statement information.

Table 10.2: GET DIAGNOSTICS statement information items		
Item	**Description**	**Data type**
DB2_GET_DIAGNOSTICS_DIAGNOSTICS	After a GET DIAGNOSTICS statement, if any error or warning occurred, this item contains all the diagnostics as a single string.	VARCHAR (32672)
DB2_LAST_ROW	After a multiple-row FETCH statement, this item contains a value of +100 if the last row in the table is in the row set that was returned.	INTEGER
DB2_NUMBER_PARAMETER_MARKERS	After a PREPARE statement, this item contains the number of parameter markers in the prepared statement.	INTEGER
DB2_NUMBER_RESULT_SETS	After a CALL statement that invokes a stored procedure, this item contains the number of result sets returned by the procedure.	INTEGER
DB2_NUMBER_ROWS	After an OPEN or FETCH statement for which the size of the result table is known, this item contains the number of rows in the result table. After a PREPARE statement, this item contains the estimated number of rows in the result table for the prepared statement. For SENSITIVE DYNAMIC cursors, this item contains the approximate number of rows.	DECIMAL (31,0)
DB2_RETURN_STATUS	After a CALL statement that invokes an SQL procedure, this item contains the return status if the procedure contains a RETURN statement.	INTEGER
DB2_SQL_ATTR_CURSOR_HOLD	After an ALLOCATE or OPEN statement, this item indicates whether the cursor can be held open across multiple units of work (Y or N).	CHAR(1)
DB2_SQL_ATTR_CURSOR_ROWSET	After an ALLOCATE or OPEN statement, this item indicates whether the cursor can use row set positioning (Y or N).	CHAR(1)
DB2_SQL_ATTR_CURSOR_SCROLLABLE	After an ALLOCATE or OPEN statement, this item indicates whether the cursor is scrollable (Y or N).	CHAR(1)
DB2_SQL_ATTR_CURSOR_SENSITIVITY	After an ALLOCATE or OPEN statement, this item indicates whether the cursor shows updates made by other processes (sensitivity A, I, or S).	CHAR(1)

Table 10.2: GET DIAGNOSTICS statement information items (continued)		
Item	**Description**	**Data type**
DB2_SQL_ATTR_CURSOR_TYPE	After an ALLOCATE or OPEN statement, this item indicates whether the cursor is declared static (S for INSENSITIVE or SENSITIVE STATIC) or dynamic (D for SENSITIVE DYNAMIC).	CHAR(1)
MORE	After any SQL statement, this item indicates whether some conditions items were discarded because of insufficient storage (Y or N).	CHAR(1)
NUMBER	After any SQL statement, this item contains the number of condition items. If no warning or error occurred, or if no previous SQL statement has been executed, the number returned is 1.	INTEGER
ROW_COUNT	After DELETE, INSERT, UPDATE, or FETCH, this item contains the number of rows that are deleted, inserted, updated, or fetched. After PREPARE, this item contains the estimated number of result rows in the prepared statement.	DECIMAL (31,0)

Table 10.3 shows the data types for GET DIAGNOSTICS items that return condition information.

Table 10.3: GET DIAGNOSTICS condition information items		
Item	**Description**	**Data type**
CATALOG_NAME	This item contains the server name of the table that owns a constraint that caused an error or that caused an access rule or check violation.	VARCHAR(128)
CONDITION_NUMBER	This item contains the number of the condition.	INTEGER
CURSOR_NAME	This item contains the name of a cursor in an invalid cursor state.	VARCHAR(128)
DB2_ERROR_CODE1	This item contains an internal error code.	INTEGER
DB2_ERROR_CODE2	This item contains an internal error code.	INTEGER
DB2_ERROR_CODE3	This item contains an internal error code.	INTEGER
DB2_ERROR_CODE4	This item contains an internal error code.	INTEGER
DB2_INTERNAL_ERROR_POINTER	For some errors, this item contains a negative value that is an internal error pointer.	INTEGER
DB2_LINE_NUMBER	Line number where an error is encountered in parsing a dynamic statement.	INTEGER
DB2_MESSAGE_ID	This item contains the message ID that corresponds to the message contained in the CHAR(10)MESSAGE_TEXT diagnostic item.	INTEGER

Table 10.3: GET DIAGNOSTICS condition information items (continued)		
Item	**Description**	**Data type**
DB2_MODULE_DETECTING_ERROR	After any SQL statement, this item indicates which module detected the error.	CHAR(8)
DB2_ORDINAL_TOKEN_*n*	After any SQL statement, this item contains the *n*th token, where *n* is a value from 1 to 100.	VARCHAR(515)
DB2_REASON_CODE	After any SQL statement, this item contains the reason code for errors that have a reason code token in the message text.	INTEGER
DB2_RETURNED_SQLCODE	After any SQL statement, this item contains the SQLCODE for the condition.	INTEGER
DB2_ROW_NUMBER	After any SQL statement that involves multiple rows, this item contains the row number on which DB2 detected the condition.	DECIMAL(31,0)
DB2_TOKEN_COUNT	After any SQL statement, this item contains the number of tokens available for the condition.	INTEGER
MESSAGE_TEXT	After any SQL statement, this item contains the message text associated with the SQLCODE.	VARCHAR (32672)
RETURNED_SQLSTATE	After any SQL statement, this item contains the SQLSTATE for the condition.	CHAR(5)
SERVER_NAME	After a CONNECT, DISCONNECT, or SET CONNECTION statement, this item contains the name of the server specified in the statement.	VARCHAR(128)

Table 10.4 shows the data types for GET DIAGNOSTICS items that return connection information.

Table 10.4: GET DIAGNOSTICS connection information items		
Item	**Description**	**Data type**
DB2_AUTHENTICATION_TYPE	This item contains the authentication type (S, C, D, E, or blank).	CHAR(1)
DB2_AUTHORIZATION_ID	This item contains the authorization ID used by the connected server.	VARCHAR(128)
DB2_CONNECTION_STATE	This item indicates whether the connection is unconnected (−1), local (0), or remote (1).	INTEGER
DB2_CONNECTION_STATUS	This item indicates whether updates can be committed for the current unit of work (1 = yes, 2 = no).	INTEGER

Table 10.4: GET DIAGNOSTICS connection information items (continued)		
Item	Description	Data type
DB2_ENCRYPTION_TYPE	This item contains one of the following values to indicate the level of encryption for the connection: A = Only the authentication tokens (authorization ID and password) are encrypted. D = All data for the connection is encrypted.	CHAR(1)
DB2_PRODUCT_ID	This item contains the DB2 product signature.	VARCHAR(8)
DB2_SERVER_CLASS_NAME	After a CONNECT or SET CONNECTION statement, this item contains the DB2 server class name.	VARCHAR(128)

The GET DIAGNOSTICS statements can prove useful and informative for your application communication. The following example shows how to use the statement to obtain a count of the number of rows that a particular statement updated.

```
EXEC SQL
   GET DIAGNOSTICS :rcount = ROW_COUNT;
```

> Using GET DIAGNOSTICS can be costly. Use it only if necessary. For example, you can obtain the number of rows returned from a multi-row fetch operation from GET DIAGNOSTICS, but interpreting the SQLCODE and SQLERRD3 fields of the SQLCA is more efficient.

Using Cursors

You use a *cursor* in an application program to retrieve multiple rows from a table or from a result set returned by a stored procedure. This section looks at how an application program can use a cursor to retrieve rows from a table.

When the SELECT statement associated with the cursor is executed, a set of rows is retrieved. The set of rows returned is referred to as the *result table* or *result set*. In an application program, we need a way to retrieve one row at a time from the result set into host variables; a cursor performs this function. A program can have several cursors open at the same time.

DECLARE Cursor

To define and identify a set of rows to be accessed with a cursor, issue a DECLARE CURSOR statement. The DECLARE CURSOR statement names a cursor and specifies a SELECT statement. The SELECT statement defines the criteria for the rows that will make up the result table. The simplest form of the DECLARE CURSOR statement is as follows:

```
EXEC SQL
    DECLARE    ECURSOR CURSOR FOR
        SELECT EMPNO, FIRSTNME, LASTNAME
        FROM   DSN8910.EMP
        WHERE  WORKDEPT = :WORKDEPT
END-EXEC.
```

Updating a Column

If any of the columns are to be updated in the rows of the identified table, include the FOR UPDATE clause. FOR UPDATE has two forms, one for when the columns to be updated are known and another for when the columns are not known. Use the following form when the columns intended for update are known.

```
EXEC SQL
    DECLARE    ECURSOR CURSOR FOR
        SELECT EMPNO, FIRSTNME, LASTNAME, SALARY
        FROM   DSN8910.EMP
        WHERE  WORKDEPT = :WORKDEPT
        FOR    UPDATE OF SALARY
END-EXEC.
```

If a cursor might be used to update any of the columns of the table, use the following form of the FOR UPDATE clause, which permits updates to any columns of the table that can be updated.

```
EXEC SQL
    DECLARE    ECURSOR CURSOR FOR
        SELECT EMPNO, FIRSTNME, LASTNAME, SALARY
        FROM   DSN8910.EMP
        WHERE  EMPNO = :EMPNO
        FOR    UPDATE
END-EXEC.
```

DB2 must do more processing when you use the FOR UPDATE clause without a column list than when you use the FOR UPDATE OF clause with a column list. Therefore, if only a few columns of a table are going to be updated, the program can run more efficiently if you include a column list.

A column of the identified table can be updated even though it is not part of the result table. In this case, there's no need to name the column in the SELECT statement. When the cursor retrieves a row (using FETCH) that contains a column value you want to update, you can use the UPDATE...WHERE CURRENT OF statement to update the row.

Some result tables—for example, the result of joining two or more tables—cannot be updated.

OPENing the Cursor

To tell DB2 that you're ready to process the first row of the result table or result set, you must issue an OPEN statement. DB2 then uses the SELECT statement within the DECLARE CURSOR statement to identify a set of rows. If the SELECT statement includes host variables, DB2 uses the current value of the variables to select the rows. The result table that satisfies the search conditions can contain zero, one, or many rows. The OPEN statement looks like this:

```
EXEC SQL
    OPEN ECURSOR
END-EXEC.
```

There is no way in DB2 to determine the number of rows that qualified during an open. An SQLCODE of +100 on the subsequent fetch, update, or delete statement identifies an empty result table or result set.

When you use them with cursors, DB2 evaluates CURRENT DATE, CURRENT TIME, and CURRENT TIMESTAMP special registers once when the OPEN statement is executed. (We provide more information about special registers later in the chapter.) DB2 uses the values returned in the registers on all subsequent FETCH statements.

Two factors influence the amount of time DB2 requires to process the OPEN statement:

- Whether DB2 must perform any sorts before it can retrieve rows from the result table

- Whether DB2 uses parallelism to process the SELECT statement associated with the cursor

Executing SQL Statements

Once a cursor is opened, one of the following SQL statements is executed using the cursor:

- FETCH

- Positioned UPDATE

- Positioned DELETE

FETCH Statements

Execute a FETCH statement for one of the following purposes:

- To copy data from a row of the result table into one or more host variables

- To position the cursor before performing a positioned UPDATE or positioned DELETE operation

The simplest form of the FETCH statement looks like this:

```
EXEC SQL
   FETCH ECURSOR
   INTO :EMPNO, :FIRSTNME, :LASTNAME, :SALARY
END-EXEC.
```

The SELECT statement within the DECLARE CURSOR statement identifies the result table from which to fetch rows, but DB2 doesn't retrieve any data until the application program executes a FETCH statement.

When the program executes the FETCH statement, DB2 uses the cursor to point to a row in the result table. That row is called the *current row*. DB2 then copies the current row contents into the program host variables you specified in the INTO clause of FETCH. This sequence is repeated for each subsequent FETCH until you've processed all the rows in the result table.

Which row DB2 points to when a FETCH statement is executed depends on whether you declare the cursor as scrollable or non-scrollable (a topic we cover later). When querying a remote subsystem with FETCH, consider using block fetch for better performance. Block fetch processes rows ahead of the current row.

•••
You cannot use block fetch when a positioned UPDATE or DELETE is performed.
•••

Positioned UPDATE

After the program has executed a FETCH statement to retrieve the current row, you can use a positioned UPDATE statement to modify the data in that row. Here is an example of a positioned UPDATE:

```
EXEC SQL
    UPDATE DSN8910.EMP
        SET SALARY = 53487
        WHERE CURRENT OF ECURSOR
END-EXEC.
```

A positioned UPDATE statement updates the row that the cursor name (ECURSOR in this case) points to. A positioned UPDATE statement must meet three conditions:

- The row cannot be updated if the update violates any unique, check, or referential constraint.

- An UPDATE statement cannot be used to modify the rows of a created temporary table. However, you can use UPDATE to modify the rows of a declared temporary table (as covered later).

- If the right side of the SET clause in the UPDATE statement contains a subselect, that subselect cannot include a correlated name for a table that is being updated.

Positioned DELETE

After the program has executed a FETCH statement to retrieve the current row, you can use a positioned DELETE statement to delete that row. Here's an example of a positioned DELETE statement:

```
EXEC SQL
   DELETE FROM DSN8910.EMP
   WHERE   CURRENT OF ECURSOR
END-EXEC.
```

A positioned DELETE statement deletes the row that the cursor points to. A positioned DELETE statement must meet three conditions:

- A DELETE statement cannot be used with a cursor to delete rows from a created global temporary table. However, you can use DELETE to delete rows from a declared temporary table.

- After a row has been deleted, you cannot update or delete another row using that cursor until you execute a FETCH statement to position the cursor on another row.

- A row cannot be deleted if the delete violates any referential constraints.

CLOSEing the Cursor

When the program is finished processing the rows of the result table, issue a CLOSE statement to close the cursor:

```
EXEC SQL
   CLOSE ECURSOR
END-EXEC.
```

This action destroys the result set that was created during the OPEN cursor.

Cursor WITH HOLD

A *held cursor*, which you declare using WITH HOLD, does not close after a COMMIT operation. A cursor that isn't declared WITH HOLD closes after a COMMIT operation. When a cursor is declared, the inclusion or exclusion of the WITH HOLD clause tells DB2 whether or not the cursor is to be held. After a COMMIT operation, a held cursor is positioned after the last retrieved row and before the next logical row of the result table to be returned.

A held cursor closes when

- a CLOSE cursor, ROLLBACK, or CONNECT statement is issued

- a Call Attach Facility (CAF) CLOSE function call or a Resource Recovery Services Attachment Facility (RRSAF) TERMINATE THREAD function call is issued

- the application program terminates

If the program terminates abnormally, the cursor position is lost. To prepare for restart, your program must reposition the cursor. The following restrictions apply to cursors declared WITH HOLD:

- Do not use DECLARE CURSOR WITH HOLD with the new user sign-on from a DB2 attachment facility because all open cursors are closed.

- Do not declare a WITH HOLD cursor in a thread that could become inactive. If you do, its locks are held indefinitely.

You also face some restrictions when using CURSOR WITH HOLD with IMS or CICS programs. (For details, see the *DB2 9 Application Programming and SQL Guide*.)

··

The use of CURSOR WITH HOLD also prevents some DB2 options that are used for performance (e.g., parallelism, drains needed for online REORG).

··

Here's a simple example of declaring a held cursor:

```
EXEC SQL
    DECLARE   ECURSOR CURSOR WITH HOLD FOR
        SELECT FIRSTNME, LASTNAME
        FROM   DSN8910.EMP
        WHERE  EMPNO = :EMPNO
END-EXEC.
```

Types of Cursors

Cursors can be scrollable or not scrollable. They can also be held or not held. The following sections discuss these characteristics in more detail.

Scrollable and Non-Scrollable

When you declare a cursor, you tell DB2 whether you want the cursor to be scrollable or non-scrollable by either including or omitting the SCROLL clause. This clause determines whether the cursor moves sequentially forward through the data set or has random access to the data set. Table 10.5 summarizes the different cursor types.

Table 10.5: Cursor characteristics				
Cursor type	**Result table**	**Visibility of own cursor's changes**	**Visibility of other cursors' changes**	**Updatability***
Non-scrollable (e.g., join, sort)	Fixed, work file	No	No	No
Non-scrollable	No work file, base table access	Yes	Yes	Yes
Insensitive scroll	Fixed, declared temporary table	No	No	No
Sensitive static scroll	Fixed, declared temporary table	Yes (inserts not allowed)	Yes (not inserts)	Yes
Sensitive dynamic scroll	No declared temporary table, base table access	Yes	Yes	Yes

*If the SELECT statement references more than one table or contains a GROUP BY or similar clause, it becomes read-only.

Using a Non-Scrollable Cursor

The simplest type of cursor is a *non-scrollable cursor*. A non-scrollable cursor always moves sequentially forward in the result table. When a cursor is opened, it is positioned before the first row in the result table. When the first FETCH is executed, the cursor is positioned on the first row. Each FETCH statement moves the cursor one row ahead.

After each FETCH statement, the cursor is positioned on the row that was fetched. After execution of a positioned UPDATE or positioned DELETE operation, the cursor stays at the current row of the result table. You cannot retrieve rows in reverse order or move to a specific position in a result table with a non-scrollable cursor.

Using a Scrollable Cursor

Scrollable cursors enable movement to any row in the result table. DB2 uses declared temporary tables to process scrollable cursors. The declaration of a scrollable cursor takes the following form:

```
EXEC SQL
    DECLARE   ECURSOR sensitivity STATIC SCROLL CURSOR FOR
        SELECT EMPNO, FIRSTNME, LASTNAME
        FROM   DSN8910.EMP
        WHERE  EMPNO = :EMPNO
END-EXEC.
```

STATIC SCROLL indicates that the cursor is scrollable and follows the static model. The sensitivity specified in the DECLARE statement indicates whether changes made to the underlying table after the cursor is opened are visible to the result table. Sensitivity can be either INSENSITIVE or SENSITIVE:

- INSENSITIVE means that no changes to the underlying table after the cursor is opened are visible to the result table.

- SENSITIVE means that some or all changes made to the underlying table after the cursor is opened are visible to the result table.

The sensitivity clause of the FETCH statement determines which changes to the underlying table are visible to the result table. When the cursor is opened, the cursor is positioned before the first row. In each FETCH statement, you include a clause to tell DB2 where to position the cursor in the result table. The FETCH clause for a scrollable cursor takes the following form:

```
EXEC SQL
    FETCH sensitivity cursor-position cursor-name
    INTO :host-variable1, :host-variable2 ...
END-EXEC.
```

Sensitivity in the FETCH statement indicates whether changes that are made to the underlying table by some means other than the cursor are visible to the result table. Sensitivity can be INSENSITIVE or SENSITIVE:

- INSENSITIVE means that changes to the underlying table are visible to the result table only when a positioned UPDATE or positioned DELETE using ECURSOR makes those changes.

- SENSITIVE means that the result table is updated when the underlying table changes.

Table 10.6 summarizes the cursor sensitivity options.

Table 10.6: Cursor sensitivity options	
Cursor sensitivity	**Result**
DECLARE C1 INSENSITIVE SCROLL FETCH INSENSITIVE	• Read-only cursor • Not aware of updates or deletes in base table
DECLARE C1 SENSITIVE STATIC SCROLL FETCH INSENSITIVE	• Updatable cursor • Aware of own updates or deletes within cursor • Other changes to base table not visible to cursor • No inserts recognized
DECLARE C1 SENSITIVE STATIC SCROLL FETCH SENSITIVE	• Updatable cursor • Aware of own updates and deletes within cursor • Sees all committed updates and deletes • No inserts recognized

Scrollable Cursor Fetching

When fetching with a scrollable cursor, you have several options. Cursor positioning becomes very flexible because you can fetch forward and backward and perform relative and absolute positioning. The following examples show several different fetching options.

```
FETCH
FETCH LAST (or FIRST)
FETCH ABSOLUTE +7
FETCH INSENSITIVE RELATIVE -3
FETCH CURRENT (or BEFORE or AFTER)
FETCH RELATIVE 2
FETCH PRIOR (or NEXT)
```

•••

In a distributed environment, you can use scrollable cursors only if you use DRDA access.

•••

Dynamic Scrollable Cursors

Dynamic scrollable cursors enable you to implement this type of cursor in your applications with better performance and more usability. Dynamic scrollable cursors permit base table access instead of requiring you to use a declared temporary table, and they don't materialize at any time. Each FETCH shows the most current activity and is sensitive to all INSERTs, UPDATEs, and DELETEs—no more delete holes and missing updates.

Dynamic scrollable cursors default to single-row fetch, but they also support multi-row fetch and positioned updates/deletes with multi-row fetch. Order is always maintained with these cursors.

The following example illustrates the syntax for defining a dynamic scrollable cursor.

```
DECLARE ECURSOR SENSITIVE DYNAMIC CURSOR
FOR SELECT EMPNO, LASTNAME, FROM EMP
```

Some SQL statements require the result sets to be placed in work files for joins. These files are considered read-only and cannot support dynamic scrolling. The new option of ASENSITIVE lets DB2 decide whether the cursor is SENSITIVE DYNAMIC or INSENSITIVE based on the complexity of the SQL statement. If the cursor is declared as ASENSITIVE and read-only, it will be INSENSITIVE; if declared as ASENSITIVE and not read-only, it will be SENSITIVE DYNAMIC.

Dynamic scrollable cursors can take advantage of backward index scans and backward sequential detection and can support both index scan access and table scan access paths.

Using Dynamic SQL

Before you decide to use dynamic SQL, devote some thought to whether using static SQL or dynamic SQL is the best technique for the application.

For most DB2 users, static SQL—embedded in a host language program and bound before the program runs—provides a straightforward, efficient path to DB2 data. Use static SQL when the SQL statements that the application needs to execute are known before runtime.

Dynamic SQL prepares and executes the SQL statements within a program while the program is running. There are four types of dynamic SQL:

- In *embedded dynamic SQL*, the application puts the SQL source in host variables and includes PREPARE and EXECUTE statements that tell DB2 to prepare and run the contents of those host variables at runtime. The programs that include embedded dynamic SQL must go through the precompile and bind steps.

- In *interactive SQL*, a user enters SQL statements through SPUFI or the command-line processor. DB2 prepares and executes these statements as dynamic SQL statements.

- *Deferred embedded SQL* statements are neither fully static nor fully dynamic. Like static statements, deferred embedded SQL statements are embedded within applications, but like dynamic statements, they are prepared at runtime. DB2 processes deferred embedded SQL statements with bind-time rules. For example, DB2 uses the authorization ID and qualifiers determined at bind time as the plan or package owner.

- With *dynamic SQL executed through ODBC functions*, the application contains ODBC function calls that pass dynamic SQL statements as arguments. There is no need to precompile and bind programs that use ODBC function calls.

Coding Dynamic SQL in Applications

Applications that use dynamic SQL employ three types of SQL statements:

- Dynamic SQL for non-SELECT statements. These statements include DELETE, INSERT, UPDATE, and MERGE.

- For execution, use either of the following SQL statement options:

  » EXECUTE IMMEDIATE

  » PREPARE and then EXECUTE

- Dynamic SQL for fixed-list SELECT statements. A SELECT statement is fixed-list if you know in advance the number and type of data items in each row of the result. For execution, use the following SQL statements:

  1. PREPARE (an SQL cursor definition)

  2. OPEN the cursor

  3. FETCH from the cursor

  4. CLOSE the cursor

- Dynamic SQL for varying-list SELECT statements. A SELECT statement is varying-list if you cannot know in advance how many data items to allow for or what their data types are.

  1. DECLARE CURSOR for the statement

  2. PREPARE the statement

  3. DESCRIBE the statement

  4. OPEN cursor

  5. FETCH using DESCRIPTOR

  6. CLOSE cursor

There are many other variations to using dynamic SQL. You can use host variables, and you can put literal data into the dynamic SQL statement. When using parameter markers in the dynamic SQL statement (to be replaced by the host variables later), you can also use the bind feature REOPT(ALWAYS), REOPT(ONCE), or REOPT(AUTO) to help the optimizer choose the right access path, based on the host variable data, at execution time.

Summary

In this chapter, we reviewed the various components of a DB2 application program. We examined how to construct a program and have it communicate with DB2. DB2 can use data in an application program by means of host variables and host structures. Using cursors, you can move through result sets of your data. These cursors must be declared and opened before fetching rows of data is possible. Scrollable and non-scrollable cursors are the two types of cursors that can be used with various options.

Additional Resources

DB2 9 Application Programming and SQL Guide (SC18-9841)
DB2 9 SQL Reference (SC18-9854)

Practice Questions

Question 1

If a DBA would like to get a count of rows returned from a multi-row fetch operation, which of the following methods would be used?

○ A. Use GET DIAGNOSTICS.

○ B. Check the SQL return code.

○ C. Check the SQLSTATE.

○ D. Perform a count in the program.

Question 2

The main difference between static scrollable cursors and dynamic scrollable cursors is which of the following?

○ A. Static cursors must be declared.

○ B. Dynamic cursors must be opened.

○ C. Dynamic cursors do not use the workfile database.

○ D. Static cursors cannot be used by pseudo-conversional CICS.

Question 3

A cursor defined WITH HOLD is released when all of the following occur except:

○ A. A CLOSE cursor, ROLLBACK, or CONNECT statement is issued.

○ B. A Call Attach Facility (CAF) CLOSE function call or an RRSAF TERMINATE THREAD function call is issued.

○ C. The application program terminates.

○ D. A commit occurs.

Question 4

Which of the following is *not* a type of dynamic SQL?

○ A. Embedded dynamic SQL

○ B. Interactive SQL

○ C. Deferred embedded SQL

○ D. Static SQL

Question 5

The following statement is referred to as which type of DELETE?

```
EXEC SQL
    DELETE FROM DSN8910.EMP
    WHERE CURRENT OF ECURSOR
END-EXEC.
```

○ A. Searched

○ B. Positioned

○ C. Selective

○ D. Mass

Answers

Question 1

The correct answer is **A**, use GET DIAGNOSTICS. By interrogating the ROW_COUNT parameter in the GET DIAGNOSTICS results, you can find out how many rows were returned from a multi-row fetch operation.

Question 2

The correct answer is **C**, dynamic cursors do not use the workfile database. The static scrollable cursors are materialized in a table space in the workfile database. The dynamic scrollable cursors don't need to materialize here because the scrolling can occur both ways against the active result set using backward index scanning.

Question 3

The correct answer is **D**, a commit occurs. A commit will not release a cursor defined WITH HOLD. The whole purpose of WITH HOLD is to hold the cursor open through a commit point so that cursors don't need to be repositioned after the commit.

Question 4

The correct answer is **D**, static SQL (because it's static, which is the opposite of dynamic). A, B, and C are all types of dynamic SQL as well as dynamic SQL executed through ODBC functions.

Question 5

The correct answer is **B**, positioned. A DELETE that is defined with a WHERE CURRENT OF cursor is known as a positioned delete because it will delete the data wherever the cursor happens to be positioned.

Binding an Application Program

In This Chapter

✔ Precompile and bind

✔ Binding and rebinding

✔ Plans and packages

✔ Removing plans and packages

✔ Authorities for plans and packages

Precompile and Bind

DB2 application programs include SQL statements. Before you can compile a program, these SQL statements must be converted into language recognized by the compiler or assembler. You use the DB2 precompiler or a host language compiler to

- replace the SQL statements in the source programs with compilable code

- create a *database request module (DBRM)*, which communicates the SQL requests to DB2 during the bind process

Once the source program has been precompiled, you create a *load module*, along with possibly one or more packages and an application plan. Creating a load module involves compiling and link-editing the modified source code that the precompiler produces. Creating a package or an application plan—a process unique to DB2—involves binding one or more DBRMs.

Figure 11.1 illustrates the program preparation process.

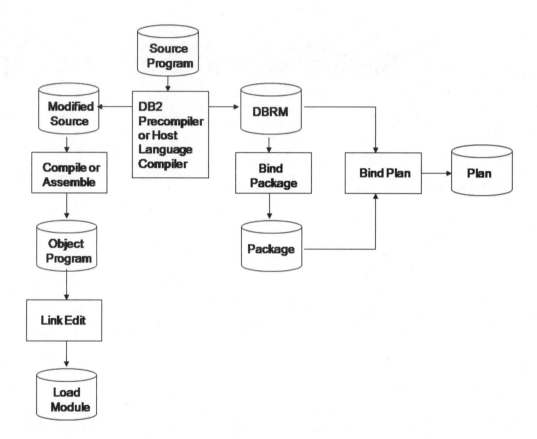

Figure 11.1: Program preparation

Precompile

The precompiler "prepares" the source program for compilation by replacing EXEC SQL with a CALL and embedding the SQL in a comment. The precompiler (which you can invoke in DB2I or in batch) acts as follows:

- Uses the included DCLGEN member

- Uses the included SQLCA member

- Looks for SQL statements and host variable definitions

- Verifies the SQL syntax

- Matches each column and table name in the SQL to the DECLARE TABLE statements contained in the DCLGEN

- Prepares the SQL for compilation or assembly in the host language

- Produces a DBRM and stores it in a partitioned data set (PDS)

- Produces a modified source and stores it in a PDS to be compiled

DB2 is not accessed during this process.

The database request module that the precompiler creates contains extracted, somewhat modified, parsed SQL source code. It can be stored as a member in a partitioned data set. The precompiler creates one DBRM for each precompile; this module then becomes the input to the bind process.

During the precompile process, the precompiler replaces the SQL statements with a call to the DSNHLI module. This call contains the necessary parameters (DBRM name, timestamp, statement number, host variable addresses, and SQLCA address) to locate the access path required to execute the SQL statement associated with the call when the DBRM and modified source are used together at execution time.

Binding

The *bind* process establishes a relationship between an application program and its relational data. This step is necessary before a program can be executed. DB2 supports two basic ways to bind a program: to a package or directly to an application plan.

If the application uses DRDA access to distribute data, you must use packages.

When a program is preprocessed for DB2, two outputs are normally produced. The first is a modified source program (to be passed to a compiler) in which the original SQL statements have been replaced with statements to invoke the appropriate DB2 interface functions. The second output, a DBRM, contains information about how DB2 will use those SQL statements. The DBRM must be bound so that all the DB2 functions used in the program can be checked for validity and authorization and so DB2 can determine a proper access path. The bind process performs the following tasks:

- Checks SQL syntax
- Checks security
- Compares column and table names against the DB2 catalog
- Builds an access path strategy for each SQL statement

We discuss these processes in more detail later.

Plans and Packages

You can bind a DBRM in a package or directly into a plan. In addition, packages can be bound into logical groups called *collections*. These packages or collections can then be bound into a plan. You can bind a package for a single SQL statement, a subset of the program, or an entire program.

A plan can be bound for multiple packages, collections, and/or DBRMs. Each package can be bound independently of a plan. If a DBRM is bound to a plan and then is re-bound, all DBRMs in the plan are re-bound as well. The output will contain the access path information for each SQL statement.

When determining the maximum size of a plan, you must consider several physical limitations, including the time required to bind the plan, the size of the environmental descriptor manager (EDM) pool, and fragmentation. The number of DBRMs you can include in a plan has no limit. However, packages provide a more flexible way to handle large numbers of DBRMs within a plan.

Packages are database objects that contain executable forms of SQL statements. They contain statements that are referenced from a DB2 application. A package corresponds to a program source module. Packages are stored in the DB2 catalog tables. The packages contain the access plan that DB2 chose during the BIND or PREPARE process. This type of bind is known as *static binding* because it is performed before the execution of the SQL statement. You cannot reference packages directly in an SQL DML statement.

Most applications that access a DB2 database will have a package or a group of packages stored (bound) in the system catalog tables. The package is the input to the BIND PLAN subcommand using the PKLIST option. To be usable, a package must be bound into a plan (packages accessed by distributed applications and stored procedures are an exception). Here's an example of a plan bind:

```
BIND PLAN (certpln) PKLIST (coll.*)
```

Plan-to-Package Ratio

It's extremely difficult to justify using one plan to contain all the packages for an installation or even for just all CICS transactions or batch jobs. Plans need to be granular. Large, cumbersome plans cause performance degradation, buffer pool problems, and EDM pool problems. In deciding the number of packages to put into a single plan, use functionality as your guide—putting all the packages that support a particular function of an online application into one plan, for example.

Advantages of Packages

Base your use of packages on the application design and objectives. Using packages provides a variety of advantages:

- **Ease of maintenance.** With packages, you don't need to bind the entire plan again if you make a change to one SQL statement. Only the package associated with the changed SQL statement needs to be bound.

- **Incremental program development.** Binding packages into package collections (discussed later) gives you the ability to add packages to an existing application plan without having to bind the entire plan again.

- **Versioning.** With versioning, you can maintain several versions of a package without requiring a separate plan for each version (and therefore separate plan names and RUN commands). (We discuss versioning further later in this section.)

- **Flexibility in using bind options.** The BIND PLAN subcommand options apply to all DBRMs bound directly to the plan. The BIND PACKAGE subcommand options apply only to the single DBRM bound to the package. The package options needn't all be the same as the plan options, nor must they match the options for other packages used by the same plan.

- **Flexibility in using name qualifiers.** You can use the QUALIFIER bind option to name a qualifier for the unqualified object names in SQL statements in a plan or package. Using packages allows different qualifiers for SQL statements in different parts of an application. For example, to redirect SQL statements from a test table to a production table, all you need is a rebind.

- **CICS flexibility.** With packages, there is no need for dynamic plan selection and the associated exit routine. A package listed within a plan is not accessed until it is executed. However, it's possible to use dynamic plan selection and packages together. Doing so can reduce the number of plans in an application and, hence, require less effort to maintain the dynamic plan exit routine.

Collections

A *collection* is a group of associated packages. If you include a collection name in the package list when a plan is bound, any package in the collection becomes available to the plan. The collection can even be empty when the plan is first bound. You can add packages to the collection later, or drop or replace existing packages, without binding the plan again.

A collection is implicitly created at the first package bind that references a named collection. The name of the package is *collection.packagename*.

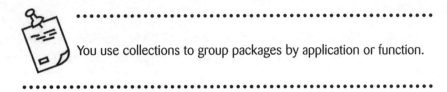

You use collections to group packages by application or function.

The CURRENT PACKAGESET special register enables package searches in specific collections and disregards any other DBRMs. The following example uses this special register to search only the DB2SAMPL collection.

```
EXEC SQL SET CURRENT PACKAGESET = 'DB2SAMPL'
```

Without the use of CURRENT PACKAGESET, all the DBRMs would be searched, and then collections would be searched.

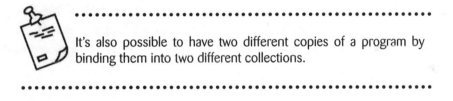

It's also possible to have two different copies of a program by binding them into two different collections.

The CURRENT PACKAGE PATH special register lets you search a list of collections.

Versioning

Maintaining several versions of a plan without using packages requires a separate plan for each version and, therefore, separate plan names and RUN commands. Isolating separate versions of a program into packages requires only one plan and helps to simplify program migration and fallback. At precompile time, the user can assign versions to the program, enabling multiple copies of the same package to exist in the DB2 system. For example, you could maintain separate development, test, and production levels of a program by binding each level of the program as a separate version of a package, all within a single plan.

Binding and Rebinding

The BIND PACKAGE subcommand lets you bind DBRMs individually. The command provides the ability to test different versions of an application without extensive rebinding.

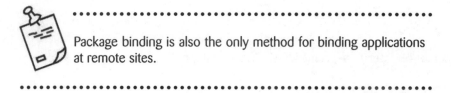

Package binding is also the only method for binding applications at remote sites.

Even when DBRMs are bound into packages, all programs must be designated in an application plan. BIND PACKAGE establishes the relationship between DB2 and all DBRMs or packages in that plan. Plans can specify explicitly named DBRMs, packages, collections of packages, or a combination of these elements. The plan contains information about the designated DBRMs or packages and provides details about the data the application program intends to use. It is stored in the DB2 catalog.

In addition to building packages and plans, the bind process

- validates the SQL statements using the DB2 catalog. During the bind process, DB2 checks the SQL statements for valid table, view, and column names. Because the bind process occurs as a separate step before program execution, errors are detected and can be corrected before the program is executed.

- verifies that the process binding the program is authorized to perform the data-accessing operations requested by your program's SQL statements. When you issue the BIND command, you can specify an authorization ID as the owner of the plan or package. The owner can be any one of the authorization IDs of the process performing the bind. The bind process determines whether the owner of the plan or package is authorized to access the data the program requests.

- selects the access paths needed to access the DB2 data that the program wants to process. In selecting an access path, DB2 considers indexes, table sizes, and other factors. DB2 considers all indexes available to access the data and decides which ones (if any) to use when selecting a path to the data. You can execute BIND PLAN and BIND PACKAGE using DB2I panels, the DSNH CLIST, or the DSN subcommands BIND PLAN and BIND PACKAGE.

Depending on how the DB2 application was designed, all DBRMs could be bound in one operation, creating only a single application plan. Or, you might bind some or all of your DBRMs into separate packages in separate operations. After that, you must still bind the entire application as a single plan, listing the included packages or collections and binding any DBRMs not already bound into packages.

Regardless of what a plan contains, the plan must be bound before the application can run.

Binding or Rebinding a Package or Plan in Use

Packages and plans are locked during binding and execution. Packages that run under a plan are not locked until the plan uses them. If you execute a plan and some packages in the package list are never executed, those packages are never locked.

There is no ability to bind or rebind a package or a plan while it is running. However, a different version of a package that is running can be bound.

Options for Binding and Rebinding

A few options are used for BINDing and REBINDing packages and plans.

- Use the BIND(ADD) option to create a new plan or package.

- Use the BIND(REPLACE) option when the program has changed.

- Use the REBIND command when the program hasn't changed but you've added an index or executed RUNSTATS (for example), and any access path changes need to be accounted for.

Several of the BIND PACKAGE and BIND PLAN options can affect your program design. For example, you can use one bind option to ensure that a package or plan can be run only from a particular CICS connection or IMS region—something you can't enforce in your code. For example:

```
BIND PLAN(CICSONLY)-
    MEMBER(CERTDBRM)-
    ACTION(ADD)-
    ISOLATION(CS)-
    OWNER(DB2USER1)-
    QUALIFIER(DB2USER1)-
    CACHESIZE(0)-
    ENABLE(CICS) CICS(CON1)
```

We discuss several other options at length in later chapters, particularly those that affect a program's use of locks, such as the ISOLATION option. Table 11.1 lists the options for the BIND and REBIND commands and the valid values for plans, packages, and trigger packages (REBIND only). (We discuss trigger packages in Chapter 15.) The options you choose are recorded in the SYSPLAN and SYSPACKAGES catalog tables.

Table 11.1: Bind and rebind options				
Option	**Valid values**	**Plan**	**Package**	**Trigger**
ACQUIRE	**USE**, ALLOCATE	X		
Determines whether to acquire resources specified in the DBRM at first access or allocation				
ACTION	**REPLACE**, ADD	X, BO	X, BO	
	REPLACE(RPLVER)		X, BO	
	REPLACE(RETAIN)	X, BO		
Determines whether the object (plan or package) replaces an existing object with same name or is new				
CACHESIZE	Value of PLAN AUTH CACHE; decimal value	X		
Determines the size (in bytes) of the authorization cache acquired in the EDM pool for the plan				
COPY	Collection-id, package-id, COPYVER		X, BO	
Determines that you are copying an existing package and names the package				
CURRENTDATA	**YES**, NO	X	X	X
Determines whether to require data currency for RO and ambiguous cursors when isolation level is CS				
CURRENTSERVER	Location-name	X		
Determines the location to connect to before running the plan				
DBPROTOCOL	**DRDA**, PRIVATE	X	X	
Specifies which protocol to use when connecting to a remote site that is identified by a three-part name				

Table 11.1: Bind and rebind options (continued)				
Option	**Valid values**	**Plan**	**Package**	**Trigger**
DEFER	DEFER(PREPARE), **NODEFER**(PREPARE)	X	X	
Determines whether to defer preparation of dynamic SQL statements that refer to remote objects or to prepare them immediately				
DEGREE	**1**, ANY	X	X	
Determines whether to attempt to run a query using parallel processing to maximize performance				
DEPLOY	(*collection-id.package-id*), **COPYVER**(*version-id*)		X	
Deploys a native SQL procedure				
DISCONNECT	**EXPLICIT**, AUTOMATIC, CONDITIONAL	X		
Determines which remote connections to destroy during COMMIT operations				
DYNAMICRULES	**RUN**, BIND, DEFINEBIND(PKG ONLY), DEFINERUN (PKG ONLY), INVOKEBIND(PKG ONLY), INVOKERUN(PKG ONLY)	X	X	
	DEFINEBIND, DEFINERUN, INVOKEBIND, INVOKERUN		X	
Determines which values apply at run time for dynamic SQL attributes				
ENABLE/ DISABLE	BATCH, CICS, DB2CALL, DLIBATCH, IMS, IMSBMP, IMSMPP, RRSAF , <u>*</u>	X	X	
	REMOTE		X	
Determines which connections can use the plan or package				
ENCODING	ASCII, EBCDIC, UNICODE, *ccsid*	X	X	
Specifies the application encoding for all static statements in the plan or package (defaults to installed selection)				
EXPLAIN	**NO**, YES	X	X	X
Determines whether to populate the PLAN_TABLE with information about the SQL statements				
FLAG	<u>I</u>, W, E, C	X	X	X
Determines what messages to display				
IMMEDIATE	**NO**, YES	X	X	
Determines whether immediate writes will be done for updates made to GBP-dependent page sets/partitions				
ISOLATION	**RR**, RS, CS, UR, NC	X	X	X
Determines how far to isolate an application from the effects of other running applications				
KEEPDYNAMIC	**NO**, YES	X	X	

Table 11.1: Bind and rebind options (continued)				
Option	Valid values	Plan	Package	Trigger
Determines whether DB2 keeps dynamic SQL statements after commit points				
LIBRARY	*dbrm-pds-name* (can be multiple for PLAN)	X, BO	X, BO	
Determines which partitioned data set to search for DBRMs listed in the member option				
MEMBER	*dbrm-member-name* (can be multiple for PLAN)	X, BO	X, BO	
Determines what DBRMs to include in the plan or package				
OPTHINT	*Hint-id*	X	X	
Controls whether query optimization hints are used for static SQL				
OPTIONS	**COMPOSITE**, COMMAND		X, BC	
Specifies which bind options to use for the new package				
OWNER	*Authorization-id*	X	X	
Determines the authorization ID or the owner of the object (plan or package)				
PACKAGE	*Location-name.collection-id. package-id (version-id)*		X	
	(*) – Rebind Only		X, RO	
Determines which package or packages to bind or rebind				
PATH	*Schema-name*, USER, *(schema-name, (USER)...)*	X	X	
Determines the SQL path that DB2 uses to resolve unqualified UDTs, functions, and stored procedure names				
PATHDEFAULT	Mutually exclusive with PATH	X	X	
Resets the PATH for a package or plan to SYSIBM, SYSFUN, SYSPROC, or a plan/package qualifier				
PKLIST or NOPKLIST	(*Location-name.collection-id. package-id...*), PKLIST only	X		
Determines which package to include for the package list in the plan				
PLAN	*Plan-name*	X		
	(*)	X, RO		
Determines which plan or plans to bind or rebind				
QUALIFIER	*Qualifier-name*	X	X	
Determines the implicit qualifier for unqualified names of objects in the plan or package				
RELEASE	**COMMIT**, DEALLOCATE	X	X	X
Determines when to release resources that the program uses, either at commit or at termination				
REOPT	ONCE, ALWAYS, AUTO, **NONE**	X	X	
Specifies whether access path should be determined at run time with host variables, parameter markers, and special registers				

Table 11.1: Bind and rebind options (continued)				
Option	Valid values	Plan	Package	Trigger
ROUNDING	CEILING, DOWN, FLOOR HALFDOWN, **HALFEVEN**, HALFUP, UP	X	X	
Specifies the rounding mode at bind time				
SQLERROR	**NOPACKAGE**, CONTINUE		X	
Determines whether to create a package if the package contains an SQL error				
SQLRULES	**DB2**, STD	X		
Determines whether a Type 2 connection can be made according to DB2 rules for an existing connection				
VALIDATE	**RUN**, BIND	X	X	
Determines whether to recheck at runtime "not found" and "not authorized" errors found at bind time				
BO = BIND only, BC = BIND COPY, RO = REBIND only, **_BOLD/UNDERSCORE_** = default				

● ●

If the values in the BIND/REBIND PACKAGE command differ from those in the BIND/REBIND PLAN, the values for BIND/REBIND PACKAGE will prevail unless the plan is more restrictive.

● ●

Preliminary Steps

Before you perform a bind:

- Determine how the DBRMs should be bound (i.e., into packages, directly into plans, or using a combination of both methods).

- Develop a naming convention and strategy for the most effective and efficient use of the plans and packages.

- Determine when the application should acquire locks on the objects it uses: either on all objects when the plan is first allocated or on each object in turn when that object is first used. (For more details about locking, see Chapter 16.)

Invalidations

If an object on which a package depends is dropped, the following results occur.

- If the package is not appended to any running plan, the package becomes invalid.

- If the package is appended to a running plan and the drop occurs outside that plan, the object is not dropped, and the package does not become invalid.

- If the package is appended to a running plan and the drop occurs within that plan, the package becomes invalid.

In all cases, the plan does not become invalid unless it has a DBRM that references the dropped object. If the package or plan becomes invalid, automatic rebind occurs the next time the package or plan is allocated.

Rebinding a Package

The way in which you specify the collection ID (*coll-id*), package ID (*pkg-id*), and version ID (*ver-id*) on the REBIND PACKAGE subcommand determines which packages are bound. REBIND PACKAGE does not apply to packages for which you do not have the BIND privilege.

An asterisk (*) used as an identifier for collections, packages, or versions does not apply to packages at remote sites. You can use the asterisk on the REBIND subcommand only for local packages. Any of the following commands rebinds all versions of all packages in all collections, at the local DB2 system, for which you have the BIND privilege.

```
REBIND PACKAGE (*)
REBIND PACKAGE (*.*)
REBIND PACKAGE (*.*.(*))
```

Either of the following commands rebinds all versions of all packages in the local collection SAMPL for which you have the BIND privilege.

```
REBIND PACKAGE (SAMPL.*)
REBIND PACKAGE (SAMPL.*.(*))
```

Either of the following commands rebinds the empty string version of the package DB2CPRG1 in all collections, at the local DB2 system, for which you have the BIND privilege.

```
REBIND PACKAGE (*.DB2CPRG1)
REBIND PACKAGE (*.DB2CPRG1.())
```

Package Lists

Using the PKLIST keyword replaces any previously specified package list. Omitting this keyword lets you use the previous package list for rebinding. Using the NOPKLIST keyword deletes any package list specified when the plan was previously bound. The following example rebinds PLANTK and changes the package list.

```
REBIND PLAN(PLANTK) PKLIST(GROUP1.*) MEMBER(TEST)
```

The next example rebinds the plan and drops the entire package list.

```
REBIND PLAN(PLANTK) NOPKLIST
```

Using information in the DB2 catalog, you can generate a list of REBIND subcommands for a set of plans or packages that cannot be described by using asterisks. You can then issue the list of subcommands through DSN.

One situation in which this technique is particularly useful is in completing a rebind operation that has terminated for lack of resources. A rebind for many objects—say, REBIND PACKAGE (*) for an ID with SYSADM authority—terminates if a needed resource becomes unavailable. As a result, some objects may be successfully re-bound, while others are not. If you repeat the subcommand, DB2 tries to rebind all the objects again. But if you generate a REBIND subcommand for each object that was not re-bound and issue those, DB2 does not repeat any work already done and is not likely to run out of resources.

Automatic Rebinding

Automatic rebind might occur if an authorized user invokes a plan or package when the attributes of the data on which the plan or package depends have changed or if the environment in which the package executes changes. Whether the automatic rebind occurs depends on the value of the field AUTO BIND on installation panel DSNTIPO. The options used for an automatic rebind are the options used during the most recent bind process.

In most cases, DB2 marks a plan or package that needs to be automatically re-bound as invalid. The following are common situations in which DB2 takes this action.

- When a package is dropped

- When a plan depends on the execute privilege of a package that is dropped

- When a table, index, or view on which the plan or package depends is dropped

- When the authorization of the owner to access any of those objects is revoked

- When the authorization to execute a stored procedure is revoked from a plan or package owner and the plan or package uses the CALL literal form to call the stored procedure

- When a table on which the plan or package depends is altered to add a TIME, TIMESTAMP, or DATE column

- When a table is altered to add a self-referencing constraint or a constraint with a delete rule of SET NULL or CASCADE

- When the limit key value of a partitioned index on which the plan or package depends is altered

- When the definition of an index on which the plan or package depends is altered from NOT PADDED to PADDED

- When the AUDIT attribute of a table on which the plan or package depends is altered

- When the length attribute of a CHAR, VARCHAR, GRAPHIC, VARGRAPHIC, BINARY, or VARBINARY column in a table on which the plan or package depends is altered

- When the data type, precision, or scale of a column in a table on which the plan or package depends is altered

- When a plan or package depends on a view that DB2 cannot regenerate after a column in the underlying table is altered

- When a created temporary table on which the plan or package depends is altered to add a column

- When a user-defined function on which the plan or package depends is altered

- When a column is renamed in a table on which a plan or package is dependent

Whether a plan or package is valid is recorded in column VALID of catalog tables SYSPLAN and SYSPACKAGE.

In the following cases, DB2 might automatically rebind a plan or package that has not been marked as invalid if the ABIND subsystem parameter is set to YES, which is the default.

- A plan or package is bound in a different release of DB2 from the release in which it was first used.

- A plan or package that was bound prior to DB2 V4.1. These will be automatically re-bound when they are run on the current release.

- A plan or package has a location dependency and runs at a location other than the one at which it was bound. This can happen when members of a data-sharing group are defined with location names and a package runs on a different member from the one on which it was bound.

DB2 marks a plan or package as *inoperative* if an automatic rebind fails. Whether a plan or package is operative is recorded in column OPERATIVE of the SYSPLAN and SYSPACKAGE catalog tables.

Whether EXPLAIN runs during automatic rebind depends on the value of the field EXPLAIN PROCESSING on installation panel DSNTIPO and on whether you specified EXPLAIN(YES). Automatic rebind fails for all EXPLAIN errors except "PLAN_TABLE not found."

The SQLCA is not available during automatic rebind; therefore, some error messages may not be available.

Migration Testing with Plans and Packages

Plans and packages provide an easy way to test access paths in production. For example, if you were migrating a DB2 database/application to a new release, you might want to investigate whether all applications using static SQL can benefit from some of the access path enhancements in the new release without impacting the way the applications are currently run. You can accomplish this by REBINDing all plans under a different name using EXPLAIN(YES), followed by a BIND PACKAGE(*) EXPLAIN(YES) into a separate collection, and then comparing the old and new access paths. This way, you can see the effect of the changes before deployment into the production environment.

Removing a Plan or Package

The only way to remove a plan or package is to use the FREE command. This command removes the object from the catalog tables, and it will no longer be available for use. This example frees all the packages in the DB2SAMPL collection:

```
FREE PACKAGE (DB2SAMPL.*)
```

Plan or Package Ownership

An application plan or a package can take many actions on many tables, all of them requiring one or more privileges. The owner of the plan or package must hold every required privilege. Another ID can execute the plan or package if it has only the EXECUTE privilege. In that way, another ID can exercise all the privileges that are used in validating the plan or package, but only within the restrictions imposed by the SQL statements in the original program.

The executing ID can use some of the owner's privileges, within limits. If the privileges are revoked from the owner, the plan or the package is invalidated. It must be re-bound, and the new owner must have the required privileges.

The BIND and REBIND subcommands create or change an application plan or a package. On either subcommand, use the OWNER option to name the owner of the resulting plan or package. Keep the following points in mind when naming an owner.

- If you use the OWNER option:
    - » Any user can name the primary or any secondary ID.

> » An ID with the BINDAGENT privilege can name the grantor of that privilege.

> » An ID with SYSCTRL or SYSADM authority can name any authorization ID on a BIND command, but not on a REBIND command.

- If you omit the OWNER option:

  > » On BIND, the primary ID becomes the owner.

  > » On REBIND, the previous owner retains ownership.

- If you use the OWNER option in a trusted context that has ROLE AS OBJECT OWNER and OWNER is specified:

  > » The role in OWNER option becomes the owner. In a trusted context, the specified OWNER must be a role.

  > » If the ROLE AS OBJECT OWNER clause is not in effect for the trusted context, the current rules for BIND and REBIND ownership apply.

- If you use the OWNER option in a trusted context that has ROLE AS OBJECT OWNER and OWNER is omitted:

  > » The role associated with the binder becomes the owner.

Unqualified Objects

A plan or package can contain SQL statements that use unqualified table and view names. For static SQL, the default qualifier for those names is the owner of the plan or package. However, you can use the QUALIFIER option of the BIND command to specify a different qualifier.

For plans or packages that contain static SQL, using the BINDAGENT privilege and the OWNER and QUALIFIER options gives you considerable flexibility in performing bind operations. For plans or packages that contain dynamic SQL, the DYNAMICRULES behavior determines how DB2 qualifies unqualified object names.

For unqualified distinct types, user-defined functions, stored procedures, and trigger names in dynamic SQL statements, DB2 finds the schema name to use as the qualifier by searching schema names in the CURRENT PATH special register. For static statements, the PATH bind option determines the path that DB2 searches to resolve unqualified distinct types, user-defined functions, stored procedures, and trigger names.

However, an exception exists for ALTER, CREATE, DROP, COMMENT ON, GRANT, and REVOKE statements. For static SQL, specify the qualifier for these statements in the QUALIFIER bind option. For dynamic SQL, the qualifier for these statements is the authorization ID of the CURRENT SQLID special register.

Plan Execution Authorization

The plan or package owner must have authorization to execute all static SQL statements that are embedded in the plan or package. These authorizations do not need to be in place when the plan or package is bound, nor do the objects that are referred to need to exist at that time.

A bind operation always checks whether a local object exists and whether the owner has the required privileges on it. Any failure results in a message. To choose whether the failure prevents the bind operation from being completed, use the VALIDATE option of BIND PLAN and BIND PACKAGE and also the SQLERROR option of BIND PACKAGE. If you let the operation be completed, the checks are made again at runtime. The corresponding checks for remote objects are always made at runtime, and authorization to execute dynamic SQL statements is also checked at runtime.

Summary

This chapter examined what it takes to compile and bind an application program to DB2 and to be able to execute that program. You must complete this process before a program can access and manipulate DB2 data. Packages and DBRMs are used to store the bound program, and the plan is the actual executable object.

We also looked at the special authorities needed to execute the plan and reviewed the various bind options for plans and packages.

Additional Resources

DB2 9 Application Programming and SQL Guide (SC18-9841)
DB2 9 Command Reference (SC18-9844)

Practice Questions

Question 1

In which of the following cases would a DBA REBIND with REOPT(AUTO)?

○ A. When using static SQL and the host variables can have many different values at runtime

○ B. When using static SQL and the host variables are specified in predicates with columns that have data skew

○ C. When using dynamic SQL and the host variables are specified in predicates with columns that have data skew

○ D. When using either dynamic or static SQL as long as the host variables are specified in predicates with columns that have data skew

Question 2

A plan is bound with ACQUIRE(USE) RELEASE(DEALLOCATE). What assumption can be made about a possible reason for using these options?

○ A. The objective is to prepare allied threads for reuse.

○ B. The objective is to defer preparation of dynamic SQL.

○ C. The objective is to have resources acquired when the thread is created.

○ D. The objective is to isolate an application from other running applications.

Question 3

In which of the following situations would a plan or package *not* be marked as invalid?

○ A. When a table, index, or view on which the plan or package depends is dropped

○ B. When the authorization of the owner to access any of those objects is revoked

○ C. When the authorization to execute a stored procedure is revoked from a plan or package owner and the plan or package uses the CALL literal form to call the stored procedure

○ D. When a trigger on a dependent table is dropped

Question 4

The bind process performs all of the following except:

○ A. Checks SQL syntax

○ B. Checks security

○ C. Allocates buffer pools

○ D. Builds access path strategy for each SQL statement

Question 5

An application program needs the highest level of concurrency possible but cannot allow for uncommitted data to be seen. What is the best isolation level to use?

○ A. RR (Repeatable Read)

○ B. RS (Read Stability)

○ C. CS (Cursor Stability)

○ D. UR (Uncommitted Read)

Answers

Question 1

The correct answer is **C**, when using dynamic SQL and the host variables are specified in predicates with columns that have data skew. If columns have a data skew that may affect access path optimization, you can use REOPT(AUTO) for dynamic SQL execution so that DB2 re-optimizes the access path at runtime if the predicates use columns and DB2 determines there is a data skew.

Question 2

The correct answer is **A**, the objective is to prepare allied threads for reuse. By using ACQUIRE(USE) RELEASE(DEALLOCATE), you will have the ability to enable thread reuse. Resources needed by the thread will be held for the duration of the thread.

Question 3

The correct answer is **D**, when a trigger on a dependent table is dropped. Dropping of a trigger on a table on which a plan or package is dependent will not cause the plan or package to become invalid. A, B, and C will all cause a plan or package to become invalid, as well as the following:

- When a table on which the plan or package depends is altered to add a TIME, TIMESTAMP, or DATE column

- When a created temporary table on which the plan or package depends is altered to add a column

- When a user-defined function on which the plan or package depends is altered

- When an index, table, or column definition changes via an ALTER

Question 4

The correct answer is **C**, allocates buffer pools. The bind process does not allocate buffer pools. In addition to A, B, and D, the bind process also compares column and table names against the DB2 catalog.

Question 5

The correct answer is **C**, CS (Cursor Stability). This isolation level is the most common and provides the best concurrency for the application program without allowing the application to read uncommitted data.

Application Program Features

In This Chapter

- ✔ Commit and rollback
- ✔ Unit of work
- ✔ Savepoints
- ✔ Temporary tables
- ✔ Fetching limited rows
- ✔ Identity columns
- ✔ Sequence objects
- ✔ Merging
- ✔ Optimistic locking

Application Program Features

All SQL programs execute as part of an *application process*. An application process involves the execution of one or more programs and is the unit to which DB2 allocates resources and locks. Different application processes might involve the execution of different programs or different executions of the same program.

The means of initiating and terminating an application process depend on the environment.

Commit, Rollback, and Savepoint

More than one application process might request access to the same data at the same time. DB2 uses locking to maintain data integrity under such conditions, preventing, for example, two application processes from updating the same row of data simultaneously. We discuss locking in detail in Chapter 16.

DB2 implicitly acquires locks to prevent uncommitted changes made by one application process from being perceived by any other. DB2 implicitly releases all locks it has acquired on behalf of an application process when that process ends, but an application process can also explicitly request locks to be released sooner.

Commit and Rollback

A *commit* operation releases locks acquired by an application process and commits the database changes the process has made. There are many good reasons to commit, including

- concurrency
- lock avoidance
- restart
- rollback/recovery
- utility processing
- resource release

As a general rule, even programs that have no concurrency problems should perform a commit at least every 10 minutes.

If you design a good batch program, commit processing is part of it. When you perform commit processing, you must identify the unit of work (UOW) in your program and also design the batch program to be restartable.

When concurrency is an issue, you probably want a commit frequency somewhere between 2 seconds and 20 seconds. A good practice is to make sure the commit frequency can be influenced from the outside. Identify a logical UOW in your program, and execute this UOW *x* number of times before doing a commit. The magic number *x* could come from a control card to your program or from a heuristic control table. This way, you can tune programs that cause concurrency problems; you can also use different settings depending on the time of day. It's a good idea to use the same design in all your programs. Software solutions are available from independent software vendors (ISVs) to take care of all commit and restart problems.

It's poor practice to commit intermittently in online transactions rather than commit at the end of the transaction. When you have a long-running (background) transaction—printing, for example—you should design your transaction so that it will reschedule itself and then terminate (doing an implicit commit). This way, all resources are released, and the transaction server can shut down in an orderly way when necessary.

DB2 also provides a way to *back out* uncommitted changes made by an application process. This action might be necessary if part of an application process fails or in a *deadlock* situation. An application process, however, can explicitly request that its database changes be backed out. This operation is called *rollback*. DB2 creates undo log records for rollbacks and creates redo log records for recovery for every row that is changed. DB2 also logs these records for changes to all affected indexes.

The interface used by an SQL program to explicitly specify commit and rollback operations depends on the environment. If your environment can include recoverable resources other than DB2 databases, you cannot use the SQL COMMIT and ROLLBACK statements. Thus, you cannot use these operations in IMS, CICS, or WebSphere environments.

Unit of Work

A unit of work, sometimes called a *logical UOW*, is a recoverable sequence of operations within an application process. At any time, an application process has a single UOW, but the life of an application process can involve many UOWs as a result of commit or full rollback operations.

A UOW is initiated when an application process is initiated. A UOW is also initiated when something other than the end of the application process ends the previous UOW. A UOW is ended by a commit operation, a full rollback operation (either explicitly initiated by the application process or implicitly initiated by DB2), or the end of an application process. A commit or rollback operation affects only the changes made to recoverable resources within the UOW.

During the time that changes (via insert, update, or delete) to data remain uncommitted, other application processes are unable to perceive those changes unless they are running with an isolation level of uncommitted read. A rollback can still back out the changes. Once committed, these database changes are accessible by other application processes and can no longer be backed out by a rollback. Locks acquired by DB2 on behalf of an application process to protect uncommitted data are held at least until the end of a UOW.

The initiation and termination of a UOW define *points of consistency* within an application process. A point of consistency in this case is a claim by the application that the data is consistent. For example, a banking transaction might involve the transfer of funds from one account to another. Such a transaction would require the funds to be subtracted from the first account and added to the second. Following the subtraction step, the data is inconsistent. Only after the funds have been added to the second account is consistency reestablished. When both steps are complete, the commit operation can be used to end the UOW, thereby making the changes available to other application processes.

Unit of Recovery

A DB2 *unit of recovery (UR)* is a recoverable sequence of operations executed by DB2 for an application process. If a UOW involves changes to other recoverable resources (e.g., MQSeries, VSAM), the UOW will be supported by those URs. If relational databases are the only recoverable resources used by the application process, the scope of the UOW and the UR are the same, and either term is accurate.

Rolling Back Work

DB2 can back out all changes or only selected changes made in a UR.
Only backing out all changes results in a point of consistency.

The SQL ROLLBACK statement without the TO SAVEPOINT clause specified causes a
full rollback operation. If such a rollback operation is executed successfully, DB2
backs out uncommitted changes to restore the data consistency that it assumes
existed when the UOW was initiated. That is, DB2 undoes the work.

Savepoints

A *savepoint* enables you to "bookmark" milestones within a transaction or UR.
An external savepoint represents the state of the data and schema at a particular
point in time. After the savepoint is set, changes the transaction makes to data and
schemas can be rolled back to the savepoint, as application logic requires, without
affecting the overall outcome of the transaction. You use the ROLLBACK statement
to restore to a savepoint.

```
EXEC SQL
SAVEPOINT SVP1 (...other options)
END-EXEC.

EXEC SQL
ROLLBACK TO SAVEPOINT SVP1
END-EXEC.
```

Savepoints are useful when a point has been reached during a unit of work and you
want to back out without undoing the entire unit of work. You can name individual
savepoints and then use ROLLBACK to roll back work to the desired point based on
the application processing requirements, skipping over individual savepoints if
necessary.

If there are outstanding savepoints, access to a remote database management system
(via DRDA or a private protocol using aliases or three-part names) is not permitted
because a savepoint's scope is within the DBMS on which it was set. DRDA access
using a CONNECT statement is allowed; however, the savepoints are local to their site.
DB2 doesn't restrict the use of aliases and three-part names to connect to a remote site
when outstanding savepoints exist at the remote site, but this use is not recommended.
There is no limit to the number of savepoints you can set.

Establishing a Savepoint

To set a savepoint, you use the SAVEPOINT statement. You can choose the name of the savepoint, so meaningful names are possible. Application logic determines whether the savepoint name needs to be reused as the application progresses or should denote a unique milestone. You can specify the UNIQUE option on the SAVEPOINT statement if you don't intend for the name to be reused. This option prevents an invoked procedure from unintentionally reusing the name. If you code a savepoint in a loop, however, you have no choice; do not use UNIQUE.

If the savepoint name identifies a savepoint that already exists within the UR and you did not create the savepoint with the UNIQUE option, the savepoint is destroyed and a new savepoint is created. Destroying a savepoint by reusing its name for another savepoint is not the same as releasing the savepoint. Reusing a savepoint name destroys only the one savepoint. Releasing a savepoint releases the named savepoint and all savepoints that were subsequently set. (We discuss releasing savepoints in more detail later.)

The following statement sets a unique savepoint named START_AGAIN. After executing this statement, the application program should check the SQL return code to verify that the savepoint was set.

```
EXEC SQL
SAVEPOINT START_AGAIN UNIQUE ON ROLLBACK RETAIN CURSORS
END-EXEC.
```

The SAVEPOINT statement sets a savepoint within a UR. You can embed this statement (as well as the ROLLBACK and RELEASE statements) in application programs, external user-defined functions, and stored procedures (i.e., defined as MODIFIES SQL DATA) or issue the statement interactively. You cannot issue SAVEPOINT from the body of a trigger. It is an executable statement that can be dynamically prepared only if DYNAMICRULES run behavior is implicitly or explicitly in effect. The syntax is as follows:

```
EXEC SQL
SAVEPOINT svptname
UNIQUE
  ON ROLLBACK RETAIN CURSORS
  ON ROLLBACK RETAIN LOCKS
END-EXEC.
```

Table 12.1 describes the elements of the SAVEPOINT syntax.

Table 12.1: SAVEPOINT syntax	
Syntax	**Description**
Svptname	Specifies a savepoint identifier that names the savepoint.
UNIQUE	Specifies that the application program cannot reuse this savepoint name within the UR. An error occurs if a savepoint with the same name as *svptname* already exists within the UR. If you do not use UNIQUE, the application can reuse this savepoint name within the UR.
ON ROLLBACK RETAIN CURSORS	Specifies that any cursors opened after the savepoint is set are not tracked and thus are not closed upon rollback to the savepoint. Even though these cursors do remain open after rollback to the savepoint, they may not be usable.
ON ROLLBACK RETAIN LOCKS	Specifies that any locks acquired after the savepoint is set are not tracked and therefore are not released upon rollback to the savepoint.

Restoring to a Savepoint

To restore to a savepoint, you use the ROLLBACK statement with the TO SAVEPOINT clause. The following example shows pseudocode for an application that sets and restores to a savepoint. The sample application makes airline reservations on a preferred date and then makes hotel reservations. If the hotel is unavailable, the application rolls back the airline reservations and repeats the process for a next-best date. Up to three dates are tried.

```
EXEC SQL SAVEPOINT START_AGAIN UNIQUE
          ON ROLLBACK RETAIN CURSORS;
   Check SQL code;
   Do i = 1 to 3 UNTIL got_reservations;
      Book_Air (dates(i),ok);
      If ok then
         Book_Hotel(dates(i),ok);
      If ok then
         got_reservations
      Else
         EXEC SQL ROLLBACK TO START_AGAIN;
      End loop;
EXEC SQL RELEASE SAVEPOINT START_AGAIN;
```

The ROLLBACK statement with the new TO SAVEPOINT option backs out data and schema changes that were made after a savepoint. Like the SAVEPOINT statement, this statement can be embedded. The skeleton syntax is as follows:

```
EXEC SQL
ROLLBACK WORK
TO SAVEPOINT svptname
END-EXEC.
```

In the skeleton syntax, ROLLBACK WORK rolls back the entire UR. All savepoints that were set within the UR are released. TO SAVEPOINT specifies that the rollback of the UR occurs only to the specified savepoint. If no savepoint name is specified, rollback is performed to the last active savepoint. The *svptname* element specifies the name of the savepoint to roll back to.

In the following example, the ROLLBACK TO SAVEPOINT statement causes the rollback to savepoint two, which causes the second and third sets of application code to be rolled back.

```
EXEC SQL
SAVEPOINT ONE ON ROLLBACK RETAIN CURSORS;
END-EXEC

First application code set...

EXEC SQL
SAVEPOINT TWO ON ROLLBACK RETAIN CURSORS;
END-EXEC.

Second application code set...

EXEC SQL
SAVEPOINT THREE ON ROLLBACK RETAIN CURSORS;
END-EXEC.

Third application code set...

EXEC SQL
RELEASE SAVEPOINT THREE;
END-EXEC.

EXEC SQL
ROLLBACK TO SAVEPOINT;
END-EXEC.
```

If the named savepoint does not exist, an error occurs. Data and schema changes made after the savepoint was set are backed out. Because changes made to global temporary tables are not logged, they are not backed out, but a warning is issued. A warning is also issued if the global temporary table is changed and an active savepoint exists. None of the following items are backed out:

- Opening or closing of cursors

- Changes in cursor positioning

- Acquisition and release of locks

- Caching of the rolled-back statements

Savepoints that are set after the one to which rollback is performed are released. The savepoint to which rollback is performed is not released. For example, in the following scenario, the ROLLBACK TO SAVEPOINT TWO statement causes savepoint three to be released, but not savepoint two.

```
EXEC SQL
SAVEPOINT ONE ON ROLLBACK RETAIN CURSORS;
END-EXEC.

First application code set...

EXEC SQL
SAVEPOINT TWO ON ROLLBACK RETAIN CURSORS;
END-EXEC.

Second application code set...

EXEC SQL
SAVEPOINT THREE ON ROLLBACK RETAIN CURSORS;
END-EXEC.

Third application code set...

EXEC SQL
ROLLBACK TO SAVEPOINT TWO;
END-EXEC.
```

Releasing a Savepoint

Releasing a savepoint uses the RELEASE SAVEPOINT statement. You cannot roll back to a savepoint after it is released. Maintaining a savepoint involves just a small amount of overhead, but it is more important to release savepoints because outstanding savepoints block any system-directed connections to remote locations. After an application no longer needs to roll back to a particular savepoint, you should release the savepoint.

The RELEASE SAVEPOINT statement releases the named savepoint and any subsequently established savepoints. Once a savepoint has been released, it is no longer maintained, and rollback to that savepoint is no longer possible. The syntax is as follows:

```
EXEC SQL
RELEASE TO
SAVEPOINT svptname
END-EXEC.
```

The savepoint identifier *svptname* identifies the savepoint to be released. If no savepoint is named, an error occurs. The named savepoint and all savepoints subsequently established by the transaction are released.

The following example releases a savepoint named START_AGAIN as well as all the savepoints subsequently set by the transaction.

```
EXEC SQL
RELEASE SAVEPOINT START_AGAIN;
END-EXEC.
```

Savepoints in a Distributed Environment

In a distributed environment, you can set savepoints only if you use DRDA access with explicit CONNECT statements. If you set a savepoint and then execute an SQL statement with a three-part name, an SQL error occurs.

The site at which a savepoint is recognized depends on whether the CONNECT statement is executed before or after the savepoint is set. For example, if an application executes the statement SET SAVEPOINT C1 at the local site before it executes a CONNECT TO S1 statement, savepoint C1 is known only at the local site. If the application executes CONNECT TO S1 before SET SAVEPOINT C1, the savepoint is known only at site S1. For more information about the CONNECT statement, see Chapter 14.

Global Transactions

Global transactions enable several UOWs to share locks if they are all participants in a unit of work. The larger unit of work is referred to as a *global transaction*. This capability provides a way to avoid deadlocks between transactions. There are several reasons that you may want to consider combining several transactions into a large transaction. For example, this approach may be an option if you're adding object-oriented (OO) interfaces on existing transactions.

This support is simply an extension of the distributed unit of work and adds the ability to share locks. Information Management System (IMS), Recoverable Resource Services (RRS), and Distributed Data Facility (DDF) transactions are supported. These transactions will be identified via a token—a global transaction ID or XID. All the URs in a global transaction must run on the same subsystem, and each part can see uncommitted updates of other parts.

The sharing of locks is limited to normal transaction locks, and an explicit LOCK TABLE statement or partition key updates could still cause deadlocks or timeouts. There are many design issues to consider before using global transactions, as well as additional risks and exposures.

Global Temporary Tables

There are occasions when a table doesn't need to exist for a long period of time. For example, you might need a table to act as a staging area for data for use by a program. To accommodate such requirements, you can use *temporary tables*. Two types of temporary tables exist: created or declared.

Created Temporary Tables

Created temporary tables (CTTs) can help improve performance in many ways. Any time you're using repetitive SQL to return a result set, producing exactly the same result each time, a CTT might provide benefit. A subquery that is used more than once is a prime example. It would be better to issue the subquery once, storing the result set rows in the CTT, and use the CTT in subsequent subqueries.

The biggest advantage of CTTs is that no logging takes place because no recovery is possible. However, no indexing occurs either, so DB2 will always use a table space scan as the access path. Also, neither an SQL UPDATE nor a DELETE can modify the data in the CTT; only INSERTs are allowed. The CTT will exist for the duration of the unit of work and will be deleted automatically when a COMMIT is issued unless the table is used in a cursor definition specifying a cursor WITH HOLD.

CTTs are useful for stored procedures. For example, a global temporary table can serve as a holding area for non-relational or non-DB2 data, such as data extracted from VSAM files. The data is held for the duration of the unit of work and can be referenced in SQL statements. This technique is particularly valuable when you need a left or full outer join that uses one DB2 table and one non-DB2 table (e.g., using VSAM data). An INSERT statement can load the temporary table with the VSAM data, and then the following SQL statement can perform the outer join.

```
EXEC SQL
SELECT * FROM T1 LEFT JOIN global-temp-name ON join predicates
END-EXEC.
```

This technique logically fits in a stored procedure so that any other process that needs the result can just execute it. The benefit is that the DB2 join algorithms, instead of a home-grown program, perform the outer join.

Another major benefit of CTTs comes in using them when a materialized set is present for a result set, view, or table expression and you need to use the materialized set more than once. You can use CTTs to hold the results of some of the tables prior to a later statement, which would combine the global temporary table with the remaining tables.

The only access path available against a CTT is a table space scan, so you should keep the size of the scan in mind when doing performance analysis. When you use a CTT in a join, the access path will generally be a merge scan join that might require sorting the CTT.

A CTT can be held longer than a unit of work when it is used inside a cursor definition that is defined WITH HOLD.

Creating a Temporary Table

A created global temporary table is created in the same manner as a normal table, through DDL, except that it is not physically created in a table space. You cannot create these tables with default values, and you cannot define unique, referential, or check constraints for them. The following example shows the creation of a created temporary table that will hold rows containing an amount and a date.

```
CREATE GLOBAL TEMPORARY TABLE SUMMARY
AMOUNT_SOLD DECIMAL(5,2) NOT NULL,
SOLD_DATE DATE NOT NULL)
```

DB2 creates an empty instance of the table at the first implicit or explicit reference to it in an SQL statement. In normal use, an INSERT would be the first statement issued. The temporary table exists only until the originating application commits, performs a rollback, or terminates, unless the table is used in a cursor using the WITH HOLD option.

Determining How Often CTTs Are Materialized

CTTs are materialized in DB2 work files. If multiple global temporary tables are being continually materialized, you could encounter a problem with the performance of all processes that use work files (e.g., sorting). To retain control over the DB2 work files, you can monitor this materialization through DB2 traces.

Performance trace, class 8, IFCID 311 contains information about CTT materialization and cursor processing. Field QW0311CI shows whether an instance of a temporary table was created in a work file. You can also see whether a cursor was opened or closed. This information will give you an idea of the amount of work occurring against the work file table space for temporary tables. If you find that a lot of activity is occurring and you feel it may be causing problems, you can also use the trace fields to determine which queries or programs are causing the materialization:

```
0017 QW0017TT  'TT'=TEMPORARY TABLE SCAN.
```

Declared Temporary Tables

Declared temporary tables (DTTs) give you the ability to declare a temporary table for use in a program. The DECLARE GLOBAL TEMPORARY TABLE statement defines a temporary table for the current session, not just for a UOW. The table description does not appear in the DB2 catalog. It is not persistent and cannot be shared (unlike a CTT).

You can embed this statement in an application program or issue it through the use of dynamic SQL statements. It is an executable statement that can also be dynamically prepared. Each session that defines a declared global temporary table of the same name has its own unique instantiation of the temporary table. When the session terminates, the temporary table is dropped.

With DTTs, some of the locking, DB2 catalog updates, and DB2 restart forward and backward log recoveries that are associated with persistent tables are avoided. No authority is required to issue the DECLARE GLOBAL TEMPORARY TABLE statement, unless the LIKE clause is used and additional authority is needed.

DTTs can be useful for applications that need to extract data from various sources and use them in SQL joins, or for data that needs to be used repetitively or kept separate from other OLTP processes. You can also use DTTs as staging areas for data that comes from various sources so that you can manipulate the data before storing it permanently in regular tables.

Here are a couple of examples of the syntax for DTTs:

```
EXEC SQL
DECLARE GLOBAL TEMPORARY TABLE SESSION.TEMPEMP
   LIKE DSN8910.EMP
INSERT INTO SESSION.TEMPEMP
   SELECT * FROM DSN8910.EMP
END-EXEC.

EXEC SQL
DECLARE GLOBAL TEMPORARY TABLE SESSION.TEMPEMP
   AS
   (SELECT * FROM DSN8910.EMP)
DEFINITION ONLY
END-EXEC.
```

Usage Considerations

You can use DTTs as a way to temporarily hold or sort data within a program. DTTs are useful for relational online analytical processing (ROLAP) and multidimensional online analytical processing (MOLAP) queries for warehouse tools and as staging areas for IMS or VSAM data so it can be SQL- and ODBC-accessible. The word SESSION must be the qualifier for a DTT; you can specify it explicitly in the table name or in the QUALIFIER BIND option on the plan or package.

DB2 logs only undo records for DTTs, and you can perform the full range of DML operations (INSERT, UPDATE, SELECT, DELETE) on them. DTTs are supported by the rollback to savepoint or last commit point. The table exists until thread termination, or, if thread reuse is being used, until it is implicitly dropped (which may or may not be desirable, depending on the application).

No locks are taken (PAGE, ROW, or TABLE) on DTTs; however, locks are taken on table space and DBD in share mode. DTTs also do not require a declared cursor to hold rows across commits.

Static SQL referencing a DTT will be incrementally bound at runtime. The cost associated with a DTT is equivalent to the cost of executing a dynamic SQL statement. High-volume transaction applications require careful evaluation if you plan to use DTTs.

Any dynamic SQL statements that reference DTTs will not be able to use the dynamic SQL cache.

Some restrictions are in force when you use declared temporary tables. DTTs do not support the following:

- LOBs or ROWIDs
- Referential integrity
- Use in a CREATE TABLE LIKE statement

- Sysplex query parallelism

- Dynamic SQL caching

- ODBC/JDBC functions that rely on the catalog definitions

- Thread reuse for DDF pool threads

- Use within triggers

Commit Options for DTTs

Declared temporary tables persist until the end of the application. To discard data or the DTT before this point, the DECLARE GLOBAL TEMPORARY TABLE statement provides alternatives. Those options are as follows:

```
ON COMMIT DELETE ROWS
     If no open cursor WITH HOLD, rows will be deleted
ON COMMIT PRESERVE ROWS
     Preserves rows, but thread reuse cannot be used
ON COMMIT DROP TABLE
     If no open cursor WITH HOLD, table is dropped
```

These options are useful for self-contained stored procedures with several DTTs and the cursors defined on them. The invokers (creators) of the DTTs can access the results and then commit and drop the DTT. The user does not need to specify the name of the DDT in this process. These features also improve DDF threads (CMSTAT=INACTIVE) because DTTs won't stop a thread from becoming inactive.

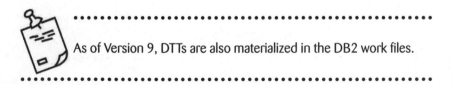

As of Version 9, DTTs are also materialized in the DB2 work files.

Fetch for Limited Rows

During cursor processing, the ability to tell DB2 to fetch only the first or top *n* rows is a requirement in many applications. There are ways to do this in SQL and the application program, but they are not the most efficient methods. For example, you could write a query as follows:

```
EXEC SQL
SELECT *
  FROM EMP A
  WHERE 5 >= (SELECT COUNT(*)
    FROM EMP B
    WHERE B.EMPNO <= A.EMPNO)
END-EXEC.
```

However, this type of query produces terrible performance because DB2 will have to read rows in proportion to the square of the numbers of table rows.

Using the FETCH FIRST clause of a fullselect, you can achieve the same functionality with improved performance because the clause sets a maximum number of rows that can be retrieved through a cursor. The application specifies that it does not want to retrieve more than some fixed number of rows, regardless of how many rows qualify for the result set.

FETCH FIRST and OPTIMIZE FOR

The OPTIMIZE FOR *n* ROWS clause, which gives the optimizer additional information about the application's intent, differs from the FETCH FIRST clause. The OPTIMIZE FOR clause can allow the entire answer set to be retrieved. In contrast, FETCH FIRST *n* ROWS ONLY stops processing after the specified number of rows, letting the application programmer directly control the size of the result table. For example, an application could enforce an implementation limit on the number of rows displayed for an online screen.

The following example shows the use of the FETCH FIRST *n* ROWS ONLY clause with the OPTIMIZE FOR *n* ROWS.

```
EXEC SQL
DECLARE FIRST_FIVE CURSOR FOR
  SELECT EMPNO
  FROM EMP
  ORDER BY EMPNO
  FETCH FIRST 5 ROWS ONLY
  OPTIMIZE FOR 5 ROWS
END-EXEC.
```

Using FETCH FIRST for Existence Checking

The FETCH FIRST clause is valid for singleton SELECTs, whereas the OPTIMIZE clause is not. This trait makes the FETCH FIRST clause a perfect solution for optimal existence checking. The application will perform a maximum of only one fetch to determine existence, and no internal second fetch for the −811 return code is required. FETCH FIRST automatically implies OPTIMIZE FOR 1 ROW and therefore discourages sequential prefetch, multi-index access, and list prefetch. This technique requires minimal coding to support singleton SELECT, and no cursor logic is required. You can code it within an application program or dynamically (e.g., Query Management Facility, DSNTEP2). The following example uses FETCH FIRST for existence checking.

```
EXEC SQL
   SELECT 1 INTO :hv-check
   FROM    TABLE
   WHERE   COL1 = :hv1
   FETCH  FIRST 1 ROW ONLY
END-EXEC.
```

Multi-Row Operations

Two types of multi-row operations are available: FETCH and INSERT. Multi-row FETCH and INSERT takes advantage of host variable arrays, which are arrays in which each element contains a value for the same column. Host variable arrays are allowed in COBOL, C++, PL/1, and (in some cases) Assembler.

The ability to perform a multi-row FETCH or INSERT can greatly improve the performance of distributed applications. It lets you FETCH or INSERT multiple rows in a single application programming interface (API) call, therefore limiting the number of statements issued. Static, dynamic, non-scrollable, and scrollable cursors support multi-row FETCH and INSERT.

Multi-Row FETCH

To implement the multi-row fetch capability, you declare a cursor with the ability to retrieve a rowset with a single FETCH statement. The FETCH then specifies the group of rows to be returned by fetching the rowset. The FETCH controls how many rows are returned. Up to 32,767 rows can make up a single rowset, but

performance testing has shown that a lower number is most efficient. Here's an
example of multi-row FETCH:

```
DECLARE CUR1 CURSOR
WITH ROWSET POSITIONING
FOR SELECT COL1, COL2 FROM TABLE1;

OPEN CUR1;

FETCH NEXT ROWSET
FOR :hv ROWS INTO :values1, :values2;
```

Multi-row FETCH is useful for queries that perform large table space scans.

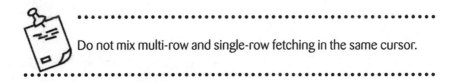

Do not mix multi-row and single-row fetching in the same cursor.

DB2 also supports positioned UPDATEs and DELETEs for cursors using multi-row
FETCH. This example performs a positioned UPDATE with a cursor defined with a
rowset:

```
UPDATE TABLE1
    SET COL1 = :newvalue
    FOR CURSOR CUR1
    FOR ROW :rownum OF ROWSET
```

Multi-Row FETCH WITH DDF

Multi-row FETCH is automatically employed for read-only queries that use DDF.
For example, a Java program using the Type 4 connection with Universal Driver
will automatically use multi-row FETCH when fetching rows from the table while
building the block to send to client. In this situation, the cursor must be read-only,
and you must specify CURRENTDATA NO on the bind with a non-ambiguous cursor
(e.g., one coded with FOR FETCH ONLY). For more information about block
fetching, see Chapter 14.

All block fetching against DB2 uses multi-row FETCH to build the blocks. Neither the requester nor the application has to do anything special. No host variable arrays are needed, and there is no requirement for FOR *n* ROWS. The blocking performed by DDF is not affected.

Block fetching using the multi-row FETCH affects the number of API calls between DDF and DBM1 and results in an automatic instant CPU savings for these applications.

Sample programs DSNTEP4 (which provides DSNTEP2-like function) and DSNTIAUL also can exploit this feature.

Multi-Row Insert

A multi-row INSERT inserts multiple rows into a table or view using values supplied in the host variable array. Each array represents multiple rows for a single column. You can specify up to 32,767 values. Here's an example of multi-row INSERT:

```
INSERT INTO TABLE1 FOR :hv ROWS
VALUES (:values1, :values2) ATOMIC
```

You can specify either ATOMIC or NOT ATOMIC CONTINUE ON SQLEXCEPTION. Your choice determines whether all changes are made if a row to be inserted fails.

ATOMIC is basically all or nothing; the inserts are treated as a single statement, so you must take care with large amounts of data because a lengthy and expensive rollback might result. In this statement, statement triggers are fired once.

The NOT ATOMIC CONTINUE ON SQLEXCEPTION option lets processing continue if errors occur. In this case, the statement level triggers are fired once for each row. Diagnostics are available for each failed row and are obtainable through GET DIAGNOSTICS statements. The SQLCODE return codes indicate whether all inserts worked (+252), some did not (–253), or all failed (–254).

Identity Columns

Identity columns provide a way to have DB2 automatically generate unique, sequential, and recoverable values for each row in a table. You define the new identity column by providing the AS IDENTITY attribute in the column definition. Each table can have only one identity column defined to it. Identity columns are ideally suited for the task of generating unique primary key values, such as employee number, order number, item number, or account number. You can also use identity columns to alleviate concurrency problems caused by application-generated sequence numbers.

An identity column value can be always generated by DB2 or be generated by default. For identity columns defined as GENERATED ALWAYS, DB2 always generates the column value. Applications cannot provide an explicit value for a column defined this way. If you define an identity column as GENERATED BY DEFAULT, an application can supply an explicit value for the column; if no value is specified, DB2 generates a value. However, only when you use GENERATED ALWAYS does DB2 guarantee the uniqueness of the identity column value. The use of GENERATED BY DEFAULT is intended for data propagation (copying the contents of an existing table or unloading and reloading a table).

Identity column counters are increased or decreased independently of the transaction. There may be gaps between generated numbers because several transactions may concurrently increment the same identity counter by inserting rows into the same table. If an application requires a consecutive range of numbers, exclusive locks should be taken on the tables that contain identity columns. Gaps in the generated identity column numbers can also appear if a transaction that generated a value for the identity column is rolled back or if a DB2 subsystem that has a range of identity values cached terminates. As a general rule, gaps in identity values shouldn't cause a lot of concern (unless you're still using preprinted forms). Additional properties of identity column values include the following:

- Values must have a numeric data type.

- Identity column values can be a data type of SMALLINT, BIGINT, INTEGER, or DECIMAL with a scale of zero (or a distinct type based on one of these types).

- You can specify the difference between consecutive values.

- The counter value for an identity column is recoverable from the DB2 log.

- Identity column values are incremented across multiple members in a data-sharing group.

- You can cache identity column values for better performance.

For information about creating identity columns and specifying options, see Chapter 4.

INSERTs and UPDATEs

You can use the DEFAULT keyword in the VALUES clause for identity columns. The keyword DEFAULT lets DB2 generate the value to be inserted into the column:

```
EXEC SQL
  INSERT INTO ACCOUNT_TRANS (ACCOUNT_NO, TYPE, LAST_NAME)
  VALUES (DEFAULT, :type, :lname)
END-EXEC.
```

DB2 always generates the value for an identity column defined as GENERATED ALWAYS. Even if you specify a value to insert, DB2 will either issue an error or ignore the value. DB2 ignores the value and generates a value for insertion if you use the OVERRIDING USER VALUE clause. Because this clause is not used in the following statement, it will produce an error.

```
EXEC SQL
  INSERT INTO ACCOUNT_TRANS (ACCOUNT_NO, TYPE, LAST_NAME)
    VALUES (:account, :type, :lname)
END-EXEC.
```

DB2 will use a specified value for identity columns defined as GENERATED BY DEFAULT. However, DB2 doesn't verify the uniqueness of the value in this situation, and the value might be a duplicate of another value in the column if no unique index is defined on the column.

The rules for an insert within a subselect are similar to those for an insert with a VALUES clause. If you want the value implicitly specified in the column list to be inserted into a table's identity column, you must first define the column of the table from which the data is being selected as GENERATED BY DEFAULT. To have DB2 ignore the value and insert a generated value into the identity column of the table being inserted into, define the identity column of the table being selected from as GENERATED ALWAYS, and include the OVERRIDING USER VALUE clause in the INSERT statement. The following example demonstrates the use of this clause.

```
EXEC SQL
   INSERT INTO ACCOUNT_TRANS OVERRIDING USER VALUE
   SELECT * FROM ACCOUNT_UPDT;
END-EXEC.
```

Updates are allowed on a value in an identity column, but only if the identity column is defined as GENERATED BY DEFAULT. DB2 does not verify the value to guarantee uniqueness during the update. You cannot make updates to identity columns defined with GENERATED ALWAYS.

You can find the last column number generated by using the following technique.

```
EXEC SQL
SET :HV = IDENTITY_VAL_LOCAL()
END-EXEC.
```

The result is returned as DECIMAL(31,0). If a commit or rollback occurred since the insert, a null is returned. We recommend storing the value after the insert and checking the return code.

Obtaining Generated Identity Columns Values

You can obtain the identity column value generated during an INSERT by using the "INSERT within a SELECT" feature. The following example uses this feature to obtain the identity column values during the insert. (Assume the table was created with an identity column on ACCT_ID generated always.)

```
SELECT ACCT_ID
FROM FINAL TABLE (INSERT INTO UID1.ACCOUNT (NAME, TYPE, BALANCE)
VALUES ('Master Card', 'Credit', 50000) )
```

Sequence Objects

A *sequence object* is a user-defined object that generates a sequence of numeric values according to the specifications in which the object was created. Sequence objects provide an incremental counter generated by DB2 and are similar to identity columns. You can think of an identity column as a special kind of sequence object; however, the sequence column is separate from the table.

Applications can use sequence object values for a variety of reasons. Their benefits include the following:

- No waits for incrementing values

- Standalone sequential-number-generating object (not tied to a table)

- Ascending or descending number generation

- Usefulness for porting applications from other DBMSs

- Ability to generate keys that can be used to coordinate keys across multiple tables (RI- or application-related)

Programming with Sequence Objects

Programming for the use of sequence objects is fairly flexible and is supported by two expressions: NEXT VALUE FOR and PREVIOUS VALUE FOR. NEXT VALUE FOR (NEXTVAL) generates and returns the next value for the sequence object. PREVIOUS VALUE FOR (PREVVAL) generates and returns the previous value for the sequence object. You can use these expressions with the following:

- SELECT and SELECT INTO

- An INSERT statement within a SELECT clause of a fullselect

- An UPDATE statement within a SET clause (searched or positioned)

- SET *host-variable*

- VALUES or VALUES INTO

- CREATE PROCEDURE, CREATE FUNCTION, and CREATE TRIGGER

The following statements demonstrate the use of NEXTVAL and PREVVAL. Assume ACCT_SEQ is defined using START WITH 10 INCREMENT BY 10.

```
SELECT NEXTVAL FOR ACCT_SEQ                    -> Returns 10
FROM SYSIBM.SYSDUMMY1
SELECT NEXTVAL FOR ACCT_SEQ                    -> Returns 20
FROM SYSIBM.SYSDUMMY1
COMMIT
SELECT PREVVAL FOR ACCT_SEQ                    -> Returns 20
FROM SYSIBM.SYSDUMMY1
...
UPDATE ACCOUNTS
SET ACCT_NO = NEXTVAL FOR ACCT_SEQ             -> Returns 30
...
INSERT INTO ACCOUNTS (ACCT_NO)
VALUES(SELECT NEXTVAL FROM ACCT_SEQ)           -> Returns 40
```

Let's review some additional considerations to keep in mind for proper use of sequence objects.

NEXT VALUE (NEXTVAL)

The NEXTVAL expression generates and returns the next value for a specified sequence. A new value is generated for a sequence when a NEXT VALUE expression specifies the name of the sequence. If multiple instances of a NEXT VALUE expression specify the same sequence name within a query, the sequence value is incremented only once for each row of the result, and all instances of NEXT VALUE return the same value for a row of the result. NEXT VALUE is a nondeterministic expression with external actions because it causes the sequence value to be incremented. This behavior can affect query performance by forcing materialization in some instances.

If the maximum value for an ascending sequence (or the minimum value for a descending sequence) of the logical range of the sequence is exceeded and the NO CYCLE option is in effect, an error results. You'll need to ALTER or DROP/CREATE to change the range or allow cycling. The result of NEXTVAL cannot be NULL, and ROLLBACK has no effect on generated values.

NEXTVAL and Cursors

Normal processing for NEXT VALUE is as follows:

```
SELECT NEXT VALUE FOR ORDER_SEQ FROM T1
```

This statement produces a result table containing as many generated values from the sequence ORDER_SEQ as the number of rows retrieved from table T1.

A reference to a NEXT VALUE expression in the SELECT statement of a cursor refers to a value that is generated for a row of the result table. A sequence value is generated for a NEXT VALUE expression each time a row is retrieved.

For DRDA blocking at a client, sequence values may get generated at the DB2 server before the processing of an application's FETCH statement.

NEXTVAL poses some considerations with cursors. First, if the client application does not explicitly FETCH all the rows that have been retrieved from the database, the application will never see all those generated but unFETCHed values of the sequence (as many as the unFETCHed rows). These generated but unFETCHed values may constitute a gap in the sequence. If it's important to prevent such a gap, you may want to use NEXT VALUE only in places where it would function without being controlled by a cursor and where block-fetching by the client will have no effect on it.

If you must use NEXT VALUE in the SELECT statement of a cursor definition, weigh the importance of preventing the gap against performance and other implications by using FETCH FOR 1 ROW ONLY clause with the SELECT statement. You could also try preventing block fetching.

PREVIOUS VALUE (PREVVAL)

PREVVAL returns the most recently generated value for the specified sequence for a previous statement within the current application process. You can reference this value repeatedly by using PREVIOUS VALUE expressions to specify the name of the sequence. If multiple instances of PREVIOUS VALUE expressions may specify the same sequence name within a single statement, they all return the same value. These values can be used only if the current application process has already

referenced a NEXT VALUE expression specifying the same sequence name.
The value persists until the next value is generated for the sequence, until the
sequence is dropped or, until the application session ends. The value is unaffected
by COMMIT or ROLLBACK statements.

PREVVAL and Cursors

DB2 evaluates a reference to the PREVIOUS VALUE expression in a SELECT statement
of a cursor at OPEN time. A reference to the PREVIOUS VALUE expression in the
SELECT statement of a cursor refers to the last value generated by this application
process for the specified sequence *before* the opening of the cursor.

Once evaluated at OPEN time, the value returned by PREVIOUS VALUE within the
body of the cursor does not change from FETCH to FETCH, even if you invoke NEXT
VALUE within the body of the cursor. If PREVIOUS VALUE is used in the SELECT
statement of a cursor while the cursor is open, the PREVIOUS VALUE value will be
the last NEXT VALUE for the sequence generated before the cursor was opened.

After the cursor is closed, the PREVIOUS VALUE value is the last NEXT VALUE
generated by the application process.

Populating Referential Relationships

You can easily populate tables that are RI-related with sequence object values. You
can use the same sequence number as a primary key value of a parent table and
primary key of a dependent table. In the following INSERT, NEXT VALUE generates a
sequence number value for the sequence object ORDER_SEQ.

```
INSERT INTO ORDERS (ORDERNO, CUSTNO) VALUES
(NEXT VALUE FOR ORDER_SEQ, 12345);
```

In this next INSERT, PREVIOUS VALUE retrieves that same value because it was the
sequence number most recently generated for that sequence object within the
current application process.

```
INSERT INTO ORDER_ITEMS (ORDERNO, PARTNO, QUANTITY) VALUES
(PREVIOUS VALUE FOR ORDER_SEQ, 987654, 2);
```

Comparing Identity Columns and Sequence Objects

As you can see, using sequence objects instead of identity columns provides many benefits. Table 12.2 provides a short comparison of the two options.

Table 12:2: Sequence objects vs. identity columns	
Sequences object	Identity column
Standalone sequence object created at user request	Internal sequence object generated/maintained and populated by DB2
Can supply values for one or more table columns	Only one per table can exist
Used by users for whatever purpose they choose	Associated with a particular table
CYCLEing will wrap around and repeat with no uniqueness consideration	CYCLEing may have a problem if a unique index is on the identity column and duplicates are created
When used to populate a table, can later be updated	Cannot be updated if GENERATED ALWAYS
Supports NEXT VALUE FOR EXPRESSION and PREVIOUS VALUE FOR EXPRESSION	Must use ID_VAL_LOCAL, and returns only most recent values in that user's commit scope
ALTER, DROP, COMMENT, GRANT/REVOKE	ALTER TABLE only (if being added to a populated table, results in REORG-pending status); cannot be removed from a table

If future designs might benefit more from sequence objects than identity columns, be careful when choosing to use identity columns. If you define identity columns on populated tables and later want to remove them, you'll need to drop and re-create the table. This requirement could be a big problem for large tables in a high-availability environment.

Merging

Applications often interface with other applications. In these situations, an application may receive a large quantity of data that applies to multiple rows of a table. In these situations, the application could perform a blind update. That is, the application simply tries to update the rows of data in the table, and if any update fails because a row is not found, the application inserts the data instead. In other situations, the application may read all the existing data, compare that data to the new incoming data, and then programmatically insert or update the table with the new data.

DB2 supports this type of processing via the MERGE statement. MERGE updates a target (table, view, or the underlying tables of a fullselect) using the specified input data. Rows in the target that match the input data are updated as specified, and rows that don't exist in the target are inserted.

Because MERGE operates against multiple rows, you can code it as ATOMIC or NOT ATOMIC. The NOT ATOMIC option enables rows that have been successfully updated or inserted to remain if others have failed. You should use the GET DIAGNOSTICS statement along with NOT ATOMIC to determine which updates or inserts have failed.

The following example shows a MERGE of rows on the employee table.

```
MERGE INTO EMP AS EXISTING_TBL
USING (VALUES (:EMPNO, :SALARY, :COMM, :BONUS)
       FOR :ROW-CNT ROWS) AS INPUT_TBL(EMPNO, SALARY, COMM, BONUS)
ON INPUT_TBL.EMPNO = EXISTING_TBL.EMPNO
WHEN MATCHED THEN
   UPDATE SET SALARY =  INPUT_TBL.SALARY,
              COMM   =  INPUT_TBL.COMM,
              BONUS  =  INPUT_TBL.BONUS
WHEN NOT MATCHED THEN
   INSERT (EMPNO, SALARY, COMM, BONUS)
   VALUES (INPUT_TBL.EMPNO, INPUT_TBL.SALARY, INPUT_TBL.COMM,
           INPUT_TBL.BONUS);
```

Optimistic Locking

With high demands for full database availability, as well as high transaction rates and levels of concurrency, reducing database locks is always desirable. With this in mind, many applications employ a technique called *optimistic locking* to achieve these higher levels of availability and concurrency. This technique traditionally involves reading data with an uncommitted read or with cursor stability. Update timestamps are maintained in all the data tables. The update timestamp is read along with the other data in a row. When a direct update is subsequently performed on the selected row, DB2 uses the timestamp to verify that no other application or user has changed the data between the point of the read and the update. This technique places additional responsibility on the application to use the timestamp on all updates, but the result is a higher level of DB2 performance and concurrency.

Let's look at a hypothetical example of optimistic locking. First, the application reads the data from a table with the intention of subsequently updating:

```
SELECT UPDATE_TS, DATA1
FROM TABLE1
WHERE KEY1 = :WS-KEY1
```

Here, the data has changed, and the update takes place:

```
UPDATE TABLE1
SET DATA1 = :WS-DATA1, UPDATE_TS = :WS-NEW-UPDATE-TS
WHERE KEY1 = :WS-KEY1
AND UPDATE_TS = :WS-UPDATE-TS
```

This technique is a common practice in many companies that use DB2.

As of DB2 9, IBM has introduced built-in support for optimistic locking via the ROW CHANGE TIMESTAMP column. When you create or alter a table, you can define a special column as a row change timestamp. DB2 will automatically update this timestamp column whenever a row of a table is updated. This built-in support for optimistic locking takes some of the responsibility (that of updating the timestamp) out of the hands of the various applications that might be updating the data.

Here's how the previous example would look when using the ROW CHANGE TIMESTAMP for optimistic locking:

```
SELECT ROW CHANGE TIMESTAMP FOR TABLE1, DATA1
FROM TABLE1
WHERE KEY1 = :WS-KEY1
```

Here, the data has changed, and the update takes place:

```
UPDATE TABLE1
SET DATA1 = :WS-DATA1
WHERE KEY1 = :WS-KEY1
AND ROW CHANGE TIMSTAMP FOR TABLE1 = :WS-UPDATE-TS
```

Summary

In this chapter, we reviewed the various features that can be used in a DB2 application program. We looked at how to define a unit of work and how to use commits, rollbacks, and savepoints to protect the integrity of the data being manipulated by the program. We discussed other features, such as temporary tables and identity columns, in terms of how to make use of them in a program. We also examined some coding techniques, such as FETCH FIRST *n* ROWS, and discussed different uses of this feature. We described two different ways of generating and using sequential numbers and compared these methods. You can use many of these features in your application programs for enhanced functionality and optimal performance.

Additional Resources

IBM DB2 9 Administration Guide (SC18-9840)
IBM DB2 9 Application Programming and SQL Guide (SC18-9841)
IBM DB2 9 SQL Reference (SC18-9854)

Practice Questions

Question 1

Which of the following is *not* a reason to perform a commit?

○ A. Concurrency

○ B. Lock avoidance

○ C. Restart

○ D. Lessen logging

Question 2

Which of the following is true about a savepoint?

○ A. It enables milestones within a transaction or UR to be bookmarked.

○ B. It commits data.

○ C. It enables a point of recovery.

○ D. It can be shared by multiple applications.

Question 3

The following statement will create which type of table?

```
CREATE GLOBAL TEMPORARY TABLE SUMMARY
AMOUNT_SOLD DECIMAL(5,2) NOT NULL,
SOLD_DATE DATE NOT NULL)
```

○ A. A declared temporary table

○ B. A created temporary table

○ C. A common table expression

○ D. A materialized query table

Question 4

The NEXTVAL and PREVVAL expressions can be used in all of the following except:

○ A. SELECT and SELECT INTO

○ B. A DELETE statement

○ C. An UPDATE statement within a SET clause (searched or positioned)

○ D. SET *host-variable*

Question 5

Which of the following is a benefit of multi-row fetch?

○ A. Lessen the number of rows returned

○ B. Lessen the number of SQL calls

○ C. Ability to code recursive fetching

○ D. Reduction in number of joins needed

Answers

Question 1

The correct answer is **D**, lessen logging. Performing commits helps with the following: concurrency, lock avoidance, restart, rollback/recovery, utility processing, and resource release. Commits do not help reduce the amount of logging performed.

Question 2

The correct answer is **A**, a savepoint enables milestones within a transaction or UR to be bookmarked. An external savepoint represents the state of the data and schema at a particular point in time. After the savepoint is set, changes made to data and schemas by the transaction can be rolled back to the savepoint as application logic requires, without affecting the overall outcome of the transaction. A savepoint does not actually commit data, and savepoints cannot be shared; they are specific to an application process.

Question 3

The correct answer is **B**, a created temporary table. DB2 supports two types of global temporary tables: created and declared. The created table is created with a CREATE statement and has its definition stored in the DB2 catalog. You create a declared temporary table in the application program using the DECLARE statement.

Question 4

The correct answer is **B**, a DELETE statement. The NEXTVAL and PREVVAL expressions can be issued in the following:

- SELECT and SELECT INTO
- An INSERT statement within a SELECT clause of a fullselect
- An UPDATE statement within a SET clause (searched or positioned)
- SET *host-variable*
- VALUES or VALUES INTO
- CREATE PROCEDURE, CREATE FUNCTION, or CREATE TRIGGER

You cannot use these expressions in a DELETE statement.

Question 5

The correct answer is **B**, lessen the number of SQL calls. The greatest benefit to multi-row FETCH is the ability to fetch up to 32,767 rows in a single API call. This technique reduces the number of SQL calls issued.

CHAPTER 13

Stored Procedures

In This Chapter

- ✔ Benefits
- ✔ Writing stored procedures
- ✔ Defining stored procedures
- ✔ Execution environment
- ✔ SQL procedures
- ✔ Developer Workbench

Stored Procedures

A *stored procedure* is essentially a program that is stored and executed within the control of the database management system. Some DBMS products limit stored procedures to a subset of SQL functionality. DB2 implements stored procedures in one of two ways: either as internal SQL procedure runtime structures or as externally compiled programs that run in specialized DB2 address spaces.

Depending on the stored procedure language and program preparation process, DB2 stored procedures can be load modules in a library, runtime structures in the DB2 system catalog, or Java programs stored in the DB2 system catalog. The DB2 server can be either the local DB2 subsystem or a remote DB2 subsystem. These programs can execute SQL statements, connect to other DB2 servers, and retrieve data from non-database sources. A stored procedure typically contains two or more SQL statements and some manipulative or logical processing in a host language. A client application program uses the SQL CALL statement to invoke a stored procedure:

```
EXEC SQL
CALL MYSP (:parm1, :parm2, :parm3)
END-EXEC.
```

Benefits

Using DB2 stored procedures has many benefits. The major advantage to stored procedures comes when they are implemented in a client/server application that must issue several remote SQL statements. The network overhead involved in sending multiple SQL commands and receiving result sets is quite significant. Proper use of stored procedures to accept a request, process that request with encapsulated SQL statements and business logic, and return a result will lessen the traffic across the network and reduce the application overhead. Figure 13.1 depicts this advantage.

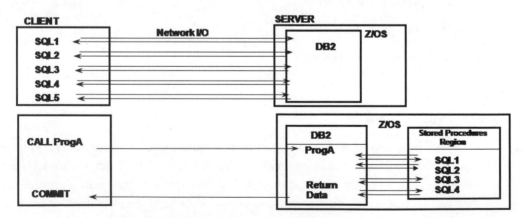

Figure 13.1: Stored procedure network improvements

Stored procedures can also provide access to data on the host server that is required to be secure. When you use a stored procedure, the client needs only the authority to execute the stored procedures; it does not need authority to the DB2 tables that the stored procedures access. Stored procedures can also help simplify development and maintenance and improve availability. By removing client dependency on the database design at the server, stored procedures enable the client code to continue to run while changes are made to the underlying databases. You can incorporate business logic into the stored procedures, minimizing changes to client code, and you can implement changes to stored procedures while the client code is still executing.

Encapsulation of core business functions is also a great way to implement stored procedures. With this approach, functions can be programmed once and executed by any and all processes required for a business process. Keep in mind that we're not suggesting the use of simple SQL statements in a stored procedure just to act as an I/O module. This should never be done with external stored procedures because the performance overhead is enormous. However, this penalty is less of an issue with native SQL procedures because the overhead associated with calling an external procedure is eliminated.

Another nice feature about using stored procedures is that you can provide access to non-DB2 data and use it in your DB2 applications. You can also use stored procedures to retrieve data from a VSAM or IMS data store to be used by a DB2 client. One way to do this is by retrieving the data into a global or declared temporary table in the stored procedure. Applications can then use SQL and result set logic for row retrieval of this data. Stored procedures also can execute a CICS transaction on behalf of a client.

In summary, the benefits of stored procedures include the following:

- Reduced network traffic
- Simplified development and maintenance
- Removal of client dependency on database design at server
- Ability to dynamically change application programs
- Ability to change and refresh code at the server
- No changes needed to client code
- Ability for client code to continue to run while changes are made
- Applications reside at the server, not the client

- Fewer global code changes at all client locations

- Reusable code

- Improved security

- No need for end-user table authority

- Processing moved away from end users

- Ability to access and update data that is not stored in DB2 (e.g., VSAM or IMS data)

- Portability across the DB2 data server family (e.g., with SQL and Java stored procedures)

Writing Stored Procedures

Programs that implement stored procedures can be written in several different languages. The currently available languages are

- Assembler

- C, C++

- COBOL

- Java

- PL/1

- REXX

- SQL Procedure Language

You can implement the calling program and the stored procedure program in different languages. For example, the client code could be COBOL, and the stored procedure could be C. The connection occurs through the DB2 thread, so individual coding doesn't matter. With the exception of REXX, the stored procedure code is compiled and stored at the server. It can contain static SQL and dynamic SQL (as well as IFI calls) and can issue DB2 commands. The stored procedure program can also access external resources such as VSAM files and even call CICS transactions.

Language Environment

You use the Language Environment product libraries to load and execute external stored procedures in one of the address spaces established by the Workload Manager (WLM), also known as *stored procedure address spaces*. When you create a stored procedure, you may pass runtime options for Language Environment to use when the stored procedure is executed. Language Environment establishes a common runtime environment for the many different languages used for building stored procedures. It provides a consistent set of interfaces for essential runtime services. When using Language Environment, you don't have to specify language-specific libraries in the JCL procedure of the WLM-established address space.

Language Environment performs several functions for DB2. It hides the differences among programming languages, provides the ability to make a stored procedure resident in the stored procedure address space, and supports many runtime options. Language Environment, along with the language compiler, gives you the ability to debug your program using the IBM Debug Tool. You can debug stored procedure programs in batch mode or interactively using the WebSphere Developer Debugger for zSeries.

You should create your external stored procedure programs to be reentrant and reusable. This approach lets Language Environment share a single copy of the program in memory. You can also use the STAY RESIDENT YES option, which keeps the program in memory for the next stored procedure call, to avoid having to retrieve the module from the load library again.

Parameters

Stored procedures usually have parameters that are passed in and possibly out. From the caller, the parameters are passed in the same manner as the commonly available CALL syntax:

```
EXEC SQL
   CALL SP1(:parm1, :parm2, :parm3)
END-EXEC.
```

Here, the parameters are host variables. Each parameter can be defined as input to the stored procedure, output from the stored procedure, or both input and output. The calling program must define appropriate storage areas for each parameter. Null values are passed by using indicator variables, as in

```
EXEC SQL
    CALL SP1(:parm1 :ind1, :parm2 :ind2, :parm3 :ind3)
END-EXEC.
```

The parameters used by the stored procedure program must match the parameters defined on the CREATE PROCEDURE statement. DB2 cannot verify that the stored procedure program handles the correct number and type of parameters, so the programmer must make sure to do this correctly. DB2 does validate the parameters specified in the calling program against the CREATE PROCEDURE statement and sets up the parameter list accordingly.

Parameter Style

The CREATE PROCEDURE statement's PARAMETER STYLE option controls the number and method of passing parameters into the stored procedure program. To illustrate the differences in parameter passing, we'll use a stored procedure program written in C and defined as follows:

```
CREATE PROCEDURE YLA.TWOTOONE
                ( IN  PARM1 CHAR(8),
                  IN  PARM2 CHAR(5),
                  OUT PARM3 CHAR(80)
                )
                EXTERNAL NAME SP1
                LANGUAGE C
                PROGRAM TYPE SUB
                PARAMETER STYLE xxxxxxx
                COLLID TEST
                STAY RESIDENT YES
                WLM ENVIRONMENT WLMENV1;
```

PARAMETER STYLE GENERAL conforms to the way DB2 passed parameters to stored procedures before Version 6. In this style, the parameters passed to the program are essentially the same parameters that are defined in the CREATE PROCEDURE statement. For this example, the function declaration would look like this:

```
void sp1(char    parm1[9],       /* Input parm1 */
         char    parm2[6],       /* Input parm2 */
         char    parm3[81],      /* Output parm3 */
         )
```

In general, C programs use a null-terminated character array to hold character string fields. DB2 handles the conversion from fixed-length character fields to null-terminated strings automatically for the stored procedure program. This is why the parameter fields in our example are one byte longer than the parameters specified on the CREATE PROCEDURE statement.

PARAMETER STYLE GENERAL WITH NULLS extends the GENERAL style to pass null indicators back and forth. The null indicators are input/output variables passed in an array, as in this example:

```
void sp1(char    parm1[9],       /* Input parm1 */
         char    parm2[6],       /* Input parm2 */
         char    parm3[81],      /* Output parm3 */
         short*  p_indparm[3]    /* Indicators for parms */
         )
```

The most compatible means of passing parameters, PARAMETER STYLE SQL, is the recommended style for new stored procedures. It is the default for all languages except Java, REXX, and SQL procedures. With the parameter style SQL specification, the parameters passed to the stored procedure program look like this:

```
void sp1(char    parm1[9],       /* Input parm1 */
         char    parm2[6],       /* Input parm2 */
         char    parm3[81],      /* Output parm3 */
         short*  p_indparm1,     /* Indicator for parm1 */
         short*  p_indparm2,     /* Indicator for parm2 */
         short*  p_indparm3,     /* Indicator for parm3 */
         char    p_sqlstate[6],  /* sqlstate to return */
         char    p_proc[28],     /* stored procedure name */
         char    p_spec[19],     /* specific name */
         char    p_diag[71],     /* message to return */
         )
```

As you can see, with parameter style SQL DB2 passes null indicators as separate variables and includes several additional parameters. The most significant of these are the p_sqlstate and p_diag parameters, which let the stored procedure program return error information to the caller without using additional output parameters. This mechanism simplifies error checking in the client programs. Any SQLSTATE value can be returned, but the following SQLSTATE values are reserved for special communication from stored procedures, user-defined functions (UDFs), and triggers.

- 00000 returns SQLCODE 0.

- 01H*xx* returns SQLCODE +462.

- 02000 returns SQLCODE +100.

- 38001 returns SQLCODE –487.

- 38002 returns SQLCODE –577.

- 38003 returns SQLCODE –751.

- 38004 returns SQLCODE –579.

- 38*yxx* returns SQLCODE –443.

The p_diag message area is limited to 70 bytes, but the caller will not receive the entire string. DB2 takes the message text from this field and appends it to the SQLERRMC field in the SQLCA. DB2 includes other information at the beginning of the SQLERRMC field, so your message may be truncated.

The last available style, PARAMETER STYLE JAVA, is used only for Java stored procedures.

DBINFO

If you desire, the stored procedure program can retrieve an additional block of information from DB2 when called. You request this information by adding the DBINFO clause to the CREATE PROCEDURE or ALTER PROCEDURE statement. When DBINFO is specified, DB2 passes the DBINFO block as the last parameter to the stored procedure program. Table 13.1 lists the information contained in this block.

Table 13.1: DBINFO block information	
Field	**Description**
Location name length	The length of the location name.
Location name	The current location name.
Authorization ID length	The length of the authorization ID.
Authorization ID	The authorization ID of the application.
Subsystem code page	A structure that provides information about the CCSIDs and encoding scheme of the subsystem.
Table qualifier length	The length of the table qualifier.
Table qualifier	The qualifier of the table that is specified in table name.
Table name length	The length of the table name.
Table name	The name of the table for a user-defined function (UDF).
Column name length	The length of the column name.
Column name	The name of the column for a UDF.
Product information	The product on which the program executes. This field has the form DSN$vvrrm$, where vv is a two-digit version identifier, rr is a two-digit release identifier, and m is a one-digit modification-level identifier.
Operating system	The operating system on which the program that invokes the UDF runs.
Number of entries in table function column list	Not used for stored procedures.
Reserved area	24 bytes.
Table function column list pointer	Not used for stored procedures.
Unique application identifier	A pointer to a string that uniquely identifies the application's connection to DB2.
Reserved area	20 bytes.

Result Sets

In addition to returning parameters, a stored procedure can return one or more result sets. A result set is a relational table implemented as a cursor from which the client program can fetch rows. This way, an ODBC client can retrieve data from DB2 without the end user requiring privileges to the underlying tables. The user need only execute privileges for the stored procedure.

Result sets from DB2 or non-relational sources can be returned from either base tables or temporary tables to clients on any DB2 server. For a stored procedure to return result sets to clients, the following must be true:

- The procedure needs to be defined for returning result sets.

- Cursors must be opened using the WITH RETURN clause.

- The DRDA client needs to support Level 3 result sets.

Client programs on platforms other than z/OS must use the DB2 Client interfaces. DB2 for z/OS does provide SQL statements that allow embedded SQL programs to also retrieve result sets.

The following is a skeleton example of coding to receive a stored procedure result set when the application program is running on the same z/OS server that is running the stored procedure.

```
EXEC SQL BEGIN DECLARE SECTION;
EXEC SQL RESULT_SET_LOCATOR VARYING locater1;
EXEC SQL END DECLARE SECTION;
EXEC SQL CALL SP1(:parm1, :parm2, …);
EXEC SQL ASSOCIATE LOCATOR (:locater1) WITH PROCEDURE SP1;
EXEC SQL ALLOCATE CSR1 CURSOR FOR RESULT SET :locater1;
EXEC SQL FETCH CSR1 INTO :acctno, :billingno;
```

To enable result sets to be returned from the stored procedure on the server, you must use the WITH RETURN clause in the cursor definition in the stored procedure, and the cursors may not be closed before the program ends. DB2 returns the rows in the result set from the opened cursors to the application program when the stored procedure ends. The following example shows the stored procedure code necessary to return the result set to the application code shown in the previous example.

```
EXEC SQL DECLARE SP_CSR1 CURSOR
                WITH RETURN FOR
              SELECT ACCT_NO, BILLING_NO
                FROM ORDER_TABLE
                WHERE ITEM = :parm1;
EXEC SQL OPEN SP_CSR1;
RETURN;
```

When returning a result set from a stored procedure, take care to avoid unintentionally closing the cursor. The cursor that the stored procedure opens will be closed if the unit of work (UOW) is terminated by a commit. This includes the commit generated internally by DB2 if you specified the COMMIT ON RETURN option during the creation of the stored procedure.

Dynamically Identifying Result Sets

From a design standpoint, most of the result sets will be of the variety we've just described. But there is a powerful way to build totally dynamic stored procedures and still be able to interface with client processes. This capability can be very significant as you move forward with Web-enabled applications that provide dynamic pages to a client.

By using the DESCRIBE PROCEDURE statement, you can retrieve all the information about a procedure's result set. This statement is not required if result sets are predefined, and it cannot be dynamically prepared. It returns information that a "dynamic" client needs to use the result sets. The SQL descriptor area (SQLDA) contains the number of result sets, with one SQLVAR entry for each result set in the stored procedure. The SQLDATA(x) field contains the result set locator value, and SQLNAME(x) contains the server application's cursor name. You invoke the DESCRIBE PROCEDURE function using either of the following methods.

```
EXEC SQL DESCRIBE PROCEDURE SP1 INTO :sqlda
EXEC SQL DESCRIBE PROCEDURE :hv INTO :sqlda
```

You can use the DESCRIBE CURSOR statement to retrieve information about a cursor that was left open inside a stored procedure and returned as a result set. This technique works for any allocated cursor but is not required for predefined result sets. This feature returns information needed by dynamic clients, such as the name, length, and type for columns contained in a result set. The output SQLDA is similar to what is produced from the DESCRIBE of a prepared statement. You invoke the DESCRIBE CURSOR function using either of the following methods:

```
DESCRIBE CURSOR SPC1 INTO sqlda
DESCRIBE CURSOR :hv INTO sqlda
```

Unit of Work

Stored procedures execute using the same logical unit of work as the client program that executes the SQL CALL statement. A stored procedure program can issue COMMIT statements. This commit impacts the entire unit of work, including any uncommitted changes the caller made before invoking the stored procedure.

COMMIT ON RETURN

In addition to issuing a commit within a stored procedure program, you can define the stored procedure to commit upon successful completion. To do so, you use the COMMIT ON RETURN clause on the CREATE PROCEDURE or ALTER PROCEDURE statement.

The COMMIT ON RETURN option for stored procedures reduces network traffic and lets locking in the stored procedure be performed on a predictable basis. Without COMMIT ON RETURN, the locks are held until the client application issues the commit. This client commit could happen some time later, and additional network messages would be required. COMMIT ON RETURN frees the locks as soon as the stored procedure ends.

As always, there are tradeoffs. You can use COMMIT ON RETURN in nested stored procedures, but DB2 ignores it in this case. The design of nested stored procedures requires some delicate planning.

Issuing COMMITs

The first instantiation of stored procedures provided for no commit at all. Then came the option to COMMIT ON RETURN to reduce network traffic. Soon after, we gained the ability to commit or roll back in a stored procedure. This latest functionality has implications only for new stored procedures or careful enhancements to existing ones; most stored procedures that exist today won't require it because they were written with the knowledge that a stored procedure was just a continuation of an existing thread. However, with more movement toward object-oriented and service-oriented programming, where stored procedures constitute one way to introduce classes and methods, this feature will have more use.

Nesting

Stored procedures, as well as triggers and UDFs, can be *nested*. That is, a stored procedure program can itself issue an SQL CALL statement or include a UDF within another SQL statement. Triggers can also call UDFs or stored procedures.

With nesting, you must plan carefully to avoid looping. DB2 imposes a limit of 16 nesting levels for stored procedures, triggers, and UDFs.

Nesting has obvious impacts for resource consumption and the scope of special registers. When you nest stored procedures, the following DB2 special registers are saved when pushing deeper and are restored when popping back up, depending on the INHERIT SPECIAL REGISTER option setting of the CREATE PROCEDURE statement (the default is to inherit the special registers from the client or caller):

- CURRENT DATE

- CURRENT DEGREE

- CURRENT PACKAGEPATH

- CURRENT PACKAGESET

- CURRENT PATH

- CURRENT RULES

- CURRENT SERVER

- CURRENT SQLID

- CURRENT TIME

- CURRENT TIMESTAMP

- CURRENT TIMEZONE

- CURRENT USER

Two important limitations also apply when nesting stored procedures:

- COMMIT ON RETURN is not executed when nested.

- Query result sets are returned to the previous nesting level only.

The application programmers, database procedural programmers, system programmers, and database administrators must communicate carefully to balance needs and to ensure that unnecessary levels, trigger cascading, and looping cannot occur.

Defining Stored Procedures

The CREATE PROCEDURE statement provides many options for creating stored procedures. Some of the main options include a parameter list, the language, and an external program name. DB2 stores the actual definition in the SYSIBM.SYSROUTINES catalog table and stores the parameter definitions in SYSIBM.SYSPARMS. The following statement demonstrates how to create a stored procedure.

```
CREATE PROCEDURE SYSPROC.MYSP1
       ( IN    PARM1  SMALLINT,
         INOUT PARM2  CHAR(10),
         OUT   CODE   INTEGER )
       EXTERNAL NAME 'CERTSP1'      -- load module name
       LANGUAGE COBOL               -- language
       PARAMETER STYLE GENERAL      -- type of parameter list
       COLLID DB2SPS                -- collection ID
       ASUTIME LIMIT 2000           -- maximum amount of SUs allowed
       STAY RESIDENT YES            -- make memory resident
       DYNAMIC RESULT SETS 3        -- 3 result sets returned
       NOT DETERMINISTIC            -- different results w/each call
       MODIFIES SQL DATA            -- Issues SQL
       WLM ENVIRONMENT MYAPPS       -- WLM environment
       PROGRAM TYPE MAIN            -- main, not subprogram
       RUN OPTIONS('TRAP(ON)')      -- specifies the LE run options
       STOP AFTER 2 FAILURES        -- stops after 2 failures
       COMMIT ON RETURN NO          -- do not commit on exit
```

To modify the options of a stored procedure, you use ALTER PROCEDURE statement:

```
ALTER PROCEDURE SYSPROC.MYSP1 STAY RESIDENT NO
```

The ALTER PROCEDURE command will be performed immediately and will take effect on next execution. When you alter an external procedure, any plans and packages that reference that stored procedure are invalidated.

Removing Stored Procedures

You remove procedures from the system by using the DROP PROCEDURE command, as in this example:

```
DROP PROCEDURE MYSPAP RESTRICT
```

This statement will drop the stored procedure unless the rules identified by the required keyword RESTRICT hold true. RESTRICT prevents the procedure from being dropped if a trigger definition contains a CALL statement with the name of the procedure.

When a procedure is directly or indirectly dropped, all privileges on the procedure are also dropped. In addition, any plans or packages that are dependent on the procedure are made inoperative.

Schema Qualification

Stored procedure names are implicitly or explicitly qualified by a schema name. If you use no schema name to qualify the procedure name, it is qualified by the following rules:

- If the CREATE PROCEDURE statement is embedded in a program, the schema name is the authorization ID specified in the QUALIFIER bind option when the plan or package was created or last re-bound. If QUALIFIER was not specified, the schema name is the owner of the plan or package.

- If the CREATE PROCEDURE statement is dynamically prepared, the schema name is the SQL authorization ID in the CURRENT SQLID special register.

When calling a stored procedure, you use the CURRENT PATH special register to identify unqualified procedure names. If no path is specified, the default path is used:

1. SYSIBM

2. SYSFUN

3. SYSPROC

4. Value of CURRENT SQLID

SYSFUN is a schema used for additional functions shipped from other servers in the DB2 product family. Although DB2 for z/OS does not have the SYSFUN schema, it can be useful to include SYSFUN in the path when doing distributed processing that involves a server that uses the SYSFUN schema.

Execution Environments

Stored procedures on z/OS execute under the control of DB2. External stored procedures execute in a workload-managed application environment.

Administration of stored procedures for z/OS includes the use of the following commands:

- START PROCEDURE and STOP PROCEDURE, which allow queuing options for callers to dynamically start and stop the ability to use or execute the stored procedure. It's also possible to start or stop procedures with the SCOPE(GROUP) option for data sharing.

- DISPLAY PROCEDURE provides the ability to display the status of a stored procedure.

The START and STOP can be issued for individual stored procedures or can include wild cards to affect multiple procedures.

The DISPLAY PROCEDURE command yields information about the status of any stored procedure that is currently started and has been executed, but it does not display any information about the individual threads using the stored procedure. For that, you must use the DISPLAY THREAD command. Here's an example:

```
-DISPLAY PROCEDURE
DSNX940I -DSNX9DIS DISPLAY PROCEDURE REPORT FOLLOWS -
PROCEDURE STATUS ACTIVE QUEUED MAXQUE TIMEOUT WLM_ENV
APPL1     STARTED   1      0      0      0
APPL2     STARTED   1      0      0      0
APPL2     STARTED   0      1      2      0
APPL5     STOPREJ   0      0      0      0
APPL6     STOPABN   0      0      0      0
PROC1     STOPQUE   0      0      0      0
DSNX9DIS DISPLAY PROCEDURE REPORT COMPLETE
```

You can issue the DISPLAY PROCEDURE, START PROCEDURE, and STOP PROCEDURE commands for full procedure names or partial names, as well as for a list of procedures. For example, the following command stops all the procedures in the SCHEMA1 and SCHEMA2 schemas.

```
-STOP PROCEDURE(SCHEMA1.*, SCHEMA2.*)
```

Workload Manager

DB2 external stored procedures run in a Workload Manager application environment. WLM can support multiple address spaces for each environment as well as manage the number of task control blocks (TCBs) within those address spaces. This support provides a complete demand-driven environment for the execution of stored procedures. For remote clients accessing a DB2 for z/OS data server, WLM can directly manage the priority of the DB2 distributed threads themselves via WLM definitions. WLM can manage the priorities and balance the workload of these distributed threads, along with other workloads on the server, and can also manage the priority of individual stored procedures.

You can have many WLM-managed environments for each DB2 subsystem, each with its own JCL. This means that the stored procedure programs for different applications can execute in different environments. You can also create separate test and quality assurance (QA) environments for the same application within the same subsystem, using different load libraries to allow for different levels of application code.

Stored procedures that execute in WLM-managed environments use the performance characteristics of the calling application. This design provides a very granular level of performance management.

The impact of program failures is limited to the execution address space, reducing the likelihood of affecting other critical stored procedures. Stored procedures that execute in WLM-managed environments use the Recoverable Resource Manager Services Attachment Facility (RRSAF) implicitly. RRS is a z/OS subsystem that is used to coordinate two-phase commits across disparate resources. RRS works cooperatively with DB2 and is required for the execution of DB2 and stored procedures. The DSNRLI interface module must be linked into the application load module, but the program must not make any DSNRLI calls. Two-phase commit is supported for any access to non-relational data updates if the data is managed by RRSAF.

Stored Procedures and WLM

WLM-established address spaces provide multiple isolated environments for external stored procedures. This architecture provides a great benefit because failures needn't affect other stored procedures. With WLM, the stored procedures also inherit the dispatching priority of the DB2 thread that issues the CALL statement. This feature enables high-priority work to have its stored procedures execute ahead of lower-priority work and associated stored procedures. The stored procedures can also run as subprograms with certain runtime options for better performance. Each WLM-managed, WLM-established space can run multiple stored procedures concurrently. The NUMTCB parameter in the JCL procedure for the WLM-established address space controls this concurrency within the address space. A system programmer can established the NUMTCB setting, or WLM itself can control it, permitting a balance between storage consumed within the address space, the number of address spaces, and the time it takes to schedule a stored procedure for execution.

Stored procedures using WLM also can have static priority assignment and dynamic workload balancing. High-priority stored procedures in WLM achieve very consistent response times, and Workload Manager provides dynamic workload balancing and distribution. WLM routes incoming requests to the WLM-established address space that is the least busy or starts a new address space if required. Once this environment has been established, the actions are fully automatic, requiring no monitoring, tuning, or operator intervention.

Another benefit WLM-managed address spaces can provide is better options for stopping runaway stored procedures. If a procedure is looping outside DB2's control, you have different alternatives for regaining control. With a runaway stored procedure in a WLM-managed application environment, you have the option to refresh the environment, which quiesces all address spaces running under that environment, starts a new address space, and routes all new requests to the new address space. Once assured that all normal work in the address space containing the runaway stored procedure has finished, you can cancel the address space. This action completely isolates all other stored procedures from failure.

An option on the stored procedure itself can also help with runaway stored procedures. You can use the ASUTIME parameter to protect against runaways. Stored procedures are normally designed for high-volume online transactions, and the

ASUTIME parameter lets you limit the resources used by stored procedures. DB2 stores the ASUTIME value in the ASUTIME column of the SYSIBM.SYSROUTINES catalog table.

By setting ASUTIME, you enable DB2 to cancel stored procedures that are in a loop. This option was designed to be used for runaway stored procedures. DB2 checks for overages on ASUTIME every 20 seconds of clock time. Therefore, the option isn't intended as a strict control on how much CPU time a stored procedure can use. That's where WLM is also beneficial. Because WLM lets you establish priorities and service goals, it gives you an additional mechanism for tight control of system resource usage. By using both ASUTIME and WLM priorities and goals, you can have total control of the stored procedures in this environment.

Program Type

Programs that run in WLM environments can be defined to execute as subprograms or main programs. Subprograms execute more efficiently but must take care to clean up resources and close files. Specify PROGRAM TYPE SUB on the CREATE PROCEDURE statement, and make sure the program is properly coded to execute as a subprogram.

Programs that run as subprograms must be dynamically fetchable. For COBOL, no real difference exists between a main program and a subprogram. PL/I subprograms may not perform I/O. C programs must be defined as fetchable, as in the following:

```
#include <sqludf.h>
#pragma linkage(sprslt,fetchable)
void sprslt (const char    parmCreator[9],
             short       * pIndCreator,
             char          p_sqlstate[6],
             char          p_proc[28],
             char          p_spec[19],
             char          p_diag[71]
          )
```

Managing WLM Environments

Administration of stored procedures used in a WLM-managed address space falls under the control of WLM. The START PROCEDURE and STOP PROCEDURE commands stop and start the procedure, but they don't cause DB2 to reload the load module. To refresh a stored procedure load module, you must use the following command from the console.

```
VARY WLM,APPLENV=wlmenv,REFRESH
```

The WLM refresh command recycles all WLM address spaces that run with that environment. New environment address spaces are started, and any new work is routed to the new address spaces. Threads executing in the existing address spaces are allowed to continue in the old environment before it is brought down.

You can start and stop the WLM environment as a whole using the following commands.

```
VARY WLM,APPLENV=wlmenv,QUIESCE
VARY WLM,APPLENV=wlmenv,RESUME
```

IBM provides a stored procedure called WLM_REFRESH that enables anyone to refresh a WLM-managed application environment without needing the authority to issue console commands.

Obtaining Diagnostic Information

The startup procedure for a WLM-managed, WLM-established address space contains a DD statement for CEEDUMP. The Language Environment writes a small diagnostic dump to CEEDUMP when a stored procedure terminates abnormally. The environment waits until the stored procedure address space terminates to print the dump output. The dump is obtained by stopping the stored procedure address space running the stored procedure.

SQL Procedure Language

The SQL Procedure Language is a procedural language that was designed for writing stored procedures. Available across the entire DB2 family, including i5/OS, it is based on the ANSI/ISO standard language SQL/PSM. Its major benefit is that users can create stored procedures very quickly, using a simple, easily understood language, without the headaches of precompilers, compilers, link editors, binding, and special authorizations. This is possible because, for the most part, DB2 manages stored procedures written using SQL Procedure Language; this support automates the process and lets programmers and users simply write the logic and pass it off to DB2.

SQL procedures provide compatibility and portability of stored procedures across the DB2 product family and eliminate platform dependency on specific languages. DB2 9 introduces native SQL procedures. With native SQL procedures, the stored procedure logic itself is built as a runtime structure and is executed within the DB2 address space. This enhancement can provide a dramatic performance improvement over external SQL procedures, as well as over external stored procedures written in other languages.

SQL procedures support multiple parameters for input, output, and returning output results sets to clients. SQL procedures are defined in the DB2 catalog, and the source can be stored there too. The following example shows an SQL procedure that was created from a client workstation using the Developer Workbench tool. It accepts one input parameter and returns a result set to the client.

```
CREATE PROCEDURE DW.SQLProc1 ( IN gender char(6) )
    SPECIFIC DW.Genders        RESULT SETS 1
    LANGUAGE SQL
P1: BEGIN
    DECLARE gender_value CHAR(1);
    DECLARE bad_gender CONDITION FOR SQLSTATE '99001';
    CASE gender
       WHEN 'MALE' THEN
           SET gender_value = 'M';
       WHEN 'FEMALE' THEN
           SET gender_value = 'F';
       ELSE SIGNAL bad_gender;
    END CASE;
    -- Declare cursor
    DECLARE cursor1 CURSOR WITH RETURN FOR
        SELECT E.EMPNO, E.LASTNAME, E.HIREDATE, D.DEPTNO,
               D.DEPTNAME
        FROM DW.DEPARTMENT D, DW.EMPLOYEE E
        WHERE E.WORKDEPT = D.DEPTNO
          AND E.SEX = :gender_value
        ORDER BY E.WORKDEPT;
    -- Cursor left open for client application
    OPEN cursor1;
END P1
```

The language itself is primarily SQL (DML and DDL) with local variables, cursors, assignment statements, flow control, and signal/resignal conditions. The real difference with the SQL Procedure Language is how it becomes a stored procedure, because all the programmer does is write a CREATE PROCEDURE...LANGUAGE SQL...*name*: BEGIN...END *name* DDL statement. All the code is in the body of the CREATE statement. The procedure body includes

- compound statements
- declaration statements
- assignment statements
- conditional statements
- iterative control structures
  - » loop
  - » repeat
  - » while
- exception handling
- calling another stored procedure

The primary language statements that show the strength of this approach are as follows:

- IF, CASE, and LEAVE
- LOOP, REPEAT, and WHILE
- FOR, CALL, and RETURN
- GET DIAGNOSTICS
- SIGNAL and RESIGNAL

Developing SQL Stored Procedures

DB2 implements SQL stored procedures as either native (running in the DB2 address space as an internal process) or external C programs. External SQL procedures were the only choice before Version 9, and prior to that release all SQL procedures were compiled into C external stored procedures. The DB2 precompiler can take an SQL procedure as input and write out a C source module. V9 introduces native SQL procedures, completely eliminating the need to create an external C program. DB2 still supports external SQL procedures, and you can still create them by specifying the FENCED or EXTERNAL option in the CREATE PROCEDURE statement. You create an SQL procedure using one of the following four methods:

- Developer Workbench (internal and external SQL procedures)
- Directly invoking DSNTPSMP (external SQL procedures)
- Define directly using DDL (internal and external SQL procedures)
- Using JCL or CLIST to prepare (external SQL procedures)

External SQL Stored Procedures

Although native SQL procedures provide superior performance in V9, external SQL procedures are still supported. DB2 automatically translates and compiles an external stored procedure as an external C program. When you build an external SQL procedure using the Developer Workbench tool (discussed later in this chapter), all the "code" is developed on the client workstation, and the completed procedure is passed to the DSNTPSMP stored procedure. DSNTPSMP is the z/OS SQL Procedure Processor—a REXX stored procedure—and it is also fully customizable. This processor invokes the following steps:

1. SQL precompile
2. C precompile
3. C compile
4. Prelink

5. Link

6. Procedure definition

7. Bind

Once the procedure is built in this fashion, it is immediately executable. The other three methods for developing an external SQL procedure basically just bypass the Developer Workbench and either directly invoke DSNTPSMP or execute the steps listed above under manual control.

DB2 Developer Workbench

The DB2 Developer Workbench is the successor to the DB2 Version 7 Stored Procedure Builder and the DB2 Version 8 Development Center. DB2 Developer Workbench is a comprehensive development environment for creating, editing, debugging, deploying, and testing DB2 stored procedures and user-defined functions (UDFs on DB2 for LUW only). You can also use DB2 Developer Workbench to develop SQLJ applications and to create, edit, and run SQL statements and XML queries.

The DB2 Developer Workbench provides a rapid, iterative development environment for building stored procedures, UDFs, structured data types, and much more. Developers can build DB2 business logic anywhere, and all DB2 platforms are supported.

The Workbench includes support for developing SQL statements, SQL and Java stored procedures, SQL scalar and table user-defined functions, MQSeries, OLE DB, XML schemas, XML queries, XML table functions, and structured data types for Enterprise JavaBean (EJB) methods and properties, as well as SQLJ applications.

From the tool, you can view live database tables, views, triggers, stored procedures, and UDFs. A quick-start launch pad guides new users through the initial set of development tasks. Some features for enhanced z/OS support include specialized SQL IDs (package owner, build owner, and secondary SQL ID) and advanced build options.

The DB2 Developer Workbench provides an excellent facility for testing and debugging stored procedures written in any language. You can use this tool to perform the following tasks:

- Create new stored procedures

- Build stored procedures on local and remote DB2 servers

- Manage, version, and migrate stored procedures across environments and even across servers

- Modify and rebuild existing stored procedures

- Run stored procedures to test their execution

Summary

Stored procedures provide a powerful mechanism for storing application code on the database server. They improve performance while enhancing application security and can support legacy data sources to DB2-based programs running on both the mainframe and other platforms. Workload Manager provides many benefits for external stored procedures and helps deliver application-defined performance. Native SQL procedures represent a major change in how DB2 for z/OS stored procedures execute, eliminating a WLM-established address space and executing within the DB2 engine itself.

Additional Resources

Developing Cross-Platform DB2 Stored Procedures: SQL Procedures and the DB2 Stored Procedure Builder (SG24-5485)
IBM DB2 9 Application Programming and SQL Guide (SC18-9841)

Practice Questions

Question 1

A stored procedure needs to access a flat file and return the data from the flat file as a result set. Once the execution of the procedure is completed, the data is no longer needed. Which type of DB2 table would be most appropriate in this situation?

○ A. A regular table

○ B. An auxiliary table

○ C. A global temporary table

○ D. A clone table

Question 2

For establishing concurrency within a WLM-managed, WLM-established address space, what is the name of the parameter used to set the number of procedures that can execute concurrently for each address space?

○ A. NUMSRB

○ B. NUMTCB

○ C. CONCUR

○ D. THRDNUM

Question 3

Which type of DB2 thread can be managed directly by WLM?

○ A. Distributed threads

○ B. Allied threads using CAF

○ C. Allied threads using RRSAF

○ D. Allied threads using TSO ATTACH

Question 4

What is the major difference between a FENCED SQL procedure and a native SQL procedure?

○ A. The fenced SQL procedure cannot modify data.

○ B. The native SQL procedure can be defined only in the Developer Workbench.

○ C. The fenced SQL procedure runs as an external C program.

○ D. The native SQL procedure cannot access temporary tables.

Question 5

A PL/I stored procedure executing as a subprogram has what limitation?

○ A. It cannot call other stored procedures.

○ B. It has to run in a WLM-established address space with NUMTCB=1.

○ C. It cannot return result sets.

○ D. It cannot issue I/O.

Answers

Question 1

The answer is **C**, a global temporary table. Global temporary tables provide a thread-independent temporary table into which the stored procedure can insert the flat file data. Once the table has data in it, a result set can be opened and returned to the client.

Question 2

The answer is **B**, NUMTCB. This parameter in the JCL for the WLM-established address space dictates the number of TCBs, or the number of procedures that the address space will run concurrently. The other parameter names listed are not valid.

Question 3

The answer is **A**, distributed threads. You can set up WLM to manage diverse workloads on a z/OS server via definitions. Those definitions include the ability to set priorities for distributed threads as well for as stored procedures.

Question 4

The answer is **C**, the fenced SQL procedure runs as an external C program. Before Version 9, all SQL procedures were compiled into C programs that were executed in a WLM-established address space. Beginning in V9, all SQL procedures by default are executed as runtime structures within the DB2 address space. However, if you use keyword FENCED or EXTERNAL, the SQL procedures are still executed as external C programs in a WLM-established address space.

Question 5

The answer is **D**, it cannot issue I/O. Subprograms provide an added level of performance in that the Language Environment linkage path is shorter. This support is a high-performance design feature. However, programmers must take extra care when coding subprograms and should be aware of some of the language limitations.

Accessing Distributed Data

In This Chapter

- ✔ CONNECT statements
- ✔ Three-part names
- ✔ DRDA
- ✔ Update coordination
- ✔ Remote query performance
- ✔ Connection pooling

Distributed Data

Using DB2's Distributed Data Facility (DDF), you can enable access to data held by other data management systems or make your own DB2 data accessible to other systems. A DB2 application program can use SQL to access data controlled by DBMSs other than the DB2 at which the application's plan is bound. This *local DB2* and the other DBMSs are called *application servers (ASs)*. Any application server other than the local DB2 is considered a *remote server (RS)*, and access to its data is a distributed operation.

DB2 provides two ways to access data at remote application servers: DRDA and DB2 private protocol access. For application servers that support the two-phase commit process, both methods enable updating data at several remote locations within the same unit of work.

The location name of the DB2 subsystem is defined during DB2 installation. The communications database (CDB) records the location name and the network address of a remote DBMS. The tables in the CDB are part of the DB2 catalog.

DRDA

Communicating between platforms introduces several issues, ranging from character conversion to definition of the actions you want executed on the other platform. Several years ago with DB2 for MVS/ESA, Version 2, Release 3, IBM introduced a set of protocols known as *Distributed Relational Database Architecture (DRDA)*. An open standard that could be licensed by other companies, DRDA provided for communications between a client (the *application requester*) and a server (the application server). The basic goals of the protocol were to maximize functionality and reduce overhead when communicating between like platforms.

DRDA achieves these goals by putting the work on the platform that receives the message. For example, the application server processes the request to fetch from a cursor, and the application requester translates the returned rows. The original DRDA specifications identified four different levels of support:

- **Remote request.** A single request to one remote DBMS. The remote request consists of one SQL statement. This level does not let you define a unit of work. Every SQL statement is an independent unit of work.

- **Remote unit of work (RUW).** A unit of work requesting services to a single remote DBMS. RUW provides integrity within a single DBMS. You can group several statements together in a single unit of work, but these statements cannot span more than one DBMS.

- **Distributed unit of work (DUW).** A unit of work requesting services to two or more DBMSs. DUW provides integrity across multiple DBMSs. However, access is to only a single DBMS in an SQL statement. The changes at all DBMSs are backed out if the execution of one SQL statement is unsuccessful.

- **Distributed request.** A request to two or more remote DBMSs residing on the same or different locations. Distributed request provides integrity across multiple locations and access to more than one location in a single SQL statement. IBM has no immediate plans to extend the DRDA architecture to include the distributed request functionality. The implementation of a standard technique to solve the distributed request problem is much more complicated because it would require the addition of optimization-related concepts such as network performance and estimation of the cost of the remote SQL component.

With DRDA (the recommended, and soon the only, method of distributed access for DB2), an application connects to a server at another location and executes packages that have been previously bound at that server. The application uses a CONNECT statement, a three-part name, or an alias (if bound with DBPROTOCOL(DRDA)) to access the server. (For more information about bind options, see Chapter 11.)

Queries can originate from any system or application that issues SQL statements as an application requester in the formats required by DRDA. DRDA access supports the execution of dynamic SQL statements and SQL statements that satisfy all of the following conditions:

- The static statements appear in a package bound to an accessible server.

- The statements are executed using that package.

- The objects involved in the execution of the statements are at the server where the package is bound. If the server is a DB2 subsystem, three-part names and aliases can be used to refer to another DB2 server.

DRDA communications conventions are invisible to DB2 applications and let a DB2 bind and rebind packages at other servers and execute the statements in those packages. For two-phase commit using System Network Architecture (SNA) connections, DB2 supports both presumed-abort and presumed-nothing protocols that are defined by DRDA. If you are using TCP/IP, only presumed abort is supported.

DB2 Private Protocol

Under *DB2 private protocol*, an older remote access method for DB2, an application program running under DB2 can refer to a table or view at another DB2. When using the private protocol method of access, the application must use an alias or three-part name to direct the SQL statement to a given location. Private protocol works only between application requesters and application servers that are both DB2 for z/OS subsystems and use SNA.

A statement is executed using DB2 private protocol access if the statement refers to objects that are not at the current server and the statement is implicitly or explicitly bound with DBPROTOCOL(PRIVATE). The current server is the DBMS to which an application is actively connected. DB2 private protocol access uses DB2 private connections. SQL INSERT, UPDATE, DELETE, and SELECT statements can be executed, with their associated SQL OPEN, FETCH, and CLOSE statements.

The location name identifies the other DB2 to the DB2 application server. A three-part name consists of a location, an authorization ID, and an object name. For example, the name NYSERVER.DB2USER1.TEST refers to a table named DB2USER1.TEST at the server whose location name is NYSERVER. Alias names have the same allowable forms as table or view names. The name can refer to a table or view at the current server or to a table or view elsewhere.

DB2 private protocol does not support many distributed functions, such as TCP/IP or stored procedures. Nor are some data types, such as large object and user-defined types, supported with this method of access. It is not the recommended method, and it is currently being phased out. DB2 9 begins the preparation for the phasing out of private protocol.

Communications Protocols

Setting up a network for use by DBMSs requires knowledge of both database management and communications. To plan and implement your network, you must put together a team of people with these skills. To communicate with other systems, DDF uses SNA or TCP/IP. VTAM is also used to control the communications and flow of data in an SNA network.

System Network Architecture

The SNA architecture describes the logical structure, formats, protocols, and operational sequences for transmitting information through networks and controlling their configuration and operation. It is one of the two main network architectures DB2 uses for network communications to enterprise servers.

Virtual Terminal Access Method

DB2 also uses VTAM to communicate with remote databases. In VTAM access, the local DB2 subsystem is assigned two names: a *location name* and a logical unit name (*LU name*). The location name distinguishes a specific DBMS in a network, so applications use this name to direct requests to the local DB2 subsystem. Other systems use different terms for a location name; for example, DB2 Connect calls this the *target database name*. DB2 uses the DRDA term *RDBNAM* to refer to non-DB2 relational database names.

TCP/IP

Transmission Control Protocol/Internet Protocol (TCP/IP) is a standard communications protocol for network communications. Previous versions of DB2 supported TCP/IP requesters, although additional software and configuration was necessary. Native TCP/IP eliminated these requirements many releases ago, enabling gateway-less connectivity to DB2 for systems running UNIX System Services.

The security aspects of TCP/IP differ from those of SNA. Unlike SNA, where it's possible to tighten security, TCP/IP makes it much easier to mimic the address you're coming from. As a result, not all features available to the SNA protocol have been implemented for TCP/IP. You can configure DDF in such a way that it performs inbound user ID translation.

Communications Database

The DB2 catalog includes the communications database, which contains several tables that hold information about connections with remote systems. These tables include

- SYSIBM.IPLIST

- SYSIBM.IPNAMES

- SYSIBM.LOCATIONS

- SYSIBM.LULIST

- SYSIBM.LUMODES

- SYSIBM.LUNAMES

- SYSIBM.MODESELECT

- SYSIBM.USERNAMES

Some of these tables must be populated before data can be requested from remote systems. If a DB2 system services only data requests, the CDB doesn't need to be populated; you can use the default values.

When sending a request, DB2 uses the LINKNAME column of the SYSIBM.LOCATIONS catalog table to determine which protocol to use.

- To receive VTAM requests, the DB2 system must have an LU name selected in installation panel DSNTIPR.

- To receive TCP/IP requests, a DRDA port and a resynchronization port must be selected in installation panel DSNTIP5. TCP/IP uses the server's port number to pass network requests to the correct DB2 subsystem. If the value in the LINKNAME column is found in the SYSIBM.IPNAMES table, DDF uses TCP/IP for DRDA connections. If the value is found in SYSIBM.LUNAMES table, SNA is used.

- If SYSIBM.LUNAMES and SYSIBM.IPNAMES contain the same name, DDF uses TCP/IP to connect to the location.

> A requester cannot connect to a given location using both SNA and TCP/IP protocols. For example, if the SYSIBM.LOCATIONS table specifies a LINKNAME of LU1 and LU1 is defined in both SYSIBM.IPNAMES and SYSIBM.LUNAMES, TCP/IP is the only protocol used to connect to LU1 from this requester for DRDA connections. For private protocol connections, the SNA protocols are used. If private protocol connections are being used, the SYSIBM.LUNAMES table must be defined for the remote location's LU name.

Gathering Configuration Information

How do you obtain the information to fill in the CDB and set up the connection with the remote system? DB2 LUW has a piece of software called the client configuration assistant, which communicates with a component on the server called the DB2 Database Administrative Server (DB2DAS). DB2DAS gives the client all the information required to define the target database. Today, DB2 for z/OS does not provide this DB2DAS, and the user has to find the required information manually. The DB2 command –DISPLAY DDF lists all the information required to set up the connection to the DB2, as shown in the following sample output.

```
DSNL080I  -DBT5 DSNLTDDF DISPLAY DDF REPORT FOLLOWS:
DSNL081I STATUS=STARTD
DSNL082I LOCATION            LUNAME              GENERICLU
DSNL083I DBT5                 TU0.BSYSDBT5        -NONE
DSNL084I IPADDR           TCPPORT RESPORT
DSNL085I 10.35.4.16        2590    2591
DSNL086I SQL     DOMAIN=t390.rpc.com
DSNL086I RESYNC DOMAIN=t390.rpc.com
DSNL090I DT=A  CONDBAT=     64 MDBAT=    64
DSNL092I ADBAT=    0 QUEDBAT=      0 IN1DBAT=  0 CONQUED=       0
DSNL093I DSCDBAT=      0 IN2CONS=      0
DSNL099I DSNLTDDF DISPLAY DDF REPORT COMPLETE
```

Without this command, you'd have to print the content of the bootstrap data set, which contains other sensitive information you may not want exposed. With the command, you can determine the status and configuration of the DDF, as well as status information for connections and threads controlled by DDF.

Communicating with a Data-Sharing Group

All the members of a DB2 data-sharing group have the same location name, but each individual member has its own specific communications parameters. There is therefore no way to define, at the application level, which member of the group should be addressed unless you defined member-specific aliases. The mapping to the group or an individual member should be defined at the level of the configuration of the client. On z/OS, that would be the definitions in the CDB; when using DB2 Connect, you define the target in the node directory.

In fact, the purpose of the data-sharing implementation is to make the entire group virtually one in order to increase the availability of the overall data-sharing group. With every new release of DB2 Connect, we see further improvements to make the routing to the data-sharing members more transparent and efficient.

At the networking level, we find solutions that let you "virtualize" the DB2 server. These enhancements include the use of SNA Advanced Program-to-Program Communications (APPC) generic resources and techniques such as TCP/IP Virtual IP Address (VIPA). Both require a considerable investment from the networking side. Another alternative is the definition of dynamic APPC application definitions. In this case, we make use of the concept of a model. The application used by DB2 is no longer defined in a static fashion but refers to a model that is active on all systems in the data-sharing group.

Member-Specific Routing

Yet another option is to use *member-specific routing* through the use of location aliases. You store this alias in the BSDS, along with a location. This approach lets you specify additional names that can be used in a connection. You can have one to eight aliases assigned, and each may listen on a different port.

The potential benefit here is the ability to segregate server work done by Parallel Sysplex and allow client systems to use a name other than the base location name for the subsystem/group. To make the entries to the BSDS, you use the DSNJU003 (Change Log Inventory) utility. Here's an example of an entry for a location alias:

```
DDF ALIAS=name1,name2:5000,name3
```

Coding Methods for Distributed Data

DB2 provides different ways to access distributed data, and there are considerations to note in preparing and binding programs that will execute statements against that data. In this part of the chapter, we review the connect options, program preparation and bind options, and additional considerations for coordinating updates.

Three-Part Names

Whether using DRDA access or DB2 private protocol access, you can use three-part table names to access data at a remote location. When you use three-part table names, you code your application the same way regardless of the access method you choose. You determine the access method when you bind the SQL statements into a package or plan. If you use DRDA access, you must bind the database request modules (DBRMs) for the SQL statements to be executed at the server into packages that reside at that server. Because platforms other than DB2 for z/OS might not support the three-part name syntax, you shouldn't code applications with three-part names if you plan to port those applications to other platforms.

In a three-part table name, the first part denotes the location. The local DB2 makes and breaks an implicit connection to a remote server as needed. An application uses a location name to construct a three-part table name in an SQL statement. It then prepares the statement and executes it dynamically (this applies to private protocol; DRDA can execute static SQL). If the statement is an INSERT, the values to be inserted are transmitted to the remote location and substituted for the parameter markers in the INSERT statement. The following overview shows how the application uses three-part names.

> *Read input values*
>
> *Do for all locations*
>
> *Read location name*
>
> *Set up statement to prepare*
>
> *Prepare statement*
>
> *Execute statement*

End loop

Commit

After the application obtains a location name—for example, SAN_JOSE—it creates the following character string.

```
INSERT INTO SAN_JOSE.DSN8910.PROJ VALUES (?,?,?,?,?,?,?,?,?)
```

The application assigns the character string to the variable INSERTX and then executes these statements:

```
EXEC SQL
PREPARE STMT1 FROM :INSERTX;
EXEC SQL
EXECUTE STMT1 USING :PROJNO, :PROJNAME, :DEPTNO, :RESPEMP,
:PRSTAFF, :PRSTDATE, :PRENDATE, :MAJPROJ;
```

To keep the data consistent at all locations, the application commits the work only when the loop has been executed for all locations. Either every location has committed the INSERT or, if a failure has prevented any location from inserting, all locations must roll back the INSERT. (If a system failure occurs during the commit process, the entire unit of work can be in doubt.)

Three-Part Names and Multiple Servers

If you use a three-part name or an alias that resolves to one location name in a statement executed at a remote server by DRDA access, and if the location name is not that of the server, the method by which the remote server accesses data at the named location depends on the value of the DBPROTOCOL bind option. If the package at the first remote server is bound with DBPROTOCOL(PRIVATE), DB2 uses DB2 private protocol access to access the second remote server. If the package at the first remote server is bound with DBPROTOCOL(DRDA), DB2 uses DRDA access to access the second remote server. We recommend that you follow these steps so that access to the second remote server is by DRDA access:

1. Rebind the package at the first remote server with DBPROTOCOL(DRDA).

2. Bind the package that contains the three-part name at the second server.

Accessing Declared Temporary Tables

You can access a remote declared temporary table using a three-part name only if you use DRDA access. However, if you combine explicit CONNECT statements and three-part names in your application, a reference to a remote declared temporary table must be a forward reference. For example, you can perform the following series of actions, which includes a forward reference to a declared temporary table.

```
EXEC SQL CONNECT TO CHICAGO; /* Connect to the remote site */
EXEC SQL
DECLARE GLOBAL TEMPORARY TABLE TEMPPROD /*Define the temporary table */
  (CHARCO CHAR(6) NOT NULL); /* at the remote site */
EXEC SQL CONNECT RESET;      /* Connect back to local site */
EXEC SQL INSERT INTO CHICAGO.SESSION.T1
(VALUES 'ABCDEF');            /* Access the temporary table */
/* at the remote site (forward reference) */
```

However, you cannot perform the following series of actions, which includes a backward reference to the declared temporary table.

```
EXEC SQL
DECLARE GLOBAL TEMPORARY TABLE TEMPPROD /* Define the temporary table */
(CHARCO CHAR(6) NOT NULL );  /* at the local site (ATLANTA)*/
EXEC SQL CONNECT TO CHICAGO; /* Connect to the remote site */
EXEC SQL INSERT INTO ATLANTA.SESSION.T1
(VALUES 'ABCDEF');            /* Cannot access temp table */
/* from the remote site (backward reference) */
```

Using Explicit CONNECT Statements

When you use explicit CONNECT statements, the application program explicitly connects to each new server. You must bind the DBRMs for the SQL statements to be executed at the server to packages that reside at that server. An application executes CONNECT for each server, and in turn the server can execute statements such as INSERTs.

In the next example, the tables to be updated each have the same name, although each is defined at a different server. The application executes the statements in a loop, with one iteration for each server. The application connects to each new server by means of a host variable in the CONNECT statement. CONNECT changes the special register CURRENT SERVER to show the location of the new server. The values to insert in the table are transmitted to a location as input host variables. The following overview shows how the application uses explicit CONNECTs.

Read input values
Do for all locations
Read location name
Connect to location
Execute insert statement
End loop
Release all
Commit

The application inserts a new location name into the variable LOCATION_NAME and executes the following statements:

```
EXEC SQL
CONNECT TO :LOCATION_NAME;
EXEC SQL
INSERT INTO DSN8710.PROJ VALUES
(:PROJNO, :PROJNAME, :DEPTNO,:RESPEMP,
:PRSTAFF, :PRSTDATE, :PRENDATE, :MAJPROJ);
```

To keep the data consistent at all locations, the application commits the work only when the loop has been executed for all locations. Either every location has committed the INSERT or, if a failure has prevented any location from inserting, all other locations must roll back the INSERT. (If a system failure occurs during the commit process, the entire unit of work can be in doubt.)

Releasing Connections

When you connect to remote locations explicitly, you can also break those connections explicitly. You have considerable flexibility in determining how long connections remain open, so the RELEASE statement differs significantly from CONNECT:

- CONNECT makes an immediate connection to exactly one remote system.

- CONNECT (type 2) does not release any current connection. (The upcoming section on precompiler options provides more information about connection types.)

- RELEASE does not immediately break a connection. The RELEASE statement labels connections for release at the next commit point. A connection so labeled is in the release-pending state and can still be used before the next commit point.

- RELEASE can specify a single connection or a set of connections for release at the next commit point.

DISCONNECT Bind Parameter

The bind parameter DISCONNECT determines which remote connections to destroy during commit operations (we discuss this parameter further below).

Preparing Programs for DRDA Access

For the most part, binding a package to run at a remote location is like binding a package to run at your local DB2. Binding a plan to run the package is like binding any other plan. For options on binding, refer to the sections on BIND options below as well as Chapter 11.

Precompiler Options

Two precompiler options are relevant to preparing a package to be run using DRDA access:

- CONNECT. Use CONNECT(2) explicitly or by default. CONNECT(1) causes your CONNECT statements to allow only the restricted function known as remote unit of work. Be particularly careful to avoid CONNECT(1) if your application updates more than one DBMS in a single unit of work.

- SQL. Use SQL(ALL) explicitly for a package that runs on a server that is not DB2 for z/OS. With this option, the precompiler accepts any statement that obeys DRDA rules. Use SQL(DB2) explicitly or by default if the server is DB2 for z/OS only. The precompiler then rejects any statement that does not obey the rules of DB2 for z/OS.

BIND PACKAGE Options

The following options of the BIND PACKAGE subcommand are relevant to binding a package to be run using DRDA access.

- *location-name*. Name the location of the server at which the package runs. The privileges needed to run the package must be granted to the owner of the package at the server. If you are not the owner, you must also have SYSADM and SYSCTRL authority or have the BINDAGENT privilege granted locally.

- **SQLERROR**. Use SQLERROR(CONTINUE) if you specified SQL(ALL)when precompiling. This combination creates a package even if the bind process finds SQL errors, such as statements that are valid on the remote server but not recognized by the precompiler. Otherwise, use SQLERROR(NOPACKAGE) explicitly or by default.

- **CURRENTDATA**. Specify CURRENTDATA(NO) to force a block fetch for ambiguous cursors. (We talk more about block fetch later in the chapter.)

- **OPTIONS**. When you make a remote copy of a package using BIND PACKAGE with the COPY option, use this option to control the default bind options DB2 uses.

  » Specify COMPOSITE (the default) to cause DB2 to use any options you specify in the BIND PACKAGE command and use the options of the copied package for all other options.

  » Specify COMMAND to cause DB2 to use the options you specify in the BIND PACKAGE command and use the defaults for the server on which the package is bound for all other options. This setting helps ensure that the server supports the options with which the package is bound.

- **DBPROTOCOL**. Use DBPROTOCOL(PRIVATE) if you want DB2 to use DB2 private protocol access to access remote data specified with three-part names. Use DBPROTOCOL(DRDA) if you want DB2 to use DRDA access to access remote data specified with three-part names. You must bind a package at all locations whose names are specified in three-part names. These values override the DATABASE PROTOCOL value on installation panel DSNTIP5. Therefore, if the DATABASE PROTOCOL setting at the requester site specifies the type of remote access you want to use for three-part names, you don't need to specify the DBPROTOCOL bind option.

BIND PLAN Options

The following options of the BIND PLAN subcommand are particularly relevant to binding a plan that uses DRDA access.

- **CURRENTSERVER.** This parameter determines the location to connect to before running the plan.

- **DISCONNECT.** For the most flexibility, use DISCONNECT(EXPLICIT) explicitly or by default. This setting requires you to use RELEASE statements in your program to explicitly end connections. However, the other values of the option are also useful. DISCONNECT(AUTOMATIC) ends all remote connections during a commit operation without the need for RELEASE statements in your program. DISCONNECT(CONDITIONAL) ends remote connections during a commit operation except when an open cursor defined as WITH HOLD is associated with the connection.

- **SQLRULES.** Use SQLRULES(DB2) explicitly or by default. SQLRULES(STD) applies the rules of the SQL standard to your CONNECT statements, so that CONNECT TO *x* is an error if you are already connected to *x*. Use STD only if you want such a statement to return an error code. If your program selects LOB data from a remote location and you bind the plan for the program with SQLRULES(DB2), the format in which you retrieve the LOB data with a cursor is restricted. After you open the cursor to retrieve the LOB data, you must retrieve all the data using either a LOB variable or a LOB locator variable. If the value of SQLRULES is STD, this restriction does not exist. If you intend to switch between LOB variables and LOB locators to retrieve data from a cursor, execute the SET SQLRULES=STD statement before you connect to the remote location.

- **CURRENTDATA.** Use CURRENTDATA(NO) to force block fetch for ambiguous cursors.

- **DBPROTOCOL.** Use DBPROTOCOL(PRIVATE) if you want DB2 to use DB2 private protocol access to access remote data specified with three-part names. Use DBPROTOCOL(DRDA) if you want DB2 to use DRDA access to access remote data specified with three-part names. You must bind a package at all locations whose names are specified in three-part names. The package value for the DBPROTOCOL option overrides the plan option. For example, if you specify DBPROTOCOL(DRDA) for a remote package and DBPROTOCOL(PRIVATE) for the plan, DB2 uses DRDA access when it accesses data at that location using a three-part name. If you don't specify any value for DBPROTOCOL, DB2 uses the value of DATABASE PROTOCOL on installation panel DSNTIP5.

Coordinating Updates

Two or more updates are coordinated if they must all commit or all roll back in the same unit of work. Updates to two or more DBMSs can be coordinated automatically if both systems implement a method called *two-phase commit*.

DB2 and IMS, and DB2 and CICS, jointly implement a two-phase commit process. You can update an IMS database and a DB2 table in the same unit of work. If a system or communications failure occurs between committing the work on IMS and on DB2, the two programs restore the two systems to a consistent point when activity resumes.

You cannot really have coordinated updates with a DBMS that does not implement two-phase commit. In the description that follows, we call such a DBMS a *restricted system*. DB2 prevents you from updating on both a restricted system and any other system in the same unit of work. In this context, update includes the statements INSERT, DELETE, UPDATE, CREATE, ALTER, DROP, GRANT, REVOKE, RENAME, COMMENT, MERGE, and LABEL.

To achieve the effect of coordinated updates with a restricted system, you must first update one system and commit that work and then update the second system and commit its work. If a failure occurs after the first update is committed and before the second is committed, no automatic provision for bringing the two systems back to a consistent point exists. Your program must assume that task.

CICS and IMS

For CICS and IMS, you cannot update at servers that don't support two-phase commit.

TSO and Batch

For TSO and batch, you can update if and only if

- no other connections exist, or
- all existing connections are to servers that are restricted to read-only operations

If these conditions are not met, you are restricted to read-only operations.

If the first connection in a logical unit of work is to a server that supports two-phase commit and there are no existing connections or only read-only connections, that server and all servers that support two-phase commit can update. However, if the first connection is to a server that does not support two-phase commit, only that server is allowed to update.

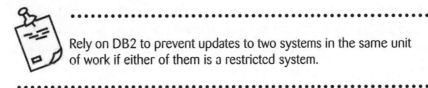

Rely on DB2 to prevent updates to two systems in the same unit of work if either of them is a restricted system.

Without Two-Phase Commit

If you're accessing a mixture of systems, some of which might be restricted, you can

- read from any of the systems at any time.
- update any one system many times in one unit of work.
- update many systems, including CICS or IMS, in one unit of work, provided none of them is a restricted system. If the first system you update in a unit of work is not restricted, any attempt to update a restricted system in that unit of work returns an error.

- update one restricted system in a unit of work, provided you don't try to update any other system in the same unit of work. If the first system you update in a unit of work is restricted, any attempt to update any other system in that unit of work returns an error.

Programming Considerations

When working with more than one location, we need to find a way to identify which DB2 holds the data we want to process. With application-directed data, before executing the SQL you identify to DB2 the location to which the SQL statement should be directed. You can do this either explicitly by coding a CONNECT statement in the application or by relying on the CURRENT SERVER register. The bind option CURRENTSERVER initially determines the value of the CURRENT SERVER register. If this bind option was not specified, CURRENT SERVER is set to blanks until you issue a CONNECT TO statement.

When you bind a package with DBPROTOCOL(DRDA) and you use a three-part name, DB2 issue the CONNECT statement under the covers. The SQLRULES bind option also determines how DB2 will handle connection management. When using SQLRULES(DB2), you can connect to a database location regardless of where you have already connected. The previous connect is simply put in the current state. However, when using SQLRULES(STD), the control is more strict. If you are already connected to a location, you should use a SET CONNECTION statement to switch between connections.

It's possible that your bind will receive errors if your program contains SQL statements that use more than one DB2. Some of the tables may not be defined at all locations or may have different definitions. It's important to bind your package with SQLERROR(CONTINUE) to allow the bind to ignore these errors. The errors won't cause any problem as long as you execute the SQL against the proper DB2. The same comment applies to the precompiler: the option SQL(ALL) causes the precompiler to flag the statements, but it doesn't prevent the creation of the DBRM.

Beware that when you use DRDA, the remote location processes the SQL statement, and the syntax rules of the target database thus apply. When using a non-z/OS target, you may encounter some differences. This point can work to your advantage, letting you exploit the full capabilities of your target database.

Application Design Options

The DRDA protocol lets an application perform any SQL statement as if the database is local to the application. When a program is connecting to a remote database and issuing several SQL statements, we notice that the application requester already performs some optimization because not all fetches seem to access the remote database. The second fetch finds the data on the client without having to access the server. This concept, called *block fetch*, sends a number of rows in one go when the context permits this to happen without creating data consistency problems.

Let's assume the client program doesn't need any interaction between the start and end. What keeps us from running the entire program, not just the SQL statements, on the server? We just invented the concept of a stored procedure. The program logic and SQL statements are ported to the database server, and the client program simply needs to connect to the database server and start the stored procedure.

Stored Procedures

In the stored procedure programming model, the application logic is moved from the client program to the database server. It is the responsibility of the database server to invoke the stored procedure program and handle the parameters flowing to and from the stored procedure. The actual implementation of the environment where the program runs depends on the platform of deployment. On z/OS, you can configure a stored procedure address space to be controlled by the Workload Manager.

If you don't need the portability of a stored procedure but want to exploit non-DB2 resources such as DL/I databases, sequential files, CICS transactions, or any other resource on z/OS, it's better to develop the stored procedure outside the scope of the Developer Workbench and use your existing application development environment.

Figure 14.1 depicts a configuration that exploits a variety of non-DB2 resources. For more information about stored procedures, see Chapter 13.

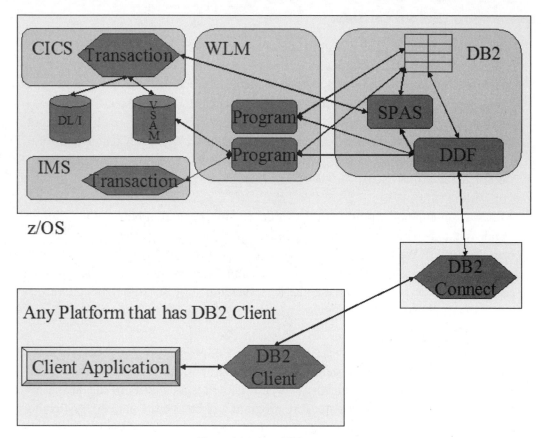

Figure 14.1: Non-DB2 resources

Remote Query Performance

There are many ways to improve the performance of remote queries. In the
following paragraphs, we take a look at some of those options.

OPTIMIZE FOR n ROWS

You can use the OPTIMIZE FOR *n* ROWS clause in distributed applications to limit
the number of rows returned in a DRDA client query block so that only a portion
of the answer set is fetched. This option can also optimize queries that fetch a large
number of rows by letting a client request multiple query blocks from a DRDA
requester in a single network transmission. You use the clause to specify the
number of query blocks to retrieve.

DB2 supports OPTIMIZE FOR *n* ROWS for result sets returned by a SELECT statement or by a stored procedure. DRDA Level 3 is implemented to give the client the ability to specify the number of extra query blocks it wants to receive (instead of the default of one at a time). Any value *n* enables the DRDA server to send multiple query blocks in a single transmission.

DB2 will send *n* number of rows of the result set in each network transmission if the result set fits in a query block. If the rows don't fit in a query block, DB2 will send extra query blocks in the same transmission, up to either the query block limit set for the server (DSNZPARM EXTRASRV) or the query block limit set by the client (DSNZPARM EXTRAREQ, which is also the value in the Distributed Data Management MAXBLKEXT parameter on the DRDA requester). You want to be cautious of these parameters because their default is 100 (query blocks per transmission). Depending on your workload mix, this setting could negatively affect the performance of your applications.

You would want to take advantage of the OPTIMIZE FOR *n* ROWS clause when the value *n* is less than the total number of rows that will fit in a DRDA query block and the application is only going to process *n* rows. You can also significantly reduce elapsed time for large query result sets by using OPTIMIZE FOR *n* ROWS when *n* is greater than the number of rows that can fit in one DRDA query block, because doing so will let the requester retrieve multiple query blocks with each network transmission.

If your DRDA application meets the following criteria, you may want to use OPTIMIZE FOR *n* ROWS.

- Read-only queries fetching a large number of rows
- SQL cursors rarely being closed before fetching an entire result set
- No statements other than FETCH used when the cursor is open
- Multiple cursors defined with OPTIMIZE FOR *n* ROWS that don't issue FETCHes

You don't want to set a large number of query blocks for cursors defined WITH HOLD because if the requester application commits while several blocks are in the network, DB2 buffers the blocks in memory. A WITH HOLD cursor also prevents a thread from going inactive.

Inactive Threads

Access threads that don't hold any cursors are known as *inactive threads*. DB2 supports two types of inactive threads: type 1 and type 2. Type 2 threads are available only for DRDA connections; they use a pool of database threads (which can be switched as needed among connections) and use less storage than type 1. You want to use type 2 inactive threads when possible.

CMTSTAT

The CMTSTAT DSNZPARM affects the creation, disconnection, re-creation, and reuse of active database access threads (DBATs) for distributed connections. For distributed applications that connect via DDF, we advise setting CMTSTAT to INACTIVE (you define this parameter in the DDF THREADS field on the DSNTIPE install panel). This setting, referred to as *DB2 inactive connection support*, lets DB2 separate the DBAT from the connection (at commit time) and reuse the DBAT to process others work while the connection is inactive. The approach is similar to a pooling behavior.

The only drawback to this technique is that it causes an accounting record to be generated when the connection becomes inactive. A large number of accounting records can flood the system management facility (SMF), but you can aggregate these records using DSNZPARMs ACCUMACC and ACCUMID.

A database access thread that is not currently processing a unit of work is called a *pooled thread*. The thread remains pooled, but its connection is released. DB2 always tries to pool database access threads, but in some cases it cannot do so. A thread can be pooled if there is

- a DRDA hop to another location

- a package bound with RELEASE(COMMIT)

- a package bound with RELEASE(DEALLOCATE)

A thread cannot be pooled if

- a held cursor, a held LOB locator, or a package bound with KEEPDYNAMIC(YES) was accessed

- a declared temporary table is active (i.e., the table wasn't explicitly dropped through the DROP TABLE statement or the ONCOMMIT DROP TABLE clause on the DECLARE GLOBAL TEMPORARY TABLE statement)

Displaying Distributed Threads

You can display distributed threads to discover information about their status using the –DISPLAY THREAD command with the LOCATION option. Here's an example of this command:

```
DISPLAY THREAD(*) TYPE(*) LOCATION(*) DETAIL
```

Distributed Application Tuning Guidelines

To ensure optimal performance of your distributed applications, keep the following guidelines in mind.

- Use stored procedures to reduce network traffic.

- Use COMMIT ON RETURN YES to issue an implicit commit for a stored procedure when a return from the CALL statement occurs.

- Commit frequently.

- The fewer SQL statements, the better.

- Use the SQL RELEASE statement to release the remote connection at commit time, and specify DISCONNECT(EXPLICIT).

- Use the CURRENT RULES of DB2 (not STD special register so DB2 can return multiple blocks of data to the program when requesting LOB data.

- Use DRDA-type connections instead of the DB2 private protocol.

Connection Pooling

The DB2 Connect product lets you connect remote clients to the DDF of DB2 for z/OS to process remote requests for data. The DB2 Connect server products, such as DB2 Connect Enterprise Edition, often provide database connections for thousands of simultaneous client requests. Establishing and severing connections to the database server can be a very resource-intensive process that adversely affects both database server and DB2 Connect server performance.

This problem is especially evident in Web environments, where each visit to a Web page can require building a new connection to the database server, performing a query, and terminating a connection. To reduce this overhead, DB2 Connect server products use *connection pooling* to maintain open connections to the database in a readily accessible pool.

Connection pooling is one of the methodologies DB2 Connect uses to map the DDF connection and manage DB2 thread resources. This technique lets subsequent connections reuse an established connection infrastructure. When a DB2 Connect instance is started, a pool of coordinating agents is created. When a connection request arrives, an agent is assigned to the request. The agent connects to the DB2 server, and a thread is created in DB2. When the application issues a disconnect request, the agent does not pass this request to the DB2 server; instead, the agent is put back into the pool. The agent in the pool still owns its connection to the DB2 server and the corresponding DB2 thread. When another application issues a connect request, the agent is assigned to the new application. To ensure secure operation, user identity information is passed along to the DB2 thread which, in turn, performs user authentication.

DB2 Connect's connection pooling provides a significant performance improvement in such environments. DB2 Connect maintains open connections to the database in an available pool. When a client requests a connection, it can be provided from this pool of ready connections. Connection pooling significantly reduces the overhead typically spent on opening and closing these connections.

Connection pooling is transparent to applications connecting to the host (z/OS) through DB2 Connect. When an application requests disconnection from the host, DB2 Connect drops the inbound connection with the application but keeps the outbound connection to the host in a pool. When a new application requests a connection, DB2 Connect uses one from the existing pool. Using the already-present connection reduces overall connection time as well as the high CPU connection cost on the host.

DB2 Connect agents can be in one of two states: active or idle. An agent is active when it is executing work for an application. Once this work is completed the agent, goes into an idle state, awaiting further work from the same or a different application. All idle agents are kept together in what is known as the *idle agent pool*.

Configuration Settings

On the DB2 z/OS host server side, several DSNZPARM help configure and manage these connections:

- **MAXDBAT.** Maximum number of distributed threads

- **POOLINAC.** Pool thread timeout

- **CONDBAT.** Maximum number of DDF threads

The DB2 Connect product also provides setting for managing the pooled connections:

- **MAXAGENTS.** Maximum number of worker agents.

- **MAX_COORDAGENTS.** Maximum number of active coordinator agents. Once this number is exceeded, new connections will fail with error SQLCODE SQL1226.

- **NUM_POOLAGENTS.** This parameter indicates the maximum number of idle agents you want the system to maintain. The agent pool includes inactive agents and idle agents. For improved performance, configure NUM_POOLAGENTS to equal the value of the MAXAGENTS parameter, or the average number of clients. Setting this parameter to 0 (zero) is equivalent to turning off the connection pooling feature.

- **NUM_INITAGENTS.** This parameter determines how many idle agents should be created at startup time. These idle agents initially will not have connections to the host database server. When a client requests a connection to the host, DB2 Connect tries to obtain an agent from among those in the pool that have a connection to the host database server. If this attempt fails, DB2 Connect tries to find an available agent in the idle pool. If the pool is empty, DB2 Connect creates a new agent.

The DB2 registry variable DB2CONNECT_IN_APP_PROCESS enables applications running on the same machine as a DB2 Connect server product to either have DB2 Connect run within the application process (the default behavior) or have the application connect to DB2 Connect and then have the host connection run within an agent. For an application to use connection pooling, the connections to the host must be made from within the DB2 Connect server product agents, and thus DB2CONNECT_IN_APP_PROCESS must be set to NO.

Summary

Access to DB2 from remote locations is a necessary part of most application environments. DB2 provides that capability through various means. You can use the Distributed Data Facility of DB2 to enable access to data held by other DBMSs or makes your DB2 data accessible to other systems. A DB2 application program can use SQL to access data at DBMSs other than the DB2 at which the application's plan is bound.

We looked at the two methods DB2 provides for accessing data at remote application servers: DRDA and DB2 private protocol access (which is being phased out in Version 9). We also looked at the use of three-part names and the DB2 CONNECT statement. We covered some of the ways to improve performance of remote queries, and discussed thread pooling and connection pooling topics in terms of use and setup.

Additional Resources

DRDA information: *http://www.opengroup.com*
IBM DB2 9 Administration Guide (SC18-9840)
IBM DB2 9 Installation Guide (GC18-9846)
IBM DB2 9 Performance Monitoring and Tuning Guide (SC18-9851)
IBM DB2 9 SQL Reference (SC18-9854)
IBM DB2 Connect Version 9 Users Guide (SC10-4229)

Open Group Technical Standard in DRDA Volume 1: Distributed Relational Database Architecture (DRDA) - Document number C911

SNA LU 6.2 Peer Protocols Reference (SC31-6808)

Practice Questions

Question 1

Which of the following DSNZPARMs is used to allow DB2 to separate the DBAT from the connection (at commit time) and reuse the DBAT to process other work while the connection is inactive?

○ A. CMTSTAT

○ B. CTHREAD

○ C. MAXDBAT

○ D. IDFORE

Question 2

When should you consider using OPTIMIZE FOR *n* ROWS for a DRDA application?

○ A. SQL cursors closed before fetching the entire result set

○ B. Multiple cursors defined with OPTIMIZE FOR *n* ROWS not issuing FETCHes

○ C. Updatable cursors

○ D. Mass insert processes

Question 3

The original DRDA specifications identified four different levels of support. Which of the following is not currently implemented?

○ A. Remote request

○ B. Remote unit of work (RUW)

○ C. Distributed unit of work (DUW)

○ D. Distributed request

Question 4

The following output is the result of which DB2 command?

```
DSNL080I  -DBT5 DSNLTDDF DISPLAY DDF REPORT FOLLOWS:
DSNL081I STATUS=STARTD
DSNL082I LOCATION            LUNAME            GENERICLU
DSNL083I DBT5               TU0.BSYSDBT5       -NONE
DSNL084I IPADDR          TCPPORT RESPORT
DSNL085I 10.35.4.16       2590     2591
DSNL086I SQL    DOMAIN=t390.rpc.com
DSNL086I RESYNC DOMAIN=t390.rpc.com
DSNL090I DT=A  CONDBAT=     64 MDBAT=    64
DSNL092I ADBAT=    0 QUEDBAT=      0 IN1DBAT=  0 CONQUED=       0
DSNL093I DSCDBAT=       0 IN2CONS=      0
DSNL099I DSNLTDDF DISPLAY DDF REPORT COMPLETE
```

O A. –DISPLAY LOCATION

O B. –DISPLAY DDF

O C. –DISPLAY THREAD

O D. –DISPLAY DISTRIBUTED

Question 5

Which of the following catalog tables is not part of the communications database (CDB)?

O A. SYSIBM.IPLIST

O B. SYSIBM.MODESELECT

O C. SYSIBM.LULIST

O D. SYSIBM.CONNECTIONS

Answers

Question 1

The correct answer is **A**, CMTSTAT. This DSNZPARM affects the creation, disconnection, re-creation, and reuse of active DBAT threads for distributed connections.

Question 2

The correct answer is **B**, when you have multiple cursors defined with OPTIMIZE FOR *n* ROWS not issuing FETCHes. Use of the clause should be considered if your application meets the following criteria:

- Read-only queries fetching a large number of rows

- SQL cursors rarely being closed before fetching the entire result set

- No statements other than FETCH used when a cursor is open

Question 3

The correct answer is **D**, distributed request. This level supports a distributed request to two or more remote DBMSs residing on the same or different locations. The implementation of a standard technique to solve the distributed request problem is quite complicated, requiring the addition of optimization-related concepts such as network performance and estimation of the cost of the remote SQL component.

Question 4

The correct answer is **B**, –DISPLAY DDF. This DB2 command lists all the information required to set up the connection to DB2.

Question 5

The correct answer is **D**, SYSBIM.CONNECTIONS. The DB2 catalog includes the communications database, which contains several tables that hold information about connections with remote systems. These tables include

- SYSIBM.IPLIST

- SYSIBM.IPNAMES

- SYSIBM.LOCATIONS

- SYSIBM.LULIST

- SYSIBM.LUMODES

- SYSIBM.LUNAMES

- SYSIBM.MODESELECT

- SYSIBM.USERNAMES

Advanced Functionality

In This Chapter

- ✔ Triggers
- ✔ User-defined functions
- ✔ Table functions
- ✔ User-defined data types (distinct types)
- ✔ Object-relational extensions
- ✔ LOBs, XML, and extenders

This chapter covers some of the more powerful features of DB2's SQL language. We discuss the extended programming features, user-defined functions, and table functions along with triggers and user-defined data types (UDTs). We also review the object-relational extensions used to support these features and take a look at how to implement and use large objects and DB2 extenders.

Triggers

A *trigger* is a set of actions that will be executed when a defined event occurs. SQL INSERT, UPDATE, and DELETE statements can be triggering events. In addition, execution of a MERGE statement can cause the activation of a trigger as a result of an underlying INSERT or UPDATE.

You define triggers for a specific table or view (for INSTEAD OF triggers). Once defined, a trigger is automatically *active*. A given table can have multiple triggers defined for it; in this case, the order of trigger activation is based on the trigger creation timestamp (i.e., the order in which the triggers were created). Triggers can be fired based on the execution of statements (INSERT, UPDATE, DELETE); based on the modification, creation, or deletion of rows; or if specific columns of a table change. DB2 stores trigger definitions in two DB2 catalog tables:

- SYSIBM.SYSTRIGGERS

    » One row for each trigger

    » TEXT column contains full text of CREATE TRIGGER statement

- SYSIBM.SYSPACKAGE

    » One row for each trigger package

    » TYPE column set to T to indicate a trigger package

Trigger Uses

Some of the uses of a trigger include the following:

- **Data validation.** Ensures that a new data value is within the proper range. This function is similar to table-check constraints but is a more flexible data-validation mechanism.

- **Data conditioning.** Implemented using triggers that fire before data record modification. This technique lets the new data value be modified or conditioned to a predefined value.

- **Data integrity.** Can be used to ensure that cross-table dependencies are maintained.

The triggered action could involve updating data records in related tables. This use is similar to referential integrity but it is a more flexible alternative.

You can also use triggers to enforce business rules, create or edit column values, validate input data, and maintain summary or cross-reference tables. Triggers enable enhanced enterprise and business functionality, faster application development, and global enforcement of business rules.

Limited only by your imagination, triggers give you a way to obtain control in order to perform an action whenever a table's data is modified. For example, a single trigger invoked by an update on a financial table could invoke a user-defined function (UDF) and/or call a stored procedure to invoke another external action, which could trigger an e-mail to a pager to notify the DBA of a serious condition. Far-fetched? No, applications such as this one are already being done.

Trigger Activation

You can define a trigger to *fire* (be activated) in one of three ways:

- A *before trigger* fires for each row in the set of affected rows before the triggering SQL statement is executed. Therefore, the trigger body sees the new data values before anything is inserted or updated into the table.

- An *after trigger* fires for each row in the set of affected rows after the statement has successfully been completed (depending on the defined granularity). Therefore, the trigger body sees the table as being in a consistent state (i.e., all transactions have been completed).

- An *instead of trigger* fires instead of the INSERT, UPDATE, or DELETE statement that activates the trigger. Unlike the other triggers, this trigger type can be defined only against a view.

Another important feature of triggers is that they can fire other triggers (or the same trigger) or other constraints. Triggers that behave this way are known as *cascading triggers*.

There is currently a safe limit to the cascading of triggers, stored procedures, and UDFs: an execution-time nesting depth of 16. This limit prevents the endless cascading that would otherwise be possible. There is a *big* performance concern here because if the 17th level is reached, an SQLCODE of –724 is set, but all 16 levels are backed out. That could be a significant problem and not something you want to see. The real issue here is processes that are executed outside the control of

DB2; such processes wouldn't be backed out, and you might have difficulty determining what was changed.

During the execution of a trigger, the new and old data values can be accessible to the trigger, depending on the nature of the trigger (before or after). By using triggers you can

- reduce the amount of application development and speed up development. Because triggers are stored in DB2 itself and are processed by DB2, you don't need to code the triggers or their actions into your applications.

- provide a global environment for your business rules. Because triggers must be defined only once and then are stored in the database, they are available to all applications executing against the database.

- reduce the maintenance of your applications. Because the trigger is handled by DB2 and is stored in the database itself, any changes to the trigger due to changes in your environment need to occur in only one, not multiple, applications.

Creating Triggers

To define a trigger, you use the CREATE TRIGGER statement, which contains many options. The primary options specify the language of the trigger and whether the trigger is a before trigger or an after trigger, a row trigger or a statement trigger, or an instead of trigger. SQL is currently the only language option, but that situation will probably change in the future.

The phrase MODE DB2SQL defines the execution mode of the trigger. You must specify this phrase for each trigger to ensure that an existing application won't be negatively impacted if DB2 adds alternative execution modes for triggers in the future. You can have up to 12 types of triggers on a single table. Figure 15.1 depicts the different trigger types.

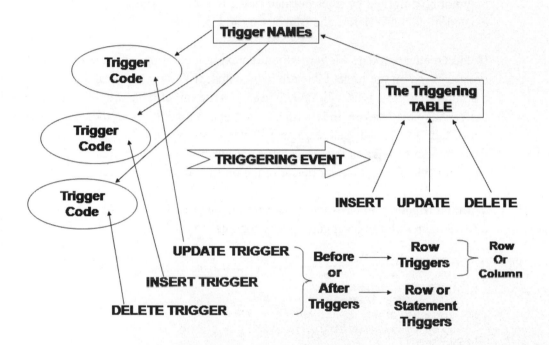

Figure 15.1: Trigger types

Triggers are invoked in the order in which you create them! DB2 records a timestamp when each trigger is created (and re-created). A DROP and (re)CREATE of a trigger can completely mess up your process by changing the order in which DB2 executes the triggers. Be careful! If the order of trigger execution matters for your process and you need to re-create one trigger, you should drop and then re-create all the triggers in the desired execution order.

When you add triggers, rows that are in violation of a newly added trigger are not rejected. When a trigger is added to a table that already has existing rows, it will not cause any triggered actions to be activated. If the trigger is designed to enforce some type of integrity constraint on the data rows in the table, those constraints may not be enforced by rules defined in the trigger (or held true) for the rows that existed in the table before the trigger was added.

If you create an update trigger without an explicit column list, packages with an update usage on the target table are invalidated. If you create an update trigger with a column list, packages with update usage on the target table are invalidated only if the package also has an update usage on at least one column in the column-name list of the CREATE TRIGGER statement. If you create an insert trigger, packages that have an insert usage on the target table are invalidated. If you create a delete trigger, packages that have a delete usage on the target table are invalidated.

Within a trigger, you have access to a lot of functionality. For example, you can use a CASE expression in a trigger, as shown here:

```
BEGIN ATOMIC
   VALUES CASE
      WHEN condition
         THEN something
      WHEN other condition
         THEN something else   END
END;
```

The best way to understand the use of triggers is to see some in action. The DB2 sample database contains many relationships that can be maintained using triggers.

After Trigger

The following example defines a trigger to add $100 to the value of the BONUS column in the EMP table when the employee has put in more than 100 work units on projects. We've named the trigger CHKBONUS. Once this trigger is created, it is active.

```
CREATE TRIGGER CHKBONUS
   AFTER INSERT ON EMPPROJACT
   REFERENCING NEW AS n
   FOR EACH ROW MODE DB2SQL
WHEN ((SELECT SUM(EMPTIME)
      FROM   EMPPROJACT
```

```
        WHERE  EMPNO = N.EMPNO) > 100)
begin atomic
UPDATE emp
  SET bonus = bonus + 100;
END!
```

The CHKBONUS trigger is an AFTER, INSERT, and FOR EACH ROW trigger. Every time a row is inserted into the EMPPROJACT table, this trigger fires. The trigger body section performs an UPDATE statement to set the value of the BONUS column for the newly inserted row. The column is populated with the current bonus plus 100 dollars.

Remember that a trigger defined against one table can modify other tables in the trigger body.

Before Trigger

A before trigger is activated before the trigger operation (INSERT, UPDATE, or DELETE) has been completed. This type of trigger is useful for three purposes:

- To condition data
- To provide default values
- To enforce data value constraints dynamically

The following before trigger ensures that any employee who is going to be assigned a management position has put in at least 100 hours on projects in that department.

```
CREATE TRIGGER CHKHOURS
  NO CASCADE BEFORE UPDATE OF MGRNO ON DEPT
  REFERENCING NEW AS N
  FOR EACH ROW MODE DB2SQL
WHEN ((SELECT SUM(A.EMPTIME)
     FROM   EMPPROJACT A
     INNER JOIN
          PROJ B
     ON    A.PROJNO = B.PROJNO
```

```
            INNER JOIN
                    DEPT C
            ON      C.DEPTNO = B.DEPTNO
            WHERE   A.EMPNO = N.MGRNO
            ) < 100)
    BEGIN ATOMIC
    SIGNAL SQLSTATE '70003'
        ('Not Enough Hours for Management!');
    END!
```

If the assigned manager has not put in the 100 hours on projects in the target department, the SQL UPDATE statement will actually fail with an SQLSTATE of 70003 and the SQL diagnostic message "Not Enough Hours for Management!"

INSTEAD OF Triggers

An INSTEAD OF trigger is a trigger that is executed instead of the INSERT, UPDATE, or DELETE statement that activates the trigger. You can define this type of trigger only against a view, and they are used to insert, update, and delete data in complex views—that is, views defined on expressions or multiple tables. Such views are often read-only; in these cases, an INSTEAD OF TRIGGER can make insert, update, and delete operations against a read-only view possible. You can define INSTEAD OF triggers not only on read-only views but on any complex view for which you want to dictate exactly how DB2 is to perform the insert, update, or delete operation against one or more of the base tables of the view.

To be able to insert, update, and delete against a complex view, you simply need to define one or more INSTEAD OF triggers. Suppose you have the following view defined within the DB2 sample database.

```
CREATE VIEW EMPV
(EMPNO, FIRSTNME, MIDINIT, LASTNAME, PHONENO, HIREDATE, DEPTNAME) AS
SELECT EMPNO, FIRSTNME, MIDINIT, LASTNAME,
        PHONENO, HIREDATE, DEPTNAME
FROM    EMP A
INNER JOIN
        DEPT B
ON      A.WORKDEPT = B.DEPTNO;
```

This view is a read-only view because it is a join between two tables. Therefore, you cannot delete from the view. If you want to be able to delete from this view, you can create an INSTEAD OF trigger to perform this operation:

```
CREATE TRIGGER EMPV_DELETE
INSTEAD OF DELETE ON EMPV
REFERENCING OLD AS OLDEMP
FOR EACH ROW MODE DB2SQL
DELETE
FROM    EMP E
WHERE   E.EMPNO = OLDEMP.EMPNO;
```

You could define similar triggers against the EMPV view to supports inserts and updates to the view.

Note that INSTEAD OF triggers can be row triggers only, and they cannot contain a WHEN condition.

Row and Statement Triggers

To understand the concept of trigger granularity, you need to understand the rows affected by the triggering operations. The set of affected rows contains all rows that are deleted, inserted, or updated by the triggering operations.

Row Triggers

You use the keyword FOR EACH ROW to activate the trigger as many times as the number of rows in the set of affected rows. This type of trigger is said to have *row granularity*. The preceding example shows a row trigger. This type of trigger is activated only if one or more rows of data change.

Statement Triggers

You use the keyword FOR EACH STATEMENT to activate the trigger once for the triggering operation. This type of trigger is said to have *statement granularity*. Use of FOR EACH STATEMENT is allowed only for AFTER triggers. A statement trigger is activated just once for each triggering statement, and it will be activated whether or not data changes. The following is an example of a statement trigger that records application-related audit information about an update.

```
CREATE TRIGGER AUDIT_A
AFTER UPDATE ON EMP
FOR EACH STATEMENT MODE DB2SQL
```

```
INSERT INTO EMPX (UID, ACTION, TS)
VALUES (CURRENT SQLID, 'U', CURRENT TIMESTAMP);
```

Transition Variables and Tables

Two constructs, transition variables and transition tables, give triggers a way to access row data as it exists before and after the triggering operation is executed.

Transition Variables

Transition variables permit row triggers to access columns of affected row data to see the row data as it existed before and after the triggering operation. To implement these variables, you include a REFERENCING clause in the definition, with OLD specifying the column values before the change and NEW specifying the column values after the change:

```
REFERENCING OLD AS OLD_ACCOUNTS
            NEW AS NEW_ACCOUNTS
```

The following example uses transition variables to replicate data from the DEPT table to the EDEPT table when an update to the DEPT table occurs. However, the trigger will only replicate the data if the LOCATION column has changed in value (selective auditing).

```
CREATE TRIGGER TR1
    AFTER UPDATE ON DEPT
    REFERENCING OLD AS OLDROW
    REFERENCING NEW AS NEWROW
    FOR EACH ROW MODE DB2SQL
WHEN (OLDROW.LOCATION <> NEWROW.LOCATION)
BEGIN ATOMIC
    INSERT INTO EDEPT
    VALUES (OLDROW.DEPTNO, OLDROW.DEPTNAME, OLDROW.MGRNO,
            OLDROW.ADMRDEPT, OLDROW.LOCATION,
            DEFAULT, CURRENT TIMESTAMP);
END!
```

Whenever an update is made to the DEPT table, the old value of the location of the department, referenced in the before trigger transition variable as OLDROW.LOCATION, is checked against the new value of the location of the department, referenced as NEWROW.LOCATION. Only when the value has changed will the trigger action be executed and the insert occur.

Transition Tables

Transition tables enable AFTER triggers to access a set of affected rows and see how they were before and after the triggering operation. As with transition variables, you implement transition tables using the REFERENCING clause in the trigger definition:

```
REFERENCING OLD_TABLE AS OLD_ACCT_TABL
          NEW_TABLE AS NEW_ACCT_TABLE
```

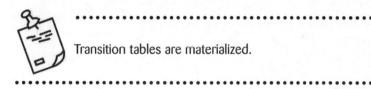

Transition tables are materialized.

Transition tables enable an SQL statement embedded in the trigger body to access the entire set of affected data in the state it was in before or after the change. In the following example, a fullselect reads the entire set of changed rows to pass qualifying data to a user-defined function.

```
CREATE TRIGGER EMPMRGR
AFTER UPDATE ON EMP
REFERENCING NEW TABLE AS NTABLE
FOR EACH STATEMENT MODE DB2SQL
BEGIN ATOMIC
   SELECT SALARYALERT(EMPNO, SALARY)
   FROM NTABLE
   WHERE SALARY > 150000;
END!
```

A trigger can also pass transition tables to stored procedures and UDFs that are invoked within the body of the trigger. Rather than passing the actual table as a parameter, the trigger passes a table locator, which can then be used to establish a cursor within the stored procedure or UDF.

A function that accepts a table as a paeameter could look like this:

```
CREATE FUNCTION SALARYALERT (TABLE LIKE EMP AS LOCATOR)
   RETURNS INTEGER
   EXTERNAL NAME SALERT
   PARAMETER STYLE DB2SQL
   LANGUAGE C;
```

The C language program would declare a cursor against the transition table by referencing the locator variable that was passed as a parameter in place of a table reference:

```
DECLARE C1 CURSOR FOR
  SELECT EMPNO, SALARY
  FROM TABLE(:LOC1 LIKE EMP)
  WHERE SALARY > 150000;
```

Once the input locator parameter is accepted into the :LOC1 variable, the cursor can be opened and processed.

Allowable Combinations

Although many different combinations of trigger options are available, not all are compatible. Table 15.1 lists the valid combinations for trigger options.

Table 15.1: Trigger option combinations

Granularity	Activation time	Trigger operation	Transition variables allowed	Transition tables allowed
ROW	BEFORE	INSERT	NEW	None
		UPDATE	OLD, NEW	
		DELETE	OLD	
	AFTER	INSERT	NEW	NEW_TABLE
		UPDATE	OLD	OLD_TABLE, NEW_TABLE
		DELETE	OLD, NEW	OLD_TABLE
	INSTEAD OF	INSERT	NEW	NEW_TABLE
		UPDATE	OLD, NEW	OLD_TABLE, NEW_TABLE
		DELETE	OLD	OLD_TABLE
STATEMENT	BEFORE	Invalid		Invalid
	AFTER	INSERT	None	NEW_TABLE
		UPDATE		OLD_TABLE, NEW_TABLE
		DELETE		OLD_TABLE

Trigger Packages

When a trigger is created, DB2 creates a *trigger package*. This package differs from the packages created for application programs (for more information about packages, see Chapter 11). Trigger packages can be re-bound locally, but you cannot bind them (this takes place automatically during creation). The package can be re-bound only with the REBIND TRIGGER PACKAGE command, and you can use this command to change subsets of default bind options (CURRENTDATA, EXPLAIN, FLAG, ISOLATION, RELEASE). You might want to rebind a trigger package for performance reasons. For example, you might want to alter the ISOLATION and CURRENTDATA options to improve concurrency or change the EXPLAIN option to YES to expose the access paths within the trigger package. For more information about the bind options, consult Chapter 11. For information about EXPLAIN, see Chapter 17.

Rebinding trigger packages after creation is also useful for picking up new access paths.

You cannot copy, free, or drop trigger packages. To delete a trigger package, issue the DROP TRIGGER SQL statement.

The qualifier of the trigger name determines the package collection. For static SQL, the authorization ID of the QUALIFIER bind option is the qualifier; for dynamic SQL, the CURRENT SQLID is the qualifier.

Trigger Invalidations

Triggers can detect and stop invalid updates in a couple of ways, by using either the SIGNAL SQLSTATE statement or the RAISE_ERROR function.

SIGNAL SQLSTATE

SIGNAL SQLSTATE is a SQL statement that causes an error to be returned to the application with a specified SQLSTATE code and a specific message to stop processing. You can use this statement only as a triggered SQL statement within a trigger, controlling it with a WHEN clause. Here's an example that demonstrates use of the SIGNAL statement:

```
WHEN NEW_ACCT.AMOUNT < (OLD_ACCT.AMOUNT)
    SIGNAL SQLSTATE '99001' ('Bad amount field')
```

RAISE_ERROR

RAISE_ERROR isn't a statement but a built-in function that causes the statement that includes it to return an error with a specific SQLSTATE, SQLCODE –438, and a message. It does basically the same thing as the SIGNAL statement, and you can use it wherever an expression can be used. The RAISE_ERROR function always returns null with an undefined data type. RAISE_ERROR is most useful in CASE expressions, especially when the CASE expression is used in a stored procedure. The next example shows a CASE expression with the RAISE_ERROR function.

```
VALUES (CASE
    WHEN NEW_ACCT.AMOUNT < OLD_ACCT.AMOUNT
    THEN RAISE_ERROR('99001', 'Bad amount field'))
```

Forcing a Rollback

If you use the SIGNAL statement to raise an error condition, a rollback will also be performed to back out the changes made by an SQL statement as well as any changes caused by the trigger, such as cascading effects resulting from a referential relationship. You can use SIGNAL in either before or after triggers. Other statements in the program can be either committed or rolled back.

Performance Issues

Recursive triggers are updates applied by a trigger that cause the same trigger to fire off again. Such triggers can easily lead to loops and can be very complex statements, but some applications require their use to handle related rows. You will need code to stop the trigger.

Ordering of multiple triggers can be an issue because triggers on the same table are activated in creation order (identified in the creation timestamp). The interaction among triggers and referential constraints can also be an issue, because the order of processing can have a significant effect on the results produced.

When you invoke stored procedures and UDFs from triggers, you face some performance and manageability concerns. Triggers can include only SQL but can call stored procedures and UDFs, which are user-written and therefore have many implications for integrity and performance. Transition tables can be passed to stored procedures and UDFs, too.

Trigger cascading occurs when a trigger can modify the triggering table or another table. Triggers can be activated at the same level or at different levels; when activated at different levels, cascading occurs. Cascading is possible only for after triggers and can occur for UDFs, stored procedures, and triggers for up to 16 levels.

Monitoring Triggers

You can use various ways to monitor the different actions of triggers. The statistics and accounting reports show statistics such as

- the number of times a trigger was activated

- the number of times a row trigger was activated

- the number of times an SQL error occurred during the execution of a triggered action

The traces yield other details. For example, IFCID 16 provides information about the materialization of a work file in support of a transition table, with TR signifying the transition table for triggers. Other information in IFCID 16 includes the depth level of the trigger (0–16), with level 0 indicating that no triggers exist. You can also find the type of SQL that invoked the trigger:

- I = INSERT

- U = INSERT into a transition table because of an update

- D = INSERT into a transition table because of a delete

The trace also reports the type of referential integrity that caused an insert into a transition table for a trigger: S for SET NULL (which can occur when the SQL type is U) or C for CASCADE DELETE (which can occur when the SQL type is D).

If a transition table had to be scanned for a trigger, you can find this occurrence in IFCID 17: TR indicates a transition-table scan for a trigger.

Catalog Information

The SYSIBM.SYSTRIGGERS catalog table contains information about the triggers defined in your databases. To find all the triggers defined on a particular table, the characteristics of each trigger, and the order in which they are executed, you can issue the following query.

```
SELECT DISTINCT SCHEMA, NAME, TRIGTIME, TRIGEVENT,
       GRANULARITY, CREATEDTS
FROM SYSIBM.SYSTRIGGERS
WHERE TBNAME = table-name
  AND TBOWNER = table-owner
ORDER BY CREATEDTS
```

You can obtain the actual text of the trigger with the following statement.

```
SELECT TEXT, SEQNO
FROM SYSIBM.SYSTRIGGERS
WHERE SCHEMA = schema_name
  AND NAME = trigger_name
ORDER BY SEQNO
```

Triggers vs. Table-Check Constraints

If a trigger and a table-check constraint can enforce the same rule, it's better to use a table-check constraint to enforce business rules. You would want to explore the use of triggers only when a constraint is not enough to enforce a business rule. Constraints and declarative RI are more useful when you have only one state to enforce in a business rule. Although triggers are more powerful than table-check constraints and can be more extensive in terms of rule enforcement, constraints can be better optimized by DB2.

DB2 enforces table-check constraints for all existing data at the time of creation and for all statements affecting the data. You define a table-check constraint on a populated table using the ALTER TABLE statement, and the value of the CURRENT RULES special register is DB2. Constraints offer a few other advantages over triggers. For example, they are written in a less procedural way than triggers and are better optimized. They prohibit any kind of statement from placing data into an invalid state, whereas a trigger applies only to a specific kind of statement, such as an update or delete.

Triggers are more powerful than check constraints because they can enforce several rules that constraints cannot. You can use triggers to capture rules that involve different states of data—for example, when you need to know the state of the data before and after a calculation.

Triggers and Declarative RI

Trigger operations may result from changes made to enforce DB2-enforced referential constraints. For example, if you're deleting a row from the EMPLOYEE table that causes propagated deletes to the PAYROLL table through referential constraints, the delete triggers defined on the PAYROLL table are subsequently executed. The delete triggers are activated as a result of the referential constraint defined on the EMPLOYEE table. This may or may not be the desired result, so you need to be aware of cascading effects when using triggers.

Performing Actions Outside a Database

Triggers can contain only SQL, but through SQL you can invoke stored procedures and UDFs. Because stored procedures and UDFs are user-written code, you can perform almost any activity from a triggered event. The action causing a trigger may need a message sent to a special place via e-mail. The trigger might be a before trigger written to handle complex referential integrity checks, which could involve checking whether data exists in another non-DB2 data store. Through the use of stored procedures and UDFs, the power of a trigger is almost unlimited.

Triggers and UDFs

User-defined functions can help centralize rules to ensure that they are enforced in the same way in current and future applications. To invoke a UDF in a trigger, you must use the VALUES clause. The following example shows how to invoke a UDF in a trigger. In this example, we use the UDF invocation to set a new table value. Although this type of action is valid for UDFs, it is not possible to pass new values or result sets back from a stored procedure call within a trigger.

```
BEGIN ATOMIC
SET NEWROW.NUMMTHS = (TOTMON(START_DATE,END_DATE));
END!
```

In the next example, PAGE_DBA is a user-written program, perhaps in C or Java, that formulates a message and then triggers a process that sends the message to a pager. By using these kinds of UDFs in triggers, it is possible for a trigger to perform any kind of task and not just be limited to SQL.

```
BEGIN ATOMIC
   VALUES(PAGE_DBA('Table spaces:' CONCAT TS.NAME,
      'needs to be reorged NOW!'));
END!
```

We discuss UDFs in more detail later in the chapter.

Triggers and Stored Procedures

Like a normal stored procedure call, the invocation of a stored procedure within a trigger is via a CALL statement. It's extremely important to note that while transition variables and tables can be passed from a trigger to a stored procedure, output parameters and result sets cannot be passed from the stored procedure back to the trigger. If you need data returned to a transition variable, you should use a UDF. Also, because error information returned in stored procedure parameters isn't processed by the trigger, it's extremely wise to use the parameter style SQL for the stored procedure. In that way, the stored procedure can return an SQLSTATE to the trigger.

The following example illustrates a stored procedure call from within the body of a trigger.

```
BEGIN ATOMIC
   CALL SPCICS1(NEWROW.ACCT_ID, NEWROW.CUST_ID, NEWROW.AMOUNT);
END!
```

Dropping Triggers

You can drop triggers using the DROP TRIGGER statement. If the table on which a trigger is defined is dropped, so is the trigger. Regardless of what caused the trigger to be dropped, the information about the trigger is removed from SYSIBM.SYSTRIGGERS and SYSIBM.SYSPACKAGE. It's a good idea to keep a copy of the trigger code so you can re-create it if the trigger is dropped.

Object-Relational Extensions

With the object extensions of DB2, you can incorporate object-oriented concepts and methodologies into your relational database by extending DB2 with richer sets of data types and functions. With these extensions, you can store instances of object-oriented data types in columns of tables and operate on them using functions in SQL statements. In addition, you can control the types of operations users can perform on those data types. The object extensions DB2 provides are

- distinct types
- UDFs
- large objects

Schemas serve as qualifiers for the object-relational extensions as well as for stored procedures. You use schemas to qualify objects within DB2, including

- user-defined data types
- UDFs
- stored procedures
- sequences
- roles
- triggers

Schemas

All the objects qualified by the same schema name can be thought of as a group of related objects. A schema name has a maximum length of eight bytes. The schema name SYSIBM is used for built-in data types and built-in functions, and SYSPROC is used for some stored procedures delivered by IBM in support of the Control Center as well as Visual Explain.

Schema Names

You can specify a schema name explicitly when referencing an object in a CREATE, ALTER, DROP, or COMMENT ON statement. If the object is unqualified and the statement is dynamically prepared, DB2 uses the SQL authorization ID contained in the CURRENT SQLID special register for the schema name of the objects.

Schema Privileges

Certain authorities are associated with schemas. Schema privileges include CREATIN, ALTERIN, and DROPIN, which, respectively, let you create, alter, or drop objects in the identified schema. If the schema name is an authorization ID, that authorization ID has these privileges implicitly.

PATH Bind Option

The PATH bind option is applicable to the BIND PLAN, BIND PACKAGE, REBIND PLAN, and REBIND PACKAGE commands. DB2 uses the list of specified schemas to resolve unqualified references to user-defined distinct types and UDFs in static SQL statements. This list is also used to resolve unqualified stored procedure names when the SQL CALL statement specifies a literal for the procedure name. The list specifies an ordered list of schemas to be searched to resolve these unqualified references.

CURRENT PATH Special Register

There is also a corresponding special register for the PATH. The SET CURRENT PATH statement changes the value of the PATH special register. DB2 uses this PATH special register the same way it uses the PATH bind option: to resolve unqualified references in dynamic SQL. The CURRENT PATH special register can also be used to resolve unqualified stored procedure names in CALL host-variable statements. You use the PATH bind option to set the initial value for this special register. SYSIBM and SYSPROC needn't be specified as part of the PATH; they are implicitly assumed as the first schema.

CURRENT SCHEMA Special Register

The CURRENT SCHEMA special register is used to qualify all unqualified object names (tables included) in dynamically prepared SQL statements. It is initially the value of CURRENT SQLID until it is changed.

User-Defined Data Types

We looked briefly at what user-defined data types are and how they are implemented using Data Definition Language in Chapter 4. In this section, we take a closer look at UDTs and some of their benefits.

By using UDTs, you can avoid writing excess code to support data typing that is not included in the DB2 product. You enable DB2 to do *strong-typing*, which says that only functions and operations defined on the UDT can be applied to instances of the UDT. This support is beneficial for applications because you don't have to code for comparison errors.

Once you define a UDT, column definitions can reference that type during the issuing of a CREATE or ALTER statement the same as they would any DB2 built-in data type. If a distinct type is specified without a schema name, DB2 resolves the distinct type using the CURRENT SCHEMA special register or by searching schemas in the current path.

UDTs enable you to use DB2 built-in data types in special ways. Built off the DB2 built-in types, UDTs let you extend these types and declare specialized usage on them. DB2 then enforces these rules by performing only the kinds of computations and comparisons you've defined for the new data type.

Defining UDTs

To use a UDT, you must first create it. You do so by using one of the DB2 built-in types as a base. You create a UDT using the CREATE TYPE statement as shown here:

```
CREATE TYPE distinct-type-name
    AS source-data-type
    WITH COMPARISONS
```

The name of the distinct type is a two-part name that must be unique within the DB2 subsystem. The qualifier is a schema name. The distinct type shares a common internal representation with its source data type. However, the distinct type is considered an independent data type that is distinct from the others.

LONG VARHCAR and LONG VARGRAPHIC cannot be used as source types.

An instance of a distinct type can be compared only with another instance of the same distinct type. The WITH COMPARISONS clause is to allow for comparison only between the same distinct type. This phrase is required if the source data type is not a LOB type, such as BLOB, CLOB, or DBCLOB. Comparisons for these types are not allowed.

If you specify WITH COMPARISONS on a distinct type with a LOB source type, you'll receive a warning message, but the comparisons are still not allowed.

Casting

Two operations are allowed on distinct types: comparisons and casting. You can compare the values of distinct types (non-LOB), or you can cast between the distinct type and the source type.

Character and arithmetic operators employed in built-in functions that are used on a source type are not automatically inherited by the distinct type. You need to create these operators and functions explicitly.

Comparison operators such as the following are allowed on UDTs.

```
=
<>
>
<
>=
<=
¬=
¬>
BETWEEN
NOT BETWEEN
IS NULL
IN
NOT IN
IS NOT NULL
```

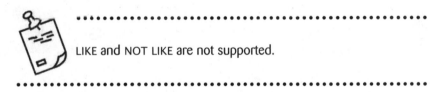

LIKE and NOT LIKE are not supported.

You use casting functions to convert instances of source data types into instances of a different data type. These functions have the name of the target data type and a single parameter, the source data type. They return the target data type. DB2 generates two cast functions when you issue the CREATE DISTINCT TYPE statement, to convert between the distinct type and its source type. The functions are created in the same schema as the distinct type.

The following example creates a UDT and then uses it both with and without casting.

```
CREATE DISTINCT TYPE EURO AS DECIMAL (9,2) WITH COMPARISONS
    EURO(DECIMAL)
    -- where EURO is the target and DECIMAL is the source
DECIMAL (EURO)
    -- where DECIMAL is the target and EURO is the source
```

```
Without casting - using the function name
   SELECT ITEM
   FROM INVENTORY
   WHERE COST > EURO (1000.00)

With casting - using cast function
   SELECT ITEM
   FROM INVENTORY
   WHERE COST > CAST (1000.00 AS EURO)
```

Constants are always considered to be source-type values.

If you want to find all items that have a cost of greater than 1,000.00 Euros, you'll need to cast because you can't compare data of type EURO with data of the source data type of the EURO, which is DECIMAL. You must use the cast function to cast data from DECIMAL to EURO. You can also use the cast function DECIMAL to cast from EURO to DECIMAL and cast the column COST to type DECIMAL. Depending on the way you choose to cast—from or to the UDT—you can use the function name notation *data-type*(*argument*) or the cast notation CAST(*argument* AS *data-type*).

Built-In Functions for UDTs

The built-in data types come with a collection of built-in functions that operate on them. Some of these functions implement operators, such as the arithmetic operators on numeric data types and the substring operators on character data types. Other functions include scalar and column functions, which we discussed in Chapter 5.

When you create a UDT, DB2 automatically creates some cast functions in support of casting between the source data type and the UDT. However, you'll need to define any other functions that are needed within the application to operate against the UDT as sourced user-defined functions. These sourced functions will operate on the UDT and duplicate the semantics of the built-in functions that work on the source type. Remember, this functionality isn't available until you've defined the UDF. Even simple operations such as addition and subtraction are not available until the UDFs to support them are defined. The following example shows how to create a sourced function.

```
CREATE FUNCTION '+' (EURO, EURO) RETURNS EURO
            SOURCE SYSIBM.'+' (DECIMAL(9,2), DECIMAL(9,2))
```

You can also give UDTs distinct semantics of their own by creating external functions that you write in a host language to operate on your UDTs.

Privileges

You must have privileges granted to use UDTs. The GRANT USAGE ON TYPE statement grants privileges to use the UDT as a column data type in a CREATE or ALTER statement or to use the UDT as a parameter in a stored procedure or UDF. GRANT EXECUTE ON enables users to cast functions on a UDT.

Catalog Information

The DB2 catalog stores information about UDTs in the following tables.

- SYSIBM.SYSDATATYPES contains a row for each UDT.
- SYSIBM.SYSROUTINES contains a row for each cast function.
- SYSIBM.SYSRESTAUTH stores authorizations for the USAGE privilege.
- SYSIBM.SYSROUTINEAUTH stores authorizations for the EXECUTE privilege.

User-Defined Functions

User-defined functions form the basis of object-relational extensions to the SQL language, along with UDTs and LOBs. Fundamentally, a database function is a relationship between a set of input data values and a result value. DB2 comes with many built-in functions; it's also possible to create your own scalar and table functions.

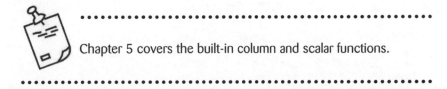

Chapter 5 covers the built-in column and scalar functions.

You can write a scalar or table UDF in a high-level programming language such as COBOL, C, C++, or Java, or you can use a single SQL expression. There are three different methods to develop UDFs:

- **External.** A UDF that you write in a supported language. An external UDF can be further categorized as a scalar or table function.

- **Sourced.** A UDF based on another scalar UDF or on a built-in scalar or column function. This concept is similar to overloading classes in object-oriented programming.

- **SQL scalar.** A scalar UDF that is based on a single SQL expression. The source code for an SQL UDF is contained entirely within the UDF definition.

External UDFs

An *external UDF* is similar to any other program written for the z/OS operating system. External UDFs may or may not contain SQL statements, Instrument Facility Interface (IFI) commands, or DB2 commands. They may be written in assembler, C, C++, COBOL, Java, or PL/I. External UDFs, once written and generated as dynamically loadable libraries or classes, must be registered with the database.

You define an external function to DB2 with a reference to a z/OS load module (or to a JAR in the case of Java) that DB2 should load when the function is invoked. The load module holds the object code for the application program that contains the logic of the external function. If the program includes SQL statements, an associated package contains the database request module (DBRM). External functions cannot be column functions.

In the following example, the congrat function is an external scalar UDF that is registered using the CREATE FUNCTION statement.

```
CREATE FUNCTION congrat(VARCHAR(30),VARCHAR(40))
    RETURNS VARCHAR(30)
    EXTERNAL NAME 'CONGRAT'
    LANGUAGE C
    PARAMETER STYLE SQL
    DETERMINISTIC
```

```
FENCED
READS SQL DATA
COLLID TEST
NO EXTERNAL ACTION
DISALLOW PARALLEL;
```

DB2 passes parameters to external UDFs in a standard manner, in much the same way it passes parameters to stored procedures. DB2 uses the following structure:

Address of parameter 1
Address of parameter 2
Address of parameter 3

. . .

Address of result 1
Address of result 2
Address of result 3

. . .

Address of parameter 1 null indicator
Address of parameter 2 null indicator
Address of parameter 3 null indicator

. . .

Address of result 1 null indicator
Address of result 2 null indicator
Address of result 3 null indicator

. . .

Address of SQLSTATE
Address of procedure name
Address of specific name
Address of message text
Address of the scratchpad (if the DDL specifies SCRATCHPAD)
Address call type indicator (if the DDL specifies FINAL CALL)
Address of DBINFO (if the DDL specifies DBINFO)

A scalar function can return only a single result parameter, while table functions return multiple result parameters, each representing a column in a row of the table being returned.

The SQLSTATE can be returned from the external UDF to DB2 to indicate a condition upon which DB2 can then act. It is highly advisable to have the UDF return an SQLSTATE to the caller. Any SQLSTATE can be returned; returned values that start with anything other than '00', '01', or '02' are error conditions. Although any SQLSTATE can be returned, the following SQLSTATEs can be used to set special application-specific conditions and result in the noted SQLCODEs.

SQLSTATE	Returned SQLCODE
01H*xx*	+462
02000	+100
38001	−487
38002	−577
38003	−751
38004	−579
38*yxx*	−443

Sourced UDFs

You register a *sourced UDF* simply by specifying the DB2 built-in source function. Sourced functions can be scalar functions or column functions, but they cannot be table functions. Sourced functions are often helpful when you need to allow the use of a built-in function on a UDT.

The following example lets us create an AVG function for the SCORE data type.

```
CREATE FUNCTION AVG (SCORE)
    RETURNS SCORE
    SOURCE SYSIBM.AVG(DECIMAL);
```

These CREATE FUNCTION statements place an entry for each UDF in the SYSIBM.SYSROUTINES catalog table and record the parameters in SYSIBM.SYSPARMS. You can query these catalog tables for information about the UDFs.

SQL Scalar UDFs

An *SQL scalar function* is a UDF in which the entire functionality of the function is a single SQL expression and is coded into the CREATE FUNCTION statement. You identify the function as an SQL scalar function by coding the LANGUAGE SQL option of the CREATE FUNCTION statement. This functionality enables you to code an expression that multiple statements commonly use and modularize that expression by storing it separately as a UDF. Any SQL statement can then reference the UDF in the same way any scalar function can be invoked. With SQL scalar functions, you can code common expressions only once and store them separately in the DB2 catalog, centralizing the coding and administration of these types of functions.

You specify the SQL expression in the RETURN clause of the CREATE FUNCTION statement. The expression can contain references to the function input parameters, as in the following example, which computes the total number of months between two dates.

```
CREATE FUNCTION TOTMON (STARTX DATE, ENDY DATE)
RETURNS INTEGER
LANGUAGE SQL
CONTAINS SQL
NO EXTERNAL ACTION
DETERMINISTIC
RETURN ABS( (YEAR(STARTX - ENDY)*12) + MONTH(STARTX - ENDY) );
```

The expressions contained in an SQL scalar UDF cannot contain references to column names or host variables. However, an SQL scalar UDF can invoke other UDFs, including external UDFs that can be SQL programs.

The source code for an SQL scalar function is actually stored in the SYSIBM.SYSVIEWS DB2 catalog table. When an SQL statement referencing an SQL scalar function is compiled, the function source from the SYSIBM.SYSVIEWS catalog table is merged into the statement. Package and plan dependencies on the SQL scalar functions, as with all UDFs, are maintained in the SYSIBM.SYSPACKDEP and SYSIBM.SYSPLANDEP tables, respectively.

Table Functions

With DB2, you can also create another type of UDF called a *table function*. A table function is a UDF that returns a table to the SQL statement that calls it. This means that a table function can be referenced only in the FROM clause of a SELECT statement. Table functions give you a way to include external data or complex processes in SQL queries. Table functions can read non-DB2 data—for instance, a file on the operating system or over the Web—tabularize it, and return the data to DB2 as a relational table that can subsequently be treated like any other relational table.

The following sample function definition accepts a customer ID parameter as input and returns a list of groups the customer belongs to, as well as some application security settings. This information is returned in the form of a table with two columns.

```
CREATE FUNCTION LISTGROUPS(CUSTID CHAR(8))
RETURNS TABLE
  (GROUP CHAR(8),
    SECSTRING CHAR(30))
EXTERNAL NAME LGROUPS
LANGUAGE C
PARAMETER STYLE SQL
NO SQL
DETERMINISTIC
NO EXTERNAL ACTION
FINAL CALL
DISALLOW PARALLEL
CARDINALITY 20;
```

If we wanted to retrieve the information about the customer:

```
SELECT A.CUSTNAME, B.GROUP, B.SECSTRING
FROM   CUST_TABLE A,
       TABLE(LISTGROUPS(A.CUSTID)) AS B;
```

Invoking User-Defined Functions

You invoke scalar UDFs in much the same way as any built-in DB2 scalar function. A function name identifies the function, and one or more parameters pass information from the invoking SQL statement to the UDF. The parameters passed can be table columns, constants, or expressions. If you pass an expression to an external UDF, DB2 resolves the expression and then passes the result to the UDF. The result of the UDF execution replaces the function invocation at execution time.

In the following example, we use the SQL scalar function TOTMON to calculate the number of months between two dates.

```
SELECT  HIREDATE, BIRTHDATE,
        TOTMON(HIREDATE, BIRTHDATE) as total_months,
FROM    EMP;
```

Here, the query selects the HIREDATE and BIRTHDATE columns from the EMP table, and the TOTMON function (previously defined in this chapter) determines the total number of months between the two dates, which were fed to the function as parameters. In this case, the TOTMON function, being an SQL scalar function, is merged with the statement during statement compilation as if the expression itself were coded within the SQL statement.

You can define a UDF as deterministic or not deterministic. A *deterministic* function is one that returns the same result from one invocation to the next if the input parameter values have not changed. Although no mechanism exists within DB2 to "store" the results of a deterministic function, the designation can impact the invoking query execution path relative to materialization. In a situation in which a table expression is nested within an SQL statement, a *non-deterministic* function *will* force the materialization of the inner query. For example:

```
SELECT  WORKDEPT, SUM(TOTAL_MONTHS), AVG(TOTAL_MONTHS)
FROM
(SELECT  WORKDEPT,
         TOTMON(HIREDATE, BIRTHDATE) as total_months,
  FROM   DSN8710.EMP) AS TAB1
GROUP BY WORKDEPT;
```

Here, if there is an index on the WORKDEPT column of the EMP table, the inner table expression called TAB1 may not be materialized but rather may be merged with the outer SELECT statement. This is possible because the TOTMON function is deterministic. If the TOTMON function was not deterministic, DB2 would have to materialize the TAB1 table expression, possibly storing it in the temporary table spaces and sorting to perform the desired aggregation. However, it's not exactly clear whether having TOTMON be deterministic is a good thing. If the TOTMON function is CPU-intensive, it may be better to materialize the result of the inner table expression because the merged TOTMON function (if it is deterministic) will actually be executed twice in the outer query, once per reference (for the SUM and AVG functions in this case).

You can reference a table function in an SQL statement anywhere that a table can normally be referenced. You identify the table function, or a nested table expression, in the query by using the TABLE keyword, as in the following example.

```
SELECT TAB1.EMPNO, TAB2.TEMPURATURE, TAB2.FORECAST
FROM   EMP, TABLE(WEATHERFUNC(CURRENT DATE)) AS TAB2
```

In this query, we use the TABLE keyword to identify a nested table expression called TAB2 that is an invocation of the table UDF called WEATHERFUNC. The query returns the employee number along with some weather information in some of the columns that are returned from the WEATHERFUNC table function. This is a fairly simple invocation of a table function.

More important, you can embed correlated references within a nested table expression. Although the weather may not be useful information to return with employee data, perhaps retrieving the resumé and credit information from an external source is. In this case, we can pass the employee number as a correlated reference into the table expression identified by the TABLE keyword and ultimately pass it into the table UDF:

```
SELECT TAB1.EMPNO, TAB2.RESUME, TAB2.CREDITINFO
FROM   EMP AS TAB1, TABLE(EMPRPT(TAB1.EMPNO)) AS TAB2
```

The TABLE keyword tells DB2 to look to the left of the keyword when attempting to resolve any otherwise irresolvable correlated references within the table expression. If we had coded the join in reverse (that is, if the invocation of the EMPRPT table UDF appeared before the EMP table in the statement), the correlated reference to the TAB1.EMPNO column would not have been resolved, and the statement would not have been compiled successfully.

The use of the TABLE keyword can be expanded beyond that of correlated references as input into table UDFs. You can use the same keyword with a nested table expression that may benefit from a correlated reference. This technique can be especially useful when the nested expression is performing an aggregation and needs to work on only a subset of the data in the table it is accessing. In the next example, we need to list the employee number and salary of each employee, along with the average salary and head count of all employees in their associated departments. This type of query is traditionally coded as a left outer join of two table expressions, the first obtaining the employee numbers and salaries and the second calculating the head count and average salary for all departments. If filtering takes place against the employee table, the entire table might be unnecessarily read to perform the aggregations.

```
SELECT    TAB1.EMPNO, TAB1.SALARY,
          TAB2.AVGSAL,TAB2.HDCOUNT
FROM
    (SELECT EMPNO, SALARY, WORKDEPT
     FROM   DSN8610.EMP
     WHERE  JOB='SALESREP') AS TAB1
LEFT OUTER JOIN
    (SELECT AVG(SALARY) AS AVGSAL,
            COUNT(*)AS HDCOUNT,
            WORKDEPT
     FROM   DSN8610.EMP
     GROUP  BY WORKDEPT) AS TAB2
ON TAB1.WORKDEPT = TAB2.WORKDEPT;
```

Here, the entire EMP table must be read in the TAB2 nested table expression to calculate the average salary and head count for all departments. This requirement is unfortunate, because we need only the departments that employ sales reps. By using the TABLE keyword and a correlated reference to TAB1 within the TAB2 expression, we can perform filtering before the aggregation:

```
SELECT    TAB1.EMPNO, TAB1.SALARY,
          TAB2.AVGSAL,TAB2.HDCOUNT
FROM      DSN8610.EMP TAB1,
  TABLE(SELECT AVG(SALARY) AS AVGSAL,
            COUNT(*) AS HDCOUNT
        FROM   DSN8610.EMP
        WHERE  WORKDEPT = TAB1.WORKDEPT) AS TAB2

WHERE TAB1.JOB = 'SALESREP';
```

Polymorphism and UDFs

DB2 UDFs subscribe to the object-oriented concept of polymorphism. Ad hoc polymorphism (better described as overloading) lets an SQL statement issue the same function against varying parameter lists and/or data types. This overloading requires you to create a unique definition for each variation of a particular function in data types or number of parameters. Polymorphism basically means "many changes," and for DB2 functions it means that many functions can have the same name. These functions are identified by their signature, which is composed of the schema name, the function name, the number of parameters, and the data types of the parameters. This approach enables you to create UDFs for all your UDTs. These sourced UDFs can assume the same name as the UDFs of built-in functions from which they are sourced, but they are unique in the system due to the data type of their parameter(s). This support also lets you define SQL or external UDFs to accommodate any variation in data type or number of parameters. For example, if you need a variation of the TOTMON function that accommodates timestamps, you could create the following function:

```
CREATE FUNCTION TOTMON (STARTX TIMESTAMP, ENDY TIMESTAMP)
RETURNS INTEGER
LANGUAGE SQL
CONTAINS SQL
NO EXTERNAL ACTION
NOT DETERMINISTIC
RETURN ABS( (YEAR(STARTX - ENDY)*12) + MONTH(STARTX - ENDY) );
```

The only thing that differs between this TOTMON function and the original TOTMON is that the input parameters here are TIMESTAMPs instead of DATEs. From the application programming point of view, this technique enables an SQL statement to issue a TOTMON function regardless of whether it is using a pair of dates or timestamps as input. However, it requires that the people responsible for deploying the UDFs do so with consistency of functionality for like-named functions.

External UDF Execution

The external scalar and table UDF programs execute in a WLM application environment, in much the same way as stored procedures. One or more WLM-established address spaces support the WLM environment. When creating an external function, you should specify the WLM keywords that name the WLM environment in which to execute; otherwise, the program defaults to the WLM environment specified at installation time. This default environment is recorded in the SYSIBM.SYSROUTINES catalog table. UDFs execute under the same thread as the invoking program and run at the same priority, using the WLM enclave processing.

Monitoring and Controlling UDFs

You can invoke UDFs in an SQL statement wherever you can use expressions or built-in functions. External UDFs, like stored procedures, run in WLM-established address spaces. DB2 external UDFs are controlled by several commands.

The START FUNCTION SPECIFIC command activates an external function that has been stopped. You cannot start built-in functions or UDFs that are sourced on another function. You can use the START FUNCTION SPECIFIC command to activate all or a specific set of stopped external functions. To activate an external function that is stopped, you would issue the following command.

```
-START FUNCTION SPECIFIC (function-name)
```

Use the SCOPE (GROUP) option on the START FUNCTION command to start a UDF on all subsystems in a data-sharing group.

The DB2 command DISPLAY FUNCTION SPECIFIC displays statistics about external UDFs that are accessed by DB2 applications. This command produces an output line for each function that a DB2 application has accessed. The information returned by this command reflects a dynamic status for a point in time and may change before another DISPLAY is issued. The command does not display information about built-in functions or UDFs that are sourced on another function. To display statistics about an external UDF accessed by DB2 applications, issue the following command.

```
-DISPLAY FUNCTION SPECIFIC (function-name)
```

The DB2 command STOP FUNCTION SPECIFIC prevents DB2 from accepting SQL statements with invocations of the specified external functions. This particular command does not prevent SQL statements with invocations of the functions from running if they have already been queued or scheduled by DB2. While the STOP FUNCTION SPECIFIC command is in effect, any attempt to execute the stopped functions is queued. You can use this command to stop access to all or a specific set of external functions.

STOP FUNCTION SPECIFIC stops an external function. Built-in functions or UDFs that are sourced on another function cannot be explicitly stopped. To activate all or a specific set of stopped external functions, use the START FUNCTION SPECIFIC command.

To prevent DB2 from accepting SQL statements with invocations of the specified functions, issue the following statement.

```
STOP FUNCTION SPECIFIC (function-name)
```

UDF Statistics

The optimizer uses statistics, if available, to estimate the costs for access paths where UDFs are used. You can update the statistics that the optimizer needs by using the SYSSTAT.FUNCTIONS catalog view. A field in the statistics report lets you view the maximum level of indirect SQL cascading, including cascading due to triggers, UDFs, or stored procedures.

Cost Information

User-defined table functions add additional access cost to the execution of an SQL statement. To select the best access path for the SQL statement, DB2 needs to know this cost factor. The total cost of the user-defined table function is determined by three components:

- The initialization cost that results from the first call processing
- The cost associated with acquiring a single row
- The final call cost that performs the clean-up processing

To determine the elapsed and CPU time spent for UDF operations, you can view an accounting report (shown in Figure 15.2).

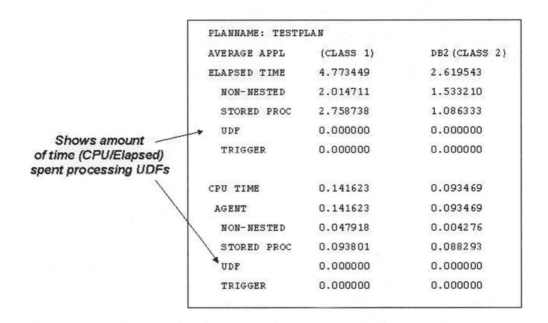

Figure 15.2: Accounting report information for UDF operations

Catalog Information

The SYSIBM.SYSROUTINES catalog table describes UDFs. To retrieve information about UDFs, you can use the following query:

```
SELECT SCHEME, NAME, FUNCTION_TYPE, PARM_COUNT
FROM SYSIBM.SYSROUTINES
WHERE ROUTINETYPE='F'
```

Large Objects

Large objects constitute the third type of object-relational extension to DB2, providing data types that can store large amounts of unstructured data.

LOB Data Types

Three DB2 data types support LOBs:

- BLOB data type (binary large object)

  » Binary strings (not associated with a CCSID)

  » Useful for storing image, voice, and sound data

- CLOB data type (character large object)

  » Strings of single-byte characters or single/double-byte characters with an associated CCSID

  » Useful if data is larger than VARCHAR allows

- DBCLOB data type (double-byte character large object)

  » Strings of double-byte characters with an associated CCSID

Each of these types can contain up to 2 GB of data, although in most cases the amount of storage for individual columns is considerably less (depending on the type of data stored). There is a large use today of the 32 K LONG VARCHAR column, which has limitations in both size and functionality. The way you store your data (LOB versus VARCHAR) really depends on the features and functionality desired, as well as the applications.

LOB Implementation

LOBs are implemented with structures that are different from normal tables and table spaces. A LOB table space must be created for each column (or each column of each partition) of a base LOB table in the same database as the base table. This table space contains the auxiliary table, which must have an auxiliary index associated with it. The LOB table space also has a different recovery scheme, optional logging, and different locking options. (We cover LOB locking in Chapter 16.) LOB table spaces cannot be compressed, so you cannot specify the COMPRESS parameter on a CREATE TABLESPACE statement for a LOB.

If a table contains a LOB column and the plan or package is bound with SQLRULES(STD), DB2 implicitly creates the LOB table space, the auxiliary table, and the auxiliary index. DB2 chooses the name and characteristics for these implicitly created objects.

It's better to develop naming standards beforehand for these objects and control their placement. This standardization is critical for management and performance.

INSERTing and LOADing LOBs

LOB loading and insertion also differs from the processes for non-LOB data. The methods are also entirely different depending on whether DB2 extenders are used. Without extenders (which we cover in more detail later), you must address some real limitations when inserting LOB data, primarily the 32 K limit and logging impacts. If the total length of the LOB column and the base table row is less than 32 K, the LOAD utility can insert the LOB column. When the limits of LOAD are exceeded, you must use SQL INSERT, MERGE or UPDATE statements. However, the SQL INSERT has its own limitations in that enough memory must be available to hold the entire value of the LOB. The constraints are the amount of memory available to the application and the amount of memory that the language in use can address. If the LOBs are all small, memory is not as much of an issue because memory and language constructs will be available. When dealing with very large LOBs, however, you can easily see the differences by comparing the C language construct with COBOL.

The following example specifies a LOB host variable using the C language:

```
SQL TYPE IS CLOB(20000K) my_clob;
is generated by DB2 as
    struct { unsigned long length;
            Char data[20960000];
          } my_clob;
```

The following COBOL language for a LOB host variable

```
01 MY-CLOB    USAGE IS SQL TYPE IS CLOB(20000K).
```

is generated by DB2 as

```
01  MY-CLOB.
    02  MY-CLOB-LENGTH    PIC 9(9) COMP.
    02  MY-CLOB-DATA.
```

```
        49  FILLER    PIC  X(32767).
        49  FILLER    PIC  X(32767).
        49  FILLER    PIC  X(32767).
  --Repeated 622 times
```

This is another area where extenders help solve the problem. When a table and column are enabled for an extender, the whole process changes. You can use an INSERT statement in the program to contain extender functions (UDFs) that enable an image, for example, to be loaded into the database directly from an external file. With the image extender, you could insert the image content into an administrative support table and then insert another record into another administrative table describing the attributes of the image, such as number of colors, thumbnail-sized version, and format characteristics (e.g., JPG, TIF). The extenders require WLM application environments to be created in support of the extender UDFs and stored procedures.

Even though the LOB data is stored in an auxiliary table, the INSERT statement specifies the base table. You can read the LOB data from a file in your DB2 program and place the data into the declared DB2 LOB variable. The INSERT statement then simply references the LOB variable. For example, if you wanted to insert employee resumés into the EMP_RESUME table, which includes a 2 MB CLOB data type to hold resumés, you declare the resumé variable in your program:

```
SQL TYPE IS CLOB(2000K) resume;
```

Then, populate the resumé variable with the CLOB data, and perform the insert:

```
EXEC SQL INSERT INTO EMP_RESUME VALUES (:EMPNO, :RESUME);
```

DB2 uses contiguous storage in data spaces to store LOBs that your program is manipulating. Because LOBs can be quite large, DB2 avoids materializing them until completely necessary. The amount of storage required depends on the size of the LOBs and the number of LOBs referenced in a statement. The storage requirements of your program and DB2 can become quite large. For this reason, you can use LOB locators to manipulate LOB data without retrieving that data from the DB2 table. You declare a LOB locator in the application program:

```
SQL TYPE IS CLOB_LOCATOR resume_loc;
```

An SQL statement can reference the locator, and the LOB is not materialized in DB2 until absolutely necessary, and it is never moved into the application memory.

```
SELECT  RESUME
INTO    :resume_loc
FROM    EMP_RESUME
WHERE   EMPNO=:empno;
```

Further SQL statements can reference the locator variable, enabling the LOB to be manipulated in various ways. One way would be by using SQL SET commands. DB2 will manipulate the LOB data within the table and only materialize the LOB as needed.

LOBs and UDTs

Being able to store LOBs and manipulate them through extenders is only part of the story. The capability also exists to define new distinct data types based on the needs of particular applications. A UDT, also known as a distinct type, provides a way to differentiate one LOB from another LOB, even for LOBs of the same base type, such as BLOB or CLOB. A UDT is not limited to objects and can be created for standard data types as well as LOBs.

Even though they are stored as LOBs (binary or character), image, video, spatial, XML, and audio objects are treated as types distinct from BLOBs and CLOBs and distinct from each other. For example, suppose an application that processes spatial data features needs a polygon data type. You can create a distinct type named POLYGON for polygon objects, as follows:

```
CREATE DISTINCT TYPE POLYGON AS BLOB (512K)
```

The polygon-type object is treated as a distinct type of object even though internally it is represented as a 512 K binary object (BLOB).

UDTs are used like SQL built-in types to describe the data stored in columns of tables. The extenders create distinct data types for the type of object they process, such as image, audio, and video, making it easier for applications to incorporate these types of objects:

```
CREATE TABLE DB2_MAG_DEMO
   (GEO_ID CHAR(6),
    EURO_ANNUAL     EURO_DOLLAR,
    OZ_ANNUAL       AUSTRALIAN_DOLLAR,
    US_ANNUAL       US_DOLLAR,
    DEMO_GRAPHIC    POLYGON)
```

Casting functions allow operations between different data types — for example, comparing a slide from a video UDT with an expression. You must cast the expression to a UDT (video in this example) for the comparison to work. Some casting functions are supplied with DB2 (CHAR, INTEGER, and so on), and others are created automatically whenever you create a UDT with the CREATE TYPE statement.

Extenders

As you've seen, the extenders in DB2 aid in the use of LOBs, the base storage for the object-relational environment. Extenders are a complete package that defines distinct data types and special functions for many types of LOBs, including image, audio, video, text, XML, and spatial objects. With this support, you don't need to worry about defining these data types and functions in your applications. You can use SQL to manipulate these data types and functions. LOBs can be relatively small to extremely large and can be cumbersome to deal with.

LOB and Extender Usage

When you use an extender for a particular LOB type, additional options actually enable the data to be stored in its native format in separate files, such as a picture that is a single JPEG file. In this example, DB2 would store the hierarchical path name in support tables that would let the extender use this indirect reference to process the actual data. The extenders also require administrative support tables that vary based on the extender used. These tables are also referred to as *metadata tables* because their content enables the extenders to appropriately handle user requests, such as inserting audio, displaying images, and so on. These tables identify base tables and columns that are enabled for the extender and reference other support tables used to hold attribute information about LOB columns. Triggers supplied by the extenders are used to update many of these support tables when underlying LOB data is inserted, updated, or deleted. At present, six extenders are available in the DB2 family: image, audio, video, text, XML, and spatial.

Applications generally use SQL to retrieve pointers to the data, with UDFs and/or stored procedures assisting with more complex and unique operations. Extender APIs will be more commonly used because all the coding is supplied for dealing with the LOBs. For applications, this is a considerable advantage, both from a "not-having-to-program-it" standpoint and by easing the pain of the learning curve. For example, when you work with the image extenders, several different formats are supported. The common ones (BMP, EPS, GIF, JPG, TIF) are provided, of course, along with more than 15 other formats. This means that if a user were browsing through a series of pictures, each LOB picture could be of a different format, but the program wouldn't have to be aware of the format differences because the extender would take care of them. The same is true of the text extender. A user could browse through a series of text documents, one in Microsoft Word format, another in WordPerfect, and so on.

But it is not browsing documents, playing a video, or streaming audio that represents the most power. It is the searching ability of the LOB extenders. For example, with the text extender, you can perform searching by soundex, synonym, thesaurus, proximity, linguistic, and several other criteria. With images, the QBIC API enables searching by image content, and this is a very extensive and powerful API.

Application programming for objects generally will require the use of the extenders. Without their use, you can do little without extensive user programming. The power of objects comes with the UDFs and API libraries that are packaged with the extenders. They permit an application to easily store, access, and manipulate any of the supported object types.

Although the current list supplies only the six extenders we mentioned, many others are in development and will be released in the future as they are completed. Application programmers will be able to use UDFs in their SQL to position to the necessary LOB and then use an API to manipulate it, such as to display a picture on the screen. So, there are really two completely different libraries to strategize from. As a simple example, without forcing it to match any particular programming language, the following pseudocode represents first storing a picture in a LOB and then displaying it on the screen.

First, insert the data into the LOB by using the DB2IMAGE extender:

```
EXEC SQL BEGIN DECLARE SECTION;
  storage_type;
EXEC SQL END DECLARE SECTION;

SET storage_type = MMDB_STORAGE_TYPE_INTERNAL

EXEC SQL INSERT INTO MY_PERSONAL_DIGITAL_PICTURES
  VALUES ('OZ TRIP 2',
          'Sydney Opera House',
          DB2IMAGE (
                CURRENT SERVER,
                'c:/My Pictures/1999/Australia/OpraHse.jpg',
                'ASIS',
                :storage_type));
```

Second, retrieve and display the data on the screen using API DBiBROWSE:

```
EXEC SQL BEGIN DECLARE SECTION;
  image_handler;
EXEC SQL END DECALRE SECTION;

EXEC SQL SELECT PICTURE INTO :image_handler
  WHERE NAME = 'Sydney Opera House';
Set return_code to DBiBROWSE("ib %s",
  MMDB_PLAY_HANDLE,
  image_handler,
  MMDB_PLAY_BI_WAIT);
```

From this pseudocode, it's easy to see that the extenders offer significant power and enable applications to be written quickly. In addition, most of the work takes place at the server, and the client is simply the recipient of all that power. When implementing extenders, keep in mind that the program will need to have enough memory available to support the use of LOBs on graphical clients.

Enabling Extenders

IBM provides a Software Developers Kit (SDK) and a client and server runtime environment with the DB2 extenders installation package. DB2 extender applications can be executed in a server machine that has the extender client runtime code (automatically installed when the server runtime code is installed) and server runtime code. Extender applications can also be run on a client machine with the client runtime code; you must ensure that a connection can be made to the server.

When storing image, audio, video, or text objects, you don't store the object in the user table but instead use an extender-created character string, referred to as a *handle*, that represents the objects, and the handle is stored in the user table. The object is actually stored in an administrative support table (or file identifier if the content is a file). The attributes and handles are also stored in these administrative tables. The extender then links the handle in the user table to the object and its attributes in the administrative tables.

Text Extenders

Text extenders bring full-text retrieval to SQL queries for searching large text documents intelligently. With the use of text extenders, you can search several thousand large text documents very quickly. You can also search based on word variations and synonyms. The documents can be stored directly in the database or in a separate file.

Files such as native word-processing documents can be searched by keywords, wildcards, phrases, and proximity. IBM has built into the text extenders a high-performance linguistic search technology, providing multiple options for searching and retrieving documents. These text searches can be integrated with normal SQL queries, enabling you to integrate into your SELECT statements the ability to perform attribute and full-text searches very easily.

The following example shows how to achieve this integration. In this example, we do a SELECT from a table that also performs a search on a specified document using a text extender called DB2TX.CONTAINS. The query searches the legal cases document to see whether the words "malpractice" and "won" appear in the same paragraph for cases occurring after January 1, 1990. LEGCSE_HANDLE refers to the column LEGCSE that contains the text document.

```
SELECT DOC_NUM, DOC_DATE
FROM LEGAL_CLAIMS
WHERE DOC_DATE > '1990-01-01'
AND DB2TX.CONTAINS
   (LEGCSE_HANDLE,
   "malpractice"
   IN SAME PARAGRAPH AS "won") = 1
```

Text extenders let applications

- search documents of several languages and formats

- perform wildcard searches using masks

- search for words that sound like the search input

- perform fuzzy searches for similar words (various spellings)

- search for specific text, synonyms, phrases, and proximity

- perform free-text searches where the input is a natural language

Indexing Text Extenders

Scans are just as undesirable in text documents as they are with our DB2 tables. We need to create indexes so that sequential scans of documents aren't necessary. By using a text index, you can speed up the searches performed on these documents.

A text index contains important words as well as a list of words known as *stop words* (such as "and" and "the"), which will not be in a text index. This list can be modified, but you'd want to do so only once, at installation time. When a request is made, the index is searched for the important terms to determine which documents contain the specified terms.

To set up a text index, you first record the text documents that need to be indexed in a log table. This process occurs when a DB2 trigger is fired during an insert, update, or delete of a column of a text document. Then, when the terms are inserted or updated in the text document, they are added to the index. If the terms are deleted from the text document, they are also deleted from the index.

There are four types of text indexes, and the type must be established before you implement columns that will use text extenders. Not all search options are available with every index type, so you want to make sure the index you use suits your criteria for searching. The four types of indexes are as follows:

- **Linguistic.** In this type of index, linguistic processing is performed during the analysis for the text when the index is created. Before a word is inserted into the index, it is reduced to its base form. Queries also use linguistic processing when searching against this index. Linguistic indexes require the least amount of space, but their searches may be longer than those executed against a precise index (described next).

- **Precise.** In this type of index, the search terms are exactly as they are in the text document and are case-sensitive. DB2 uses the same processing for the query search terms, so they must match exactly. You can broaden the search by using masks. Precise indexes provide a more precise search, and the retrieval and indexing is fast; however, they require more storage space.

- **Dual.** Dual indexes are combinations of linguistic and precise indexes. They let the user decide which type of search to use. This type of index requires the most amount of disk space. It is slower for searching and indexing than the linguistic indexes and is not recommended for a large number of text documents.

- **Ngram.** The Ngram index is used primarily for indexing double-byte character set (DBCS) documents; it analyzes text by parsing sets of characters. This index type also supports fuzzy searches.

When creating tables that will support the ability to search text using extenders, you must consider a few design options. You can create one text index for all text columns in the table, or you can have several different text indexes, one for each text column. Using separate indexes for each text column offers the most flexibility in terms of support for your searches. It also gives you other options, such as how frequently the index is updated and where it is stored. One common index is easier to maintain but is less flexible. If your indexes are large, consider storing them on separate disks, especially if you expect to have concurrent access to the indexes.

You can also define multiple indexes on a single text column. You may want to take this approach if you need the ability to allow different types of searches on a text column. Just like other DB2 indexes, these indexes will need to be reorganized. If you have a text column that is continually updated, you'll need to reorganize it. However, when using these indexes, the text extender automatically reorganizes them in the background. Despite this feature, you still may have to reorganize an index manually every so often, depending on its volatility. You do so with the REORGANIZE INDEX command. To see whether an index needs reorganization, issue the GET INDEX STATUS command.

Frequency of Index Updates

When text documents are added, deleted, or changed, their content must be synchronized with the index. This information is automatically stored by triggers in a log table, and the documents will be indexed the next time an index update is executed.

You can update the indexes immediately using the UPDATE INDEX command, but having the update performed automatically on a periodic basis is easier. This time-based information is kept in an environment variable called DB2TXUPDATEFREQ, which provides default settings that can be changed during execution of the ENABLE TEXT COLUMN or ENABLE TEXT TABLE commands. For an existing index, you can use the CHANGE INDEX SETTINGS command to change the variable settings.

The variable for determining when indexing should occur is based on the minimum number of queued text documents in the log table; when this minimum is reached, the index is updated. Because updating indexes is a resource-intensive and time-consuming task, be sure to set this frequency carefully.

Catalog View for Text Extenders

A catalog view is created for each subsystem when you run the ENABLE SERVER command. This view, DB2TX.TEXTINDEXES, contains information about the tables and the columns that have been enabled for the text extender. The entries are made during table, column, or external file enablement. If these objects are disabled, the row is removed.

You can view the entries in the catalog view using SQL. The view lets you see information such as how often the indexes are scheduled for updates, whether you have a multiple-index table, and index type.

Image, Audio, and Video Extenders

The DB2 video extender can store as many as three representative frames per shot. By displaying the frames, you get a quick, yet effective, view of a video's content. The DB2 video extender provides sample programs that demonstrate how to build and display a video storyboard.

Video storyboards let you preview videos before you download and view them. This practice can save you time and reduce video traffic on the network. When image data is placed into a table using the DB2IMAGE UDFs, many processes are performed for the application automatically. The following code demonstrates using this function.

```
EXEC SQL INSERT INTO CONSULTANTS VALUES(
    :cons_id,
    :cons_name,
    DB2IMAGE(
        CURRENT SERVER,
        '/RYC/images/current.bmp'
        'ASIS',
        MMDB_STORAGE_TYPE_INTERNAL,
        :cons_picture_tag);
```

In this example, the DB2IMAGE function reads all the attributes of the image (height, width, colors, layers, pixels, and more) from the source image file header—in this case, file current.bmp. All the input is of a standard supported format, and all graphic files contain header information about the structure of the content. The function then creates a unique handle for the image and records all the information in the support table for administrative control of the image. This table contains

- the handle for the image

- a timestamp

- the image size in bytes

- the comment contained in :cons_picture_tag

- the content of the image

The content of the image source file is inserted into the LOB table as a BLOB. No conversion takes place, and the image is stored in its native format. A record in the administrative table contains all the image-specific attributes, such as the number of colors in the image, as well as a thumbnail-sized version of the image.

The example uses the storage type constant MMDB_STORAGE_TYPE_INTERNAL to store the image into a database table as a BLOB. By using the extenders, we could have stored it elsewhere. If you wanted to store the object and have its content remain in the original file on the server, you'd specify the constant MMDB_STORAGE_TYPE_EXTERNAL.

Just because you're using LOBs doesn't mean they have to be in DB2-managed tables. The administrative support table for image extenders tells where the LOB is actually stored. (This functionality requires Open Edition support services on the z/OS system.) From a performance perspective, there are many considerations as to where the LOB is stored, how it is used, where it is materialized, and so on.

XML Extender

DB2 9 offers XML as a data type as well as functions and XPath features that let XML be stored and retrieved directly from DB2. XML data can now be fully integrated with a DB2 database system, and DB2 functionality provides direct access to this XML data. The XML data is stored separately from the relational data, but the application is oblivious to this distinction. Because the XML column data type provides storage for XML data in DB2 tables, many common database operations work with XML data, including the creation of tables, indexes, and triggers as well as inserting, updating, and deleting XML documents.

The XML extender existed before the release of DB2 for z/OS Version 9. This extender enables the creation, administration, and access of XML document within a relational data store. The extender remains useful for pre-V9 implementations as well as for any implementation that prefers the storage of XML data in a relational manner.

Summary

In this chapter, we talked about very powerful DB2 and SQL features, such as UDFs and triggers. These features can reduce the amount of application development time and maintenance. You can use these features to encapsulate code into one place for use by many applications.

DB2 implements some object-relational functions, such LOB support, UDTs, and UDFs. These features also provide great flexibility and power for applications. LOBs, of course, give you the ability to stored large amounts and different types of data, such as multimedia, enabling the ability to develop very sophisticated applications.

Additional Resources

IBM DB2 9 Administration Guide (SC18-9840)
IBM DB2 9 Application Programming and SQL Guide (SC18-9841)
IBM DB2 9 SQL Reference (SC18-9854)

Practice Questions

Question 1

Assume the following statements are issued in order:

```
CREATE DISTINCT TYPE MONEY AS DECIMAL(9,2);
COMMIT;

SELECT CAST(1.5 AS MONEY) + CAST(1.5 AS DEC(9,2)) FROM
    SYSIBM.SYSDUMMY1;
```

Which of the following statements is true?

○ A. The value 3.0 is returned as a DECIMAL (9,2).

○ B. The statement fails because the data types are incompatible.

○ C. The statement fails because no "+" function exists to add MONEY.

○ D. The value 3.0 is returned as MONEY because DECIMAL (9,2) is promoted to MONEY.

Question 2

What type of user-defined function is created in the following definition?

```
CREATE FUNCTION TOTMON (STARTX DATE, ENDY DATE)
RETURNS INTEGER
LANGUAGE SQL
CONTAINS SQL
NO EXTERNAL ACTION
DETERMINISTIC
RETURN ABS( (YEAR(STARTX - ENDY)*12) + MONTH(STARTX - ENDY) );
```

○ A. A sourced UDF

○ B. An external table UDF

○ C. An external scalar UDF

○ D. An SQL sourced UDF

Question 3

When you create a LOB table space, which of the following options of the CREATE TABLESPACE statement *cannot* be specified?

○ A. CLOSE YES

○ B. COMPRESS YES

○ C. LOCKSIZE ANY

○ D. LOG YES

Question 4

Three after triggers (TRIG1, TRIG2, and TRIG3) have been created on the same table and are designed to run in sequential order, TRIG1 through TRIG3. The WHEN search condition for TRIG2 is incorrect and must be recoded. What is the appropriate action?

○ A. Alter trigger TRIG2, and correct the SQL.

○ B. Drop and re-create TRIG2 and TRIG3 after correcting the SQL.

○ C. Drop and re-create TRIG1 and TRIG2 after correcting the SQL.

○ D. Rebind triggers TRIG1, TRIG2, and TRIG3 after correcting the SQL in TRIG2.

Question 5

A special situation exists in which whenever a delete operation is performed against a certain table, a single row containing the user ID needs to be recorded in an audit table. That is, any time a DELETE is issued against the table, that action must be recorded in the audit table. Which type of trigger would best serve this purpose?

○ A. A before delete row trigger

○ B. An after delete row trigger

○ C. An after delete statement trigger

○ D. An INSTEAD OF trigger

Answers

Question 1

The answer is **C**, the statement fails because no addition function exists for the MONEY type. Although DB2 automatically creates casting functions between the distinct type and its source data type, you have to create user-defined sourced functions that operate against the new type before they can be used.

Question 2

The answer is **D**, an SQL sourced UDF. External functions are user-written programs, similar to stored procedures, and are identified by the EXTERNAL keyword. While a sourced function is based on an existing function, an SQL sourced function is based on a single SQL expression.

Question 3

The answer is **B**, COMPRESS YES. LOB table spaces differ in several ways from regular table spaces. One of the ways they differ is that a LOB table space cannot be compressed.

Question 4

The answer is **B**, drop and re-create TRIG2 and TRIG3 after correcting the SQL. When similar triggers are created against a table, they are executed in the order in which they were created. Because these are all after triggers, they logically fire at the same time. DB2, however, executes them in the order they were defined.

Question 5

The answer is **C**, an after delete statement trigger. This type of trigger serves the purpose best because the action needs to be recorded, and if no data changes, the row trigger won't fire. Also, the action is to record a row containing the user ID of the delete. Because a statement trigger fires only once for a statement, it will accomplish the task of adding only a single row to the audit table no matter how many rows are deleted.

Locking and Concurrency

In This Chapter

✔ Locking data

✔ Lock attributes

✔ Avoiding locks

✔ Claims and drains

✔ Escalation and promotion

✔ Designing for concurrency

It would be easy to have one process simply lock all the data while using it, but that practice, of course, would mean other applications couldn't access the data during this time. *Concurrency*, the ability for multiple applications to access the same data at the same time, needs to be allowed but also controlled to prevent lost updates, access to uncommitted data, and unrepeatable reads (data changing between reads).

We need to achieve a balance for maximum concurrency of all processes. DB2 provides many controls to help us achieve maximum concurrency while maintaining the integrity of our data. These tools range from the parameters with which we bind our programs, to DDL options for the creation of objects, to subsystem-level parameters.

DB2 uses locks to control concurrency within a database—that is, to manage simultaneous access to a resource by more than one user (a process also referred to as *serialization*). Locks also block access to uncommitted data, which prevents updates from becoming lost (part of data integrity) and lets a user see the same data, without the data ever changing, within a period of processing called a *commit scope*.

From a performance standpoint, everything that happens in DB2 has a tradeoff. In locking, the tradeoff is between concurrency and performance because more concurrency imposes a higher cost of CPU use due to lock management. In some cases, DB2 may override the designed locking strategy because processes hold locked resources that exceed the site-established thresholds. However, only certain combinations of parameters cause this override to occur.

Locking Data

DB2 uses transaction locking (via the Internal Resource Lock Manager, or IRLM), latches, and other non-IRLM mechanisms to control concurrency and access of SQL statements and utilities. These mechanisms are there to associate a resource with a process so that other processes can't access the same resource when doing so would cause lost updates and access to uncommitted data.

In general, a process holds a lock on manipulated data until it completes its work. This way, it ensures that other processes don't gain access to data that has been changed but not committed. Another use of locking is for repeatable read, when an application needs to reread data that must still be in the same state as it was when it was initially read. There are also user options to avoid locking and permit access to uncommitted data and system settings and mechanisms to provide for lock avoidance when it would not cause a data integrity problem.

Not all objects need to have locks acquired on them to establish concurrency. The following objects can be locked:

- User tables
- Catalog tables
- Directory tables

Indexes are not locked, because their serialization is controlled by latches and concurrency is controlled by data locking. Drains and claims are also used to control utilities and DB2 commands. Draining lets utilities and commands acquire partial or full control of a needed object with minimal interruption to concurrent access.

DB2 often needs to access data in the catalog, and the data being read or updated must be locked. During plan binding, the Skeleton Cursor Table (SKCT) is locked, and during a package bind, the Skeleton Package Table (SKPT) is locked. During DDL activity, the Database Descriptor (DBD) will be locked.

Lock Attributes

Locks should be viewed as having the following characteristics:

- **Size.** How much data is locked
- **Mode.** Whether others are allowed to read and/or update the locked object
- **Duration.** How long the lock is held

Each of these attributes plays a role in the acquisition and release of a lock. Understanding these attributes can help you use them wisely and avoid contention.

Depending on lock mode, more than one type of lock can exist for a specific user for a particular table space. For example, locks might be held on the table space, table, page, and row simultaneously for a particular user. Each lock has its own mode.

Lock Sizes

Locks can be taken on various objects in DB2, and the size of the lock determines how much of the total object is locked. The following objects can be locked in DB2:

- Non-LOB data
  - » Table space: Lock the entire table space.
  - » Table: Only segmented table spaces permit an individual table to be locked.

- Partition: Lock only a partition.

- Page: Lock an individual page in a table.

- Row: Lock an individual row in a table.

- LOB data

  » LOB locks

- XML data

  » XML lock

Table Space and Table Locks

Table space and table locks are the most encompassing locks, and, of course, they allow for the least amount of concurrency between users. Table locks in a simple table space may lock data in other tables because the rows can be intermingled on different pages. In a segmented table space, the pages with rows from a single table will be locked and won't affect other tables in the table space. For more information about simple and segmented table spaces, see Chapter 4.

Partition or Universal Table Space Locking

When a partitioned table space is accessed, DB2 can choose to lock only a partition of the table space. DB2 takes locks on the individual partition instead of the entire table space and does not escalate locks to the table space level but rather to the partition level.

In a few instances, DB2 may not be able to take partition-level locks:

- When the plan or package is bound with ACQUIRE(ALLOCATE)

- When the table space is defined with LOCKSIZE TABLESPACE

- When the LOCK TABLE statement is used without the PART option

Page Locks

Page locking is usually the lock size of choice for best concurrency. This type of locking lets DB2 lock only a single page of data, whether it is a 4 K, 8 K, 16 K, or 32 K page. Page locks for a table in a simple table space may lock rows of more than one table if the rows are intermingled on the page. Page locks for tables in a segmented table space will lock the rows of only one table.

Row Locks

DB2 supports row-level locking, and if applications are experiencing a lot of concurrency problems, you might consider this alternative. However, you shouldn't use row-level locking as a fix for what could be an issue of physical design or application design. Row-level locking should be employed when multiple applications need a page of data simultaneously and each user's interest is on different rows. If the interest is on the same row, row-level locking buys you nothing. Use row-level locking only if the increased cost (concurrency and wait-time overhead) of locking is tolerable and you can definitely justify the benefit.

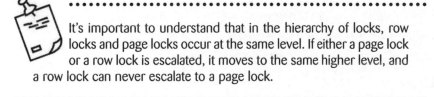

It's important to understand that in the hierarchy of locks, row locks and page locks occur at the same level. If either a page lock or a row lock is escalated, it moves to the same higher level, and a row lock can never escalate to a page lock.

LOB Locks

DB2 provides an additional lock mode for LOBs called a LOB lock. LOB locks have different characteristics from regular locks. No concept of row or page locking exists with a LOB. LOB locking is not at all like the traditional transaction-level locking. Because LOBs are in an associated object, concurrency between the base table and the LOB must be maintained at all times, even if the base table is using UR (uncommitted read). A LOB lock still needs to be held on the LOB to provide consistency and, most important, to maintain space in the LOB table space.

Locks on LOBs are taken when an INSERT or UPDATE operation requires them, and they are released immediately at the completion of the operation. LOB locks are not held for SELECT and DELETE operations. In the case of an application that uses the uncommitted read option, a LOB lock might be acquired, but only to test the LOB for completeness. The lock is released immediately after it is acquired.

Locks on LOB table spaces are acquired when they are needed; that is, the ACQUIRE option of BIND has no effect on when the table space lock on the LOB table space is taken. A combination of factors determine when the release of the table space lock occurs:

- The RELEASE option of bind
- Whether the SQL statement is static or dynamic
- Whether there are held cursors or held locators

When the RELEASE option is COMMIT, the lock is released at the next commit point unless held cursors or held locators exist. If the RELEASE option is DEALLOCATE, the lock is released when the object is deallocated (i.e., when the application ends). The BIND option has no effect on dynamic SQL statements, which always use RELEASE(COMMIT) unless you use dynamic statement caching.

XML Locks

DB2 stores XML column values in a separate XML table space. An application that reads or updates a row in a table that contains XML columns might use lock avoidance or obtain transaction locks on the base table. If an XML column is updated or read, the application might also acquire transaction locks on the XML table space and XML values that are stored in the XML table space. A lock that is taken on an XML value in an XML table space is called an XML lock. In addition to the XML locks, page locks are also acquired on pages in the XML table space. During insert, update, and delete operations, exclusive (X) page locks are acquired; during fetch processing, including uncommitted read and lock avoidance, share (S) page locks are acquired. In summary, the main purpose of XML locks is to manage the space used by XML data and ensure that XML readers don't read partially updated XML data.

LOCK TABLE Statement

Some situations may call for the ability to exclusively lock a table or partition. There is one SQL statement that can override locking at any time: the LOCK TABLE IN EXCLUSIVE MODE statement. A typical reason to override locking is if you want to take a snapshot of data and be able to access a table without any other concurrent processes changing data. You can give other processes read-only access to the table by using the LOCK TABLE IN SHARE MODE statement. This is different from repeatable read (RR) isolation because RR prevents changes only from rows or pages that you've already accessed. You can prevent all other access with LOCK TABLE IN EXCLUSIVE MODE.

The LOCK TABLE and LOCK TABLESPACE statements can be used only to get a lock, in either share mode or exclusive mode. The lock is acquired when the SQL statement is executed. Its release depends on the previous settings of the ACQUIRE and RELEASE parameters. The table or table space lock is released at thread deallocation if RELEASE(DEALLOCATE) was specified in the options when the program was bound. The lock also can be released at either COMMIT or ROLLBACK time if the RELEASE(COMMIT) option was specified at bind time. Despite the type of locking held when the SQL LOCK TABLE statement was issued, when the COMMIT or ROLLBACK is issued, the system falls back to page-level locking unless another SQL LOCK TABLE statement is issued. A user or application must constantly reissue the SQL LOCK TABLE statement after the commit or rollback when RELEASE(COMMIT) has been specified if locking is still needed at the table or table space level.

You can also use the LOCK TABLE IN EXCLUSIVE MODE statement to avoid additional overhead if you're updating a large portion of a table. This approach can be more efficient because when you prevent concurrent accesses to the data, DB2 avoids the overhead of locking and unlocking each page during updates.

You can prevent timeouts as well by using either the LOCK TABLE IN EXCLUSIVE or the LOCK TABLE IN SHARE MODE statement. This technique lets you process the data quickly without the possibility of having to contend for locks with other applications.

If you need further granularity, you can choose to lock only the partition, as seen in the following example:

```
LOCK TABLE CERTTB PART 1 IN EXCLUSIVE MODE
```

This example would take an X lock on PART 1 regardless of any other locks held on other partitions in the table space.

SKIP LOCKED DATA

The SKIPPED LOCKED DATA option lets a transaction skip rows that are incompatibly locked by other transactions. This option can help improve the performance of some applications by eliminating lock wait time. You should use this technique only for applications that don't require unavailable or uncommitted data. Transactions using this option will not read or modify data that is unavailable, uncommitted, or held by locks.

You can specify the SKIP LOCKED DATA option in a SELECT, SELECT INTO, PREPARE, searched UPDATE, or searched DELETE statement. You can also use it with the UNLOAD utility. The option works with isolation level CS or RS. It is ignored for isolation levels UR and RR.

The next example returns a count of only the rows that are not uncommitted (if no index exists on CUST_NO).

```
SELECT COUNT(*)
FROM CUSTOMER
WHERE CUST_NO >= 500
SKIP LOCKED DATA
```

Lock Modes

DB2 provides six lock modes:

- IS (intent share)

- S (share)

- IX (intent exclusive)

- U (update)

- SIX (share with intent exclusive)

- X (exclusive)

Modes are easy to understand using a simple formula: If the table or table space lock has an I in it, which stands for intent, then row or page locks are in use on the individual pages. In all other cases, the table or table space lock is the only lock used.

An intent lock acts as an indicator to DB2 to identify what is occurring within the table or table space. Some locking is beyond the control of the programmer and designer, while other locks can be controlled to a degree. Table 16.1 lists the compatibility of the different lock modes for table spaces, tables, and partitions. Table 16.2 lists the compatibilities for pages and rows.

Table 16.1: Lock mode compatibility for table spaces, tables, and partitions						
Lock mode	**IS**	**IX**	**S**	**U**	**SIX**	**X**
IS	Yes	Yes	Yes	Yes	Yes	No
IX	Yes	Yes	No	No	No	No
S	Yes	No	Yes	Yes	No	No
U	Yes	No	Yes	No	No	No
SIX	Yes	No	No	No	No	No
X	No	No	No	No	No	No

Table 16.2: Lock mode compatibility for pages and rows			
Lock mode	**S**	**U**	**X**
S	Yes	Yes	No
U	Yes	No	No
X	No	No	No

Table or Table Space Locks

When page or row locks are in use, the table or table space lock will be one of the following:

- IS
  - » Lock owner wants to read only (may lock pages/rows).
  - » Allow read of lock owner's pages/rows and read/update of all other pages/rows.

- » Lock owner has share locks on the pages.

- » Other users can still read and update.

- IX

  - » Lock owner wants to update (may lock pages/rows).

  - » Allow read/update of all other pages/rows.

  - » Lock owner can have share, update, or exclusive locks on the pages/rows.

  - » Other users can still read and update.

- SIX

  - » Lock owner wants to read (will not lock pages/rows).

  - » Lock owner wants to update (may lock pages/rows).

  - » Allow read of all other pages/rows.

  - » Lock owner can have share, update, or exclusive locks on the pages/rows.

  - » Other users can still read, but no other user can update.

● ●

SIX is not a common lock. This mode usually occurs when an IX lock already exists and a share has to be acquired.

● ●

When row and page locks are not is use, the table/table space lock will be one of the following:

- S

  - » Lock owner wants to read only.

  - » Others are allowed to read only.

  - » No one can update.

- U

  - » Lock owner wants to read with possibility of update.

  - » Others are allowed to read only.

  - » No other user can update.

- X

  - » Lock owner wants to update.

  - » Other access is not allowed.

  - » User needs exclusive use of the table or table space/partition.

  - » No other user is allowed.

Page or Row Locks

Page or row locks can be one of three types:

- S

  - » Restricts other users to read-only use of this page/row.

  - » S or U locks can be acquired by other users.

  - » Using SELECT or FETCH without update intent will acquire this lock.

- U

  - » Lets the user go to the actual update step if required.

  - » Other applications can get S locks but nothing else.

- X

  - » User has updated the data on the page/row, and no other user can get any page/row lock on the page/row

The DML statement determines the lock mode as follows:

Statement	Lock mode
SELECT. . .	S
SELECT. . .FOR UPDATE OF. . .	U
UPDATE/DELETE/INSERT	X

DB2 does not allow update (UPDATE, INSERT, or DELETE) of uncommitted changes by other users. Reading of uncommitted data is allowed only if an isolation level of UR is specified in the SQL WITH clause or as a BIND option.

Lock Durations

The lock duration is the length of time a lock can be held by a requester. The duration can affect both application performance and object availability.

Table, Table Space, and Partition Lock Durations

The values you specify for the BIND operation's ACQUIRE and RELEASE parameters determine the duration of table, table space, and partition locks.

- ACQUIRE determines when table, table space, or partition locks are taken.

  » ALLOCATE: When the first SQL statement is issued, the maximum required lock is taken on all the objects in the plan or package.

  » USE: When an SQL statement is issued, the required lock is taken on the objects involved in the SQL statement.

- RELEASE determines when table, table space, or partition locks are released.

  » DEALLOCATE: The lock is released at the end of the program.

  » COMMIT: The lock is released at commit.

Page or Row Lock Durations

The duration of a lock defines the actual length of time that the lock will be held (the period between acquiring and releasing the lock). You can control how long locks are held through various means, such as commit scopes, program bind parameters, and system parameters. You, of course, want to maximize concurrency, so you shouldn't hold locks longer than necessary (using a large lock for the duration of the process), but you don't want to incur too much memory and CPU overhead by taking an excessive number of smaller locks (such as taking several row locks over a period of time for the same process).

Isolation levels are set when a program is bound or when specified in an individual SQL statement using the WITH ISOLATION clause. The isolation levels directly affect the duration for which locks are held. You can set the following isolation levels either at bind time or in an individual SQL statement:

- UR (uncommitted read)
- CS (cursor stability)
- RS (read stability)
- RR (repeatable read)

Of these levels, cursor stability, read stability, and repeatable read have to do with lock durations, while uncommitted read has to do with overriding locks.

Cursor Stability

The cursor stability level of program isolation can hold a lock on the row or page (depending on the lock size defined) only if the cursor is actually positioned on that row or page. The lock is released when the cursor moves to a new row or page but is held until a commit is issued if changes are being made to the data. This option provides the maximum concurrency for applications that are accessing the same data, but it cannot allow uncommitted reads.

Read Stability

The read stability option holds locks on all rows or pages qualified by stage 1 predicates for the application until the commit is issued. Nonqualified rows or pages, even though touched, are not locked, as with the RR option. Uncommitted changes of other applications cannot be read, but if an application issues the same query again, any data changed or inserted by other applications will be read because RS allows other applications to insert new rows or update rows that could fall within the range of the query. This option is less restrictive but similar in function to repeatable read.

Repeatable Read

The repeatable read isolation level holds a lock on all rows or pages touched by an application program since the last commit was issued, whether or not all those rows or pages satisfied the query. It holds these locks until the next commit point, which ensures that if the application needs to read the data again, the values will be the same (no other process can update the locked data). This option is the most restrictive in terms of concurrency of applications and is the default isolation level.

Uncommitted Read

The uncommitted read option tells DB2 not to take any locks and to ignore other locks and allow read access to the locked data. It lets an application run concurrently with other processes (except mass deletes and utilities that drain all claim classes).

Table 16.3 compares the different isolation levels.

Table 16.3: DB2 isolation level comparisons				
Access by other applications	UR	CS	RS	RR
Can the application see uncommitted changes made by other application processes?	Yes	No	No	No
Can the application update uncommitted changes made by other application processes?	No	No	No	No
Can the re-execution of a statement be affected by other application processes?	Yes	Yes	Yes	No
Can updated rows be updated by other application processes?	No	No	No	No
Can updated rows be read by other application processes that are running at an isolation level other than UR?	No	No	No	No
Can updated rows be read by other application processes that are running at the UR isolation level?	Yes	Yes	Yes	Yes
Can accessed rows be read by other application processes?	Yes	Yes	Yes	Yes

Share Lock Duration

Using SELECT or FETCH without update intent acquires an S (share) lock. This lock is released for plans bound with CS when

- a TSO, CAF, or batch process issues an SQL COMMIT or ROLLBACK
- an IMS process issues the next SYNCH or ROLB
- a CICS synch point or rollback call occurs
- a non-cursor SQL statement is completed without update
- the cursor position moves to a new row/page without update
- the cursor is closed

Using the cursor WITH HOLD option holds the lock over COMMIT or ROLLBACK processes in TSO and CAF. If no COMMIT is used in the program, the locks are held until the cursor is closed. It's important to understand that the lock will be held on the previous row/page until DB2 obtains the lock on the new one.

Update Lock Duration

A FETCH on a cursor that specifies FOR UPDATE OF acquires a U (update) lock. UPDATE and DELETE statements without a cursor also acquire this lock. UPDATE and DELETE statements cause an implicit SELECT to occur first, matching the conditions in the WHERE clause. During this SELECT, DB2 places a U lock on the accessed page, before completing the UPDATE or DELETE. DB2 releases the lock for plans bound with CS when

- a TSO, CAF, or batch process issues an SQL COMMIT or ROLLBACK
- an IMS process issues the next SYNCH or ROLB
- the next synch point or rollback call occurs in CICS
- a non-cursor SQL statement is completed without update
- the cursor position moves to a new page without update
- the cursor is closed without an update having occurred

Using the cursor WITH HOLD option holds the lock over COMMIT and ROLLBACK. However, the COMMIT will demote the U lock back to an S lock. If an update is to occur, the lock will be promoted to an X lock before the data page is changed.

Exclusive Lock Duration

X (exclusive) locks are released when

- a TSO, CAF, or batch process issues an SQL COMMIT or ROLLBACK

- an IMS process issues the next SYNCH or ROLB

- the next synch point or rollback call occurs in CICS

The lock is held over COMMIT and ROLLBACK in TSO and CAF when you use the cursor WITH HOLD option. However, the COMMIT will demote the X lock back to an S lock.

Avoiding Locks

You can avoid page and row locking at execution time by letting the system use *lock avoidance* mechanisms. DB2 can test to see whether a row or page has committed data on it. If it does, no lock is required on the data at all. Lock avoidance is valid only for read-only or ambiguous cursors and requires a combination of events and settings to occur. First, the statement must be a read-only or an ambiguous cursor along with the proper isolation level and the appropriate CURRENTDATA setting. The best setting for maximum lock avoidance is an isolation level of CS, either as a bind parameter or on the individual SQL statement, with CURRENTDATA set to NO as a bind option.

Lock avoidance is the default for most uses because it removes a lot of locking overhead. DB2 executes a small instruction set to determine whether an IRLM lock is truly needed for read-only cursors or ambiguous cursors.

Page and row locking can also be overridden at bind time or execution time. You can override locking for read-only cursors (not ambiguous cursors) by using the UR isolation level at bind time or on the individual statement level, as shown here:

```
EXEC SQL SELECT ... WITH ISOLATION UR
```

An SQL SELECT statement is considered to be read-only when it uses any of the following operations and clauses:

- JOIN
- SELECT DISTINCT
- GROUP BY
- ORDER BY
- UNION
- UNION ALL
- SELECT of a column function
- FOR FETCH ONLY (FOR READ ONLY)
- SELECT FROM non-updatable catalog table

If the SELECT statement does not incorporate any of the above, it is said to be *ambiguous*, meaning that DB2 does not know for sure whether modifying DML will be issued against the cursor. The CURRENTDATA setting of NO tells DB2 that the ambiguous cursor is read-only. If the statement is targeted by updating SQL, you'll receive an error. Table 16.4 shows the circumstances when locking is avoided or overridden.

Isolation level	CURRENTDATA	Cursor type	Avoid locks on returned data	Avoid locks on rejected data
UR	n/a	Read-only	n/a	n/a
CS	YES	Read-only	No	Yes
		Updatable	No	Yes
		Ambiguous	No	Yes
	NO	Read-only	Yes	Yes
		Updatable	No	Yes
		Ambiguous	Yes	Yes
RS	n/a	Read-only	No	Yes
		Updatable	No	Yes
		Ambiguous	No	Yes
RR	n/a	Read-only	No	No
		Updatable	No	No
		Ambiguous	No	No

Table 16.4: Lock avoidance determination

If your program is bound with ISOLATION(UR), mass deleters cannot run concurrently with your program.

Determining Whether Lock Avoidance Is Used

To determine whether your application is getting lock avoidance, you can run a performance trace class 6, IFCID 214. This trace provides information about whether lock avoidance was used for a particular page set in a unit of work. Field QW0218PC will contain either a Y or an N indicating its use. IFCID 223 in trace class 7 includes more detailed information about the use of lock avoidance on a particular resource.

System Parameters

Table 16.5 lists some system parameters (DSNZPARMs and IRLM PROC) that let you control various aspects of locking.

Table 16.5: System parameters for locking	
Parameter	**Description**
DEADLOK (IRLM parm)	Specifies the time, in seconds or milliseconds, of the local deadlock detection cycle. DB2 interprets values between 1 and 5 as seconds and interprets values between 100 and 5000 as milliseconds. This parameter also specifies the number of local deadlock cycles that must expire before the IRLM performs global deadlock detection processing (data sharing).
EVALUNC	Controls predicate evaluation for UR and RS isolation levels.
IRLMRWT	Specifies the number of seconds a transaction will wait for a lock before a timeout is detected. The IRLM uses this setting for timeout and deadlock detection. Most shops accept the default of 60 seconds, but in some high-performance situations where detection must occur sooner (so the applications don't incur excessive lock wait times), a lower number is used. If timeouts or deadlocks are hit often, the application is reviewed and tuned.
LRDRTHLD	Can be used to proactively identify reader threads that have exceeded the user-specified time limit threshold without COMMIT. When this value is non-zero, DB2 records the time a task holds a read claim. When passed a specified number of minutes, this parameter causes an IFCID 313 record to be written.
NUMLKTS	Represents the maximum number of locks on an object. If you turn off lock escalation (LOCKMAX 0), you'll need to increase this number. If you're using LOCKMAX SYSTEM, the NUMLKTS value will be the value for SYSTEM.
NUMLKUS	Specifies the maximum number of page or row locks that a single application can hold concurrently on all table spaces. This includes data pages, index pages, and rows. If you specify 0, no limit is imposed on the number of locks. You want to be careful with 0 because if you turn off lock escalation and don't commit frequently enough, you could run into storage problems (DB2 uses 250 bytes for each lock).
RRULOCK	Specifies whether to use the U (update) lock when using RR (repeatable read) or RS (read stability) isolation to access a table.
SKIPUNCI	Skips uncommitted insert for packages bound as CS (cursor stability) or RR (repeatable read).
URCHKTH	Specifies the number of checkpoints that should occur before a message is issued identifying a long-running unit of work. This parameter is used to find long-running units of work that are not committing.
URLGWTH	Specifies the number of log records to be written by an uncommitted unit of recovery before DB2 issues a warning message.
XLKUPDLT	Specifies the locking method to use when a searched UPDATE or DELETE is performed. The default, NO, best for concurrency; it tells DB2 to use an S or a U lock when scanning qualifying rows and to upgrade to an X lock when it finds a qualifying row. The YES value is useful in a data-sharing environment when the searches involve an index because it takes an X lock on qualifying rows or pages.

Claims and Drains

DB2 uses claim and drain locks to control currency between SQL processes and utilities, with partition independence being a major focus. Utilities and SQL can concurrently access and update different partitions, including different logical partitions of non-partitioned indexes.

A logical partition refers to the set of index entries that point to rows in a particular data partition. Logical partitions exist only in non-partitioned indexes of partitioned tables. An index entry belongs to one and only one logical partition.

Claims

When an application first accesses an object within a unit of work, it makes a *claim* on the object. It releases the claim at the next commit point. Unlike a transaction lock, the claim cannot persist past the commit point. To access the object in the next unit of work, the application must make a new claim. Claims can be acquired on

- a simple, segmented, or universal table space

- an index space

- a data partition

- an index partition

Table 16.6 describes the three claim classes: write, repeatable read, and cursor stability.

Table 16.6: Claim classes					
Claim class	Isolation level	Allows reading?	Allows updating?	Allows inserting?	Allows deleting?
Write	Any	Yes	Yes	Yes	Yes
Repeatable read	RR	Yes	No	No	No
Cursor stability	CS	Yes	No	No	No

Claims are released at COMMIT except for utilities and cursors defined WITH HOLD still positioned on an object. All SQL processes are claimers, but only occasionally is a utility a claimer (e.g., online load resume).

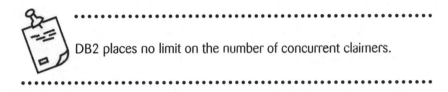

DB2 places no limit on the number of concurrent claimers.

Drains

DB2 uses *drain locks* to serialize access to partitions and page sets among utilities, commands, and SQL applications. The drain is initiated at any time, but the actual takeover of an object occurs only when all access to the object has been quiesced. The drain process acquires a lock to prevent subsequent access from occurring until the lock is released.

To drain a resource, a utility or command first acquires a drain lock and then waits until all claimers of a particular class on the resource are released. When all claims on the resource in a claim class are released, the resource is considered drained. A utility trying to take over can time out if a long-running SQL process doesn't release the claim quickly enough.

A utility that needs only read-only access will drain on the write class, which will prevent any new updating claimers. A utility that needs to change data will drain all claim classes.

Locking Issues and Problems

Too much locking can be a problem at times, resulting in suspensions, timeouts, or even deadlocks. Let's take a look at how these situations can occur.

Timeouts and Deadlocks

While waiting for a lock, a process can exceed an allowable amount of wait time that has been established. A systemwide option determines the maximum time a process can wait before it receives a "resource unavailable" error. This value, called the *resource timeout value*, is calculated by the following formula:

1. Divide RESOURCE TIMEOUT by DEADLOCK TIME.

2. Round up the result to the next largest integer.

3. Multiply this integer by DEADLOCK TIME.

4. Multiply the result by the appropriate resource timeout factor (shown in Table 16.7).

Table 16.7: Timeout factors	
Component	**Factor**
IMS MPP, IMS Fast Path Message Processing, CICS, DB2 QMF, CAF, TSO batch and online, RRSAF, global transactions	1
BIND	3
IMS BMP	4
IMS Fast Path	6
Utility	Utility timeout
STOP DATABASE command	10
Retained locks for all types	0

The result is the timeout value that is always greater than or equal to the RESOURCE TIMEOUT. When the timeout value has been reached, the requesting task is informed of the unavailable resource. Several conditions can cause a process to exceed a timeout value, and each returns a different message to a different location.

Another system parameter, DEADLOCK TIME, determines the time interval between two successive scans for a deadlock (the default is 1 second). For every deadlock interval, the IRLM verifies whether deadlock situations exist. In those cases, DB2 informs the task (usually the one that made the fewest changes) that a deadlock has occurred. The other tasks continue without any problems.

The main causes of a timeout are

- a program holding a lock has not freed it soon enough

- a deadlock between DB2 and a non-DB2 resource

The main causes of deadlocks are

- two hot (i.e., constantly used) pages
- lock escalation
- one hot page, promotion from S to X lock, and FOR UPDATE OF missing on the cursor

When a timeout or deadlock occurs, error codes and messages are sent as follows.

- To the application program:
  - » –911 = "The current unit of work has been rolled back due to deadlock or timeout, Reason [*reason-code*], Type of resource [*resource-type*], and Resource name [*resource-name*]."

    The reason code indicates whether a timeout or a deadlock has occurred. The application is rolled back to the previous commit. On receipt of the –911 return code, the application should terminate or retry.

  - » –913 = "Unsuccessful execution caused by deadlock or timeout, Reason [*reason-code*], Type of resource [*resource-type*], and Resource name [*resource-name*]."

    The reason code indicates whether a timeout or a deadlock has occurred. The current unit of work *has not been rolled back*. The application should either commit or roll back. Then the application should terminate or retry.

- To the console:
  - » DSNT376I message
  - » DSNT500I message

Coding Retry Logic for Locking Errors

A –911 SQL return code means that a deadlock or a timeout occurred and DB2 has issued a successful ROLLBACK to the last commit point. If the rollback was not successful, the application receives a –913 SQL return code signifying that a rollback was not performed. With a –913 return code, the application needs to issue a ROLLBACK before proceeding with any other SQL.

When a –911 condition occurs, the choice of whether to use retry logic depends on the individual application. If a large amount of work has been rolled back and other, non-DB2 files are present, it may be difficult to reposition everything and retry the unit of work. With most –911 situations, a restart process (vendor-supplied or user-written) is generally easier than a programmatic reposition and retry. If a small amount of work was lost, you could perform a simple retry up to some fixed number of times. It's important not to retry with a breakpoint because the source of the problem that caused the negative codes might still exist.

Lock Promotion and Escalation

Under certain circumstances, DB2 may change the locks acquired during execution of SQL statements based on the number or type of locks being held. In this section, we look at the implications of lock escalation and lock promotion.

Lock Escalation

Lock escalation can occur when the number of held locks reaches the LOCKMAX value set on the CREATE TABLESPACE statement. At this time, DB2 releases all held locks in favor of taking a more comprehensive lock. In other words, it releases several page or row locks to escalate to a table or table space lock. DB2 tries to balance the number of locks on objects based on the amount of concurrent access. The LOCKMAX option then further determines whether and when escalation occurs.

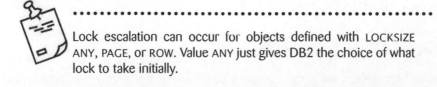

Lock escalation can occur for objects defined with LOCKSIZE ANY, PAGE, or ROW. Value ANY just gives DB2 the choice of what lock to take initially.

The LOCKMAX value defines how many locks can be held simultaneously on an object. When the number of held locks reaches the specified value, DB2 escalates the locks. If you use LOCKSIZE ANY, LOCKMAX defaults to the value SYSTEM, which means it uses the number set by the NUMLKTS DSNZPARM. Otherwise, the option defaults to 0 for specific object locks such as page, row, table, and table space.

You can turn off lock escalation by setting LOCKMAX to 0. If you choose this approach, be sure the applications that access the objects are committing frequently, and adjust DSNZPARM NUMLKTS to permit more locks to be taken. Otherwise, you risk hitting negative SQL codes when you reach the maximum number of locks (without escalation, you can hold more, smaller locks). Lock escalation is there to protect you from taking excessive system resources, so if you turn it off, you need to control it. If you are CPU-bound, turning off lock escalation may be unwise because DB2 will take longer to traverse long chains of locks and IRLM latch activity will require more CPU.

The DB2 console log provides details about lock escalation activity, identified by the DSNI031I message. This message indicates the resource that experienced the escalation and contains details about the new state of the lock. Figure 16.1 shows a sample message.

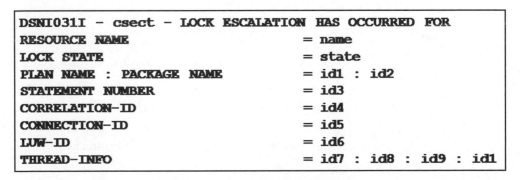

Figure 16.1: Sample DSNI031I message

Lock Promotion

The lock mode that will be used for a table, table space, or table space partition during execution of an SQL statement is reflected in column TSLOCKMODE of the PLAN_TABLE populated by EXPLAIN if DB2 can determine the isolation at bind time. The SQL statement uses this mode for the table or table space lock if and only of a preceding SQL statement has not raised the lock mode. For example, assume an SQL SELECT statement has a TSLOCKMODE of IS. If, during execution, DB2 promotes the lock to the more restrictive IX mode, that is the mode a subsequent SELECT statement will use. This process, called *lock promotion*, generally isn't a concern—just a fact.

Database and Application Design for Concurrency

In this section, we provide some advice about how to design your database and applications for maximum concurrency.

Database Design

Keep the following recommendations in mind as you design your database, before the physical implementation of the tables and table spaces. Changing the database after the data is in use will be difficult.

- Use segmented or universal table spaces, not simple ones.
  - » To keep rows of different tables on different pages, so page locks lock rows for only one table
- Use LOCKSIZE parameters appropriately.
  - » To minimize the amount of locked data unless the application requires exclusive access
- Consider spacing out rows for small tables with heavy concurrent access by using MAXROWS = 1. (Row-level lock can also help in this situation, but its overhead is greater, especially in a data-sharing environment.)
- Use partitioning where possible.
  - » To reduce contention and increase parallel activity for batch processes
  - » To reduce overhead in data sharing by enabling the use of affinity routing to different partitions
  - » To permit locks to be taken on individual partitions

- Use Data Partitioned Secondary Indexes (DPSI).

  » To promote partition independence and lessen contention for utilities

- Consider using LOCKMAX 0 to turn off lock escalation in high-volume environments. (You'll need to increase NUMLKTS and make sure applications commit frequently.)

- Use volatile tables.

  » To reduce contention (because an index will also be used to access the data by applications that always access the data in the same order)

- Have an adequate number of databases.

  » To reduce DBD locking if DDL, DCL, and utility execution is high for objects in the same database

- Use sequence objects.

  » To provide better number generation without the overhead of using a single control table

Application Design

The following recommendations can help you achieve the best concurrency by reducing the number of locks an application takes.

- Access tables in the same order to prevent applications from deadlocking.

- Have commits in the applications. With a proper commit strategy, you can reduce contention, achieve lock avoidance, reduce rollback time for an application, reduced elapsed time for system restart, and allow other processes (e.g., online REORG) to interrupt.

- Code retry logic for deadlocks.

- Bind with appropriate parameters.

- Use CURRENTDATA(NO) and ISOLATION(CS) to let DB2 attempt lock avoidance. These options will also allow locks to be released as soon as possible.

- Use ACQUIRE(USE) to take locks when necessary.

- Use uncommitted read where appropriate (best to use at statement level).

- Close all cursors as soon as possible to allow locks and resources to be freed.

- Consider using SKIP LOCKED DATA if applicable.

- Be careful with multi-row inserts with positioned updates and deletes because they can expand the unit of work.

- Use optimistic locking, and test whether another transaction has changed the underlying data source column since the last read operation. To do so, define a column in the table with FOR EACH ROW ON UPDATE AS ROW CHANGE TIMESTAMP and use the timestamp for comparison during the update. The following example shows this usage:

```
SELECT PKG_ID, PKG_DESC, ROW CHANGE TIMESTAMP FOR PKG_TBL
FROM PKG_TBL
WHERE PKG_ID     = :PKG-ID WITH UR
  . . . row modified by application
UPDATE PKG_TBL
SET PKG_DESC     = :PKG-DESC
WHERE  PKG_ID    = :PKG_ID
AND ROW CHANGE TIMESTAMP FOR PKG_TBL = :UPD-TSP
```

For additional examples of optimistic locking, see Chapter 12.

Lock Monitoring

Several tools are available for monitoring lock activity in DB2:

- Explain

- Optimization Service Center (OSC)

- Accounting and statistics reports

- DISPLAY command

- Traces

Explain

When using the EXPLAIN utility to see what access path DB2 will choose, you can also view what object locks are planned for the query. (Chapter 17 describes how to run EXPLAIN.) The PLAN_TABLE will contain a column named TSLOCKMODE, which shows the initial lock mode for the table. This mode applies to the table or table space (depending on the value of LOCKSIZE and whether the table space is simple or segmented).

Accounting and Statistics Reports

Using the accounting and statistics reports produced by a DB2 monitoring tool, you can review locking activity.

To ensure that the correct information is available for the reports, you should always have statistics classes 1, 3, and 4 and accounting classes 1 and 3.

These reports let you view counters for timeouts, deadlocks, suspensions, escalation, lock/unlock requests, and claim/drain requests. The following example shows the accounting trace output for an application. The statistics report would show similar counts, by subsystem, plus information about events per second/thread/commit.

```
LOCKING                     TOTAL
_____         _____
TIMEOUTS                    1
DEADLOCKS                   0
ESCAL. (SHAR)               0
ESCAL. (EXCL)               0
MAX PG/ROW LCK HELD         5
LOCK REQUEST                0
UNLOCK REQST                0
QUERY REQST                 0
CHANGE REQST                0
OTHER REQST                 0
LOCK SUSPENS.               2
IRLM LATCH SUSPENS          0
OTHER SUSPENS               0
TOTAL SUSPENS               2
```

```
DRAIN/CLAIM              TOTAL
----------------         -----
DRAIN REQST                 0
DRAIN FAILED                0
CLAIM REQST                 5
CLAIM FAILED                0
```

Displaying Locks

To investigate application concurrency problems, you can display the locks that are being held. By using the –DISPLAY DATABASE (*dbname*) SPACE (*tsname*) LOCKS command, you can see many properties about a given lock, as shown in Figure 16.2.

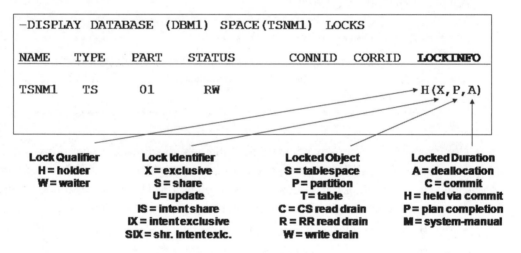

Figure 16.2: –DISPLAY DATABASE LOCKS command output

Traces

You can use DB2 traces to trace and record subsystem data and events, including locking information. A statistics trace class 3 provides information about deadlocks and timeouts, and an accounting trace class 3 shows the elapsed time divided into various waits, such as the duration of suspensions due to waits for locks and latches or waits for I/O. There are also more details in performance traces (classes 6, 7, and 17). You can use these trace classes to help monitor and tune locking contention problems.

Summary

In this chapter, we discussed how concurrency (serialization) is controlled. To protect the data as it is being modified, rules are established and the changes are grouped into units of work. The updated data is made permanent by the COMMIT statement or removed by the ROLLBACK statement. The isolation level, the lock size, and the rules of lock duration determine the rules of concurrency.

DB2 implements the isolation-level semantics of data access by implicitly acquiring locks on behalf of applications. Applications can decide to lock a resource for exclusive or share modes. The resources that can be locked are the row, page, table, table space, LOB, and partition.

If a requested lock is more restrictive and another application already has the resource locked, a wait on the release of the lock occurs. System-wide parameters for both resource timeout and deadlocks dictate the amount of time an application will wait.

If multiple applications require access to data that is held by other applications, a deadlock scenario can occur. DB2 will detect the occurrence of any deadlocks and force one of the transactions to roll back. Every requested lock requires memory in the IRLM, and the amount of lock storage is configurable using IRLM parameters.

We also discussed many opportunities for avoiding excessive locks and lock problems. These opportunities come through proper database and application designs.

Additional Resources

IBM DB2 9 Administration Guide (SC18-9840)
IBM DB2 9 Application Programming and SQL Guide (SC18-9841)
IBM DB2 9 Command Reference (SC18-9844)

Practice Questions

Question 1

If you want to find out information about locks being held on a table space, which of the following commands would you use?

○ A. –DISPLAY LOCKS

○ B. –DISPLAY DATABASE (*dbname*) LOCKS

○ C. –DISPLAY TABLESPACE (*tsname*) LOCKS

○ D. –DISPLAY GROUP

Question 2

To reduce the amount of time DB2 waits for a resource before a timeout occurs, which of the following DSNZPARMs should be changed?

○ A. NUMLKTS

○ B. NUMLKUS

○ C. IRLMRWT

○ D. SKIPUNCI

Question 3

An application wants to skip data that is currently locked by another application. The application doesn't have the need to see uncommitted or unavailable data. Which option could be used on the SELECT statement?

○ A. SKIP LOCKED DATA

○ B. FOR FETCH ONLY

○ C. FETCH FIRST *n* ROWS

○ D. OPTIMIZE FOR *n* ROWS

Question 4

If you need to diagnose locking-contention problems in an application, which trace class would be useful?

○ A. Accounting Trace Class 3

○ B. Statistics Trace Class 2

○ C. Accounting Trace Class 2

○ D. Statistics Trace Class 1

Question 5

Which of the following is *not* a valid lock mode?

○ A. Update

○ B. Share Intent Exclusive

○ C. Exclusive

○ D. Insert

Answers

Question 1

The correct answer is **B**, The –DISPLAY DATABASE command with the LOCKS option shows you the locks being held on the table spaces in the specified database.

Question 2

The correct answer is **C**, IRLMRWT. This DSNZPARM specifies the number of seconds a transaction will wait for a lock before a timeout is detected. The IRLM uses this value for timeout detection.

Question 3

The correct answer is **A**, SKIP LOCKED DATA. You can use this option on a SELECT statement to let the transaction skip data that has an incompatible lock held by another application. You should use this option only if the transaction can tolerate seeing somewhat less than accurate data.

Question 4

The correct answer is **A**, Accounting Trace Class 3. You use this trace class to show the elapsed time divided into various waits, such as the duration of suspensions due to waits for locks and latches or waits for I/O.

Question 5

The correct answer is **D**, Insert. There is no lock mode known as Insert. would take an exclusive lock on the page.

Performance Monitoring and Tuning

In This Chapter

- ✔ SQL monitoring and tuning
- ✔ Optimization
- ✔ Using EXPLAIN
- ✔ Exploiting indexes
- ✔ Database monitoring
- ✔ Tracing
- ✔ Memory tuning
- ✔ Problem determination

Tuning DB2 queries is critical to performance. You need to understand how the DB2 optimizer works and how to create the best possible indexes for your queries. The other part of the picture is determining whether DB2 is using the best index and is performing joins and other operations effectively. DB2 provides several tools to help with these tasks.

In addition to properly monitoring and tuning SQL, you need to monitor the applications that use DB2 and the DB2 subsystems themselves for performance. When used properly, a variety of DB2 tools and facilities can be extremely critical for overall application and system tuning.

Access Paths and Optimization

If you want to know how DB2 will execute a query, you must analyze its access path, or the way it retrieves data from a specific table. Often times, unexpected decreases in performance (e.g., excessive GETPAGEs) are the result of a change in the access path. The DB2 EXPLAIN facility provides information about how DB2 accesses the data to process SQL statements.

You should understand at a high level how the DB2 database engine processes SQL statements: DB2 analyzes each SQL statement for syntax and examines the DB2 catalog for the objects referenced in the statement; then it determines how to process the statement either during a static bind or during prepare (when a statement is executed dynamically). The method used to retrieve data from tables is called the *access plan*.

The component within DB2 that determines the access plan to be used is known as the *optimizer*. During the static preparation of a SQL statement, the SQL compiler is called on to generate an access plan. The access plan contains the data access strategy, including index usage, sort methods, locking semantics, and join methods.

The executable form of the SQL statement is stored in the system tables when you execute a BIND command. The access module is called a *database request module (DBRM)*, which can then be bound into a package. For more information about packages, see Chapter 11.

Sometimes, the complete statement isn't known until execution time. In this case, the compiler is invoked during program execution to generate an access plan for the query that the database manager can use to access the data. Such a SQL statement is called a *dynamic SQL statement*. The access plans for dynamic SQL statements are not stored in the system catalog. They can be cached in memory in the dynamic SQL cache and will not be re-prepared if the access plans for the dynamic SQL statements already exist in the dynamic SQL cache.

EXPLAIN

The EXPLAIN facility produces information about the following:

- A plan, package, or SQL statement when it is bound. The output appears in a table you create, called PLAN_TABLE, which is also called the *plan table*.

For experienced users, you can use the plan table to give optimization hints (discussed later) to DB2.

- The details of an access plan, such as whether a predicate is stage 1 or stage 2, the filter factor and number of rows returned, and whether partitions have been eliminated.

- An estimated cost of executing an SQL SELECT, INSERT, MERGE, UPDATE, or DELETE statement. The output appears in a table you create, called DSN_STATEMNT_TABLE, which is also known as the *statement table*.

- User-defined functions referred to in the statement, including the specific name and schema. The output appears in a table you create, called DSN_FUNCTION_TABLE, also called the *function table*.

- Statements cached in the system, including information about the quantity of executions within the statement cache as well as the resources required to execute the statements. This information is stored in the *statement cache table* and is populated by a special form of the EXPLAIN statement.

- Detailed information about the predicates, filtering, sorting, partition elimination, and parallel operations within a statement. This information is provided via a number of optional tables that can be created by the DB2 Optimization Service Center or manually. These tables, if they exist, are populated by the EXPLAIN facility.

Let's take a closer look at the data contained in these tables, as well as the DB2 Optimization Service Center product, and how to use this data to improve query performance.

Gathering Explain Data

There are three ways to populate the explain tables:

- Executing the SQL EXPLAIN statement. You can populate PLAN_TABLE and the other explain tables by executing the SQL statement EXPLAIN. In the statement, specify a single explainable SQL statement in the FOR clause. You can execute EXPLAIN either statically from an application program or dynamically using Query Management Facility (QMF) or SPUFI.

- Binding with the option EXPLAIN(YES). You can populate PLAN_TABLE and the other explain tables by binding a package with the EXPLAIN(YES) option for a program with static embedded SQL statements.

- Executing EXPLAIN via the Optimization Service Center.

Before you can use EXPLAIN, you must create at least the PLAN_TABLE table to hold the statement's results. The DB2 sample library provides a copy of the statements needed to create the table, under the member name DSNTESC. (Unless you need the information they provide, you needn't create a function table or a statement table to use EXPLAIN.) The additional explain tables are optional and typically are created automatically when you use the Optimization Service Center product.

DB2 does not automatically delete rows from the plan table. To clear the table of obsolete rows, use DELETE, just as you would to delete rows from any table.

Examining Explain Data

EXPLAINs populate the PLAN_TABLE table, and from there you must interpret the data and act accordingly. Table 17.1 describes the columns in the plan table.

Table 17.1: PLAN_TABLE columns	
Column name	Description
QUERYNO	A number intended to identify the statement being explained. For a row produced by an EXPLAIN statement, specify the number in the QUERYNO clause. For a row produced by non-EXPLAIN statements, specify the number using the QUERYNO clause, which is an optional part of the SELECT, INSERT, UPDATE, and DELETE statement syntax. Otherwise, DB2 assigns a number based on the line number of the SQL statement in the source program.
	FETCH statements do not each have an individual QUERYNO assigned to them. Instead, DB2 uses the QUERYNO of the DECLARE CURSOR statement for all corresponding FETCH statements for that cursor.
	When the values of QUERYNO are based on the statement number in the source program, values greater than 32,767 are reported as 0. Hence, in a very long program, the value is not guaranteed to be unique. If QUERYNO is not unique, use the value of TIMESTAMP, which is always unique.

Table 17.1: PLAN_TABLE columns (continued)	
Column name	**Description**
QBLOCKNO	A number that identifies each query block within a query. The value of the numbers are not in any particular order, nor are they necessarily consecutive.
APPLNAME	The name of the application plan for the row. Applies only to embedded EXPLAIN statements executed from a plan or to statements explained when binding a plan. Blank if not applicable.
PROGNAME	The name of the program or package containing the statement being explained. For statements explained dynamically, such as with QMF or SPUFI, the associated plan/package is listed. Blank if not applicable.
PLANNO	The number of the step in which the query indicated in QBLOCKNO was processed. This column indicates the order in which the steps were executed.
METHOD	A number (0, 1, 2, 3, or 4) that indicates the join method used for the step: 0 = First table accessed, continuation of previous table accessed, or not used. 1 = Nested loop join. For each row of the present composite table, matching rows of a new table are found and joined. 2 = Merge scan join. The present composite table and the new tables are scanned in the order of the join columns, and matching rows are joined. 3 = Sorts needed by ORDER BY, GROUP BY, SELECT DISTINCT, UNION, a quantified predicate, or an IN predicate. This step does not access a new table. 4 = Hybrid join. The current composite table is scanned in the order of the join-column rows of the new table. The new table is accessed using list prefetch.
CREATOR	The creator of the new table accessed in this step; blank if METHOD is 3.
TNAME	The name of a table, materialized query table, created or declared temporary table, materialized view, or materialized table expression. The value is blank if METHOD is 3. The column can also contain the name of a table in the form DSNWFQB(*qblockno*). DSNWFQB(*qblockno*) is used to represent the intermediate result of a UNION ALL, an INTERSECT ALL, an EXCEPT ALL, or an outer join that is materialized. If a view is merged, the name of the view does not appear. UDSN_BIM_TBL(qblockno) is used to represent the work file of a star join dimension table.
TABNO	IBM use only.
ACCESSTYPE	The method of accessing the new table: DI = By an intersection of multiple DOCID lists to return the final DOCID list. DU = By a union of multiple DOCID lists to return the final DOCID list. DX = By an XML index scan of the index named in ACCESSNAME to return a DOCID list. E = By direct row using a row change timestamp column. I = By an index (identified in ACCESSCREATOR and ACCESSNAME).

Table 17.1: PLAN_TABLE columns (continued)	
Column name	**Description**
ACCESSTYPE	I1 = By a one-fetch index scan.
	M = By a multiple index scan (followed by MX, MI, or MU).
	MX = By an index scan on the index named in ACCESSNAME. When the access method MX follows the access method DX, DI, or DU, the table is accessed by the DOCID index using the DOCID list returned by DX, DI, or DU.
	MI = By an intersection of multiple indexes.
	MU = By a union of multiple indexes.
	N = By an index scan when the matching predicate contains the IN keyword.
	P = By a dynamic index ANDing scan.
	R = By a table space scan.
	RW = By a work file scan of the result of a materialized user-defined table function.
	V = By buffers for an INSERT statement within a SELECT.
	Blank = Not applicable to the current row.
MATCHCOLS	For ACCESSTYPE I, I1, N, MX, or DX, the number of index keys used in an index scan; otherwise, 0.
ACCESSCREATOR	For ACCESSTYPE I, I1, N, MX, or DX, the creator of the index; otherwise, blank.
ACCESSNAME	For ACCESSTYPE I, I1, N, MX, or DX, the name of the index; for ACCESSTYPE P, DSNPJW(*mixopseqno*) is the starting pair-wise join leg in MIXOPSEQNO; otherwise, blank.
INDEXONLY	Whether access to an index alone is enough to carry out the step, or whether data, too, must be accessed. Y = Yes; N = No.
SORTN_UNIQ	Whether the new table is sorted to remove duplicate rows. Y = Yes; N = No.
SORTN_JOIN	Whether the new table is sorted for join method 2 or 4. Y = Yes; N = No.
SORTN_ORDERBY	Whether the new table is sorted for ORDER BY. Y = Yes; N = No.
SORTN_GROUPBY	Whether the new table is sorted for GROUP BY. Y = Yes; N = No.
SORTC_UNIQ	Whether the composite table is sorted to remove duplicate rows. Y = Yes; N = No.
SORTC_JOIN	Whether the composite table is sorted for join method 1, 2, or 4. Y = Yes; N = No.
SORTC_ORDERBY	Whether the composite table is sorted for an ORDER BY clause or a quantified predicate. Y = Yes; N = No.
SORTC_GROUPBY	Whether the composite table is sorted for a GROUP BY clause. Y = Yes; N = No.

Table 17.1: PLAN_TABLE columns (continued)	
Column name	**Description**
TSLOCKMODE	An indication of the mode of lock to be acquired on the new table or its table space or table space partitions. If the isolation can be determined at bind time, the values are: IS = Intent share lock IX = Intent exclusive lock S = Share lock U = Update lock X = Exclusive lock SIX = Share with intent exclusive lock N = UR isolation; no lock If the isolation cannot be determined at bind time, the lock mode determined by the isolation at runtime is shown by the following values. NS = For UR isolation, no lock; for CS, RS, or RR, an S lock. NIS = For UR isolation, no lock; for CS, RS, or RR, an IS lock. NSS = For UR isolation, no lock; for CS or RS, an IS lock; for RR, an S lock. SS = For UR, CS, or RS isolation, an IS lock; for RR, an S lock. The data in this column is right-justified. For example, IX appears as a blank followed by I followed by X. If the column contains a blank, no lock is acquired. If the access method in the ACCESSTYPE column is DX, DI, or DU, no latches are acquired on the XML index page, and no lock is acquired on the new base table data page or row, nor on the XML table and the corresponding table spaces. The value of TSLOCKMODE is blank in this case.
TIMESTAMP	Usually, the time at which the row is processed, to the last 0.01 second. If necessary, DB2 adds 0.01 second to the value to ensure that rows for two successive queries have different values.
REMARKS	A field into which you can insert any character string of 254 or fewer characters.
PREFETCH	Whether data pages are to be read in advance by prefetch: D = Optimizer expects dynamic prefetch S = Pure sequential prefetch L = Prefetch through a page list Blank = Unknown at bind time or no prefetch
COLUMN_FN_EVAL	When a SQL aggregate function is evaluated: R = While the data is being read from the table or index S = While performing a sort to satisfy a GROUP BY clause Blank = After data retrieval after any sorts

Table 17.1: PLAN_TABLE columns (continued)	
Column name	**Description**
MIXOPSEQ	The sequence number of a step in a multiple index operation:
	1, 2, . . . n = For the steps of the multiple index procedure (ACCESSTYPE is MX, MI, MU, DX, DI, or DU)
	0 = For any other rows
VERSION	The version identifier for the package. Applies only to an embedded EXPLAIN statement executed from a package or to a statement that is explained when binding a package. Blank if not applicable.
COLLID	The collection ID for the package. Applies only to an embedded EXPLAIN statement executed from a package or to a statement that is explained when binding a package. Blank if not applicable. The value DSNDYNAMICSQLCACHE indicates that the row is for a cached statement.
ACCESS_DEGREE	The number of parallel tasks or operations activated by a query. This value is determined at bind time; the actual number of parallel operations used at execution time could differ. The column contains 0 if there is a host variable.
ACCESS_PGROUP_ID	The identifier of the parallel group for accessing the new table. A parallel group is a set of consecutive operations, executed in parallel, that have the same number of parallel tasks. This value is determined at bind time; it could change at execution time.
JOIN_DEGREE	The number of parallel operations or tasks used in joining the composite table with the new table. This value is determined at bind time and can be 0 if there is a host variable. The actual number of parallel operations or tasks used at execution time could be different.
JOIN_PGROUP_ID	The identifier of the parallel group for joining the composite table with the new table. This value is determined at bind time; it could change at execution time.
SORTC_PGROUP_ID	The parallel group identifier for the parallel sort of the composite table.
SORTN_PGROUP_ID	The parallel group identifier for the parallel sort of the new table.
PARALLELISM_MODE	The kind of parallelism, if any, that is used at bind time:
	I = Query I/O parallelism
	C = Query CP parallelism
	X = Sysplex query parallelism
MERGE_JOIN_COLS	The number of columns that are joined during a merge scan join (Method = 2).
CORRELATION_NAME	The correlation name of a table or view that is specified in the statement. If there is no correlation name, the column is blank.
PAGE_RANGE	Whether the table qualifies for page range screening, so that plans scan only the partitions that are needed. Y = Yes; blank = No.

Table 17.1: PLAN_TABLE columns (continued)	
Column name	**Description**
JOIN_TYPE	The type of an outer join:
	F = Full outer join
	L = Left outer join
	S = Star join
	Blank = Inner join or no join
	RIGHT OUTER JOIN converts to a LEFT OUTER JOIN when you use it, so that JOIN_TYPE contains L.
GROUP_MEMBER	The member name of the DB2 that executed EXPLAIN. The column is blank if the DB2 subsystem was not in a data-sharing environment when EXPLAIN was executed.
IBM_SERVICE_DATA	IBM use only.
WHEN_OPTIMIZE	When the access path was determined:
	blank = At bind time, using a default filter factor for any host variables, parameter markers, or special registers.
	B = At bind time, using a default filter factor for any host variables, parameter markers, or special registers; however, the statement is reoptimized at runtime using input variable values for input host variables, parameter markers, or special registers. The bind option REOPT(ALWAYS), REOPT(ONCE), or REOPT(AUTO), must be specified for reoptimization to occur.
	R = At runtime, using input variables for any host variables, parameter markers, or special registers. The bind option REOPT(ALWAYS), REOPT(ONCE), or REOPT(AUTO) must be specified for this to occur.
QBLOCK_TYPF	For each query block, the type of SQL operation performed. For the outermost query, the column identifies the statement type. Possible values:
	SELECT = SELECT
	INSERT = INSERT
	UPDATE = UPDATE
	DELETE = DELETE
	SELUPD = SELECT with FOR UPDATE OF
	DELCUR = DELETE WHERE CURRENT OF CURSOR
	UPDCUR = UPDATE WHERE CURRENT OF CURSOR
	CORSUB = Correlated subquery
	NCOSUB = Noncorrelated subquery
	TABLEX = Table expression
	TRIGGR = WHEN clause on CREATE TRIGGER

Table 17.1: PLAN_TABLE columns (continued)	
Column name	**Description**
QBLOCK_TYPE	UNION = UNION UNIONA = UNION ALL INTERS = INTERSECT INTERA = INTERSECT ALL EXCEPT = EXCEPT EXCEPTA = EXCEPT ALL
BIND_TIME	For non-cached static SQL statements, the time at which the plan or package for the statement or query block was bound. For cached static and dynamic statements, the time at which the statement entered the cache. For non-cached static, cached static, and cached dynamic statements, this is a full-precision timestamp value. For non-cached dynamic SQL statements, this is the value contained in the TIMESTAMP column of PLAN_TABLE appended by four zeroes.
OPTHINT	A string that you use to identify this row as an optimization hint for DB2. DB2 uses this row as input when choosing an access path.
HINT_USED	If DB2 used one of your optimization hints, it puts the identifier for that hint (the value in OPTHINT) in this column.
PRIMARY_ ACCESSTYPE	Indicates whether direct row access will be attempted first: D = DB2 will try to use direct row access. If it cannot use direct row access at runtime, it uses the access path described in the ACCESSTYPE column of PLAN_TABLE. T = The base table or result file is materialized into a work file, and the work file is accessed via sparse index access. If a base table is involved, ACCESSTYPE indicates how the base table is accessed. Blank = DB2 will not try to use direct row access.
PARENT_QBLOCK	Number that indicates the QBLOCKNO of the parent query.
TABLE_TYPE	The type of new table: B = Buffers for SELECT from INSERT, SELECT from UPDATE, SELECT from MERGE, or SELECT from DELETE statement. C = Common table expression F = Table function M = Materialized query table Q = Temporary intermediate result table (not materialized). For the name of the view or nested table expression, a value of Q indicates that the materialization was virtual and not actual. Materialization can be virtual when the view or nested table expression definition contains a UNION ALL that is not distributed.

Table 17.1: PLAN_TABLE columns (continued)	
Column name	**Description**
TABLE_TYPE	R = Recursive common table expression
	S = Subquery (correlated or non-correlated)
	T = Table
	W = Work file
	The value of the column is null if the query uses GROUP BY, ORDER BY, or DISTINCT, which requires an implicit sort.
TABLE_ENCODE	The encoding scheme of the table. If the table has a single CCSID set, possible values are:
	A = ASCII
	E = EBCDIC
	U = Unicode
	M = The table contains multiple CCSID sets.
TABLE_SCCSID	The SBCS CCSID value of the table. If column TABLE_ENCODE is M, the value is 0.
TABLE_MCCSID	The mixed CCSID value of the table. If column TABLE_ENCODE is M, the value is 0.
TABLE_DCCSID	The DBCS CCSID value of the table. If column TABLE_ENCODE is M, the value is 0.
ROUTINE_ID	IBM use only.
CTREF	If the referenced table is a common table expression, the value is the top-level query block number
STMTTOKEN	A user-specified statement token.
PARENT_PLANNO	Corresponds to the plan number in the parent query block where a correlated subquery is involved. Or, for non-correlated subqueries, corresponds to the plan number in the parent query block that represents the work file for the subquery.

Access Path Evaluation

Next, let's review how to examine some of the most useful data in the plan table and determine what the DB2 optimizer is using to access the data.

Index Access

The following paragraphs describe the different types of index access and how they are represented in the plan table.

Index Access (ACCESSTYPE is I, I1, N, MX, or DX)

If column ACCESSTYPE in the plan table has the value I, I1, N, MX, or DX, DB2 uses an index to access the table named in column TNAME. Columns ACCESSCREATOR and ACCESSNAME identify the index.

Multiple Index Access (ACCESSTYPE = M)

An ACCESSTYPE value of M indicates that DB2 uses a set of indexes to access a single table. A group of rows in the plan table contain information about the multiple index access. The rows are numbered in column MIXOPSEQ in the order of execution of steps in the multiple index access. (If you retrieve the rows in order by MIXOPSEQ, the result is similar to postfix arithmetic notation.)

Number of Matching Index (MATCHCOLS = *n*)

If the plan table's MATCHCOLS column value is 0, the access method is called a *non-matching index scan*, and all the index keys and their row identifiers (RIDs) are read. If MATCHCOLS is greater than 0, the access method is a *matching index scan*: the query uses predicates that match the index columns.

In general, the matching predicates on the leading index columns are equal or IN predicates. The predicate that matches the final index column can be an equal, IN, or range predicate (<, <=, >, >=, LIKE, or BETWEEN). The following example illustrates matching predicates.

```
SELECT *
FROM EMP
WHERE JOBCODE = '5'
AND LOCATION ='CA'
AND SALARY > 60000
AND AGE > 21;

INDEX XEMP5 on (JOBCODE,LOCATION,SALARY,AGE)
```

The index XEMP5 is the chosen access path for this query, with MATCHCOLS = 3. Two equal predicates are specified on the first two columns, and a range predicate is on the third column. Although the index contains four columns, only three of them can be considered matching columns.

At most, one IN predicate can be a matching predicate; the exception, however, is a non-correlated IN subquery. IN-list predicates cannot be matching predicates for MX access or list prefetch.

Increasing the number of matching columns can help query performance; however, if the column that is added is highly correlated to the existing columns, it may not provide much of a benefit in terms of filtering.

Only Boolean term predicates can use matching index access on a single index.

Index-Only Access (INDEXONLY = Y)

When the value of the plan table's INDEXONLY column is Y, DB2 uses *index-only access*. For a SELECT operation, all the columns needed for the query can be found in the index, and DB2 does not access the table. For an UPDATE or DELETE operation, only the index is required to read the selected row.

If access is by more than one index, INDEXONLY is Y for a step with access type MX, because the data pages are not actually accessed until all the steps for intersection (MI) or union (MU) take place.

Table Access

The following paragraphs summarize the different types of table accesses and how they are represented in the plan table.

Table Space Scan (ACCESSTYPE = R, PREFETCH = S)

DB2 most often uses a table space scan (R = relational scan) for one of the following reasons:

- Access is through a created global temporary table (index access is not possible for created global temporary tables).

- A matching index scan is not possible because an index is not available or no predicates match the index columns.

- A high percentage of the rows in the table are returned. In this case, an index isn't really useful because most rows need to be read anyway.

- The indexes that have matching predicates have low cluster ratios and are therefore efficient only for small amounts of data.

Assume that table DSN8910.EMP has no index on the BONUS column. The following an example illustrates a table space scan.

```
SELECT * FROM DSN8910.EMP WHERE BONUS > 5000;
```

In this case, at least every row in the EMP table must be examined to determine whether the value of BONUS matches the given range.

DB2 can also show a table space scan against a work file temporary table during complex query operations. For certain complex queries, DB2 has to materialize nested table expressions. This requirement is typically the case when the query in the nested table expression needs to be sorted or aggregated. A DISTINCT or a GROUP BY will result in the materialization of a nested table expression, as will the placement of a non-deterministic function, such as the RAND() function. The plan table will show one or more query blocks for the nested table expression and then, within another query block, a table space scan against the temporary work file table. The ACCESS_TYPE will be R, and the TABLE_TYPE will be T for a table named "B". The following query materializes and sorts the nested table expression and then scans it as part of a merge scan join (described later in this section).

```
SELECT A.C1, B.C2
FROM T1 A
LEFT OUTER JOIN
(SELECT DISTINCT C1, C2
FROM T2
WHERE C4 = :ws-C4) AS B
ON      A.C1 = B.C1
AND A.C3 = :ws-C3;
```

Prefetching (PREFETCH = D, L, S, or Blank)

Prefetching is a method of determining in advance that a set of data pages is about to be used and then reading the entire set into a buffer with a single asynchronous I/O operation.

If the value of the PREFETCH column is D, the optimizer is expecting *dynamic prefetch*. Dynamic prefetch occurs when DB2 detects that a reader is reading pages in a sequential manner. Once sequential processing is detected, DB2 begins dynamically prefetching data into memory. It will continue to monitor the pattern of access, turning dynamic prefetch on or off as needed.

If PREFETCH is S, the method is called *sequential prefetch*. The data pages that are read in advance are sequential. A table space scan always uses sequential prefetch. An index scan might not use it.

If PREFETCH is L, the method is called *list prefetch*. One or more indexes are used to select the RIDs for a list of data pages to be read in advance; the pages need not be sequential. Usually, the RIDs are sorted. The exception is the case of a hybrid join (METHOD = 4) when the value of column SORTN_JOIN is N.

If PREFETCH is blank, DB2 does not choose prefetching as an access method at bind or prepare time. However, depending on the pattern of the page access, data can be prefetched at execution time through a process called *sequential detection* (also known as *dynamic prefetch*).

> DB2 always and only attempts to use sequential prefetch for a table space scan. For a segmented table space, if DB2 determines that less than four pages will be read at runtime, sequential prefetch is disabled. The OPTIMIZE FOR 1 ROW option also potentially disables sequential and list prefetch at bind time.

Limited Partition Scanning (PAGE_RANGE = Y)

DB2 can limit the number of partitions scanned for data access. The query must provide the leading columns of the partitioning key. The following example limits the search for the name of the employee by providing the high and low number of the employee number, therefore limiting the number of partitions to be scanned (assuming the limit key for the partitions is on EMPNO).

```
SELECT FIRSTNME
FROM EMP
WHERE EMPNO BETWEEN :low AND :high
```

SORT (SORTN_*xxx* and SORTC_*yyy*)

The plan table shows the reasons a sort was invoked. Those reasons could include a sort of data rows or a sort of RIDs in a RID list. Column SORTN_JOIN indicates that the new table of a join is sorted before the join. (For a hybrid join, this is a sort of the RID list.) When SORTN_JOIN and SORTC_JOIN are both Y, DB2 performs two sorts for the join. The sorts for joins are indicated on the same row as the new table access.

A sort of the composite table for a join (SORTC_JOIN) is beneficial in avoiding death by random I/O. Providing cluster ratio for an index and keycard statistics for multicolumn cardinalities gives DB2 the information to determine whether a query will suffer from excessive synchronous I/O. In this case, sorting the composite for a nested loop or sorting both (if required) for a sort merge or hybrid join can provide sequential access to the data.

Column SORTC_UNIQ indicates the use of a sort to remove duplicates, as might be needed by a SELECT statement with DISTINCT or UNION. SORTC_ORDERBY usually indicates a sort for an ORDER BY clause. But SORTC_UNIQ and SORTC_ORDERBY also indicate when the results of a non-correlated subquery are sorted, both to remove duplicates and to order the results. A SORTC_GROUPBY value of Y would indicate a sort for processing a GROUP BY clause.

If more than one SORTC indicator is set to Y on the same explain output line, DB2 is actually performing one sort to accomplish two tasks, such as sorting for uniqueness and ordering. This point does not apply to SORTN_JOIN and SORTC_JOIN, as one sort is for the composite and one is for the new table.

To perform list prefetch, DB2 sorts RIDs into ascending page-number order. The plan table usually doesn't indicate a RID sort, but DB2 normally performs a RID sort whenever list prefetch is used. The only exception to this rule is when a hybrid join is performed and a single, highly clustered index is used on the inner table. In this case, the SORTN_JOIN value is N, indicating that the RID list for the inner table was not sorted.

Nested Loop Join (METHOD = 1)

DB2 can use a *nested loop join* for all types of joins (inner or outer). For a nested loop join, DB2 scans the composite (outer) table. For each row in that table that qualifies (by satisfying the predicates on the table), DB2 searches for matching rows of the new (inner) table. It concatenates any it finds with the current row of the composite table. If no rows match the current row, then:

- For an inner join, DB2 discards the current row.

- For an outer join, DB2 concatenates a row of null values.

- Stage 1 and stage 2 predicates can eliminate unqualified rows before the physical joining of rows occurs.

A loop join is often used in the following cases:

- The outer table is small.

- Predicates with small filter factors reduce the number of qualifying rows in the outer table.

- An efficient, highly clustered index exists on the join columns of the inner table, or DB2 can dynamically create a sparse index on the inner table and use that index for subsequent access.

- The number of data pages accessed in the inner table is small.

The nested loop join repetitively accesses the inner table. That is, DB2 scans the outer table once and accesses the inner table as many times as the number of qualifying rows in the outer table. Hence, the nested loop join is usually the most efficient join method when the values of the join column passed to the inner table are in sequence and the index on the join column of the inner table is clustered, or if the number of rows retrieved in the inner table through the index is small. If the tables are not clustered in the same sequence, DB2 can sort the composite to match the sequence of the inner table. Accesses to the inner table can then use sequential or dynamic prefetch.

Nested Loop Join with Sparse Index (METHOD = 1, PRIMARY_ACCESSTYPE = T)

Your plan table might show a nested loop join that includes a sort on the new table with an indication of sparse index access (PRIMARY_ACCESSTYPE = T). These settings indicate that DB2 dynamically creates a sparse index on the inner table. Nested loop join with sparse index has the following performance advantages:

- Access to the inner table is more efficient when the inner table has no efficient index on the join columns.

- A sort of the composite table is avoided when the composite table is relatively large.

Merge Scan Join (METHOD = 2)

A *merge scan join* (also known as a *merge join* or a *sort merge join*) requires one or more predicates of the form TABLE1.COL1 = TABLE2.COL2, where the two columns have the same data type, length, and null attributes. If the null attributes don't match, the maximum number of merge join columns is 1. The exception is a full outer join, which permits mismatching null attributes.

Join columns cannot be matching columns for a merge scan join. Instead, these columns are listed as MERGE_JOIN_COLS in the plan table. Local predicates can be matching predicates and will be applied before the join.

DB2 scans both tables in the order of the join columns. If no efficient indexes on the join columns provide the order, DB2 might sort the outer table, the inner table, or both. The inner table is put into a work file; the outer table is put into a work file only if it must be sorted. When a row of the outer table matches a row of the inner table, DB2 returns the combined rows. A merge scan join is often used in these circumstances:

- The qualifying rows of the inner and outer table are large, and the join predicate provides little filtering—that is, in a many-to-many join.

- The tables are large and have no indexes with matching columns.

- Few columns are selected on inner tables. This is the case when a DB2 sort is used. The fewer the columns to be sorted, the more efficient the sort.

DB2 always chooses a merge scan join for a full outer join.

Hybrid Join (METHOD = 4)

The *hybrid join* method (METHOD = 4) applies only to an inner join and requires an index on the join column of the inner table. The method requires obtaining RIDs in the order needed to use list prefetch. In the successive steps, DB2 does the following:

1. Scans the outer table (OUTER).

2. Joins the outer table using RIDs from the index on the inner table. The result is the phase 1 intermediate table. DB2 scans the index of the inner table for every row of the outer table.

3. Sorts the data in the outer table and the RIDs, creating a sorted RID list and the phase 2 intermediate table. The sort is indicated by a value of Y in column SORTN_JOIN of the plan table. If the index on the inner table is highly clustered, DB2 can skip this sort; the value in SORTN_JOIN is then N.

4. Retrieves the data from the inner table using list prefetch.

5. Concatenates the data from the inner table and the phase 2 intermediate table to create the final composite table.

A join is often used if

- a non-clustered index (or indexes) is used on the join columns of the inner table

- the outer table has duplicate qualifying rows

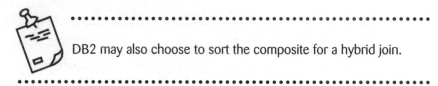

DB2 may also choose to sort the composite for a hybrid join.

Star Join (METHOD = 0, 1; JOIN TYPE = S)

A join is the access path used in processing a *star schema*, which is a logical database design included in many data-warehouse and decision-support applications. A star schema consists of a *fact table* and a number of *dimension tables* that are connected to it. Each dimension table contains several values that are given an ID, which the fact table uses instead of all the values. You can think of the fact table, which is much larger than the dimension tables, as being in the center surrounded by dimension tables; the result resembles a star formation.

To access the data in a star schema, you write SELECT statements that include join operations between the fact table and the dimension tables; no join operations exist between dimension tables. A query must satisfy several conditions before it qualifies for the star join access path. The first requirement is detection of the fact table. Given that the access path objective is efficient access to the fact table, it's important for the fact table to be identified correctly.

The first fact table detection algorithm is known as the *unique index check*. Beginning outside-in, the optimizer evaluates each set of join predicates. For each set of join predicates between two tables, the table with a unique index on the join predicates is considered to be the parent in a parent–child relationship. As DB2 continues outside-in, the table without any further children (and which therefore only has parents) is considered to be the fact table.

The second fact table detection algorithm is based on the values of the STARJOIN DSNZPARM:

- **ENABLE.** Star join is enabled, and the fact table is 25 times larger than the largest dimension table.

- **DISABLE.** Star join is disabled (the default).

- **1.** The fact table will be the largest table in the star join query.

- **2–32, 768.** The specified number *n* represents the ratio between the fact table and the largest dimension table. The fact table must be *n* times larger than the largest dimension table.

The third fact table detection algorithm is the *topology check*, whereby the fact table is considered to be the table with the greatest number of join predicates in the query.

Once the optimizer identifies the fact table using any of the three detection algorithms, the following conditions must be met for DB2 to use the star join technique:

- The number of tables in the query block must be at least 10 (you can change this setting using DSNZPARM SJTABLES).

- All join predicates are between the fact table and the dimension tables or within tables of the same dimension (*snowflake schema*).

- All join predicates between the fact and dimension tables must be equijoin (equal join) predicates.

- All join predicates between the fact and dimension tables must be Boolean term predicates (fact-to-dimension join predicates cannot be ORed).

- A local predicate on a dimension table cannot be ORed with a local predicate of another dimension table.

- A single fact table column cannot be joined to columns of different dimension tables in join predicates. For example, fact table column F1 cannot be joined to column D1 of dimension table T1 and also joined to column D2 of dimension table T2.

- No correlated subqueries exists across dimensions.

- The data type and length of both sides of a join predicate are the same between the fact and dimension tables.

- Dimensions cannot be a table function.

- After DB2 simplifies join operations, no outer join operations can exist between the fact and dimension tables.

A successful match on all of these star schema detection rules immediately qualifies the query for star join optimization. A failure on any of these rules for a fact table results in evaluation of the next fact table detection algorithm. A failure of these rules for all three fact table detection algorithms causes DB2 to optimize the query using standard dynamic programming (exhaustive search) techniques or algorithms.

When star join is performed, it is identified by an S in the JOIN_TYPE column of PLAN_TABLE, but only for dimension tables that are accessed before the fact table.

For a star schema, even though the intersection of all dimensions with the fact table can produce a small result set, the predicates applied to one single dimension table are typically insufficient to reduce the enormous number of fact table rows.

If a join based on related tables (dimension to fact table) does not provide adequate performance, an alternative is to join unrelated tables. Joining of unrelated tables results in a Cartesian product, whereby every row of the first table is joined with every row of the second.

Performing a Cartesian join of all dimension tables before accessing the fact table may not be efficient. DB2 must decide how many dimension tables to access first to provide the greatest level of filtering of fact table rows using available indexes. This can be a delicate balance because further Cartesian products will produce a massive increase in the size of the intermediate result sets. On the other hand, minimal prejoining of unrelated dimension tables may not provide adequate filtering for the join to the fact table. For an efficient Cartesian process, DB2 employs a logical rather than a physical Cartesian of the dimension tables. Each dimension or snowflake (further normalized dimension) covered by the chosen fact table index is accessed independently before the fact table. Each qualifying dimension (and snowflake) has all local predicates applied, with the result sorted into join column order and finally materialized into its own separate work file.

If many of the dimensions involve snowflakes, this preprocessing and materialization significantly reduces the number of overall tables joined because the snowflake is resolved into a single dimension.

Rather than requiring the physical work file storage involved in a physical Cartesian, DB2 simulates a Cartesian by repositioning itself within each work file to potentially join all possible combinations to the central fact table. The sequence of this simulated Cartesian join respects the column order of the selected fact table index.

The sparseness of data within the fact table implies that a significant number of values generated by the Cartesian process are not to be found by a join to the fact table. To minimize the CPU overhead of joining unnecessarily derived rows to the fact table, DB2 uses an index key feedback loop to return the next highest key value whenever it encounters a not-found condition.

A hit on the fact table index returns the matching fact table row. A miss returns the next valid fact table index key so that the data manager can reposition itself within the dimension work files, thus skipping composite rows with no possibility of obtaining a fact table match.

To further improve the performance of the join to the fact table, the entire join is pushed down to data manager (stage 1), but only for star join access from the composite (dimensions) to the fact table. This approach ensures a reduced path length because rows no longer need to be returned to relational data services RDS (stage 2) for the join to occur. The join method used by this process is a nested loop join.

Parallelism Usage (PARALLELISM_MODE = I, C, or X)

Parallel processing applies only to read-only queries. The mode values are

- I for parallel I/O operations
- C for parallel central processor (CP) operations
- X for Sysplex query parallelism

Non-null values in columns ACCESS_DEGREE and JOIN_DEGREE of the plan table indicate to what degree (number of concurrent processes) DB2 plans to use parallel operations. However, this decision can change at runtime. We discuss parallelism in more detail later in the chapter.

Interpreting Access for Subqueries

The EXPLAIN output in the plan table might show the position and order in which some subqueries are executed. The subqueries are indicated by a row in the plan table with TNAME="DSNWFQB(*nn*)", where *nn* is the query block number associated with the subquery, and TABLETYPE='S'. For correlated subqueries, the plan table's PARENT_PLANNO column corresponds to the plan number in the parent query block where the correlated subquery is invoked. For non-correlated subqueries, this column corresponds to the plan number in the parent query block that represents the work file for the subquery.

The non-correlated form of the following subquery produces the EXPLAIN output shown below.

```
SELECT *
FROM T1
WHERE T1.C2 IN (SELECT T2.C2 FROM T2, T3 WHERE T2.C1 = T3.C1);
```

QBNO	PLANNO	METHOD	TNAME	AC TYPE	MC	AC NAME	SC_JN	PAR_QB	PAR_PNO	QB TYPE	TB TYPE
1	1	0	DSNFW QB (02)	R	0		N	0	0	SELECT	S
1	2	1	T1	I	1	T1_1X_C2	Y	0	0	SELECT	T
2	1	0	T2	R	0		N	1	1	NCOSUB	T
2	2	1	T3	I	1	T3_X_C1	N	1	1	NCOSUB	T

In this example, the row corresponding to QBNO=2 and PLANNO=1 has PARENT_PLANNO (abbreviated in the table as PAR_PNO) = 1 and PARENT_QBNO (abbreviated as PAR_QB) = 1. This means that the row corresponding to QBNO=1 and PLANNO=1 is the parent row. The sequence of execution flows from parent to child, then back to parent after the child rows are exhausted. In this case, that means the sequence of execution is (QBNO, PLANNO): (1,1), (2,1), (2,2), (1,2).

The following correlated subquery produces the EXPLAIN output shown below.

```
SELECT *
FROM T1
WHERE EXISTS
(SELECT 1 FROM T2, T3 WHERE T2.C1 = T3.C1 AND T2.C2 = T1.C2)
```

QBNO	PLANNO	METHOD	TNAME	AC TYPE	MC	AC NAME	SC_JN	PAR_QB	PAR_PNO	QB TYPE	TB TYPE
1	1	0	T1	R	0		N	0	0	SELECT	T
2	1	1	T2	I	1	T2_IX_C2	N	1	1	CORSUB	T
2	2	1	T3	I	1	T3_IX_C1	N	1	1	CORSUB	T

Optional Tables Populated by EXPLAIN

DB2's EXPLAIN facility can optionally populate a variety of other tables in addition to PLAN_TABLE. These other tables provide a wealth of additional specifics about how SQL queries are executed. These tables can be created via the DB2 Optimization Service Center (discussed in more detail later) or manually. They are intended to be used by the EXPLAIN facility and various optimization tools, such as the Optimization Service Center.

The easiest way to view the contents of these optional tables is via the Optimization Service Center, but you can also query the tables independently. The Optimization Service Center is not required to create and populate these tables.

DSN_STATEMNT_TABLE

When you run EXPLAIN, the facility also populates the statement table, DSN_STATEMNT_TABLE (if it exists). Some of this table's columns resemble those in PLAN_TABLE; others are new and relate only to the statement cost. The following columns are unique to the statement table.

Column name	Description
STMT_TYPE	Type of SQL statement
COST_CATEGORY	How much information was available

PROCMS	Estimated processor cost in milliseconds
PROCSU	Estimated processor cost in service units
REASON	Reasons COST_CATEGORY may be inaccurate

The COST_CATEGORY determination is affected by factors such as number of tables, number of rows in the tables, column cardinality, cluster ratio, first key cardinality, full key cardinality, number of leaf pages, number of index levels, host variables, special registers, triggers, UDFs, RI, LOBs, and expressions. Table 17.2 describes the complete contents of the statement table.

Table 17.2: DSN_STATEMNT_TABLE columns	
Column name	**Description**
QUERYNO	A number intended to identify the statement being explained. If QUERYNO is not unique, the value of EXPLAIN_TIME is unique.
APPLNAME	The name of the application plan for the row, or blank.
PROGNAME	The name of the program or package containing the statement being explained, or blank.
COLLID	The collection ID for the package. Applies only to an embedded EXPLAIN statement executed from a package or to a statement that is being explained when binding a package. Blank is not applicable. The value DSNDYNAMICSQLCACHE indicates that the row is for a cached statement.
GROUP_MEMBER	The member name of the DB2 that executed EXPLAIN, or blank.
EXPLAIN_TIME	The time at which the statement is processed. This time is the same as the BIND_TIME column in PLAN_TABLE.
STMT_TYPE	The type of statement being explained: SELECT = SELECT INSERT = INSERT UPDATE = UPDATE DELETE = DELETE SELUPD = SELECT with FOR UPDATE OF DELCUR = DELETE WHERE CURRENT OF CURSOR UPDCUR = UPDATE WHERE CURRENT OF CURSOR
COST_CATEGORY	Indicates whether DB2 was forced to use default values when making its estimates: A = DB2 had enough information to make a cost estimate without using default values. B = Some condition exists for which DB2 was forced to use default values. See the values in REASON to determine why DB2 was unable to put this estimate in cost category A.

Table 17.2: DSN_STATEMNT_TABLE columns (contiuned)	
Column name	**Description**
PROCMS	The estimated processor cost in milliseconds for the SQL statement, rounded up to the next integer value. The maximum value for this cost is 2,147,483,647 milliseconds, which is equivalent to approximately 24.8 days. If the estimated value exceeds this maximum, the column reports the maximum value.
PROCSU	The estimated processor cost in service units for the SQL statement, rounded up to the next integer value. The maximum value for this cost is 2,147,483,647 service units. If the estimated value exceeds this maximum, the column reports the maximum value.
REASON	A string that indicates the reasons for putting an estimate into cost category B:
	HAVING CLAUSE: A subselect in the SQL statement contains a HAVING clause.
	HOST VARIABLES: The statement uses host variables, parameter markers, or special registers.
	REFERENTIAL CONSTRAINTS: Referential constraints of the type CASCADE or SET NULL exist on the target table of a DELETE statement.
	TABLE CARDINALITY: The cardinality statistics are missing for one or more of the tables used in the statement.
	UDF: The statement uses user-defined functions.
	TRIGGERS: Triggers are defined on the target table of an INSERT, UPDATE, or DELETE statement.
	MATERIALIZATION: Statistics are missing because the statement uses materialized views or nested table expressions.
STMT_ENCODE	The encoding scheme of the statement. If the statement represents a single CCSID set, possible values are:
	A = ASCII
	E = EBCDIC
	U = Unicode
	If the statement has multiple CCSID sets, the column value is M.
TOTAL_COST	The overall estimated cost of the statement. This cost should be used only for reference purposes.

DSN_FUNCTION_TABLE

The function table, DSN_FUNCTION_TABLE, contains information about the cost of user-defined functions used in a SQL statement. (Chapter 15 discusses UDFs.) Table 17.3 summarizes the contents of DSN_FUNCTION_TABLE.

Table 17.3: DSN_FUNCTION_TABLE columns	
Column name	**Description**
QUERYNO	A number intended to identify the statement being explained. If QUERYNO is not unique, the value of EXPLAIN_TIME is unique.
APPLNAME	The name of the application plan for the row, or blank.
PROGNAME	The name of the program or package containing the statement being explained, or blank.
COLLID	The collection ID for the package, or blank.
GROUP_MEMBER	The member name of the DB2 that executed EXPLAIN, or blank.
EXPLAIN_TIME	The time at which the statement is processed. This time is the same as the BIND_TIME column in PLAN_TABLE.
SCHEMA_NAME	The schema name of the function invoked in the explained statement.
FUNCTION_NAME	The name of the function invoked in the explained statement.
SPEC_FUNC_ID	The specific name of the function invoked in the explained statement.
FUNCTION_TYPE	The type of function invoked in the explained statement: SU = Scalar function TU = Table function
VIEW_CREATOR	If the function specified in the FUNCTION_NAME column is referenced in a view definition, the creator of the view. Otherwise, blank.
VIEW_NAME	If the function specified in the FUNCTION_NAME column is referenced in a view definition, the name of the view. Otherwise, blank.
PATH	The value of the SQL path that was used to resolve the schema name of the function.
FUNCTION_TEXT	The text of the function reference (the function name and parameters). If the function reference is more than 1,500 bytes, this column contains the first 1,500 bytes. For functions specified in fixed notation, FUNCTION_TEXT contains only the function name. For example, for a function named /, which overloads the SQL divide operator, if the function reference is A/B, FUNCTION_TEXT contains only /, not A/B.

DSN_STATEMENT_CACHE_TABLE

The statement cache table, DSN_STATEMENT_CACHE_TABLE, contains information about the SQL statements in the statement cache. This information is captured as the result of an EXPLAIN STATEMENT CACHE ALL statement. The table contains numerous execution-time statistics about dynamic SQL statements, including the number of pages, sorts, and rows processed by the query. Table 17.4 describes the columns in the statement cache table.

Table 17.4: DSN_STATEMENT_CACHE_TABLE columns	
Column name	**Description**
STMT_ID	An EDM unique token.
STMT_TOKEN	A user-provided identification string.
COLLID	Collection ID; value is DSNDYNAMICSQLCACHE.
PROGRAM_NAME	Name of package or DBRM that performed the initial PREPARE.
INV_DROPALT	Invalidated by DROP/ALTER.
INV_REVOKE	Invalidated by REVOKE.
INV_LRU	Removed from cache by LRU.
INV_RUNSTATS	Invalidated by RUNSTATS.
CACHED_TS	Timestamp when statement was cached.
USERS	Number of current users of statement. These are the users that have prepared or executed the statement during their current unit of work.
COPIES	Number of copies of statement owned by all threads in the system.
LINES	Precompiler line number from the initial PREPARE.
PRIMAUTH	Primary authorization ID of the user that did the initial PREPARE.
CURSQLID	CURRENT SQLID of the user that did the initial prepare.
BIND_QUALIFIER	Bind object qualifier for unqualified table names.
BIND_ISO	ISOLATION bind option: UR = Uncommitted read CS = Cursor stability RS = Read stability RR = Repeatable read
BIND_C	DATA CURRENTDATA bind option: Y = CURRENTDATA(YES) N = CURRENTDATA(NO)
BIND_DYNRL	DYNAMICRULES bind option: B = DYNAMICRULES(BIND) R = DYNAMICRULES(RUN)
BIND_DEGRE	CURRENT DEGREE value: A = ANY 1 = 1
BIND_SQLRL	CURRENT RULES value: D = DB2 S = SQL
BIND_CHOLD	Cursor WITH HOLD bind option: Y = Initial PREPARE was done for a cursor WITH HOLD N = Initial PREPARE was not done for a cursor WITH HOLD

Column name	Description
Table 17.4: DSN_STATEMENT_CACHE_TABLE columns (continued)	
STAT_TS	Timestamp of stats when IFCID 318 is started.
STAT_EXEC	Number of executions of statement. For a cursor statement, this value is the number of OPENs.
STAT_GPAG	Number of getpage operations performed for statement.
STAT_SYNR	Number of synchronous buffer reads performed for statement.
STAT_WRIT	Number of buffer write operations performed for statement.
STAT_EROW	Number of rows examined for statement.
STAT_PROW	Number of rows processed for statement.
STAT_SORT	Number of sorts performed for statement.
STAT_INDX	Number of index scans performed for statement.
STAT_RSCN	Number of table space scans performed for statement.
STAT_PGRP	Number of parallel groups created for statement.
STAT_ELAP	Accumulated elapsed time used for statement.
STAT_CPU	Accumulated CPU time used for statement.
STAT_SUS_SYNIO	Accumulated wait time for synchronous I/O.
STAT_SUS_LOCK	Accumulated wait time for lock and latch requests.
STAT_SUS_SWIT	Accumulated wait time for synchronous execution unit switch.
STAT_SUS_GLCK	Accumulated wait time for global locks.
STAT_SUS_OTHR	Accumulated wait time for read activity done by another thread.
STAT_SUS_OTHW	Accumulated wait time for write activity done by another thread.
STAT_RIDLIMT	Number of times a RID list wasn't used because the number of RIDs would have exceeded one or more DB2 limits.
STAT_RIDSTOR	Number of times a RID list wasn't used because not enough storage was available to hold the list of RIDs.
EXPLAIN_TS	When the statement cache table is populated.
SCHEMA	CURRENT SCHEMA value.
STMT_TEXT	Statement text.
STMT_ROWID	Statement ROWID.
BIND_RA_TOT	The total number of REBIND commands that have been issued for the dynamic statement because of the REOPT(AUTO) option.
BIND_RO_TYPE	The current specification of the REOPT option for the statement: N = REOPT(NONE) 1 = REOPT(ONCE) or its equivalent A = REOPT(AUTO) or its equivalent 0 = The current plan is deemed optimal and there is no need for REOPT(AUTO)

DSN_PREDICAT_TABLE

The *predicate table*, DSN_PREDICAT_TABLE, contains information about all the predicates in a query. Table 17.5 lists the contents of the predicate table.

Table 17.5: DSN_PREDICAT_TABLE columns	
Column name	**Description**
QUERYNO	A number used to help identify the query being explained. It is not a unique identifier. Using a negative number will cause problems. The possible sources are: • The statement line number in the program • The QUERYNO clause • The EXPLAIN statement • The EDM unique token in the statement cache
QBLOCKNO	A number used to identify each query block within a query.
APPLNAME	The application plan name.
PROGNAME	The program name (binding an application) or the package name (binding a package).
PREDNO	A number used to identify a predicate within a query.
TYPE	A string used to indicate the type or the operation of the predicate. The possible values are: AND OR EQUAL RANGE BETWEEN IN LIKE NOT LIKE EXISTS NOT EXIST SUBQUERY HAVING OTHERS

Column name	Description
Table 17.5: DSN_PREDICAT_TABLE columns (continued)	
LEFT_HAND_SIDE	If the left-hand side (LHS) of the predicate is a table column (LHS_TABNO > 0, this column indicates the column name. Other possible values are: VALUE COLEXP NONCOLEXP CORSUB NONCORSUB SUBQUERY EXPRESSION Blanks
LEFT_HAND_PNO	
LHS_TABNO	If the LHS of the predicate is a table column, this column indicates a number that uniquely identifies the corresponding table reference within a query.
LHS_QBNO	If the LHS of the predicate is a table column, this column indicates a number that uniquely identifies the corresponding table reference within a query.
RIGHT_HAND_SIDE	If the right-hand side (RHS) of the predicate is a table column (RHS_TABNO > 0), this column indicates the column name. Other possible values are: VALUE COLEXP NONCOLEXP CORSUB NONCORSUB SUBQUERY EXPRESSION Blanks
RIGHT_HAND_PNO	If the predicate is a compound predicate (AND/OR), this column indicates the second child predicate. However, this column is not reliable when the predicate tree consolidation happens.
RHS_TABNO	If the RHS of the predicate is a table column, this column indicates a number that uniquely identifies the corresponding table reference within a query.
RHS_QBNO	If the RHS of the predicate is a subquery, this column indicates a number that uniquely identifies the corresponding query block within a query.
FILTER_FACTOR	The estimated filter factor.
BOOLEAN_TERM	Whether this predicate can be used to determine the truth value of the whole WHERE clause.
SEARCHARG	Whether this predicate can be processed by data manager (DM) stage 1. If it cannot, the relational data service (RDS) stage 2 needs to be used to take care of it, which is more costly.

Table 17.5: DSN_PREDICAT_TABLE columns (continued)	
Column name	**Description**
AFTER_JOIN	Indicates the predicate evaluation phase: A = After join D = During join Blank = Not applicable
ADDED_PRED	Whether the predicate is generated by transitive closure, which means DB2 can generate additional predicates to provide more information for access path selection, when the set of predicates that belong to a query logically imply other predicates.
REDUNDANT_PRED	Whether the predicate is a redundant predicate, which means evaluation of other predicates in the query already determines the result that the predicate provides.
DIRECT_ACCESS	Whether the predicate is direct access, which means one can navigate directly to the row through ROWID.
KEYFIELD	Whether the predicate includes the index key column of the involved table.
EXPLAIN_TIME	The EXPLAIN timestamp.
CATEGORY	IBM internal use only.
CATEGORY_B	IBM internal use only.
PRED_ENCODE	IBM internal use only.
PRED_CCSID	IBM internal use only.
PRED_MCCSID	IBM internal use only.
MARKER	Whether the predicate includes host variables, parameter markers, or special registers.
PARENT_PNO	The parent predicate number. If this predicate is a root predicate within a query block, this column is 0.
NEGATION	Whether the predicate is negated via NOT.
LITERALS	The literal value or literal values separated by colon symbols.
CLAUSE	The clause where the predicate exists: HAVING = HAVING clause ON = ON clause WHERE = WHERE clause
GROUP_MEMBER	The member name of the DB2 that executed EXPLAIN. The column is blank if the DB2 subsystem was not in a data-sharing environment when EXPLAIN was executed.

DSN_STRUCT_TABLE

The *structure table*, DSN_STRUCT_TABLE, contains information about the query blocks in a query. Table 17.6 lists the contents of the structure table.

Table 17.6: DSN_STRUCT_TABLE columns	
Column name	**Description**
QUERYNO	A number used to help identify the query being explained. It is not a unique identifier. Using a negative number will cause problems. The possible sources are: • The statement line number in the program • The QUERYNO clause • The EXPLAIN statement • The EDM unique token in the statement cache
QBLOCKNO	A number used to identify each query block within a query.
APPLNAME	The application plan name.
PROGNAME	The program name (binding an application) or the package name (binding a package).
PARENT	The parent query block number of the current query block in the structure of SQL text; this is the same as the PARENT_QBLOCKNO in the PLAN_TABLE.
ROWCOUNT	The estimated number of rows returned by RDS (query cardinality).
ATOPEN	Whether the query block is moved up for do-at-open processing. The value is Y if done-at-open or N otherwise.
CONTEXT	This column indicates the context of the current query block. The possible values are: TOP LEVEL UNION UNION ALL PREDICATE TABLE EXP UNKNOWN
ORDERNO	This column is currently not used.
DOATOPEN_PARENT	The parent query block number of the current query block. Do-at-open parent if the query block is done-at-open, this value may differ from the PARENT_QBLOCKNO in the PLAN_TABLE.
QBLOCK_TYPE	The type of the current query block: SELECT INSERT UPDATE DELETE SELUPD

Table 17.6: DSN_STRUCT_TABLE columns (contiued)	
Column name	**Description**
QBLOCK_TYPE	DELCUR
	UPDCUR
	CORSUB
	NCOSUB
	TABLEX
	TRIGGR
	UNION
	UNIONA
	CTE
	This column is equivalent to the QBLOCK_TYPE column in PLAN_TABLE, except for CTE.
EXPLAIN_TIME	The EXPLAIN timestamp.
QUERY_STAGE	IBM internal use only.
GROUP_MEMBER	The member name of the DB2 subsystem that executed EXPLAIN. The column is blank if the DB2 subsystem was not in a data-sharing environment when EXPLAIN was executed.

DSN_PGROUP_TABLE

The *parallel group table*, DSN_PGROUP_TABLE, contains information about the parallel groups in a query. Table 17.7 lists the contents of the parallel group table.

Table 17.7: DSN_PGROUP_TABLE columns	
Column name	**Description**
QUERYNO	A number used to help identify the query being explained. It is not a unique identifier. Using a negative number will cause problems. The possible sources are: • The statement line number in the program • The QUERYNO clause • The EXPLAIN statement • The EDM unique token in the statement cache
QBLOCKNO	A number used to identify each query block within a query.
PLANNAME	The application plan name.
COLLID	The collection ID for the package.
PROGNAME	The program name (binding an application) or the package name (binding a package).

Table 17.7: DSN_PGROUP_TABLE columns (contiued)	
Column name	**Description**
EXPLAIN_TIME	The explain timestamp.
VERSION	The version identifier for the package.
GROUPID	The parallel group identifier within the current query block.
FIRSTPLAN	The plan number of the first contributing mini-plan associated within this parallel group.
LASTPLAN	The plan number of the last mini-plan associated with this parallel group.
CPUCOST	The estimated CPU cost of this parallel group in milliseconds.
IOCOST	The estimated total I/O cost of this parallel group in milliseconds.
BESTTIME	The estimated elapsed time for each parallel task for this parallel group.
DEGREE	The degree of parallelism for this parallel group determined at bind time. The maximum parallelism degree if the table space is large is 255; otherwise, 64.
MODE	The parallel mode: I = I/O parallelism C = CPU parallelism X = Multiple CPU Sysplex parallelism (highest level) N = No parallelism
REASON	The reason for downgrading parallelism mode.
LOCALCPU	The number of CPUs currently online when preparing the query.
TOTALCPU	The total number of CPUs in Sysplex. LOCALCPU and TOTALCPU are different only for the DB2 coordinator in a Sysplex.
FIRSTBASE	The table number of the table that on which partitioning is performed.
LARGETS	Value is Y if the table space is large in this group.
PARTKIND	The partitioning type: L = Logical partitioning P = Physical partitioning
GROUPTYPE	Indicates what operations this parallel group contains: table access, join, or sort (A, AJ, or AJS).
ORDER	The ordering requirement of this parallel group: N = No order. Results need no ordering. T = Natural order. Ordering is required but results already ordered if accessed via index. K = Key order. Ordering achieved by sort. Results ordered by sort key. This value applies only to parallel sort.

Table 17.7: DSN_PGROUP_TABLE columns (continued)	
Column name	**Description**
STYLE	The input/output format style of this parallel group. Blank for I/O parallelism. For other modes: RIRO = Records IN, Records OUT WIRO = Work file IN, Records OUT WIWO = Work file IN, Work file OUT
RANGEKIND	The range type: K = Key range P = Page range
NKEYCOLS	The number of interesting key columns—that is, the number of columns that will participate in the key operation for this parallel group.
LOWBOUND	The low bound of the parallel group.
HIGHBOUND	The high bound of the parallel group.
LOWKEY	The low key of range if partitioned by key range.
HIGHKEY	The high key of range if partitioned by key range.
FIRSTPAGE	The first page in range if partitioned by page range.
LASTPAGE	The last page in range if partitioned by page range.
GROUP_MEMBER	IBM internal use only.
HOST_REASON	IBM internal use only.
PARA_TYPE	IBM internal use only.
PART_INNER	IBM internal use only.
GRNU_KEYRNG	IBM internal use only.
OPEN_KEYRNG	IBM internal use only.

DSN_PTASK_TABLE

The *parallel task table*, DSN_PTASK_TABLE, contains information about the parallel tasks in a query. Table 17.8 lists the contents of the parallel task table.

Table 17.8: DSN_PTASK_TABLE columns	
Column name	**Description**
QUERYNO	A number used to help identify the query being explained. It is not a unique identifier. Using a negative number will cause problems. The possible sources are: • The statement line number in the program • The QUERYNO clause • The EXPLAIN statement • The EDM unique token in the statement cache

Table 17.8: DSN_PTASK_TABLE columns (contiuned)	
Column name	**Description**
QBLOCKNO	A number used to identify each query block within a query.
APPLNAME	The application plan name.
PROGNAME	The program name (binding an application) or the package name (binding a package).
LPTNO	The parallel task number.
KEYCOLID	The key columns ID (KEY range only).
DPSI	Indicates whether a data partition secondary index (DPSI) is used.
LPTLOKEY	The low key value for this key column for this parallel task (KEY range only).
LPTHIKEY	The high key value for this key column for this parallel task (KEY range only).
LPTLOPAG	The low page information if partitioned by page range.
LPTLHIPAG	The high page information if partitioned by page range.
LPTLOPG#	The lower bound page number for this parallel task (page range or DPSI enabled only).
LPTHIPG#	The upper bound page number for this parallel task (page range or DPSI enabled only).
LPTLOPT#	The lower bound partition number for this parallel task (page range or DPSI enabled only).
KEYCOLDT	The data type for this key column (KEY range only).
KEYCOLPREC	The precision/length for this key column (KEY range only).
KEYCOLSCAL	The scale for this key column (KEY range with decimal data type only).
EXPLAIN_TIME	The EXPLAIN timestamp.
GROUP_MEMBER	The member name of the DB2 that executed EXPLAIN. The column is blank if the DB2 subsystem was not in a data-sharing environment when EXPLAIN was executed.

DSN_FILTER_TABLE

The *filter table*, DSN_FILTER_TABLE, contains information about how predicates are used during query processing. Table 17.9 lists the contents of the filter table.

Table 17.9: DSN_FILTER_TABLE columns	
Column name	Description
QUERYNO	A number used to help identify the query being explained. It is not a unique identifier. Using a negative number will cause problems. The possible sources are: • The statement line number in the program • The QUERYNO clause • The EXPLAIN statement • The EDM unique token in the statement cache
QBLOCKNO	A number used to identify each query block within a query.
PLANNO	A number used to identify each mini-plan within a query block.
APPLNAME	The application plan name.
PROGNAME	The program name (binding an application) or the package name (binding a package).
COLLID	The collection ID for the package.
ORDERNO	The sequence number of evaluation. Indicates the order in which the predicate is applied within each stage
PREDNO	A number used to identify a predicate within a query.
STAGE	Indicates at which stage the predicate is evaluated. The possible values are: • Matching • Screening • Stage 1 • Stage 2
ORDER_CLASS	IBM internal use only.
EXPLAIN_TIME	The EXPLAIN timestamp.
MIXOPSEQ	IBM internal use only.
REEVAL	IBM internal use only.
GROUP_MEMBER	The member name of the DB2 subsystem that executed EXPLAIN. The column is blank if the DB2 subsystem was not in a data-sharing environment when EXPLAIN was executed.

DSN_DETCOST_TABLE

The *detailed cost table*, DSN_DETCOST_TABLE, contains information about detailed cost estimation of the mini-plans in a query. Table 17.10 lists the contents of the detailed cost table.

Table 17.10 intentionally omits several columns of the DSN_DETCOST_TABLE that are all "IBM internal use only." For the full list of detailed cost table columns, see the DB2 Performance Monitoring and Tuning Guide.

Table 17.10: DSN_DETCOST_TABLE columns	
Column name	**Description**
QUERYNO	A number used to help identify the query being explained. It is not a unique identifier. Using a negative number will cause problems. The possible sources are: • The statement line number in the program • The QUERYNO clause • The EXPLAIN statement • The EDM unique token in the statement cache
QBLOCKNO	A number used to identify each query block within a query.
PLANNO	A number used to identify each mini-plan within a query block.
APPLNAME	The application plan name.
PROGNAME	The program name (binding an application) or the package name (binding a package).
OPENIO	The Do-at-open I/O cost for the non-correlated subquery.
OPENCPU	The Do-at-open CPU cost for the non-correlated subquery.
OPENCOST	The Do-at-open total cost for the non-correlated subquery.
DMIO	IBM internal use only.
DMCPU	IBM internal use only.
DMTOT	IBM internal use only.
SUBQIO	IBM internal use only.
SUBQCOST	IBM internal use only.
BASEIO	IBM internal use only.
BASECPU	IBM internal use only.
BASETOT	IBM internal use only.
ONECOMPROWS	The number of rows qualified after applying local predicates.
IMLEAF	IBM internal use only.
IMIO	IBM internal use only.
IMPREFH	IBM internal use only.
IMMPRED	IBM internal use only.
IMFF	The filter factor of matching predicates only.
IMSRPRED	IBM internal use only.

Table 17.10: DSN_DETCOST_TABLE columns (continued)	
Column name	**Description**
IMFFADJ	The filter factor of matching and screening predicates.
IMSCANCST	IBM internal use only.
IMREDSORT	IBM internal use only.
IMMERGCST	IBM internal use only.
IMCPU	IBM internal use only.
IMTOT	IBM internal use only.
IMSEQNO	IBM internal use only.
DMPEREFH	IBM internal use only.
DMCLUDIO	IBM internal use only.
DMPREDS	IBM internal use only.
DMSROWS	IBM internal use only.
DMSCANCST	IBM internal use only.
DMROWS	The number of data manager rows returned (after all stage 1 predicates are applied).
DMCOLS	The number of data manager columns.
RDSROWCST	IBM internal use only.
DMPAGECST	IBM internal use only.
DMDATAIO	IBM internal use only.
DMDATACPU	IBM internal use only.
RDSROW	The number of RDS rows returned (after all stage 1 and stage 2 predicates are applied).
SNCOLS	The number of columns as sort input for a new table.
SNROWS	The number of rows as sort input for a new table.
SNRUNS	The number of runs generated for a sort of a new table.
SNMERGES	The number of merges needed during a sort.
SNIOCOST	IBM internal use only.
SNCPUCOST	IBM internal use only.
SNCOST	IBM internal use only.
SNCSANIO	IBM internal use only.
SNSCANCPU	IBM internal use only.
SNCCOLS	The number of columns as sort input for a composite table.
SCROWS	The number of rows as sort input for a composite table.
SCRECSZ	The record size for a composite table.
SCPAGES	The page size for a composite table.

Table 17.10: DSN_DETCOST_TABLE columns (continued)	
Column name	Description
SCRUNS	The number of runs generated during the sort of a composite table.
SCMERGES	The number of merges needed during a sort of a composite table.
SCIOCOST	IBM internal use only.
SCCPUCOST	IBM internal use only.
SCCOST	IBM internal use only.
SCSCANIO	IBM internal use only.
SCSCANCPU	IBM internal use only.
SCSCANCOST	IBM internal use only.
COMPCARD	The total composite cardinality.
COMPIOCOST	IBM internal use only.
COMPCPUCOST	IBM internal use only.
COMPCOST	The total cost.
JOINCOLS	IBM internal use only.
EXPLAIN_TIME	The EXPLAIN timestamp.
GROUP_MEMBER	The member name of the DB2 subsystem that executed EXPLAIN. The column is blank if the DB2 subsystem was not in a data-sharing environment when EXPLAIN was executed.

DSN_SORT_TABLE

The *sort table*, DSN_SORT_TABLE, contains information about sort operations required for a query. Table 17.11 lists the contents of the sort table.

Table 17.11: DSN_SRT_TABLE columns	
Column name	Description
QUERYNO	A number used to help identify the query being explained. It is not a unique identifier. Using a negative number will cause problems. The possible sources are: • The statement line number in the program • The QUERYNO clause • The EXPLAIN statement • The EDM unique token in the statement cache
QBLOCKNO	A number used to identify each query block within a query.
PLANNO	A number used to identify each mini-plan within a query block.

Table 17.11: DSN_SRT_TABLE columns (continued)	
Column name	**Description**
APPLNAME	The application plan name.
PROGNAME	The program name (binding an application) or the package name (binding a package).
COLLID	The collection ID for the package.
SORTC	Indicates the reasons for sort of the composite table, using a bitmap of the following values: G = Group By O = Order By J = Join U = Uniqueness
SORTN	Indicates the reasons for sort of the Composite table. Using a bitmap of the following values: G = Group By O = Order By J = Join U = Uniqueness
SORTNO	The sequence of the sort.
KEYSIZE	The sum of the lengths of the sort keys.
ORDERCLASS	IBM internal use only.
EXPLAIN_TIME	The EXPLAIN timestamp.
GROUP_MEMBER	The member name of the DB2 subsystem that executed EXPLAIN. The column is blank if the DB2 subsystem was not in a data-sharing environment when EXPLAIN was executed.

DSN_SORTKEY_TABLE

The *sort key* table, DSN_SORTKEY_TABLE, contains information about sort keys for all the sorts required by a query. Table 17.12 lists the contents of the sort key table.

Table 17.12: DSN_SORTKEY_TABLE columns	
Column name	**Description**
QUERYNO	A number used to help identify the query being explained. It is not a unique identifier. Using a negative number will cause problems. The possible sources are: • The statement line number in the program • The QUERYNO clause • The EXPLAIN statement • The EDM unique token in the statement cache
QBLOCKNO	A number used to identify each query block within a query.
PLANNO	A number used to identify each mini-plan within a query block.
APPLNAME	The application plan name.
PROGNAME	The program name (binding an application) or the package name (binding a package).
COLLID	The collection ID for the package.
SORTNO	The sequence number of the sort.
ORDERNO	The sequence of the sort key.
EXPTYPE	The type of the sort key. The possible values are: COL EXP QRY
TEXT	The sort key text; can be a column name, a scalar subquery, or 'Record ID'.
TABNO	A number that uniquely identifies the corresponding table reference within a query.
COLNO	A number that uniquely identifies the corresponding column within a query. Applicable only when the sort key is a column.
DATATYPE	The data type of the sort key. The possible values are: HEXADECIMAL CHARACTER PACKED FIELD FIXED(31) FIXED(15) DATE TIME VARCHAR PACKED FLD FLOAT

Table 17.12: DSN_SORTKEY_TABLE columns (contiuned)	
Column name	**Description**
DATATYPE	TIMESTAMP
	UNKNOWN DATA TYPE
LENGTH	The length of the sort key.
CCSID	IBM internal use only.
ORDERCLASS	IBM internal use only.
EXPLAIN_TIME	The EXPLAIN timestamp.
GROUP_MEMBER	The member name of the DB2 subsystem that executed EXPLAIN. The column is blank if the DB2 subsystem was not in a data-sharing environment when EXPLAIN was executed.

DSN_PGRANGE_TABLE

The *page range* table, DSN_PGRANGE_TABLE, contains information about qualified partitions for all page range scans in a query. This information is more detailed than the PAGE_RANGE column of PLAN_TABLE, and it includes information about when partitions are eliminated even when the query is scanning an index. Table 17.13 lists the contents of the page range table.

Table 17.13: DSN_PGRANGE_TABLE columns	
Column name	**Description**
QUERYNO	The query number, a number used to help identify the query being explained. It is not a unique identifier. Using a negative number will cause problems. The possible sources are: • The statement line number in the program • The QUERYNO clause • The EXPLAIN statement • The EDM unique token in the statement cache
QBLOCKNO	A number used to identify each query block within a query.
RANGE	The sequence number of the current page range.
FIRSTPART	The starting partition in the current page range.
LASTPART	The ending partition in the current page range.
NUMPARTS	The number of partitions in the current page range.
EXPLAIN_TIME	The EXPLAIN timestamp.
GROUP_MEMBER	The member name of the DB2 subsystem that executed EXPLAIN. The column is blank if the DB2 subsystem was not in a data-sharing environment when EXPLAIN was executed.

DSN_VIEWREF_TABLE

The *view reference table*, DSN_VIEWREF_TABLE, contains information about all the views and materialized query tables used to process a query. Table 17.14 lists the contents of the view reference table.

Table 17.14: DSN_VIEWREF_TABLE columns	
Column name	**Description**
QUERYNO	A number used to help identify the query being explained. It is not a unique identifier. Using a negative number will cause problems. The possible sources are: • The statement line number in the program • The QUERYNO clause • The EXPLAIN statement • The EDM unique token in the statement cache
APPLNAME	The application plan name.
PROGNAME	The program name (binding an application) or the package name (binding a package).
VERSION	The version identifier for the package. Applies only to an embedded EXPLAIN statement that is executed from a package or to a statement that is explained when binding a package. Blank if not applicable. The value DSNDYNAMICSQLCACHE indicates that the row is for a cached statement.
CREATOR	Authorization ID of the owner of the object.
NAME	Name of the object.
TYPE	The type of the object: • V = View • R = MQT that has been used to replace the base table for rewrite • M = MQT
MQTUSE	IBM internal use only.
EXPLAIN_TIME	The EXPLAIN timestamp.
GROUP_MEMBER	The member name of the DB2 subsystem that executed EXPLAIN. The column is blank if the DB2 subsystem was not in a data-sharing environment when EXPLAIN was executed.

DSN_QUERY_TABLE

The *query table*, DSN_QUERY_TABLE, contains information about an SQL statement and displays the statement before and after query transformation in XML. Table 17.15 lists the contents of the query table.

Table 17.15: DSN_QUERY_TABLE columns	
Column name	Description
QUERYNO	A number used to help identify the query being explained. It is not a unique identifier. Using a negative number will cause problems. The possible sources are: • The statement line number in the program • QUERYNO clause • The EXPLAIN statement • The EDM unique token in the statement cache
TYPE	The type of the data in the NODE_DATA column.
QUERY_STAGE	The stage during query transformation when this row is populated.
SEQNO	The sequence number for this row if NODE_DATA exceeds the size of its column
NODE_DATA	The XML data containing the SQL statement and its query block, table, and column information.
EXPLAIN_TIME	The EXPLAIN timestamp.
QUERY_ROWID	The ROWID of the statement.
GROUP_MEMBER	The member name of the DB2 subsystem that executed EXPLAIN. The column is blank if the DB2 subsystem was not in a data-sharing environment when EXPLAIN was executed.
HASHKEY	The hash value of the contents in NODE_DATA.
HASH_PRED	When NODE_DATA contains an SQL statement, this column indicates whether the statement contains a parameter marker literal, a non-parameter marker literal, or no predicates.

Explain Table Querying and the Optimization Service Center

DB2 9's Optimization Service Center (OSC) is a workstation-based tool that lets you easily interact with DB2 EXPLAIN and the explain tables to analyze SQL statements, objects, statistics, the statement cache, and workloads. The OSC replaces the Visual Explain product that was available with Version 8.

The OSC provides DBAs with a rich set of autonomic tools that help optimize query performance and workloads. You can use OSC to identify and analyze problem SQL statements and to receive expert advice about statistics you can gather to improve the performance of problematic and poorly performing SQL statements on a DB2 subsystem. Using the OSC, you can

- snap the statement cache

- collect statistics information

- analyze indexes

- group statements into workloads

- monitor workloads

- invoke EXPLAIN for dynamic SQL statements

- provide DB2 catalog statistics for referenced objects of an access path or for a group of statements

Using the OSC, you can automatically gather information from EXPLAIN and view graphical depictions of the access plans DB2 chooses for your SQL queries and statements. Such graphs eliminate the need to manually interpret EXPLAIN information and clearly illustrate the relationships between database objects (e.g., tables and indexes) and operations (e.g., table space scans and sorts). You can use this information to help you perform the following tasks:

- Determine the access path that DB2 chooses for a query

- Design databases, indexes, and application programs

- Decide when to rebind an application

The Optimization Service Center also lets you snap the information from the statement cache and view the contents of the statement cache table. You can import queries into the OSC from the DB2 system catalog, as well as from files or programs. You can group statements into workloads and monitor and analyze those workloads together.

Although the Optimization Service Center is by far the easiest way to view the contents of the explain tables, the explain tables are populated via the EXPLAIN statement for the user executing EXPLAIN. You can access these tables using normal SQL queries. Although most people are used to querying the plan table, it does not provide the details of the remaining explain tables. The additional explain tables can be joined to the PLAN_TABLE table for a query and indexed via the query number and explain timestamp. The Service SQL feature lets you easily package EXPLAIN statement information for reporting problems to IBM for service.

In addition, the OSC provides

- an easy-to-understand display of a selected access path

- suggestions for changing a SQL statement

- a subsystem parameter browser with keyword find capabilities

- a graphical interface for creating optimization hints

Guidelines for Using Explain Output

There are numerous many ways in which analyzing the explain data can help you to tune your queries and environment. For example, analyzing the explain data can help you determine whether indexes are being used or verify that the type of access is appropriate for the application.

Verifying Index Use

Creating appropriate indexes can significantly benefit performance. Using the explain output, you can determine whether the indexes you've created to help a specific set of queries are in fact being used. In the explain output, look for index use in the following areas:

- Join predicates

- Local predicates

- GROUP BY clauses

- ORDER BY clauses

- The SELECT list

You can also use EXPLAIN to evaluate whether DB2 can use a different index instead of an existing index or no index at all. After creating a new index, collect statistics for that index using the RUNSTATS utility, and rebind the query.

Over time, you may notice, through the explain data, that instead of an index scan, DB2 is now using a table scan. This behavior can result from a change in the clustering of the table data. If the index that was previously being used now has a low cluster ratio, take these steps:

1. Reorganize your table to cluster the data according to that index.

2. Use RUNSTATS to update the catalog statistics.

3. Rebind the query.

4. Reexamine the explain output to determine whether reorganizing the table has affected the access plan.

The more indexes you have, the more important it is to collect accurate and detailed statistics. Good statistics help DB2 differentiate between indexes for access path selection. Increasing the number of indexes increases the potential access paths that DB2 must evaluate. If the statistics don't adequately distinguish each index for DB2, it may choose a less efficient access path.

Checking Application Access

You can use the explain output to look for types of access to the data that, as a rule, aren't optimal for the type of application being executed.

For example, OLTP applications are prime candidates to use matching index scans with range-delimiting predicates because they tend to return only a few rows in their queries, using an equality predicate against a key column. If your OLTP queries are using a table scan or a non-matching index scan, you may want to analyze the explain data to determine why a matching index scan wasn't used.

Explain data can also be useful for analyzing access by read-only queries. The search criteria for a read-only query may be vague, causing a large number of rows to qualify. If the user usually looks only at a few screens of the output data, he or she may be trying to ensure that the entire answer set needn't be computed before some results are returned. In this case, the user's goals are different from the basic operating principle of the optimizer, which tries to minimize resource consumption for the entire query, not just the first few screens of data.

For example, if the explain output shows that the access plan used both merge scan join and sort operators, the entire answer set will be materialized in a temporary table before any rows are returned to the application. In this case, you might try to change the access plan by using the OPTIMIZE FOR clause on the SELECT statement. The value specified for the OPTIMIZE clause should represent the number of rows to be processed by the application. In this way, the optimizer can attempt to choose an access plan that doesn't produce the entire answer set in a temporary table before returning the first rows to the application.

Access Path Optimization Hints

DB2 provides a facility for giving optimization *hints*, or instructions about how DB2 should process a query. Setting the installation parameter OPTHINTS to YES enables DB2 to use optimization hints. Optimization hints are useful in the following situations:

- When you want to ensure consistent response times across rebinds and across release migrations (or maintenance releases)

- When you want to temporarily bypass the access path chosen by DB2

The process of providing hints to DB2 is relatively simple, but determining what those hints should be is not.

The facility for implementing access path hints involves many tasks, and the subsystem where the query will be bound must be enabled for hints. The Optimization Service Center lets you create hints graphically. When you use optimization hints, you must

- modify the SQL to use the hint

- update a plan table with the desired access path information or use an existing access path

- Change the bind options for the affected packages (OPTHINT parameter)

Even after you've established a hint, it's not always possible for the optimizer to use it. As part of the normal bind process, the optimizer evaluates the hint to determine whether it is valid. You should have measures in place to make sure rebinds don't change the process because although the hint may help prevent a change in access path during a rebind, it is no guarantee. As long as the hint is valid, DB2 will use it to maintain the access path across rebinds. For this reason, you shouldn't use hints unless all else fails in establishing an acceptable access path.

Catalog Statistics

DB2 maintains information about the data in your tables as well as about the organization of tables, table spaces, indexes, and more. This information is retained in the DB2 system catalog and is often referred to as the *catalog statistics*. DB2's cost-based optimizer uses catalog statistics to help determine the proper access path for a query. Accurate catalog statistics are a must for proper performance. You collect this information using the RUNSTATS utility, which you can use to gather a variety of types of statistics.

Filter Factors and Catalog Statistics

To determine optimal access paths, DB2 needs an accurate estimate of the number of rows that qualify after applying each predicate. When a query involves multiple tables, filtering affects the cost of join order and join method as well. Catalog tables SYSIBM.SYSCOLUMNS and SYSIBM.SYSCOLDIST are the main sources of statistics for calculating predicate filter factors.

Column COLCARDF of the SYSCOLUMNS table indicates whether statistics exist for a column. A positive value is an estimate of the column's *cardinality*—that is, the number of distinct values in the column. A COLCARDF value of –1 results in the use of default statistics. The COLCARDF value generated by the RUNSTATS TABLESPACE command is an estimate determined by a sampling method. If you know a more accurate number for COLCARDF, you can supply it by updating the catalog. If the column is the first column of an index, the value generated by RUNSTATS INDEX is exact.

Columns in table SYSCOLDIST contain statistics about the *frequency*, or distribution, of values for a single column. This table can also contain statistics about the cardinality of a group of columns and the frequency of values for that group. When frequency statistics don't exist, DB2 assumes that the data is uniformly distributed and that all values in the column occur with the same frequency. If the data is skewed, this assumption can lead to an inaccurate estimate of the number of qualifying rows, which in turn can result in performance problems.

For example, assume that a column (AGE_CATEGORY) contains five distinct values (COLCARDF=5), each of which occurs with the following frequencies:

AGE_CATEGORY value	Frequency of value
INFANT	5 percent
CHILD	15 percent
ADOLESCENT	25 percent
ADULT	40 percent
SENIOR	15 percent

Without this frequency information, DB2 would use a default filter factor of 1/5 (1/COLCARDF), or 20 percent, to estimate the number of rows that qualify for predicate AGE_CATEGORY=ADULT. However, the actual frequency of that age category is 40 percent. Thus, the number of qualifying rows would be underestimated by 50 percent.

When collecting statistics about indexes, you can specify the RUNSTATS utility's KEYCARD option to collect cardinality statistics on the specified indexes. You can also use the FREQVAL option with KEYCARD to specify whether RUNSTATS should collect distribution statistics and for how many concatenated index columns. By default, RUNSTATS collects distribution statistics on the first column of each index for the 10 most frequently occurring values. The utility also collects FIRSTKEYCARDF and FULLKEYCARDF statistics by default.

When collecting statistics at the table level, you can use the COLUMN option of RUNSTATS to collect cardinality statistics on just the columns you specify. The COLGROUP option lets you specify a group of columns for which to collect cardinality statistics. If you use the FREQVAL option with COLGROUP, you can also collect distribution statistics for the column group.

To limit the resources required to gather statistics, you need to collect only column cardinality and frequency statistics that have changed. For example, a column on GENDER is likely to have a COLCARDF of 2, with M and F as the possible values. It's unlikely that the cardinality for this column ever changes. Depending on the volatility of the data, the distribution of the values in the column might not change often either.

If query performance is unsatisfactory, consider the following actions:

- Collect cardinality statistics on all columns used as predicates in a WHERE clause.

- Collect frequencies for all columns with a low cardinality that are used as COL *op constant* predicates.

- Collect frequencies for a column when the column can contain default data, the default data is skewed, and the column is used as a COL *op constant* predicate.

- Collect KEYCARD on all candidate indexes.

- Collect column group statistics on all join columns.

LOW2KEY and HIGH2KEY columns in the catalog tables are limited to storing the first 2,000 bytes of a key value. If the column is nullable, values are limited to 1,999 bytes.

The closer the value of column SYSINDEXES.CLUSTERRATIOF is to 100 percent (a value of 1), the more closely the ordering of the index entries matches the physical ordering of the table rows.

For more information about using the RUNSTATS utility, see Chapter 7 and the "RUNSTATS" section of the *IBM DB2 9 Utility Guide and Reference*.

Histogram Statistics

Histogram statistics enable DB2 to improve access path selection by estimating predicate selectivity from value-distribution statistics that are collected over the entire range of values in a data set. RUNSTATS cannot collect histogram statistics on randomized key columns.

DB2 chooses the best access path for a query based on predicate selectivity estimation, which in turn relies heavily on data distribution statistics. Histogram statistics summarize data distribution on an interval scale by dividing the entire range of possible values within a data set into a number of intervals.

DB2 creates *equal-depth* histogram statistics, meaning that it divides the whole range of values into intervals that each contain about the same percentage of the total number of rows. The following columns in a histogram statistics table define an interval:

Column	Description
QUANTILENO	An ordinary sequence number that identifies the interval
HIGHVALUE	The value that serves as the upper bound for the interval
LOWVALUE	A value that serves as the lower bound for the interval

Note the following characteristics of histogram statistics intervals:

- Each interval includes approximately the same number, or percentage, of the rows. A highly frequent single value might occupy an interval by itself.

- A single value is never broken into more than one interval, meaning that the maximum number of intervals is equal to the number of distinct values on the column. The maximum number of intervals cannot exceed 100, the maximum number that DB2 supports.

- Adjacent intervals sometime skip values that don't appear in the table, especially when doing so avoids a large range of skipped values within an interval. For example, if a value has a 1 percent frequency, placing it in the seventh interval would balance the percentage of rows in the sixth and seventh intervals; however, doing so would introduce a large skipped range to the seventh interval.

- HIGHVALUE and LOWVALUE can be inclusive or exclusive, but an interval generally represents a non-overlapped value range.

- NULL values, if any exist, occupy a single interval.

Histogram statistics provide an advantage over frequency distribution statistics in that the histogram covers the range over the entire domain of values, while distribution statistics describe only the *n* most or least frequent values, with column cardinality minus the occurring values used to determine the filter factor for any remaining equals predicates. However, histogram statistics provide the greatest advantage for range predicates across skewed data values. For example, the following query would benefit the most from histogram statistics if the YRS_OF_EXPERIENCE column has skewed values.

```
SELECT T1.EMPID
FROM IBM_EMPLOYEE T1, IBM_OPENJOBS T2
WHERE T1.SPECIALTY = T2.AREA
AND T1.YRS_OF_EXPERIENCE > T2.YRS_OF_EXPERIENCE;
```

Statistics for Partitioned Table Spaces

For a partitioned table space, DB2 keeps statistics separately by partition and also collectively for the entire table space. Table 17.16 shows the catalog tables that contain statistics by partition and, for each one, lists the table that contains the corresponding aggregate statistics.

Table 17.16: Statistics tables for partitioned table spaces	
Statistics by partition are in	**Aggregate statistics are in**
SYSTABSTATS	SYSTABLES
SYSINDEXSTATS	SYSINDEXES
SYSCOLSTATS	SYSCOLUMNS
SYSCOLDISTSTATS	SYSCOLDIST
SYSKEYTARGETSTATS	SYSKEYTARGETS
SYSKEYTGTDISTSTATS	SYSKEYTGTDIST

If you run RUNSTATS for separate partitions of a table space, DB2 uses the results to update the aggregate statistics for the entire table space. You should either run RUNSTATS once on the entire object before collecting statistics on separate partitions or use the appropriate option to ensure that the statistics are aggregated appropriately, especially if some partitions are not loaded with data.

Using Statistics to Model a Production Environment

The DB2 catalog includes statistics that the optimizer uses in calculating the costs of SQL to determine the best access path to pick. When you build a test environment, it's often helpful to copy statistics from a production environment or to update the statistics to an approximation of what production might be like. Table 17.17 lists the catalog statistics that can be updated and are also used by the optimizer in access path selection.

Many other statistics used for access path selection cannot be updated by the user. The best way to update statistics is by using the RUNSTATS utility. Copying statistics from production to test is an effective method for estimating production access paths. However, updating catalog statistics for access path influence is extremely risky.

Table 17.17: Updatable catalog statistics used in access path selection	
Table	**Statistics**
SYSIBM.SYSCOLDIST	CARDF
	COLGROUPCOLNO
	COLVALUE
	FREQUENCYF
	HIGHVALUE
	LOWVALUE
	NUMCOLUMNS
	QUANTILENO
	TYPE
SYSIBM.SYSCOLDISTSTATS	HIGHVALUE
	QUANTILENO
SYSIBM.SYSCOLUMNS	COLCARDF
	HIGH2KEY
	LOW2KEY
SYSIBM.SYSINDEXES	CLUSTERRATIOF
	FIRSTKEYCARDF
	FULLKEYCARDF
	NLEAF
	NLEVELS
	DATAREPEATFACTORF
SYSIBM.SYSINDEXSTATS	DATAREPEATFACTORF
SYSIBM.SYSKEYTARGETS	HIGH2KEY
	LOW2KEY
	STATS_FORMAT

Table 17.17: Updatable catalog statistics used in access path selection (continued)	
Table	**Statistics**
SYSIBM.SYSKEYTARGETSTATS	HIGHKEY
	HIGH2KEY
	LOWKEY
	LOW2KEY
	STATS_FORMAT
SYSIBM.SYSKEYTGTDIST	CARDF
	KEYGROUPKEYNO
	KEYVALUE
	FREQUENCYF
	HIGHVALUE
	LOWVALUE
	NUMKEYS
	QUANTILENO
	TYPE
SYSIBM.SYSKEYTGTDISTSTATS	HIGHVALUE
	LOWVALUE
	QUANTILENO
SYSIBM.SYSROUTINES	CARDINALITY
	INITIAL_INSTS
	INITIAL_IOS
	INSTS_PER_INVOC
	IOS_PER_INVOC
SYSIBM.SYSTABLES	CARDF
	NPAGES
	NPAGESF
	PCTROWCOMP
SYSIBM.SYSTABLESPACE	NACTIVE
SYSIBM.SYSTABSTATS	CARDF
	NPAGES

Predicate Types

DB2 processes the predicates in a query based on the stage at which it can apply each predicate as well as on the order in which the predicates are coded. (Recall the three types of predicates: indexable, stage 1, and stage 2.) The way a predicate is coded determines when it can be evaluated and when DB2 can use an index. DB2 applies the following criteria in processing query predicates.

1. Indexable predicates are applied first.

   » Matching predicates on index key columns are evaluated in index key order when the index is accessed.

      ■ All equal predicates and IN list of one value

      ■ All range predicates and column IS NOT NULL

      ■ All other predicate types

   » Index screening.

      ■ All equal predicates and IN list of one value

      ■ All range predicates and column IS NOT NULL

      ■ All other predicate types

2. Other stage 1 data predicates are applied next and are evaluated after data page access.

   » All equal predicates and IN list of one value

   » All range predicates and column IS NOT NULL

   » All other predicate types

3. The stage 2 predicates are applied on the returned data rows.

   » All equal predicates and IN list of one value

   » All range predicates and column IS NOT NULL

4. All remaining predicates are evaluated in the order in which they appear in the query.

Indexable Predicates

Indexable predicate types match index entries when the index is used for the access path. These predicates may or may not be index matching predicates; it all depends on the indexes that are available and the access path chosen at bind time. For example, if the employee table has an index on the column LASTNAME, the following predicate can be an index matching predicate (and is stage 1):

```
SELECT *
FROM EMP
WHERE LASTNAME = 'LAWSON';
```

The next example shows a predicate (IS NOT DISTINCT FROM) that considers null values as equals and is a stage 1 indexable predicate.

```
SELECT DEPTNO, DEPTNAME, MGRNO, ADMRDEPT
FROM DEPT
WHERE MGRNO IS NOT DISTINCT FROM '000010';
```

Although it's desirable to have all index matching predicates, we can't index every single column in every table for every combination of predicates. There has to be a balance between managing the indexes and query performance.

Stage 1 Predicates

Stage 1 predicates can be processed within the stage 1 portion of the DB2 engine (also known as the *DM component*). This is where DB2 accesses tables and indexes. The previous example of an indexable predicate is a stage 1 predicate. Stage 1 predicates are very efficient, and you should strive to use them when performance is a concern. Many predicates are stage 1. Many are indexable, but some are not. The following example uses a stage 1 predicate that is not indexable.

```
SELECT DEPTNO, DEPTNAME, MGRNO, ADMRDEPT
FROM DEPT
WHERE DEPTNO <> 'D01';
```

Stage 2 Predicates

Stage 2 predicates are processed within the stage 2 portion of the DB2 engine (also known as the *RDS component*). In simple terms, this part of the engine is the place where DB2 applies scalar functions and sorts. Another simplified way to think about stage 2 predicates is that the stage 2 engine is unaware of indexes and tables. For that reason, stage 2 predicates don't limit the range of data retrieved from disk but can still filter data before it is returned to the query. If your predicates are simple, as in the indexable example above, they are likely to be stage 1 predicates. If you move more logic into the predicates themselves, they may be stage 2.

For example, the following query employs a scalar function against a column value, using what is known as a *type of columns* expression. Because DB2 processes scalar functions in the stage 2 engine, the predicate is a stage 2 predicate. DB2 cannot use an index for data access, and it will have to move the data from stage 1 to stage 2 to filter the data.

```
SELECT *
FROM EMP
WHERE SUBSTR(LASTNAME,1,1) = 'L';
```

For more information about stage 1 and stage 2 predicates, see Chapter 6.

Designing Indexes and SQL for Performance

In the following paragraphs, we review the different access paths provided by indexes. You should ensure that indexes are in place to provide the best access path possible for critical queries. When predicates in a query match index columns and DB2 uses the index to access the table, the predicates used to match the index are known as *index matching predicates*.

Indexes for Efficient Access

To achieve efficient access, DB2 uses the following index access paths (represented by the noted PLAN_TABLE column values).

- Matching index scan (MATCHCOLS > 0)

- Index screening

- Non-matching index scan (ACCESSTYPE = I and MATCHCOLS = 0)

- IN-list index scan (ACCESSTYPE = N)

- Multiple index access (ACCESSTYPE is M, MX, MI, MU, DX, DI, or DU)

- One-fetch access (ACCESSTYPE = I1)

- Index-only access (INDEXONLY = Y)

- Equal unique index (MATCHCOLS = *number of index columns*)

Matching Index Scan (MATCHCOLS > 0)

In a matching index scan, predicates are specified on either the leading or all of the index key columns. These predicates provide filtering; only specific index pages and data pages need to be accessed. If the degree of filtering is high, the matching index scan is efficient.

DB2 applies index matching predicates in the sequence of the index columns. Therefore, coding sequence isn't important for this type of predicate. DB2 evaluates WHERE clause predicates in the following order.

1. Indexed predicates

2. Matching predicates

3. Index screening predicates

4. Stage 1 predicates

5. Stage 2 predicates

Excluding index matching predicates, within each stage (screening, stage 1, or stage 2), DB2 generally applies predicates in the following sequence.

1. All equal predicates (and IS NULL)

2. All range predicates (and IS NOT NULL)

3. All other predicates

The final rule for predicate evaluation dictates that within each of the preceding guidelines, DB2 evaluates predicates in the sequence in which they are coded. This gives the programmer some control over predicate execution, and therefore the programmer should code the most restrictive predicates first.

Index Screening

In *index screening*, predicates are specified on index key columns but are not part of the matching columns. Such predicates improve subsequent data-page access by reducing the number of rows that qualify during the index search. For example, with an index on table T (C1,C2,C3,C4) in the following SQL statement, C3 > 0 and C4 = 2 are index screening predicates, while C1 = 1 is a matching index predicate.

```
SELECT * FROM T
WHERE C1 = 1
AND C3 >0 AND C4 = 2
AND C5 = 8;
```

Non-Matching Index Scan (ACCESSTYPE = I and MATCHCOLS = 0)

In a *non-matching index scan*, no matching columns are in the index. Hence, DB2 must examine all the index keys. Because a non-matching index scan usually doesn't provide strong filtering, only a few cases provide an efficient access path if subsequent data pages must also be accessed. If the access path is index-only, a non-matching index scan may prove beneficial, especially if the index is smaller than the table space.

> An index-only non-matching index scan may not always be more efficient than a table space scan. A table space may be smaller than an index if the number of index keys is large or if the table space is compressed. Also, assuming both are of similar size, an index scan may be less efficient because the scan must follow the leaf page pointer chain, which may not be sequential due to index page splits.

IN-List Index Scan (ACCESSTYPE = N)

An *IN-list index scan* is a special case of the matching index scan in which a single indexable IN predicate serves as a matching equal predicate. You can regard the IN-list index scan as a series of matching index scans, with the values in the IN predicate being used for each matching index scan. The following example has an index on (C1,C2,C3,C4) and might use an IN-list index scan.

```
SELECT * FROM T
WHERE C1 = 1 AND C2 IN (1,2,3)
AND C3 > 0 AND C4 < 100;
```

This example could result in an ACCESSTYPE = N and MATCHCOLS = 3 (C1,C2,C3). C4 would be an index screening predicate.

●●

IN list predicates cannot be matching predicates for MX access or list prefetch.

●●

Multiple Index Access (ACCESSTYPE is M, MX, MI, MU, DX, DI, or DU)

Multiple index access uses more than one index to access a table. It is a good access path when

- no single index provides efficient access

- a combination of index accesses provides efficient access

RID lists are constructed for each of the indexes involved. The unions (OR conditions) or intersections (AND conditions) of the RID lists produce a final list of qualified RIDs that DB2 uses to retrieve the result rows, using list prefetch. You can consider multiple index access as an extension to list prefetch with more complex RID retrieval operations in its first phase. The complex operators are union and intersection.

DB2 may choose multiple index access for the following query.

```
SELECT * FROM EMP
WHERE (AGE = 34) OR
(JOB = 'MANAGER');
```

For this query, assume

- EMP is a table with columns EMPNO, EMPNAME, DEPT, JOB, AGE, and SAL

- EMPX1 is an index on EMP with key column AGE

- EMPX2 is an index on EMP with key column JOB

If DB2 chooses multiple index access for this query, both the EMPX1 and EMPX2 indexes will be used, the RIDs corresponding to the matching key values collected and sorted, and those RID lists UNIONed in support of the OR.

One-Fetch Access (ACCESSTYPE = I1)

One-fetch index access requires retrieving only one row. It is the best possible access path and is chosen whenever it is available. It applies to a statement with a MIN or MAX column function: the order of the index lets a single row give the result of the function. Either an ascending or a descending index can be used to satisfy a MIN or MAX function using one-fetch index access.

Index-Only Access (INDEXONLY = Y)

With *index-only access*, the access path doesn't require any data pages because the access information is available in the index. Conversely, when an SQL statement requests a column that is not in the index, updates any column in the table, or deletes a row, DB2 has to access the associated data pages. Because the index is generally smaller than the table itself, an index-only access path usually processes the data efficiently.

> The number of levels of the index can determine whether DB2 will choose index-only access instead of index and data access via a different index. Assume index IX1 has four levels and provides an index-only access path and that IX2 has three levels and is not index-only. DB2 may choose IX2 and access the data pages because both access paths result in four potential I/Os.

Equal Unique Index (MATCHCOLS = Number of Index Columns)

An index that is fully matched and unique, and in which all matching predicates are equal predicates, is called an *equal unique index* case. This case guarantees that DB2 retrieves only one row. If no one-fetch index access is available, equal unique index is considered the most efficient access over all other indexes that are not "equal unique." (The uniqueness of an index is determined by whether it was defined as unique.) Sometimes, DB2 can determine that an index that isn't fully matching is actually an equal unique index case. This assessment is based on the existence of another unique index with a subset of the key columns.

Using Indexes to Help Avoid Sorts

As well as providing selective access to data, indexes can order data, sometimes eliminating the need for sorting. DB2 can avoid some sorts if index keys are in the order needed by ORDER BY, GROUP BY, a join operation, or DISTINCT in a column function. A DISTINCT sort can also be avoided if a unique index exists on the selected columns and/or WHERE clause columns. In other cases, as when list prefetch is used, the index provides no useful ordering, and the selected data might have to be sorted.

When it is absolutely necessary to prevent a sort, consider creating an index on the column or columns necessary to provide that ordering. Consider also using the clause OPTIMIZE FOR 1 ROW to discourage DB2 from choosing a sort for the access path. Consider this query:

```
SELECT C1,C2,C3 FROM T
WHERE C1 > 1
ORDER BY C1 OPTIMIZE FOR 1 ROW;
```

An ascending index on C1 or an index on (C1,C2,C3) could eliminate a sort.

> OPTIMIZE FOR 1 ROW has implications other than avoiding a sort, and you should therefore use it only when necessary. Consider specifying a value that represents the number of rows that are required to be processed by the application.

Not all sorts are inefficient. For example, if the index that provides ordering is not an efficient one and many rows qualify, using another access path to retrieve and then sort the data could be more efficient than employing the inefficient, ordering index.

DB2 can backward-scan an index and avoid a sort on queries that can use this feature. This method works if the index is the exact opposite of the queries. DB2 will be able to avoid a sort in both of the following examples, which assume an index on (COL1 ASC, COL2 DESC).

```
SELECT COL1, COL2
FROM T
ORDER BY COL1 ASC, COL2 DESC

SELECT COL1, COL2
FROM T
ORDER BY COL1 DESC, COL2 ASC
```

Dynamic SQL

Dynamic SQL performance is critical for many applications, but it is a bit harder to guarantee and tune than static SQL. A few tips can help you get the best performance for dynamic SQL:

- Reorganize the DB2 catalog.

- Reorganize the application table space and indexes.

- Use dynamic statement caching.

- Use bind parameters REOPT (discussed below) and KEEPDYNAMIC (discussed in Chapter 11).

- Use SET CURRENT DEGREE = 'ANY' to attempt parallelism.

The dynamic SQL cache is important to the performance of dynamic SQL because statements in the cache don't need to be re-prepared. To pick up new statistics for objects used in dynamic SQL, you must refresh the dynamic SQL. To do so, execute RUNSTATS on the objects on which the query is dependent. You can also refresh by using RUNSTATS NONE REPORT NO if you don't want to update catalog statistics or report on changes.

Runtime Reoptimization

DB2 normally determines the access path in one of two ways:

- During the BIND process for static embedded SQL

- During statement preparation for dynamic SQL

In most situations, the optimizer chooses an efficient access path. There are, however, situations in which it may be better to determine the access path at statement execution time. Take, for example, a table with column C1. If the values for column C1 are evenly distributed from 1 to 100, the following assumptions can be made:

- WHERE C1 > 10 will return about 90 percent of the data from the table.

- WHERE C1 > 95 will return about 5 percent of the data.

- WHERE C1 > ? will return an unknown percentage of the data.

- WHERE C1 > :H will return an unknown percentage of the data.

In the first two cases, where literal values are used, DB2 can make assumptions about the distribution of the data (or use distribution statistics if they are available) and use those assumptions to determine the best access path. In the second two cases, DB2 has no idea what the input values are and has to use default values and formulas to determine the best access path.

In situations where the input values can have a dramatic effect on the access path, or in situations in which the data values for a column referenced in a WHERE clause are skewed, the query may benefit from *runtime reoptimization*. You can implement runtime reoptimization for static or dynamic SQL through the use of bind parameters or via the REOPTEXT subsystem parameter.

Runtime Reoptimization for Static SQL

Runtime reoptimization for static SQL is beneficial for queries that use host variables, when those host variable values are for range predicates that can dramatically influence the access path, and for queries that use host variables against columns that have skewed values. The REOPT(ALWAYS) bind parameter implements runtime reoptimization for static SQL. This bind parameter tells DB2 that for each statement in the DBRM (within a plan) or package, the statement should be re-bound at execution time, using the host-variable data values to calculate the access path. So, all statements within that plan or package will be re-bound at execution time. This step can dramatically improve the performance for queries that can benefit, but it can also add significant incremental bind costs for statements that don't really benefit from this setting. For this reason, it may be best when using this bind parameter to isolate the statement that can benefit within its own program, thus limiting the runtime reoptimization to only the statement that will benefit.

Runtime Reoptimization for Dynamic SQL

For dynamic SQL, there are two major ways to influence the runtime reoptimization: via bind parameters or via the REOPTEXT subsystem parameter.

BIND Parameters for Runtime Reoptimization of Dynamic SQL

Three reoptimization settings can influence the access path, and when the access path is determined, for dynamic SQL:

- **REOPT(ALWAYS).** As with static SQL, this setting causes the dynamic SQL to re-determine the access path for each statement execution. This step is important for dynamic statements that use parameter markers that vary greatly for range predicates as well as for dynamic statements that use parameter markers against columns whose value distribution is skewed. This re-determination also causes the access path to not be reused in the dynamic statement cache and can lead to additional incremental bind costs for dynamic statements that really can't benefit from the runtime reoptimization.

- **REOPT(ONCE).** This setting works like REOPT(ALWAYS), except that the reoptimization occurs only the first time the statement is executed. In other words, on the first execution of the statement, DB2 uses the values of the host variables referenced by the parameter markers to determine the access path. That access path will be reused for additional executions until the statement is invalidated or removed from the dynamic statement cache and needs to be prepared again.

- **REOPT(AUTO).** This setting works like REOPT(ALWAYS) for dynamic SQL, except that it is smart enough to know when the host variables referenced by the parameter markers change. When those values change, DB2 will recognize whether the changes in the values are dramatic enough to influence the access path; if they are, DB2 will perform an incremental bind and re-determine the access path.

Setting Dynamic SQL Reoptimization at the Subsystem Level

If you want to apply runtime reoptimization to all dynamic SQL at a subsystem level, you can use the REOPTEXT subsystem parameter. This parameter causes all dynamic SQL that uses parameter markers to be reoptimized according to the rules of the REOPT(AUTO) bind parameter for any statements that are not executed under packages (or plans) bound with the REOPT(NONE), REOPT(ALWAYS), or REOPT(ONCE) bind parameters.

Query Parallelism

To reduce elapsed time for a query, DB2 can give a query with parallel resources, such as several I/O paths or processors. By taking advantage of these resources, queries can run in a shorter period of time, enabling more work to be pushed through the system. Parallelism can help improve the performance of I/O and CPU bound read-only queries. It can help queries that are reading large amounts of data, regardless of the filtration.

Some overhead in terms of CPU is associated with the use of parallelism. DB2 scales processor-intensive work across all available processors. Parallelism can average less than 1 percent additional CPU overhead for long-running queries and less than 10 percent for short-running queries. Even if you select query parallelism at bind or prepare time, there is no guarantee that it will be used at execution time. DB2 may reduce or eliminate the degree of parallelism if it determines at runtime that insufficient resources (memory, CPU, and so on) exist to support the parallelism. You can use the DB2 Accounting Report to determine whether parallelism was used at the thread level, and you can use a DB2 performance trace to determine the actual degree of parallelism used for a query.

I/O and CPU Parallelism (PARALLELISM_MODE = I or C)

DB2 can use two different methods to achieve query parallelism: I/O or CPU. With I/O parallelism, the goal is to move elapsed time toward CPU time by splitting data access into equal, sequential prefetch streams to bring I/O time down to estimated CPU time. If CPU is estimated at one second and I/O at three seconds, the three I/O parallel streams of approximately equal size will be started. Each I/O stream should cost about one second. This type of parallelism is implemented with a round-robin type of GET paging. With current releases of DB2, I/O parallelism is very infrequently chosen; instead, the preferred method is CPU parallelism.

The goal of CPU parallelism is to move elapsed time toward CPU time by splitting queries into multiple equal, smaller queries and processing those queries in multiple execution units, or parallel tasks. At execution time, DB2 considers the number of CPUs available, and if there are not enough CPUs to support the degree of parallelism initially chosen by the optimizer, the degree will be degraded.

DB2 parallelism is decided both at the time of the bind and at runtime. If parallelism is not chosen at bind time, there is no possibility of it being chosen at runtime. Even if parallelism is chosen at bind time, it may not be used at runtime due to several factors. If insufficient space exists in the virtual buffer pool to support the requested degree of parallelism, DB2 can reduce the degree from that chosen at bind time, or it can turn off parallelism altogether. An SQL query that uses host variables can prevent DB2 from determining which partitions will qualify in a query; therefore, the degree of parallelism chosen will be decided at runtime. If the machine on which DB2 is running doesn't have hardware sort at runtime, parallelism will be disabled. If DB2 determines that an ambiguous cursor can be updated, parallelism will be disabled. If parallelism is disabled, the query doesn't fail; DB2 simply uses a sequential plan to access the data.

During BIND or PREPARE, DB2 chooses the access path best suited to the query and then does a post-optimization step to identify the sections of the access path that will benefit most from parallelism. It then identifies the part of the actual query that can be executed in parallel and finally determines the degree of parallelism to be used.

Queries Best-Suited for Parallelism

Queries with the following characteristics can take advantage of parallelism:

- Long-running, read-only queries, both static and dynamic SQL, from both local and remote sites, and that use either private or DRDA protocols

- Table space scans and index scans

- Joins

- Nested loop

- Merge scan

- Hybrid without sort on new tables

- Sorts

- Aggregate functions

Queries that will process large amounts of data against partitioned table space are excellent candidates for parallelism. There are only a few places where DB2 won't consider using parallelism:

- Queries that use materialization of views

- Queries that perform materialization because of nested table expressions

- Queries that use multi-index access to return a DOCID list

- Queries that use an XML data type

The following circumstances will cause only Sysplex parallelism not to be considered:

- Queries with list prefetch and multiple index access

- Queries performing direct row access via a RID

- Queries accessing a table with a security ID column

- Queries accessing LOB data

Parallelism should not be used if a system is already CPU-constrained because parallelism would only add to the problem in most situations.

CPU parallelism cannot be used when a cursor is defined WITH HOLD, because this cursor's use is potentially interrupted by a commit, which causes a stoppage in processing.

Short-running queries usually won't see a great benefit from parallelism (in general, a short-running query is one that is subsecond). But how often are long-running queries separated from short-running queries? Well, if you're trying to obtain the benefits of parallelism without placing unnecessary overhead where it doesn't belong, you'll need to give consideration to this type of granularity of processing. You could separate the long-running queries into a separate package and bind the package using DEGREE(ANY) in a different collection; then use the SET CURRENT PACKAGESET statement to switch between the package and a program bound with DEGREE(1) for shorter queries that are better off run sequentially. Or, you could set the macro SPRMPTH to disable parallelism for short-running queries. The default value for SPRMPTH is 120, which causes parallelism to be disabled for any query with an estimated cost of less than 120 milliseconds; parallelism is enabled for any query above this threshold. For dynamic SQL, you could consider use of the SET CURRENT DEGREE statement to switch parallelism on and off. Also, for dynamic queries, you can use the resource limit facility to disable the various types of parallelism for certain users, plans, packages, collections, or locations.

Sysplex Query Parallelism (PARALLELISM_MODE = X)

Sysplex query parallelism works in much the same multitasking way as CPU parallelism; in addition, it gives us the ability to take a complex query and run it across multiple members in a data-sharing group. Sysplex query parallelism is best used with isolation level UR (uncommitted read) to avoid excess lock propagation.

In this scenario, a query is issued by a coordinator, who sends the query to the assistant members in the group. The members then process the data and return it to the coordinator either via a work file (the coordinator will read each assistant's work files) or by cross-system coupling facility (XCF) links when a work file is not necessary.

Elements of Performance

Performance is the way a computer system behaves given a particular workload. We measure performance in terms of the system's response time, throughput, and availability. Performance is affected by the resources available and how well those resources are utilized.

You should undertake performance tuning when you want to improve the cost–benefit ratio of your system. Specific situations include the following:

- You want to process a larger, more demanding workload without increasing processing costs that may include having to acquire additional hardware.

- You want to obtain faster system response time or higher throughput without increasing processing costs.

- You want to reduce processing costs without negatively affecting service to the client(s).

Translating performance from technical terms into economic terms is difficult. Performance tuning costs money in terms of labor and machine resources, so you need to weigh the cost of tuning against the benefits that tuning may or may not deliver.

Some of these benefits, including reduced resource use and the ability to add more users to the system, are tangible, whereas other benefits, such as increased customer satisfaction, are less tangible from a monetary perspective.

Tuning Guidelines

In developing an overall approach to performance tuning, keep the following guidelines in mind.

- *Remember the law of diminishing returns.* Your greatest performance benefits usually come from your initial efforts. Further changes generally produce smaller and smaller benefits while requiring greater effort.

- *Do not tune just for the sake of tuning.* Tune to relieve identified constraints. If you tune resources that are not the primary cause of performance problems, your efforts can have little or no effect on response time until you've relieved the major constraints, and they can actually make subsequent tuning work more difficult. If there is any significant improvement potential, it lies in improving the performance of the resources that are major factors in the response time.

- *Consider the whole system.* You can never tune one parameter or system in isolation. Before you make any adjustment, consider how it will affect the system as a whole.

- *Change one parameter at a time.* Do not change more than one performance tuning parameter at a time. Even if you are sure that all the changes will be beneficial, you'll have no way of evaluating how much each change has contributed. You also cannot effectively judge the tradeoff you've made by changing more than one parameter at a time. Every time you adjust a parameter to improve one area, you almost always affect at least one other area that you may not have considered.

- *Measure and reconfigure by levels.* For the same reasons that you should change only one parameter at a time, tune one level of your system at a time. You can use the following list of levels within a system as a guide:

  » Hardware

  » Operating system

  » Application server and requester

  » Database

  » SQL statements

  » Application programs

- *Check for hardware and software problems.* You may be able to correct some performance problems by applying service to your hardware, your software, or both. Don't spend excessive time monitoring and tuning your system when simply applying service may be the solution to the problem.

- *Understand the problem before upgrading hardware.* Even if it seems that an additional storage or processor resource could immediately improve performance, take the time to understand where the bottlenecks are. You may spend money on added disk storage only to find that you don't have the processor resource to exploit it.

- *Put fallback procedures in place before you start tuning.* Because you're making changes to an existing system, you must be prepared to back out those changes if they don't have the desired effect or if they have a negative effect on the system.

It's important to take into consideration the cost of detailed performance analysis (i.e., running traces), as well as the time needed to perform the analysis, because the process of detailed performance analysis can be costly.

Performance Improvement Process

Monitoring and tuning a database and its applications should be performed using the following basic process:

1. Establish performance indicators.

2. Define performance objectives.

3. Develop a performance monitoring plan.

4. Implement the plan.

5. Analyze the measurements. Determine whether the objectives have been met. If so, consider reducing the number of measurements to keep the amount of resources consumed for monitoring to a minimum.

6. Determine the major constraints in the system.

7. Decide where you can afford to make tradeoffs and which resources can bear an additional load. Most tuning activities involve tradeoffs among system resources and various elements of performance.

8. Adjust the configuration of the system. If you think that it is feasible to change more than one tuning option, implement one at a time.

9. Based on the results, start another iteration of the monitoring cycle.

You may want to go through this process for periodic monitoring or when significant changes occur to the system, to the workload taken on by the system, or to both.

How Much Can You Tune a System?

There are limits to how much you can improve the efficiency of a system. Think about how much time and money you should spend on improving system performance and how much the spending of additional time and money will help the users of the system.

Your system may perform adequately without any tuning at all, but it probably won't perform to its potential. Each database is unique. As soon as you develop your own database and applications for it, investigate the tuning parameters available and learn how you can customize their settings to reflect your situation.

In some circumstances, there will be only a small benefit from tuning a system. In most circumstances, however, the benefit may be significant.

If your system encounters performance bottlenecks, tuning will likely be effective. If you're close to the performance limits and you increase the number of users on the system by about 10 percent, the response time may rise by much more than 10 percent. In this situation, you will need to determine how to counterbalance the degradation in performance by tuning your system. However, there is a point beyond which tuning cannot help. At that point, you should consider revising your goals and expectations within that environment. Or, you should change your system environment by considering more disk storage, faster or additional processors, more memory, or faster networking solutions.

A Less Formal Approach

If you don't have enough time to set performance objectives and to monitor and tune in a comprehensive manner, you can address performance by listening to your users. Find out whether they are having performance-related problems. You can usually locate the problem, or determine where to start looking for the problem, by asking a few simple questions. For example, you can ask your users:

- What do you mean by slow response? Is it 10 *percent* slower or 10 *times* slower than you expect it to be?

- When did you notice the problem? Is it recent, or has it always been there?

- Do you know of other users who are complaining of the same problem? Are those complaining one or two individuals or a whole group?

- Are the problems you are experiencing related to a specific transaction or application program?

- Do your problems appear during regular periods, such as at lunch hour, or are they continuous?

Database Monitoring

Database monitoring should be an ongoing, proactive process. You have a variety of ways to monitor DB2, including specialized monitoring software and traces.

Online and Batch Performance Monitors

Many performance analysis tools are available for both the DB2 subsystem and applications. Their primary objective is to report DB2 instrumentation data in a form that is easy to understand and analyze. The IBM product offering is the IBM Tivoli OMEGAMON XE for DB2 Performance Expert for z/OS. This product includes the OMEGAMON DB2 Performance Monitor (DB2 PM) and presents its instrumentation data in the following ways.

The Batch reports present the data you select in comprehensive reports or graphs that contain system-wide and application-related information for both single DB2 subsystems and DB2 members of a data-sharing group. You can combine instrumentation data from several different DB2 locations into one report. You can use these reports to examine performance problems and trends over a period of time:

- The Online Monitor gives a current "snapshot" view of a running DB2 subsystem, including applications that are running. Its history function displays information about subsystem and application activity in the recent past.

- The Statistics reports provide an excellent source of information, such as buffer pools, EDM pools, RID processing, and logging, all at a subsystem level.

- The Accounting reports provide information about applications for specific time periods. These reports are the most popular, most useful reports for ongoing analysis, trend analysis, and predictive monitoring.

More specific reports are also available, such as the Lock Detail Analysis report for monitoring locking problems. These more detailed reports require additional traces to be turned on, and you should use them only for problem analysis rather than run them on a continual basis. Both the Accounting and the Statistics reports have long and short versions; which version you use depends on the amount of detail needed for analysis.

The online portion of the DB2 OMEGAMON PM product has a very user-friendly interface. From here, you can monitor all your DB2 subsystems and your data-sharing environment. Figure 17.1 gives you a look at the main screen, and Figure 17.2 shows detail for a thread.

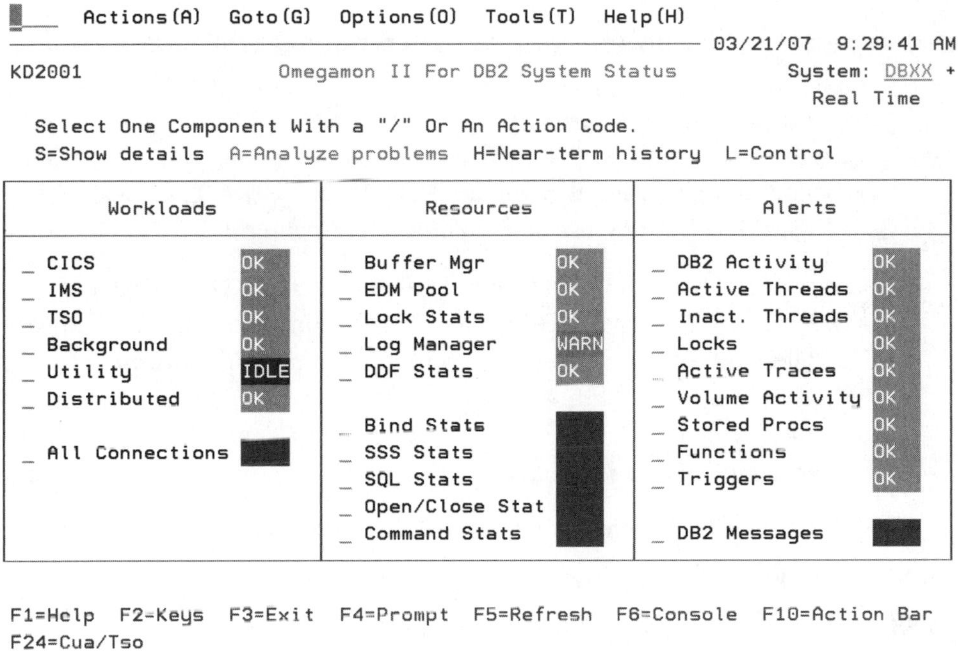

```
■___   Actions(A)  Goto(G)  Options(O)  Tools(T)  Help(H)
                                           ── 03/21/07  9:29:41 AM
   KD2001            Omegamon II For DB2 System Status    System: DBXX +
                                                        Real Time

      Select One Component With a "/" Or An Action Code.
      S=Show details  A=Analyze problems  H=Near-term history  L=Control

   ┌──────────────────┬───────────────────────┬─────────────────────────┐
   │    Workloads      │      Resources        │        Alerts           │
   │                   │                       │                         │
   │  _ CICS      OK   │  _ Buffer Mgr   OK    │  _ DB2 Activity    OK   │
   │  _ IMS       OK   │  _ EDM Pool     OK    │  _ Active Threads  OK   │
   │  _ TSO       OK   │  _ Lock Stats   OK    │  _ Inact. Threads  OK   │
   │  _ Background OK  │  _ Log Manager  WARN  │  _ Locks           OK   │
   │  _ Utility   IDLE │  _ DDF Stats    OK    │  _ Active Traces   OK   │
   │  _ Distributed OK │                       │  _ Volume Activity OK   │
   │                   │  _ Bind Stats         │  _ Stored Procs    OK   │
   │  _ All Connections│  _ SSS Stats          │  _ Functions       OK   │
   │                   │  _ SQL Stats          │  _ Triggers        OK   │
   │                   │  _ Open/Close Stat    │                         │
   │                   │  _ Command Stats      │  _ DB2 Messages         │
   └──────────────────┴───────────────────────┴─────────────────────────┘

   F1=Help  F2-Keys  F3=Exit  F4=Prompt  F5=Refresh  F6=Console  F10=Action Bar
   F24=Cua/Tso
```

Figure 17.1: OMEGAMON main screen

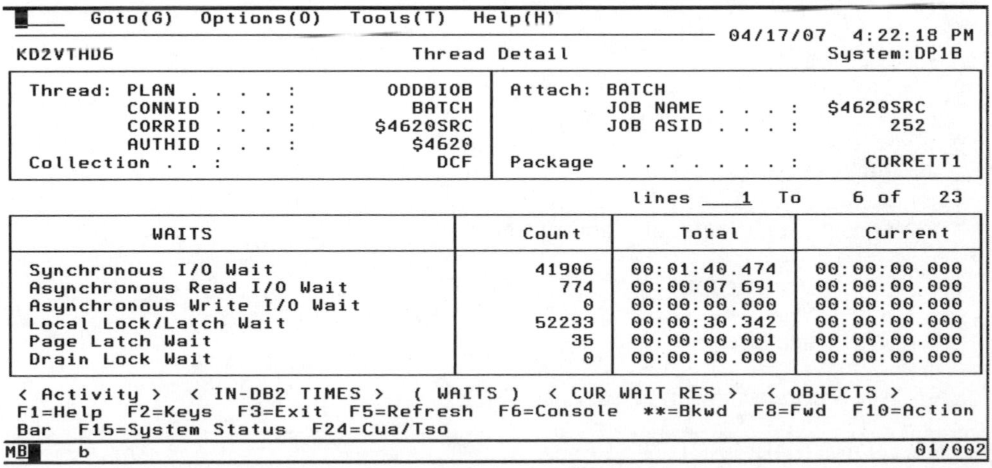

```
■___   Goto(G)  Options(O)  Tools(T)  Help(H)
                                           ── 04/17/07  4:22:18 PM
   KD2VTHD6                  Thread Detail            System:DP1B
   ┌─────────────────────────────────────┬───────────────────────────────────┐
   │ Thread: PLAN . . . . :  ODDBIOB      │ Attach: BATCH                     │
   │         CONNID . . . :    BATCH      │         JOB NAME . . . :  $4620SRC│
   │         CORRID . . . :  $4620SRC     │         JOB ASID . . . :      252 │
   │         AUTHID . . . :    $4620      │                                   │
   │ Collection . . . :         DCF       │ Package . . . . . . . :  CDRRETT1 │
   └─────────────────────────────────────┴───────────────────────────────────┘
                                          lines ___1 To    6 of    23
   ┌────────────────────────────────┬───────┬─────────────┬─────────────┐
   │             WAITS              │ Count │    Total    │   Current   │
   ├────────────────────────────────┼───────┼─────────────┼─────────────┤
   │ Synchronous I/O Wait           │ 41906 │ 00:01:40.474│ 00:00:00.000│
   │ Asynchronous Read I/O Wait     │   774 │ 00:00:07.691│ 00:00:00.000│
   │ Asynchronous Write I/O Wait    │     0 │ 00:00:00.000│ 00:00:00.000│
   │ Local Lock/Latch Wait          │ 52233 │ 00:00:30.342│ 00:00:00.000│
   │ Page Latch Wait                │    35 │ 00:00:00.001│ 00:00:00.000│
   │ Drain Lock Wait                │     0 │ 00:00:00.000│ 00:00:00.000│
   └────────────────────────────────┴───────┴─────────────┴─────────────┘
   < Activity >  < IN-DB2 TIMES >  ( WAITS )  < CUR WAIT RES >  < OBJECTS >
   F1=Help  F2=Keys  F3=Exit  F5=Refresh  F6=Console  **=Bkwd  F8=Fwd  F10=Action
   Bar  F15=System Status  F24=Cua/Tso
   MB■   b                                                        01/002
```

Figure 17.2: OMEGAMON thread detail screen

Resource Limit Facility

DB2's resource limit facility (governor) lets you perform the following activities:

- Set warning and error thresholds by which the governor can inform users (via your application programs) that a certain processing limit might be exceeded for aparticular dynamic SELECT, INSERT, UPDATE, or DELETE statement. This activity is called *predictive governing*.

- Stop a currently executing dynamic SQL statement (SELECT, INSERT, UPDATE, or DELETE) that exceeds the processor limit you've specified for that statement. This activity is sometimes called *reactive governing* to differentiate its function from that of predictive governing. The resource limit facility does not control static SQL statements, whether or not they are executed locally or remotely.

- Restrict bind and rebind activities to avoid performance impacts on production data.

- Restrict particular parallelism modes for dynamic queries.

Tracing Problems in DB2

DB2 provides a variety of traces that you can use for problem determination:

- DB2 trace
- IMS attachment facility trace
- CICS trace
- Three TSO attachment facility traces
- CAF trace stream
- RRS trace stream
- MVS component trace used for IRLM
- ODBC/JDBC/SQLJ/CLI trace

In this section, we look at DB2 traces. For information about other trace capabilities, consult the appropriate product documentation.

DB2 Traces

DB2 Trace lets you trace and record subsystem data and events. There are five different types of trace, and DB2 Trace can record six types of data: statistics, accounting, audit, performance, monitor, and global. The tables provided later in this chapter indicate which instrumentation facility IDs (IFCIDs) are activated for the different types of trace, the classes within those trace types, and the information each IFCID returns. The trace records are written using generalized trace facility (GTF) or system measurement facility (SMF) records or OPx buffers. We now take a look at the types of data DB2 collects for each trace class.

Statistics

The data collected in the statistics trace lets you conduct DB2 capacity planning and tune the entire set of DB2 programs. The statistics trace reports information about how much of the DB2 system services and database services are used. This system-wide trace should not be used for charge-back accounting. Use the information the statistics trace provides to plan DB2 capacity or to tune the entire set of active DB2 programs.

Statistics trace classes 1, 3, 4, 5, and 6 are the default classes for the statistics trace if you specified YES for the SMF STATISTICS field in panel DSNTIPN. If you start the statistics trace using the START TRACE command, class 1 is the default class.

- Class 1 provides information about system services and database statistics. It also includes the system parameters that were in effect when the trace was started and information about DB2 virtual storage usage.

- Class 3 provides information about deadlocks and timeouts.

- Class 4 provides information about exceptional conditions.

- Class 5 provides information about data sharing.

- Class 6 provides storage information for the DBM1 address space.

If you specified YES for SMF STATISTICS on the tracing panel (DSNTIPN), the statistics trace starts automatically when you start DB2, sending classes 1, 3, 4, 5, and 6 statistics data to SMF. SMF records statistics data in SMF type 100 and 102 records. IFCIDs 0001, 0002, 0202, and 0230 are of SMF type 100. All other IFCIDs in statistics trace classes are of SMF type 102.

From panel DSNTIPN, you can also control the statistics collection interval (using the STATISTICS TIME field). The statistics trace is written on an interval basis, and you can control the exact time when statistics traces are taken.

Accounting

The accounting trace provides data you can use to assign DB2 costs to individual authorization IDs and to tune individual programs. This trace provides information related to application programs, including details such as

- start and stop times

- number of commits and aborts

- number of times certain SQL statements are issued

- number of buffer pool requests

- counts of certain locking events

- processor resources consumed

- thread wait times for various events

- RID pool processing

- distributed processing

- resource limit facility statistics

Accounting times are usually the prime indicator of a performance problem, and most often they should be the starting point for analysis. DB2 times are classified as follows:

- **Class 1.** This shows the time the application spent since connecting to DB2, including time spent outside DB2.

- **Class 2.** This shows the elapsed time spent in DB2. It is divided into CPU time and waiting time.

- **Class 3.** This elapsed time is divided into various waits, such as the duration of suspensions due to waits for locks and latches or waits for I/O.

DB2 Trace starts collecting this data at successful thread allocations to DB2 and writes a completed record when the thread terminates or when the authorization ID changes. Having the accounting trace active is critical for proper performance monitoring, analysis, and tuning. When an application connects to DB2, it is executing across address spaces, which are shared by perhaps thousands of users across many address spaces. The accounting trace provides information about the time spent within DB2, as well as the overall application time. Class 2 time is a component of class 1 time, and class 3 time a component of class 2 time. For example, DB2 remote connections that cannot become inactive at commit will show high class 1 times but low class 1 CPU time and low class 2 time. If there is high class 1 time as well as high class 2 and 3 times, this could indicate a problem waiting for a resource, such as a lock or I/O. If the trace shows a high class 2 time that cannot be accounted for in CPU or class 3 time consumed, this may be an indication that the machine is CPU-constrained. You can expose this information via online monitors or via a DB2 Accounting Report.

Several DB2 components accumulate accounting data for class 1 (the default) during normal execution. This data is then collected at the end of the accounting period; it does not involve as much overhead as individual event tracing.

On the other hand, when you start class 2, 3, 7, or 8, many additional trace points are activated. DB2 Trace traces every occurrence of these events internally, but the traces aren't written to any external destination. Rather, the accounting facility uses these traces to compute the additional total statistics that appear in the accounting record when you activate class 2 or class 3. Accounting class 1 must be active to externalize the information.

For you to turn on accounting for packages and DBRMs, accounting trace classes 1 and 7 must be active. Although you can turn on class 7 while a plan is being executed, accounting trace information is only gathered for packages or DBRMs executed after class 7 is activated. Activate accounting trace class 8 with class 1 to collect information about the amount of time an agent was suspended in DB2 for each executed package. If you've activated accounting trace classes 2 and 3, minimal additional performance cost is incurred for activating accounting trace classes 7 and 8.

If you want information from either or both accounting class 2 and class 3, be sure to activate class 2 and/or 3 before your application starts. If you activate these classes while the application is running, the times gathered by DB2 trace are only from the time the class was activated.

Accounting trace class 5 provides information about the amount of elapsed time and task control block (TCB) time an agent spent in DB2 processing instrumentation facility interface (IFI) requests. If an agent did not issue any IFI requests, these fields are not included in the accounting record.

If you specified YES for SMF ACCOUNTING on the tracing panel, the accounting trace starts automatically when you start DB2 and sends IFCIDs that are of SMF type 101 to SMF.

Performance

The performance trace provides information about a variety of DB2 events, including events related to distributed data processing. You can use this information to further identify a suspected problem or to tune DB2 programs and resources for individual users or for DB2 as a whole.

To trace performance data, you must use the –START TRACE(PERFM) command; performance traces cannot be automatically started. Performance traces are expensive to run and consume a lot of CPU. They also collect a large volume of information. Performance traces are usually run via an online monitor tool, or you can send the output to SMF and then analyze it using a monitor reporting tool or send it to IBM for analysis.

Because performance traces can consume a lot of resources and generate a great deal of data, you can set several options when starting the trace to balance the information desired with the resources consumed. You can limit the trace data collected by plan, package, trace class, and even IFCID.

The following example limits the trace data collected to a specific package and class; it is looking for a particular SQL statement within the package that is consuming a lot of CPU. This trace balances the need for the information with the conservation of the resources required to run the trace.

```
-STA TRA(PERFM) CLASS(3) TDATA(CPU) PKGPROG(PROG1)
```

The IFCID table presented later lists some of the events that a performance trace records, depending on the trace classes and/or IFCIDs set by the START TRACE command. This record includes events such as

- beginning an end of a commit or rollback
- start of a select, insert, update, or delete
- start and end of a sort
- start and end to a user routine, such as a stored procedure
- start and end of a trigger activation

Audit

The audit trace provides data that can help monitor DB2 security and access to data to ensure that data access is allowed only for authorized purposes. On the CREATE TABLE or ALTER TABLE statement, you can specify whether a table is to be audited and in what manner; you can also audit security information, such as any access denials, grants, or revokes for the table. The default causes no auditing to take place. If you specified YES for AUDIT TRACE on the tracing panel, audit trace class 1 starts automatically when you start DB2. By default, DB2 sends audit data to SMF.

Monitor

The monitor trace records data for online monitoring with user-written programs. This trace type has several predefined classes; the following are used explicitly for monitoring.

- Class 1 (the default) allows any application program to issue an IFI READS request to the IFI facility. If monitor class 1 is inactive, a READS request is denied. Activating class 1 has a minimal impact on performance.

- Class 2 collects processor and elapsed time information. The information can be obtained by issuing a READS request for IFCID 0147 or 0148. In addition, monitor trace class 2 information is available in the accounting record, IFCID 0003. Monitor class 2 is equivalent to accounting class 2 and results in equivalent overhead. Monitor class 2 times appear in IFCIDs 0147, 0148, and 0003 if either monitor trace class 2 or accounting class 2 is active.

- Class 3 activates DB2 wait timing and saves information about the resource causing the wait. You can obtain the information by issuing a READS request for IFCID 0147 or 0148. In addition, monitor trace class 3 information is available in the accounting record, IFCID 0003. As with monitor class 2, monitor class 3 overhead is equivalent to accounting class 3 overhead. When monitor trace class 3 is active, DB2 can calculate the duration of a class 3 event, such as when an agent is suspended due to an unavailable lock. Monitor class 3 times appear in IFCIDs 0147, 0148, and 0003 if either monitor class 3 or accounting class 3 is active.

- Class 5 traces the amount of time spent processing IFI requests.

- Class 7 traces the amount of time an agent spent in DB2 to process each package. If monitor trace class 2 is active, activating class 7 has minimal performance impact.

- Class 8 traces the amount of time an agent was suspended in DB2 for each executed package. If monitor trace class 3 is active, activating class 8 has minimal impact.

Invoking Traces

Traces can be started automatically via the DB2 install panel options, or you can stop and start them dynamically by using the TRACE commands:

- START TRACE invokes one or more types of trace.

- DISPLAY TRACE displays the trace options that are in effect.

- STOP TRACE stops any trace that was started by either the START TRACE command or the parameters specified when installing or migrating.

- MODIFY TRACE changes the trace events (IFCIDs) being traced for a specified active trace. Several parameters let you further qualify the scope of a trace. Specific events within a trace type as well as events within specific DB2 plans, authorization IDs, resource manager IDs, and locations, can be traced. You can also control the destination to which trace data is sent.

Trace Classes

It's important to have the appropriate classes always gathering information about your DB2 subsystem and its activity. It is a general recommendation that you have SMF accounting class 1, 2, and 3 and SMF statistics class 1, 3, and 4 (1 and 3 at a minimum) selected during normal execution. Any other trace classes should not be run constantly because they cause excessive overhead if run for long periods of time.

When you execute other traces, is it wise to time the trace to only the IFCIDs necessary for the appropriate performance analysis or problem diagnosis. In addition, you should run these traces for only short periods of time. Here is an example of limiting a trace:

```
-START TRACE(P) CLASS(30) IFCID(0221) PLANNAME(CERTPLA)
```

This example limits a performance trace to class 8 with IFCID 221, which is used to view the actual degree of parallelism at runtime.

IFCIDs

Tables 17.18 through 17. 22 show the various IFCIDs that are started for each different type of class within a trace.

Table 17.18: Accounting trace		
Class	IFCID	Description
1	3	All accounting
	106	System parameters in effect
	239	Overflow for package accounting
2	200	UDF entry/exit signal
	232	DB2 thread entry/exit signal
3	6	Beginning of a read I/O operation
	7	CC after read I/O operation
	8	Beginning of synchronous write I/O
	9	CC of sync or async write I/O
	32	Beginning of wait for log manager
	33	End of wait for log manager
	44	Lock suspend or identify call IRLM
	45	Lock resume
	51	Shared latch resume; serviceability
	52	Shared latch wait, serviceability
	56	Exclusive latch wait; serviceability
	57	Exclusive latch resume. serviceability
	117	Begin thread wait time for log I/O
	118	End thread wait time for log I/O
	127	Agent ready to suspend page wait
	128	Page requester resumed by I/O initialization
	170	Suspend for sync EXEC.N unit switch
	171	Resume agent waiting DB2 service task
	174	Begin archive log mode (QUIESCE)
	175	End archive log mode (QUIESCE)
	213	Beginning of wait for claim request
	214	End of wait for claim request
	215	Beginning of wait for drain request
	216	End of wait for drain request
	226	Beginning of suspend for page latch
	227	End of suspend for page latch
	242	Begin wait for scheduled stored procedure
	313	Messages for long-running URs
4	151	User-defined accounting trace

Class	IFCID	Description
		Table 17.18: Accounting trace (continued)
Class	**IFCID**	**Description**
5	187	Entry to and exit from IFI
7	232	DB2 thread entry/exit signal
	232	For package- or DBRM-level accounting
	240	Event signal for package accounting
8	6	Beginning of a read I/O operation
	7	CC after read I/O operation
	8	Beginning of synchronous write I/O
	9	CC of sync or async write I/O
	32	Beginning of wait for log manager
	33	End of wait for log manager
	44	Lock suspend or identify call IRLM
	45	Lock resume
	51	Shared latch resume; serviceability
	52	Shared latch wait; serviceability
	56	Exclusive latch wait; serviceablilty
	57	Exclusive latch resume; serviceability
	117	Begin thread wait time for log I/O
	118	End thread wait time for log I/O
	127	Agent ready to suspend page wait
	128	Page requestor resumed by I/O initialization
	170	Suspend for sync EXEC.N unit switch
	171	Resume agent waiting DB2 service task
	174	Begin archive log mode (QUIESCE)
	175	End archive log mode (QUIESCE)
	213	Beginning of wait for claim request
	214	End of wait for claim request
	215	Beginning of wait for drain request
	216	End of wait for drain request
	226	Beginning of suspend for page latch
	227	End of suspend for page latch
	241	Begin/end suspension of package or DBRM
	242	Begin wait for scheduled stored procedure
	243	End wait for scheduled stored procedure
	329	Asynchronous GBP requests
10	239	Package detail

Table 17.19: Audit trace

Class	IFCID	Description
1	140	Authorization failures
2	141	Explicit grants and revokes
3	142	Creates, alters, drops audit
4	143	First attempted write audited object
5	144	First attempted read audited object
6	145	Audit log record of some SQL statements
7	55	Issuance of set current SQLID
	83	End identify request
	87	Ending of sign-on request
	169	Distributed authorization ID translation
	312	DCE Security
	319	Audit trail for security processing
8	23	Utility start information
	24	Utility object or phase change
	25	Utility end information
	219	Listdef data set information
	220	Utility output data set information
9	146	User-defined audit trace

Table 17.20: Monitor trace

Class	IFCID	Description
1	1	System services
	2	Database services
	106	System parameters in effect
	124	Current SQL statement
	129	Virtual storage access method (VSAM) (CI) -DB2 recover log
	147	Summary thread status record
	148	Detailed thread status record
	149	Lock information for a resource
	150	Lock information for an agent IFCID
	202	System parameters
	230	Data-sharing global statistics
	254	Group buffer pool use

Table 17.20: Monitor trace (continued)		
Class	**IFCID**	**Description**
	306	Log record retrieval
	316	Prepared statement cache statistics
	317	Prepared statement cache statement text
2	232	DB2 thread entry exit signal
3	6	Beginning of a read I/O operation
	7	CC after read I/O operation
	8	Beginning of synchronous write I/O
	9	CC of sync or async write I/O
	32	Beginning of wait for log manager
	33	End of wait for log manager
	44	Lock suspend or identify call IRLM
	45	Lock resume
	51	Shared latch resume; serviceability
	52	Shared latch wait; serviceability
	56	Exclusive latch wait; serviceability
	57	Exclusive latch resume; serviceability
	117	Begin thread wait time for log I/O
	118	End thread wait time for log I/O
	127	Agent ready to suspend page wait
	128	Page requester resumed by I/O initialization
	170	Suspend for sync EXEC unit switch
	171	Resume agent waiting DB2 service task
	174	Begin archive log mode (QUIESCE)
	175	End archive log mode (QUIESCE)
	213	Beginning of wait for claim request
	214	End of wait for claim request
	215	Beginning of wait for drain request
	216	End of wait for drain request
	226	Beginning of suspend for page latch
	227	End of suspend for page latch
	242	Begin wait for scheduled stored procedure
	243	End wait for scheduled stored procedure
	329	Asynchronous GBP requests
4	155	User-defined monitor trace
5	187	Entry or exit to IFI

Class	IFCID	Description
\multicolumn{3}{l}{*Table 17.20: Monitor trace (continued)*}		
6	185	Data capture information
7	232	DB2 thread entry/exit signal
	232	For package- or DBRM-level accounting
	240	Event signal for package accounting
8	6	Beginning of a read I/O operation
	7	CC after read I/O operation
	8	Beginning of synchronous write I/O
	9	CC of sync or async write I/O
	32	Begin of wait for log manager
	33	End of wait for log manager
	44	Lock suspend or identify call IRLM
	45	Lock resume
	51	Shared latch resume; serviceability
	52	Shared latch wait; serviceability
	56	Exclusive latch wait; serviceability
	57	Exclusive latch resume; serviceability
	117	Begin thread wait time for log I/O
	118	End thread wait time for log I/O
	127	Agent ready to suspend page wait
	128	Page requester resumed by I/O initialization
	170	Suspend for sync EXEC unit switch
	171	Resume agent waiting DB2 service task
	174	Begin archive log mode (QUIESCE)
	175	End archive log mode (QUIESCE)
	213	Beginning of wait for claim request
	214	End of wait for claim request
	215	Beginning of wait for drain request
	216	End of wait for drain request
	226	Beginning of suspend for page latch
	227	End of suspend for page latch
	241	Begin/end suspension of pack/DBRM
	242	Begin wait for scheduled stored procedure
	243	End wait for scheduled stored procedure

Table 17.21: Performance trace		
Class	IFCID	Description
1	1	System services
	2	Database services
	31	EDM pool full condition
	42	Checkpoint started
	43	Checkpoint ended
	76	Beginning of an end memory request
	77	End of an end memory request
	78	Beginning of an end task request
	79	End of an end task request
	102	Detection of short on storage
	103	Setting off of short on storage
	105	Internal DBID OBID to DB/TS
	106	System parameters in effect
	107	Dataset open/close information
	153	User-defined except-condition trace
2	3	All accounting
	68	Beginning of a rollback request
	69	End of a rollback request
	70	Begin commit phase 2 request
	71	End commit phase 2 request
	72	Beginning of create thread request
	73	End of a create thread request
	74	Beginning of terminate thread request
	75	End of a terminate thread request
	80	Beginning of an establish exit request
	81	End of an establish exit request
	82	Begin identify request
	83	End identify request
	84	Begin phase 1 commit request
	85	End phase 1 commit request
	86	Beginning of sign-on request
	87	End of sign-on request
	88	Beginning of sync request
	89	Ending of sync request

Class	IFCID	Description
		Table 17.21: Performance trace (contiuned)
	106	System parameters in effect
	174	Begin archive log mode (QUIESCE)
	175	End archive log mode (QUIESCE)
3	22	Mini-plans generated
	53	Commit, rollback, or error
	55	Issuance of set current SQLID
	58	End of SQL statement execution
	59	Start of FETCHSQL statement execution
	60	Start of SELECTSQL statement execution
	61	Start of INSERT, UPDATE, OR DELETE SQL
	62	Start of DDL statement execution
	63	SQL statement to be parsed
	64	Start PREPARE SQL statement exec
	65	Start open cursor static or dynamic SQL
	66	Start close cursor static or dynamic SQL
	92	Start access method services
	95	Sort started
	96	Sort ended
	97	Access method services command completion
	106	System parameters in effect
	112	Attributes plan after thread allocation
	177	Successful package allocation
	233	Start/end call to user routine
	237	Set current degree information
	272	Associate locators information
	273	Allocate cursor information
	324	Function resolution information
	325	Start/end trigger activation
4	6	Beginning of a read I/O operation
	7	Completion code after read I/O
	8	Beginning of synchronous write I/O
	9	CC of sync or async write I/O
	10	Beginning of async write I/O
	29	Start EDM I/O request; load DBD or CT
	30	End of EDM I/O request

Table 17.21: Performance trace (contiuned)		
Class	**IFCID**	**Description**
	105	Internal DBID OBID to DB/TS
	106	System parameters in effect
	107	Dataset open/close information
	127	Agent ready to suspend page wait
	128	Page requester resumed by I/O initialization
	226	Begin of suspend for page latch
	227	End of suspend for page latch
5	32	Begin of wait for log manager
	33	End of wait for log manager
	34	Log manager wait for read I/O begin
	35	Log manager wait for read I/O end
	36	Log manager wait for non-I/O begin
	37	Log manager wait for non-I/O end
	38	Log manager wait act log write begin
	39	Log mgr wait act log write I/O end
	40	Log manager archive write I/O begin
	41	Log manager archive write I/O end
	104	Log data set mapping
	106	System parameters in effect
	114	Start archive read I/O wait
	115	End read archive I/O wait on DASD
	116	End read archive I/O wait on tape
	117	Begin archive read
	118	End archive read
	119	BSDS write I/O beginning
	120	BSDS write I/O end
	228	Start archive allocation wait
	229	End archive allocation wait
6	20	Locking summary
	44	Lock suspend or an ID; call to IRLM
	45	Lock resume
	105	Internal DBID OBID to DB/TS
	106	System parameters in effect
	107	Data set open/close information
	172	Units of work involved in deadlock
	196	Lock timeout details

Class	IFCID	Description
		Table 17.21: Performance trace (contiuned)
	213	Beginning of wait for drain lock
	214	End of wait for drain lock
	218	Summary of lock avoidance technique
7	21	Detail lock request on return from IRLM
	105	Internal DBID OBID to DB/TS
	106	System parameters in effect
	107	Dataset open/close information
	199	Buffer pool dataset statistics
	223	Detail of lock avoidance technique
8	13	Input to hash scan
	14	End of hash scan
	15	Input matching or non-matching index scan
	16	Input to the first insert
	17	Input to sequential scan
	18	End index scan, insert, or sequential scan
	105	Internal DBID OBID to DB/TS
	106	System parameters in effect
	107	Data set open/close information
	125	Rid list processing usage
	221	Parallel degree for parallel group
	222	Parallel group elapsed time
	231	Parallel group completion
	305	Table check constraints
	311	Temporary tables
9	26	Work file obtained for sort
	27	Number of ordered records sort run
	28	Detailed sort information
	95	Sort started
	96	Sort ended
	106	System parameters in effect
10	23	Utility start information
	24	Utility object or phase change
	25	Utility end information
	90	Command text of entered DB2 command
	91	Completion status of a DB2 command
	105	Internal DBID OBID to DB/TS

Class	IFCID	Description
	106	System parameters in effect
	107	Data set open/close information
	108	Beginning of bind/rebind
	109	End of bind/rebind
	110	Beginning of free plan
	111	End of free plan
	201	Status before/after alter buffer pool
	219	Listdef data set information
	220	Utility output data set information
	256	Attributes before/after alter buffer pool
11	46	Agent begin execution unit switch
	47	New SRB execution unit started
	48	New SRB execution unit completed
	49	Begin new TCB
	50	End new TCB
	51	Shared latch resume
	52	Shared latch wait
	56	Exclusive latch wait
	57	Exclusive latch resume
	93	Suspend was called
	94	Event resumed
	106	System parameters in effect
	113	Attributes plan after agent allocation
12	98	Begin getmain/freemain (nonpool)
	99	End getmain/freemain (nonpool)
	100	Begin getmain/freemain (pool)
	101	End getmain/freemain (pool)
	106	System parameters in effect
13	11	Results of a validation exit call
	12	Results edit exit call encode record
	19	Results edit exit call decode a row
	105	Internal DBID OBID to DB/TS
	106	System parameters in effect
	107	Data set open/close information
14	67	Start of accounting collection
	106	System parameters in effect

Table 17.21: Performance trace (contiuned)

Class	IFCID	Description
		Table 17.21: Performance trace (contiuned)
	121	Entry allocating DB2 connection
	122	Exit allocating DB2 connection
15	154	User-defined routine condition performed
16	157	DRDS interface with RDS RDI call types
	158	DRDS interface with conversation manager
	159	DRDS requesting location data
	160	Requesting agent data
	161	Serving agent data
	162	Distributed transaction manager request agent data
	163	Distributed transaction manager response agent data
	167	Conversation allocation request queued
	183	DRDS RDS/SCC interface data
17	211	Information about claims
	212	Information about drains
	213	Beginning of wait for drain lock
	214	End of wait for drain lock
	215	Beginning of wait of claim count to 0
	216	End of claim count to go to 0
20	249	EDM pool DBD invalidation
	250	Group buffer pool continued/discontinued
	251	P-lock operations
	256	Alter buffer pool command
	257	Details of IRLM notify request
	261	Group buffer pool checkpoint
	262	Group buffer pool cast-out threshold processing
	267	Begin CF structure rebuild/expand/contract
	268	End CF structure rebuild/expand/contract
	329	Asynchronous GBP request
21	255	Buffer refresh due to XI
	259	P-lock request/negotiation request
	263	Page set and partition cast-out data
	314	Authorization exit parameters
	327	Language environment runtime information

Table 17.22: Statistics trace		
Class	**IFCID**	**Description**
1	1	System services
	2	Database services
	105	Internal DBID OBID to DB/TS
	106	System parameters in effect
	202	Buffer pool attributes
2	152	User-defined statistics trace
3	172	Units of work involved in deadlock
	196	Lock timeout details
	250	Connect/disconnect from GBP
	258	Data set extend information
	330	Active log shortage
	335	Stalled system event notification
4	191	Data capture for DDIS errors
	192	DDM-level 6a header errors
	193	UOW disposition/SQLCODE mismatch
	194	Invalid SNA FMH5 received
	195	First failure data capture for DRDS
	203	Heuristic decision occurred
	204	Partner cold start detected
	205	Incorrect log name/sync parameters
	206	SNA compare states protocol error
	207	Heuristic damage occurred
	208	SNA sync point protocol error
	209	Sync point communication failure
	210	Log name changed on warm start
	235	Conditional restart data loss
	236	Exchange log names protocol error
	238	DB2 restart error
	267	Start of CF structure rebuild
	268	End of CF structure rebuild
5	230	Data sharing global statistics
7	326	Workload manager delay monitor support

Continuous Performance Monitoring

For monitoring the basic load of the system, try continually running classes 1, 3, 4, and 6 of the DB2 statistics trace and classes 1 and 3 of the DB2 accounting trace. In the data you collect, look for statistics or counts that differ from past records. Pay special attention to peak periods of activity, both of any new application and of the system as a whole. Running accounting class 2 as well as class 1 lets you separate DB2 times from application times.

Running with CICS without the open transaction environment (OTE) entails less need to run with accounting class 2. Application and non-DB2 processing take place under the CICS main task control block. Because SQL activity takes place under the SQL TCB, the class 1 and class 2 times are generally close. The CICS attachment work is spread across class 1, class 2, and time spent processing outside of DB2. Class 1 time thus reports on the SQL TCB time and some of the CICS attachment. If you're concerned about class 2 overhead and you use CICS, you can generally run without turning on accounting class 2.

Statistics and accounting information can be very helpful for application and database designers. Consider putting this information into a performance warehouse so that all the personnel who need the information can analyze the data more easily. Information collected on a continuous basis can be stored in this warehouse and then queried to determine potential performance problems. For example, a data warehouse environment in which queries are running 24X7 may experience a general degradation in performance over time. If we have a warehouse of performance information gathered from the statistics and accounting traces, we can query this performance warehouse to track and report on the consumption of elapsed time and CPU by plans and packages over time. This analysis could help determine which applications and database objects are experiencing the degradation.

Periodic Performance Monitoring

A typical periodic monitoring interval of about 10 minutes provides information about the workload achieved, resources used, and significant changes to the system. In effect, you take "snapshots" at peak loads and under normal conditions. Monitor peak periods when constraints and response-time problems are more pronounced.

The current peak is also a good indicator of the future average. You might have to monitor more frequently at first to confirm that expected peaks correspond with actual ones. Do not base conclusions on one or two monitoring periods but on data from several days, representing different periods.

Both continuous and periodic monitoring serve to check system throughput, utilized resources (processor, I/Os, and storage), changes to the system, and significant exceptions that might affect system performance. You might notice that subsystem response is becoming increasingly sluggish or that more applications fail from lack of resources (such as from locking contention or concurrency limits). You also might notice an increase in the processor time DB2 is using, even though subsystem responses seem normal. In any case, if the subsystem continues to perform acceptably and you aren't having any problems, DB2 might not need additional tuning.

For periodic monitoring, gather information from z/OS, the transaction manager (IMS, CICS, or WebSphere), the network, the distributed application platforms (e.g., Windows, UNIX, or Linux), DB2 Connect, and DB2 itself. To compare the different results from each source, monitor each for the same period of time. Because the monitoring tools require resources, you need to consider the overhead for using these tools.

Detailed Performance Monitoring

Add detailed monitoring to periodic monitoring when you discover or suspect a problem. Use it also to investigate areas not covered periodically. To keep the cost of the detailed monitoring low, limit the information to the specific application and data as much as possible.

If you have a performance problem, first verify that faulty design of an application or database isn't the cause. If you suspect a problem in application design, consult the "Designing a DB2 Database Application" topic in the *DB2 Application Programming and SQL Guide*. For information about database design, see "Designing a Database: Advanced Topics" in the *DB2 Administration Guide*.

If you believe that the problem is caused by the choice of system parameters, I/O device assignments, or other factors, begin monitoring DB2 to collect data about its internal activity. A good place to start would be with a DB2 Statistics Report.

If you have access path problems, you can examine a DB2 Accounting Report or use the EXPLAIN facility or the Optimization Service Center to diagnose the problem.

Exception Performance Monitoring

Exception monitoring looks for specific exceptional values or events, such as very high response times or deadlocks. Perform exception monitoring for response-time and concurrency problems. Online monitors are best-suited for exception monitoring. For example, with IBM Tivoli OMEGAMON XE, exception monitoring is available in both batch reporting and the online monitor.

Using DISPLAY Commands

Much of the information you can obtain from the Accounting and Statistics reports can also be obtained using the DISPLAY command. This command can show you details about current activity in the subsystem. There are several types of DISPLAYs:

- DISPLAY ARCHIVE
- DISPLAY BUFFERPOOL
- DISPLAY DATABASE
- DISPLAY FUNCTION SPECIFIC
- DISPLAY GROUP
- DISPLAY GROUPBUFFERPOOL
- DISPLAY LOCATION
- DISPLAY LOG
- DISPLAY PROCEDURE
- DISPLAY RLIMIT

- DISPLAY THREAD

- DISPLAY TRACE

- DISPLAY UTILITY

You can also view this type of information in the DB2 Control Center.

For more information about the options on the DISPLAY command, consult the *IBM DB2 9 Command Reference.*

Buffer Pools

Buffer pools are areas of virtual storage that temporarily store pages of table spaces or indexes. When a program accesses a row of a table, DB2 places the page containing that row in a buffer. When a program changes a row of a table, DB2 must write the data in the buffer back to disk (eventually), normally either at a DB2 system checkpoint or at a write threshold. Each write threshold is either a vertical threshold at the page set level or a horizontal threshold at the buffer pool level.

The way buffer pools work is fairly simple by design, but tuning these simple operations can make all the difference in the world to application performance. The data manager issues GETPAGE requests to the buffer manager, which hopefully can satisfy the request from the buffer pool instead of having to retrieve the page from disk. We often trade CPU for I/O to manage our buffer pools efficiently. Buffer pools are maintained by the subsystem, but individual buffer pool design and use should be by object granularity and in some cases also by application.

DB2 buffer pool management by design provides the ability to ALTER and DISPLAY buffer pool information dynamically without requiring a bounce of the DB2 subsystem. This feature improves availability by letting you dynamically create new buffer pools when necessary and also dynamically change and delete buffer pools. You may find you need to ALTER buffer pools a couple times during the day because of varying workload characteristics. We'll discuss this requirement when we look at tuning the buffer pool thresholds.

Initial buffer pool definitions are set at installation/migration but are often hard to configure at this time because the application process against the objects usually isn't detailed at installation. Regardless of the installation settings, however, you can use an ALTER statement any time after the install to add or delete buffer pools, resize buffer pools, or change any thresholds.

DB2 stores the buffer pool definitions in the bootstrap data set (BSDS), and you can move objects between buffer pools by using an ALTER INDEX or ALTER TABLESPACE statement and a subsequent STOP/START command of the object.

Pages

Virtual buffer pools contain three types of pages:

- *Available pages*, which are pages on an available queue (LRU, FIFO, MRU) for stealing.

- *In-Use pages*, which are pages currently in use by a process and unavailable for stealing. In-Use counts don't indicate the size of the buffer pool, but this count can help determine residency for initial sizing.

- *Updated pages*, which are pages that are not "in-use" and not available for stealing. These pages are considered "dirty pages" in a buffer pool waiting to be externalized.

There are four page sizes and several buffer pools to support each size:

Page size	Buffer pool
4K	BP0–BP49
8K	BP8K0–BP8K9
16K	BP16K0–BP16K9
32K	BP32K0–BP32K9

Work file table space pages are only 4 K or 32 K.

Asynchronous page writes per I/O will change with each page size accordingly:

Page size	Writes per I/O
4K	32
8K	16
16K	8
32K	4

With these new page sizes, you can achieve better hit ratios and reduce I/O because more rows can fit on a page. For instance, if you have a 2,200-byte row (for a data warehouse, perhaps), a 4 K page would be able to hold only one row, but if you used an 8 K page, three rows could fit on a page, one more than if you used 4 K pages and potentially one less lock. However, you don't want to use these new page sizes as a band-aid for what may be a poor design. Consider decreasing the row size based on usage to get more rows per page.

The DSNZPARM DSVCI permits the control interval to match to the actual page size.

Virtual Buffer Pools

You can have up to 80 virtual buffer pools, a limit that allows for up to fifty 4 K–page buffer pools (BP0–BP49), up to ten 32 K–page buffer pools (BP32K–BP32K9), up to ten 8 K–page buffer pools, and up to ten 16 K–page buffer pools. The physical memory available on your system limits the size of the buffer pools, with a maximum size for all buffer pools of 1 TB. It doesn't take additional resources to search a large pool versus a small pool. If you exceed the system's available memory, the system will start swapping pages from physical memory to disk, a consequence that can severely impact performance.

Buffer Pool Queue Management

DB2 processes pages used in the buffer pools in two categories: random (pages read one at a time) and sequential (pages read via prefetch). These pages are queued separately: in a Random Least Recently Used (LRU) queue or a Sequential Least Recently Used (SLRU) queue (prefetch steals only from this queue). Parameter VPSEQT (Sequential Steal Threshold) on the ALTER BUFFERPOOL statement controls the percentage of each queue in a buffer pool. This setting becomes a hard threshold to adjust and often requires two values—for example, one setting for batch processing and another for online processing. The way we process data between batch and online processes often differs. Batch is usually more sequentially processed, whereas online is processed more randomly.

DB2 breaks up these queues into multiple LRU chains. This way, queue management incurs less overhead because the latch that is taken at the head of the queue (actually on the hash control block that keeps the order of the pages on the queue) will be latched less because the queues are smaller. Multiple subpools are created for a large virtual buffer pool, and the threshold is controlled by DB2, not to exceed 4,000 virtual buffer pool (VBP) buffers in each subpool. The LRU queue is managed within each of the subpools to reduce buffer pool latch contention when the degree of concurrency is high. Stealing of these buffers occurs in a round-robin fashion through the subpools.

You can use first-in, first-out (FIFO) processing instead of the default of LRU. With this method, the oldest pages are moved out regardless. This alternative decreases the cost of doing a GETPAGE operation and reduces internal latch contention for high concurrency. You would only use this option where little or no I/O occurs and the table space or index is resident in the buffer pool. You would have separate buffer pools with LRU and FIFO objects, set via the ALTER BUFFERPOOL command with a new PGSTEAL option setting of FIFO. (LRU is the PGSTEAL option default.)

I/O Requests and Externalization

Synchronous reads are physical pages that are read in one page per I/O. *Synchronous writes* are pages written one page per I/O. You want to limit synchronous reads and writes to only what is truly necessary, meaning small in occurrence and number. Otherwise, you may start to see buffer pool stress (too many checkpoints, for example). DB2 will begin to use synchronous writes if the Immediate Write (IWTH) threshold is reached (more about this threshold later) or if two system checkpoints pass without a page being written that has been updated and not yet committed.

Asynchronous reads are several pages read per I/O for prefetch operations such as sequential prefetch, dynamic prefetch, or list prefetch. *Asynchronous writes* are several pages written per I/O for operations such as deferred writes.

DB2 externalizes pages to disk when any of the following events occurs:

- DWQT threshold is reached

- VDWQT threshold is reached

- Data set is physically closed or switched from R/W to R/O

- DB2 takes a checkpoint (LOGLOAD or CHKFREQ is reached)

- QUIESCE (WRITE YES) utility is executed

- Page is at the top of the LRU chain, and another update is required of the same page by another process

You want to control page externalization via the DWQT and VDWQT thresholds on the ALTER statement for best performance and to avoid surges in I/O. You don't want page externalization to be controlled by DB2 system checkpoints because too many pages would be written to disk at one time, causing I/O queuing delays, increased response time, and I/O spikes. During a checkpoint, all updated pages in the buffer pools are externalized to disk, and the checkpoint is recorded in the log (except for the work files).

Checkpoints and Page Externalization

DB2 checkpoints are controlled through the DSNZPARM CHKFREQ. The CHKFREQ parameter specifies either the number of minutes between checkpoints, using a value of 1 to 60, or the number of log records written between DB2 checkpoints, using a value of 200 to 16000000. The default value is 500000. You may need different settings for this parameter depending on workload; for example, you may want it higher during batch processing. However, CHKFREQ is a hard parameter to set often because it requires a bounce of the DB2 subsystem to take effect.

Recognizing the importance of the ability to change this parameter based on workloads, IBM introduced the –SET LOG CHKTIME command, which you can use to dynamically set the CHKFREQ parameter. Other options added to the –SET LOG command let you SUSPEND and RESUME logging for a DB2 subsystem. SUSPEND causes a system checkpoint to be taken in a non–data-sharing environment. By obtaining the log-write latch, this action prevents further log records from being created and causes any unwritten log buffers to be written to disk. Also, the BSDS will be updated with the high-written RBA. All further database updates are prevented either until update activity is resumed by a –SET LOG command to RESUME logging or until a –STOP DB2 command is issued. These are single-subsystem–only commands, so you must enter them for each member when running in a data-sharing environment.

In general terms, during online processing, DB2 should checkpoint about every five to 10 minutes, or you can use some other value based on investigative analysis of the impact on restart time after a failure. Two real concerns impact how often you take checkpoints:

- The cost and disruption of the checkpoints

- The restart time for the subsystem after a crash

The costs and disruption of DB2 checkpoints are often overstated. Although a DB2 checkpoint is a tiny hiccup, it does not prevent processing from proceeding. Having a CHKFREQ setting that is too high along with large buffer pools and high thresholds, such as the defaults, can cause enough I/O to make the checkpoint disruptive. In trying to control checkpoints, some users increase the CHKFREQ value and make the checkpoints less frequent but, in effect, actually make them much more disruptive. The situation is corrected by reducing the amount written and increasing the checkpoint frequency, which yields much better performance and availability. It is not only possible but does occur at some installations that a checkpoint every minute does not impact performance or availability. The write efficiency at DB2 checkpoints is the key factor to observe to determine whether you can reduce CHKFREQ. If the write thresholds (DWQT/VDQWT) are doing their job, there is less work to perform at each checkpoint. Using the write thresholds to cause I/O to be performed in a level, non-disruptive fashion is also helpful for the non-volatile storage in storage controllers.

However, even if you have your write thresholds (DWQT/VDQWT) set properly, as well as your checkpoints, you could still see an unwanted write problem. This could occur if you don't have your log data sets properly sized. If the active log data sets are too small, active log switches will occur often. When an active log switch takes place, DB2 takes a checkpoint automatically. Therefore, the logs could be driving excessive checkpoint processing, resulting in constant writes. This situation would prevent you from achieving a high ratio of pages written per I/O because the deferred write queue would not be allowed to fill as it should.

Sizing

The ALTER statement's VPSIZE parameter determines buffer pool sizes. This parameter sets the number of pages to be used for the virtual pool. DB2 can handle large buffer pools efficiently as long as enough real memory is available. If insufficient real storage exists to back the requested buffer pool storage, paging can result. Paging can occur when the buffer pool size exceeds the available real memory on the z/OS image. DB2 limits the total amount of storage allocated for buffer pools to approximately twice the amount of real storage (although less is recommended). A maximum of 1 TB total is supported for all buffer pools (provided the real storage is available).

To size buffer pools, it's helpful to know the residency rate of the pages for the object(s) in the buffer pool.

Sequential vs. Random Processing

The VPSEQT parameter specifies the percentage of the virtual buffer pool that can be used for sequentially accessed pages. This setting is intended to prevent sequential data from using all the buffer pool and to reserve some space for random processing. Possible values are 0 to 100 (percent), with a default of 80. That value would indicate that 80 percent of the buffer pool is to be set aside for sequential processing and 20 percent for random processing. Set this parameter according to how objects in the buffer pool are processed.

One tuning option often used is to alter VPSEQT to 0 to set the pool up for just random use. When VPSEQT is 0, the SLRU is no longer valid, and the buffer pool is now totally random. Because only the LRU will be used, all pages on the SLRU must be freed. This setting will also disable prefetch operations in the buffer pool, which is beneficial for certain strategies. However, this approach poses problems for certain buffer pools, as we'll explain later.

Writes

Parameter DWQT (Deferred Write Threshold), also known as the Horizontal Deferred Write Threshold, is the percentage threshold that determines when DB2 starts turning on write engines to begin deferred writes (32 pages per asynchronous I/O). The value can be from 0 to 90. When the threshold is reached, write engines (up to 600 write engines as of this publication) begin writing pages out to disk. Running out of write engines can occur if the write thresholds are not set to keep a constant flow of updated pages being written to disk. If this situation is uncommon, it is okay, but if it occurs daily, you have a tuning opportunity. DB2 turns on these write engines, basically one vertical page set queue at a time, until a 10 percent reverse threshold is met. When DB2 runs out of write engines, the statistics reports record the event in the WRITE ENGINES NOT AVAILABLE indicator.

Setting the DWQT threshold to a high value can help improve the hit ratio for updated pages, but a high value will also increase I/O time when deferred write engines begin. You can use a low value to reduce I/O length for deferred write engines, although this setting will increase the number of deferred writes. You should set this threshold based on the way your applications reference the data.

If you choose to set DWQT to 0 (zero), so that all objects defined to the buffer pool are scheduled to be written immediately to disk, DB2 actually uses its own internal calculations to determine exactly how many changed pages can exist in the buffer pool before it is written to disk.

DB2 still writes 32 pages per I/O, but it will take 40 dirty pages (updated pages) to trigger the threshold so that the highly re-referenced updated pages, such as space map pages, remain in the buffer pool.

When implementing large objects, you should use a separate buffer pool, and it should not be shared (backed by a group buffer pool in a data-sharing environment). Set parameter DWQT to 0 so that for LOBs with LOG NO, force-at-commit processing occurs, and the updates flow to disk continually instead of in surges of writes. For LOBs defined with LOG YES, DB2 can use deferred writes and avoid massive surges at checkpoints.

The DWQT threshold works at a buffer pool level for controlling writes of pages to the buffer pools, but for a more efficient write process, you'll want to control writes at the page set/partition level. Parameter VDWQT (vertical deferred write threshold) provides this control, specifying the percentage threshold that determines when DB2 starts turning on write engines and begins the deferred writes for a given data set. This setting helps keep a particular page set/partition from monopolizing the entire buffer pool with its updated pages. The value can be 0 to 90, with a default of 10. The VDWQT value should always be less than the DWQT value.

A good rule of thumb for setting the VDWQT is that if less than 10 pages are written per I/O, set the threshold to 0. You may also want to set it to 0 to trickle-write the data out to disk. It's normally best to keep this value low to prevent heavily updated page sets from dominating the section of the deferred write area. Either a percentage of pages or an actual number of pages (from 0 to 9999) can be specified for VDWQT. You must set the percentage to 0 to use the number specified. Set VDWQT to 0,0 to have the system use MIN(32,1) for good trickle I/O.

If you set VDWQT to 0, 32 pages are still written per I/O, but it will take 40 dirty pages (updated pages) to trigger the threshold, letting the highly re-referenced updated pages, such as space map pages, remain in the buffer pool.

It's a good idea to set VDWQT using a number rather than a percentage because if someone increases the buffer pool, more pages for a particular page set can now occupy the buffer pool, and this situation may not always be optimal or what you want.

When looking at any performance report that shows the amount of activity for the VDWQT and the DWQT, you would want to see the VDWQT being triggered most of the time (VERTIC.DEFER.WRITE THRESHOLD) and the DWQT much less often (HORIZ.DEFER.WRITE THRESHOLD). We can provide no general ratios because that would depend on the both the activity and the number of objects in the buffer pools. The bottom line is that you want to control I/O by the VDWQT, with the DWQT watching for and controlling activity across the entire pool and in general writing out rapidly queuing-up pages. This approach also helps limit the amount of I/O that a checkpoint would have to perform.

Parallelism

Parameter VPPSEQT (Virtual Pool Parallel Sequential Threshold) specifies the percentage of the VPSEQT setting that DB2 can use for parallel operations. Possible values are 0 to 100, with a default of 50. Setting VPPSEQT to 0 disables parallelism for objects in that particular buffer pool. This setting can be useful for buffer pools that cannot support parallel operations.

Parameter VPXPSEQT (Virtual Pool Sysplex Parallel Sequential Threshold) specifies the percentage of the VPPSEQT to use for inbound queries. It, too, defaults to 50 percent. A setting of 0 disables Sysplex query parallelism originating from the member to which the pool is allocated. This setting is normally used in affinity data-sharing environments, to prevent inbound resource consumption of work files and buffer pools.

Stealing Method

The VPSTEAL threshold lets you choose a queuing method for the buffer pools. The default is LRU, but FIFO is also an option. This option turns off the overhead for maintaining the queue and may be useful for objects that can completely fit in the buffer pool or if the hit ratio is less than 1 percent.

Page Fixing

You can use the PGFIX keyword with the ALTER BUFFERPOOL command to fix a buffer pool in real storage for an extended period of time. The PGFIX keyword has the following options:

- **PGFIX(YES).** The buffer pool is fixed in real storage for the long term. Page buffers are fixed when they are first used, and they remain fixed.

- **PGFIX(NO).** The buffer pool is not fixed in real storage for the long term. Page buffers are fixed and unfixed in real storage, permitting paging to disk. PGFIX(NO) is the default option.

The recommendation is to use PGFIX(YES) for buffer pools with a high I/O rate (i.e., a high number of pages read or written). For buffer pools with zero I/O, such as some read-only data or some indexes with a nearly 100 percent hit ratio, PGFIX(YES) is not recommended. In these cases, PGFIX(YES) provides no performance advantage.

Internal Thresholds

The following thresholds represent a percent of unavailable pages to total pages, where unavailable means either updated or in use by a process.

Sequential Prefetch Threshold

The Sequential Prefetch Threshold (SPTH) is checked before a prefetch operation is scheduled and during buffer allocation for a previously scheduled prefetch. If the SPTH threshold is exceeded, prefetch either will not be scheduled or will be canceled. The Statistics Report indicator PREFETCH DISABLED - NO BUFFER is incremented every time a virtual buffer pool reaches 90 percent of active unavailable pages, disabling sequential prefetch. This value should always be zero; a non-zero value is a clear indication that you are probably experiencing degraded performance due to all prefetch being disabled. To eliminate this problem, you may want to increase the size of the buffer pool (VPSIZE). Another option may be to have more frequent commits in the application programs to free pages in the buffer pool because this will put the pages on the write queues.

Data Manager Threshold

The Data Manager Threshold (DMTH), also referred to as the Buffer Critical Threshold, occurs when 95 percent of all buffer pages are unavailable (in use). The Buffer Manager will request all threads to release any possible pages immediately. This occurs if you set GETPAGE/RELPAGE processing by row instead of page. After a GETPAGE and single row is processed, a RELPAGE is issued. This causes CPU to become high for objects in the buffer pool, and I/O sensitive transaction can suffer. This can happen if the buffer pool is too small. You can observe when this occurs by seeing a non-zero value in the DM THRESHOLD REACHED indicator on a statistics report. This threshold is checked every time a page is read or updated. If it is not reached, DB2 will access the page in the virtual pool once for each page (no matter how many rows are used). If the threshold has been reached, DB2 will access the page in the virtual pool once for every *row* on the page that is retrieved or updated, which can lead to serious performance degradation.

Immediate Write Threshold

The Immediate Write Threshold (IWTH) is reached when 97.5 percent of buffers are unavailable (in use). If this threshold is reached, synchronous writes begin, presenting a performance problem. For example, if there are 100 rows in a page and there are 100 updates, 100 synchronous writes will occur, one by one for each row. Synchronous writes are not concurrent with SQL but serial, so the application will be waiting while the writes occur (including 100 log writes, which must occur first). This causes large increases in I/O time. It is not recorded explicitly in a statistic reports, but DB2 will appear to be hung and you'll see synchronous writes start to occur when this threshold is reached. Be careful with some monitors that send exception messages to the console when synchronous writes occur and refer to it as "IWTH reached," but not all synchronous writes are caused by this threshold being reached. This is simply being reported incorrectly.

> When looking at some performance reports, be aware that the IWTH counter can also be incremented when dirty pages on the write queue have been re-referenced, causing a synchronous I/O before the new process could use the page. This threshold counter can also be incremented if more than two checkpoints occur before an updated page is written because this situation causes a synchronous I/O to write out the page.

Virtual Pool Design Strategies

Your use of separate buffer pools should be based on their usage by the applications (such as buffer pools for objects that are randomly accessed vs. those that are sequentially accessed). Each pool will have its own unique settings, and the type of processing may even differ between the batch cycle and the online day. These are very generic breakouts just for this example. Actual definitions would be much finer-tuned and less generic. Here is a more detailed example of buffer pool object breakouts:

Buffer pool	Purpose
BP0	Catalog and directory (DB2 use only)
BP1	Work files (sort)

BP2	Code and reference tables (heavily accessed)
BP3	Small tables, heavily updated (transaction tables, work tables)
BP4	Basic tables
BP5	Basic indexes
BP6	Special for large, clustered, range-scanned table
BP7	Special for master table full index (random searched table)
BP8	Special for an entire database for a special application
BP9	Derived tables and "saved" tables for ad hoc querying
BP10	Staging tables (edit tables for short-lived data)
BP11	Staging indexes (edit tables for short-lived data)
BP12	Vendor tool/utility objects

Tuning with the –DISPLAY BUFFER POOL Command

In several cases, you can tune the buffer pools effectively using the –DISPLAY BUFFERPOOL command. When a tool isn't available for tuning, you can use these steps to help tune buffer pools:

1. Use the command, and view statistics.

2. Make changes (i.e., to thresholds, size, object placement)

3. Use the command again during processing, and view statistics.

4. Measure statistics.

The output from the –DISPLAY BUFFER POOL command contains valuable information, such as prefetch information (sequential, list, dynamic requests) pages read, prefetch I/O, and disablement (no buffer, no engine). The incremental detail display shifts the time frame every time you perform a new display.

RID Pool

The Row Identifier pool is used for storing and sorting RIDs for operations such as

- list prefetch

- multiple index access

- hybrid joins

- enforcing unique keys while updating multiple rows

The optimizer looks at the RID pool for prefetch and RID use. The full use of RID POOL is possible for any single user at runtime. Runtime can result in a table space scan being performed if not enough space is available in the RID. For example, if you want to retrieve 10,000 rows from a 100,000,000-row table and no RID pool is available, a scan of 100,000,000 rows would occur, at any time and without external notification. The optimizer assumes physical I/O will be less with a large pool.

Sizing

The default size of the RID pool is currently 8 MB with a maximum size of 10,000 MB. The MAXRBLK installation parameter controls RID pool size. You could set the RID pool size to 0 to disable the types of operations that use the RID pool, and DB2 would not choose access paths that the RID pool supports. DB2 creates the RID pool at start-up time, but no space is allocated until RID storage is actually needed. Space is then allocated in 32 K blocks as needed, until the maximum size specified on installation panel DSNTIPC is reached.

There are a few guidelines for setting the RID pool size. You should have as large a RID pool as required because it is a benefit for processing and performance degradation can result if the RID pool is too small. A good rule of thumb for sizing the RID pool is as follows:

# of concurrent RID processing activities X average # of RIDs X 2 X 5 bytes per RID

Statistics to Monitor

There are three statistics to monitor for RID pool problems.

RIDs Over the RDS Limit

This statistic reports the number of times list prefetch is turned off because the RID list built for a single set of index entries is greater than 25 percent of the number of rows in the table. If this is the case, DB2 determines that instead of using list prefetch to satisfy a query, it would be more efficient to perform a table space scan, which may or may not be good depending on the size of the table accessed. Increasing the size of the RID pool will *not* help in this case. This is an application issue for access paths and needs to be evaluated for queries using list prefetch.

There is one critical issue regarding this type of failure. The 25 percent threshold is actually stored in the package/plan at bind time; therefore, it may no longer match the real 25 percent value and in fact could be far less. It's important to know what packages/plans are using list prefetch and on what tables. If the underlying tables are growing, you should rebind the packages/plans that rely on them after running the RUNSTATS utility to update the statistics. Key correlation statistics and better information about skewed distribution of data can also provide better statistics for access path selection and may help avoid this problem. (For more information about data correlation statistics, see Chapter 7.)

RIDS Over the DM Limit

This situation occurs when more than 28 million RIDs were required to satisfy a query. There is currently a 28 million RID limit in DB2. The consequences of hitting this limit can be fallback to a table space scan. To control this, you have a couple of options:

- Fix the index by doing something creative.

- Add an additional index better suited for filtering.

- Force list prefetch off and use another index.

- Rewrite the query.

- Maybe it just requires a table space scan.

Insufficient Pool Size

This indicates that the RID pool is too small.

The Sort Pool

DB2 performs sorts in two phases:

1. During initialization, DB2 builds ordered sets of *runs* from the given input.

2. During merge, DB2 merges the runs together.

At start-up, DB2 allocates a sort pool in the private area of the DBM1 address space. DB2 uses a special sorting technique called a *tournament sort*. During the sorting processes it is not uncommon for this algorithm to produce logical work files called *runs*, which are intermediate sets of ordered data. If the sort pool is large enough, the sort is completed in that area. More often than not, the sort cannot be completed in the sort pool, and the runs are moved into the work file database, especially if there are many rows to sort. DB2 merges these runs later to complete the sort. When a work file database is used to hold the pages that make up the sort runs, you could experience performance degradation if the pages get externalized to the physical work files because DB2 will have to read them back in later to complete the sort.

Sort Pool Size

The sort pool size defaults to 2 MB unless specified. It can range in size from 240 K to 128 MB and is set with an installation DSNZPARM. The larger the sort pool (sort work area), the fewer sort runs produced. If the sort pool is large enough, DB2 may not use the buffer pools and sort work files. If buffer pools and the work file database are not used, the better performance will be due to reduced I/O. You want to size the sort pool and work file database large because you don't want sorts to have pages being written to disk.

The EDM Pool

The Environmental Descriptor Manager (EDM) pool consists of three components, each of which resides in its own separate storage and contains many items, including the following:

-   EDM pool

» CTs—cursor tables (copies of the SKCTs)

» PTs—package tables (copies of the SKPTs)

» authorization cache block for each plan

■ except those with CACHESIZE set to 0

- EDM skeleton pool

» SKCTs—skeleton cursor tables

» SKPTs—skeleton package tables

- EDM DBD cache

» DBDs – database descriptors

- EDM statement cache

» skeletons of dynamic SQL for CACHE DYNAMIC SQL

EDM Pool Size

If the EDM pool is too small, you'll see increased I/O activity in the following DB2 table spaces, which support the DB2 directory:

- DSNDB01.DBD01

- DSNDB01.SPT01

- DSNDB01.SCT02

Your main goal for the EDM pool is to limit the I/O against the directory and catalog. If the pool is too small, you will also see increased response times due to the loading of the SKCTs, SKPTs, and DBDs and re-preparing the dynamic SQL statements because they could not remained cached. By correctly sizing the EDM pools, you can keep unnecessary I/Os from accumulating for a transaction. If a SKCT, SKPT, or DBD must be reloaded into the EDM pool, additional I/O is required. This can happen if the pool pages are stolen because the EDM pool is too small. Pages in the pool are maintained on an LRU queue, and the least recently used pages are stolen if required. You can use a DB2 performance monitor statistics report to track the statistics concerning the use of the EDM pools.

If a new application is migrating to the environment, it may be helpful to look in SYSIBM.SYSPACKAGES to get an idea of the number of packages that may have to exist in the EDM pool and thus determine the size.

Efficiency

The following ratios can help you determine whether your EDM pool is efficient. Think of these values as EDM pool hit ratios.

- CT requests vs. CTs not in EDM pool

- PT requests vs. PTs not in EDM pool

- DBD requests vs. DBDs not in EDM pool

What you want is a value of 5 for each of the above (1 out of 5). An 80 percent hit ratio is what you are aiming for.

Dynamic SQL Caching

If you're going to use dynamic SQL caching, you need to pay attention to the EDM statement cache pool size. Cached statements are not backed by disk, and if this pool's pages are stolen and the statement is reused, the statement will have to be prepared again. Static plans and packages can be flushed from EDM by LRU but are backed by disk and can be retrieved when used again. Statistics to help monitor cache use and trace fields that show the effectiveness of the cache can be seen on the Statistics Long Report. In addition, you can snap the dynamic statement cache by using the EXPLAIN STMTCACHE ALL explain statement. The results of this statement are placed in the DSN_STATEMENT_CACHE_TABLE described earlier in this chapter.

In addition to the global dynamic statement caching in a subsystem, an application can cache statements at the thread level via the KEEPDYNAMIC(YES) bind parameter in combination with not re-preparing the statements. In these situations, the statements are cached at the thread level in thread storage as well as at the global level. As long as there is no shortage of virtual storage, the local application thread level cache is the most efficient storage for the prepared statements. You can use the MAXKEEPD subsystem parameter to limit the amount of thread storage consumed by applications caching dynamic SQL at the thread level.

Logging

Every system has some component that will eventually become the final bottleneck. Logging is not to be overlooked when trying to get transactions through the systems in a high-performance environment. You can tune and refine logging, but the synchronous I/O associated with logging and commits will always be there.

Log Reads

When DB2 needs to read from the log, it's important that the reads perform well because reads are normally performed during recovery, restarts, and rollbacks—processes that you don't want taking forever. You'll need to dedicate an input buffer for every process that requests a log read. DB2 will first look for the record in the log output buffer. If it finds the record there, it can apply it directly from the output buffer. If the record is not in the output buffer, DB2 will look for it in the active log data set and then in the archive log data set. When found, the record is moved to the input buffer so the requesting process can read it. You can monitor the successes of reads from the output buffers and active logs in the statistics report. These reads are the better performers. If the record must be read in from the archive log, processing time will be extended. For this reason, it's important to have large output buffers and active logs.

Log Writes

Applications move log records to the log output buffer using two methods: no wait or force. The "no wait" method moves the log record to the output buffer and returns control to the application; however, if no output buffers are available, the application will wait. If this happens, the statistics report will have a non-zero value for UNAVAILABLE ACTIVE LOG BUFF. This means that DB2 had to wait to externalize log records because there were no available output log buffers. The statistics report records successful moves without a wait as NO WAIT requests.

A force occurs at commit time, and the application will wait during this process, which is considered a synchronous write. Log records are then written from the output buffers to the active log data sets on disk either synchronously or asynchronously. To know how often this happens, you can check the WRITE OUTPUT LOG BUFFERS indicator in the statistics report.

To improve the performance of the log writes, you have a few options. First, you can increase the number of output buffers available for writing active log data sets by changing an installation parameter (OUTBUFF). You'd want to increase this setting if you're seeing unavailable buffers. Providing a large buffer will improve performance for log reads and writes.

Summary

Understanding the DB2 database environment is an important part of any database administrator's job. Various facilities are available to help you gain this understanding. There are several ways to analyze the database activity. Graphical monitoring tools, such as Omegamon and the Optimization Service Center, can be used with DB2 9.

The DB2 optimizer is one of the most advanced in the relational database industry. The optimizer generates an access plan during query compilation. Access paths are stored in the system catalog tables for static SQL applications. Access paths for dynamic SQL statements are generated at query execution time and stored in memory.

To gain an understanding of the access path (strategy) chosen by the DB2 optimizer, you can use the EXPLAIN utility. EXPLAIN populates the explain tables with detailed information about the SQL statements. You can query these tables to determine the plan information regarding use of indexes and other database resources. A graphical version of the access path can be examined using the Optimization Service Center. The ability to determine whether an SQL access path is appropriate is critical for the best performance of DB2 queries.

Understanding the performance of the DB2 database management system, its databases, and active applications in a dynamic environment requires monitoring. This means that a database administrator should gather information about the use of the database. An application programmer may also require SQL statement execution information. We discussed how to gather database information using DB2's monitoring facilities and reviewed information regarding SQL statement processing.

We also reviewed the various DB2 facilities for monitoring and gathering information for input into the tuning process, along with the EXPLAIN process, trace, commands, and other tools used to monitor DB2 database objects and SQL statements. You can use these tools to

- understand user and application activity within DB2

- better understand how an SQL statement is processed

- determine the sources and causes of problems

- tune buffer pool and system parameters

- improve database and application performance

We also looked at other performance topics, such as how to use DB2 traces and IFCIDs to help diagnose problems in DB2 and how to monitor statistics. We discussed various areas of memory, including buffer pools, the RID pool, the EDM pool, the sort pool, and dynamic SQL caching.

Additional Resources

IBM DB2 9 Administration Guide (SC18-9840)
IBM DB2 9 Application Programming and SQL Guide (SC18-9841)
IBM DB2 9 Command Reference (SC18-9844)
IBM DB2 9 Performance Monitoring and Tuning Guide (SC18-9851)
IBM DB2 9 SQL Reference (SC18-9854)

Practice Questions

Question 1

Which of the following types of performance monitoring would best be used to determine why there is general performance degradation in a data warehouse environment (high query usage, low update/insert and delete activity) over time? This environment runs 24X7 with no predictable workload pattern. Assume a performance database is used for reporting purposes where the collection of accounting and statistics data is stored.

○ A. Track and report on DBM1 virtual storage utilization over time.

○ B. Track and report on the number of timeouts and deadlocks over time.

○ C. Track and report on the average CPU and average elapsed time for plans and packages over time.

○ D. Track and report on the plans and packages that use more than two seconds of CPU time or one hour of elapsed time.

Question 2

Which of the following statistics is used for access path selection?

○ A. HIGH2KEY

○ B. ORGRATIO

○ C. AVGKEYLEN

○ D. PERCACTIVE

Question 3

What is the main difference between the deferred write threshold (DWQT) and the vertical deferred write threshold (VDWQT)?

○ A. The DWQT threshold applies to pages with LOB data, whereas the VDWQT threshold applies to pages containing mixed data.

○ B. The DWQT threshold deals with a fixed number of buffers, whereas the VDWQT threshold deals with a variable number of buffers.

○ C. The DWQT threshold is used only with sort/work buffer pools, whereas the VDWQT threshold can be used with buffers associated with any type of table spaces.

○ D. The DWQT threshold applies to all updated (unavailable) pages in the entire buffer pool, whereas the VDWQT threshold applies to the number of updated (unavailable) pages for a single page set.

Question 4

The PLAN_TABLE results from an explain of an SQL statement show the following column values: JOIN_METHOD = 1, MATCHCOLS = 2, and ACCESS_TYPE = I1. What is the access path chosen for this SQL statement?

- O A. Merge scan join, matching on two index columns, using a sparse index
- O B. Hybrid join, matching on two index columns, using one fetch index scan
- O C. Nested loop join, matching two columns in the table, using index-only access
- O D. Nested loop join, matching on two index columns, using one fetch index scan

Question 5

In which of the following explain tables can the number of rows processed by a dynamic SQL statement be found?

- O A. PLAN_TABLE
- O B. DSN_STATEMNT_TABLE
- O C. DSN_FUNCTION_TABLE
- O D. DSN_STATEMENT_CACHE_TABLE

Answers

Question 1

The answer is **C**, track and report on the average CPU and average elapsed time for plans and packages over time. In a 24X7 environment with an unpredictable workload, a continuous monitoring technique may be best. The accounting and statistics data that is collected can be put into a performance warehouse database and queried over time to help determine the problem plans and packages.

Question 2

The answer is **A**, HIGH2KEY. While the other statistics provide information about the organization and size of the data, only HIGH2KEY, which represents the high key value, is used by the optimizer.

Question 3

The answer is **D**. VDWQT applies to a page set, and DWQT applies to the entire buffer pool. These are important settings, especially with large buffer pools and large page sets (e.g., table spaces, partitions), to ensure that writes are distributed over time rather than at system checkpoints.

Question 4

The answer is **D**, a nested loop join, matching on two index columns with one fetch index scan. PLAN_TABLE is the most valuable resource for determining an efficient query access path. Understanding the contents of the plan table is an important skill.

Question 5

The answer is **D**. The statement cache table is populated via the EXPLAIN STMTCACHE ALL statement or from the Optimization Service Center. The table can then be queried to determine the runtime performance of statements in the statement cache.

A

DB2 Sample Database

This appendix contains an entity relationship diagram (ERD) and the SQL Data Definition Language (DDL) for the DB2 sample database objects used as examples in this book.

The ERD (Figure A.1) depicts the relationships between the tables, as well as the columns in the tables. Bold columns are required, and the other columns are nullable. Primary keys are indicated by **PK**, foreign keys with **FK**, and unique constraints with a **U**.

The sample DDL that follows the ERD (Listing A.1) is a portion of the DDL contained in the SDSNSAMP sample library's members DSNTEJ1 and DSNTEJ7. The results of queries in this book may differ from your actual results.

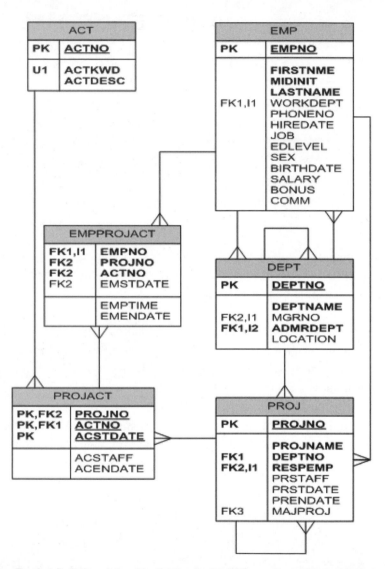

Figure A.1: Entity relationship diagram for the DB2 sample database objects

```
-- CREATION OF THE STOGROUP FOR OUR OBJECTS,
-- USING SMS SO SPECIFYING VOLUME *
CREATE STOGROUP DSN8G910
  VOLUMES (*)
  VCAT  DSNC910;
```

Listing A.1: DDL for the DB2 sample database objects (part 1 of 8)

```
--NEXT THE DATABASE IS CREATED FOR OUR BASE
--TABLES
CREATE DATABASE DSN8D91A
  STOGROUP DSN8G910
  BUFFERPOOL BP0
  CCSID EBCDIC;

--TABLES WITH BLOBS ARE IN A SEPARATE DATABASE
CREATE DATABASE DSN8D91L
  STOGROUP  DSN8G910
  BUFFERPOOL  BP0
  CCSID  EBCDIC;

--THE TABLE SPACE DEFINITIONS WILL BE SHOWN
--TOGETHER WITH THEIR TABLES AND INDEXES.
--SOME FOREIGN KEY DEFINITIONS ARE IN THE TABLE
--DDL; OTHERWISE THEY COME LAST VIA ALTERS

--TABLE SPACE DEFINITION FOR DEPT
CREATE TABLESPACE DSN8S91D
  IN DSN8D91A
  USING STOGROUP DSN8G910
            PRIQTY 20
            SECQTY 20
            ERASE NO
  LOCKSIZE PAGE LOCKMAX SYSTEM
  BUFFERPOOL BP0
  CLOSE NO
  CCSID EBCDIC;

--TABLE DEFINITION FOR DEPT
CREATE TABLE DSN8910.DEPT
      (DEPTNO   CHAR(3)        NOT NULL,
       DEPTNAME VARCHAR(36)    NOT NULL,
       MGRNO    CHAR(6)                 ,
       ADMRDEPT CHAR(3)        NOT NULL,
       LOCATION CHAR(16)                ,
       PRIMARY KEY(DEPTNO))
IN DSN8D91A.DSN8S91D
CCSID EBCDIC;

--INDEX DEFINITIONS FOR DEPT
CREATE UNIQUE INDEX DSN8910.XDEPT1
      ON DSN8910.DEPT
          (DEPTNO   ASC)
      USING STOGROUP DSN8G910
              PRIQTY 12
              ERASE NO
      BUFFERPOOL BP0
      CLOSE NO;
```

Listing A.1: DDL for the DB2 sample database objects (part 2 of 8)

```
CREATE INDEX DSN8910.XDEPT2
        ON DSN8910.DEPT
            (MGRNO    ASC)
        USING STOGROUP DSN8G910
                   PRIQTY 12
                   ERASE NO
        BUFFERPOOL BP0
        CLOSE NO;

CREATE INDEX DSN8910.XDEPT3
        ON DSN8910.DEPT
            (ADMRDEPT ASC)
        USING STOGROUP DSN8G910
                   PRIQTY 12
                   ERASE NO
        BUFFERPOOL BP0
        CLOSE NO;

--TABLE SPACE DEFINITION FOR EMP
CREATE TABLESPACE DSN8S91E
    IN DSN8D91A
    USING STOGROUP DSN8G910
               PRIQTY 20
               SECQTY 20
               ERASE NO
    NUMPARTS 4
        (PART 1 USING STOGROUP DSN8G910
                           PRIQTY 12
                           SECQTY 12,
         PART 3 USING STOGROUP DSN8G910
                           PRIQTY 12
                           SECQTY 12)
    LOCKSIZE PAGE LOCKMAX SYSTEM
    BUFFERPOOL BP0
    CLOSE NO
    COMPRESS YES
    CCSID EBCDIC;

--TABLE DEFINITION FOR EMP
CREATE TABLE DSN8910.EMP
        (EMPNO     CHAR(6)         NOT NULL,
         FIRSTNME  VARCHAR(12)     NOT NULL,
         MIDINIT   CHAR(1)         NOT NULL,
         LASTNAME  VARCHAR(15)     NOT NULL,
         WORKDEPT  CHAR(3)                    ,
         PHONENO   CHAR(4) CONSTRAINT NUMBER CHECK
          (PHONENO >= '0000' AND PHONENO <= '9999'),
         HIREDATE  DATE NOT NULL WITH DEFAULT      ,
```

Listing A.1: DDL for the DB2 sample database objects (part 3 of 8)

```
            JOB        CHAR(8)                    ,
            EDLEVEL    SMALLINT                   ,
            SEX        CHAR(1)                    ,
            BIRTHDATE  DATE                       ,
            SALARY     DECIMAL(9, 2)              ,
            BONUS      DECIMAL(9, 2)              ,
            COMM       DECIMAL(9, 2)              ,
            PRIMARY KEY(EMPNO),
            FOREIGN KEY RED (WORKDEPT) REFERENCES DSN8910.DEPT
                ON DELETE SET NULL)
  EDITPROC   DSN8EAE1
  IN DSN8D91A.DSN8S91E
  CCSID EBCDIC;

--INDEX DEFINITIONS FOR EMP
CREATE UNIQUE INDEX DSN8910.XEMP1
        ON DSN8910.EMP
            (EMPNO     ASC)
        USING STOGROUP DSN8G910
                PRIQTY 12
                ERASE NO
        CLUSTER
          (PART 1 VALUES('099999'),
           PART 2 VALUES('199999'),
           PART 3 VALUES('299999'),
           PART 4 VALUES('999999'))
        BUFFERPOOL BP0
        CLOSE NO;

CREATE INDEX DSN8910.XEMP2
        ON DSN8910.EMP
            (WORKDEPT ASC)
        USING STOGROUP DSN8G910
                PRIQTY 12
                ERASE NO
        BUFFERPOOL BP0
        CLOSE NO;

--TABLE SPACE DEFINITION FOR PROJ
CREATE TABLESPACE DSN8S91P
  IN DSN8D91A
  USING STOGROUP DSN8G910
            PRIQTY 160
            SECQTY 80
  SEGSIZE 4
  LOCKSIZE ROW
  BUFFERPOOL BP0
  CLOSE NO
  CCSID EBCDIC;
```

Listing A.1: DDL for the DB2 sample database objects (part 4 of 8)

```
--TABLE DEFINITION FOR PROJ
CREATE TABLE DSN8910.PROJ
      (PROJNO   CHAR(6) PRIMARY KEY NOT NULL,
       PROJNAME VARCHAR(24)    NOT NULL WITH DEFAULT
        'PROJECT NAME UNDEFINED',
       DEPTNO   CHAR(3)         NOT NULL REFERENCES
         DSN8910.DEPT ON DELETE RESTRICT,
       RESPEMP  CHAR(6)         NOT NULL REFERENCES
         DSN8910.EMP ON DELETE RESTRICT,
       PRSTAFF  DECIMAL(5, 2)           ,
       PRSTDATE DATE                    ,
       PRENDATE DATE                    ,
       MAJPROJ  CHAR(6))
IN DSN8D91A.DSN8S91P
CCSID EBCDIC;

--INDEX DEFINITIONS FOR PROJ
CREATE UNIQUE INDEX DSN8910.XPROJ1
      ON DSN8910.PROJ
          (PROJNO   ASC)
      USING STOGROUP DSN8G910
                PRIQTY 12
                ERASE NO
      BUFFERPOOL BP0
      CLOSE NO;

CREATE INDEX DSN8910.XPROJ2
      ON DSN8910.PROJ
          (RESPEMP  ASC)
      USING STOGROUP DSN8G910
                PRIQTY 12
                ERASE NO
      BUFFERPOOL BP0
      CLOSE NO;

--TABLE SPACE DEFINITION FOR ACT
--AND FOR EMPPROJACT
CREATE TABLESPACE DSN8S91P
  IN DSN8D91A
  USING STOGROUP DSN8G910
            PRIQTY 160
            SECQTY 80
  SEGSIZE 4
  LOCKSIZE ROW
  BUFFERPOOL BP0
  CLOSE NO
  CCSID EBCDIC;
```

Listing A.1: DDL for the DB2 sample database objects (part 5 of 8)

```
--TABLE DEFINITION FOR ACT
CREATE TABLE DSN8910.ACT
        (ACTNO     SMALLINT      NOT NULL,
         ACTKWD    CHAR(6)       NOT NULL,
         ACTDESC   VARCHAR(20)   NOT NULL,
PRIMARY KEY(ACTNO))
IN DSN8D91A.DSN8S91P
CCSID EBCDIC;

CREATE UNIQUE INDEX DSN8910.XACT1
        ON DSN8910.ACT
          (ACTNO     ASC)
        USING STOGROUP DSN8G910
                 PRIQTY 12
                 ERASE NO
        BUFFERPOOL BP0
        CLOSE NO;

CREATE UNIQUE INDEX DSN8910.XACT2
        ON DSN8910.ACT
          (ACTKWD    ASC)
        USING STOGROUP DSN8G910
                 PRIQTY 12
                 ERASE NO
        BUFFERPOOL BP0
        CLOSE NO;

--TABLE DEFINITION FOR EMPPROJACT
CREATE TABLE DSN8910.EMPPROJACT
        (EMPNO     CHAR(6)        NOT NULL,
         PROJNO    CHAR(6)        NOT NULL,
         ACTNO     SMALLINT       NOT NULL,
         EMPTIME   DECIMAL(5, 2)           ,
         EMSTDATE  DATE                    ,
         EMENDATE  DATE                    ,
          FOREIGN KEY REPAPA (PROJNO, ACTNO, EMSTDATE)
          REFERENCES DSN8910.PROJACT
          ON DELETE RESTRICT,
          FOREIGN KEY REPAE (EMPNO) REFERENCES DSN8910.EMP
          ON DELETE RESTRICT)
IN DSN8D91A.DSN8S91P
CCSID EBCDIC;

--INDEX DEFINITIONS FOR EMPPROJACT
CREATE UNIQUE INDEX DSN8910.XEMPPROJACT1
        ON DSN8910.EMPPROJACT
          (PROJNO    ASC,
           ACTNO     ASC,
```

Listing A.1: DDL for the DB2 sample database objects (part 6 of 8)

```
                EMSTDATE ASC,
                EMPNO    ASC)
        USING STOGROUP DSN8G910
                 PRIQTY 12
                 ERASE NO
        BUFFERPOOL BP0
        CLOSE NO;

CREATE INDEX DSN8910.XEMPPROJACT2
        ON DSN8910.EMPPROJACT
          (EMPNO    ASC)
        USING STOGROUP DSN8G910
                 PRIQTY 12
                 ERASE NO
        BUFFERPOOL BP0
        CLOSE NO;

--ADDITIONAL FOREIGN KEY DEFINITIONS
ALTER TABLE DSN8910.DEPT
   FOREIGN KEY RDD (ADMRDEPT) REFERENCES DSN8910.DEPT
     ON DELETE CASCADE;
ALTER TABLE DSN8910.DEPT
   FOREIGN KEY RDE (MGRNO) REFERENCES DSN8910.EMP
     ON DELETE SET NULL;
ALTER TABLE DSN8910.PROJ
   FOREIGN KEY RPP (MAJPROJ) REFERENCES DSN8910.PROJ
     ON DELETE CASCADE;


--TABLE SPACE DEFINITION FOR EMP_PHOTO_RESUME
CREATE TABLESPACE  DSN8S91B
      IN  DSN8D91L
    USING STOGROUP  DSN8G910
          PRIQTY  20
          SECQTY  20
    ERASE  NO
    LOCKSIZE  PAGE
    LOCKMAX  SYSTEM
    BUFFERPOOL  BP0
    CLOSE  NO
    CCSID  EBCDIC;

--TABLE DEFINITION FOR EMP_PHOTO_RESUME
CREATE TABLE  DSN8910.EMP_PHOTO_RESUME
      (EMPNO         CHAR( 06 )   NOT NULL,
       EMP_ROWID     ROWID NOT NULL GENERATED ALWAYS,
       PSEG_PHOTO    BLOB( 500K ),
       BMP_PHOTO     BLOB( 100K ),
       RESUME        CLOB(  5K ),
```

Listing A.1: DDL for the DB2 sample database objects (part 7 of 8)

```
          PRIMARY KEY  ( EMPNO ) )
IN  DSN8D91L.DSN8S91B
CCSID  EBCDIC;

--LOB TABLE SPACES, AUX TABLES, AND INDEXES FOR EMP_PHOTO_RESUME
CREATE LOB TABLESPACE  DSN8S91L
IN  DSN8D91L
LOG  NO;

CREATE AUX TABLE  DSN8910.AUX_PSEG_PHOTO
IN  DSN8D91L.DSN8S91L
STORES  DSN8910.EMP_PHOTO_RESUME
COLUMN  PSEG_PHOTO;

CREATE UNIQUE INDEX  DSN8910.XAUX_PSEG_PHOTO
ON  DSN8910.AUX PSEG_PHOTO;

CREATE LOB TABLESPACE  DSN8S91M
IN  DSN8D91L
LOG  NO;

CREATE AUX TABLE  DSN8910.AUX_BMP_PHOTO
IN  DSN8D91L.DSN8S91M
STORES  DSN8910.EMP_PHOTO_RESUME
COLUMN  BMP_PHOTO;

CREATE UNIQUE INDEX  DSN8910.XAUX_BMP_PHOTO
ON  DSN8910.AUX_BMP_PHOTO;

CREATE LOB TABLESPACE  DSN8S91N
IN  DSN8D91L
LOG  NO;

CREATE AUX TABLE  DSN8910.AUX_EMP_RESUME
IN  DSN8D91L.DSN8S91N
STORES  DSN8910.EMP_PHOTO_RESUME
COLUMN  RESUME;

CREATE UNIQUE INDEX  DSN8910.XAUX_EMP_RESUME
ON  DSN8910.AUX_EMP_RESUME;
```

Listing A.1: DDL for the DB2 sample database objects (part 8 of 8)

Sample Exam Questions

In this appendix, we provide you with a sample test. There are questions covering all chapters. You'll find the answers in Appendix C, along with brief explanations and a chapter of reference. Take the exam here, and then check your answers in Appendix C. The questions are written in a very similar fashion to those on the actual test. These questions are focused toward the 732 exam, with only a few focused toward the 730 exam. Read the question and answers twice; sometimes, you may find that the most obvious answer may not be the correct one. Good luck!

Practice Questions

Question 1

Which of the following is the name of the type of relationship between two tables in which the primary key columns of the parent table are inherited by and become a subset of the primary key columns of the child table?

○ A.   Recursive

○ B.   Identifying

○ C.   Independent

○ D.   Associative

Question 2

Which of the following products is required for a DB2 for z/OS application to be able to connect to a remote DB2 data server?

○ A.   DB2 RunTime Client

○ B.   DB2 Connect Enterprise Edition for z/OS

○ C.   DB2 for z/OS

○ D.   DB2 Control Center

Question 3

A DBA needs to issue a DB2 command. Which of the following options will allow this?

○ A.   SPUFI

○ B.   Trigger

○ C.   z/OS console

○ D.   An SQL statement

Question 4

The NEXTVAL and PREVVAL expressions can be used in all of the following except:

○ A.   SELECT and SELECT INTO

○ B.   A DELETE statement

○ C.   An UPDATE statement within a SET clause (searched or positioned)

○ D.   SET *host-variable*

Question 5

When reviewing a statistics report, a DBA notices that about 20 timeouts occurred in a 24-hour period. The DBA is unsure how long each user is actually waiting before a timeout error message is issued. How can this information be determined?

○ A. By looking at the NUMLKTS DSNZPARM

○ B. By observing the value of the IRLMRWT DSNZPARM

○ C. By selecting from SYSIBM.SYSTABLESPACE and observing the LOCKMAX value

○ D. By looking at the total wait time in the accounting report for each plan

Question 6

If you need to diagnose locking-contention problems in an application, which trace class would be useful?

○ A. Accounting Trace Class 3

○ B. Statistics Trace Class 2

○ C. Accounting Trace Class 2

○ D. Statistics Trace Class 1

Question 7

What is the recommended priority setting for the DB2 address spaces?

○ A. IRLM, MSTR, DBM1

○ B. DB2 performance monitors, IRLM, MSTR

○ C. IRLM, DBM1, MSTR

○ D. CICS, IRLM, DBM1

Question 8

DBA1 needs to be able to create tables in a database and be able to run periodic REORGs. However, DBA1 is not permitted to access the data or manipulate it. Which of the following authorities would be the most appropriate?

○ A. SYSADM

○ B. DBADM

○ C. DBCTRL

○ D. DBMAINT

Question 9

Which of the following structures should *not* exist in the coupling facility of a data-sharing group?

○ A.   Lock structure

○ B.   Global buffer pool(s)

○ C.   Virtual buffer pool(s)

○ D.   Shared communications area (SCA)

Question 10

A user ID is required to attach a client to the current application/process connection to enable client application testing of native SQL or Java procedures that are executed within the session. Which of the following system privileges is required?

○ A.   TRACE

○ B.   MONITOR1

○ C.   MONITOR2

○ D.   DEBUGSESSION

Question 11

An application program needs the highest level of concurrency possible but cannot allow for uncommitted data to be seen. What is the best isolation level to use?

○ A.   RR (Repeatable Read)

○ B.   RS (Read Stability)

○ C.   CS (Cursor Stability)

○ D.   UR (Uncommitted Read)

Question 12

A DBA wants to create a new plan using the BIND PLAN PKLIST option and specifying individual packages. What authority/privilege must the DBA have for the operation to be successful?

○ A.   COPY to copy the individual packages

○ B.   EXECUTE authority on each package specified in the PKLIST

○ C.   CREATE IN to name the collection containing the individual packages

○ D.   BINDAGENT to bind all the individual packages on behalf of their owner

Question 13

To reduce the amount of time DB2 waits for a resource before a timeout occurs, which of the following DSNZPARMs should be changed?

○ A.   NUMLKTS

○ B.   NUMLKUS

○ C.   IRLMRWT

○ D.   SKIPUNCI

Question 14

The bind process performs all of the following except:

○ A.   Checks SQL syntax

○ B.   Checks security

○ C.   Allocates buffer pools

○ D.   Builds access path strategy for each SQL statement

Question 15

Which of the following options is the most plausible reason for a DROP INDEX failing?

○ A.   The table was defined with restrict on drop.

○ B.   The index has no extents left.

○ C.   A unique key constraint exists.

○ D.   The DEFER keyword was not specified.

Question 16

In which of the following situations would a plan or package *not* be marked as invalid?

○ A.   When a table, index, or view on which the plan or package depends is dropped

○ B.   When the authorization of the owner to access any of those objects is revoked

○ C.   When the authorization to execute a stored procedure is revoked from a plan or package owner and the plan or package uses the CALL literal form to call the stored procedure

○ D.   When a trigger on a dependent table is dropped

Question 17

If you want to find out information about locks being held on a table space, which of the following commands would you use?

○ A.   DISPLAY LOCKS

○ B.   DISPLAY DATABASE (*dbname*) LOCKS

○ C.   DISPLAY TABLESPACE (*tsname*) LOCKS

○ D.   DISPLAY GROUP

Question 18

The following output is the result of which DB2 command?

```
DSNL080I  -DBT5 DSNLTDDF DISPLAY DDF REPORT FOLLOWS:
DSNL081I STATUS=STARTD
DSNL082I LOCATION              LUNAME              GENERICLU
DSNL083I DBT5                  TU0.BSYSDBT5        -NONE
DSNL084I IPADDR        TCPPORT RESPORT
DSNL085I 10.35.4.16     2590    2591
DSNL086I SQL    DOMAIN=t390.rpc.com
DSNL086I RESYNC DOMAIN=t390.rpc.com
DSNL090I DT=A   CONDBAT=     64 MDBAT=    64
DSNL092I ADBAT=     0 QUEDBAT=       0 IN1DBAT= 0 CONQUED=      0
DSNL093I DSCDBAT=       0 IN2CONS=       0
DSNL099I DSNLTDDF DISPLAY DDF REPORT COMPLETE
```

○ A.   DISPLAY LOCATION

○ B.   DISPLAY DDF

○ C.   DISPLAY THREAD

○ D.   DISPLAY DISTRIBUTED

Question 19

Three after triggers (TRIG1, TRIG2, and TRIG3) have been created on the same table and are designed to run in sequential order, TRIG1 through TRIG3. The WHEN search condition for TRIG2 is incorrect and must be recoded. What is the appropriate action?

○ A.   Alter trigger TRIG2, and correct the SQL.

○ B.   Drop and re-create TRIG2 and TRIG3 after correcting the SQL.

○ C.   Drop and re-create TRIG1 and TRIG2 after correcting the SQL.

○ D.   Rebind triggers TRIG1, TRIG2, and TRIG3 after correcting the SQL in TRIG2.

Question 20

Which clause would be used to create a partition-by-growth table space?

○ A. The DSSIZE MAX clause

○ B. The NUMPARTS MAX clause

○ C. The NUMPARTS 4096 clause

○ D. The MAXPARTITIONS clause

Question 21

In which of the following explain tables can the number of rows processed by a dynamic SQL statement be found?

○ A. PLAN_TABLE

○ B. DSN_STATEMNT_TABLE

○ C. DSN_FUNCTION_TABLE

○ D. DSN_STATEMENT_CACHE_TABLE

Question 22

The primary space allocation on a DB2-managed segmented table space named MYTS1 in database MYDB needs to be increased from 50 MB to 60 MB. Which of the following sequences of steps should you take to change the primary space quantity and allocate the additional space?

○ A. ALTER TABLESPACE MYDB.MYTS1 PRIQTY 60000;

○ B. ALTER TABLESPACE MYDB.MYTS1 PRIQTY 60000;
REORG TABLESPACE MYDB.MYTS1

○ C. -STOP DATABASE(MYDB) SPACENAM(MYTS1
ALTER TABLESPACE MYDB.MYTS1 PRIQTY 60000;

○ D. -STOP DATABASE(MYDB) SPACENAM(MYTS1)
ALTER TABLESPACE MYDB.MYTS1 PRIQTY 60000;
REORG TABLESPACE MYDB.MYTS1 REUSE

Question 23

An application wants to skip data that is currently locked by another application. The application doesn't have the need to see uncommitted or unavailable data. Which option could be used on the SELECT statement?

○ A. SKIP LOCKED DATA

○ B. FOR FETCH ONLY

○ C. FETCH FIRST *n* ROWS

○ D. OPTIMIZE FOR *n* ROWS

Question 24

Given that an environment that uses EBCDIC as the default encoding scheme doesn't support mixed and graphic data and has a table TEST.TABLE1 in ASCII format, the DBA issues the following SQL statement:

```
SELECT * FROM TEST.TABLE1 WHERE COL1 = X'26'
```

Which of the following encoding schemes will be used for the value that is compared with COL1?

○ A. CCSID

○ B. EBCDIC

○ C. ASCII

○ D. UNICODE

Question 25

A view is considered to be "read-only" if the view definition

○ A. contains an ORDER BY clause

○ B. contains a scalar fullselect

○ C. references more than one table in the first FROM clause

○ D. contains a subquery referencing a table in the first FROM clause

Question 26

Assume the following table definition:

```
CREATE TABLE DSN8910.DEPT
        (DEPTNO    CHAR(3)        NOT NULL,
         DEPTNAME  VARCHAR(36)    NOT NULL,
         MGRNO     CHAR(6)                ,
         ADMRDEPT  CHAR(3)        NOT NULL,
         LOCATION  CHAR(16)               ,
         PRIMARY KEY(DEPTNO))
```

```
   IN DSN8D91A.DSN8S91D
   CCSID EBCDIC;
```

If the manager is being replaced and the location reset in every department with a department number that starts with the letter D, which of the following statements would be correct?

- ○ A. UPDATE DEPT SET (MGRNO = NULL; LOCATION=NULL) WHERE DEPTNO LIKE 'D%'
- ○ B. UPDATE DEPT SET (MGRNO, LOCATION) = (NULL, NULL) WHERE DEPTNO LIKE 'D%'
- ○ C. UPDATE DEPT SET MGRNO = NULL, SET LOCATION = NULL WHERE DEPTNO LIKE 'D%'
- ○ D. UPDATE DEPT SET (MGRNO = NULL), (LOCATION = NULL) WHERE DEPTNO LIKE 'D%'

Question 27

If a coupling facility that contains the group buffer pool structures fails, which is the best option to help lessen the duration of the outage?

- ○ A. Use ARM.
- ○ B. Use group buffer pool duplexing.
- ○ C. Use lock structure duplexing.
- ○ D. Remove the pages.

Question 28

Which of the following statements will count only the unique occurrences of the department number in the employee table?

- ○ A. SELECT COUNT(UNIQUE WORKDEPT) FROM EMP
- ○ B. SELECT COUNT(DISTINCT WORKDEPT) FROM EMP
- ○ C. SELECT COUNT(WORKDEPT) UNIQUE FROM EMP
- ○ D. SELECT COUNT(WORKDEPT) DISTINCT FROM EMP

Question 29

Which of the following clauses will sort the EMP table in order of department descending and then last name ascending:

- ○ A. SORT BY WORKDEPT, LASTNAME
- ○ B. SORT BY WORKDEPT DESC, LASTNAME ASC
- ○ C. ORDER BY WORKDEPT DESC, LASTNAME ASC
- ○ D. ORDER BY LASTNAME, WORKDEPT DESC

Question 30

Which of the following is *not* a type of dynamic SQL?

○ A. Embedded dynamic SQL

○ B. Interactive SQL

○ C. Deferred embedded SQL

○ D. Static SQL

Question 31

Given the following join coded with implicit join syntax, which of the four choices represent the correct explicit join syntax supporting the same query?

```
SELECT E.EMPNO, E.FIRSTNME, E.LASTNAME, D.DEPTNAME
FROM    DSN8910.EMP E, DSN8910.DEPT D
WHERE   E.WORKDEPT = D.DEPTNO
AND     E.WORKDEPT IN ('A00', 'C01')
```

○ A.
```
SELECT E.EMPNO, E.FIRSTNME, E.LASTNAME, D.DEPTNAME
FROM   DSN8910.EMP E
FULL OUTER JOIN
       DSN8910.DEPT D
ON     E.WORKDEPT = D.DEPTNO
WHERE E.WORKDEPT IN ('A00', 'C01')
```

○ B.
```
SELECT E.EMPNO, E.FIRSTNME, E.LASTNAME, D.DEPTNAME
FROM   DSN8910.EMP E
LEFT JOIN
       DSN8910.DEPT D
ON     E.WORKDEPT = D.DEPTNO
WHERE E.WORKDEPT IN ('A00', 'C01')
```

○ C.
```
SELECT E.EMPNO, E.FIRSTNME, E.LASTNAME, D.DEPTNAME
FROM   DSN8910.EMP E
INNER JOIN ON E.WORKDEPT = D.DEPTNO
       DSN8910.DEPT D
WHERE E.WORKDEPT IN ('A00', 'C01')
```

○ D.
```
SELECT E.EMPNO, E.FIRSTNME, E.LASTNAME, D.DEPTNAME
FROM   DSN8910.EMP E
INNER JOIN
       DSN8910.DEPT D
ON     E.WORKDEPT = D.DEPTNO
AND    E.WORKDEPT IN 'A00', 'C01'
```

Question 32

Given the CASE expression

```
CASE
        WHEN  EDLEVEL  <  15  THEN  'SECONDARY'
        WHEN  EDLEVEL  <=  19  THEN  'COLLEGE'
        ELSE
        'POST  GRADUATE'
    END  AS  SCHOOLING
```

and the values 19, 10, 15, and 22 for EDLEVEL, what will the resulting rows contain?

○ A. COLLEGE, SECONDARY, SECONDARY, POST GRADUATE

○ B. POST GRADUATE, COLLEGE, SECONDARY, POST GRADUATE

○ C. COLLEGE, SECONDARY, COLLEGE, POST GRADUATE

○ D. COLLEGE, SECONDARY, SECONDARY, POST GRADUATE

Question 33

Which of the following queries will return data from the first table, TABLE1, only when those rows don't exist in the second table, TABLE2, also eliminating any duplicates in the resulting rows?

○ A. SELECT COL1, COL2
       FROM   TABLE1
       UNION
       SELECT COL1, COL2
       FROM   TABLE2

○ B. SELECT COL1, COL2
       FROM   TABLE1
       EXCEPT ALL
       SELECT COL1, COL2
       FROM   TABLE2

○ C. SELECT COL1, COL2
       FROM   TABLE1
       NOT EXISTS
       SELECT COL1, COL2
       FROM   TABLE2

○ D. SELECT COL1, COL2
       FROM   TABLE1
       EXCEPT
       SELECT COL1, COL2
       FROM   TABLE2

Question 34

Given the following XML document and XPath expression in an XMLQUERY function, what will the output look like?

```
<customerinfo xmlns="http://posample.org" Cid="1000"><name>Kathy
Smith</name><addr country="Canada"><street>5
Rosewood</street><city>Toronto</city><prov-state>Ontario</prov-
state><pcode-zip>M6W 1E6</pcode-zip></addr><phone type="work">
416-555-1358</phone></customerinfo>

SELECT XMLQUERY('declare default element namespace
"http://posample.org"; $d/customerinfo/phone' passing INFO as "d")
as PHONE
FROM     DSN8910.CUSTOMER
WHERE    CID = 1000;
```

- ○ A. 416-555-1358
- ○ B. <phone xmlns="http://posample.org" type="work">
  416-555-1358</phone>
- ○ C. <416-555-1358/>
- ○ D. Nothing is returned.

Question 35

Given that you need to return a list of sales reps, along with the number of employees and total salary for the departments in which they work, which of the following statements would actually be successful?

- ○ A. SELECT   TAB1.EMPNO, TAB1.SALARY,
  TAB2.AVGSAL,TAB2.HDCOUNT
  FROM   DSN8910.EMP TAB1,
  (SELECT   AVG(SALARY) AS AVGSAL,
  COUNT(*) AS HDCOUNT
  FROM   DSN8910.EMP
  WHERE   WORKDEPT = TAB1.WORKDEPT) AS TAB2
  WHERE   TAB1.JOB = 'SALESREP';
- ○ B. SELECT   TAB1.EMPNO, TAB1.SALARY,
  TAB2.AVGSAL,TAB2.HDCOUNT
  FROM   DSN8910.EMP TAB1,
  TABLE(SELECT   AVG(SALARY) AS AVGSAL,
  COUNT(*) AS HDCOUNT
  FROM   DSN8910.EMP
  WHERE   WORKDEPT = TAB1.WORKDEPT) AS TAB2
  WHERE TAB1.JOB = 'SALESREP';

```
○ C.  SELECT   TAB1.EMPNO, TAB1.SALARY,
                TAB2.AVGSAL,TAB2.HDCOUNT
        FROM     DSN8910.EMP TAB1,
          (SELECT    AVG(SALARY) AS AVGSAL,
                     COUNT(*) AS HDCOUNT
          FROM      DSN8910.EMP
          WHERE     WORKDEPT = (SELECT WORKDEPT
                                   FROM    DSN8910.EMP
                                   WHERE   WORKDEPT=TAB1.WORKDEPT)
          )   AS TAB2
        WHERE    TAB1.JOB = 'SALESREP';

○ D.  SELECT   TAB1.EMPNO, TAB1.SALARY,
                TAB2.AVGSAL,TAB2.HDCOUNT
        FROM     DSN8910.EMP TAB1,
          TABLE(SELECT   AVG(SALARY) AS AVGSAL,
                     COUNT(*) AS HDCOUNT
              FROM    DSN8910.EMP E) AS TAB2
        WHERE    TAB1.JOB = 'SALESREP'
        AND       TAB1.WORKDEPT = E.WORKDEPT;
```

Question 36

A DBA wants to know the object descriptor (OBD) of a table space. Which utility provides this information?

○ A. REPAIR

○ B. DSN1PRNT

○ C. DSN1COMP

○ D. DIAGNOSE

Question 37

Which of the following utilities would you use to identify orphaned records in DSNDB06.SYSGROUP?

○ A. DSN1CHKR

○ B. DSN1PRNT

○ C. DIAGNOSE

○ D. CHECK DATA

Question 38

Which statistics does the following statement collect?

```
RUNSTATS TABLESPACE DSN8D81A.DSN8S81E
REPORT YES
UPDATE ALL
```

○ A. Table space statistics

○ B. Table space and index statistics

○ C. Table space and column statistics

○ D. Table space and histogram statistics

Question 39

Which of the following DSNZPARMs is used to allow DB2 to separate the DBAT from the connection (at commit time) and reuse the DBAT to process other work while the connection is inactive?

○ A. CMTSTAT

○ B. CTHREAD

○ C. MAXDBAT

○ D. IDFORE

Question 40

A non-partitioned index in RECP status has pages from the logical partition in the logical page list. Which command or utility could you use to manually resolve the pages in the logical page list?

○ A. -RECOVER INDOUBT ACTION(COMMIT) ID(*)

○ B. RECOVER INDEXSPACE db1.ix1 ERROR RANGE

○ C. -START DATABASE(db1) SPACENAM(ix1) ACCESS(RO)

○ D. REBUILD INDEXSPACE (db1.ix1 PART 3) SCOPE PENDING

Question 41

Which of the following statements is correct regarding the recovery of the DB2 catalog and directory at a disaster recovery site?

- ○ A. SYSADM authority is required to RECOVER DSNDB06.SYSUSER.
- ○ B. RECOVER will not use the logs when recovering DSNDB06.SYSCOPY if it was not updated after the image copy was made.
- ○ C. DSNDB01.DBD01 must be recovered after DSNDB06.SYSCOPY for the RECOVER utility to obtain the image copy information.
- ○ D. After the indexes for SYSDBASE and SYSUSER have been rebuilt, all remaining catalog and directory table spaces can be recovered in a single RECOVER utility statement.

Question 42

When the RECOVER utility is recovering a list of objects and the recovery base is created by the BACKUP SYSTEM utility, which of the following will occur?

- ○ A. Objects that have a dump copy will be recovered in parallel.
- ○ B. RECOVER will do backup processing in order to use a dump copy if the FlashCopy isn't usable.
- ○ C. Some objects will be recovered from a FlashCopy, and some will be recovered from a dump copy.
- ○ D. Objects will be restored from a FlashCopy, if it exists, even if the FROMDUMP keyword is specified.

Question 43

A data-sharing environment contains two members (DB21 and DB22) on separate LPARs (L1 and L2) with two coupling facilities (CF1 and CF2). CF1 contains the lock and SCA structures, and CF2 contains the group buffer pool structures. The GBPs are not duplexed. Assume that all the structures can reside on either CF1 or CF2 based on the CRFM policy PREFLIST and parameter AUTOREC is set to YES.

CF2 fails and is no longer available to DB21 or DB22. What action is necessary to minimize loss of data availability to the application?

- ○ A. Manually rebuild the GBP structures on CF1.
- ○ B. Stop members DB21 and DB22 and initiate a group restart.
- ○ C. No action is needed. Each member performs automatic GRECP recovery.
- ○ D. No action is needed. The GBP structures are automatically rebuilt in CF2.

Question 44

Which of the following items are registered in the coupling facility in a data-sharing environment?

- ○ A. Logs
- ○ B. Work files
- ○ C. EDM pool entries
- ○ D. Locks

Question 45

Which of the following is *not a benefit* of a data-sharing environment?

- ○ A. Continuous availability
- ○ B. Configuration flexibility
- ○ C. Concurrent read/write access to the same data
- ○ D. No need for image copies

Question 46

If a DBA would like to get a count of rows returned from a multi-row fetch operation, which of the following methods would be used?

- ○ A. Use GET DIAGNOSTICS.
- ○ B. Check the SQL return code.
- ○ C. Check the SQLSTATE.
- ○ D. Perform a count in the program.

Question 47

The main difference between static scrollable cursors and dynamic scrollable cursors is which of the following?

- ○ A. Static cursors must be declared.
- ○ B. Dynamic cursors must be opened.
- ○ C. Dynamic cursors do not use the workfile database.
- ○ D. Static cursors cannot be used by pseudo-conversional CICS.

Question 48

The following statement is referred to as which type of DELETE?

```
EXEC SQL
    DELETE FROM DSN8910.EMP
    WHERE CURRENT OF FCURSOR
END-EXEC.
```

○ A. Searched

○ B. Positioned

○ C. Selective

○ D. Mass

Question 49

In which of the following cases would a DBA REBIND with REOPT(AUTO)?

○ A. When using static SQL and the host variables can have many different values at runtime

○ B. When using static SQL and the host variables are specified in predicates with columns that have data skew

○ C. When using dynamic SQL and the host variables are specified in predicates with columns that have data skew

○ D. When using either dynamic or static SQL as long as the host variables are specified in predicates with columns that have data skew

Question 50

Which of the following entry-level DB2 products can be installed and run on a server with up to four CPUs?

○ A. DB2 Express Edition

○ B. DB2 Personal Edition

○ C. DB2 Workgroup Edition

○ D. DB2 Enterprise Edition

Question 51

Which of the following statements is true regarding postponed units of recovery?

○ A. Individual URs being processed by postponed recovery cannot be canceled separately.

○ B. Use of the –RECOVER POSTPONED CANCEL command while postponed abort threads are backing out causes all data base objects that were in use by postponed abort URs to be put in recover pending.

○ C. Using system parameters LBACKOUT=AUTO and BACKODUR=1, any incomplete UR older than 1 checkpoint found during restart of a failed DB2 system will be processed after end restart as a postponed abort UR.

○ D. If a DB2 system fails during backout of a postponed abort UR, subsequent restart of the DB2 system will cause the postponed abort backout to pick up starting with the last log record applied during the last postponed abort recovery.

Question 52

Assume the following query:

```
SELECT FIRSTNME, MIDINIT, LASTNAME, EMPNO, WORKDEPT, PROJNO,
PROJNAME, DEPTNO
FROM DSN8910.EMP, DSN8910.PROJ
```

If the EMP table contains two rows and the PROJ table contains four rows, how many rows does this query return?

○ A. Four

○ B. Eight

○ C. Six

○ D. Two

Question 53

A plan is bound with ACQUIRE(USE) RELEASE(DEALLOCATE). What assumption can be made about a possible reason for using these options?

○ A. The objective is to prepare allied threads for reuse.

○ B. The objective is to defer preparation of dynamic SQL.

○ C. The objective is to have resources acquired when the thread is created.

○ D. The objective is to isolate an application from other running applications.

Question 54

To limit exposure for an application, a company creates an APP1 trusted context and an APP1_DBA role. DBA1 was assigned to this role and all the objects. What happens if DBA1 leaves the company and the ID is removed?

○ A.   The objects and privileges of the role are untouched.

○ B.   All privileges need to be re-granted.

○ C.   All dependent privileges are cascade revoked.

○ D.   The objects need to be dropped and re-created.

Question 55

Which of the following is *not* a reason to perform a commit?

○ A.   Concurrency

○ B.   Lock avoidance

○ C.   Restart

○ D.   Lessen logging

Question 56

Which of the following is true about a savepoint?

○ A.   It enables milestones within a transaction or UR to be bookmarked.

○ B.   It commits data.

○ C.   It enables a point of recovery.

○ D.   It can be shared by multiple applications.

Question 57

Which of the following utilities can be used to check the data consistency of indexes on the DB2 catalog?

○ A.   DSN1CHKR

○ B.   DSN1COPY

○ C.   CHECK DATA

○ D.   CHECK INDEX

Question 58

Which of the following is true for compatibility mode*?

○ A. DB2 can fall back to V8.

○ B. Data-sharing groups can have V8 members.

○ C. Changes made to the catalog during migration are undone.

○ D. Objects created in DB2 9 new-function mode can still be accessed.

Question 59

The following statement will create which type of table?

```
CREATE GLOBAL TEMPORARY TABLE SUMMARY
AMOUNT_SOLD DECIMAL(5,2) NOT NULL,
SOLD_DATE DATE NOT NULL)
```

○ A. A declared temporary table

○ B. A created temporary table

○ C. A common table expression

○ D. A materialized query table

Question 60

A cursor defined WITH HOLD is released when all of the following occur except:

○ A. A CLOSE cursor, ROLLBACK, or CONNECT statement is issued.

○ B. A Call Attach Facility (CAF) CLOSE function call or an RRSAF TERMINATE THREAD function call is issued.

○ C. The application program terminates.

○ D. A commit occurs.

Question 61

Which of the following is a benefit of multi-row fetch?

○ A. Lessen the number of rows returned

○ B. Lessen the number of SQL calls

○ C. Ability to code recursive fetching

○ D. Reduction in number of joins needed

Question 62

A stored procedure needs to access a flat file and return the data from the flat file as a result set. Once the execution of the procedure is completed, the data is no longer needed. Which type of DB2 table would be most appropriate in this situation?

○ A. A regular table

○ B. An auxiliary table

○ C. A global temporary table

○ D. A clone table

Question 63

For establishing concurrency within a WLM-managed, WLM-established address space, what is the name of the parameter used to set the number of procedures that can execute concurrently for each address space?

○ A. NUMSRB

○ B. NUMTCB

○ C. CONCUR

○ D. THRDNUM

Question 64

Which of the following options is not a phase of the DB2 REORG utility?

○ A. LOG

○ B. SORT

○ C. UNLOAD

○ D. ENFORCE

Question 65

Which type of DB2 thread can be managed directly by WLM?

○ A. Distributed threads

○ B. Allied threads using CAF

○ C. Allied threads using RRSAF

○ D. Allied threads using TSO ATTACH

Question 66

Which level of authority is required to revoke a privilege that another ID has granted?

- ○ A. DBADM
- ○ B. DBCTRL
- ○ C. SYSOPR
- ○ D. SYSCTRL

Question 67

Which of the following tools can make recommendations for indexes and/or MQTs to improve the performance of DB2 applications?

- ○ A. Visual Explain
- ○ B. Tivoli System Automation
- ○ C. Configuration Assistant
- ○ D. Design Advisor

Question 68

A PL/I stored procedure executing as a subprogram has what limitation?

- ○ A. It cannot call other stored procedures.
- ○ B. It has to run in a WLM-established address space with NUMTCB=1.
- ○ C. It cannot return result sets.
- ○ D. It cannot issue I/O.

Question 69

When should you consider using OPTIMIZE FOR *n* ROWS for a DRDA application?

- ○ A. SQL cursors closed before fetching the entire result set
- ○ B. Multiple cursors defined with OPTIMIZE FOR *n* ROWS not issuing FETCHes
- ○ C. Updatable cursors
- ○ D. Mass insert processes

Question 70

The original DRDA specifications identified four different levels of support. Which of the following is not currently implemented?

○ A.   Remote request

○ B.   Remote unit of work (RUW)

○ C.   Distributed unit of work (DUW)

○ D.   Distributed request

Question 71

Which of the following catalog tables is not part of the communications database (CDB)?

○ A.   SYSIBM.IPLIST

○ B.   SYSIBM.MODESELECT

○ C.   SYSIBM.LULIST

○ D.   SYSIBM.CONNECTIONS

Question 72

Assume the following statements are issued in order:

```
CREATE DISTINCT TYPE MONEY AS DECIMAL(9,2);
COMMIT;

SELECT CAST(1.5 AS MONEY) + CAST(1.5 AS DEC(9,2)) FROM
    SYSIBM.SYSDUMMY1;
```

Which of the following statements is true?

○ A.   The value 3.0 is returned as a DECIMAL(9,2).

○ B.   The statement fails because the data types are incompatible.

○ C.   The statement fails because no "+" function exists to add MONEY.

○ D.   The value 3.0 is returned as MONEY because DECIMAL(9,2) is promoted to MONEY.

Question 73

Consider the following scenario for application table space DB1.TS1.

1. Full copy made at RBA 0010000
2. Updates
3. Full copy made at RBA 0040000
4. Updates
5. Incremental copy made at RBA 0070000
6. Updates

The full copy made at point 3 has an I/O error and cannot be used. Which of the following RECOVER statements will recover the DB1.TS1 table space to the current point in time?

- A. RECOVER TABLESPACE DB1.TS1 TOLASTCOPY
- B. RECOVER TABLESPACE DB1.TS1 TOLOGPOINT CURRENT
- C. RECOVER TABLESPACE DB1.TS1 TOLOGPOINT X'0070000'
- D. RECOVER TABLESPACE DB1.TS1 RESTOREBEFORE X'0040000'

Question 74

What is the major difference between a FENCED SQL procedure and a native SQL procedure?

- A. The fenced SQL procedure cannot modify data.
- B. The native SQL procedure can be defined only in the Developer Workbench.
- C. The fenced SQL procedure runs as an external C program.
- D. The native SQL procedure cannot access temporary tables.

Question 75

What is the emphasis and strength of the DB2 Data Warehouse Edition offering?

- A. Backup and recovery
- B. Queries
- C. Transactions
- D. Security

Question 76

What type of user-defined function is created in the following definition?

```
CREATE FUNCTION TOTMON (STARTX DATE, ENDY DATE)
RETURNS INTEGER
LANGUAGE SQL
CONTAINS SQL
NO EXTERNAL ACTION
DETERMINISTIC
RETURN ABS( (YEAR(STARTX - ENDY)*12) + MONTH(STARTX - ENDY) );
```

○ A. A sourced UDF

○ B. An external table UDF

○ C. An external scalar UDF

○ D. An SQL sourced UDF

Question 77

Which of the following tools can be used to view the result of Control Center actions?

○ A. Journal

○ B. Task Center

○ C. Activity Monitor

○ D. Command Line Processor

Question 78

When you create a LOB table space, which of the following options of the CREATE TABLESPACE statement *cannot* be specified?

○ A. CLOSE YES

○ B. COMPRESS YES

○ C. LOCKSIZE ANY

○ D. LOG YES

Question 79

What is one main difference between the DB2 catalog and the DB2 directory?

○ A. The directory doesn't need to be backed up.

○ B. The catalog can be accessed using SQL.

○ C. The catalog is in BP0.

○ D. The directory consist of tables.

Question 80

Which of the following types of performance monitoring would best be used to determine
why there is general performance degradation in a data warehouse environment (high
query usage, low update/insert and delete activity) over time? This environment runs 24X7
with no predictable workload pattern. Assume a performance database is used for reporting
purposes where the collection of accounting and statistics data is stored.

○ A. Track and report on DBM1 virtual storage utilization over time.

○ B. Track and report on the number of timeouts and deadlocks over time.

○ C. Track and report on the average CPU and average elapsed time for plans
and packages over time.

○ D. Track and report on the plans and packages that use more than two
seconds of CPU time or one hour of elapsed time.

Question 81

A special situation exists in which whenever a delete operation is performed against a
certain table, a single row containing the user ID needs to be recorded in an audit table.
That is, any time a DELETE is issued against the table, that action must be recorded in the
audit table. Which type of trigger would best serve this purpose?

○ A. A before DELETE row trigger

○ B. An after DELETE row trigger

○ C. An after DELETE statement trigger

○ D. An INSTEAD OF trigger

Question 82

Which of the following is *not* a valid lock mode?

○ A. Update

○ B. Share Intent Exclusive

○ C. Exclusive

○ D. Insert

Question 83

Which of the following statistics is used for access path selection?

○ A. HIGH2KEY

○ B. ORGRATIO

○ C. AVGKEYLEN

○ D. PERCACTIVE

Question 84

What is the main difference between the deferred write threshold (DWQT) and the vertical deferred write threshold (VDWQT)?

○ A. The DWQT threshold applies to pages with LOB data, whereas the VDWQT threshold applies to pages containing mixed data.

○ B. The DWQT threshold deals with a fixed number of buffers, whereas the VDWQT threshold deals with a variable number of buffers.

○ C. The DWQT threshold is used only with sort/work buffer pools, whereas the VDWQT threshold can be used with buffers associated with any type of table spaces.

○ D. The DWQT threshold applies to all updated (unavailable) pages in the entire buffer pool, whereas the VDWQT threshold applies to the number of updated (unavailable) pages for a single page set.

Question 85

The PLAN_TABLE results from an explain of an SQL statement show the following column values: JOIN_METHOD = 1, MATCHCOLS = 2, and ACCESS_TYPE = I1. What is the access path chosen for this SQL statement?

○ A. Merge scan join, matching on two index columns, using a sparse index

○ B. Hybrid join, matching on two index columns, using one fetch index scan

○ C. Nested loop join, matching two columns in the table, using index-only access

○ D. Nested loop join, matching on two index columns, using one fetch index scan

Sample Exam Answers

In this appendix, we give the answers to the sample exam questions in Appendix B. In addition to providing some information about the answer, we note the chapter in which you can find more information about the topic in the question.

Question 1

The answer is **B**, identifying. **(Chapter 4 – Database Objects)**

Question 2

The answer is **C**, DB2 for z/OS. The DB2 for z/OS product comes complete with the ability to connect to remote data servers and databases. **(Chapter 1 – DB2 Product Fundamentals)**

Question 3

The correct answer is **C**, a z/OS console. You can issue the command START DB2 only from a z/OS console (or APF-authorized program passing it to the console). All other DB2 commands can be issued from

- a z/OS console or z/OS application program
- a TSO terminal session
- a DB2I panel
- an IMS terminal
- a CICS terminal
- an APF-authorized program
- an IFI application program

(Chapter 2 – Environment)

Question 4

The correct answer is **B**, a DELETE statement. The NEXTVAL and PREVVAL expressions can be issued in the following:

- SELECT and SELECT INTO
- An INSERT statement within a SELECT clause of a fullselect
- An UPDATE statement within a SET clause (searched or positioned)
- SET *host-variable*
- VALUES or VALUES INTO
- CREATE PROCEDURE, CREATE FUNCTION, or CREATE TRIGGER

You cannot use these expressions in a DELETE statement.
(Chapter 12 – Application Program Features)

Question 5

The correct answer is **B**, by observing the value of the IRLMRWT DSNZPARM. The IRLMRWT parameter specifies the number of seconds an application will wait before it times out. **(Chapter 2 – Environment)**

Question 6

The correct answer is **A**, Accounting Trace Class 3. You use this trace class to show the elapsed time divided into various waits, such as the duration of suspensions due to waits for locks and latches or waits for I/O. **(Chapter 16 – Locking and Concurrency)**

Question 7

The correct answer is **C**: IRLM, DBM1, MSTR. A complete list or recommended address space prioritization is a follows:

- MVS monitor with IRLM capabilities
- IRLM
- DB2 performance monitors
- DBM1
- MSTR
- CICS

(Chapter 2 – Environment)

Question 8

The correct answer is **C**, DBCTRL. This authority will let DBA1 create tables in a specified database as well as run some utilities, such as REORG, on the table spaces in the database. This authority does not permit SQL Data Manipulation Language (DML) to be executed against the objects in the database. **(Chapter 3 – Access and Security)**

Question 9

The correct answer is **C**, virtual buffer pool(s). Virtual buffer pools still exist on each DB2 subsystem (member). The other options are all structures defined in the coupling facility. **(Chapter 9 – Data Sharing)**

Question 10

The correct answer is **D**, DEBUGSESSION. This is a new privilege with DB2 9 that provides the ability to control debug session activity for native SQL and Java stored procedures. **(Chapter 3 – Access and Security)**

Question 11

The correct answer is **C**, CS (Cursor Stability). This isolation level is the most common and provides the best concurrency for the application program without allowing the application to read uncommitted data. **(Chapter 11 – Binding an Application Program)**

Question 12

The correct answer is **B**, EXECUTE authority on each package specified in the PKLIST. To be able to create a new plan with packages, you must have EXECUTE authority on the packages in the PKLIST. **(Chapter 3 – Access and Security)**

Question 13

The correct answer is **C**, IRLMRWT. This DSNZPARM specifies the number of seconds a transaction will wait for a lock before a timeout is detected. The IRLM uses this value for timeout detection. **(Chapter 16 – Locking and Concurrency)**

Question 14

The correct answer is **C**, allocates buffer pools. The bind process does not allocate buffer pools. In addition to A, B, and D, the bind process also compares column and table names against the DB2 catalog. **(Chapter 11 – Binding an Application Program)**

Question 15

The answer is **C**, a unique constraint exists. Whenever a primary key constraint or a unique key constraint is defined on a table, a unique index must exist to support the constraint. If the index being dropped is the last unique index in support of a unique constraint or primary key, that index cannot be dropped until the primary key is dropped or the unique constraint is dropped. **(Chapter 4 – Database Objects)**

Question 16

The correct answer is **D**, when a trigger on a dependent table is dropped. Dropping of a trigger on a table on which a plan or package is dependent will not cause the plan or package to become invalid. A, B, and C will all cause a plan or package to become invalid, as well as the following:

- When a table on which the plan or package depends is altered to add a TIME, TIMESTAMP, or DATE column

- When a created temporary table on which the plan or package depends is altered to add a column

- When a user-defined function on which the plan or package depends is altered

- When an index, table, or column definition changes via an ALTER

(Chapter 11 – Binding an Application Program)

Question 17

The correct answer is **B**. The –DISPLAY DATABASE command with the LOCKS option shows you the locks being held on the table spaces in the specified database. **(Chapter 16 – Locking and Concurrency)**

Question 18

The correct answer is **B**, –DISPLAY DDF. This DB2 command lists all the information required to set up the connection to DB2. **(Chapter 14 – Accessing Distributed Data)**

Question 19

The answer is **B**, drop and re-create TRIG2 and TRIG3 after correcting the SQL. When similar triggers are created against a table, they are executed in the order in which they were created. Because these are all after triggers, they logically fire at the same time. DB2, however, executes them in the order they were defined. **(Chapter 15 – Advanced Functionality)**

Question 20

The answer is **D**, the MAXPARTITIONS clause. Two types of universal table spaces exist: partition-by-growth and range-partitioned. While the MAXPARTITIONS clause designates a partition-by-growth table space, the combination of NUMPARTS and SEGSIZE designates a range-partitioned universal table space. NUMPARTS alone creates a partitioned table space, and SEGSIZE alone creates a segmented table space. **(Chapter 4 –Database Objects)**

Question 21

The answer is **D**. The statement cache table is populated via the EXPLAIN STMTCACHE ALL statement or from the Optimization Service Center. The table can then be queried to determine the runtime performance of statements in the statement cache.
(Chapter 17 – Performance Monitoring and Tuning)

Question 22

The answer is **B**. The primary space allocation indicates the initial size of the VSAM data set (or sets) supporting the table space. Once this initial space is allocated, it can be changed, but the change won't be effective until the primary space is reallocated. This will happen only if the underlying VSAM data set is deleted and redefined. This will happen during a REORG or LOAD REPLACE, but only if the data set isn't reused.
(Chapter 4 – Database Objects)

Question 23

The correct answer is **A**, SKIP LOCKED DATA. You can use this option on a SELECT statement to let the transaction skip data that has an incompatible lock held by another application. You should use this option only if the transaction can tolerate seeing somewhat less than accurate data. **(Chapter 16 – Locking and Concurrency)**

Question 24

The answer is **C**, ASCII. Comparisons on the data server are always in the encoding scheme defined for the table. Likewise, sorting on columns in an ORDER BY depends on the encoding scheme of the table. **(Chapter 4 – Database Objects)**

Question 25

The answer is **C**, references more than one table in the first FROM clause.
(Chapter 5 – Retrieving and Manipulating Database Objects)

Question 26

The answer is **B**. This statement demonstrates the proper representation of a row expression.
(Chapter 5 – Retrieving and Manipulating Database Objects)

Question 27

The correct answer is **B**, use group buffer pool duplexing. By enabling this feature, you can minimize the outage in the event of a coupling facility failure because you won't have to wait for the primary structure to be rebuilt in the surviving coupling facility. The secondary structure will take over. **(Chapter 9 – Data Sharing)**

Question 28

The answer is **B**. The DISTINCT clause will eliminate null values as well as any duplicate values for the WORKDEPT column, so the COUNT function will count only the resulting distinct (i.e., unique) values. **(Chapter 5 – Manipulating Database Objects)**

Question 29

The answer is **C**. The order of the columns specified in the ORDER BY clause dictates the order of the columns in the sort, so you must specify the WORKDEPT column first. The default ordering is ASC (ascending). **(Chapter 5 – Manipulating Database Objects)**

Question 30

The correct answer is **D**, static SQL (because it's static, which is the opposite of dynamic). A, B, and C are all types of dynamic SQL as well as dynamic SQL executed through ODBC functions. **(Chapter 10 – Using SQL in an Application Program)**

Question 31

The answer is **D**. The proper format for an explicit join is table name, JOIN clause, ON clause. This pattern continues until all joins are specified; a WHERE clause can then be used. An implicit join can be only an inner join, and so the explicit format should specify INNER JOIN or, optionally, just the word JOIN, which implies inner. **(Chapter 6 – Advanced SQL Coding)**

Question 32

The answer is **C**: COLLEGE, SECONDARY, COLLEGE, POST GRADUATE. CASE expressions are powerful tools for performing data conversions, whether it be report writing, data analysis, grouping, or even for performance to avoid multiple passes through the data.
(Chapter 6 – Advanced SQL Coding)

Question 33

The answer is **D**. The EXCEPT will return only those rows in the first subselect that are not in the second subselect. In addition, EXCEPT ALL allows duplicate values to be returned, while EXCEPT or EXCEPT DISTINCT eliminates the duplicates. **(Chapter 6 – Advanced SQL Coding)**

Question 34

The answer is **B**. The XMLQUERY or XQuery db-fn:xmlcolumn function returns a well-formed XML element pulled out of a document. **(Chapter 6 – Advanced SQL Coding)**

Question 35

The answer is **B**. To make a correlated reference from inside a nested table expression to outside the nested table expression, the nested table expression must be preceded with the TABLE keyword. Also, the correlated reference only works from inside the table expression to outside the table expression. You cannot make references outside the table expression to tables inside the table expression. **(Chapter 6 – Advanced SQL Coding)**

Question 36

The correct answer is **D**, DIAGNOSE. The DIAGNOSE utility generates information useful in diagnosing problems. Some of the information this utility can output includes the following:

- ODB of the table space and/or index space
- Records from the SYSIBM.SYSUTIL catalog table
- Module entry point lists (MEPLs)
- Utilities available on the subsystem
- Database exception table (DBET)

(Chapter 7 – Maintaining Data)

Question 37

The correct answer is **A**, DSN1CHKR. The DSN1CHKR utility verifies the integrity of DB2 directory and catalog table spaces. The utility scans the specified table space for broken links, broken hash chains, and records that aren't part of any link or chain. In other words, it helps find orphaned records in the catalog and directory. **(Chapter 7 – Maintaining Data)**

Question 38

The correct answer is **A**, table space statistics. Only the statistics for the table space will be collected with the given syntax because the INDEX parameter and the COLUMN parameters were excluded. Also, the example does not specify use of histogram statistics with the HISTOGRAM option. **(Chapter 7 – Maintaining Data)**

Question 39

The correct answer is **A**, CMTSTAT. This DSNZPARM affects the creation, disconnection, re-creation, and reuse of active DBAT threads for distributed connections. **(Chapter 14 – Accessing Distributed Data)**

Question 40

The correct answer is **C**. The –START DATABASE command is the way to remove pages from the logical page list. **(Chapter 8 – Recovery and Restart)**

Question 41

The correct answer is **D**. There is a predetermined order for recovery of the catalog and directory due to dependencies. However, after SYSDBASE and SYSUSER have had their indexes rebuilt, all table spaces/indexes after that can be handled in single RECOVER statement. **(Chapter 8 – Recovery and Restart)**

Question 42

The correct answer is **A**, objects that have a dump copy will be recovered in parallel. If objects in a list to be recovered require a system-level backup that has been dumped to tape as its recovery base (i.e., the FROMDUMP option has been specified), the DB2 RECOVER utility invokes DFSMShsm to restore the data sets for the objects in parallel, with the degree of parallelism being capped by the maximum number of tasks that can be started by the RECOVER. DFSMShsm restores the data sets in parallel based on its install options. **(Chapter 8 – Recovery and Restart)**

Question 43

The correct answer is **C**, no action is needed because each member performs automatic GRECP recovery. The members will perform automatic GRECP recovery of the pages that existed in the group buffer pools when CF2 became unavailable. Because GBP duplexing was not turned on and CF1 was listed in the PREFLIST with AUTOREC on, the rebuild will occur automatically in the surviving coupling facility (CF1). **(Chapter 9 – Data Sharing)**

Question 44

The correct answer is **D**, locks. Locks can be registered in the coupling facility. The other items—logs, work files, and EDM pool entries—are all still associated with a single subsystem and are not found in the coupling facility. **(Chapter 9 – Data Sharing)**

Question 45

The correct answer is **D**, no need for image copies. A data-sharing environment can provide the means for continuous availability, configuration flexibility, and concurrent read/write access to data. However, it does not have the ability to replace normal backup and recovery practices, including the need to do image copies. **(Chapter 9 – Data Sharing)**

Question 46

The correct answer is **A**, use GET DIAGNOSTICS. By interrogating the ROW_COUNT parameter in the GET DIAGNOSTICS results, you can find out how many rows were returned from a multi-row fetch operation. **(Chapter 10 – Using SQL in an Application Program)**

Question 47

The correct answer is **C**, dynamic cursors do not use the workfile database. The static scrollable cursors are materialized in a table space in the workfile database. The dynamic scrollable cursors don't need to materialize here because the scrolling can occur both ways against the active result set using backward index scanning. **(Chapter 10 – Using SQL in an Application Program)**

Question 48

The correct answer is **B**, positioned. A DELETE that is defined with a WHERE CURRENT OF cursor is known as a positioned delete because it will delete the data wherever the cursor happens to be positioned. **(Chapter 10 – Using SQL in an Application Program)**

Question 49

The correct answer is **C**, when using dynamic SQL and the host variables are specified in predicates with columns that have data skew. If columns have a data skew that may affect access path optimization, you can use REOPT(AUTO) for dynamic SQL execution so that DB2 re-optimizes the access path at runtime if the predicates use columns and DB2 determines there is a data skew. **(Chapter 11 – Binding an Application Program)**

Question 50

The answer is **C**, DB2 Workgroup Edition. While both the Express Edition and the Workgroup Edition provide a robust, full-functional data server, the Express Edition is limited to two CPUs, and the Workgroup Edition is limited to four. There is no CPU limit for the Enterprise Edition. **(Chapter 1 – DB2 Product Fundamentals)**

Question 51

The correct answer is **A**. The individuals URs being processed by postponed recovery cannot be canceled separately. **(Chapter 8 – Recovery and Restart)**

Question 52

The answer is **B**, eight rows will be returned. The query contains no join predicate, so it is a Cartesian product, which is every row from the first table joined to every row from the second table. **(Chapter 5 – Retrieving and Manipulating Database Objects)**

Question 53

The correct answer is **A**, the objective is to prepare allied threads for reuse. By using ACQUIRE(USE) RELEASE(DEALLOCATE), you will have the ability to enable thread reuse. Resources needed by the thread will be held for the duration of the thread. **(Chapter 11 – Binding an Application Program)**

Question 54

The correct answer is **A**, the objects and privileges of the role are untouched. One benefit of roles is the fact that if the ID assigned to the role is removed, nothing happens to the objects or privileges assigned to the role. **(Chapter 3 – Access and Security)**

Question 55

The correct answer is **D**, lessen logging. Performing commits helps with the following: concurrency, lock avoidance, restart, rollback/recovery, utility processing, and resource release. Commits do not help reduce the amount of logging performed. **(Chapter 12 – Application Program Features)**

Question 56

The correct answer is **A**, a savepoint enables milestones within a transaction or UR to be bookmarked. An external savepoint represents the state of the data and schema at a particular point in time. After the savepoint is set, changes made to data and schemas by the transaction can be rolled back to the savepoint as application logic requires, without affecting the overall outcome of the transaction. A savepoint does not actually commit data, and savepoints cannot be shared; they are specific to an application process. **(Chapter 12 – Application Program Features)**

Question 57

The correct answer is **D**, CHECK INDEX. You can use this utility to check the data consistency of the indexes in the DB2 catalog. **(Chapter 7 – Maintaining Data)**

Question 58

The correct answer is **D**, objects created in DB2 9 new-function mode can still be accessed. The * indicates that at one time the DB2 subsystem or data-sharing group was in enabling-new-function mode, enabling-new-function mode*, or new-function mode. Objects that were created in enabling-new-function mode or new-function mode can still be accessed. Data-sharing groups cannot have any Version 8 members, and you cannot fall back to Version 8 from compatibility mode* or coexist with a Version 8 system. **(Chapter 2 – Environment)**

Question 59

The correct answer is **B**, a created temporary table. DB2 supports two types of global temporary tables: created and declared. The created table is created with a CREATE statement and has its definition stored in the DB2 catalog. You create a declared temporary table in the application program using the DECLARE statement. **(Chapter 12 – Application Program Features)**

Question 60

The correct answer is **D**, a commit occurs. A commit will not release a cursor defined WITH HOLD. The whole purpose of WITH HOLD is to hold the cursor open through a commit point so that cursors don't need to be repositioned after the commit. **(Chapter 10 – Using SQL in an Application Program)**

Question 61

The correct answer is **B**, lessen the number of SQL calls. The greatest benefit to multi-row fetch is the ability to fetch up to 32,767 rows in a single API call. This technique reduces the number of SQL calls issued. **(Chapter 12 – Application Program Features)**

Question 62

The answer is **C**, a global temporary table. Global temporary tables provide a thread-independent temporary table into which the stored procedure can insert the flat file data. Once the table has data in it, a result set can be opened and returned to the client. **(Chapter 13 – Stored Procedures)**

Question 63

The answer is **B**, NUMTCB. This parameter in the JCL for the WLM-established address space dictates the number of TCBs, or the number of procedures that the address space will run concurrently. The other parameter names listed are not valid. **(Chapter 13 – Stored Procedures)**

Question 64

The correct answer is **D**, ENFORCE. The ENFORCE phase is not included in the REORG utility. The phases in the REORG utility are as follows:

1. UTILINIT
2. UNLOAD
3. RELOAD
4. SORT

5. BUILD

6. SORTBLD

7. LOG

8. SWITCH

9. UTILTERM

(Chapter 7 – Maintaining Data)

Question 65

The answer is **A**, distributed threads. You can set up WLM to manage diverse workloads on a z/OS server via definitions. Those definitions include the ability to set priorities for distributed threads as well as for stored procedures. **(Chapter 13 – Stored Procedures)**

Question 66

The correct answer is **D**, SYSCTRL. This is the only level of authority that can revoke a privilege granted by another ID. **(Chapter 3 – Access and Security)**

Question 67

The answer is **D**, the Design Advisor. The Configuration Assistant aids in setting up connections to DB2 data servers. Tivoli System Automation helps monitor and configure system settings. Visual Explain can expose an access path and can recommend RUNSTATS, but it doesn't suggest database changes. **(Chapter 1 – DB2 Product Fundamentals)**

Question 68

The answer is **D**, it cannot issue I/O. Subprograms provide an added level of performance in that the Language Environment linkage path is shorter. This support is a high-performance design feature. However, programmers must take extra care when coding subprograms and should be aware of some of the language limitations. **(Chapter 13 – Stored Procedures)**

Question 69

The correct answer is **B**, when you have multiple cursors defined with OPTIMIZE FOR *n* ROWS not issuing FETCHes. Use of the clause should be considered if your application meets the following criteria:

- Read-only queries fetching a large number of rows
- SQL cursors rarely being closed before fetching the entire result set
- No statements other than FETCH used when a cursor is open

(Chapter 14 – Accessing Distributed Data)

Question 70

The correct answer is **D**, distributed request. This level supports a distributed request to two or more remote DBMSs residing on the same or different locations. The implementation of a standard technique to solve the distributed request problem is quite complicated, requiring the addition of optimization-related concepts such as network performance and estimation of the cost of the remote SQL component. **(Chapter 14 – Accessing Distributed Data)**

Question 71

The correct answer is **D**, SYSBIM.CONNECTIONS. The DB2 catalog includes the communications database, which contains several tables that hold information about connections with remote systems. These tables include

- SYSIBM.IPLIST
- SYSIBM.IPNAMES
- SYSIBM.LOCATIONS
- SYSIBM.LULIST
- SYSIBM.LUMODES
- SYSIBM.LUNAMES
- SYSIBM.MODESELECT
- SYSIBM.USERNAMES

(Chapter 14 – Accessing Distributed Data)

Question 72

The answer is **C**, the statement fails because no addition function exists for the MONEY type. Although DB2 automatically creates casting functions between the distinct type and its source data type, you have to create user-defined sourced functions that operate against the new type before they can be used. **(Chapter 15 – Advanced Functionality)**

Question 73

The correct answer is **D**. RESTOREBEFORE X'*byte-string*' specifies that RECOVER is to search for an image copy, concurrent copy, or system-level backup (if YES has been specified for SYSTEM-LEVEL BACKUPS on install panel DSNTIP6) with an RBA or LRSN value earlier than the specified X'*byte-string*' value to use in the RESTORE phase. To avoid specific image copies, concurrent copies, or system-level backups with matching or more recent RBA or LRSN values in START_RBA, the RECOVER utility applies the log records and restores the object to its current state or to the specified TORBA or TOLOGPOINT value. DB2 compares the RESTOREBEFORE value with the RBA or LRSN value in the START_RBA column in the

SYSIBM.SYSCOPY record for those copies. For system-level backups, the RESTOREBEFORE value is compared with the data complete LRSN. If you specify a TORBA or TOLOGPOINT value with the RESTOREBEFORE option, the RBA or LRSN value for RESTOREBEFORE must be lower than the specified TORBA or TOLOGPOINT value. If you specify RESTOREBEFORE, you cannot specify TOCOPY, TOLASTCOPY, or TOLASTFULLCOPY. **(Chapter 8 – Recovery and Restart)**

Question 74

The answer is **C**, the fenced SQL procedure runs as an external C program. Before Version 9, all SQL procedures were compiled into C programs that were executed in a WLM-established address space. Beginning in V9, all SQL procedures by default are executed as runtime structures within the DB2 address space. However, if you use keyword FENCED or EXTERNAL, the SQL procedures are still executed as external C programs in a WLM-established address space. **(Chapter 13 – Stored Procedures)**

Question 75

The answer is **B**, queries. While a database designed for OLTP focuses on the performance of small units of work and specific granular transactions, a warehouse is designed for optimal query performance of large queries. DB2 DWE provides the tools for this application. **(Chapter 1 – DB2 Product Fundamentals)**

Question 76

The answer is **D**, an SQL sourced UDF. External functions are user-written programs, similar to stored procedures, and are identified by the EXTERNAL keyword. While a sourced function is based on an existing function, an SQL sourced function is based on a single SQL expression. **(Chapter 15 – Advanced Functionality)**

Question 77

The answer is **A**, the Journal. You use the Task Center to run or to schedule database operations (scripts) to run at specific times. The Activity Monitor monitors application performance and concurrency. The Command Line Processor provides a simple interface for entering database commands, CLP commands, and SQL statements. **(Chapter 1 – DB2 Product Fundamentals)**

Question 78

The answer is **B**, COMPRESS YES. LOB table spaces differ in several ways from regular table spaces. One of the ways they differ is that a LOB table space cannot be compressed. **(Chapter 4 – Database Objects; Chapter 15 – Advanced Functionality)**

Question 79

The correct answer is **B**, the catalog can be accessed using SQL. You can query the DB2 catalog using standard SQL statements. **(Chapter 2 – Environment)**

Question 80

The answer is **C**, track and report on the average CPU and average elapsed time for plans and packages over time. In a 24X7 environment with an unpredictable workload, a continuous monitoring technique may be best. The accounting and statistics data that is collected can be put into a performance warehouse database and queried over time to help determine the problem plans and packages. **(Chapter 17 – Performance Monitoring and Tuning)**

Question 81

The answer is **C**, an after DELETE statement trigger. This type of trigger serves the purpose best because the action needs to be recorded, and if no data changes, the row trigger won't fire. Also, the action is to record a row containing the user ID of the delete. Because a statement trigger fires only once for a statement, it will accomplish the task of adding only a single row to the audit table no matter how many rows are deleted. **(Chapter 15 – Advanced Functionality)**

Question 82

The correct answer is **D**, Insert. There is no lock mode known as Insert. INSERTs would take an exclusive lock on the page. **(Chapter 16 – Locking and Concurrency)**

Question 83

The answer is **A**, HIGH2KEY. While the other statistics provide information about the organization and size of the data, only HIGH2KEY, which represents the high key value, is used by the optimizer. **(Chapter 17 – Performance Monitoring and Tuning)**

Question 84

The answer is **D**. VDWQT applies to a page set, and DWQT applies to the entire buffer pool. These are important settings, especially with large buffer pools and large page sets (e.g., table spaces, partitions), to ensure that writes are distributed over time rather than at system checkpoints. **(Chapter 17 – Performance Monitoring and Tuning)**

Question 85

The answer is **D**, a nested loop join, matching on two index columns with one fetch index scan. PLAN_TABLE is the most valuable resource for determining an efficient query access path. Understanding the contents of the plan table is an important skill. **(Chapter 17 – Performance Monitoring and Tuning)**

A P P E N D I X **D**

References

IBM DB2 9 Administration Guide (SC18-9840)

IBM DB2 9 Application Programming and SQL Guide (SC18-9841)

IBM DB2 9 Application Programming Guide and Reference for Java (SC18-9842)

IBM DB2 9 Codes (GC18-9843)

IBM DB2 9 Command Reference (SC18-9844)

IBM DB2 9 Connect Users Guide (SC10-4229)

IBM DB2 9 Data Sharing: Planning and Administration (SC18-9845)

IBM DB2 9 Installation Guide (GC18-9846)

IBM DB2 9 Messages (GC18-9849)

IBM DB2 9 Performance Monitoring and Tuning Guide (SC18-9851)

IBM DB2 9 RACF Access Control Module (SC18-9852)

IBM DB2 9 Reference for Remote DRDA Requesters and Servers (SC18-9853)

IBM DB2 9 Reference Summary (SX26-3854)

IBM DB2 9 SQL Reference (SC18-9854)

IBM DB2 9 Utility Guide (SC18-9885)

IBM DB2 9 XML Extender Administration and Programming (SC18-9857)

IBM DB2 9 XML Guide (SC18-9858)

To view these IBM references online, go to http://www-306.ibm.com/software/data/db2/zos/v9books.html.

Index

A

ABEND command, 69t

ABEXP, 60t

ABIND, 60t

access control, 16, 99–**137**. *See also*
security

  Application Transparent Transport
  Layer Security (AT-TLS) and,
  104–105

  audits in, 100

  authentication and, 99

  authorities and. *See* authorities

  authorization and, 99

  authorization IDs in, 105, 106–107,
  136

  catalog table information on, 129, 130t

  CICS and, 103–104, 136

  confidentiality and, 100

  data integrity and, 99

  data set protection and, 105

  denial of service attacks and, 105

  DSNR resource class and, 101

  exit routines and, for authorization
  control, 102

  EXPLAIN and, 804–805

  explicit privileges and, 112

  IMS and, 103–104, 136

  Integrated Cryptographic Service
  Facility (ICSF) and, 105

  Kerberos and, 104, 136

  local, 103

  logical terminal (LTERMs) and,
  103–104

  multilevel security and, 131

  object access and, 105–130. *See
  also* specific objects

  PassTickets for, 103

  passwords and, 103

  performing tasks on behalf of another
  in, DBADM and, 111–112

  PERMIT command and, 102

  privileges and. *See* privileges

  RACF and, 136

  remote, 103

  Remote Access Control Facility
  (RACF) and, 101, 104, 105, 106

  restrictive/advisory states and,
  417–418, 419–422t

  roles and, 107, 109, 136, 140

  Secure Sockets Layer (SSL) and,
  104–105

  SecureWay and, 104

  security threats and, 99

  SQL IDs and, SET CURRENT for,
  107

  stem integrity in, 100

  subsystem and, 100–105

  trusted connections and, 108

  trusted contexts and, 107–108,
  109–110, 137

  views for, 130

ACCESS DATABASE command, 70t

Access Method Services (AMS),
REORG utility, 372–373

access paths, 389–390, 756, 765–803.
See also access plans

  catalog statistics used in selection
  of, 810, 811–812t

  optimization hints for, 805

  performance issues and, 815–816

access plans, 756. *See also* access paths

  dimension tables and, 774

  DSNZPARM and, 774–777

  fact table and, 774

  hybrid joins and, METHOD, 773–774

  indexes and, 765–767

  merge scan join and, METHOD,
  772–773

  nested loop joins and,
  METHOD/PRIMARY_ACCES
  STYPE 771–772

  parallelism and
  (PARALLELISM_MODE),
  777–778

  partition scans and,
  PAGE_RANGE, 769–770

  prefetching, PREFETCH and, 769

  SORT, SORTN, SORTC and,
  770–771

  star joins and, METHOD/JOIN
  TYPE, 774–777

  subqueries and, 778–779, 778t, 779t

  table spaces, 767–768

  tables and, 767–768

  topology check and, 775

  unique index check and, 774

accessing distributed data. *See*
distributed data

accounting

  performance issues and, 832

  trace for, 836–838, 842–843t

ACCUMACC, 60t

ACCUMUID, 60t

Activity Monitor, 33, 37

adaptive memory allocation, 11, 12

ADD CLONE keywords, 147–148, 213

ADD CONSTRAINT, 179

ADD_MONTHS, 164

address spaces, 39, 40–42, **41**, 96

  allied, 43, 44

  attachment facilities and, 45–46

  database services (DSAS), 41,
  42–43, 92